1980

UNDERSTANDING ADOLESCENCE

UNDERSTANDING ADOLESCENCE

CURRENT DEVELOPMENTS IN ADOLESCENT PSYCHOLOGY

Fourth Edition

JAMES F. ADAMS
Temple University

Allyn and Bacon, Inc.
Boston · London · Sydney · Toronto

Production Editor: Charleen Akullian
Series Editor: Miggy Hopkins

Library of Congress Cataloging in Publication Data

Adams, James Frederick, 1927-
    Understanding adolescence.

    Includes index.
    1. Adolescent Psychology.   I. Title.
BF724.A25   1980   155.5   79-23928
ISBN 0-205-06931-2

Printed in the United States of America.

TO OUR ADOLESCENTS
Past—Present—Future

Robert B. Adams

Dorothy Adams Vanderhorst

James E. Adams, II

Kathleen T. Helppie

Bruce A. Helppie

Charles E. Helppie, III

Eric H. Eichorn

Debbie E. Hamachek

Dan E. Hamachek

Paul F. Grotevant

David F. Gallagher

Beth Marie Gallagher

Lisa C. Mansfield

Abigail K. Mansfield

David K. Nichols

James E. Nichols

Frank H. Palmer

Elizabeth Wright

Jenifer Wright

Melanie Wright

Kennedy W. Wright

Serena L. Stein

Jamie Welch

Dawn S. Biedler

Louise C. Keely

Shari A. Wagner

Byrne E. Lovell

Jeff T. Lovell

Vickey J. Lovell

Meg B. Lovell

Helen Havighurst Berk

Ruth Havighurst Neff

Dorothy Havighurst Kucera

James P. Havighurst

Walter M. Havighurst

Charles R. Cross

Catherine F. Cross

John O. Crites, Jr.

Jerald L. Crites

CONTENTS

Preface xi

1 · UNDERSTANDING ADOLESCENCE 1
James F. Adams

2 · THEORIES OF ADOLESCENCE 30
Judith Gallatin

3 · BIOLOGICAL DEVELOPMENT 54
Dorothy H. Eichorn

4 · PSYCHOLOGY AND DEVELOPMENT
OF THE ADOLESCENT SELF 78
Don E. Hamachek

5 · PERSONALITY DEVELOPMENT 110
Harold D. Grotevant

6 · COGNITIVE DEVELOPMENT
IN ADOLESCENCE 135
Jeanette M. Gallagher and Richard S. Mansfield

7 · INDIVIDUAL DIFFERENCES
IN INTELLIGENCE   164
Robert C. Nichols

8 · MORAL DEVELOPMENT
AND MORAL BEHAVIOR   207
Myra Windmiller

9 · SEX ROLE DEVELOPMENT
AND THE ADOLESCENT   229
Aletha Huston-Stein and Renate L. Welch

10 · ADOLESCENT SEXUALITY   262
Carol A. Wagner

11 · EDUCATIONAL INSTITUTIONS
AND YOUTH   308
Lloyd Lovell

12 · SUBCULTURES OF ADOLESCENTS
IN THE UNITED STATES   334
Robert J. Havighurst

13 · PSYCHOLOGICAL PERSPECTIVES ON DRUGS
AND YOUTH   360
Herbert J. Cross and Randall R. Kleinhesselink

14 · CAREER DEVELOPMENT   395
John O. Crites

15 · IN CONCLUSION   421
James F. Adams

Author Index   437
Subject Index   443

PREFACE

Organizing a book on the topic of adolescence is a fascinating as well as a thought-provoking task. Since the first edition of this book in 1968, an increasing awareness of national and international problems has spread throughout the youth culture of the United States (and the world). The priorities of our country continue to be examined as the adults and the youth of today realize that humankind faces the possibility of extinction through the exhaustion of the world's resources (minerals, petroleum, water, etc.). Concern with population and pollution has increased tremendously within the last few years, and we are being asked to balance shortages of energy resources against the public desire to continue to decrease the level of pollution. We have also become aware that the issues of peace and poverty are very directly related to the ecological problems of the world. Adolescents who read the first edition of this book are now, as adults, facing the task of reordering national and world priorities if they wish to salvage an earth that is slowly dying—still largely unnoticed.

Understanding Adolescence was planned for those who are interested in understanding the problems of youth today. It contains a number of chapters that are traditional in nature as well as additional chapters that focus on the immediate present. It is probable that this book could be read, with profit, by any interested and concerned adult; but it has been written, in particular, for individuals who are preparing for their future role of parents, teachers, psychologists, social workers, and, most importantly, responsible citizens.

I am indebted to many individuals who, over the years, have stimulated my interest in adolescence, not the least of whom are my own children, who have moved through adolescence into adulthood (and added another generation to the family—I think I am resisting being called a grandfather) since the first edition of this book. Most young people of the adolescent age group do not like the term *adolescent*. Since there seems to be no other word that describes this age adequately (I once suggested "elderly children"), we will continue to use the term; all the adolescents to whom I have spoken do agree that *understanding* would help. Most of all, I am indebted to the authors who have contributed their work to this book. Many areas of psychology have become too involved for a single person to cover with comprehensiveness and integrity. Whatever merit the book may have will be found in their contributions.

1

UNDERSTANDING ADOLESCENTS

James F. Adams

Adolescence has been considered from a variety of viewpoints. In the main, it has been approached from a consideration of physiological and hormonal development, social influences, economic determination, or emotional development. Often it is considered from a combination of approaches, usually including physiological and hormonal maturation. We know, for example, that puberty (the time when a young person becomes capable of reproduction) usually occurs sometime between the ages of 10 and 15. For some, this period is considered to be the onset of adolescence. Most certainly it is a part of adolescent development.

Historically, one can say the period of adolescence—if it existed at all—frequently was very short in duration. In past centuries, primitive, agrarian, and urban cultures needed the contributions of their youth at a very early age. In these cultures, children went from childhood to the responsibilities of adulthood with scarcely a pause for what we now call adolescence. The short life spans of adults, as well as economic and social pressures, often forced the age of adult responsibility downward.

It is only within the last hundred years or so that adolescence, as a focus of interest and study, has blossomed forth into the literature in great quantities. G. Stanley Hall (Ross, 1972; Gallatin, 1975), at the turn of the twentieth century, launched the increasing flood of research that has continued unabated to the present time. Why, we might ask, has this happened? Perhaps the simplest explanation is that due to increased life spans, technological and industrial developments, and exploding populations, we have much less need for the contributions of our youth. Their contributions to society are no longer economically important. We do not need their sexual reproductive capacities because the world is already overpopulated. In 1974, when many in the United States were talking of having reached zero population growth (at about 220 million), the population actually increased by 1,600,000; and the population of the world passed the 4 billion mark in the middle of 1975 (United Nations, 1974; U.S. Department of Commerce, 1975).

Personal and national decisions with respect to childbearing and immigration, will have a marked impact on the lives of adolescents in the future. Occupational and employment opportunities are directly affected by these decisions. Figure 1.1 shows how the total fertility rate (TFR) in 1978 and a net immigration rate of 1.2 million individuals since 1975 will result in a population of 330 million in the United States in the year 2025 (Option A). It should be obvious that increased attention will need to be fo-

---

James F. Adams is Professor of Psychology at Temple University. In addition to this book and its earlier editions, he has edited or written *Problems in Counseling: A Case Study Approach; Counseling and Guidance: A Summary View;* and *Human Behavior in a Changing Society.* He has also written chapters on adolescence in several encyclopedias and published numerous journal articles on such topics as counseling, adolescent psychology, psychological testing, and the history of psychology.

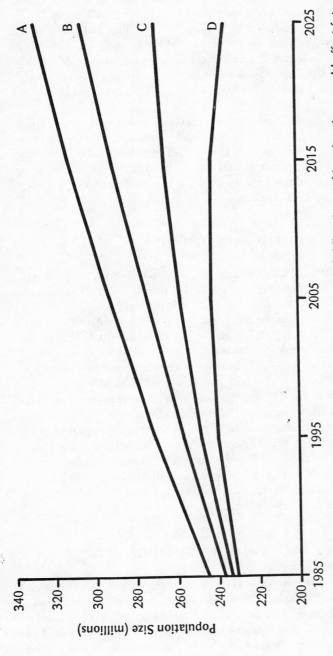

How Many People? Options in this figure show how decisions today, on childbearing and immigration, would affect future population levels. Actual net immigration into the U.S. is not known. There is a net *legal* immigration of 300,000 to 400,000 a year, plus uncounted *illegal* immigrations of hundreds of thousands. **Option A** assumes a total fertility rate (TFR) of 1.8 children per woman (current rate in 1978) and annual net immigration of 1.2 million since 1975. **Option B** assumes a slight increase in childbearing to a TFR of 2.1, plus annual net immigration of 400,000. **Option C** assumes a TFR of 1.8 and annual net immigration of 400,000 since 1975. **Option D** assumes decreased childbearing to a TFR of 1.6 plus a decrease of net immigration to 150,000 by 1985.

Figure 1.1 How Many People Will Be Living in the United States Over the Next 50 Years? *(Source:* Zero Population Growth, Inc., 1346 Connecticut Ave., N. W., Washington, D. C. 20036. Used by permission.)

3

cused on this topic. There is some hopeful evidence (Tsui & Bogue, 1978) that the world's fertility rate is beginning to drop. Between 1968 and 1975, there was a decline from 4.6 to 4.1 births per woman. This is attributed to the impact of family planning on the less developed countries. Assuming this trend continues, Tsui and Bogue project a world population of 5.8 billion by the turn of the century—an optimistic projection as the World Bank estimates 6 billion and the United Nations 6.3 billion (Tsui & Bogue, 1978).

In addition to population increases, mechanization and automation are likely to continue to leave us with vast and increasing reservoirs of unemployed workers. This will extend the period of adolescence for many young people. We have, in short, *created* a prolonged period of adolescence in the industrialized societies of the world. It is the adolescents of our own society who are the topic of this book.

ADOLESCENCE DEFINED

Adolescence can be defined as a holding period in which education, maturation, and waiting are the major tasks to be faced. For this reason, it scarcely seems profitable to define the adolescent period as being tied in with age. Adolescence, as a meaningful concept, is best considered within a broad framework of the total development of the individual. When the child begins to feel less need for the security of familial supervision and protection, when physiological and hormonal development begins to approximate adult maturity, and when psychological maturity moves the child in the direction of becoming responsible in society, adolescence has begun. It should be readily apparent that in using these criteria, individual age differences for determining the onset of adolescence can be expected. It should be equally apparent that the termination of adolescence, for some, may never occur. To be *mature*, defined as being a contributing, relatively self-sufficient member of society, is a goal we all strive for. Some are more successful than others in reaching this goal. These variable years of development are considered the adolescent years.

THE EXPLOSION OF KNOWLEDGE

There was a time when the world was moving along at a reasonably slow pace. The task of growing from childhood to adulthood could be accomplished with temporal leisure. Children had time to be children, and adolescents had their years of development but with few of the pressures they encounter today. We are now faced with this fact of life: Science has moved us forward so fast that our capabilities of adaptation cannot keep up with the pace. While the rate at which knowledge is increasing is difficult to estimate, its acceleration and the accompanying tempo of life have reached frightening speeds.

For children born today, it has been estimated that, by the time they graduate from college, the fund of the world's knowledge will have increased fourfold. When these same children reach 50 years of age, the world's knowledge will have increased 32 times, and 97% of everything known in the world will have been learned since they were born (Toffler, 1970).

My own field of psychology is an excellent example of what is occurring in science as a whole. For the year 1960, the *Psychological Abstracts* listed 8,532 contributions to the psychological literature. By 1970, the total had increased to 21,722; by 1974, 25,558; and by 1978, 26,271. While it would appear that we are reaching a plateau (at least for the time being) of the published research in psychology, it would be no exaggeration to say that if I have some inkling of 10% of what is occurring in my profession, I should consider myself fortunate. It is just impossible for a scientist today to be broadly conversant within his own field of specialization. And when you consider the knowledge coming from related fields, it becomes a Herculean task! Let me give you an interesting example.

AGE OF MENARCHE

The age of menarche is the time at which a girl has her first menstrual period. Escomel in 1939 (cited in Masterson, 1967) described the case of Lina Medina whose onset of menstruation occurred at 9½ *months* and who delivered a 300-gram son by cesarean section at the age of 5 years, 8 months. With rare exceptions such as this, you might expect that the age of menarche would be relatively the same for girls all over the world. In fact, this is not so. The average age of menarche for white girls in the United States is 12.8 (MacMahon, 1974). Contrast this with the average age of 18.0 for the Bundi girls of New Guinea (Malcolm, 1970). Before I attempt to explain this difference of over five years, let me first comment on the sources of information on the topic.

I had rather expected psychologists would be interested in menarche as a stage of human development. A computer search revealed psychological interest focused almost entirely on the lower animals. In identifying the literature, I found myself turning to medical, anthropological, physical educational, and world statistical resources. I identified articles in more than 15 languages and from over 40 countries. The most surprising fact, for me at least, was that many of the scientific disciplines that showed an interest in menarche were relatively unaware of what the other disciplines were doing. Of the over 300 articles I collected, I observed remarkably little cross-referencing or any attempts to explain some rather puzzling findings by turning to the available knowledge from other subject areas. Let us now consider a little of what is known about the age of menarche.

Methods of Research

Research on menarche has been of interest for well over 100 years (Diers, 1974). One method to determine the time of menarche has been to ask mature women to remember the age at which they experienced their first menstrual period. As might be expected, errors in memory make this procedure somewhat suspect. Another way to examine the topic is through a longitudinal approach. Here a number of girls, none of whom have yet menstruated, are followed over a number of years with a record being kept of their first menstruation. One difficulty with this procedure is the length of time it takes. A procedure that avoids these problems is the *Status Quo* method which is evaluated by the means of probit or logit analysis (Finney, 1971). Girls at varying age levels (beginning prior to the expected age of menarche and extending past the expected age of menarche) are asked, "Have you had your first menstrual period?" A line is fitted to the increasing percentages of girls who answer yes. From this line the mean or median age of menarche is computed. Figure 1.2 will give you an indication of the range of ages that have been reported from almost 80 studies from many countries using this method.

Factors Related to the Age of Menarche

A number of different variables may influence the age of menarche. Severe nutritional deprivation would appear to be the best explanation for the delayed age of the Bundi girls (Gajdusek, 1970) although altitude may also be a factor (Wurst, 1962; Valšík, Štukovský & Bernatova, 1963). Girls who live in higher altitudes tend to have a later menarche. Genetic factors play a role; monozygotic (identical) twins' age of menarche is closer than dizygotic (fraternal) twins (Hiernaux, 1972). A frequent finding is that urban girls have an earlier menarche than rural girls (e.g., Attallah, 1978). Climate does not appear to be a factor (Ellis, 1950; Levine, 1953) although it was once thought to be influential. The number of siblings in a family is related to menarcheal age. An only child has an earlier menarche than girls from families with multiple siblings (Roberts, Danskin & Chinn, 1975). It appears that the age of menarche is different between black and white girls in the U.S. MacMahon (1974) has found a mean age for blacks of 12.52 and for whites of 12.8 years. As these figures are representative of almost 23 million girls between the ages of 6 and 17, it is likely they reveal a true dif-

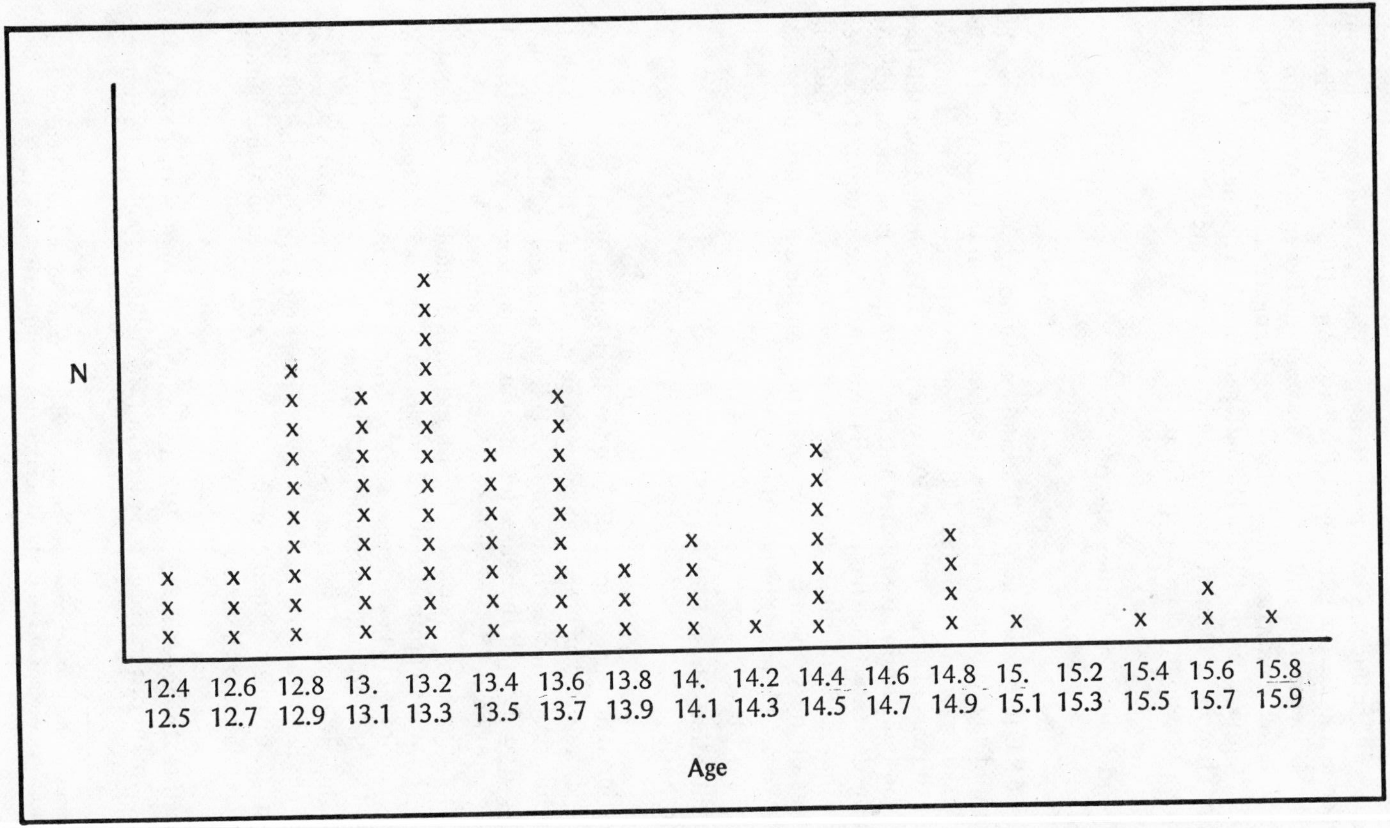

N

12.4 12.6 12.8 13. 13.2 13.4 13.6 13.8 14. 14.2 14.4 14.6 14.8 15. 15.2 15.4 15.6 15.8
12.5 12.7 12.9 13.1 13.3 13.5 13.7 13.9 14.1 14.3 14.5 14.7 14.9 15.1 15.3 15.5 15.7 15.9

Age

Figure 1.2 Age of Menarche Across Cultures.
Note. Includes means and medians (probit and logit analysis) found by the Status Quo Method. Each "x" represents a study.

7

ference. Other findings have been that girls of stouter body build have an earlier menarche than thin girls (Neyzi & Alp, 1975), and girls from a higher socioeconomic status tend to have an earlier menarche than girls from a lower socioeconomic status (Lee, Chang & Chan, 1963; Roberts, Chinn, Girjia & Singh, 1977). This latter finding has not held up in all societies (Jenicek & Demirjian, 1974) which may indicate that factors other than socioeconomic class are involved.

A Trend Toward an Earlier Age of Menarche

One of the interesting and well-documented findings of researchers who have studied menarche is that the age of menarche in industrialized societies has decreased over the last 100 years on the average of about 4 months every 10 years (Tanner, 1968, 1970).[1] Scientists have puzzled over this fact with most attributing it to better nutrition and health care. In considering that the decrease in age has paralleled the industrial revolution, it occurred to me that modern industrial societies may have contributed something in the way of stress which may have an impact on the age of first menstruation. We shall look at this hypothesis next.

A Stimulation-Stress Factor (SSF) Hypothesis

The stimulation-stress factor (SSF) refers to the multiplicity and intensity of the stimuli to which an infant is exposed early in life. It would include such things as crowding, handling, noise, light, and smells—all things that are received through the senses (or the frustration in *not* receiving stimuli when there is a need to organize one's environment—such as the frustration that might be experienced by a blind girl). It should be remembered that SSF can be both pleasant and unpleasant. We would expect the fondling of an infant to be pleasant. The construct of SSF has some similarities to the General Adaptation Syndrome of Hans Selye (Selye, 1976, 1978).

I shall attempt to show that SSF is related to early menarche as well as to the physiological acceleration of several other factors such as height and weight. To do this, we shall examine a sampling of the animal and human research related to the issue.

Supporting Animal Research. It is a common observation that the handling of infant rats increases their weight (McClelland, 1956) and advances

---

[1] Apparently, in a number of countries, this trend has come to an end. There has been no noticeable decrease in age in the United States over the last 30 years.

sexual maturity (Morton, Denenberg & Zarrow, 1963). In addition, rats that are taken from the mother and handled live longer than nonhandled rats when subjected to deprivation of food and water (Weininger, 1956; Denenberg & Karas, 1959; Denenberg, 1962). Levine (1958) has further found that rats that were stressed by handling as pups were better able to handle stress as adults.

I shall mention only one other animal study, one that has resulted in a rather surprising finding. Wilen and Naftolin (1976) have found that Rhesus monkeys have had a decrease in the age of menarche over the last 50 years. Being curious, I called several directors of primate centers to ask if they had been feeding the monkeys better. Their response was that they had not fed monkeys better: decreases in funds had cut down the fresh foods they were able to provide for their colonies. A second question concerning inoculations produced an affirmative answer: blood studies (withdrawing blood via hypodermic needles) and inoculations were on the increase. This latter item will strike a responsive cord for the reader in a few moments.

Supporting Human Research. Moriyama, Kashiwazaki, Takemoto and Suzuki (1977) report that they observed a decrease in the age of menarche in Japan following World War II. We should note that this has occurred in an environment with substantial stress in a post-war recovery period.

In stressful situations, other physiological effects have been observed: Landauer and Whiting (1964) report that in societies where infants have their heads or limbs "repeatedly molded or stretched, or where their ears, noses, or lips were pierced, where they were circumcised, vaccinated, inoculated, or had tribal marks cut or burned in their skin, the mean adult male stature was over two inches greater than in those societies where these customs were not practiced" (p. 1018). Gunders (1961) found that the separation of children from their mother in infancy was associated with greater height. Whiting (1974), again with primitive people, notes that earlier menarche is associated with infant stress. On a related topic, Gunders and Whiting (1968) report that infants born in a hospital (more stress?) have a faster growth rate than infants born at home.

Corah, Anthony, Painter, Stern, and Thurston (1965) report that at the age of 7, children who were anoxic at birth (deprived of oxygen), weigh more and are taller than their controls who had a normal delivery; and, Whiting, Landauer, and Jones (1968) found that the adult stature of individuals inoculated prior to the age of 2 was significantly greater than individuals who had not been inoculated.

Let us look at some other odds and ends of research that begin to make sense if we posit an SSF. Zacharias and Wurtman (1954, 1969) discovered that blind girls have an earlier age of menarche than do sighted girls. Malina and Chumlea (1977) report a similar finding for deaf girls. Spitz (1946) notes that infants in a hospital where they receive a minimum of handling have a mortality rate of 37% whereas the mortality rate for infants who are handled by their mothers or others is zero.

You will also remember that urban girls have an earlier menarche than rural girls. We might expect an urban environment to be more stressful than a rural environment. In addition, an only child has an earlier menarche than girls in a family with multiple siblings. Would you agree that more attention is focused by parents on an only child? One last puzzling finding I shall report to you is that dark-haired girls have a later menarche than do light-haired girls (Bolk, 1926; Ley, 1938). I wonder if it is possible that blond-haired girls receive greater attention because there are fewer of them in many geographical areas.

A Word of Caution. I have spent a considerable amount of time on menarche for several reasons. First, it is an event that has been studied in great detail and it is an important developmental stage in every female's life. Second, it is a good example of how the complexities and disciplinary isolation of scientific areas make communication or the transmission of knowledge difficult. Much of what I have reported continues to be unknown to many of the scientists who are interested in the topic of menarche. Lastly, it is a good example of how hypotheses are formed in science to explain a group of seemingly unrelated facts. And it is at this point that I suggest that you exercise a bit of caution. In hypothesizing a stimulation-stress factor to explain certain facts, I am utilizing a questionable procedure. Because certain factors seemingly go together does *not* necessarily mean that one causes another to occur. To become a more reasonable hypothesis, the SSF needs to be much more thoroughly researched. For example, I would predict in the Corah et al. (1965) study of anoxic infants that the girls in the study would have an earlier age of menarche. The Bolk (1926) and Ley (1938) findings that dark-haired girls have a later menarche than light-haired girls could be checked by observing the reactions of adults and other children to blond-haired girl infants. Do blond-haired children, in fact, receive more attention early in life? Of course, one must also ask if there are better explanations than the SSF to explain the curious reports on the age of menarche?

For now we have spent sufficient time on this one aspect of adolescent development. Next, let us broaden our scope and focus on the adolescent in our modern society.

THE STRESSES OF A MODERN SOCIETY

Adolescents of today, who have not yet reached an age when it is necessary to specialize, who are not being overwhelmed by the vast frontiers of expanding knowledge, and who are not yet forced to earn a living, are still faced with some rather real stresses in our modern world. To make the period even more difficult, the phase is viewed by many adults as a period of maladjustment to home and society. Psychologists and psychiatrists may inadvertently contribute to this view as they call attention to the disturbed young people who pass through their offices. Surprisingly enough, most adolescents make remarkably good adjustments to a frequently difficult environment.

But some young people do exhibit stresses and strains as they are growing up; these young people are the ones magnified by the news media as being the typical product of their times. The image often projected by the media is that all adolescents are having emotional difficulties, are hooked on drugs, or are involved in undemocratic protests with unreasonable requests. It is forgotten that the great majority of young people grow up rather enjoying new experiences and new challenges and presenting few difficulties for their parents and their neighbors. The key to providing an environment within which most young people will reach adulthood with a minimum of stress and strain is *mature understanding*. By this I mean that teachers, concerned adults, or parents should keep a balance on their own emotions as they attempt to be empathic with their adolescents.

I wonder if you have ever stopped to consider that there is no such thing as a professional parent. We are all amateurs in our roles of rearing children. By the time we have learned a little, our children are grown and we have already made our mistakes (and also, we hope, had our triumphs). Reading about the raising of children can prove to be helpful; certainly Spock (1946) has influenced several generations of parents. Although this literature may have been written by experts (educators, physicians, psychiatrists, psychologists, and sociologists), we should remember that when it comes to being parents, we too are amateurs. Rearing one, two, or three children is just as personal with us as it is with you. We share, in spite of our professional training, the same fears, misgivings, joys, and hopes for our children. What we can contribute from our various disciplines is an objectivity about other people's children—not our own. Many of the writers of this book have spent their lives studying and trying to understand children and adolescents. All of us would quickly admit that having our own children has had a humbling effect on our expertise. However, by controlled study and observation, much has been learned that is true with respect to young people in general and occasionally to young people specifically. This knowledge should make you a more intelligent parent, teacher, or adult when it comes to working with or understanding the adolescent. In addition, the same information should provide the adolescent with greater self-understanding. One of the basic needs in growing toward maturity is to discover that many of the concerns you have are shared by others, that many of the difficulties you are encountering have been encountered and solved by others.

Let us turn our discussion to a more personal vein of thought. Let us assume that as a present or future parent you have adolescents in your home. Your children have become more or less independent young adults—adolescents. Day by day you wonder if you have prepared them adequately for the new world they are facing. You find yourself concentrating on many of the minutiae of growing up. You may become suddenly concerned with their table manners (which you, too, have been neglecting), and they, just as suddenly, become totally unconcerned. You find that there are times when they are affectionate and that there are times when they go their own way without seeming to need that closeness that you once had together. As a parent, you try to comfort yourself with some old cliche such as "The love of a parent for a child is the one love that should grow toward separation." It does not help much.

In short, you are a little confused with respect to this new state of affairs. Then you suddenly become acutely aware of teenage problems and they take on a new meaning. You hear of gang wars, drinking, and pot parties (Sadava, 1975). Your adolescents are covering their rooms with posters that imply thinking that you do not entirely understand. A young girl down the street is killed in an automobile accident, and a friend of your son's commits suicide. School grades become more important as the possibility of going to college approaches. You find out that your daughter has been smoking when she is with her friends. A neighbor's 16-year-old girl becomes pregnant (Johnson, 1974; Juhasz, 1974). You read that suicide rates have gone up on college campuses and that boys and girls are living together in the same residence halls. You ask yourself if you have raised your son or daughter to cope with these pressures. You hope that you have, but a strong element of doubt exists in your mind. Guess what? You are a normal parent. It is now that you need that mature understanding mentioned earlier. Let us turn to a consideration of adolescents themselves in an attempt to refresh your memory of what adolescents are all about.

THE ADOLESCENT

Adolescents stand on the threshold of adult responsibility. They are beginning to think for themselves and to question the wisdom of their parents. They find that there are major issues in the destiny of the world with which their parents are relatively unconcerned. They attend a conference on pollution problems and leave the conference more polluted than they found it (Norman, 1971). There is an inconsistency to their behavior that adults do not understand. Sometimes adolescents find that their parents are not very receptive to discussing the issues that concern them; these issues range all the way from environmental destruction to what time they should be home at night. They look at their school and teachers critically. They find that no one in the adult world is perfect, including their parents. Yet their high idealism makes it difficult for them to accept imperfection.

The adolescents find a discrepancy between what they have been taught is right and how people actually conduct themselves. These young people live in a world of high hopes and aspirations (which they have difficulty in meeting themselves), but they find that others, the adults, do not share either their enthusiasm or ideals.

They read such writers as Hesse (1951), Teilhard de Chardin (1969, 1971), and Camus (1961) in an attempt to reach some conclusion about the nature of people (and themselves). Or they may withdraw from any attempt at a reasoned approach to the nature of people in general and seek their own identity with their peers. In either case, they have not found the answers to their questions within their everyday environment.

The Adolescent and Educational Institutions

The adolescent may turn to educational institutions to find the answers. It doesn't take too much of an investigation to find that education might better be called *hedgeucation*. They hear that learning for learning's sake is to be greatly admired; but they observe that what adults are really interested in are grades. They find that educators are great at *hedging* when they ask questions. Democracy, supposedly, should give people freedom to choose their own governments. Why then, they ask, does this country try to enforce its style of living on other countries? Why is supporting corrupt foreign governments more important than eliminating, or at least trying to eliminate, poverty in the United States? Why does their school organize its teaching around the College Boards when it tells its students it is preparing them for enlightened citizenship? What is so important about teaching calculus in the ninth grade? Just what is education anyway?

All their friends are going to college; well, at least most of them. They hear their fathers say, "Where else can they do less harm for four years?" They read that keeping young people in school is important because it keeps them out of the labor market. The counselor tells them that it is important to go to college because they are likely to earn a quarter of a million dollars more in their lifetime (this, by the way, is no longer true). Is this what education is for—to make money? Why can't or won't adults give a straight, honest, meaningful answer? Is it that they have no answer?

I wonder why we are so surprised when adolescents decide to ignore the adult world and build their own peer-group culture. Fortunately for us, many adolescents do not withdraw but work for positive change. Universities throughout the country have felt the impact of concerned students who have insisted on meaningful and relevant education. I think that it would be safe to estimate that 90% of the innovations occurring in higher education in the last 20 years were a direct result of the pressures exerted by students on their institutions. This is not to say that all their efforts have been positive; they, too, have made mistakes. When viewed in retrospect, however, the changes that occurred—frequently with great misgivings on the part of educators—opened up a new era of willingness to change. We now realize that education is a process of change and that youth have given us the stimulus to move out of our conservative positions on topics as varied as grading, government, and curricula.

Personal Concerns of Adolescents

On top of all the foregoing considerations, adolescents also have their own personal concerns. Socially they may be very ill at ease, but they are learning to converse as equals in both an adult and a heterosexual peer world. They wish to be accepted by the girls and boys of their peer group. There is much verbal fencing and trying on of roles for size. Well over one-fourth of adolescents' major problems focus on interpersonal relationships, emotions, growing maturity, and their families. Girls have more problems in these areas than do boys. These problems are well illustrated by Renee Gettys who writes of this period in her development:

> When all my girlfriends started growing noticeably, I was still very small. I, therefore, had a harder time playing games such as "tag" which involved running, hitting or stretching (as in basketball). Although my physical appearance was not as mature as my girlfriends, I too wanted older boyfriends. I had a problem with this however, because I was not as physically mature as my girlfriends and therefore was not considered to be as attractive to the older boys. I was then stuck somewhere in between. The boys my age seemed very unattractive to me and the older boys felt that I was too young. I then stayed away from the parties given by both groups (older and younger males) and was very unhappy for awhile. What made things worse was that I really didn't understand the reasons for my problems. This stage was very uncomfortable for me and a lot of others like me. It is one of those periods where the real problem can really only be worked out by the passing of time. (From a personal communication to the author.)

About the same proportion of problems exist for the adolescent in their school environment, except that there the boys have a greater concentration of difficulties (Adams, 1964). As we consider the personal problems of adolescents, let us bear in mind that we are not emphasizing the *problem* aspect as being the private property of the adolescent. Children and adults also have personal problems. The spotlight is really on those matters that are of *concern* to this age group.

A Focus on Parents

Our adolescent typically finds that the adults (parents being the most important representatives of this group) are strangely reticent to recognize their newly assumed maturity. When they act mature, parents convey to them that they are still children. Adults use a double-barreled shotgun on their adolescents; they point one barrel at them when their behavior is considered childish; they use the other barrel when adolescents are asking for recognition of developing maturity.

I think it is reasonable for the adults to shoulder the burden of understanding. As we learn more about the world of the adolescent, we should be able to aid them better in their transition into the complex adult world. As a function of understanding, we should become more secure and efficient in our desire to help youth whether we are parents, educators, politicians, or concerned adults.

This is not to imply that *understanding* will ever completely insure our feelings of security as adults or parents. Living itself is not a secure proposition at best, and there are no final proven answers to most of the important issues of life.

The Meanings of Words and Concepts

One of my sons introduced me to a book with which I was totally unfamiliar. It is entitled *The Devil's Dictionary* (begun in 1881), by Ambrose Bierce.[2] In our relationships with adolescents (and people in general), his definitions are priceless. Consider the following examples:

Absurdity   A statement or belief manifestly inconsistent with one's own opinion.

Accuse   To affirm another's guilt or unworth; most commonly as a justification of ourselves for having wronged him.

Acknowledge   To confess. Acknowledgment of one another's faults is the highest duty imposed by our love of the truth.

Admonition   Gentle reproof as with a meat-axe. Friendly warning.

Age   That period of life in which we compound for the vices that we still cherish by reviling those that we have no longer the enterprise to commit.

---

[2] Ambrose Bierce, *The Devil's Dictionary* (New York: Hill and Wang, 1957). Used by permission.

Alone   In bad company.

Battle   A method of untying with the teeth a political knot that would not yield to the tongue.

Brain   An apparatus with which we think we think.

Christian   One who believes that the New Testament is a divinely inspired book admirably suited to the spiritual needs of his neighbor.

Comfort   A state of mind produced by contemplation of a neighbor's uneasiness.

Conversation   A fair for the display of the minor mental commodities, each exhibitor being too intent upon the arrangement of his own wares to observe those of his neighbor.

Friendship   A ship big enough to carry two in fair weather, but only one in foul.

Impartial   Unable to perceive any promise of a personal advantage from espousing either side of controversy or adopting either of two conflicting opinions.

Ultimatum   In diplomacy, a last demand before resorting to concessions.

As growth into adulthood occurs, the adolescent finds there is a difference in the way Webster defines words and the way in which they are often used. The adolescent must, sooner or later, learn that the world is a most imperfect place. This task is more difficult for some adolescents than for others. It is particularly difficult when we adults raise our children as if society maintained the principles we teach them. Undoubtedly society would be far worse if we did not raise our children in this manner, but it can be a difficult and embittering process that they go through when they discover that all of life is not based upon love and respect for each other. I am not suggesting that we should teach our children differently, but rather that we inform them of the frailty of human nature while we are encouraging them to live up to their fullest potential, and pointing out their responsibility to leave the world a little better than they found it.

Internalization of Standards

Many of the familial problems, which are of great importance for the adolescent, are a result of conflicts over behavioral standards. Every adult, at one time or another, has had an adolescent object to recommended behavioral principles by saying, "So-'n-so's parents don't make him" (or make her), or, "It isn't fair," or, "Give me a good reason." What they are reflecting is an attempt to cope with one of the most difficult tasks of life, which is, internalizing a set of personal standards that stand at least relatively independent of the influences of society. Consider the words of 15-year-old Debbie Deliere (killed in an automobile accident): "I must reach for a goal

16

reached only by a few, but this makes me an individual. . . . I must make my own decision. I can either continue striving for the goals I place in front of myself, or I can go along with 'The Crowd.' Do what they want and go where they want. But then I am a fake."[3]

We become quite adept in using the psychological mechanisms of rationalization to justify our own unacceptable behaviors. Much of our middle-class society is a society of tranquilizers and sleeping pills, yet we object to our youth compounding our errors with additional drug experimentation—and quite correctly so. Attempting to escape from the realities of life does not make those realities less real or more palatable, and because there are many evils in the world does not mean that we should add to the collection from our own experiences.

Peer Approval. The adolescent has an additional problem: the need for peer approval. As they move into adulthood, they gain much of their security from their companions within their own age group whose standards and behavior are most important to them. If they lose peer approval and sanction, they stand by themselves. This is difficult to do during a period in which they are moving away from the security of the home and in the direction of complete independence. It is quite likely that adolescents will agree that they should have their own standards to live by; that they should stand on their own two feet without parental admonition for support. The uncomfortable fact is that they may yet lack the internal strength to follow their own ideals. It is much easier for an adolescent to say "My parents told me I had to be home by eleven," than it is to say "I think I should be home by eleven." Adults need to exercise tolerance and understanding during this phase. If there has been an overall pattern of mutual trust among family members (Peck, 1958), it is likely that adolescents will be moved in a positive direction by their parents' suggestion.

The Need for Self-Expression

One of the interesting phenomena of our times is the increasing number of adolescents, both male and female, who are turning to prose and poetry as a means of expressing their inner feelings. Writers such as Kahlil Gibran (*The Prophet; Tears and Laughter*) have captured the emotions of young people with the beauty that can be expressed through the written word. Poetry is a medium through which many of the innermost thoughts of youth are revealed. The work of McKuen is an excellent example of this type of poetry (1971, 1972). Adolescents' thoughts portray the way in which they

---

[3] *The San Juan Star,* March 30, 1972, p. 41.

would like the world to be; through their poetry, they ask for understanding. They share their poetry with each other and with interested adults.

Music, frequently at a decibel level that produces adult howls of discomfort, is another mode of expression and sometimes a type of escape from painful reality. The words of today's songs focus on a plea for the positive elements in life, such as peace and human understanding. The protests are against a deviant society, against the establishment, and against the rules that prohibit individuals from "doing their own thing." The musical sounds take adolescents away from their immediate problems and bathe them in an aura of their emotional reactions. Their musical "trips" may become a means of tolerating what they may consider a difficult world.

It is probable that never in the history of the world has more music been produced by so many individuals with so little talent. Talent is not a prerequisite; the ability to express one's self is. Most youth firmly believe that they have the "talent" to become a successful musician. They create their own inner music as they listen to others. They attempt self-expression through music in the same manner as they do through poetry. Individualized music has never been a major part of our culture (as, for example, in Latin countries), but it is rapidly becoming so.

Why this youth movement into poetry and music? I think that there is a sadly simple explanation: We have, by and large, walled youth out from participation within their own society.

In the agricultural societies of the past, individuals were considered adults when they were old enough to till the soil and to marry; that is, when they were economically independent. They participated much more fully within their communities. Today many of our youth are not economically self-sufficient until they reach their twenties, if then. But their minds have been educated, and they grasp the issues that inundate the world. These problems have become so great in magnitude that they are creating desperation within the young (as they should within the old).

There is nothing more frustrating for an adult than to know what is wrong in a situation and yet to be stymied from initiating the solution. If this is true for the adult, think of how much greater magnification the problem assumes in the eyes of youth, for whom patience is a still-to-be-developed virtue.

Developing Sexuality

There are a number of very normal biological needs that are a part of every human being. Most of these needs are satisfied in an unprohibited manner; e.g., no one objects to our breathing, drinking water, eating, or eliminating our waste products. However, when we reach the area of sex, the meeting of needs is not so simple. It is the only biological need for which society claims a restrictive right.

To be fulfilled completely, human sexual needs involve two individuals, both of whom are extremely vulnerable in their interpretations of the meaning of the sexual act. Procreation, which has always been considered a major function of intercourse, is relatively minor when compared with the significance of the emotional communication that should occur in the sexual union. Marriages are seldom satisfactory when there is poor sexual-psychological adjustment. Couples who do not converse meaningfully in their daily contacts become increasingly distant if their sexual contacts become merely an expression of physiological pleasure. Sexual relationships can provide the closest and most meaningful approach to unity that two people will ever experience.

The adolescent's sexual needs cannot be ignored. Sex, like many other human experiences, is a learning experience. Our society has hastened the learning process by the emphasis it places on heterosexual contacts at an early age. If society insists that children learn to dance together in the elementary school, then it should not be surprising when those children become sexually involved during their junior high school or high school years. If we were preparing our youth for meaningful lasting sexual relationships upon graduation from high school, the learning experiences we provide would be admirable. As it is, most of our adolescents must put off marriage, and the responsibilities that should accompany sexual relationships, for a prolonged period of time.

Even more unfortunate is the fact that many adolescents are unable to tolerate the waiting period. They desperately need the human closeness that the sexual experience can provide. The speed with which our industrialized society has developed has removed many of the possibilities for human involvement and companionship available to many of us as we were growing to maturity (Toffler, 1970). The average family in the United States remains in one locality about the same length of time that a student spends in college or in a four-year high school.

In addition to the lack of geographical stability of the average family, the pressures and the frightening realities facing our aware youth as they move toward adult status make a close relationship with at least one other human being almost a necessity. It is scarcely surprising that adolescents turn to their peers of the opposite sex for their emotional and physiological needs. In many respects it may not be desirable, but in every respect it should be understandable. If we want premarital sex to decrease, we must first look toward changing the society that produces the situations that cause the need for the sexual involvement. In addition, we should give adolescents both an intellectual and an emotional understanding of the implications of the sexual relationship.

NATIONAL AND INTERNATIONAL ISSUES
CONCERNING ADOLESCENTS

A number of years ago (Adams, 1963), I canvassed some 4,000 adolescents on their feelings concerning the problems of their country. Approximately two-thirds of their responses focused on the international scene. Our adolescents did not restrict their horizons to the internal problems of the United States, although they were cognizant of these problems. At the time I conducted these studies, I cannot recall one adolescent who mentioned pollution as a problem of major magnitude, and only 1% mentioned the population explosion as a concern. The area of greatest concern had to do with racial tensions, with a minor focus on education, crime, and the economic welfare of the country.

A study conducted during the summer of 1974 by the Grey Marketing and Research Department provides an interesting contrast with my earlier work, although the two studies are by no means similar in design or procedures. This study employed a sample of 400 high school students, chosen to be representative in geographical location and to reflect both the metropolitan and nonmetropolitan composition of the country. In Table 1.1, the responses of these students to the importance of certain social issues are compared with adults' ratings on the same issues.

The number one item of both youth and adults, *corruption in government*, can be explained by the fact that the questions were asked during the summer of 1974 at the height of the Watergate trials. The only discrepancy of three rank orders is found for *pollution of environment*, which was ranked third by youth and sixth by adults. While both youth and adults are concerned with *drug abuse*, it is scarcely surprising that adults view it as a more serious problem. There is really remarkable similarity of the ranks assigned by both adolescents and adults, with perhaps a greater disparity in how strongly they feel about these issues. It is quite obvious that youth and adults are tuned into most, if not all, of the social issues of today. However, as we well know, there is quite a difference between social concern and social action.

An Emerging National Problem: Alcohol and Youth

Little public recognition has been given to a youth problem that is assuming major proportions. The consumption of alcoholic beverages in the youth culture is beginning to skyrocket—largely unnoticed. Apparently adults are so happy to see a decrease in the use of "hard" drugs by youth

TABLE 1.1 *Adolescent and Adult Concern with Social Issues*

ADOLESCENTS			ADULTS	
PERCENT[a]	RANK	SOCIAL ISSUE[b]	PERCENT[a]	RANK
78	1	Corruption in government	83	1
76	2	Crime in streets*	82	3
76	3	Pollution of environment*	69	6
72	4	Drug abuse**	83	2
71	5	Drunk driving	76	5
64	6	Inflation**	82	4
63	7	Energy crisis	65	8
62	8	Alcoholism	67	7
50	9	Racial conflicts	50	10
45	10	Unemployment**	56	9

Note. Adapted from Grey Marketing and Research Department, A strategic study for communication programs on alcohol and highway safety (Washington, D.C.: Office of Pedestrian and Driver Programs, National Highway Traffic Safety Administration, U.S. Department of Transportation, #10300BR606, November, 1974).

[a] Percent rating "extremely" or "very" important.

[b] The authors of this study did not report the numbers of adults who participated; however, if we can assume that they are equal in numbers to the approximately 400 adolescents, rho (the rank order correlation) between the rankings of the adults and adolescents = .82 < .01. Using chi square as a test of homogeneity to determine whether the differences between the percentages of adults and adolescents who rated the items as "Extremely" or "Very" important could have occurred by chance reveals that in those items marked with (*), $p < .05$ and in those items marked with (**), $p < .01$.

that they are not overly concerned with drinking behavior, which they may consider to be more "normal" by adult standards. The Grey Marketing and Research Department study, referred to earlier, reports some rather startling statistics on youth drinking behavior. Fifty percent of the high school youth they surveyed reported that they had been in an alcohol-related situation (ARS) at least one or more times in the previous month. Of this group, 6% reported that they had been drunk at least one time in the past month (19% two or three times and 15% four or more times). In comparing these youth with adults, it is interesting to note that they surpass adults in their consumption of alcohol on any one day in the past week. Eleven percent of ARS adults and 14% of ARS youth reported nine or more drinks on any one day; 28% of ARS adults and 29% of ARS youth reported four to eight drinks.

The ARS youth group is not a fringe element of the youth group in the population but draws from all age, class, and student types. They are somewhat older but 25% are fifteen years of age or younger. There are slightly more males, but four out of ten are females. These students are quite similar to other students in grades and activities.

TABLE 1.2 *Life-Style Portrait of Youth Who Drink versus Youth Who Seldom Drink* [a]

THOSE WHO DRINK ARE HIGHER THAN THOSE WHO SELDOM DRINK ON: (PERCENT HIGHER)		THOSE WHO DRINK ARE LOWER THAN THOSE WHO SELDOM DRINK ON: (PERCENT LOWER)
26	Sociability	
25	Liberalistic	
22	Impulsivity	
14	Autonomy	
12	Aggression	
6	Noninvolvement with people	
5	Family alienation	
1	Hostility	
	Social alienation	1
	Acceptance of social order	3
	Dominance	3
	Need for social recognition	6
	Hopelessness	7
	Supportiveness of friends	11
	Helpfulness to others	13
	Cautiousness	24
	Respect for law	52

Note. Adapted from Grey Marketing and Research Department, A strategic study for communication programs on alcohol and highway safety (Washington, D.C.: Office of Pedestrian and Driver Programs, National Highway Traffic Safety Administration, U.S. Department of Transportation, #10300BR606, November, 1974).

[a] Youth who drink defined as those who consume one or more drinks per month; those who do not drink defined as less than one drink or those who do not drink at all.

Table 1.2 reveals a life-style or personality portrait of ARS youth as compared with non-ARS youth. The authors of the study interpret their findings as follows:

> When compared with the [non-ARS] group, [these] young people tend to be a good deal more social and group oriented. They like to be with a group of their peers in most of their social activities. In terms of their social and civic attitudes, they are more likely to be liberal and permissive and feel their current social environment is overly restrictive and authoritarian in its attitudes toward young people. Their involvement in drinking tends to be very much of a social activity. It is actuated not

so much by antisocial attitudes but rather by their greater degree of impulsivity and desire to experiment with new experiences. Their willingness to do this is reinforced by their greater degree of self-confidence and ability to make their own decisions about what they want to do. With regard to their likelihood of controlling the behavior of other members of their social group, these [ARS] involved high school students display no tendency toward helping or supporting their friends. In this sense, the social group in which they participate is probably not very commitment-oriented and most of the students are reluctant to take the lead in attempting to influence the behavior of others. This is so even in situations which are risky from the standpoint of legal difficulties or actual personal danger to members of the group. (Grey Marketing and Research Department, 1974, pp. 25–26)

Quite aside from the fact that alcohol plays a role in 52% of all highway deaths, the signs of social detachment in these young people are disturbing. Remember that we are discussing *50% of the high-school-age population*. It would appear that alcohol is rapidly replacing "hard" drugs on the youth scene, and the likelihood of abuse in this area should be just as frightening to both youth and adults. The prospect of physical and psychological damage is every bit as real.

I do not think entering into this area legalistically is a realistic solution if we can profit from our experiences in the area of drug abuse. We do need to educate youth on the use and dangers of alcohol and, perhaps more importantly, attempt to remove the impression that drinking makes one an adult. It is unfortunate that our society, in contrast to a Latin culture, for example, seems committed to the notion that alcohol is needed to socialize. In a Latin country, there is no need to have an excuse to socialize, and the use of alcohol (while frequent) is decidedly secondary and kept much more in perspective. It is seen not as a medium for attaining adult status but as a natural part of the social environment that is not denied youth but used in moderation during the growing-up years.

The needed solution to social detachment in young people is to incorporate our youth in a more meaningful way within our family units and within our society.

GREATER INVOLVEMENT OF YOUTH

In the history of our country, the sector of youth involvement has been pitifully small. Our nation has built educational systems that have insured better-educated and more aware young people than can be found in any other nation of the world. Yet we have effectively locked youth out from active participation in the development of those agencies of society with which they are intimately involved. With the major exception of universities, where youth have forced the issue, it would be safe to say that young people have been ignored as a resource that could contribute much in the development of their society.

By ignoring the possibilities of participation by adolescents in their developing years, we have been, as a nation, the losers in two senses: we have not had the benefits of their contributions in their younger years, and we have thereby discouraged their participation in their adult years. Most of us were raised in an era when "children should be seen but not heard." Consider how few of us are now involved in community, state, and national government. Yet all of us complain about the quality of our national leaders and the directions in which they are moving society.

We just cannot fall back on the cliché that age and wisdom are synonymous. There is too much evidence to the contrary. In fact, age tends to produce a desire for stability and a fear of change, regardless of the evils that are perpetuated. Youth are willing to risk, to dare, and to change, and to change again if necesary. Their very impatience is a desirable quality in many instances. I have been continually impressed by the contributions of the young people with whom I have served. While their elders would sit around and discuss the difficulties of needed changes, they would say, "Let's make the change and worry about the difficulties later. We can always try something else if this doesn't work." Of course, not all their ideas were good ideas, but has our record been so much better?

What I am suggesting is that we involve our adolescents in all the meaningful sectors of life, as full-fledged participants wherever possible. They should be represented on school boards, on city councils, and on advisory committees to governors and presidents. They should be strongly represented on most university committees and should be represented on boards of trustees in their colleges. They should be challenged to participate to the fullest possible extent in all the phases of society that touch them personally.

Is there an alternative? Most certainly there is. We can continue to go in the directions we are currently pursuing. We can continue to watch our society and civilization self-destruct. We can continue to watch selfish interest groups in our country destroy our air and water and land. It seems to me that a better alternative is to involve our youth in helping us to change our priorities and to salvage a nation that still has great untapped resources—its youth.

SUMMARY

In our modern industrial society, we have prolonged the period of adolescence due to advanced technologies and uncontrolled population expansion. A thoughtful analysis of what the population of the United States should be has yet to be developed. An increase in the population is likely to prolong the period of adolescence even further as industry continues to use fewer workers to accomplish the same goals. On the world level, the situation would appear to be even more severe: More societies will have unemployed youth in greater and greater numbers.

The age in which our adolescents live is an age that is moving along with amazing speed. Science is developing at a pace that makes it even difficult for scientists to stay abreast of their fields of expertise. I have attempted to illustrate this by presenting a sampling of the vast literature that has accumulated on the topic of menarche. In addition, a stimulation-stress factor hypothesis has been presented in an attempt to explain a number of the curious findings that are cited in the menarche research.

This introductory chapter also gives the reader a look at a number of the developmental problems that adolescents encounter as they move in the direction of maturity. Our adolescents are becoming more aware of the issues facing their society during the same period in which they are solidifying their personal identity. This presents problems where the understanding adult can lend a helping hand. While science has contributed a vast storehouse of knowledge with respect to human maturation, each of us must look within ourselves to find our identities, to find a meaning for our existence. The adolescent seeks answers in different ways: some give up the quest; some withdraw; but the majority wish to make their personal contribution to a better world.

I have suggested that we should involve aware and service-oriented adolescents in all phases of our society. We can ill afford to lose their contributions during their youth, or the training that involvement will provide to our future leaders. In the process, meaning will be added to the adolescent quest for identity. The contributing potentials of the young have never been tapped as a national resource, and we need their energy and assistance channeled into society's development. Giving the 18-year-old the right to vote is not enough; we need to encourage all youth to become involved.

In the remainder of this book, the reader will find topics relevant to an understanding of today's adolescent. Such current topics as moral development, adolescent sexuality, drug abuse, and the problems of adolescent subcultures will be found. In addition, the more traditional topics relating to biological, cognitive, personality, and career development are available. At the conclusion of each chapter, the interested reader will find suggestions for further reading in order to explore each topic in greater depth. Let me also call to your attention the last chapter in the book, a summarizing chapter, in which questions are raised for further thought, consideration, and discussion and should be considered in conjunction with the separate chapters as they are read. It is my hope that you will find your exposure to *Understanding Adolescence* a pleasant one and that you will come away from the experience with an increased appreciation of this important period in life.

SUGGESTIONS FOR FURTHER READING

EDITORS OF HERON HOUSE. *The book of numbers.* New York: A & W Publishers, 1978.

ERIKSON, E. H. *Identity: Youth and crisis.* New York: Norton, 1968.

ESMAN, A. H. (Ed.). *The psychology of adolescence.* New York: International Universities Press, 1975.

GORDON, S. *The sexual adolescent.* Belmont, Calif.: Wadsworth, 1973.

HARTUP, W. W. Adolescent peer relations: A look to the future. In J. P. Hill & F. J. Monks (Eds.), *Adolescence and youth in prospect.* Atlantic Highlands, N.Y.: Humanities Press, 1977.

RASHKIS, H. A:, & TASHJIAN, L. D. *Understanding your parents.* Philadelphia: George F. Stickley, 1978.

BIBLIOGRAPHY

ADAMS, J. F. Adolescent opinions on national problems. *Personnel and Guidance Journal,* 1963, *42,* 497–500.

ADAMS, J. F. Adolescent personal problems as a function of age and sex. *Journal of Genetic Psychology,* 1964, *104,* 207–214.

ATTALLAH, N. L. Age at menarche of schoolgirls in Egypt. *Annals of Human Biology,* 1978, *5,* 185–189.

BIERCE, A. *The devil's dictionary.* New York: Hill & Wang, 1957.

CAMUS, A. *Resistance, rebellion and death.* New York: Knopf, 1961.

BOLK, L. Untersuchungen über die Menarche bei der neiderländischen Bevölkerung. *Zeitschrift für Geburtshülfe und Gynäkologie,* 1926, *89,* 364–380.

CORAH, N. L., ANTHONY, E. J., PAINTER, P., STERN, J. A., & THURSTON, D. Effects of perinatal anoxia after seven years. *Psychological Monographs,* 1965, *79* (Whole No. 596).

DENENBERG, V. H. The effects of early experience. In E. S. E. Hafez (Ed.), *The behavior of domestic animals.* Baltimore: Williams & Wilkins, 1962.

DENENBERG, V. H., & KARAS, G. G. Effects of differential infantile handling upon weight gain and mortality in the rat and mouse. *Science,* 1959, *130,* 629–630.

DIERS, C. J. Historical trends in the age at menarche and menopause. *Psychological Reports,* 1974, *34,* 931–937.

ELLIS, W. B. Age of puberty in the tropics. *British Medical Journal,* 1950, *1,* 85–89.

ESCOMEL, E. La plus jeune mère du monde. *La Presse Medicale,* 1939, *47,* 875.

FINNEY, D. J. *Probit analysis* (3rd ed.). London: Cambridge University Press, 1971.

GAJDUSEK, D. C. Physiological and psychological characteristics of stone age man. *Engineering and Science,* 1970, *33,* No. 6, 26–62.

GALLATIN, J. E. *Adolescence and individuality.* New York: Harper & Row, 1975.

GREY MARKETING AND RESEARCH DEPARTMENT. A strategic study for communication programs on alcohol and highway safety. Washington, D.C.: Office of Pedestrian and Driver Programs, National Highway Traffic Safety Administration, U.S. Department of Transportation, 10300BR606, November, 1974.

GUNDERS, S. M. *The effects of periodic separation from the mother during infancy upon growth and development.* Unpublished doctoral dissertation, Harvard University, 1961.

GUNDERS, S. M. & WHITING, J. W. M. Mother infant separation and physical growth. *Ethnology,* 1968, *7,* 196–206.

HESSE, H. *Siddhartha.* New York: New Directions, 1951.

HIERNAUX, J. Ethnic differences in growth and development. *Eugenics Quarterly,* 1972, *15,* 12–21.

JENICEK, M., & DEMIRJIAN, A. Age of menarche in French Canadian girls. *Annals of Human Biology,* 1974, *1,* 339–346.

JOHNSON, C. L. Attitudes toward premarital sex and family planning for single-never-pregnant teenage girls. *Adolescence,* 1974, *9,* 255–262.

JUHASZ, A. M. The unmarried adolescent parent. *Adolescence,* 1974, *9,* 263–272.

LANDAUER, T. K., & WHITING, J. W. M. Infantile stimulation and adult stature in males. *American Anthropologist,* 1964, *66,* 1007–1028.

LEE, M. M. C., CHANG, K. S. F., and CHAN, M. M. C. Sexual maturation of Chinese girls in Hong Kong. *Pediatrics,* 1963, *32,* 389–398.

LEVINE, S. Noxious stimulation in infant and adult rats and consummatory behavior. *Journal of Comparative and Physiological Psychology,* 1958, *51,* 230–233.

LEVINE, V. E. Studies in physiological anthropology. III. The age of onset of menstruation of the Alaskan Eskimo. *American Journal of Physical Anthropology,* 1953, *11,* 252.

LEY, L. Über die Menarche der Frau un Ihre Bezeihungen zur Pigmentation: Untersuchungen an Schulkindern der Stadt Mainz. *Archiv für Gynäkologie,* 1938, *165,* 489–503.

MACMAHON, B. Age at menarche: United States. *Vital and Health Statistics,* Series 11, No. 133. Washington, D.C.: U.S. Department of Health, Education, and Welfare, 1974.

MALCOLM, L. A. Growth and development of the Bundi child of the New Guinea Highlands. *Human Biology,* 1970, *42,* 292–328.

MALINA, R. M., & CHUMLEA, C. Age at menarche in deaf girls. *Annals of Human Biology,* 1977, *4,* 485–488.

MASTERSON, J. G. True precocious puberty. *Annals of New York Academy of Sciences,* 1967, *42,* 779–782.

McCLELLAND, W. J. Differential handling and weight gain in the albino rat. *Canadian Journal of Psychology,* 1956, *10,* 19–22.

McKUEN, R. *Fields of wonder.* New York: Cheval Books, 1971.

McKUEN, R. *And to each season.* New York: Simon & Schuster, 1972.

MORIYAMA, M., KASHIWAZAKI, H., TAKEMOTO, T., & SUZUKI, T. A secular trend in age at menarche in Sendai city and its surroundings. *Tohoku Journal of Experimental Medicine,* 1977, *123,* 393–394.

MORTON, J. R. C., DENENBERG, V. H., & ZARROW, M. X. Modification of sexual development through stimulation in infancy. *Endocrinology*, 1963, *72*, 439–442.

NEYZI, O., & ALP, H. Relationship between body build and age of menarche in a group of girls of heterogeneous socioeconomic background. *Nutrition Reports International*, 1975, *12*, 27–34.

NORMAN, G. Project survival. In Editors of *Playboy: Project survival.* Chicago: HMH Publishing Co., 1971.

PECK, R. F. Family patterns correlated with adolescent personality structure. *Journal of Abnormal and Social Psychology*, 1958, *57*, 347–350.

ROBERTS, D. F., DANSKIN, M. J., & CHINN, S. Menarcheal age in Northumberland. *Acta Paediatricia Scandinavia*, 1971, *60*, 158–164.

ROBERTS, D. F., CHINN, S., GIRIJA, B., & SINGH, H. D. A study of menarcheal age in India. *Annals of Human Biology*, 1977, *4*, 171–177.

ROSS, D. G. *Stanley Hall: The psychologist as prophet.* Chicago: University of Chicago Press, 1972.

SADAVA, S. W. Research approaches in illicit drug use: A critical review. *Genetic Psychology Monographs*, 1975, *91*, 3–59.

SELYE, H. "They all looked sick to me." *Human Behavior*, February, 1978, 58–63.

SELYE, H. *The stress of life.* New York: McGraw-Hill, 1976.

SPITZ, R. A. Hospitalism: A follow-up report. In Anna Freud (Ed.), *Psychoanalytic study of the child* (Vol. 2). New York: International University Press, 1946.

SPOCK, B. *The commonsense book of baby and child care.* New York: Duell, Sloan & Pearce, 1946.

TANNER, J. M. Earlier maturation in man. *Scientific American*, 1968, *218*, 21–27.

TANNER, J. M. Physical growth. In P. H. Mussen (Ed.), *Carmichael's manual of child psychology* (Vol. 1). New York: Wiley, 1970.

TEILHARD DE CHARDIN, P. *How I believe.* New York: Harper & Row, 1969.

TEILHARD DE CHARDIN, P. *Human energy.* New York: Harcourt, Brace Jovanovich, 1971.

TOFFLER, A. *Future shock.* New York: Random House, 1970.

TSUI, A. A., & BOGUE, D. J. Declining world fertility: Trends, causes, implications. *Population Bulletin:* A publication of the Population Reference Bureau, Inc., 1978, *33* (Whole No. 4).

UNITED NATIONS. *World and regional population prospects.* New York: United Nations, World Population Conference Background Paper, E/CONF. 60/CBP, April 16, 1974.

U.S. DEPARTMENT OF COMMERCE. *News.* Washington, D.C.: Bureau of the Census, Social and Economic Administration, U.S. Department of Commerce, January 1, 1975.

VALŠÍK, J. A., ŠTUKOVSKÝ, R., & BERNATOVA, L. Quelques facteurs géographiques et sociaux ayant une influence sur l'âge de la puberte. *Biotypologie*, 1963, *23*, 109–121.

WEININGER, O. The effects of early experience on behavior and growth characteristics. *Journal of Comparative and Physiological Psychology*, 1956, *49*, 1–9.

WHITING, J. W. M. Menarcheal age and infant stress in humans. In F. A. Beach (Ed.), *Sex and behavior*, Huntington, N.Y.: Robert E. Krieger, 1974.

WHITING, J. W. M., LANDAUER, T. K., & JONES, T. M. Infantile immunization and adult stature. *Child Development*, 1968, *39*, 59–67.

WILEN, R., & NAFTOLIN, F. Age, weight and weight gain in the individual pubertal female rhesus monkey (Macaca mulatta). *Biology of Reproduction*, 1976, *15*, 356–360.

WURST, F. Beruf der Eltern und Wohnstatte in ihren Einfluss auf die körperliche un geistige Entwicklung des Kindes. *Zeitschrift für Ärztliche Fortbildung*, 1962, *55*, 211–214.

ZACHARIAS, L., & WURTMAN, R. J. Blindness: Its relation to age of menarche. *Science*, 1954, *144*, 1154–1155.

ZACHARIAS, L., & WURTMAN, R. J. Blindness and menarche. *Obstetrics and Gynecology*, 1969, *33*, 603–608.

2

THEORIES OF ADOLESCENCE

Judith Gallatin

et's begin this chapter with a brief quiz. Answer yes or no: Is adolescence always a period of storm and stress? When I was teaching psychology of adolescence, I used to include this question in a survey I distributed at the beginning of the semester. Judging from about a decade of experience, I have a hunch that you mentally answered "yes" just now and agreed that adolescence is a period of storm and stress. If you *did* answer "yes," you have lots of company. About two-thirds of my former students said the same thing, and I have to admit that the prevailing image of adolescence is a fairly tempestuous one. Newspapers, TV programs, and how-to-parent books all give you the impression that the typical teenager is a creature to be reckoned with—moody, impulsive, conflict-ridden, and rebellious. As it turns out, a great many professionals agree with this assessment, including those who have devised *theories* of adolescent development.

On the other hand, if you answer "no," you may be in the minority, but you're not necessarily alone. Some experts on the subject don't believe that adolescence is always stormy and stressful. A few even sharply criticize their colleagues for perpetuating a "myth" (Bandura, 1964; Adelson, 1970). In this chapter, I'll be comparing a number of theories on both sides. What I hope you'll gain from my review is a sense of some of the major issues in adolescent psychology.

G. STANLEY HALL'S RECAPITULATION THEORY

G. Stanley Hall is usually given credit for introducing the notion of adolescent turmoil into psychology, and his own life reveals a number of contradictions. Born in 1844 to a poor, rural family he nevertheless managed to have a distinguished career. After taking part of his education in Germany, he returned to the United States, earned the first PhD in psychology ever awarded by an American university, and eventually became the first president of the American Psychological Association.

Hall was unquestionably something of a prude. For example, he rejected Freud's theory of infantile sexuality out of hand. Nonetheless, Hall greatly admired Freud and was instrumental in bringing him to America for his only series of lectures in this country. Also, Hall was a deeply religious man but was also almost entranced with Darwin's theory of evolu-

Judith Gallatin, formerly a professor of psychology at Eastern Michigan University, is currently an author and consultant with Helppie and Gallatin of Portland, Oregon. She is the author or coauthor of *Adolescence and Individuality, Disordered Lives: Abnormal Psychology in Perspective, Adolescent Political Thought,* and *Childhood and Change: Perspectives on Child and Adolescent Development* as well as several articles on the development of political socialization during adolescence.

tion. As a psychologist, Hall wanted to formulate a set of principles that would explain the various stages of human development. Accordingly, he turned to Darwin for assistance. You will see shortly that this passion for Darwin was probably Hall's undoing.

Darwin's influence on Hall was actually mediated by the nineteenth-century biologist, Ernst Haeckel. As you probably know, Darwin speculated that human beings had evolved over millions of years from lower forms of life—apelike, monkeylike, birdlike, reptilelike, all the way down to a probable one-celled organism. Haeckel was responsible for publicizing many of Darwin's ideas, and he also applied the theory of evolution to pre-natal development. He specialized in studying embryos and, on the basis of his work, concluded there was a link between *ontogeny*, the stages that an organism passes through while still in the womb or shell, and *phylogeny*, the stages that the organism's ancestors passed through as they evolved. To put it succinctly, ontogeny was supposed to "recapitulate" phylogeny.

Hall followed Haeckel's lead and took what seemed to be a logical next step, applying Darwin's theory to the *postnatal* development of human beings. The various phases of childhood, Hall reasoned, corresponded to various phases in human evolution. During early infancy, he suggested, children were repeating a "monkeylike" stage in the history of their species. In contrast to this, during the years of middle childhood, they resembled a more advanced but still rather primitive forerunner of civilized people, perhaps a tribe that had managed to support itself through hunting and fishing. And finally adolescence was supposed to repeat a stage midway between savagery and civilization, when the still-primitive human being had begun to fashion the rudiments of a culture.

Indeed, because he believed that adolescence represented a brief repetition of a critical stage in human *evolution,* Hall concluded that adolescence was also the most crucial period in the human *life cycle.* Before puberty, Hall argued, development was more or less automatic. Children would recapitulate the more primitive stages of evolution no matter what anyone did. They were oblivious, Hall asserted, to any outside influences. With adolescents, it was a different story. Because they resembled a "transitional" human being, adolescents were supposed to be more flexible and sensitive than children, more responsive to the various institutions of society.

So impressed was Hall with this theory of adolescence that he published two massive volumes of research on the period, a masterwork entitled *Adolescence: Its Psychology and Its Relations to Physiology, Anthropology, Sociology, Sex, Crime, Religion, and Education* (1904). The book is often cited, but few psychologists have read it from cover to cover, and the title helps to explain why. Hall jumps from topic to topic, reeling off a bewildering array of statistics and pausing frequently to deliver sermons on anything that strikes his fancy.

Nonetheless, *Adolescence* had a substantial impact on adolescent psychology. Since he believed that the teenager was a cross between a savage and a civilized person, Hall characterized adolescence as a period of storm and stress. The adolescent's more primitive impulses and his more humane ones would inevitably come into conflict, Hall reasoned. Or, as the old moralist himself put it, "The forces of sin and those of virtue never struggle so hotly for possession of the youthful soul" (Hall, 1904, II, p. 83). As I have already indicated, this notion of "adolescent turmoil" was readily and widely accepted.

Hall's other, and in my opinion more significant, contributions are less well known. Despite his disorganization, Hall did manage to identify the major aspects of adolescence. A few of the chapter headings in his two-volume study may have a faintly antiquated ring, but most of them— "Growth in Height and Weight," "Sexual Development," "Adolescent Love," "Social Instincts and Institutions," "Intellectual Development and Education," "Juvenile Faults, Immoralities, and Crimes," "Diseases of Body and Mind"—resemble many a modern day textbook. Then, too, Hall included two separate chapters on feminine psychology. His views would not be wildly popular with advocates of Women's Liberation—he believed that "in any ideal community the greatest possible number of women must be devoted to maternity and marriage" (1904, II, p. 576). But he at least recognized that the male and female adolescent developed along rather different lines.

Most important of all, however, Hall viewed adolescence as the period for developing a sense of individuality. The teenage years might be agonizingly stormy and stressful, but they could serve as a kind of rebirth as well. If youngsters were pulled one way by their "baser instincts," they were also becoming aware of their society and culture for the first time. Unlike children, whom Hall likened to a very low form of humanity, adolescents could be educated and molded. They could appreciate art, science, and religion. They were capable of higher feelings. They could reason and be reasoned with. Accordingly, Hall concluded, adolescents were also ready to put their lives into some sort of perspective. Now that they could truly become a part of their culture, they could begin to perceive their place in that culture. Hall remarked, "In adolescence, individuation is suddenly augmented and begins to sense its limits to the race which the Fates prescribe" (1904, II, p. 58).

As we shall see, in attributing this sort of significance to adolescence, Hall anticipated the contemporary theorist Erik Erikson. Unfortunately, Hall's own theory was resoundingly discredited soon after it appeared in print, and some of his more sensitive insights never received the attention they deserved. His failure to organize his material was undoubtedly an important element in his fall from favor. His insistence on linking human development with evolution was another. Edward Thorndike, who was himself to become a leading figure in psychology, exposed the fatal weaknesses in Hall's theory. It was impossible, Thorndike (1904) declared, to explain the behavior of a two-year-old child by claiming that the child was "recapitulating" a monkey-like stage. A two-year-old human being, Thorndike pointed out, already possessed skills that made the child far superior to any near relatives in the animal kingdom. Where, then, was the connection between evolution and human development?

As devastating as such criticisms were, the true cause of Hall's decline was probably more a matter of historical accident than anything else. Hall believed that the course of childhood was fixed by nature and heredity—that it was a kind of passive unfolding. He therefore thought it was perfectly reasonable to concentrate most of his energies as a researcher on adolescence. From his point of view, adolescence was a much more critical period than childhood. Ironically, due to events on both sides of the Atlantic, most psychologists were shortly to conclude just the opposite—childhood came to be viewed as much more important than adolescence! In the United States, John Watson, one of the architects of behaviorism, argued that *environment* rather than heredity was the key force in personality development. Rather than being slaves to their genes, human infants could be influenced and molded from the very first moment of birth, Watson declared, and he performed experiments to prove it. Gallatin (1980) gives a detailed account of these studies. In Vienna, Sigmund Freud, the inventor of psychoanalysis, concluded that sexuality was the most compelling motive in life, and he proceeded to trace the roots of adult sexuality far back into infancy. Eventually, behaviorists and psychoanalysts again became interested in adolescence; but for decades the study of childhood overshadowed the study of adolescence.

THE PSYCHOANALYTIC THEORY OF ADOLESCENT DEVELOPMENT

Oddly enough, despite the fact that Freudians have never been terribly interested in adolescence, their accounts of the period have been much more influential than Hall's. They do, as you may already have gathered, believe adolescence is a less significant stage than childhood—and their conviction forces me to back up just a bit at this point. Without knowing something about the psychoanalytic theory of childhood, you can't understand the psychoanalytic theory of adolescence.

According to Freud, as I've noted, sexuality is the dominant motive in life. He pictured the human infant as a virtual bundle of sexual impulses. These drives (Freud referred to them in a kind of theoretical shorthand as the *id*) emerge in sequence in a series of *psychosexual stages*. During the first of these, the oral stage, children are supposed to be concerned primarily with activities like eating and sucking, activities that will later be translated into erotic pursuits like kissing. This stage gives way to another in which anal impulses predominate, and finally, around the age of three or so, children allegedly enter into the phallic period. During this third phase of infantile sexuality, children are supposed to focus upon their genitals and become preoccupied with the pleasure they provide. As a related development, children are also supposed to become strongly attached to the parent of the opposite sex and to begin harboring feelings of hostility toward the parent of the same sex. Indeed, Freud theorized that at the height of this "Oedipus complex," the little boy actually wants to do away with his father and have his mother exclusively to himself, the converse being true for the little girl.

Such wishes are, of course, doomed to disappointment, and more than that, they create a dreadful conflict for the child. Finally, because of the child's fear that he or she will be severely punished for these intentions (the little boy is supposed to grow especially concerned about being castrated), the child represses Oedipal conflicts, banishing them from awareness and entering into a relatively tranquil period of "latency." Freud admitted (1924, 1931) that his account applied more often to boys than to girls.

In the psychoanalytic scheme of things, latency takes up the years between ages 5 or 6 and 12. Its comparative peace and quiet are abruptly shattered by the approach of puberty, and the youngster enters into adolescence with all the sexual conflicts of early childhood threatening to erupt once again. The physiological changes associated with puberty strain the defenses that adolescents have erected against their own sexuality, and the result is a great deal of storm and stress.

Here you may have detected a certain similarity between Hall's account of adolescence and the psychoanalytic version. Both employ the principle of recapitulation to explain the turmoil of the teenage years. However, Hall thought that adolescent storm and stress resulted from the repetition of a critical stage in human evolution, whereas psychoanalytic theory points instead to the resurgence of infantile sexuality.

I think you can now understand why Freud himself largely neglected adolescence. He assumed that the conflicts of early childhood reappeared at puberty—but obviously, if the adolescent's conflicts simply mirrored those of infancy, then adolescence itself could not be a very important period of development. Indeed, if it had not been for Anna Freud, Sigmund Freud's daughter, psychoanalytic theory might never have had much to say about adolescence. As it happens, Anna Freud did manage to modify the psychoanalytic position somewhat.

Although Anna Freud (1936, 1958) agrees that the experiences of early childhood have far more impact upon the adult personality than those of adolescence, she nonetheless believes that puberty ushers in some notable adjustments. There is a difference, she insists, between the problems the teenager must cope with and the dilemmas that confront the small child. If children get into difficulties, she observes, it is usually because they have collided with their parents on some point. Children repress their Oedipal fantasies, for example, chiefly because they are afraid something dreadful will happen to them if they do not. For adolescents, the conflict is much more highly *internalized*. To be sure, adolescents know they may be punished for giving into their newly aroused sexual impulses, but they have also learned to feel guilty about these impulses. Furthermore, Anna Freud admits, adolescents *do* have to overcome their childhood inhibitions about sex to some extent. The culture may pressure them to exercise restraint, but they will be adults one day after all. And as adults they can enjoy a degree of sexual gratification—even if they have to wait until they are out of their teens and safely married.

In contrast to small children, adolescents must gradually undo some of their previous training and figure out how to satisfy their sexual impulses without offending public morality. This isn't exactly an easy task, according to Anna Freud. Throughout the long years of latency, youngsters have had a tight rein on their sexual drives. When these drives erupt again at puberty, the adolescent must find some new and novel ways of defending against them. Perhaps the most obvious way young people can protect themselves against temptation is by repudiating *all* of life's pleasures. Freud notes that there are adolescents who pass through a distinctly *ascetic* phase, denying themselves any form of enjoyment because anything pleasurable has somehow acquired sexual connotations.

Teenagers may also try to gain distance from their inner conflicts by *intellectualizing* them. Some adolescents, Anna Freud remarks (1936, p. 159), appear to perform truly astonishing feats of intelligence:

> They will argue the case for free love or marriage and the family life, a free-lance existence or the adoption of a profession, roving or settling down, or discuss philosophical problems such as religion or free thought, or different political systems, such as revolution versus submission to authority or friendship in all of its forms.

Closer examination reveals that these flashes of brilliance are "defensive" rather than genuine. The issues that adolescents have suddenly become so fond of debating *represent opposing sides of their own internal conflicts,* disguised and raised to an intellectual plane. "Once more," Anna Freud declares, "the point at issue is how to relate the instinctual side of human nature to the rest of life, how to decide between putting sexual impulses into practice and renouncing them, between liberty and restraint, between revolt against and submission to authority" (1936, p. 161). By casting this struggle in the form of a philosophical argument, youngsters avoid having to face their sexual conflicts directly—and not so incidentally avoid feeling a lot of guilt and anxiety as well.

Finally, as a third defensive measure, adolescence is supposed to be marked by some startling changes in *identification.* During the early infantile period, children allegedly resolve their Oedipal conflicts by identifying with their parents, particularly the parent of the same sex. Instead of opposing and competing with his father—a hazardous undertaking in view of the father's superior strength and size—the little boy tries to imitate him, a maneuver that permits the child to gain some control over his feelings of guilt and hostility. Although the details are fuzzier, the little girl is supposed to identify with her mother, too. In any case, the resurgence of infantile sexuality during adolescence creates fresh problems for teenagers and their parents. When the sexual drives make their second entrance on the scene at puberty, it is thought that the youngster starts to experience desire once again for the parent of the opposite sex and begins to resent the parent of the same sex.

The safest way for an adolescent to insulate himself from these forbidden fantasies, Anna Freud suggests, is to withdraw emotionally from his mother and father. "From this time on," she observes, "he will live with the members of his family as though with strangers" (1936, p. 166). But the parents have, after all, been a major source of support and affection throughout childhood, so breaking with them leaves youngsters feeling depressed and empty. They need new relationships to replace what they have lost, and consequently, they begin to look outside the family, hoping to find other people with whom to identify. For most youngsters, this search is supposed to be somewhat frantic. According to Anna Freud, they flit from friendship to friendship and crush to crush, transforming today's bosom buddy into tomorrow's pet enemy. Such flightiness is only to be expected, she insists, it is merely another outward sign of the conflict and upheaval that are occurring within. Indeed, Freud is quite emphatic on this point. She believes (1958) that turmoil is an inevitable and *necessary* part of adolescence. Without it, she declares, the youngster cannot make the adjustments required to become a mature adult.

As I've noted, this characterization of adolescence, with all its drama and romance, is the accepted one. It seems to be almost as popular today with psychologists as it is with the media and the lay public. Theorists from a wide variety of backgrounds (learning theory, interpersonal theory, Lewinian theory, cultural anthropology) assume that the adolescent (the American adolescent, at least) undergoes severe storm and stress while making the transition to adulthood. The *explanations* may differ, but the assumptions are really fairly similar.

A LEARNING THEORY APPROACH TO
ADOLESCENCE

McCandless (1970) has attempted to apply the principles of social learning theory to adolescent development. Although he warns his audience not to be too carried away by the notion of storm and stress, his description of adolescence is still not too different from Anna Freud's or G. Stanley Hall's.

McCandless assumes that human behavior is governed by drives. Like the Freudians, he believes that sexuality is an important force in life, but he also identifies a number of other influences, namely frustration and aggression, anxiety, curiosity, and dependence. It is not clear, McCandless admits, whether these drives are learned or innate, but all of them serve to energize people and help them *select* and *direct* their behavior. All of these drives are also certainly affected by learning. Human beings learn to recognize cues that tell them whether they are feeling aggressive, anxious, curious, dependent, or sexy. By a process of trial and error, they also discover which behaviors will satisfy a particular drive (the selective function of drive) and how to pursue those behaviors (the directive function).

In McCandless's opinion, teenagers undergo considerable strain during adolescence because of the way in which the culture handles a number of these drives. For instance, adolescents (particularly adolescent males, according to McCandless) experience a heightened level of sexual drive because of the biological changes that accompany puberty. However, McCandless observes, our society does very little to help them select the appropriate outlets for this drive. If anything, it discourages them from seeking direct satisfaction. To be sure, the culture looks the other way a bit more for boys than it does for girls, but youngsters of both sexes are generally encouraged to refrain from sexual activity until they are married (or at least out of their teens). That the expectation of our culture is not fulfilled, is amply demonstrated in Wagner's chapter on sexual development.

Dependency can be an equally troublesome drive during adolescence—although for somewhat different reasons. Children are encouraged to develop a degree of dependency on adults: parents, teachers, clergy, what have you. However, at adolescence, youngsters begin to be confronted by some rather contradictory demands. The same culture that has promoted their dependency now expects them to become increasingly *independent* and autonomous, presumably so that they can assume the responsibilities that accompany adulthood. Once again, McCandless suggests that boys may suffer more cross-pressures on this account than girls do. But in any case, when either of these drives (sex or dependency) is thwarted, the adolescent is likely to experience a certain amount of stress (what McCandless calls "a heightening of the anxiety drive").

The Concept of Discontinuity

Hall, Freud, and McCandless might explain adolescent turmoil a little differently, but by now I think you can begin to detect a common theme. For all three theorists, the watchword seems to be *discontinuity*. In Hall's view, adolescence is turbulent because it signals a sharp break with childhood. It is a period of unique sensibilities and equally unique temptations. Anna Freud points to the clash between the adolescent's newly awakened sexual impulses and the guilt that has become associated with them. And McCandless, as we have just seen, emphasizes the contradiction between the teenagers' previous learning and the new expectations that society has suddenly imposed on them. Indeed, most theories that portray adolescence as a period of storm and stress contain some variant of the discontinuity theme.

SULLIVAN'S INTERPERSONAL THEORY

Sullivan's is undoubtedly one of the most interesting and also most neglected of the theories discussed in this chapter. Although he was much influenced by psychoanalysis, Sullivan eventually grew disenchanted with it. Psychoanalytic theory, he decided, placed far too much emphasis on sex. On the basis of his work with severely disturbed patients, Sullivan concluded that the *satisfaction of certain interpersonal needs* was more important. What human beings seek more than anything else, Sullivan declares (1953a, 1953b), is security, and he describes this craving for security as "the need to be free of anxiety."

Anxiety arises almost inevitably out of the initial dependence and helplessness of human infants. Because they must rely so much on other people for survival and well-being, the infants are peculiarly sensitive to the moods and general attitudes of others. Sooner or later, Sullivan suggests, the person caring for the child, most likely the mother, becomes upset about something and, in a mysterious, nonverbal way, communicates these feelings. Perhaps it has to do with the way a mother touches; perhaps it is a change in a father's expression, but, whatever the cause, the infant senses that something is drastically wrong and experiences the profoundly unpleasant emotion called anxiety. This feeling is so dreadful that the infant will do almost anything to escape it. Infants quickly learn that certain of their own activities provoke responses from a parent that in turn will make the infant anxious. As a consequence, they learn to refrain from those activities as a way of avoiding anxiety.

As dissatisfied as he may have been with psychoanalytic theory, Sullivan recognized that in American society the infant's *sexual* activities were particularly likely to provoke anxiety. In many households, he notes (1953a), the mother discovers her supposedly innocent little baby boy playing with himself (often before he has even outgrown his cradle), and she is horrified by what she sees. She communicates her displeasure to the infant, thereby encouraging him to develop a kind of "phobia" about sex.

The easiest way for children to avoid feeling anxious about sexual matters is to avoid having anything to do with them in the first place. Consequently, they lose touch with their own sexuality. This sets the scene for some terrific "collisions between needs" during adolescence. Sooner or later, every youngster undergoes puberty and is made aware, whether they like it or not, of their genitals. The genitals, in fact, become the source of intense pleasure, and sexual release becomes a powerful motive in its own right. However, since the adolescent has acquired so many inhibitions about sex, this need to be free of anxiety clashes painfully with the need to satisfy what Sullivan calls the "lust dynamism."

To make matters worse, adolescents begin to perceive that they are expected (eventually at least) to form an intimate relationship with a person of the opposite sex—and that the genitals, formerly the source of so much anxiety, are supposed to figure prominently in this relationship. To compound the problem still further, all sorts of stereotypes about people of the opposite sex are acquired, which leaves one not *knowing* how to relate to them. And as a final complication, parents, who may have left their adolescents alone to some extent while they were still just interested in same-sex friends, will probably decide to get into the act. Because of their *own* anxieties, parents have a tendency to respond rather harshly if their teenager shows any signs of preoccupation with the opposite sex:

> One of the most potent instruments used in this particular is ridicule; many an adolescent has been ridiculed practically into very severe anxiety by parents who just do not want him to become, as they think of it, an adult interested in such things as sex, which may get him diseased or what not, or may result in marriage and his leaving home. (Sullivan, 1953b, p. 268)

Nor can teenagers relieve their tensions by steering clear of the opposite sex and trying to satisfy their "lustful feelings" on their own. According to Sullivan, American society disapproves of this kind of behavior too:

> Now this activity, commonly called masturbation, has in general been rather severely condemned in every culture that generally imposes marked restrictions on freedom of sexual development. That's very neat, you see; it means that adolescence is going to be hell whatever you do, unless you have wonderful preparation for being different—in which case you may get into trouble for being different. (1953b, p. 270)

Interestingly enough, just like the other theorists we have discussed so far, Sullivan observes that this account applies better to boys than to girls. In fact, he admits quite candidly that he knows very little about female adolescents.

LEWIN'S FIELD THEORY

At the risk of becoming repetitious, I should also point out that Kurt Lewin's (1939) field theory is often included among the "storm and stress" or "discontinuity" theories of adolescent development. What we observe as behavior, Lewin claims, is actually the result of *interactions* between people and their respective environments. There are, he suggests, a vast array of personal factors (e.g., age, intelligence, specific talents, sex) and environmental factors (e.g., family relationships, neighborhood friends, authorities) to take into account. All of these interacting factors make up what is called the *life space*. Within this life space, people identify various goals or valences, some of which are positive and attract them, others of which are negative and repel them.

During infancy, the life space is rather simple and the goals and valences are few. However, as human beings mature and add to their store of experiences, their life space becomes differentiated into more and more separate *regions,* and it is up to each individual to organize and make sense of them all. The personal and environmental factors in an individual's life space do not remain stationary; they are obviously in a constant state of flux. When they change gradually, organizing and integrating them is not an unduly demanding task. However, Lewin believes that during periods of rapid change, people undergo considerable stress, and he considers adolescence to be just such a period. Suddenly and without warning, teenagers are compelled to cope with a host of physical changes and are confronted with a new set of expectations and demands. They outgrow their clothes at an astonishing rate, they experience puberty, and they begin to perceive the necessity for formulating a set of life goals. These changes alone would produce a good deal of discontinuity during adolescence.

To complicate matters still further, there are other sources of strain. Lewin believes that during adolescence the life space becomes distorted. Teenagers find themselves between two worlds, "marginal" human beings, so to speak. There is no simple and direct connection between the behaviors they have learned in childhood and those they will engage in as adults. As teenagers, they can no longer pout, whine, and cling. But neither can they console themselves with "adult activities" like drinking, driving, sexual relations, or even holding down a full-time job—at least not until relatively late in adolescence. They are forced to give up the goals and valences of childhood before they can really "locomote" toward those of adulthood; and the resulting dislocation makes for considerable conflict and stress.

ANTHROPOLOGICAL THEORY

Anthropologists have also theorized about adolescent development, and many of them have displayed a certain fondness for the "discontinuity hypothesis." Margaret Mead is perhaps the best known member of this group, and she seems, at first glance, to be a rather unlikely candidate. Mead (1928) created something of a stir when she first published her research on Samoan culture. One of her more striking conclusions was the suggestion that adolescence needn't *always* be a period of storm and stress. She claimed that the Samoan girls she had observed appeared to pass through adolescence placidly and unperturbed:

> With the exception of a few cases . . . adolescence represented no period of crisis or stress, but was instead an orderly developing of a set of slowly maturing interests and activities. The girls' minds were perplexed by no conflicts, troubled by no philosophical inquiries, beset by no remote ambitions. To live as a girl with many lovers as long as possible and then to marry in one's own village and have many children, these were uniform and satisfying ambitions. (Mead, 1961, p. 120)

Mead's assessment of American youngsters was quite different, however. American youngsters, she conceded, *did* experience great stress during adolescence. Why the contrast? Mead's explanation touches upon some themes that by now will be all too familiar to you. In Samoa, she asserts, taboos on sexual behavior are largely absent. Youngsters learn about sex early in childhood, and they are not expected to refrain from sexual activity before marriage. American teenagers, on the other hand, have been encouraged to inhibit their sexuality and to refrain from sexual activity even after they reach puberty. Thus, their awakening sexual feelings inevitably clash (i.e., become discontinuous) with prevailing cultural standards, and the equally inevitable result is storm and stress. Another anthropologist who expresses much the same view is Ruth Benedict (1954).

A Resumé

This might be a good place to stop and take stock. What conclusions can we draw at this point? As I've been hinting all along, it's obvious that a good many theorists regard adolescence as a period of turmoil, and I should add that my review hasn't been exhaustive by any means. I could have brought a number of other theorists—Remplein, Gesell, Kroh, Barker—into the picture. Virtually all of them employ some variant of what I've been calling the *discontinuity hypothesis,* and all of them point to puberty (or rather the sexual feelings that accompany puberty) as a major source of conflict. Some theorists also cite other features of adolescence to explain the alleged agonies of the American teenager: contradictory expectations, inconsistent learning, ambiguities of status, and so forth.

The Clash Between Theory and Data

Now for the surprise. When it comes to studying adolescent development, we can uncover plenty of discontinuity all right, but it's mainly a discontinuity between *theory* and *fact.* It amazes me that so many theories portray adolescence as a period of storm and stress when there is so little evidence to support this point of view. Of course, research on the subject is not exactly abundant, but the existing studies suggest that storm and stress during adolescence is the exception rather than the norm. Researchers who have actually talked to teenagers (Bandura & Walters, 1959; Douvan & Adelson, 1966; Offer, 1969; Offer & Offer, 1975) agree that adolescence may be a period of considerable readjustment, but they reject the notion that it is always turbulent. More or less normal teenagers, it turns out, do not experience profound inner turmoil, do not hate their parents, and do not stage wholesale rebellions against society. Furthermore, youngsters who do become disturbed have some fairly good reasons for feeling distressed. Their families are typically just as stormy and conflict-ridden as they are (Weiner, 1970; Jacobs, 1971; Offer & Offer, 1975; Gallatin, 1980). In the face of such findings, it's no wonder that Adelson (1964, 1970) describes the whole idea of adolescent storm and stress as a myth.

If these findings are valid (and I'm strongly inclined to accept them), we have another problem on our hands. Are there theorists who portray adolescence as something other than a period of turbulence and turmoil? Fortunately for the field, I believe we can locate several.

PIAGET'S COGNITIVE THEORY

Some people might disagree with me, but I think Piaget belongs in the "anti-storm and stress" camp. Unlike most of the theorists we have considered so far, Piaget concentrates on a single aspect of human life: the "growth of intelligence." In so doing, he has devised an enormously influential theory of cognitive development; and you may wish to read chapter 6 by Gallagher and Mansfield for a more detailed discussion of Piaget's contributions.

43

Piaget asserts that intelligence unfolds in four distinct phases between childhood and adolescence. During the first of these, the sensorimotor stage, children display a type of thinking that is notably limited and primitive. Although they are acquiring numerous basic skills, the only mental problems they can solve are those which can be acted out bodily (hence the term *sensorimotor*). This phase is followed by an intuitive stage, which lasts roughly from the ages of two to seven. During the intuitive stage, children make a major advance: they learn to speak and can now communicate and reason much more efficiently. However, they still have a tendency to approach problems "intuitively," rather than puzzling them out systematically. Unaware of certain principles of constancy, they judge situations by the *look of things*. For example, during the intuitive stage, children will say that you can alter the amount of clay in a particular lump simply by changing its shape.

In contrast to this, when children enter the third phase of mental development, the stage of concrete operations, they have a much better understanding of what Piaget calls "conservation of mass." They recognize that as long as you don't add or subtract anything to it, a lump contains the same amount of clay, no matter what you do to its shape. However, children who have attained the stage of concrete operations are still limited in some respects. When confronted with a complex puzzle, they have difficulty envisioning *all* the possible solutions and may "get stuck" on one or two strategies. Indeed, the ability to ponder and weigh various alternatives is one of the hallmarks of the fourth and final phase of cognitive development, the stage of formal operations. Only during this stage, at age twelve or so, do youngsters begin to evaluate problems in a truly systematic manner.

For our purposes, the most significant aspect of Piaget's theory is his belief that the capacity for formal thought develops *gradually* rather than abruptly. This highest form of mental activity, he declares, appears at the beginning of adolescence and represents a logical extension of the previous stages:

> The eruption of this new kind of thinking in the form of general ideas and abstract constructions, is actually much less sudden than it would seem. It develops in relatively continuous fashion from the concrete thinking of middle childhood. The turning point occurs at about the age of twelve, after which there is rapid progress in the direction of free reflection no longer directly attached to external reality. (1967, p. 61)

Given Piaget's position on cognitive development, namely that it is a comparatively smooth, continuous process, I think we can assume that he would take a similar stand on the issue of adolescent turmoil. I suspect he would reject the view that adolescence absolutely *has* to be a time of great storm and stress. You certainly don't get the impression from his description of cognitive development that adolescence is the least bit more turbulent than any other period of life.

LEARNING THEORY REVISITED

A more obvious example of the "anti-storm and stress" school is Albert Bandura (1964). Like McCandless, Bandura is basically a social learning theorist. Unlike McCandless, he objects to the concept of adolescent turmoil. On the basis of his own research, he concludes that teenagers who come from stable, loving families (and he seems to believe that such families are in the majority) have a relatively easy time during adolescence. By the time they reach puberty, Bandura insists, such youngsters have been so well socialized, i.e., "reinforced" so often for conforming and conventional behavior, that even sex does not present much of a problem. Normal teenagers may express some anxiety about the whole matter and wish they had more reliable information, but most identify readily with their parents' (often restrictive) standards of conduct (see chapter 4).

Youngsters who do experience turmoil during adolescence—and Bandura acknowledges that there are some—are said to be "poorly socialized." An aggressive young troublemaker is not simply suffering normal growing pains but is instead a victim of faulty learning habits. His parents have not provided him with the proper training. As proof, Bandura notes that the aggressive teenagers in his study (Bandura & Walters, 1959) invariably came from unstable and conflict-ridden homes, homes in which fights and arguments were lamentably common.

SPRANGER'S GEISTESWISSENSCHAFTLICHE THEORY OF ADOLESCENCE

Eduard Spranger (1955) is another theorist who deserves to be brought into the controversy over adolescent storm and stress. Spranger was a German psychologist and his most important work has apparently not been translated into English. Fortunately, Muuss (1975) has included Spranger in his anthology and provides us with a competent summary of his theory. According to Muuss, Spranger was a disciple of the German philosopher, Dilthey, a man who held the rather interesting view that psychology was not a "true science." This, incidentally, is the origin of the somewhat ponderous German term *geisteswissenschaft*, which means, translated very literally, "thought science." Because each human being is unique in at least some respects, Dilthey claimed, psychology could not hope to formulate laws of cause and effect like the ones found in physics. With so many different human types, psychologists could not possibly outline a set of principles that would account for every separate person's behavior.

Spranger incorporated this concept of human uniqueness into his theory of adolescent development, and it shows up prominently when he turns to the issue of storm and stress. Must adolescence be turbulent? In answering this question, Spranger advances a theory of *individual variability*. He identifies three patterns of growth that may emerge during adolescence. Youngsters who follow the first pattern are afflicted with the by now familiar (and controversial) storm and stress. For them, the transition from childhood to adulthood is every bit as painful (and romantic) as popular writers have described it. On the other hand, there are youngsters who pass through adolescence largely unscathed, and their adolescence is representative of a slow, continuous pattern of development. These teenagers move quietly and peacefully into adult life without visible signs of conflict or distress. Finally, there is a pattern that seems to be a cross between the other two, a kind of dynamic variation. Adolescents who display this pattern of growth participate directly in their own development. They may experience crises but they overcome them by consciously and actively trying to master them. In short, Spranger believes that adolescence may or may not be stressful, depending on the *type* of young person under consideration.

Interestingly enough, some recent research findings provide tentative support for this theory. In a follow-up study of his original research with adolescent boys (1969), Offer (1975) concludes that there are basically three developmental routes through adolescence: *continuous growth, surgent growth*, and *tumultuous growth*. I scarcely need to point out that the resemblance to Spranger's theoretical model is quite striking.

ERIKSON'S PSYCHOSOCIAL THEORY

Another theory that has no difficulty accommodating the actual research on adolescence is Erik Erikson's. As I have indicated elsewhere (Gallatin, 1975), I believe that Erikson's theory of adolescent development is the most comprehensive yet devised. Since his work is extremely well known, you may already be familiar with his concept of *identity crisis*. But I sometimes worry that his great popularity may have obscured his most important contributions to adolescent psychology.

Like Sullivan, Erikson was originally trained as a psychoanalyst and, also like Sullivan, he has attempted to modify Freudian theory. However, his reworking of Freudian theory has been less radical, which may explain why he has been more widely accepted than Sullivan.

Erikson's initial encounters with psychoanalysis were notably intimate and direct. While he was in his mid-twenties, an old friend of his, Peter

Blos, invited him to Vienna, the center of Freudian thought. A new school was being established, one that would operate according to psychoanalytic principles, and Erikson was asked if he might be interested in teaching there.

Erikson accepted the position and almost at once began to come into contact with some of the leading lights of psychoanalysis, among them Anna Freud. She was in fact so impressed with Erikson that she encouraged him to become an analyst and she herself served as his training therapist.

Subsequently, Erikson emigrated to the United States, set up a practice and eventually joined the faculties of several distinguished universities. In the late 1930s he took a number of field trips with a close friend of his who was an anthropologist, and during World War II he was a consultant to the American armed forces. Both of these experiences convinced him that psychoanalytic theory was too restrictive in some respects, and he set about to revise it. The *psychosocial* theory that he formulated places special emphasis on adolescence. It also resembles all the other theories we have reviewed, including G. Stanley Hall's.

Like Sullivan, Erikson concluded that psychoanalysis concentrated too much on infantile sexuality. Instead of discarding the concept, however, he enlarged it. During infancy, Erikson observes, children are indeed bent upon satisfying certain psychosexual impulses, but these impulses are only part of a much broader picture. They are important in their own right, but they also reflect various *modalities*—ways of interacting with the outside world. To give you an example, Erikson agrees that during what Freud called the oral phase, children are intensely preoccupied with obtaining oral gratification. Eating, sucking, biting and the like are all unquestionably significant activities. However, says Erikson, look at all the other things children are up to during this stage. They seem, he notes, to be relating to the world in an "oral" manner—"drinking in" a great many perceptions, "absorbing" a host of tactile sensations, visual images, noises, and smells. Their orality, then, reflects a general attitude of passivity and receptiveness, a willingness to "take in." Of course, in recognizing drives other than the purely sexual ones, Erikson resembles the social learning theorists, McCandless and Bandura.

The Concept of Nuclear Conflict

Because they are so helpless and dependent during early infancy, children are confronted with a rather specific developmental challenge—what Erikson calls a *nuclear conflict* or *normative crisis*. If their development is to proceed in a healthy fashion, they must acquire a *sense of trust* in those who care for them. If, on the other hand, they *mistrust* their caretakers too much, their progress can be fearfully impeded. Coping with and successfully resolving the clash between trust and mistrust is thus the infant's first major task in life, and according to Erikson, there are a number of other challenges ahead.

Indeed, Erikson envisions the human life cycle as a series of nuclear conflicts (eight in all), the celebrated *Eight Ages of Man*. In addition to *basic trust* vs. *mistrust,* he describes the nuclear conflict that corresponds to the Freudian anal period as *autonomy* vs. *shame* and *doubt.* Similarly, for the phallic period, the Eriksonian equivalent is *initiative* vs. *guilt;* for latency (middle childhood), *industry* vs. *inferiority;* and for adolescence, *identity* vs. *identity confusion.* Erikson also extends the boundaries of psychoanalytic theory by describing the three nuclear conflicts of adulthood. In order to have a satisfying existence, the young adult must resolve the crisis of *intimacy* vs. *isolation;* the middle-aged person must find a solution to the conflict of *generativity* vs. *stagnation,* and the elderly individual must balance *integrity* vs. *despair.*

Mindful of his anthropological training, Erikson asserts that the way in which these conflicts are resolved varies somewhat from culture to culture. In this he resembles both Mead and Lewin. But since he also believes that each person is just a little unique, Erikson implies that each human being resolves the basic nuclear conflicts a bit differently. At this point, you may want to recall that we've encountered the notion of "individual uniqueness" before—in Spranger's theory.

Our chief concern, of course, is what Erikson has to say about adolescence. Judging from the amount of space he has devoted to describing it (1950, 1959, 1968), Erikson regards adolescence as a period of special significance. Because of the point at which it occurs in the human life cycle, adolescence is supposed to recapitulate all the preceding nuclear conflicts of childhood and to anticipate all those of adulthood. It is, in other words, a *pivotal* stage. As they enter their teens, youngsters begin to perceive what they have already become and also to recognize what they *could* become. As a consequence, Erikson believes that the nuclear conflict of adolescence—*identity* vs. *identity confusion*—is made up of seven subsidiary conflicts, each of which harks back to a previous conflict or foreshadows a future one.

Let's see how adolescence recalls Erikson's first four ages of man. To begin with, teenagers try to overcome their sense of *time confusion* by achieving a sense of *temporal perspective,* a struggle which mirrors the original nuclear conflict of *basic trust* vs. *mistrust.* Similarly, their attempts to master adolescent *self-consciousness* by acquiring a measure of *self-certainty* bring to mind the earlier conflict of *autonomy* vs. *shame* and *doubt.* To avoid locking themselves into a set of rigidly prescribed roles (*role fixation*), adolescents must feel free to test out and to experiment (*role experimentation*), thus recalling the younger child's tussles with *initiative* and *guilt.* And in trying to overcome any feelings of *work paralysis* by building up a healthy sense of *ap-*

prenticeship, adolescents resemble school-age children who pit their *industry* against a sense of *inferiority.*

Now let's see how adolescence anticipates the three nuclear conflicts of adulthood. The crisis between *intimacy* and *isolation* is foreshadowed in the youngster's attempts to define his or her sexual identity (*sexual polarization* vs. *bisexual confusion*). By trying to locate a special niche in society, out of all the possible niches they might occupy (*leadership* and *followership* vs. *authority confusion*), adolescents prepare themselves for the conflict of *generativity* vs. *stagnation.* And finally, in fashioning their own unique set of values out of all the competing ideologies available (*ideological commitment* vs. *confusion of values*), teenagers anticipate the ultimate struggle between *integrity* and *despair.*

The Concept of Identity

If all goes well, an adolescent's attempts to resolve his multifaceted conflict result in a health sense of *identity* (as opposed to a sense of *identity confusion*). But what *is* an identity? Erikson complains (1968) that the term has become almost too popular (it is fashionable these days for people to claim that they are in the throes of an "identity crisis"), but he expresses doubt that the concept is very well understood. He also admits that he himself is in part responsible for anv public misconception, for he has purposely allowed the definition of identity to remain somewhat vague. If we take a close look at it, however, the concept appears to bear an intriguing resemblance to Hall's "sense of individuality." Erikson refers to identity in various ways as "an unconscious striving for continuity of experience," a feeling of "solidarity with group ideals," and most significantly for our purposes, "a conscious sense of individual uniqueness" (1968, p. 208). This last definition is the one that seems to predominate when Erikson actually writes about identity. "Individually speaking," he remarks,

> ... identity includes, but is more than, the sum of all successive identifications of those earlier years when the child wanted to be, and often was forced to become, like the people he depended on. *Identity is a unique product,* which now meets a crisis to be solved only in new identifications with age mates and with leader figures outside of the family. (1968, p. 87, italics added)

During adolescence, in other words, youngsters are supposed to become capable of perceiving themselves rather differently than they did in childhood. They may well be aware of the traits they have in common with other people (presumably this is what Erikson means when he speaks of identity including "the sum of all successive identifications"), but they can also recognize traits that are peculiar to them alone. Hall, of course, observed that adolescents differed from children in being able to view themselves as autonomous human beings, each with his or her own special and unique destiny in life. Now that you have a nodding acquaintance with Erikson, I think you can appreciate Hall more and see how far ahead of his times he was in some respects.

Erikson, however, explains much more plausibly than Hall *why* the crystallization of identity can occur only during adolescence. It has to do with the maturation of the mind; only at adolescence do youngsters have the *intellectual* skills to take stock of what they have become and to begin determining their eventual fate in life. It's no accident if this sounds like Piaget. Erikson refers explicitly to Piaget in some of his more recent work. Equally important, only at adolescence do youngsters experience serious *pressures*—pressures that impel them to define themselves more sharply. The arrival of puberty rather forcefully makes them aware of their own sexuality; their parents encourage them to become more independent and responsible; their teachers suggest that they begin to think about the kind of work they might be suited for. As Erikson himself puts it, identity "has its own *developmental period,* before which it could not come to crisis because the somatic, cognitive, and social preconditions are not yet given" (1970, p. 732).

Erikson's position on the issue of adolescent storm and stress also differs from Hall's. Because Erikson believes (like Spranger) that each individual is unique and that, even with the same culture, no two people ever develop in quite the same fashion, he suggests that adolescence is a highly individual matter as well. Teenagers in any given society may face many of the same problems but each resolves these problems just a bit differently. Hence adolescence *may* be turbulent and conflict-ridden—but then again it may not. Erikson remarks, "The task to be performed here by the young person and his society is formidable. *It necessitates in different individuals and in different societies, great variations in the duration, intensity, and ritualization of adolescence"* (1968, p. 155, italics added).

Feminine Psychology: A Persistent Problem

As attractive as it is, Erikson's theory is not an airtight account of adolescent development. Like the other theories we have reviewed, it contains a significant flaw. All in all, Erikson's description of adolescent development has a decidedly masculine ring to it. If we examine our own culture, we discover that the adolescent *male* experiences strong pressures to define himself. He is expected to achieve a sense of self-certainty, to decide upon a line of work, and to initiate sexual relationships. His destiny depends on himself, but I wonder if this model applies as well to the adolescent female. Traditionally, at least, her destiny has been highly dependent upon that of the man she will meet and marry, a circumstance that leaves her eyeing the future with more uncertainty.

Douvan and Adelson (1966), in fact, present evidence that boys actually do develop a firmer sense of identity during adolescence than their female counterparts. The boys in Douvan and Adelson's intensive study to a greater extent than the girls, seemed to be fashioning their own moral code, formulating realistic educational plans, and orienting themselves to a particular occupation. Girls remained much fuzzier about the future, presumably because almost all of them assumed they would marry; and the impact that this event would have on their lives was still somewhat uncertain. A more recent and very interesting but rather impressionistic study (Konopka, 1976) does little to dispel this picture of feminine haziness.

Of course, women are becoming more self-aware and are entering the labor force in increasing numbers. It remains to be seen what influence social changes like these will have on female adolescents. Will more of them begin defining themselves as individuals rather than vaguely assuming that marriage and motherhood will do the defining for them? As yet, no one seems to have researched this question in depth. There are relatively few intensive studies of adolescent development in general (let alone studies of adolescent girls), and this fact brings me to my final point.

Theories of adolescence do not exist in a vacuum, although they are often treated as if they did. Ideally, specialists ought to verify or disconfirm such theories, rather than respond to them as if they had been etched in stone and handed down from Mt. Sinai. Because few psychologists have ever attempted to find out whether adolescence truly is a period of turmoil, the image of adolescent storm and stress persists in the public mind. In generation after generation, the popular media have warned parents to steel themselves for the "difficult years" and to expect their teenagers to withdraw from them, and rebel against them. Ironically, I suspect that many teenagers have concluded they were "abnormal" because they remained comparatively happy and well adjusted during adolescence.

In this connection, I will never forget how many times my mother, a psychiatric social worker, expressed astonishment that I had "never rebelled" during adolescence. My conformity, self-discipline, and general air of obedience ran contrary to everything she had ever heard about teenagers, she assured me. Almost certainly, she predicted, I would have to go back and do my "acting out" at some later date.

SUMMARY

Although this review has been selective, numerous theories of adolescent development have been discussed. We have reviewed representatives of recapitulation theory, psychoanalysis, interpersonal theory, learning theory, field theory, anthropology, Piagetian theory, *geisteswissenschaftliche*

(Spranger's) theory, and Erikson's theory. What this review reveals, I think, is that most theorists describe the same constellation of events during adolescence: sexual development, intellectual maturation, increasing autonomy, and so forth. However, they seem to divide over a single critical issue. Some of them—the majority, in fact—assume that in Western culture the characteristic changes of adolescence are inevitably accompanied by great storm and stress. Others (most notably Spranger and Erikson) argue that human beings are too variable to make such a sweeping generalization. They suggest that adolescence may or may not be stormy, depending upon *which* adolescent and *which* culture you are referring to.

As is no doubt evident by now, I personally favor the "individual variability" model. Research on adolescence, as we have seen, seems to indicate that the period is *not* necessarily one of severe turmoil. Of all the theories discussed, Erikson's theory is the most adequate. Comprehensive and flexible, it integrates several different points of view (psychoanalytic, interpersonal, anthropological), and incorporates various ideas from Hall, McCandless, Lewin, Piaget, Spranger, and Bandura. Erikson's theory also focuses on what I am convinced is the most critical and definitive feature of adolescence—the development of a sense of identity. G. Stanley Hall, of course, advanced a similar notion, but he was unable to elaborate on it very convincingly in his theory of adolescence.

Finally, I have identified two major problems in adolescent psychology: the lack of intensive research on teenagers and the absence of an adequate theory of feminine development. Needless to say, I hope these problems will be remedied in the future—perhaps by some of you who are currently reading this book.

SUGGESTIONS FOR FURTHER READING

BANDURA, A. The stormy decade: Fact or fiction? *Psychology in the Schools,* 1964, *1,* 224-231.
DOUVAN, E., & ADELSON, J. *The adolescent experience.* New York: Wiley, 1966.
ERIKSON, E. *Identity: Youth and crisis.* New York: Norton, 1968.
GALLATIN, J. *Adolescence and individuality: A conceptual approach to adolescent psychology.* New York: Harper & Row, 1975.
KONOPKA, G. *Young girls.* Englewood Cliffs, N.J.: Prentice-Hall, 1976.
MUUSS, R. *Theories of adolescence* (3rd ed.). New York: Random House, 1975.

BIBLIOGRAPHY

ADELSON, J. The mystique of adolescence. *Psychiatry,* 1964, *27,* 1-5.
ADELSON, J. What generation gap? *New York Times Magazine,* January 18, 1970, 10 ff.

BANDURA, A. The stormy decade: Fact or fiction? *Psychology in the Schools,* 1964, *1,* 224–231.

BANDURA, A., & WALTERS, R. H. *Adolescent aggression.* New York: Ronald, 1959.

BENEDICT, R. Continuities and discontinuities in cultural conditioning. In W. Martin & C. Stendler (Eds.), *Readings in child development.* New York: Harcourt-Brace, 1954.

DOUVAN, E., & ADELSON, J. *The adolescent experience.* New York: Wiley, 1966.

ERIKSON, E. Autobiographic notes on the identity crisis. *Daedalus,* 1970, *99,* 730–759.

ERIKSON, E. *Childhood and society.* New York: Norton, 1950.

ERIKSON, E. Identity and the life cycle. *Psychological Issues,* 1959, *1,* 1–171.

ERIKSON, E. *Identity: Youth and crisis.* New York: Norton, 1968.

FREUD, A. Adolescence. *Psychoanalytic Study of the Child,* 1958, *13,* 255–278.

FREUD, A. *The writings of Anna Freud* (Vol. II) *The ego and mechanisms of defense* (Rev. ed. 1936). New York: International Universities Press, 1966.

FREUD, S. The passing of the oedipus complex. (1924) *Collected papers* (Vol. II). London: Hogarth, 1950.

FREUD, S. Female sexuality. (1931) *Collected papers* (Vol. V). London: Hogarth, 1952.

GALLATIN, J. *Adolescence and individuality: A conceptual approach to adolescent psychology.* New York: Harper & Row, 1975.

GALLATIN, J. *Disordered lives: Abnormal psychology in perspective.* 1980.

HALL, G. S. *Adolescence: Its psychology and its relations to physiology, anthropology, sociology, sex, crime, religion, and education.* New York: Appleton, 1904.

JACOBS, J. *Adolescent suicide.* New York: Wiley, 1971.

KONOPKA, G. *Young girls: A portrait of adolescence.* Englewood Cliffs, N.J.: Prentice-Hall, 1976.

LEWIN, K. Field theory and experiment in social psychology: Concepts and methods. *American Journal of Sociology,* 1939, *44,* 868–897.

McCANDLESS, B. R. *Adolescents: Behavior and development.* Hinsdale, Ill.: Dryden Press, 1970.

MEAD, M. *Coming of age in Samoa.* New York: William Morrow, 1961.

MUUSS, R. *Theories of adolescence* (3rd ed.). New York: Random House, 1975.

OFFER, D. *The psychological world of the teenager.* New York: Basic Books, 1969.

PIAGET, J. *Six psychological studies.* New York: Random House, 1967.

SPRANGER, E. *Psychologie des jugendalters* (24th ed.). Heidelberg: Quelle and Meyer, 1955.

SULLIVAN, H. S. *Conceptions of modern psychiatry.* New York: Norton, 1953. (a)

SULLIVAN, H. S. *The interpersonal theory of psychiatry.* New York: Norton, 1953. (b)

THORNDIKE, E. L. The newest psychology. *Educational Review,* 1904, *28,* 217–227.

WEINER, I. *Psychological disturbance in adolescence.* New York: Wiley, 1970.

3

BIOLOGICAL DEVELOPMENT

Dorothy H. Eichorn

Changes in the size and shape of the human body and in the underlying chemical and physiological processes occur continuously throughout life. However, the *rate* of change is most rapid during the prenatal and early postnatal phases. It declines gradually across the remainder of the life course except for one major reversal—the period we call the *adolescent growth spurt.*

Between conception and early postnatal life, a single cell is transformed into a complex being many thousand times larger, and develops from a parasite dwelling in water to an air-breather, independently carrying on all the physiological functions necessary to stay alive. But the functions necessary to sustain individual life are not sufficient to maintain the future life of the species. Biologically, adolescence is the period during which the development of the structures and processes needed to perform this normal adult biological function is completed. Because the chemical substances that trigger this development are carried by the blood to all parts of the body, they filter into the fluids surrounding every cell. Almost all kinds of cells are stimulated to increased growth by one or more of these chemicals, so the adolescent growth spurt is *general,* that is, it occurs in almost all tissues and organs. However, not all cells respond to the same degree. Thus, by the time the adolescent growth spurt ends, the relative size of different organs and body dimensions has changed. The child is now an adult in appearance as well as internal function. Tadpole to frog or cocoon to butterfly may be a more dramatic metamorphosis, but the slower human transformation from child to adult is equally impressive.

NEURAL-HORMONAL BASIS OF ADOLESCENCE

The chemical substances that trigger sexual maturation and other aspects of adolescent biological development are several of the *hormones* secreted by *endocrine* glands. A gland is a group of cells specialized for secretion or excretion. If secretion is through one particular opening or channel, the gland is called an exocrine, or duct, gland. When secretion is instead simply through cell walls directly into the blood stream or lymphatic system (a group of vessels that drain lymph fluid from cells and transport it to the blood stream), the gland is called endocrine, or ductless. Some hormones

Dorothy H. Eichorn is Associate Director of the Institute of Human Development at the University of California, Berkeley. She is also the Executive Officer of the Society for Research in Child Development and has served on the Panel on Youth of the President's Scientific Advisory Committee; she coedited the report of that committee which has appeared as *Youth: Transition to Adulthood.* Her publications on the physiological and physical development in youth include numerous journal articles, chapters in books, and material for encyclopedias.

are secreted continuously, although the amount may vary with age or other circumstances; others are secreted only in response to certain stimuli.

A number of different endocrine glands, many of which secrete more than one hormone, are located in different parts of the body. Those most distinctively involved in the phenomena of adolescence are the *pituitary gland,* located at the base of the brain, the *sex glands* in the gonads (ovaries of the female and testes of the male), and the *cortex of the adrenal gland*—the outer part of a paired gland, one of which lies over each kidney. All of these glands themselves undergo an adolescent growth spurt, and the spurt in the anterior pituitary is particularly marked in girls.

The pituitary gland, although small, is divided into several lobes; the anterior lobe is often called the "master gland" because it secretes a number of different *tropic* hormones (those that stimulate the activity of other endocrine glands). Among these are the gonadotropins—follicle-stimulating hormone (FSH), luteinizing hormone (LH), and interstitial cell-stimulating hormone (ICSH). FSH stimulates development of the follicles within the female ovaries, resulting in the production of mature eggs or ova, and of the seminiferous tubules in the male testes that produce sperm. In the female, secretion of estrogens and progesterone by the ovaries is stimulated by LH; whereas in the male, it is ICSH that stimulates the production of testosterone by the Leydig cells in the testes and the final stages of maturation of sperm in the seminiferous tubules.

Estrogens (female sex hormones) and androgens (male sex hormones) are known collectively as the sex steroids because of their chemical configuration. Both groups of hormones are secreted by both sexes; the adrenal cortex is believed to be the principal source of androgens in the female and of estrogens in the male. The sex difference in the relative amounts of these hormones secreted arises from the secretion of large amounts of estrogens by the ovaries in the female and of large amounts of androgens by the testes in the male.

Although the anterior pituitary is called the "master gland," its secretory activity is in fact the result of complex interactions with the blood levels of hormones from its "target" glands and with the central nervous system. Two different patterns of gonadotropin secretion occur in both sexes, and a third pattern is found only in females between puberty and menopause. The first pattern is an inhibitory, or negative, feedback mechanism that develops early in fetal life, first in relation to a gonadotropin secreted by the placenta and later in relation to FSH, and probably LH, secreted by the fetal pituitary. When blood levels of the sex steroids are low, the secretion of gonadotropins increases. Conversely, when the blood levels of gonadotropins rise to a certain level, secretion is inhibited. This is the basic pattern of interaction in males, in female children, and one of the patterns in females after puberty.

The "set-point" for inhibition of secretion of gonadotropins by the anterior pituitary is controlled by the central nervous system. Until puberty, this set-point is very low, that is, the anterior pituitary is very sensitive to circulating levels of estrogens and androgens, so secretion of gonadotropins is inhibited by very low levels of sex steroids in the blood. Although the mechanism is not well understood, decreased sensitivity to sex steroids occurs when neurosecretory neurons within the hypothalamus (a part of the brain lying close to the pituitary) produce and release LRF (luteinizing hormone releasing factor). In turn, synthesis of this factor is affected by cells within the hypothalamus that are linked to the limbic system, a part of the brain closely involved with emotions.

The second pattern of gonadotropin secretion found in both sexes is intermittent or episodic. Thus far it has been found only after puberty. Although the mechanism is not understood, it too is mediated by the central nervous system but is independent of the blood levels of sex steroids.

Between puberty and menopause, a third pattern occurs in women. This one is cyclic, related to the ovulatory cycle, and operates by a positive rather than inhibitory feedback mechanism. As the amount of estrogen released into the blood by the ovaries increases, a level is reached that stimulates the simultaneous release of LH and FSH.

Four other hormones that influence growth and maturation throughout the developmental period should also be mentioned. The thyroid gland is located in the neck just below the larynx (or "voice box"). It too shows an adolescent growth spurt, particularly in boys, and usually reaches its greatest size sometime between mid-adolescence and early adulthood (about age 20). Thyroid hormone increases metabolic rate and hence the rate of growth and maturation of all tissues. If thyroid secretion is deficient, growth is not only slowed but distorted, especially in infancy and early childhood. The four parathyroids are embedded in the thyroid but are independent glands. These glands show not only a growth spurt but also a change in cellular composition during adolescence. Because parathyroid hormone is one of the most important factors in the metabolism of calcium and phosphorus, this hormone is essential for normal growth and maturation of the bones.

Growth hormone, one of the hormones secreted by the pituitary gland, also influences skeletal growth and the metabolism of nutrients, particularly amino acids (the building blocks of proteins) and glucose (simple sugar). Its secretion is not constant; instead, secretion is controlled by such stimuli as physical exercise, emotional arousal, and the blood levels of nutrients. It is activated when blood sugar levels fall rapidly and when amino acid levels rise. If growth hormone deficiency or excess occurs before growth in height is completed, growth is slowed down or speeded up symmetrically so a person is unusually short or tall but normally proportioned. After growth in the length of bones has ceased, excess growth hormone will result in deformities because the bones then can grow only by becoming thicker.

Without sufficient sugar to fuel the conversion of food into new tissue, growth is slowed. The hormone insulin, secreted by certain cells in the pancreas, promotes the transfer of sugar from the blood into the cells. These secretory cells, called the islets of Langerhans, also show an adolescent growth spurt in size and weight.

MATURATIONAL AGE

From shortly after the time that secretion of gonadotropins and gonadal hormones begins to increase markedly through late adolescence, "maturational age" determined on any of a variety of scales correlates more highly with maturation than does chronological age. Further, the variation observed within and between sexes in the age at which various adolescent phenomena occur is markedly reduced if the data are plotted by maturational age rather than birth age.

The sequences of pubic hair, testicular growth, and breast development constitute several means of assessing maturation age (see Table 3.1). Three others, however, are much more widely used, in part because they provide continuous scales with equal intervals and in part because rating body hair, breasts, or testicles requires that the part of the body involved be nude. Also for years it has been believed that skeletal growth is more closely associated with primary sexual maturation than is the development of secondary sexual characteristics. Although there are data to suggest that this may not be true (Marshall, 1974), the other advantages of scales based on skeletal growth are so useful that they will probably continue to be used.

Frequent and direct measures of growth in height form the criterion for scaling on the basis of *age deviation* from *peak height velocity*. The age at which the peak occurs is taken as the zero point, and chronological years before and after this point are designated as minus one, two, and so on, or plus one, two, and so on. For example, suppose that the peak growth in height for a boy occurred exactly at 14 years. Then 13 years would be −1, 12 would be −2, 11 would be −3, 14 would be +1, and so on. Age at menarche (first menstrual period) is also often used as the zero point in girls.

A third system is determination of skeletal or bone age from X-rays of the hand and wrist. These standards have been developed by securing such X-rays from large groups of children at consecutive ages from early infancy through "skeletal maturity." The latter is said to occur when the long bones in the arms, legs, fingers, and toes fuse with growth centers called epiphyses, which until fusion were separate units near the ends of the long bones. Also the individual bones of the wrist, ankle, and knee go through complex changes in shape as well as size. Although rating systems vary in

TABLE 3.1 *Developmental Stages of the Breasts, Penis, Testes, and Scrotum, and Pubic Hair*

STAGE NUMBER	BREASTS	PENIS, TESTES AND SCROTUM	PUBIC HAIR
1 (Preadolescent)	Elevation of papilla only	Same as in early childhood	None: any hair same as that on abdomen
2	Breast buds; areolar diameter enlarged; elevation of breast and papilla as small mound	Little or no enlargement of penis; testes and scrotum slightly larger, skin of scrotum reddened, texture changed	Sparse hair, only slightly pigmented; straight or only slightly curled; mostly along labia or at base of penis
3	Breast and areola more enlarged and elevated, but no separation of contours	Penis slightly larger, mainly in length; testes and scrotum larger	Sparse hair over junction of pubes; courser, more curly, considerably darker
4	Areola and papilla constitute a second mound above contour of breast	Penis larger, glans broader and more developed; testes and scrotum larger, scrotal skin darker	Hairy area considerably smaller than adult; none yet on medial surface of thighs; hair of adult type
5 (Mature)	Only papilla projects; areola has receded to general contour of breast	Mature in shape and size	Hair adult in type and amount; has spread to medial surface of thighs; distribution is horizontal—classic "feminine" pattern
6 (reached in only about 10% of women, but 80% of men)			Hair spreads up linea albea or other areas above inverse triangle

Note. Adapted from text in Tanner, 1969

the degree to which changes in individual bones are separately rated, the general principle is the same: the X-ray of an individual child is compared with a standard set exemplifying the average development at each age. Because skeletal maturation occurs at a faster rate in girls, separate standards should be used for each sex.

Two examples will suffice to illustrate the differences in variation between or within sexes when a maturational rather than chronological age scale is used. First, increased FSH secretion begins to be detected about a year earlier in girls than in boys. However, if the data are plotted against skeletal age, this increase is found to occur at about a skeletal age of 7 years in both sexes (Grumbach, 1975). Second, among a normal probability sample of girls, the standard deviation (a measure of variability within the group) for age at menarche is about 1 chronological year but only 6 months in terms of age deviation from peak height velocity or age deviation from menarche (Tanner, 1969; Faust, 1977).

SEXUAL MATURATION

The term adolescence is derived from the present participle of a verb meaning to grow up, hence it means "growing up." Growing up in the sense of becoming *sexually mature* is the essence of biological adolescence, so we will consider this process first. Growing up in the sense of becoming taller and heavier is secondary; indeed a small percentage of persons become sexually mature while very young and of small overall size. For example, complete adolescent biological development has been seen as early as 1 to 2 years old in cases with brain tumors (Weinberger & Grant, 1941; Troland & Brown, 1948; Seckel, 1950). In one widely cited case, a girl who had been menstruating since she was a year old was delivered of a full-term baby by cesarean section v·hen she was 5 years, 8 months old (Escomel, 1939). This unusual phenomenon is called *puberty praecox* (precocious puberty) and can result either from injuries to the central nervous system or simply as an extreme of the normal developmental continuum. Study of such cases, as well as of persons with genetic disorders of the sex chromosomes, has aided our understanding of the mechanisms of more normal development.

Two related facts that these cases make clear are (1) the central nervous system plays an important role in the initiation of sexual maturation; whereas, (2) the sensitivity of the sexual "end organs," the testes and the ovaries, does not. The latter will respond with appropriate development even in infancy if the proper hormonal stimuli are provided.

Reproductive System

The primary sex organs are the gonads and accessory structures that contribute to the production and delivery of mature ova and sperm. Many of the structures we tend to associate with sexual maturity, e.g., breasts or pubic hair (the term *pubescence* comes from a Latin word meaning "becoming hairy"), are in fact, *secondary* characteristics in that they are not essential for reproduction. Lactation, the production of milk, is possible with quite immature-looking breasts. Features such as pubic hair or rounded hips tend to be "releasers" or stimulators for sexual behavior among sexually mature persons, especially experienced ones, but they are not necessary for either sexual behavior or fertility.

Preadolescent Development

It is also important to understand that sexual development is completed during adolescence; it begins very early in prenatal life. The kinds of sex chromosomes the individual will have are determined at fertilization, the union of the ovum and sperm. Ova contain only female (X) chromosomes; some sperm contain X chromosomes, others contain male (Y) chromosomes. The cells of each normal individual contain a single pair of chromosomes—either two X's or an X and a Y. If a human being's cells contain *only* X chromosomes, regardless of whether the number is one or more, development is female, although it will usually be abnormal to some degree if more than two X's are present. If one or more Y's are present, differentiation will be male although abnormalities will usually occur in the presence of either excess Y's or excess X's. These statements must be modified if abnormal amounts of hormones of the opposite sex are introduced, for example, by injections, by transfer from the mother during pregnancy, or from tumors in the adrenal gland.

Until about the seventh week after fertilization, human gonadal tissue looks the same in both males and females. At around that age, the testicular tissue can be recognized in males. In about two weeks, the Leydig cells that secrete testosterone appear in this tissue and multiply rapidly until around the sixth month, probably in response to a gonadotropin secreted by the placenta. Judged by the amount secreted in the mother's urine, secretion of this gonadotropic hormone rises until the eighth to tenth week after fertilization and then decreases to quite low levels by the end of the fourth month after fertilization.

Becoming female seems to be the basic nature of human embryonic tissue because if no Y chromosomes are present, the "seventh week" changes do not occur. Instead, about a week later, the gonadal tissue becomes an ovary; and near the twelfth week after fertilization, the external genitals become recognizably female. These developments seem to occur without a hormonal stimulus.

In both sexes, at about 18 weeks after fertilization, neurosecretions similar to LRF can be detected around the blood vessels in the hypothalamus, and various pituitary hormones can be detected even earlier. It is these observations that led to the inference mentioned earlier that the inhibitory, or negative, feedback mechanism observed in both sexes during childhood and adolescence is established early in fetal life.

Both experiments with animals and observations on cases of atypical sexual development in human infants and children strongly suggest that an important phase of sexual development, the "sexing of the brain," takes place around the time of birth or at least during infancy. In the rat, a truly critical period occurs during the first five days after birth. To understand the importance of this phase, two sets of facts must be known. First, not only the anterior pituitary but also cells in certain areas of the brain take up sex hormones. Second, experiments show that in all mammals that have been studied in this way, biological, and to a considerable extent, behavioral, maleness is a function of some change in the hypothalamus, not in the endocrine glands. The critical experimental is to remove the pituitary gland of a male and implant instead the pituitary of a female. Once the necessary blood circulation has been reestablished, that "female" pituitary will secrete male gonadotropins in a male pattern. Analogously, if a "male" pituitary gland is substituted in a female, it will secrete all the female gonadotropins and in the cyclic female pattern.

Now back to experiments with rats in the critical perinatal period. Testosterone secreted by the Leydig cells in the testes during the first two or three days after birth stimulates differentiation of a male hypothalamus (and probably some other brain tissues). If testosterone is injected into the animal before birth or after the fifth postnatal day, this differentiation does not occur. Even one dose of estrogens during this period will interfere with normal male differentiation. Similarly, if a female rat receives one injection of testosterone during these few days, she will be sterile as an adult because the endocrinological and ovulatory cycles never become established. Further, she will not show female sexual behavior even if nonfunctional ovaries are removed and the normal hormonal cycle is introduced via hormonal therapy. She will behave like a male, however, if her ovaries are removed and testosterone is injected—an evidence that her brain was "sexed as a male" during those early few days. Analogous manipulations in the male do interfere with complete expression of male sexual behavior but the effect is less extreme, indicating that the brain had already been "sexed" by the early secretion of testosterone.

The higher up the phylogenetic scale an animal group is, the less rigidly is its behavior controlled by hormonal levels and patterns (Ford & Beach, 1951). Nevertheless, instances of hormonal therapy administered during pregnancy and other cases of atypical development indicate that the basic patterns of human sexual differentiation during the prenatal period and early infancy operate in similar fashion.

After a short perinatal period during which the Leydig cells of the human male infant are quite prominent and actively secrete testosterone (or, in the female, the ovaries secrete estrogen), a number of years of quiescence are observed. The Leydig cells almost completely disappear; androgens, estrogens, and gonadotropins are secreted only at very low levels; the anterior pituitary, as noted earlier, is very unresponsive to the low levels of gonadal hormones; the testes and accessory primary male organs show almost no growth after age two years, and the ovaries and uterus grow very slowly. However, the stage is set for the adolescent drama.

THE ADOLESCENT SEQUENCE

Certain developmental sequences seem so deeply rooted in the genetic constitution of all human beings that they are rarely violated if the person is viable (likely to stay alive). One example is the major patterns of embryonic differentiation; another is the early motor sequences of rolling over, sitting up, standing, and walking. A third is the adolescent sequence. However, in all of these, individual, sex, and group (ethnic, nutritional) differences in *timing* are observed (the later the developmental stage, the greater the absolute amounts of time involved). Timing differences include not only *when* a particular development begins but also how long it takes to complete it and the interval of time between different parts of the sequence. Many illustrations of these statements will be seen in the following discussion, so two examples, one general and one specific, will suffice here. In general, all new phases of development occur earlier in females, and from the prenatal period, when the differences are measured in days or weeks through adolescence, when they are of the order of two years, females increase their lead. A specific example is that stages of breast or penis development may follow one another in quite rapid succession or be stretched out over more than the average number of years.

The first signs of sexual maturation can be detected only by chemical analyses of blood or urine, and they occur at younger ages than we customarily associate with adolescence. Depending upon the individual, his or her sex, and the hormone in question, secretion of gonadal hormones and gonadotropins begins to rise sometime between 6 and 10 or 11 years. Much of the earlier phases of the increases in androgens and estrogens may reflect secretion from the adrenal cortex rather than from the primary gonads. Perhaps increased secretion of steroidal hormones by the adrenal cortex stimulates maturation of the hypothalamus-pituitary-gonadal interaction. At least recent data suggest that this may be one of the mechanisms (Ducharme, Alberti, Forest, De Peretti, Sempé & Bertrand, 1974). In girls, blood levels of FSH seem to increase sooner than do blood levels of LH, whereas in boys the early increases may occur simultaneously, with FSH then increasing more rapidly (Grumbach, 1975). However, wide variations occur both within and between studies. Internal changes, such as maturation of the seminiferous tubules in the testes, begin before external signs, such as increased volume of the testes, are observable. The growth spurt of organs such as the testis and penis of the male and ovary and uterus of the female follow.

63

Although the growth spurt in the volume of the testes typically begins about a year before that in the size of the penis, development to adult size takes longer for the testis (about 4½ years) than for the penis (about 3½ years). "Locker room" comparisons seem inevitable, and anxieties about the size of the penis generally are more common. In fact, however, the size of these organs, particularly the penis, bears no particular relation to fertility or to the sexual satisfaction of either male or female. Wagner, in chapter 10, considers adolescent sexuality within the context of its meaning to adolescents and its implications for sex education. I shall keep my focus on the biological development in this chapter.

Among boys, the earlier external signs of sexual maturation include not only accelerated growth of the scrotum and testes but also accelerated growth in height and the appearance of unpigmented pubic hair. For girls, the first signs are the unpigmented pubic hair and the appearance of breast buds; typically the height spurt does not begin until about a year later. Whether or not pubic hair is the first external sign in either sex depends on whether one uses direct observation or photographs. Rating scales of development that are based on photographs place the appearance of pubic hair later than those based on direct observation because the early unpigmented hair does not show up in photographs—pubic hair or other hair on the body can be seen in photographs only after it darkens.

Several scales for rating the development of pubic and axillary (underarm) hair and of testis, penis, and breast development have been devised. Because these are often used in studies relating physiological and physical development or biological and behavioral development, examples of three scales now in common use are given in Table 3.1. The stages specified there are also useful in simplifying the description of the normal range of ages at which these manifestations occur and the sequence of their development.

Accelerated growth of the ovaries typically begins between 7 and 9 years, and the age range for the first appearance of pubic hair is 8-14, of breast buds, 8-13, and of the height spurt in girls, 9½-14½. Menarche (the initiation of menstrual periods) is fairly late in the sequence, the median age in the United States now being about 12 years, 9 months. Table 3.2 shows the age range observed in a large national probability sample. Usually the peak of the height spurt in girls occurs during the year before menarche. In the most frequently observed pattern, stages 2, 3, and 4 of breast development follow each other rapidly, all three occurring on the average between 11 and 12 years, whereas the average age for reaching the final stage (number 5) is about 13½. However, some completely grown women fully capable of nursing never reach stage 5. Similarly, the stages of pubic hair development usually are not spaced evenly. Typical ages are shortly after 11 for stage 2, 11½ for stage 3, 12 for stage 4, and 14 for stage 5. Again, some women never develop the most advanced pattern.

Analogous milestones for boys are 10-13¼ for the start of the growth

TABLE 3.2 *Percentage of Girls Whose Menstrual Periods Had Started, by Race and Age: United States*

AGE[a]	ALL RACES[b]	WHITE	BLACK
Six-nine years	0.2	0.2	0.2
Ten years	1.2	0.8	4.0
Eleven years	12.8	11.6	21.3
Twelve years	43.3	41.7	51.2
Thirteen years	73.2	72.9	74.1
Fourteen years	91.7	91.4	93.5
Fifteen years	98.3	98.2	98.7
Sixteen-seventeen years	99.7	99.6	100.0

Note. From Brian MacMahon. Age at menarche: United States. *Vital and Health Statistics,* Series 11, No. 133. Washington: U.S. Department of Health, Education and Welfare, 1974.

[a] Age at last birthday.

[b] Includes data for "other races," which are not shown separately.

spurt in the volume of the testes, 11–14½ for the penis, 10½–16 for the height spurt, and 10–15 years for stage 2 of pubic hair development. Penis growth typically ceases between 13½ and 16½, and testicular growth between 14½ and 18. Typical ages for stages 3, 4, and 5 of pubic hair are 13½, 14, and 15 years 9 months. The peak of the height spurt most frequently is seen shortly before 14; this is also about the age of the first ejaculation of semen (range about 11–16), although behavior, such as masturbation, is one of the factors associated with this phenomenon when it is first observed. Erection of the penis occurs even in infants; sexual maturity is not necessary.

Maturation of Reproductive Capacity

Within the testes, the essential development is the production of mature sperm. After FSH stimulates maturation of the seminiferous tubules, primitive *spermatogonia* in the tubules go through cell division, producing additional spermatogonia as well as spermatocytes, each of which divides into two smaller *secondary spermatocytes.* The latter first appear on the average about age 12–13. Secretion of ICSH by the anterior pituitary is required before the spermatocytes undergo the last cell division and become *spermatids,* which then mature into *spermatozoa,* the fully developed male sperm cells. Sperm next travel through several accessory organs. Among the more important are the *vas deferens,* where sperm are stored, and the *seminal vesicle* and *prostate gland,* which contribute to the *seminal fluid* that helps keep sperm alive and highly mobile. The prostate gland is one that grows rapidly during the early "nonvisible" stages of pubescence, and the first ejaculation, which may not contain mature sperm, contains seminal fluid. Another set of glands, *Cowper's glands,* produce a fluid that also promotes the passage of sperm through the urethra in the penis. This fluid usually appears on the external surface of the penis soon after sexual arousal and before ejaculation. However, it sometimes contains live sperm, so impregnation is possible even when the penis is removed from the vagina before ejaculation.

The increase in the size of the uterus during adolescence is relatively greater than that in the size of the ovaries, probably because the latter show more growth during childhood. At birth, the ovaries contain some 200,000 to 400,000 *follicles,* each of which has the potential to develop into an ovum. However, by menarche the number has dwindled to about 10,000. The vagina, uterus, and ovaries undergo maturational changes in addition to an increase in size, and the folds of tissue, the labia minora (small inner folds) and labia majora (large outer folds) surrounding the vaginal opening become much larger. The *clitoris* is the erectile tissue in females that is the anatomical homologue of the penis in males. Like the penis, it is capable of erection during childhood, but it enlarges during adolescence, and its supply of blood vessels, which are responsible for erection, increases.

The essential maturational change, however, is the production and release of mature ova, a complex process known as the *ovulatory cycle.* During the first half of this cycle, FSH secreted by the anterior pituitary stimulates the maturation of, usually, only one follicle in one ovary (multiple births occur when more than one follicle develops into a mature ovum and two or more are fertilized). Once the maturation is complete, the ovum literally bursts forth from the ovary (ovulation) and moves into and down one of the *Fallopian tubes.* Meanwhile, the lining of the uterine wall has been growing and undergoing chemical changes that prepare it for the implantation and nourishment of a fertilized ovum. Shortly before ovulation occurs, secretion of estrogens by the ovarian follicle (which has been building up during the previous 12–14 days) reaches a peak, and LH begins to be secreted by the anterior pituitary. This synchronous release of LH and FSH following an extended period of rising estrogen levels is called the preovulatory LH surge, and is the *positive* feedback system discussed early in this chapter. It is not established until adolescence and ceases to be operative after the menopause (cessation of the ovulatory and menstrual cycles). Through the *negative* feedback system, the rising levels of estrogens inhibit further secretion of FSH by the anterior pituitary and hence the maturation of another follicle into an ovum. During the latter half of the ovulatory or menstrual cycle, the anterior pituitary continues to secrete LH, which stimulates the growth of follicular cells remaining after the ovum has erupted. These cells form the *corpus luteum,* which is also an endocrine gland, secreting progesterone, a hormone that stimulates the further development of the uterine wall for the implantation of a fertilized ovum. If the mature ovum is not fertilized, the level of estrogen secretion slowly subsides while the amount of progesterone being secreted by the corpus luteum first increases and then decreases as the corpus luteum disintegrates. The temporary lining of the uterus is then shed (the blood and cells from this process constitute the menstrual flow), and the whole cycle then begins again.

Early menstrual cycles may be anovulatory, that is, the amount of hormones secreted is not sufficient to produce mature ova. Until the intricate endocrine mechanisms are well integrated and the response of uterine tissue appropriate, these early periods may also be irregular and the menstrual flow scant. Further, similar phenomena—irregularity and absence of ovulation—may occur at any time between puberty and menopause as a result of either physical conditions, such as poor nutrition, or emotional stress. Because these facts have been known and reported in textbooks for years, many persons assume that all early menstrual cycles are anovulatory and that pregnancy is highly unlikely. There is interesting data that provides evidence to the contrary. Not only may the earliest menstrual periods be regular and ovulatory (Borsos, Takács & Smid, 1977), but also ovulation and ovulatory cycles, and, hence, the ability to become pregnant, sometimes precede the appearance of menstrual flow (Odell & Swerdloff, 1975). Pregnancies also occur after apparent menopause, i.e., after menstrual periods have ceased. Finally, although ovulation usually occurs mid-cycle, data on groups of women indicate that fertilization appears to have occurred on every possible day of the cycle. Obviously, no completely "safe" age nor a completely "safe" period during a cycle exists; the likelihood of impregnation is a matter of statistical probabilities.

PHYSICAL DEVELOPMENT

From an average of about 24 centimeters (9.6 inches) during the first year, the annual rate of growth in height decelerates quite steeply until early adolescence, when the rate begins to climb steeply again. At the adolescent peak of velocity, the annual rate is over 10 centimeters among boys and over 9 centimeters in girls. However, the growth in length is not equal in different segments of the body. Eichorn (1973) has summarized the pattern of changes, with some emphasis on boys. Faust (1977) has published a monograph giving more detail on girls.

Accelerated growth begins later in the trunk than in the legs, but because the total increase in the trunk is greater, body proportions change in the direction of a higher trunk/leg length ratio. Peak growth in chest and hip breadth usually occur about four months after that in leg length. A few months later, shoulder breadth reaches its maximum growth rate followed by trunk length and chest depth. Total hip growth is greater in girls than boys, while the reverse is true of chest and shoulder dimensions.

About 98% of maximal height is attained by the average boy at 17.5 (the average girl reaches this point at 15.5), with small increments continuing into the late twenties. The apex of weight gain is about six months later than the peak of height growth, although gains continue at a more gradual pace to the mid-fifties. About three months after peak growth in boys, muscular growth reaches its apex. However, their apex of dynametric strength comes much later (about 14 months after the height peak), and their capacity to increase strength through exercise does not reach a maximum until age 25 to 35. Although it is not true that the adolescent boy "outgrows his strength," there does appear to be "a period of about a year when a boy, having completed his physical growth, does not have the strength of a young adult of the same body size and shape" (Tanner, 1962, p. 204). About the time of the boy's spurt in strength, his motor coordination also improves markedly. Performance of simple and complex motor tasks, including athletic feats, improves into the thirties, but evidence for an adolescent spurt is lacking. Increases in strength and in motor coordination and performance occur earlier in girls than in boys but are not, on the average, as great.

Some two years after pubic hair growth begins, axillary hair first appears, as does facial hair in boys. Other body hair may also appear at this time but often is delayed until considerably later. The mustache and beard follow a definite sequence of appearance, and the final state—hair along the side and lower border of the chin—rarely takes place until the development of pubic hair and the genitalia is complete.

Concomitant with or preceding these external manifestations are changes in internal organs, body biochemistry and composition, and physiological function. Lymphoid tissue decreases steeply throughout adolescence after reaching its peak at age 10 to 12. Subcutaneous fat has a curvilinear growth curve. The brain and other portions of the nervous system grow rapidly during early childhood but seem to share little in the adolescent growth spurt. However, gradual maturing of function is suggested by dendritic growth in the brain, by continued myelination of some nerve tracts, and by some physiological measures, for example, faster reaction times and further maturing of the electroencephalogram (EEG).

Accompanying enlargement of the larynx is deepening of the voice in both sexes. Growth of the larynx is greater in boys, as is their voice change, but the process is gradual, beginning when penis growth is almost completed and often continuing until near the end of adolescence.

PHYSIOLOGICAL DEVELOPMENT

Most of the internal organs, including the heart and lungs, participate in the adolescent growth, and many of these organs also undergo changes in composition and biochemical reactions. Such developments reflect the need for more oxygen and more "fuel" to meet the metabolic demands of faster growth. In turn, various measures of physiologic function show altered levels.

Metabolic rate, which had been decreasing since infancy and will resume its decline after adolescence, may slow its rate of decline or even show an increase particularly in boys. Probably the temporary change in pattern would be even greater were it not the case that metabolic efficiency improves during adolescence, e.g., in exchange of oxygen and carbon dioxide in the lungs. With increased lung and chest size, vital capacity increases and the blood is also able to carry more oxygen because of an increase in red blood cells, again, particularly in boys. When metabolic rate is plotted against maturational rather than chronological age, an early adolescent increase followed by a leveling off at adult levels can also be detected in girls (Shock, 1943).

Respiratory rate, pulse rate, and body temperature also decline from infancy through adulthood and may also show temporary slowing or reversal in adolescence, particularly if plotted against maturational age (Shock, 1943: Eichorn, 1970). These measures tend to have low positive correlations both with each other and with metabolic rate.

Blood volume increases with age because of its correlation with increases in body size. The relationship to weight is linear, but the correlation with age, height, and surface area are not. At greater heights or ages, for example, there is a larger increase in blood volume than would be predicted from a linear relationship (Eichorn, 1970). In part, the increase in blood volume is a function of the increase in number of red cells, and this relationship is reflected in the marked increase in both among boys during adolescence. Blood volume also seems to be greater in persons with larger amounts of muscle relative to fat and bone. Boys have a greater increase in muscle mass during adolescence than do girls, whereas the amount of fat tissue is relatively greater in girls. These tissue differences probably also help to account for the sex difference in blood volume that is established at adolescence and retained in adulthood.

During adolescence, a sex difference in blood pressure also becomes established and is maintained until late middle age (Eichorn, 1970; Roberts & Maurer, 1977b). The sex difference in blood volume may play a role here, but many other factors also affect blood pressure. Peripheral resistance is one major factor, and peripheral resistance increases with age. In part, this increased resistance has an "unhealthy" basis. That is, fat accumulates along the walls of the blood vessels, increasing the friction of blood flow. Such accumulation begins early and may be quite marked by late adolescence. On the other hand, lesser resistance in younger individuals may be a function of less adequate ability to constrict the blood vessels and the lesser development of the peripheral blood vessels, which contribute to overall resistance. Further, the larger, stronger muscle of the older heart is able to expel the blood from the heart with greater force. Muscular differences as well as differences in blood volume and possibly in other factors influencing blood pressure probably underlie the sex difference.

Across the life span, blood pressure rises gradually, and some acceleration of this trend may occur at adolescence. Among girls, an adolescent acceleration usually is not noticeable in group data unless they are plotted against maturational age (Shock, 1943). However, an acceleration for boys can often be seen even in chronological age curves (see, for example, Roberts & Maurer, 1977b.)

HEALTH

Within the last twenty years, a great amount of data on the health status of adolescents in the United States has become available from the survey programs of the National Center for Health Statistics. People aged 12–17 were examined in one of the "cycles" of the Health Examination Survey, conducted between 1966 and 1970. Earlier surveys included persons over 18 (1960–1962) and in the age range 6–11 (1963–1965). Subsequently the first Health and Nutrition Examination covering the age range 1–74 was done in 1971–1974. Each of these surveys was based on a large national probability sample stratified by geographic areas and socioeconomic status. Both sexes and various ethnic groups were included. For the first time, therefore, we have a broad and reliable picture of the health and nutritional status of the country and good cross-sectional standards against which to evaluate individuals. Unfortunately, "secular" trends (changes occurring across historical time) may occur and render some of these norms inappropriate for later generations. Thus repetitions of such surveys from time to time are advisable.

Analyses of data from these surveys have been, and are continuing to be, reported, primarily in *Vital and Health Statistics,* published by the U.S. Department of Health, Education and Welfare. (A majority of the publications to date that include adolescent data are listed in the bibliography at the end of this chapter, although they may not be referred to directly in the discussion.) Only a small sampling of the findings can be summarized here, but interested readers should be able to find these publications in university libraries; they may also be ordered at low cost from the U.S. Government Printing Office.

> Each youth in the sample was administered a 3-hour single-visit examination in a mobile examination center constructed specially for the survey. The examination focused primarily on growth and development

and on adolescent health. It included examinations by a physician and a dentist, several tests administered by a psychologist, and a variety of additional tests and measurements performed by health technicians.

Several questionnaires were employed to supplement the information obtained by direct examination. Among them were a household questionnaire administered by an interviewer from the U.S. Bureau of the Census to obtain demographic and socioeconomic information; two medical histories for each youth, one completed by a parent and the other by the youth himself; and a health behavior questionnaire completed by the youth at the examination center. For those youths enrolled in school, additional questionnaire information was requested from school officials regarding grade placement, absenteeism, disciplinary problems, grades skipped or repeated, and health, academic, or adjustment problems that required special resources or facilities. A teacher's rating of each youth's behavior, ability, and academic performance was also sought. In addition, a birth certificate was obtained to verify each youth's age and to gain other information relating to the youth at birth. All information in the survey was collected under an assurance of confidentiality. (Scanlon, 1975, p. 1)

Given these various types of data, it is possible to look at relationships among measures and to examine differences among sexes, regions of the country, ethnic groups, handicapped and nonhandicapped youngsters, and so on. Further, because a sizeable number of the children examined in the survey of ages 6–11 also by chance were included in the random sampling done for the 12–17 year survey, some longitudinal data are available to supplement the cross-sectional information.

As was true of all age groups sampled, most of the adolescents considered themselves to be healthy. The proportions reported were: health excellent (26.6%), very good (33.2%), good (36.7%), fair (4.2%), and poor (0.4%). However, the incidence of poor or fair health reported increased slightly with age, and about 10% of the adolescents said they had a health problem that they might want to discuss with a physician. "Boys were more likely than girls to report excellent health, and there were proportionately more girls than boys among the 4 percent of the youths who considered themselves in fair health" (Scanlon, 1975, p. 3). The proportion of black youths reporting that they would like to consult with a physician (13.8%) was significantly larger than for whites (9.7%).

In the year prior to the examination, somewhat more youths had visited a physician for a checkup (48%) than for actual medical treatment (43%). Considerable awareness of some symptoms likely to be associated with serious illness was shown by the fact that a great majority (over 70%) of the youngsters stated they would definitely want to consult a physician if they had such symptoms as blood in their urine or bowel movements or a lump in the stomach. As might be expected, more youngsters from high income families (66%) than from low (35%) had had a physical checkup during the previous year. Higher education of the parents and urban as opposed to rural residence were also associated with higher proportions who had had a physical checkup.

Agreement between parents and youths on health questions that both were asked was fairly good, for example, identical responses occurred on 58 of 100 items. Agreement was 8% higher for girls than for boys and better for youths scoring higher on intelligence and achievement tests than for the less able. In general, parents considered their adolescents to be in better health than the adolescents themselves did, but parents worried more about their offspring's health problems. Adolescents also reported considerably more nervousness than their parents recognized (or at least reported). One disturbing finding was that parents of adolescents judged their offspring to be in better health than did parents of the children surveyed in the previous cycle, but the physicians' findings were exactly reversed. That is, the physicians found more symptoms of ill health. Perhaps parents attend more closely to the health of younger children, or have closer contact with their children while young. Both this finding and the fact that less than half of the adolescents surveyed had visited a physician for a checkup in the past year suggest a need for more attention to the health problems of adolescents.

This survey, like less representative ones done many years ago in the adolescent studies at the Institute of Human Development, showed that acne, height and weight, and other aspects of physical appearance (e.g., temporary swelling of the breasts in boys) cause psychological distress. For example, over 80% of both males and females reported being "bothered" by their acne (Roberts & Ludford, 1976). The incidence of acne increased rapidly between 12 and 17 years, particularly in boys. When related to maturational age, mild acne showed an earlier rise, leveling off in the middle of adolescent maturation, whereas the incidence of severe acne showed its greatest increase from mid- to late adolescence. Severe acne was more common in boys. The steroidal hormones are the primary culprits in acne, and the higher levels of androgen secretion in boys probably account for the sex difference. Acne was also slightly more common among those rated as being in poor or fair health either by themselves or their parents. Also those who reported, or were reported as, eating too much or too little were more likely to have acne (Hamachek, in chapter 4, discusses the impact of such problems as acne on the self-concept of the adolescent).

Nutrition is, of course, related to both growth and health. The most commonly found dietary lack among adolescents in the United States is iron but both undernutrition as judged by caloric intake and overnutrition as judged by obesity occur with disturbing frequency (Abraham, Carroll, Dresser & Johnson, 1977).

─────────── SUMMARY ───────────

Biologically, adolescence is the period of transition from the sexual immaturity of childhood to the sexual maturation of adulthood. This maturation of the reproductive system is accompanied by marked changes in secondary sexual characteristics and in the size, composition, and function of most of the tissues of the body. At no time in the life span are individual differences within a sex so marked. Further, marked differences between the sexes become established. During this period, the developmental status of the two sexes becomes markedly out of joint.

Both individual and sex differences during adolescence have important implications for behavior. Some of the suggested readings discuss these in detail. Let us close here with a few summary examples. The peak growth in height of girls precedes that of boys by about 2½ years. Indeed, almost all girls complete their adolescent growth by the time the boys' peak occurs. From about 11 to 14, the average girl is taller than the average boy, and from 9 or 10 to about 14½ she is also heavier. Within each sex there are early, average, and late maturers. Differences among late and early maturers are so great that, for example, one 14-year-old boy may have reached his adult size while another has yet to begin his adolescent development. At age 15, early maturing boys exceed late maturers by about 8 inches and 30 pounds.

Yet youths of the same chronological age are in the same classroom, so a class of 12-year-olds is likely to contain some girls who are completely mature, and a class of 16-year-olds is likely to have some boys who are still quite immature. Many interest patterns and behaviors of adolescents are more congruent with their maturational age than with their chronological age. Consider the problems that this maturational mix makes for both pupils and teachers. The reader will find these problems discussed in more detail later in the book. Individual differences in maturation can elicit feelings of both pride and discomfort in the adolescent who is going through the various stages of biological development.

SUGGESTIONS FOR FURTHER READING

CLAUSEN, J. A. The social meaning of differential physical and sexual maturation. In S. E. Dragastin & G. H. Elder, Jr. (Eds.), *Adolescence in the life cycle.* New York: Wiley, 1975.

EICHORN, D. H. Adolescence. In D. L. Sills (Ed.), *International encyclopedia of the social sciences* (Vol. 1). New York: Macmillan and Free Press, 1968.

EICHORN, D. H. Asynchronizations in adolescent development. In S. E. Dragastin & G. H. Elder, Jr. (Eds.), *Adolescence in the life cycle.* New York: Wiley, 1975.

McKIGNEY, J. I., & MUNRO, H. N. (Eds.), *Nutrient requirements in adolescence.* Cambridge, Mass.: MIT Press, 1975.

STOLZ, H. R., & STOLZ, L. M. *Somatic development of adolescent boys.* New York: Macmillan, 1951.

TANNER, J. M. Physical growth. In P. H. Mussen (Ed.), *Carmichael's manual of child psychology* (Vol. 1). New York: Wiley, 1970.

BIBLIOGRAPHY

ABRAHAM, S., CARROLL, M. D., DRESSER, C. M., & JOHNSON, C. L. Dietary intake findings. *Vital and Health Statistics,* Series 11, No. 202. Washington, D.C.: Department of Health, Education, and Welfare, 1977.

ABRAHAM, S., CARROLL, M. D., DRESSER, C. M., & JOHNSON, C. L. Dietary intake of persons 1–74 years of age in the United States. *Advance Data,* 1977, No. 8, U.S. Department of Health, Education, and Welfare.

ABRAHAM, S., LOWENSTEIN, F. W., & O'CONNELL, D. E. Preliminary findings of the first health and nutrition examination survey, United States, 1971–1972: anthropometric and clinical findings. No. (HRA) 75-1229, U.S. Department of Health, Education, and Welfare, 1975.

BERENBERG, S. R. *Puberty: Biologic and psychosocial components.* Leiden: H. E. Stenfert Kroese B. V., 1975.

BORSOS, A., TAKÁCS, I., & SMID, I. Endocrine and somatic background of the perimenarche. In O. G. Eiben (Ed.), *Growth and development physique, Symposia biologica Hungarica 20.* Budapest: Akadëmiai Kiadó, 1977.

CHILMAN, G. S. *Adolescent sexuality in a changing American society.* DHEW Publication No. (NIH) 79–1426. Washington, D.C.: U.S. Department of Health, Education, and Welfare, 1979.

COLEMAN, J. S., BREMNER, R. H. CLARK, B. R., DAVIS, J. B., EICHORN, D. H., GRILICHES, Z., KETT, J. F., RYDER, N. B., DOERING, Z. B., & MAYS, J. M. *Youth: Transition to adulthood.* Chicago: University of Chicago Press, 1974.

CYPRESS, B. K. Office visits for hypertension, National Ambulatory Medical Care Survey: United States, January 1975–December 1976. *Advance Data,* 1978, No. 28, U.S. Department of Health, Education, and Welfare.

DUCHARME, J. R., ALBERTI, G., FOREST, M. G., DePERETTI, E., SEMPÉ, M., & BERTRAND, J. Pubertal pattern of plasma androgens and estrogens from childhood through adolescence. *Acta Paediatrica Scandinavica,* 1974, *63,* 342–352.

EICHORN, D. H. Adolescence. In D. L. Sills (Ed.), *International encyclopedia of the social sciences* (Vol. 1). New York: Macmillan and Free Press, 1968.

EICHORN, D. H. Physiological development. In P. H. Mussen (Ed.), *Carmichael's manual of child psychology* (Vol. 1). New York: Wiley, 1970.

EICHORN, D. H. Biological, psychological, and socio-cultural aspects of adolescence and youth. In J. S. Coleman et al. (Eds.), *Youth: Transition to adulthood.* Washington, D.C.: U.S. Government Printing Office, 1973.

EICHORN, D. H. Asynchronizations in adolescent development. In S. E. Dragastin & G. H. Elder, Jr. (Eds.), *Adolescence in the life cycle.* New York: Wiley, 1975.

ESCOMEL, E. La plus jeune mère du monde. *La Presse Medicale,* 1939, *47,* 875.

EZZATI, T. Ambulatory care utilization patterns of children and young adults. *Vital and Health Statistics,* Series 13, No. 39. Washington D.C.: U.S. Department of Health, Education, and Welfare, 1978.

FAUST, M. S. Somatic development of adolescent girls. *Monographs of the Society for Research in Child Development,* 1977, *42,* Serial No. 169.

FORD, C. S., & BEACH, F. A. *Patterns of sexual behavior.* New York: Harper, 1951.

GRUMBACH, M. M. Onset of puberty. In S. R. Berenberg (Ed.), *Puberty: Biologic and psychosocial components.* Leiden: H. E. Stenfert Kroese B. V., 1975.

HAMILL, P. V. V., DRIZD, T. A., JOHNSON, C. L., REED, R. B., & ROCHE, A. F. NCHS growth curves for children birth–18 years. *Vital and Health Statistics,* Series 11, No. 165. Washington, D.C.: Department of Health, Education, and Welfare, 1977.

HEALD, F., LEVY, P. S., HAMILL, P. V. V., & ROWLAND, M. Hematocrit values of youth 12–17 years. *Vital and Health Statistics,* Series 11, No. 146. Washington, D.C.: U.S. Department of Health, Education, and Welfare, 1974.

JOHNSON, M. L. T., & ROBERTS, J. Prevalence of dermatological disease among persons 1–74 years of age: United States. *Advance Data,* 1977, No. 4, U.S. Department of Health, Education, and Welfare.

JOHNSTON, F. E., HAMILL, P. V. V., & LEMESHOW, S. Skinfold thickness of youths 12–17 years, United States. *Vital and Health Statistics,* Series 11, No. 132. Washington, D.C.: Department of Health, Education, and Welfare, 1974.

KELLY, J. E., & HARVEY, C. R. Decayed, missing, and filled teeth among youths 12–17 years. *Vital and Health Statistics,* Series 11, No. 144. Washington, D.C.: U.S. Department of Health, Education, and Welfare, 1974.

KELLY, J. E., & HARVEY, C. R. An assessment of the occlusion of the teeth of youths 12–17 years. *Vital and Health Statistics,* Series 11, No. 162. Washington, D.C.: U.S. Department of Health, Education, and Welfare, 1977.

LEVY, P. S., HAMILL, P. V. V., HEALD, F., & ROWLAND, M. Serum uric acid values of youths 12–17 years. *Vital and Health Statistics,* Series 11, No. 152. Washington, D.C.: U.S. Department of Health, Education, and Welfare, 1975.

LEVY, P. S., HAMILL, P. V. V., HEALD, F., & ROWLAND, M. Total serum cholesterol values of youths 12–17 years. *Vital and Health Statistics,* Series 11, No. 156. Washington, D.C.: U.S. Department of Health, Education, and Welfare, 1976.

MACMAHON, B. Age at menarche: United States. *Vital and Health Statistics,* Series 11, No. 133. Washington, D.C.: U.S. Department of Health, Education, and Welfare, 1974.

MARSHALL, W. A. Interrelationships of skeletal maturation, sexual development and somatic growth in man. *Annals of Human Biology,* 1974, *1,* 29–40.

ODELL, W. D., & SWERDLOFF, R. S. Maturation of sexual function. In S. R. Berenberg (Ed.), *Puberty: Biologic and psychosocial components.* Leiden: H. E. Stenfert Kroese B. V., 1975.

OLIVER, L. I. The association of health attitudes and perceptions of youths 12–17 years of age with those of their parents. *Vital and Health Statistics,* Series 11, No. 161. Washington, D.C.: U.S. Department of Health, Education, and Welfare, 1977.

PYLE, S. I., WATERHOUSE, A. M., & GREULICH, W. W. *A radiographic standard of reference for the growing hand and wrist.* Chicago: Year Book Medical Publishers, 1971.

ROBERTS, J. Eye examination findings among youths 12–17 years: United States. *Vital and Health Statistics,* Series 11, No. 155. Washington, D.C.: U.S. Department of Health, Education, and Welfare, 1975.

ROBERTS, J., & AHUJA, E. M. Hearing levels of youths 12–17 years: United States. *Vital and Health Statistics,* Series 11, No. 145. Washington, D.C.: U.S. Department of Health, Education, and Welfare, 1975.

ROBERTS, J., & AHUJA, E. M. Hearing sensitivity and related medical findings among youths 12–17 years: United States. *Vital and Health Statistics,* Series 11, No. 145. Washington, D.C.: U.S. Department of Health, Education, and Welfare, 1975.

ROBERTS, J., & LUDFORD, J. Skin conditions of youths. *Vital and Health Statistics,* Series 11, No. 157. Washington, D.C.: U.S. Department of Health, Education, and Welfare, 1976.

ROBERTS, J., & LUDFORD, J. Monocular visual acuity of persons 4–74 years: United States, 1971–1972. *Vital and Health Statistics,* Series 11, No. 201. Washington, D.C.: U.S. Department of Health, Education, and Welfare, 1977.

ROBERTS, J., & MAURER, K. Blood pressure levels of persons 6–74 years: United States, 1971–1974. *Vital and Health Statistics,* Series 11, No. 203. Washington, D.C.: U.S. Department of Health, Education, and Welfare, 1977. (a)

ROBERTS, J., & MAURER, K. Blood pressure of youths 12–17 years: United States. *Vital and Health Statistics,* Series 11, No. 163. Washington, D.C.: U.S. Department of Health, Education, and Welfare, 1977. (b)

ROBERTS, J., & ROWLAND, M. Refraction status and motility defects of persons 4–74 years: United States, 1971–1972. *Vital and Health Statistics,* Series 11, No. 206. Washington, D.C.: U.S. Department of Health, Education, and Welfare, 1978.

ROBERTS, J., & SLABY, D. Refraction status of youths 12–17 years: United States. *Vital and Health Statistics,* Series 11, No. 148. Washington, D.C.: U.S. Department of Health, Education, and Welfare, 1974.

ROCHE, A. F., ROBERTS, J., & HAMILL, P. V. V. Skeletal maturity of youths 12–17 years. *Vital and Health Statistics,* Series 11, No. 160. Washington, D.C.: U.S. Department of Health, Education, and Welfare, 1976.

ROCHE, A. F., ROBERTS, J., & HAMILL, P. V. V. Skeletal maturity of youths 12–17 years: Racial, geographic area, and socioeconomic differentials. *Vital and Health Statistics,* Series 11, No. 167. Washington, D.C.: Department of Health, Education, and Welfare, 1974.

SANCHEZ, M. J. Periodontal disease among youths 12–17 years. *Vital and Health Statistics,* Series 11, No. 141. Washington, D.C.: U.S. Department of Health, Education, and Welfare, 1974.

SANCHEZ, M. J. Oral hygiene among youths 12–16 years. *Vital and Health Statistics,* Series 11, No. 151. Washington, D.C.: U.S. Department of Health, Education, and Welfare, 1975.

SCANLON, J. Self-reported health behavior and attitudes of youths 12–17 years: United States. *Vital and Health Statistics,* Series 11, No. 147. Washington, D.C.: Department of Health, Education, and Welfare, 1975.

SECKEL, H. P. G. Sex examples of precocious sexual development. II. Studies in growth and maturation. *American Journal of the Diseases of Children,* 1950, *79,* 278–309.

SHOCK, N. W. The effect of menarche on basal physiological functions in girls. *American Journal of Physiology,* 1943, *139,* 288–292.

SLABY, D., & ROBERTS, J. Color vision deficiences in youths: United States. *Vital and Health Statistics,* Series 11, No. 134. Washington, D.C.: U.S. Department of Health, Education, and Welfare, 1974.

TANNER, J. M. *Growth at adolescence* (2nd ed.). Oxford: Blackwell, 1962.

TANNER, J. M. Growth and endocrinology of the adolescent. In L. Gardner (Ed.), *Endocrine and genetic diseases of childhood.* Philadelphia: Saunders, 1969.

TANNER, J. M. Physical growth. In P. H. Mussen (Ed.), *Carmichael's manual of child psychology* (Vol. 1). New York: Wiley, 1970.

4

PSYCHOLOGY AND DEVELOPMENT OF THE ADOLESCENT SELF

Don E. Hamachek

Adolescence is a very special time in the human life cycle. It is a time for finishing the task of growing up and for starting the business of growing away. It is a collage of emotional happenings, intellectual changes, and physical maturity spread over a 5 to 7 year time span. Its events are simultaneously exciting and exhilarating, yet scarey and confusing. There is virtually no aspect of an adolescent's physical, social, emotional, or intellectual self that is not subject to modification. With the exception of the first several years of life, during the adolescent years a person experiences more growth and maturational changes than at any other time during the life cycle. Consider some examples. Between the ages of 11 and 18, and depending on whether the adolescent is a boy or a girl, his or her height may increase by as much as 25% and weight may double what it was at age 10. Hair begins growing all over the body, acne and blackheads appear as a consequence of overactive, oil secreting sebaceous glands, and facial features change for better or for worse as the nose and chin assume their final adult proportions.

On the social front, friendships grow deeper and more profound, cliques develop, crowds form, and boy–girl relationships grow increasingly more exciting and tempting, but a little scarey too, as the complex chemistry of awakening sexuality stirs new motivations.

The emotional life of the typical adolescent is a series of fluctuating ups and downs, with the ups being very up and the downs being very down. Nothing, for example, is more exhilarating than being in love for the first time, and nothing is more despairing than falling out of love for the first time. Lacking an experimental base against which to measure their emotional highs and lows, things usually seem much better or a whole lot worse than they really are. Only time and more experience with life can help here. Intellectually, the typical adolescent shifts from thinking primarily in "here and now" terms to the more mature cognitive ability of making logical deductions from abstract hypothetical events. It is a time for raising such questions as: what am I, how am I coming across to others, how did I get to be this way in the first place, and what will I do with my life? Actually the adolescent years are not so much a time of creating a self as they are a time for discovering the self that's already there.

Don E. Hamachek is Professor of Counseling, Personnel Services and Educational Psychology at Michigan State University. Among the books that he has edited or written are *Encounters with the Self; Human Dynamics in Psychology and Education; Behavior Dynamics in Teaching, Learning, and Growth;* and *The Self in Growth, Teaching, and Learning.* He has also contributed a sizable number of journal articles on topics such as the self-concept, child-rearing, teaching practices, and human behavior.

WHAT DO WE MEAN BY ADOLESCENCE?

Adolescence is such a commonly accepted growth stage in Western culture that most people consider it an inevitable and predictable fact of life that has been around since the beginning of time. Not so. As it turns out, adolescence is neither a universal happening nor does it have lengthy historical credentials (Kett, 1977). The Greeks and the Romans, for example, did not view it as a separate growth stage, except for the relatively short 1- to 2-year period it took to change from sexual immaturity to sexual maturity. Although the Roman emperor Claudius was regarded by his relatives in the Claudian and Julian families as somewhat dull and slow in developing, he was nonetheless married at 12 and a high priest at 13.

The leap from childhood straight into adulthood with no adolescent apprenticeship was typical not only of classical cultures, but also characteristic of the Middle Ages and the Renaissance. For example, Philip Aries (1962), who has traced the history of adolescence, notes that in the 1300s and 1400s elementary-age boys frequently went to school armed with sabers. Thus, age has not always been a criterion for deciding what growing youngsters could do or what they should be taught. Aries (1962) has further observed that pupils in some of the French primary grades in the 1670s ranged in age from 9 to 17. Those in the highest grades were anywhere between 12 and 20. For both those who went to school and those who did not, 7 years old was considered to be the age of adulthood in most early Western cultures. For example, within certain hunting cultures, childhood terminates by age 8; within certain agrarian cultures it ceases anywhere between 8 and 12 (Landis, 1945). Only within our contemporary Western culture is this period we call adolescence viewed as an extension of childhood dependency.

In a purely physical sense, adolescence is indeed a universal phenomenon. What varies are the meanings and expectations that different cultures and various subcultures place on growing youngsters as they move through this growth stage. In terms of physical development, adolescence commences with the prepubertal growth spurt and ends with the attainment of full physical maturity.

In a purely psychological sense, adolescence refers more to a state of mind, an attitude, a life-style that begins with puberty and ends when one is relatively independent of parental control. You have probably noted from your own experiences that the cessation of adolescence varies from individual to individual. For some, psychological adolescence is terminated when they are about eighteen, while for others psychological adolescence persists into their twenties or thirties or, sadly enough, even later.

You can see that there is an emphasis on the idea of attaining a higher level of physical and psychological maturity during adolescence. This is consistent, by the way, with the Latin word *adolescere* from which adolescence is derived, meaning "to grow" or "to grow into maturity." This growth toward maturity may be complex and difficult or it may be a period that one goes through with surprisingly few complications.

All in all, we can reasonably conclude that adolescence begins with signs of sexual maturity in both physical and social development and ends when the individual becomes self-supporting, responsible, and accepted in most ways by the peers toward whom he or she looks for approval, recognition, and advice. I want to emphasize the importance of shifting one's needs for approval, recognition, and advice to the peer group because one of the major symptoms of a persisting *psychological* adolescence, particularly when physical adolescence has been completed, is a continued dependence on one's parents as a major source of approval, recognition, and guidance. Twenty-five-year-old adults who persist in calling their parents every time they have a rift with their spouse or who continue to live with their parents even though they are financially able to support themselves could very well be psychologically adolescent in their dependency and their inability to think for themselves.

A major achievement of adolescence, and one that usually signals its conclusion, is the capacity and willingness of a growing youngster to fall out with his or her parents, which is the necessary first step of falling in love with another person, or making one's way as an individual single person. An important route to doing this is through the accomplishment of certain developmental tasks.

MAJOR DEVELOPMENTAL TASKS OF ADOLESCENCE

The adolescent self does not mature simply because a developing youngster grows older and taller. Rather, maturity grows out of certain interpersonal experiences and educational outcomes or accomplishments. Havighurst (1972) has coined the term *developmental tasks* to describe certain rather specific "tasks" that developing youth must accomplish at various stages of growth in order to reach the next level of development. A developmental task, then, is an event that occurs at a certain point in an individual's life, and its successful achievement spurs that person to further growth and probable success with later tasks. Conversely, failure to master the tasks associated with a particular stage of growth can lead to disapproval by society and difficulty with later tasks.

The major developmental tasks confronting the adolescent boy and girl include the following:

Achieving new and more mature relations with age mates of both sexes.
Achieving a masculine or feminine social role.

Accepting one's physique and using the body effectively.
Achieving emotional independence from parents and other adults.
Achieving assurance of economic independence.
Selecting and preparing for an occupation.
Preparing for marriage and family life.
Developing intellectual skills and concepts necessary for civic competence.
Desiring and achieving socially responsible behavior.
Acquiring a set of values and an ethnic system as a guide to behavior.

In a sense, these ten developmental tasks are the prerequisite learnings and accomplishments necessary for successful adult living. Each task, in its own way, contributes to the adolescents' maturing sense of self, of who they are, of what they want to be, and how they can best achieve their goals. Unless, for example, adolescents achieve greater maturity and confidence in their relationships with the opposite sex during adolescence, it becomes increasingly difficult to acquire these qualities as they move into adulthood.

Just as there are some individuals who remain psychological adolescents most of their lives, there are others who, unfortunately enough, scramble headlong into adulthood without completely working through the tasks of adolescence. An example of this is the boy who drops out of school before either emotionally or educationally ready for economic independence. Another example is that of two teenagers who marry before they understand themselves (or others) well enough to know that the person they are marrying is really the one they can live with in an intimate relationship. Conger's (1977) review of research related to adolescent marriages led to the startling finding that, in the first five years of marriage, the divorce rate of both men and women who marry younger than age 20 is more than twice that of those who marry at later ages, and that this rate remains consistently higher throughout life.

One unhappily married 23-year-old woman, espoused since she and her husband were 18, expressed her feelings about it this way during a counseling session:

> When Bill and I got married right after high school it was great. We dated each other all through high school and never really considered dating others. Marriage just seemed a natural outgrowth of our relationship. But now, I don't know, it's sorta like we've missed out on something—at least I feel that way and I think he does, too. Isn't it stupid? Here we've been married 5 years and we feel that we're into something we weren't ready for in the first place.

This young woman is saying what many young adults (and an increasing number of older adults) feel as they look back over their adolescent years, namely, the wish to have had a broader range of experiences with a greater number of persons while the opportunities were available. Adolescence comes but once, and there's no way to go back to it.

The developmental tasks of adolescence are not simply hurdles that must be jumped in some mechanical way. They are, in a deeper sense, highly personalized experiences, each of which help adolescents to define themselves as individuals and to develop a recognizable and reasonably predictable "self" from which both a self-concept and feelings of self-esteem can grow.

WHAT IS THE SELF?

The term *self,* as it will be used here, is that part of each of us of which we are aware. It is the sum total of all that a person can consciously call his or her being. *Self-concept* refers to that particular cluster of ideas and attitudes we have about our awareness at any given moment in time. Or, another way of looking at it is to view our self-concept as the organized cognitive structure derived from experiences of our own self. Thus, out of our awareness of ourselves grows the ideas (concepts) of the kind of person we see ourselves as being. Self-concept, then, is the cognitive aspect of the self.

Self-esteem, on the other hand, is the affective dimension of the self. Not only do we have certain ideas about who we are, but we have certain *feelings* about who we are. Self-esteem, then, refers quite literally to the extent to which we admire or value the self. Out of all of this emerges what is commonly referred to as *personality.* Different people have different levels of awareness of the self, different ideas about themselves as persons, and, as a consequence, different ways for expressing what we interpret as their personality.

The self can be reflected through one's personality in many different ways. It may be Sally's assertiveness or Sandy's shyness. It may be Robert's braggadocio or Richard's quiet confidence. It can be one person's open candor and another person's guarded secrecy. Each of us has a certain self-image constructed from the "sort of person I am."

The self can be best understood if it is viewed as a social phenomenon growing within a larger framework of comparative interpersonal relationships. That is, one's sense of self is nurtured not only by what one would ideally like to be but also by how one views one's self as actually performing in relation to other people. We live in a social world, and it is no surprise that the self is very much a social product.

Comparison of one's self with others is an important and ongoing process that allows the adolescent boy and girl to check the self they would like to be against the social reality of what they can more realistically expect to be and do. This is a process that continues throughout life, but it has more energy and intensity during the adolescent years. A major force behind this increased intensity is the adolescent's growing egocentrism.

ADOLESCENT EGOCENTRISM AS RELATED TO DEVELOPMENT OF THE SELF

It is a well-accepted fact that adolescents go through a very intense period of preoccupation with themselves. This is a rather unusual kind of preoccupation, and it grows directly from what Inhelder and Piaget (1958) have identified as the adolescent's maturing ability to think abstractly and to make hypotheses. (See chapter 6 by Gallagher and Mansfield on cognitive development.) Suppose we said to a group of 7 and 8 year olds: "Let's suppose that for one day all boys could be girls and all girls could be boys and let's imagine what would happen." You would probably find that many would say: "But we can't do that—boys are boys and girls are girls." Adolescents, on the other hand, could easily accept this contrary-to-fact hypothesis and begin to conceptualize what some outcomes might be. The shift away from the specific, tangible, black and white thinking associated with the concrete-operational stage of the elementary school years to the propositional or formal operations period of the adolescent years (Forman & Kuschner, 1977) enables adolescents not only to see themselves but to *imagine* themselves.

Elkind (1967) suggested that it is this capacity to take account of other people's thought that is the crux of adolescent egocentrism. The reason this is an unusual type of egocentrism is that adolescents are typically so concerned with themselves that they fail to differentiate between their own cognitive preoccupations and what others are thinking. Accordingly, adolescents assume that others are as consumed with their behavior and appearance as they are themselves. In this sense, Elkind reasons that the adolescent is continually constructing, or reacting to, an imaginary audience. There seems to be a good bit of truth in this observation. I know it rings a bell in my own memories as an adolescent boy, and it squares with my work with adolescents in classroom and clinical settings. I recall, for example, a 14-year-old girl's description of how she prepared herself to come into a group: "I try to get a picture in my head of how people will look at me and how they will feel about me. I don't know why I do that, but it seems that the less certain I feel about myself the more I worry about how others will feel about me." This feeling of uncertain acceptance seems characteristic of many adolescents and helps explain why they might create an imaginary audience against which to try themselves out.

Elkind (1967) speculates that the egocentrism of adolescence decreases by age 16 or so, as the imaginary audience is increasingly replaced by the reactions of the real audience. The imaginary audience may be a figment of the adolescent's cognitive projections, but we would be wise to remember that, to the adolescent, the imagined audience is quite real. The imaginary audience is a way to test a growing, changing, emerging self against possible hypothetical reactions to it. This kind of testing helps adolescents not only to understand themselves, but to gradually differentiate between their own self-perceptions and the perceptions others have of them.

THE SELF BEGINS ITS DEVELOPMENT PRIOR TO ADOLESCENCE

The concept that the self begins its development prior to adolescence is a critical one because it is crucial that parents and teachers have a deep appreciation of how important a youngster's early years are to his or her developing sense of self. As it turns out, adolescence is *not* a time when dramatic shifts take place in how youngsters feel about themselves.

Adolescence is a time when the self expands and matures. Quite literally, it builds on the foundation laid during the first twelve or so years of life. This is not to suggest that radical changes don't sometimes occur, but it is to suggest that waiting until adolescence to change a youngster may be to wait too long. Nothing mystical will happen to resolve an aggressive 6th-grade boy's explosive rage or a shy, frightened 7th-grade girl's terror of others *just because* they enter the adolescent years. Research related to the stability of self-concept over time is rather clear and consistent in pointing to the fact that a growing youngster's sense of self tends to continue in the direction it started *if the basic experiences and significant others remain essentially the same* (Kagen & Moss, 1960; Piers & Davis, 1964; Bronson, 1966; Goodenough & Karp, 1967; Mischel, 1969; Bachman, O'Malley & Johnston, 1978; Hamachek, 1978; Jersild, Brook & Brook, 1978).

THE SELF-CONCEPT CAN ALWAYS CHANGE

Impressive as the evidence may seem for early determination of personality and for its stability over time, there are also reasons for believing that one's self-concept can change. The findings do not suggest that the self is *completely* formed during early childhood. Also, even though a general personality trend may be established quite early, the manner in which it is expressed may continue to be quite susceptible to change. My own personal experience as a psychotherapist is quite consistent with a large body of clinical literature (Corsini, 1965; Mueller, 1973) that strongly indicates that youth and adults can change both their behaviors and feelings about themselves at any point in time.

Although psychologists are pretty much in agreement that the influence of the early years is important, the experiences of adolescence and later years are also important in either reinforcing or changing the character structure tentatively shaped during the early years. For example, after a thorough review of the empirical literature, one psychologist (Orlansky, 1949, p. 35) concluded that "events subsequent to the first year or two of life have the power to confirm or deny the personality of the growing infant, to perpetuate or remake it, depending on whether the circumstances of later childhood perpetuate or alter the situation in which the child was reared."

This seems to me a hopeful and optimistic viewpoint for those who move in the world of adolescents, in their various roles as professionals or parents. It suggests that, as the adolescent self is being crystallized, it is also going through a period of revision and refinement. This means that parents, teachers, and other professionals, who care enough to make a difference, can, through the medium of a meaningful relationship, be significant and positive forces in helping adolescents grow in healthy and self-actualizing ways.

All in all, the typical adolescent's concept of self is a tenuous, fragile thing. Arriving at a more mature definition of the self is a major undertaking. Indeed, it seems at times like a terribly bewildering experience, an idea one adolescent girl (Williams, 1972, p. 642) expressed by asking:

> *How do you tell anyone:*
> *This is me.*
> *I am this and that*
> *and—then—again—*
> *I am not?*
> *Can you put down*
> *in black and white*
> *why you are as you are*
> *if sometimes it is not clear to you*
> *that you are at all?*

Williams raises an issue that is no doubt characteristic of practically all adolescents, namely, a certain amount of uncertainty about the self.

THE MORE UNCERTAIN THE ADOLESCENT SELF THE MORE SUSCEPTIBLE IT IS TO CHANGE

Some adolescents have not had the sort of positive life experiences that provided the emotional footings on which the foundation for a stable, consistent self-concept could be constructed. As psychiatrist Erik Erikson

(1963, 1968) has observed, youngsters who grow up with a sense of mistrust, feelings of shame and doubt about themselves, feelings of guilt about their behavior, and a sense of inferiority about their abilities are exceptionally good candidates for experiencing more than the usual amount of identity confusion during adolescence. Adolescent *A*, whose childhood provided a rich foundation of positive social interaction, self-respect, and self-confidence, uses adolescence as a time to *refine* the self that has already been started. Adolescent *B*, whose childhood provided little in the way of expectations to live up to or too few adult models to look up to, or perhaps too few rules to follow may be more apt to use adolescence as a time to *define* a self that never really got started to begin with.

It is the adolescents who tend to fit into this latter category who may be most susceptible to having their self-concepts manipulated and changed. There is, for example, evidence to suggest that adolescents who are most alienated from themselves and from their significant others are also most apt to be influenced by various countercultural movements such as the Children of God, the Divine Light Mission, the Unification Church, and the Hare Krishna (Carroll, 1973; Robbins, Anthony & Curtis, 1975). Research (Harder, Richardson & Simmons, 1972) indicates that youth who are most susceptible to the persuasion by propaganda (some call it brainwashing) used by these various religious movements are inclined to come from unhappy homes, to have experimented widely with drugs, and to score low on tests measuring such qualities as self-confidence and personal adjustment. They are ripe for someone else's version of who they are and how to live their lives. Under these conditions, an adolescent's definition of self is sometimes sold to the most persuasive bidder. An example of this can be found in the words of sophomore college student Allison Scott, who joined a nomadic religious commune that called itself simply the *Body*. As Allison describes herself:

> I thought I wanted to become a nurse, but I wasn't sure. I thought Christianity meant a lot to me, but I wasn't sure of that either. I guess I was kind of desperately looking for somebody who had firm yes-and-no answers, somebody who was sure about things and could make me sure. I had never known anything like the Body before, but I couldn't stay away. I kept going back and asking questions, and they always knew the answers—I mean they really knew them. (Gunther, 1976, p. 23)

Adolescents who seek their sense of self and personal identity in countercultural groups frequently reflect a state of self-concept confusion and uncertainty. Psychiatrist James Brussel has observed that youth who join oddball cults are usually in that kind of state. He goes on to observe, "They have no strong beliefs that can be violated—and what's more, they're desperately looking for somebody to tell them what to believe. They want some firm, easy-to-understand code, with an assertive personality to back it up . . ." (cited in Gunther, 1976, p. 27).

It is perhaps worth noting that mystical and religious cults seem to do their most successful recruiting among college freshmen and seniors. Both of these groups are making major transitions. Freshmen are moving away from parents and home for the first time, and many feel scared and bewildered. Seniors are preparing to step out into the world of jobs and responsibilities where they have to prove themselves as adults. Both freshman and senior classes may have candidates ripe for the tempting offerings of certain religious cults that promise definitive answers, a protecting and structured environment, and a "father" who is the judge of right and wrong. What is there about the adolescents' homes that prepares them or does not prepare them for decision making in the adult world?

IMPACT OF PARENTS ON THE ADOLESCENT'S GROWING SELF

A major developmental task of adolescence is that of moving toward greater self-sufficiency and self-direction. Both clinical evidence and empirical research make it abundantly clear that parents greatly influence the achievement of that task. Although adolescent boys and girls are continually prodded toward adulthood, parents sometimes behave as if their reaching it is in some remote and far-off future. As one frustrated sixteen-year-old boy expressed it: "You know, I think my parents want me to be independent and think for myself, but apparently not while I'm living at home." Discrepancies frequently occur between parents and youth in how the adolescent self is perceived. Perhaps the observation that adulthood comes about two years later than the adolescent claims, and about two years earlier than their parents are ready to admit is more accurate than we realize.

The fact is that most parents do not easily let go of their emerging adolescents, a reality that has both good and bad points. The positive side is that the adolescent boy and girl must work harder and withstand stiffer challenges to prove to their parents and to *themselves* that they really can make it on their own and that their self-concepts are sturdy enough to withstand both the responsibilities and setbacks accompanying independent adult living. The negative side is that parents who hang on too tightly can cause a young person struggling to be free to either feel guilty ("My parents need me so—how can I leave them?") or inadequate ("They don't trust me on my own—maybe I'm not able enough."). As Douvan and Adelson (1966) point out in the results of their study of a large number of adolescents, either too much or too little involvement can inhibit the adolescent's achievement of independence. If parents are too little involved, the security necessary for self-direction is underdeveloped. On the other hand, too much involvement may generate dependency needs which interfere with the growth of autonomy.

Child-Rearing Styles and Their Differential Expressions

No question about it, parents have a strong impact on an adolescent's growing self. However, the kind of impact, the intensity of it, indeed, whether it is healthy or unhealthy depends largely on the sort of parenting style to which an adolescent is exposed. Research has shown that there are many different child-rearing styles, and each has its own particular characteristics and consequences.

Consider, for example, the seven different parenting styles distinguished by Elder (1962) in his study involving over 7400 adolescents:

Autocratic No allowance is provided for the youth to express his views on a subject nor for him to assert leadership or initiative in self government.

Authoritarian Although the adolescent contributes to the solution of problems, his parents always decide issues according to their own judgment.

Democratic The adolescent contributes freely to discussion of issues relevant to his behavior, and may even make his own decisions; however, in all instances the final decision is either formulated by parents or meets their approval.

Equalitarian This type of structure represents minimal role differentiation. Parents and the adolescent are involved to a similar degree in making decisions pertaining to the adolescent's behavior.

Permissive The adolescent assumes a more active and influential position in formulating decisions which concern him than do his parents.

Laissez-Faire The position of the adolescent in relation to that of his parents in decision making is clearly more differentiated in terms of power and activity. In this type of relationship the youth has the option of either subscribing to or disregarding parental wishes in making his decisions.

Ignoring This type of structure, if it can be legitimately considered as such, represents actual parental divorcement from directing the adolescent's behavior.

As the parent-child relationships move from the autocratic to the ignoring type one can see a gradual increase in the freedom adolescents experience for making their own decisions and a concurrent decrease in the decisions made by their parents for them.

These relationship styles represent variations in the allocation of both communication and control between parents of the adolescent. In the autocratic structure, it is primarily from parent to child and parent over child, while in the permissive structure it is primarily from child to parent and child over parent.

How did the 7400 adolescents respond to these varying patterns of parent-child relationships? It was found that those exposed to *democratic* practices considered their parents most fair (approximately 95% for both mother and father). Equalitarian parents ranked second; autocratic parents ranked lowest. These results are consistent with other research reports (Dusek, 1977; Lambert, Rothschild, Altland & Green, 1978), which, together, support what common sense and experience have been teaching us for years—namely, democratic relationships between parents and adolescents tend to encourage identification and closeness, whereas autocratic relationships tend to foster resentment and distance.

In order for adolescents to develop self-concepts that allow them to be reasonably self-reliant, adaptable, creative, and self-disciplined individuals, there must be as many opportunities as possible for incorporating these qualities during the growth years. A youngster growing up in either a very authoritarian or very permissive house gets shortchanged in this regard. The late Margaret Mead's (1970, p. 904) anthropological studies of family life have spanned the globe over the past forty years and offer some good reasons about why this may be so:

> Authoritarian control and permissive noncontrol may both shield the child from the opportunity to engage in vigorous interaction with people. Demands which cannot be met or no demands, suppression of conflict or sidestepping of conflict, refusal to help or too much help, unrealistically high or low standards, all may curb or understimulate the child so that he fails to achieve the knowledge and experience which could realistically reduce his dependence upon the outside world. The authoritarian and permissive parent may both create, in different ways, a climate in which the child is not desensitized to the anxiety associated with non-conformity. Both models minimize dissent, the former by suppression and the latter by diversion or indulgence. To learn how to dissent, the child may need a strongly held position from which to diverge and then be allowed under some circumstances to pay the price for nonconformity by being punished. Spirited give and take within the home, if accompanied by respect and warmth, may teach the child how to express aggression in self-serving and prosocial causes and to accept the partially unpleasant consequences of such actions.

A Balance Between Parental Warmth and Firmness Is Important

You might ask: "Is there a reasonable balance between too much control and too little control?" Apparently there is. The best kind of parenting for adolescents is that which combines just the right mixture of being tough and being permissive. The qualities of *explicit warmth and caring* are important ingredients in that mixture. For example, Baumrind (1977) has noted from her research that it is a combination of parental *warmth* and firm *discipline* that is likely to produce a self-reliant, self-controlled, adequate-feeling youngster. Coopersmith's (1967) research also supports this observation. He found that the most notable antecedents to high self-esteem among youngsters were directly related to parental behavior and the consequences of the rules and regulations that parents establish. As an illustration, he observed that definite and consistently enforced limits on behavior were associated with high self-esteem; that families that maintained clear limits utilized less drastic forms of punishments; and that parents producing children with high self-esteem cared deeply about their children and were not afraid to show it.

We might also add here that not only did parents of high self-esteem youth have attitudes of total or near total acceptance of their children (which does not mean that they accepted or even tolerated all of their behaviors) but they also allowed considerable flexibility within established limits.

Differences Between Warm-Restrictive and Warm-Controlling Parents

It is not enough, however, to say that sufficient amounts of parental warmth are the answer to facilitating a healthy self-concept among adolescent youth. It depends on what factors are combined with the warmth. For example, *restrictive* control is associated with the use of extensive proscriptions and prescriptions covering practically all areas of an adolescent's life. These severely limit the adolescents' autonomy to test themselves out in new ways and to learn new skills. There are many "no's," "keep off" signs, and "don't touch" signals in the life of an adolescent. *Firm control* is different in the sense that the emphasis is less apt to be one that says, "You will be bad if you don't mind" and more apt to be one that says, "I *expect* you to be good." There is a firm and consistent enforcement of the rules, effective resistance against the adolescent's demands, and generally more guiding and showing as opposed to the ordering and telling behavior of restrictive-controlling parents.

Effects of Different Parenting Styles on Self-Concept Development

What kind of self-feelings are likely to be associated with each parenting style? Becker (1964) reported that warm-*restrictive* parents tended to have passive, fearful, dependent children who were generally well behaved. (It is difficult for a passive, fearful, dependent child *not* to behave.) Baumrind (1977) found, however, that warm-*controlling* (in contrast to warm-*restrictive*) parents were likely to have youngsters who feel responsible, assertive, self-reliant, and independent.

Rather than concluding that one particular child-rearing style is better than the rest, we need to recognize that there are both desirable and undesirable aspects associated with any style we might consider. As an example, although fearless, curious, and self-directed adolescents are likely to come from homes in which a psychological climate of democracy and openness prevails, these same youths are also inclined to be aggressive, rebellious, and nonconforming. This is no better illustrated than in Mantell's (1974) investigation of family differences between 25 Green Berets and 25 war resisters. The Special Forces soldiers (Green Berets) were much more likely to have come from homes that were more authoritarian in the sense of stressing obedience and conformity. War resisters, on the other hand, were more likely to come from homes that encourage questioning authority (parents) and independent thinking. I am not suggesting that either one or the other is bad or good—it depends on your values. I bring this to your attention to illustrate further the dramatic effect that parent-child relationships can have on the thinking, behavior, and self-feelings of youth.

Identification with Parents Is an Important Factor

The extent to which boys and girls identify with their parents can affect, for better or for worse, both their interpersonal relationships and feelings about themselves. As a case in point, there is evidence to indicate that a boy's adjustment during adolescence depends to some extent on the sort of affectional ties he has with his father. In an interesting cross-cultural study (Mussen, Young, Caddini & Morante, 1963), it was found that adolescent boys who received little in the way of affection from their fathers were less secure, less self-confident, and less well-adjusted than boys whose fathers were more affectionate. Barclay and Cusumano (1967) have observed that male adolescents without fathers tend to be more passive and less self-reliant than those with fathers. Other research (Heilbrun, 1965, 1970) has revealed that older adolescent males who identified with their fathers were better adjusted and had a stronger sexual identity (more certain about their "maleness") than males who were less identified with their fathers. All in all, it appears that the more masculine boys are closer to their fathers and, as Matteson's (1975) review of the research shows, masculine boys are more apt to be better adjusted, more contented, happier, and smoother in social functioning than less masculine boys.

Just as a healthy sense of self is encouraged as a boy is able to identify with his father so, too, is this the case for a girl's identification with her mother. Mussen and Rutherford (1963) noted that the highly feminine girls in their sample were more likely than girls low in femininity to perceive their mothers as significantly warmer, more nurturing, and more affectionate. We might note here that parental warmth is an important factor in a youngster's identification with a parent because it allows the child to be emotionally close to the parent, a quite necessary prerequisite to becoming *like* the parent. In addition, a warm parent is very likely a *rewarding* parent—the kind of parents, for example, capable of making their children feel good about being around them.

Other research has bound that adolescent girls who see themselves as confident, wise, reasonable, and self-controlled also feel close to their mothers. In contrast, those who felt more distant from their mothers tended to perceive themselves as rebellious, impulsive, touchy, and tactless (Block, 1963). Mother cannot do it all; fathers are important too. Following a thorough review of research literature, Biller and Weiss (1970) concluded that warm, rewarding father-daughter relationships played a vital role in helping a girl to value her femininity and to move toward a positive acceptance of herself as a woman. Research by Hetherington (1973) supports these conclusions, as do Wagner's comments on adolescents who are responsible in the use of their sexuality (see chapter 10).

Seymour Fisher (1972) has found that highly orgasmic married women are more likely to have been raised by men who were "real fathers" to their daughters—that is, men who were dependable, caring, demanding, and insistent that their daughters meet certain moral standards and expectations. Implicit in this seems to be the idea that a strong, dependable masculine father is able to lay the sort of trust groundwork that will be necessary in his daughter's subsequent adult relationships with men. The same seems to be true for the adolescent boy. If he is identified with his father but shares mutually warm feelings with his mother, his relationships to women are more likely to be comfortable and pleasant (Hamachek, 1978).

It may be that once the adolescent boy (or girl) is explicitly and warmly accepted by his father (or her mother), in a mutually caring relationship, then they are free to develop relationships with others without undue concern about whether they are acceptable or lovable. A more primary relationship with a closer significant other has already taught them that they are.

A certain amount of cross-sex identification (see chapter 9) is an important aspect of the adolescent's overall self-concept development. Sargent's (1977) compilation of research points to a conclusion that makes very good sense these days, namely, boys need less of the traits associated with stereotypic masculinity, and girls need less of the restrictiveness associated with stereotypic femininity. Thus boys should be exposed to the kind of maternal warmth we take for granted in raising girls, and girls should have the kind of freedom to explore we encourage in boys.

On the whole, the main trend during the adolescent years as far as influence of parents is concerned is toward a more thorough internalization of parental values, even though there may be considerable hassling about particular points (Troll, Neugarten & Kraines, 1969). This generalization is especially true for girls, who are more apt to be identified with the parental point of view.

In fact, the influence of parents on an adolescent's developing self extends well into adult life. It is not uncommon that those adolescents who battle their parents' beliefs and values so ferociously in their teens come to adopt those same beliefs and values as their own as they enter their twenties (Bath & Lewis, 1962). Others retain undercurrents of bitterness toward their parents, and still others acquire a deeper feeling of respect. Actually, the alleged gulf between adolescents and their parents—the so-called generation gap— is not so large as may once have been the case. National surveys (Yankelovich, 1969; Harris, 1971) involving younger and older adolescents and their parents reveal that approximately two out of three young people and seven out of ten parents agree that the generation gap has been exaggerated. Four out of five adolescents stated that their parents had "lived up to their own ideals," and an additional three out of four adolescents stated that they were in general agreement with their parents' ideals.

Parents are incredibly important. They are primary reference sources for a growing youngster's attitudes, values, and beliefs about life generally and about his or her own sense of self and personal worth specifically. Peers are also important, an idea to which we turn next.

IMPACT OF PEER RELATIONSHIPS ON THE ADOLESCENT'S GROWING SELF

You may recall from your own experience that relationships to age-mates become increasingly important during the adolescent years. Peer group influence hits a peak around middle adolescence and begins to decline after that, when young people begin to go their separate ways. However, during the junior high and high school years, adolescents have a society or "youth culture" of their own, overlapping with, and yet separate from, the larger society in which they live.

There is little question but that the peer group has an enormous impact on an adolescent's developing sense of self. Why does the adolescent peer culture succeed in having such an influence on the behavior and self-attitudes of young people? Medinnus and Johnson (1969, p. 709) think it may be for some of the following reasons:

It succeeds because it is dangerous and exciting and it requires real skills . . . because it is *not* based on such things as class distinctions, which are contrary to our expressed-adult values system but not to our actual behavior; because it *is* based on the idea that the individual should be judged in terms of personal attributes and accomplishments; because it is in many ways more humane and accepting of individual differences than adult cultural values; because it is concerned with expanding self-awareness at a time when people have few means of discovering themselves; because it is against sham; and because it fulfills the needs of young people better than does adult culture.

Functions of the Peer Group

Ausubel (1954) has listed seven basic functions the peer group serves during adolescence. In somewhat modified form, in view of research which has appeared since Ausubel wrote, these functions are as follows:

A Replacement for Family.   To some extent, the peer group takes the place of the family; that is, a youngster can feel a certain status, or lack of it, quite independent of who his or her family is. As you might suspect, this is invaluable preparation for adulthood because it gives one a chance for more objective feedback than parents can usually provide.

A Stabilizing Influence.   Peer group membership is a useful stabilizer during a period of rapid transition. In light of the incredible endocrinal, developmental, and social changes that occur during the brief period of adolescence, it is comforting to know that others are going through the same thing. As one 16-year-old boy put it, "I hate these dumb pimples, but I'd hate them more if I was the only one who had them."

A Source of Self-Esteem.   The peer group can be an important source of self-esteem, in the sense of being important to someone outside the primary family unit. Of course it can work the other way, too, particularly for the adolescent who is isolated or scapegoated.

A Source for Behavioral Standards.   Ausubel takes more or less for granted an issue over which there is some disagreement—namely, that adolescents allow their peer group the authority to set standards. The reasoning is that adolescents thereby affirm their own right to self-determination, since the peer group basically represents what they value in the first place.

This may be, but the evidence does not suggest that the impact of the peer group is any more intense than the influence of the family. For example, Kandel, Lessor, Roberts and Weiss (1970), in a review of the literature, make it clear that belonging to the peer group or the family is not an either-or situation for adolescents. What is more likely is that they belong to *both* the family and the peer group. Although the adolescent moves initially in the direction of the more liberal peer group, there is evidence to suggest that, for basic life decisions, the standards of the family carry more weight than the peer group when the two are in conflict (Coleman, 1965; Douvan & Adelson, 1966; Levitt & Edwards, 1970; Gordon, 1975; McKinney, Fitzgerald & Strommen, 1977). Indeed, Brittain's (1963) research findings on the relative influence of parents and peers on adolescent girls' decision making strongly suggests that for the more important decisions— such as taking a part-time job or reporting an adult who has damaged property—they are more likely to turn to parents for advice. For less important decisions—such as how to dress for a football game or party—they are more likely to turn to their friends. So you can see that the family's influence is quite significant.

However, where parental warmth and a sense of "equal rights" within the home are at a minimum, as is sometimes the case, the peer group may provide both the security and the models that adolescents need. We can say with some certainty that the greater the wall between adolescents and their families, the more attractive the peer culture becomes, and the more they will turn to it for support and identity. It has been noted for instance, that "the peer-oriented child is more a product of parental disregard than of the attractiveness of the peer group—that he turns to his age-mates less by choice than by default" (Condry, Siman & Bronfenbrenner, 1968).

There Is Security in Numbers. The peer group insulates and protects adolescents, to some extent, from the coercions that adults are likely to impose on young people. When adolescents say something on the order of "Well, everyone else is going (or doing it, or wearing it, or whatever), why can't I?" they are raising what has become an almost universal wail of defensive protest designed to implore restricting adults to change their minds. As you can imagine (or remember from your own adolescent years), there is a certain safety in lodging this protest while holding membership within the security of one's peer group. Being able to say that "everyone" is doing it is a much more persuasive statement than "he" or "she" is doing it.

Opportunities for Practice by Doing. Another thing the peer group provides is an opportunity to practice by doing. Dating, participation in extracurricular activities, bull sessions about life, sex, future goals, and the world generally are all important rehearsal experiences for becoming an adult. As one practices by doing, the peer group is a source of instant feedback; it is an audience of self-proclaimed critics watching for flaws in the performance of their own kind and in themselves. Feedback from peers is important because it is objective (sometimes unmercifully so) and it provides cues and information that can be used to modify and refine adolescents' maturing concepts of who they are as persons.

Opportunities for Modeling.   Particularly for disadvantaged youngsters, the peer group offers a psychosocial moratorium that many parents simply cannot provide. Hoffman and Saltzstein (1967), in research relating parental discipline to a child's moral development, found that there was substantial modeling of their parents among middle-class youngsters but almost none among lower socioeconomic status subjects. It may very well be that lower socioeconomic youth are more psychologically dependent on their peers and thus use them more extensively for models.

Peer Acceptance and Social Adjustment

Being liked and being accepted are important at any age, but they seem particularly crucial during the adolescent years. Sometimes the dependence on group approval is so severe that it seems something on the order of a "popularity neurosis." No matter how interested in their own group various clusters of boys and girls seem to be, at a deeper level they are really proclaiming and advertising how interesting *they* are. Individuals within any given peer group may be busy politicking and making time, but so is everyone else. In a sense, they are all campaigning for office, for the esteem and acclaim and recognition that will tell them where they finished in the voting. Actually, the adolescent's concern about getting along with people or having a "good personality" is sometimes less a search for inner strength and more a search for the skills that will gain him or her approval and acceptance whether it be in making the varsity team, playing a musical instrument, getting high grades, developing into the class clown, or being active in extracurricular activities.

The adolescent's need to be liked and accepted is no different than similar needs existing in all of us no matter what age we happen to be. It's just that the typical adolescent boy's and girl's need is more intensified because each is still refining the "personality they will be" and needs as much encouragement and approval along the way as possible.

Factors Influencing Acceptance by Peers

Many factors affect an adolescent's rejection or acceptance by peers, the more important ones being intelligence and ability, special talents, socioeconomic status, and ethnic-group membership.

Although some adolescents feel that being "too smart" is detrimental to social acceptance, reseach reveals that intelligence is positively and significantly related to peer acceptance (Hallworth, Davis & Camston, 1965). Intelligence by itself does not cause either acceptance or rejection. It is, rather, a person's relationships. Intellectual snobs are no more apt to experience peer approval than are their peers of lesser ability who either withdraw into a shell of seclusion or strike out in angry frustration.

Popularity and self-confidence are typically more accessible to members of the culturally dominant majority in most peer groups. As you might guess, the primary reason for this is that through their great numbers they tend to set the norms. Not only are members of socioeconomically deprived subgroups less likely to be accepted by their more economically favored peers, but, surprisingly, they are less likely to be accepted by youths in their own socioeconomic bracket as well (Conger, 1973).

Results of a similar sort are usually found with ethnic minorities (Brody, 1968). However, with the increasing emphasis on ethnic pride and cultural traditions, this picture is beginning to change. It appears that acceptance and popularity for one's own ethnic group is increasing rapidly, particularly among adolescents and young adults (Hraba & Grant, 1970). Havighurst discusses several groups of these youth later within chapter 12.

Youth Culture a Medium for Growth

All in all, the peer and the youth culture provide the medium within which the adolescent secures an identity, however tentative it may be. Because adolescents must separate themselves from their parents, they must, initially at least, reject parental dictates and, occasionally, parental values. Why does this happen? As any one of us can probably testify, "achieving" an identity is an active process, not one of passively purchasing the achievement of others. Typical adolescents are driven by a strong need to become who *they* are, not who their parents are. In order to do this, adolescents go through a stage of being less like their parents and more like their peers. Unfortunately, some parents overreact to this shift in affiliation by behaving as though their youngsters had sworn a blood allegiance to a group of youthful desperadoes bent on burning all parents at the stake. Nothing could be further from the truth. It is simply a necessary phase which all adolescents go through (just as each of us did) in finding themselves.

Another reason the peer group is an important medium for the adolescent's total socialization and self-definition is due to adults' neglect of providing clear landmarks and systematic steps to autonomy. Not surprisingly, adolescents constitute their own society. What has been the result of this? Well, what we end up with is a youth culture that provides a series of eccentric, substitute vehicles toward the achievement of independence and maturity. What is important is that the adolescent peer culture develops its own criteria of good and bad, right and wrong, successful and unsuccessful, and thereby offers its own series of demarcations to identify.

Adolescence is the time and the youth culture is the place in normal growth when developing youngsters begin to question all those things—parents, religion, education, self, you name it—that they had heretofore simply accepted on faith. Association with and feedback from peers help them do this.

IMPACT OF PHYSICAL DEVELOPMENT AND APPEARANCE ON THE ADOLESCENT SELF

Physical development and appearance are very much related to how adolescents feel about themselves. Between the years of 12 to 16, both boys and girls must cope with the fastest and most dramatic changes their bodies have undergone since the first year of life. Not only does the body grow faster, but it changes in its general proportions. Girls begin to add fatty tissue, which results in a more rounded figure, while boys begin to add muscle tissue, which results in a more angular and broader appearance. To complicate matters, different parts of the body grow at different rates. As a result, boys frequently trip over their own feet, which typically zoom ahead to full size as the rest of the body struggles to catch up; girls may look bottom-heavy when hips develop faster than the shoulders, and both boys and girls may think their facial features are a bit odd when the nose reaches its adult proportions before the jawbone has finished growing (Dwyer & Mayer, 1968–69). The physical aspects of growing up during adolescence are further complicated by the fact that physical maturation occurs at different rates not only *between* boys and girls, but *among* boys and girls (see chapter 3 on physiological development).

In a very real sense, the adolescents' sense of self is closely associated with the perceptions they have of their own bodies. Unlike the early years when physical changes went on without awareness, adolescents are in the quite self-conscious position of being both the objects of change and the spectators of its consequences. And they may be fascinated or horrified by the physical changes they see happening before their very eyes. After all, when one's body changes, one is not really one's self anymore. A new self—at least a new physical self—emerges. Growing youth are not able to finalize what and who they are until they are able to see how they will develop. In an important and lasting way, the adolescent's genetic unfolding will have a strong influence on his or her psychological feelings.

The Effect of Physical Appearance on
Self-Other Perceptions

The most material and visible part of the self is our physical body. Like any other object in our physical environment, our bodies are perceived through the various senses. Occupying as it does a substantial portion of our visual and auditory fields, we see and hear a lot of ourselves.

This being the case, it is not surprising to find a considerable amount of evidence to suggest that one's appearance is an important determiner of self-esteem among both men and women (Lerner, 1969). In another series of studies (Secord & Jourard, 1953; Jourard & Secord, 1955), it was found that feelings about one's body were commensurate with the feelings one had about one as a total person. That is, negative feelings about the body were related to negative feelings about the self, and vice versa.

Other researchers have demonstrated that a physically attractive person is generally attributed to have more favorable personal qualities (Miller, 1970; Berscheid & Walster, 1972); he or she is viewed as having greater social power (Sigall, Page & Brown, 1971; Wilson & Nias, 1976), and all other things being equal, physically attractive individuals are liked better than unattractive individuals (Byrne, London & Reeves, 1968; Snyder, Berscheid & Tanke, 1977).

The importance of physical attractiveness was nicely demonstrated in a clever study (Walster, Aronson, Abraham & Roltman, 1966) of college freshmen who took part in a computer-matched blind-date dance. While filling out applications for dates, the students were rated for physical attractiveness by two male and two female observers. During the dance intermission, the freshmen were interviewed regarding their desire to date their partners again. Four to six months later a follow-up was conducted to determine how frequently the couples had actually dated or asked the other for a date. The researchers had hypothesized that the freshmen would seek partners near their own level of attractiveness and with similar personality traits. This turned out not to be the case. What they found was that the only significant determinant of how much a partner was liked, was desired as a future date, and was actually asked out was his or her physical attractiveness.

This is not to suggest that only physically attractive individuals have fine personal qualities or more social power or are more likable. It is, however, to suggest that physical appearance is linked to self-esteem to the extent that it influences feedback from others, which can be positive or negative. This is a particularly important point to consider as we try to understand the development and dynamics of the adolescent self. While we might agree that intelligence, kindness, personality variables, and so forth may be equally, or even more desirable than appearance alone, these qualities are not as easily accessible to observers. It is the immediate availability of information about appearance that contributes to its importance in first-impression feelings and exchanges. As it turns out, not only does each of us have certain perceptions about our physical appearance that influences our thinking and feelings about ourselves but so too do others have certain perceptions that influence their feelings and feedback about us.

Body image, appearance, and self-esteem do seem to be related. Indeed, research has shown that how one feels about one's self is related not only to total appearance but also to the rate and pace of growth as one moves through the developmental years.

Since the effects of early or late growth are different for boys than they are for girls, perhaps we can more clearly see these differences if we separate the two and examine them one at a time.

Effect of Early versus Late Maturation in Boys

Highly significant and classical growth studies have emerged from the Institute of Human Development at the University of California. One of these studies, conducted by Jones and Bayley (1950), focused on 16 boys who were the most accelerated growers and on 16 boys who were the most consistently slow growers for a 4½-year period between the ages of 12 and 17. Keep in mind that we're looking at the two extremes on a growth continuum.

Many significant differences between the two groups were found. For example, when rated by adults, the slower growing boys were judged as lower in physical attractiveness, less masculine, less well-groomed, more animated, more affected, and more tense. They did not, however, differ from the more advanced boys in ratings of popularity, leadership, prestige, or social affect on the group. They were also considered to be less mature in heterosexual social relations.

When rated by their peers, the slower growers were judged to be more restless, more talkative, and more bossy. In addition, peer ratings showed them to be less popular, less likely to be leaders, more attention-seeking, and less confident in class situations, and significantly, perhaps, shorter on a sense of humor about themselves.

In contrast, boys who were physically accelerated were usually more accepted and were treated as more mature by adults and by peers. They were more matter-of-fact about themselves; and although they had less need to strive for status and recognition, it was from their ranks that the outstanding student leaders were chosen. The investigators concluded, "The findings give clear evidence of the effect of physical maturing on behavior. Perhaps of greater importance, however, is the repeated demonstration of the multiplicity of factors, psychological and cultural patterns" (p. 146). We might mention here that research by Weatherly (1964) found that boys who mature at an average age had about as many relative advantages as those who mature early.

In a study designed to see if there were any differences between the self-conceptions, motivations, and interpersonal attitudes of late- and early-maturing boys (Mussen & Jones, 1957), it was found that boys who mature late in adolescence are more likely to be insecure and dependent. In addition, they more frequently behave in childish, affected, attention-getting ways.

These findings are consistent with those in another study reported by Mussen and Jones (1958) in which they investigated the motivations of late- and early-maturing boys. In general, they discovered that high drives for social acceptance and for aggression are more characteristic of the slower-growing than the faster-growing boys. This may suggest that a later maturer's high needs for social visibility may stem from feelings of insecurity and dependence. It is as if these boys were saying in many different ways, "Hey, look at me!"

Looking at the total picture, we can see that the rate of physical maturing may affect self-concept development specifically and personality development generally in crucially important ways. We can reasonably infer that adult and peer attitudes toward the adolescent, as well as their treatment and acceptance of him, are related to some extent to his perceived physical status. This suggests that the sociopsychological environment in which a late-maturer grows may be significantly less rewarding and more detrimental to positive self-feelings than that of his early-maturing peers.

All in all, the early-maturing boy is likely to have a better time of it both in terms of certain physical advantages and in terms of a more positive self-concept as he moves through his adolescent years.

Effect of Early versus Late Maturation in Girls

Although the outcome of early maturation has fairly consistent advantages for boys, the picture for girls is more complex. On the whole, research suggests that differences between early- and late-maturing girls may not be so dramatic. In addition, the advantages or disadvantages of early versus late maturation may vary over time. As Faust (1960, p. 98) noted from her investigation of factors that influenced the prestige of adolescent girls:

> . . . for girls neither physical acceleration or physical retardation is consistently advantageous. It is not until the junior high school years that

the early-maturing girl "comes into her own." Until that time her pre-cocious development is somewhat detrimental to her social status. The adjustments which inevitably must be made to losses and gains in status during the adolescent period may be partly a function of this discontinuity in the relationship between developmental maturity and prestige during the adolescent period.

Weatherly (1964, p. 1209) concluded from his research that "for girls as opposed to boys, the rate of physical maturation is a much less influential variable mediating personality development." Why should this be? One possible reason may be related to the fact that the cultural sex-role prescription for males in our society is relatively clear and is one that places a high value upon attributes associated with physical strength, coordination, and athletic prowess. For girls, however, the feminine sex-role prescription is less definite and stereotyped and is, therefore, not so likely to be connected to any specific pattern of physical attributes. In addition, whereas people seem to respond more to a boy's or a man's total physical makeup, the response to a girl's physical makeup is apt to be more specific. For example, one girl's pretty face may be enough to win her many signs of approval. Another girl may have very plain facial features but her extremely attractive figure may win her feelings of social approval. Another way of stating it, I suppose, would be to suggest that when it comes to the physical side of the self, at least, girls tend to be judged more in terms of how they look and boys more in terms of how they perform. If this is true, then a tentative speculation about why it is that the rate of physical maturation has less dramatic effect on girls than boys is that girls have greater flexibility for altering or changing their looks than boys do for altering or changing their performances.

We might add here that it is precisely this kind of attention to a girl's "outer person" that is becoming increasingly more upsetting to larger segments of younger and older women who wish to be perceived and evaluated more in terms of their competencies and abilities rather than their looks. There seems to be slow but steady progress in destereotyping what young girls and women are supposed to be. Indeed, one of the healthy outgrowths of the women's liberation movement seems to be a gradual shift in social expectations away from traditional, stereotyped views about what constitutes masculine and feminine behavior to a more realistic stance that recognizes that a girl can be strong and assertive without being masculine and that a boy can be warm and sensitive without being effeminate.

SUMMARY

The adolescent self is a tenuous, fragile feeling state that not uncommonly is marked by what seems to be sudden shifts in emphasis, direction, and expression. When we talk about the adolescent "style," we refer to a kind of experimental personality style that may change, chameleon-like, on a moment's notice, depending on the strength of current social fads. Persons who either work with or are the parents of adolescent youth would do well to keep in mind that a teenager must necessarily experience a great deal of changing and growing during the adolescent years. Sometimes we forget this and act as if the normal signals and stresses of growing up were symptoms of personality malfunction and disorder.

Actually adolescence is not a time when dramatic shifts occur in a youngster's personality structure. Rather, it is a time when the self expands and matures. This is not to say that radical changes don't sometimes occur, but it is to suggest that an adolescent's emotional energy is spent not so much on changing the self, but on developing and refining the one that's already there. This is not so apt to be true for adolescents who take a poorly defined self into the adolescent years. For them, the task is not so much one of refining a sense of self, but of finding one that fits.

Parents continue to play an incredibly important part in the adolescent's growing sense of self. They then become unwitting victims of the conflict waged between an adolescent's urge to sometimes be the younger child-like self and the desire to achieve a more mature, adult-like self. For a period, it is confusing to both parent and adolescent. As the typical adolescent shifts in and out of the younger and older self, parents are confused in knowing which self to respond to. Only time can take care of this and wise adults know that adolescence is not only a time for growing up, but for growing away, too.

An important aspect of developing a healthy self-image is the quality of the relationship existing between the adolescent boy or girl and the parent of the same sex. Empirical research and clinical evidence point time and again to the fact that emotionally healthy self-other attitudes are most likely to occur when sons and daughters experience the parents of the same sex taking an active part in the child-rearing process.

Peers are also important to the adolescent's developing sense of self, but in different ways and for different reasons. Membership in a peer group can be a stabilizing influence insofar as it: offers a replacement for the family while the "moving away" is taking place; provides a certain security in numbers as adolescents try themselves in new ways; provides a reference source of "OK—not OK" behavior, against which adolescents can measure themselves; and offers opportunities for "practice by doing" and for using others as models from whom to learn new behavior patterns.

Physical development and the rate at which one grows are interrelated aspects that have a strong bearing on an adolescent boy or girl's self-feeling. Whether maturing takes place too fast or too slowly or, for that matter, hardly at all, it can be a source of agonizing self-consciousness. In general, research has shown that boys and girls who mature early are more apt to have a positive self-concept than whose who mature late. This tends to be more true for boys than for girls.

Adolescence is both a psychological and physical growth stage. The personality style or "self" we see expressed during adolescence is not unrelated to the adult self which will emerge from it. Generally speaking, the adolescent self will continue to develop in the direction it starts and will be influenced by physical growth and development and by parental and peer values.

SUGGESTIONS FOR FURTHER READING

AUSUBEL, D. P., MONTEMAYOR, R., & SUAJIAN, P. *Theory and problems of adolescent development* (2nd ed.). New York: Grune & Stratton, 1977.

DREYFUS, E. A. *Adolescence: Theory and experience.* Columbus, Ohio: Charles E. Merrill, 1976.

GUARDO, C. J. *The adolescent as individual: Issues and insights.* New York: Harper & Row, 1975.

KATCHADOURIAN, H. *The biology of adolescence.* San Francisco: W. H. Freeman, 1977.

PEREZ, J. F., & COHEN, A. I. *Mom and dad are me.* Monterey, Calif.: Brooks/Cole, 1969.

WHITE, K. M., & SPEISMAN, J. C. *Adolescence.* Monterey, Calif.: Brooks/Cole, 1977.

BIBLIOGRAPHY

ARIS, P. *Centuries of childhood.* Translated by R. Baldick. New York: Alfred A. Knopf, 1962.

ARONSON, E. *The social animal.* San Francisco: W. H. Freeman, 1972.

ARONSON, E. (Ed.). *Readings about the social animal.* San Francisco: W. H. Freeman, 1976.

AUSUBEL, D. P. *Theory and problems of adolescent development.* New York: Grune & Stratton, 1954.

BACHMAN, J. G., O'MALLEY, P. M., & JOHNSTON, J. *Adolescence to adulthood: Change and stability in the lives of young men.* Ann Arbor, Mich.: Institute for Social Research, University of Michigan, 1978.

BARCLAY, A., & CUSUMANO, D. R. Father absence, cross-sex identity, and field-dependent behavior in male adolescents. *Child Development,* 1967, *38,* 243–250.

BATH, J. A., & LEWIS, E. L. Attitudes of young female adults toward some areas of parent-adolescent conflict. *Journal of Genetic Psychology,* 1962, *100,* 241–253.

BAUMRIND, D. What research is teaching us about the differences between authoritative and authoritarian child-rearing styles. In D. E. Hamachek (Ed.),

Human dynamics in psychology and education (3rd ed.). Boston: Allyn and Bacon, 1977.

BECKER, W. C. Consequences of different kinds of parental discipline. In M. L. Hoffman & L. W. Hoffman (Eds.), *Review of Child Development Research* (Vol. 1). New York: Russell Sage Foundation, 1964.

BERSCHEID, E., & WALSTER, E. Beauty and the best. *Psychology Today,* 1972, *5,* 42–46.

BRODY, E. B. *Minority group adolescents in the United States.* Baltimore: Williams & Wilkins, 1968.

BILLER, H. B., & WEISS, S. D. The father-daughter relationship and the personality development of the female. *Journal of Genetic Psychology,* 1970, *116,* 79–93.

BLOCK, J., & TURULA, E. Identification, ego control, and rebellion. *Child Development,* 1963, *34,* 945–953.

BRITTAIN, C. V. Adolescent choices and parent-peer cross pressures. *American Sociological Review,* 1963, *23,* 385–391.

BRONSON, W. C. Central orientations: A study of behavior organization from childhood to adolescence. *Child Development,* 1966, *37,* 125–155.

BYRNE, D., LONDON, O., & REEVES, K. The effects of physical attractiveness, sex, and attitude similarity on interpersonal attractions. *Journal of Personality,* 1968, *36,* 259–271.

CARROLL, J. W. Transcendence and mystery in the counter-culture. *Religion in Life,* 1973, *42,* 361–375.

CONGER, J. J. *Adolescence and youth: Psychological development in a changing world.* New York: Harper & Row, 1973.

CONGER, J. J. *Adolescence and youth* (2nd ed.). New York: Harper & Row, 1977.

COOPERSMITH, S. *The antecedents to self-esteem.* San Francisco: W. H. Freeman, 1967.

CORSINI, R. J. Counseling and psychotherapy. In E. F. Borgatta & W. W. Lambert (Eds.), *Handbook and personality theory and research.* Skokie, Ill.: Rand McNally, 1965.

CONDRY, J. C., JR., SIMAN, M. L., & BRONFENBRENNER, U. *Characteristics of peer- and adult-oriented children.* Unpublished manuscript, Department of Child Development, Cornell University, 1968.

DOUVAN, E., & ADELSON, J. *The adolescent experience.* New York: Wiley, 1966.

DUSEK, J. B. *Adolescent development and behavior.* Chicago: Science Research Associates, 1977.

DWYER, J., & MAYER, J. Psychological effects of variations in physical appearance during adolescence. *Adolescence,* 1968–69, *3,* 353–380.

ELDER, G. H., JR. Structural variations in the child rearing relationship. *Sociometry,* 1962, *25,* 241–262.

ELKIND, D. Egocentrism in adolescence. *Child Development,* 1967, *38,* 1025–1034.

ERIKSON, E. *Childhood and society* (2nd ed.). New York: W. W. Norton, 1963.

ERIKSON, E. *Identity: Youth and crisis.* New York: W. W. Norton, 1968.

FAUST, M. S. Developmental maturity as a determinant in prestige in adolescent girls. *Child Development,* 1960, *31,* 173–184.

FISHER, S. *The female orgasm: Psychology, physiology, and fantasy.* New York: Basic Books, 1972.

FORMAN, G. E., & KUSCHNER, D. S. *The child's construction of knowledge: Piaget for teaching children.* Monterey, Calif.: Brooks/Cole, 1977.

GORDON, I. J. *Human development: A transactional perspective.* New York: Harper & Row, 1975.

GUNTHER, M. Brainwashing: Persuasion by propaganda. *Today's Health,* February, 1976, 22–27.

HALLWORTH, H. J., DAVIS, H., & CAMSTON, C. Some adolescents' perceptions of adolescent personality. *Journal of Social Psychology,* 1965, *4,* 81–89.

HAMACHEK, D. E. *Encounters with the self* (2nd ed.). New York: Holt, Rinehart and Winston, 1978.

HARDER, M. W., RICHARDSON, J. T., & SIMMONS, R. B. Jesus people. *Psychology Today,* December, 1972, *6,* 45–50, 110–113.

HARRIS, L. Change, yes—upheaval, no. *Life,* January 8, 1971, 22–27.

HAVIGHURST, R. J. *Developmental tasks and education* (3rd ed.). New York: David McKay, 1972.

HEILBRUN, A. B., JR. The measurement of identification. *Child Development,* 1965, *36,* 11–127.

HEILBRUN, A. B., JR. Identification and behavioral ineffectiveness during late adolescence. In E. D. Evans (Ed.), *Adolescents: Reading in behavior and development.* New York: Holt, Rinehart & Winston, 1970.

HETHERINGTON, E. M. Girls without fathers. *Psychology Today,* February, 1973, 47–52.

HRABA, J., & GRANT, G. Black is beautiful: A re-examination of racial preference and identification. *Journal of Personality and Social Psychology,* 1970, *16,* 398–402.

INHELDER, B., & PIAGET, J. *The growth of logical thinking from childhood to adolescence.* New York: Basic Books, 1958.

JERSILD, A. T., BROOK, J. S., & BROOK, D. W. *The psychology of adolescence* (3rd ed.). New York: Macmillan, 1978.

JONES, M. C., & BAYLEY, N. Physical maturing among boys as related to behavior. *Journal of Educational Psychology,* 1950, *41,* 129–148.

JOURARD, S. M., & SECORD, P. F. Body-cathexis and personality. *British Journal of Psychology,* 1955, *46,* 130–138.

KAGEN, J., & MOSS, H. A. The stability of passive and dependent behavior from childhood through adulthood. *Child Development,* 1960, *31,* 577–591.

KANDEL, D., LESSER, G., ROBERTS, G. H., & WEISS, R. The concept of the adolescent subculture. In R. Purnell (Ed.), *Adolescents and the high school.* New York: Holt, Rinehart & Winston, 1970.

KETT, J. F. *Rites of passages: Adolescence in America, 1970 to the present.* New York: Basic Books, 1977.

LAMBERT, B. G., ROTHSCHILD, B. F., ALTLAND, R., & GREEN, L. B. *Adolescence: Transition from childhood to maturity* (2nd ed.). Monterey, Calif.: Brooks/Cole, 1978.

LANDIS, P. H. *Adolescence and youth.* New York: McGraw-Hill, 1945.

LERNER, R. M. The development of stereotyped expectancies of body-build relations. *Child Development,* 1969, *30,* 137–141.

LEVITT, E. E., & EDWARDS, J. A. A multivariate study of correlative factors in youth cigarette smoking. *Developmental Psychology,* 1970, *2,* 5–11.

MATTESON, D. R. *Adolescence today: Sex roles and the search for identity.* Homewood, Ill.: Dorsey Press, 1975.

McFILL, E. L., & COLEMAN, J. Family and peer influence in college plans of high school students. *Sociology of Education,* 1965, *38,* 112–116.

McKINNEY, J. P., FITZGERALD, H. E., & STROMMEN, E. *Developmental psychology: The adolescent and the young adult.* Homewood, Ill.: Dorsey Press, 1977.

MEAD, M. *Culture and commitment: A study of the generation gap.* New York: Doubleday, 1970.

MEDINNUS, G. R., & JOHNSON, R. C. *Child and adolescent psychology.* New York: Wiley, 1969.

MILLER, A. G. Role of physical attractiveness in impression formation. *Psychonomic Science,* 1970, *19,* 241–243.

MISCHEL, W. Continuity and change in personality. *American Psychologist,* 1969, *24,* 1012–1018.

MUELLER, W. J. *Avenues to understanding: The dynamics of therapeutic interactions.* New York: Appleton-Century-Crofts, 1973.

MUSSEN, P. H., & JONES, M. C. Self conceptions, motivations, and interpersonal attitudes of late- and early-maturing boys. *Child Development,* 1958, *29,* 61–67.

MUSSEN, P. H., & JONES, M. C. The behavior-inferred motivations of late- and early-maturing boys. *Child Development,* 1958, *29,* 61–67.

MUSSEN, P., & RUTHERFORD, E. Parent-child relations and parental personality in relation to young children's sex role preference. *Child Development,* 1963, *34,* 589–607.

MUSSEN, P. H., YOUNG, H., CADDINI, R., & MORANTE, L. The influence of father-son relationships on adolescent personality and attitudes. *Journal of Child Psychology and Psychiatry,* 1963, *29,* 61–67.

ORLANSKY, H. Infant care and personality. *Psychological Bulletin,* 1949, *46,* 1–48.

PIERS, E. V., & DAVIS, D. B. Age and other correlates of self-concept in children. *Journal of Educational Psychology,* 1964, *55,* 91–95.

ROBBINS, T., ANTHONY, D., & CURTIS, T. Youth culture religious movements: Evaluating the integrative hypothesis. *Sociological Review,* 1975, *16,* 48–64.

SARGENT, A. G. *Beyond sex roles.* St. Paul, Minn.: West Publishing Co., 1977.

SECORD, P. F., & JOURARD, S. M. The appraisal of body-cathexis: Body-cathexis and the self. *Journal of Consulting Psychology,* 1953, *17,* 343–347.

SIGALL, H., PAGE, R., & BROWN, A. C. Effort expenditure as a function of evaluation and evaluator effectiveness. *Representative Research in Social Psychology,* 1971, *2,* 19–25.

SNYDER, M., BERSCHEID, E., & TANKE, E. D. Social perception and interpersonal behavior: On the self-fulfilling nature of social stereotypes. *Journal of Personality and Social Psychology,* 1977, *35,* 656–666.

TROLL, L. E., NEUGARTEN, B. L., & KRAINES, R. J. Similarities in values and other personality characteristics in college students and their parents. *Merrill-Palmer Quarterly of Behavior and Development,* 1969, *15,* 323–336.

TURNER, R. H. *Family interaction.* New York: Wiley, 1969.

WALSTER, E., ARONSON, V., ABRAHAM, D., & ROLTMAN, L. The importance of physical attractiveness in dating behavior. *Journal of Personality and Social Psychology,* 1966, *4,* 508–516.

WEATHERLY, D. Self-perceived rate of physical maturation and personality in late adolescence. *Child Development,* 1964, *4,* 1197–1240.

WILLIAMS, J. Chronology of a self. In D.E. Hamachek (Ed.), *Human dynamics in psychology and education* (2nd ed.). Boston: Allyn and Bacon, 1972.

WILSON, G., & NIAS, D. Beauty can't be beat. *Psychology Today,* September, 1976, 96–99.

WITKIN, H., GOODENOUGH, D. R., & KARP, S. A. Stability of cognitive style from childhood to young adulthood. *Journal of Personality and Social Psychology,* 1967, *7,* 291–300.

YANKELOVICH, D. *Generations apart.* New York: Columbia Broadcasting System, 1969.

5

PERSONALITY DEVELOPMENT

Harold D. Grotevant

Imagine that you are in a dark room in which a very large painting hangs on one wall. Although you want to be able to see and appreciate the entire canvas, you only have a small flashlight. Since it is obviously too weak to illuminate the entire work, your only option is to examine the painting in segments, hoping to construct the total sense of the art work in your mind after you have looked at all the parts.

The psychologist interested in understanding personality faces a very similar dilemma. The complexity of human personality forms a canvas that is extensive in scope. However, the theories and methods that are available for exploring the canvas limit our ability to understand the whole. Although broad-ranging personality theories have emerged from time to time in the history of psychology (Hall & Lindzey, 1978), none of them currently seems totally adequate to explain the intricate entity we call personality.

Although this is certainly a thorny problem to solve, various approaches have developed. The most common approach currently in use is to segment the domain of personality into parts, which are then studied separately. Consequently, individual researchers focus on fairly narrow domains of behavior; some are interested in sex-role development, others in self-concept, some in moral development, others in attitudes, and so on. Efforts at integrating these diverse materials are few and far between.

When discussions of personality focus solely on one area of behavior at a time, it is easy to lose a sense of the integrated nature of personality and development. Much of the personality research being conducted today fails to consider other aspects of the individual, such as cognitive ability, genetic inheritance, physical development, or cultural influence. Although research on human development does seem to be moving toward a more holistic or integrated view of the person (Achenbach, 1978), we still have a considerable distance to go.

DEVELOPMENTAL PERSPECTIVES

In this chapter, I shall attempt to shed some light on the canvas of adolescent personality development. As I do so, the discussion will be guided by four perspectives.

Harold D. Grotevant is Assistant Professor of Home Economics and of Psychology at the University of Texas at Austin. He has written a number of articles on such topics as family influences on personality, vocational interests, and intellectual development in adolescence.

Development Is Integrated

The adolescent described in these pages is experiencing developmental change in several domains at the same time (physical, cognitive, personality, emotional, etc.). In order to understand this person adequately, it will be necessary to attempt to describe the ways in which development in one area affects his or her behavior in other domains.

Personality Develops As the Adolescent Actively Deals with Five Specific Developmental Tasks

Five developmental tasks face the American adolescent of today: adjustment to the physical changes experienced in adolescence and the new feelings associated with sexual maturity; transformation in the relationship with parents (e.g., Hill & Steinberg, 1977); development of effective relationships with peers of the same and opposite sex; preparation for a vocation; and, most important, development of a sense of *identity* (Conger, 1977). The adolescent will be decribed as an active agent in his or her own development. The way in which these developmental tasks are completed will influence how well the individual is equipped to deal with the next set of challenges posed by young adulthood.

Development Can Only Be Understood by Studying the Interplay over Time Between the Changing Individual and His or Her Changing Social Environment

Neither the individual nor the environment remains static or unchanging. Personality development can best be understood in terms of both the relatively internal changes taking place (such a physical and cognitive changes) and the new social demands or challenges facing the adolescent.

The Adolescent Years Are Experienced Differently in Different Cultures

The discussion of adolescence presented in this chapter is most relevant to middle class American youth. The bulk of the theoretical and research literature on adolescence has virtually ignored lower class young people. Cross-cultural studies of adolescence (e.g., Mead, 1961), however, have taught us that young people in other cultures face different options and opportunities that profoundly affect their development during the adolescent years. Within our own culture there are important subcultures where this is also true. A number of these subcultures are discussed in chapter 12 by Havighurst.

These four perspectives will be developed and illustrated as two issues facing adolescents are discussed: identify formation and vocational interest development. Each of these aspects of the developing personality provides a vehicle through which we can study the interplay of the changing individual and his or her changing social environment and expectations. Later in the chapter, issues concerning the continuity and predictability of personality will be examined. The chapter will conclude with a discussion of abnormal development in adolescence.

IDENTITY FORMATION

Adolescence is a period of rapid and extensive change. From within, the adolescent experiences significant changes both in body and mind. Thinking that was previously focused on the "here and now" expands into the world of possibilities and hypotheses. At the same time, parents, teachers, and peers are coming to have new expectations about the adolescent's social and intellectual capabilities and responsibilities. In addition, the American adolescent is faced with a large variety of options regarding careers and life-styles from which he or she must fashion a future.

As these internal and external changes take place, the adolescent is virtually forced to reevaluate and reorganize the skills, abilities, and identifications of childhood into a new coherent framework or structure called *identity*. As this identity develops, the adolescent becomes more aware of his or her own strengths and weaknesses. At the same time, there is increasing awareness both of the adolescent's own uniqueness and distinctiveness as well as of ways in which he or she is similar to other people. To the adolescent, identity is experienced as "a *subjective sense* of an *invigorating sameness* and *continuity*" (Erikson, 1968, p. 19). The following autobiographical statement of a mature young adult illustrates this sense of self-knowledge that Erikson describes:

> To me this is what politics is all about: getting people to think critically about themselves and others in such a way that they become willing to change....
> I foresee politics in my future, probably as my future. Yet when people ask me whether I like politics I often equivocate. At times I love it—I enjoy waking people up. At other times I fear it—I don't want to alienate my apolitical friends by being too critical or solely political. Yet ultimately I am political because I think it is right to care—being politi-

cal is not so much a matter of leading the life I enjoy as living the life I believe in. (Goethals & Klos, 1976, p. 207–208)

James Marcia (1966) has developed an interview that operationalizes and tests Erikson's theoretical statements about identity. The interview reveals the presence or absence of *crisis* (active decision making) and *commitment* (certainty of a decision) in two areas: occupational choice and a philosophical-political-religious belief system (ideology).

Identity Status

The way in which an adolescent combines elements of crisis and commitment in responding to the interview determines his or her *identity status.* Marcia (1966, 1976, 1980) has described four identity statuses. *Identity Achievement* adolescents show that they have experienced a period of active decision making at some point in time (about their occupational plans, for example) and that they have made a fairly firm commitment to a particular choice. *Foreclosure* adolescents appear to have made a commitment to an occupational choice or an ideology, but they did not actively consider a number of alternatives before making the commitment. Foreclosed adolescents often make the same choices as their parents or other adult role models have made, usually without questioning the suitability of the choice for themselves (Marcia, 1976). Individuals who are currently involved in the active decision-making process but who have vague or general commitments are in the *Moratorium* identity status. Finally, *Identity Diffusion* adolescents show little evidence of commitment, although they may or may not have experienced a period of active decision making in the past.

The identity statuses may be best illustrated with examples of responses that students might give the following question: "Have you ever had any doubts about your religious beliefs?" An Identity Achiever might answer: "Yeah, I even started wondering whether or not there was a god. I've pretty much resolved that now, though. The way it seems to me is. . . ." A Moratorium adolescent might reply: "Yes, I guess I'm going through that now. I just don't see how there can be a god and yet so much evil in the world or. . . ." A Foreclosed subject might answer: "No, not really, our family is pretty much in agreement on these things." Finally, an Identity Diffused adolescent might respond: "Oh, I don't know. I guess so. Everyone goes through some sort of stage like that. But it really doesn't bother me much. I figure one's about as good as the other!" (Marcia, 1966, p. 553).

Identity status follows a reasonably predictable course over the four years of college. Waterman, Geary, and Waterman (1974) administered Marcia's identity interview to 92 male undergraduates at the beginning and end of their freshman year and to 53 of the original subjects at the end of their senior year. Identity status was scored separately for occupational choice and ideology. In the occupational choice area, there was a significant decrease in the number of Moratorium adolescents from the freshman to senior year. While 8 freshmen had been classified as Moratorium, none of them remained in this status by their senior year. There was also a significant increase in the number of Identity Achievers from the freshman (7 subjects) to the senior year (19 subjects). A similar increase in the number of Identity Achievers was found in the area of ideology. Overall, Identity Achievement was found to be the most stable of the four identity statuses (see also Hauser, 1976).

Although this general trend toward Identity Achievement has been described in contemporary college populations, there is no guarantee that all individuals will reach this development level. A recent report of identity status in adult males (who had a son in college) revealed that 57% of the fathers were Foreclosures while only 13% were Identity Achievers (Waterman & Waterman, 1976). Cultural explanations for this surprising finding will be examined later in this chapter.

Cognitive Influences on Identity Formation

As discussed in chapter 6, adolescent thought seems quite different from that of younger chidren. The adolescent can think about possibilities, think through hypotheses, think ahead, think about thinking, and think beyond old limits (Keating, 1980). These new capabilities not only allow but also force the adolescent to deal with forming an identity. The old childhood "me" is now only one of a set of all possible "me's." In other words, it is these new powers of thought that allow Identity Achievement (generation and exploration of possibilities followed by commitment) to take place.

Erikson's explanation of identity formation further illustrates the cognitive component involved in the complex activity through which the adolescent defines himself (1968, pp. 22–23).

> ... in psychological terms, identity formation employs a process of simultaneous reflection and observation, a process taking place on all levels of mental functioning, by which the individual judges himself in the light of what he perceives to be the way in which others judge him in comparison to themselves and to a typology significant to them; while he judges their way of judging him in the light of how he perceives himself in comparison to them and to types that have become relevant to him.

It seems reasonable to expect that the cognitive skills of adolescents would have some impact on how well they could deal with the complex process Erikson described. While the developing cognitive abilities of adolescents *allow* identity to form, they also complicate the picture. For example, we know that young adolescents are particularly *egocentric*. They have a difficult time distinguishing between their own thoughts or concerns and the thoughts of others. Consequently, they feel that other people are as concerned about their rapid physical changes, for example, as they are themselves. Because they feel that they are constantly being observed or talked about by others, they are reacting to an *imaginary audience* (Elkind, 1967). Another manifestation of this egocentrism is seen in the *personal fable* (Elkind, 1967). Adolescents believe that their experiences and feelings are unique: "No one else could have ever felt this way before."

As the adolescent matures cognitively, his or her own thoughts become more differentiated or distinguishable from the thoughts of others. Only then can the adolescent truly become an Identity Achiever: one who has considered different options for his or her own life and who has made a commitment based on that active consideration.

Marcia (1980) has suggested that formal operational thinking, for example, the set of cognitive abilities hypothesized by Inhelder and Piaget (1958) to develop in adolescents, may be a necessary but not sufficient condition for identity achievement. In other words, being able to reason in formal operational terms does not guarantee that you will be an Identity Achiever. However, all Identity Achievers should be able to use formal operational strategies. The small quantity of reseach attempting to test this possible link between cognitive ability and identity has not met with much success. Part of the problem stems from the simplistic assumption that any measure of formal operations should be related to any measure of identity. Future researchers will need to specify more carefully which aspects of formal operations should be related to which aspects of identity (Hill & Palmquist, 1978). It is clear that some of the difficulty lies in measuring those aspects of adolescent thinking that are important to personality (for more detail, see chapter 6 in this text and Keating, 1980).

Family Influences on Identity Formation

We have explored the way in which the internal cognitive changes of adolescence may affect identity formation. However, influences external to the adolescent, especially his or her family, also affect the quest for identity. Several studies using paper and pencil reports of parental behavior (Cross & Allen, 1970; Jordan, 1970, 1972) and one study observing family interaction (Matteson, 1974) have attempted to relate parental behavior and identity status.

In these studies, the parents of *Foreclosed* adolescents were seen in positive terms by their children. They were perceived as child-centered and spent the most time with their children. Jordan (1972; as cited in Marcia,

1976) noted that the relationships between Foreclosed adolescents and their parents could almost be called a "love affair." When these families were asked to solve a problem together, the atmosphere was one of mutual encouragement in which the adolescent played an active role but the father spoke the most.

Relations between *Moratorium* adolescents and their parents were described as ambivalent. In the problem-solving session, these families devoted the least effort to clarifying reality and had adolescents who were least submissive to their parents. Jordan (1972; as cited in Marcia, 1976) suggested that the adolescent's personal turmoil was responsible for the confusion and conflict in the home. In other words, the adolescent's own personality can have a profound effect on parental behavior. Bell and Harper (1977) give a more detailed discussion of child effects on adults.

The parents of *Diffusion* adolescents were found to be the most indifferent, rejecting, and detached. When solving a problem together, these families did not encourage their adolescent to participate, had the lowest interactions, and had fathers who showed little leadership.

Both parents of *Identity Achievers* were seen as positively involved with their adolescents, although somewhat detached and rejecting (Jordan, 1972; as cited in Marcia, 1976). It may be that Identity Achievement requires a certain degree of *separateness* from parents in order for the adolescent to explore and make commitments that are truly his or her own (Wagner's chapter focuses on this issue in the area of developing sexuality). Extremely close parent-adolescent relationships are associated with Foreclosure (i.e., lack of exploration but commitment to parental goals).

It must be pointed out that these studies assessed family interaction patterns and identity status at approximately the same time. It is highly likely that the interaction patterns of the family will change somewhat as the adolescent moves from one identity status to another. No research has yet been focused on this issue; although we have already stated the fundamental perspective that both the individual and his or her social environment constantly undergo change.

VOCATIONAL INTEREST DEVELOPMENT

Another way in which some investigators have tried to understand personality is by studying *vocational interests* of adolescents. Of all possible occupations, hobbies, activities, and school subjects, which combination attracts your attention? In which ones do you enjoy participating? Interests are often tested by providing a long list of possible activities and asking whether the individual would like, dislike, or be indifferent to participating in each one.

Whether one prefers to be a truck driver, an artist, a secretary, or an engineer clearly reflects the individual's personality. Someone with a high activity level who enjoys extensive contact with people may feel very unsatisfied as a solitary, long-distance truck driver. On the other hand, a quiet, shy individual who works best alone would probably find sales work both frustrating and difficult.

Holland's Theory of Personality

John Holland (1966, 1973) has developed a theory of personality based on vocational interests. He has proposed that one's personality can be accurately described as a profile or combination of six interest styles. Persons with *realistic* interests are practical, rugged, and aggressive; they enjoy working outdoors, with machines, or with their hands. *Investigative* individuals are scientifically oriented and like to think through problems. *Artistic* persons enjoy self-expressive or creative activities or enjoy appreciating the creative work of others. The *social* person is responsible, humanistic, cooperative, and concerned with the welfare of others. *Enterprising* individuals enjoy leading, dominating, or persuading others. Persons with *conventional* interests prefer highly structured or systematized activities that involve working with words or numbers.

According to Holland's (1966, 1973) theory, each individual's personality combines these six interest styles into a distinctive profile or pattern. This profile is obtained by calculating a score on each scale from the results of an interest inventory and then ordering the six interest styles from highest to lowest. For example, the highest three interests of psychologists are typically investigative (I), artistic (A), and social (S), in that order (Campbell, 1974). The highest three interests of guidance counselors are the same, but in a different order (SAI instead IAS). In other words, although individuals in both occupations share similar interests, psychologists are most interested in the problem-solving aspect of their work and guidance counselors are most interested in helping people. Realistic and investigative interests are the highest two for both surgeons and auto mechanics. However, the surgeon (IR) has highest interest in problem solving; the mechanic (RI) has the most interest in working with his hands.

As adolescents mature, two things happen to their vocational interests. First, they become more *differentiated*. In other words, likes and dislikes develop into stronger, more well-defined patterns. Quite often, counselors are faced with the difficult situation of offering guidance to an adolescent with a "flat" interest profile—a profile that shows no strong preferences for any interest area. Through additional testing or interviewing, the counselor will often try to pinpoint a few areas of potential interest and then suggest that the adolescent find out more about them. The counselor might suggest some books to read, some courses to take, or some individuals in the community to contact. There is no substitute for first-hand experience with an occupation to find out whether you really like it. Crites, in chapter 14 on career development, discusses this process in some detail.

After interests become differentiated, they begin to *stabilize*. Although the age at which interests become fairly stable will vary from individual to individual, interest patterns of late adolescents are generally very predictive of adult interests (Strong, 1943). Although interest profiles are relatively stable after late adolescence, it is likely that the antecedents of mature interests are identifiable earlier in childhood. Tyler (1964) studied a group of children longitudinally from the first through twelfth grades. She found that boys with scientific interests as high school seniors had distinctive personality profiles and interest preferences at age ten. Unfortunately, the only in-depth analyses she presented were for scientific interests in boys and for career versus noncareer interests in girls.

Cognitive Influences on Interest Development

I proposed earlier that the new modes of thinking available to adolescents facilitate the process of forming an identity. Since occupational choice is one of the key elements of identity, and since vocational interests are major inputs to occupational choice, I further suggest that adolescent cognitive ability influences interest development.

The data to support this assertion are not abundant. However, as I stated earlier, past research has typically tried to study the adolescent in parts—either the cognitive part, the physical part, the social part, or the personality part. Since few investigators have tried to see the adolescent as a whole, there is little research attempting to relate cognitive and personality development. Two studies, however, are relevant to this discussion.

Crites (1969) presented a graph based on Ginzberg, Ginsburg, Axelrad, and Herma's (1951) theory of occupational choice that showed an expected linear decrease in the number of vocational choices expressed by adolescents from ages 10 to 16. He superimposed another curve on this graph drawn from data obtained in a longitudinal study of boys and girls by Gesell, Ilg, and Ames (1956). Gesell et al. found a downward trend in the number of expressed vocational choices from ages 10 to 13, followed by a marked increase at age 14 and a relatively slower decrease to age 16. Crites (1969) felt that the jump at age 14 took place when adolescents began to see that fantasy career choices were no longer possible. They therefore had to reevaluate occupational plans, entering a time of uncertainty and indecision.

It also seems reasonable to propose a more cognitive explanation of this finding. The adolescent who is becoming able to use the new modes of thinking discussed earlier may be generating a number of vocational choices that had never been considered before. The task of later adolescence, then, becomes one of testing these possibilities against the realities of one's own abilities, interests, and temperament. Of course, this cognitive explanation is confounded with a change taking place in the adolescent's environment. Increasing age brings with it increased exposure to new information about careers, whether it comes through experience with part-time jobs, career days at school, television, movies, or many other possible sources. The adolescent is also faced with increased social expectations from parents and teachers as they react to his or her maturing body. Adolescents may perceive more pressure from adults to make choices and commitments, especially as the end of high school approaches.

A second study also suggests that the relation between cognitive development and interest development may be well worth pursuing (Fox, Pasternak, & Peiser, 1976). Gifted boys in the seventh grade (as measured by the Scholastic Aptitude Test) had more mature and more predictive interest profiles than intellectually average ninth grade boys. In other words, the cognitive and personality segments of the adolescent were not operating independently of each other.

Family Influences on Vocational Interests

The adolescent's interests are influenced not only by the relatively internal cognitive changes being experienced but also by external agents such as the family. The family seems to have an especially strong influence on adolescent interests in at least two ways: genetic similarity of parents and their offspring, and the similarity of the mother's and father's interests to each other.

In biologically related families, influences due to genetic similarity of parents and children are confounded with similarity of their home environment (see chapter 7 by Nichols). In order to determine whether genetic resemblance makes any contribution to interest similarity, behavior geneticists have studied "experiments of nature," such as twins and adoptive families. Twin studies (Carter, 1932; Roberts & Johansson, 1974; Loehlin & Nichols, 1976) and a study of adoptive families (Grotevant, Scarr, & Weinberg, 1977, 1978) have converged on the same conclusion: genetic relatedness does appear to make a contribution to interest similarity. In general, identical twins (who share 100% of their genes) have more similar vocational interests than fraternal twins (who share only 50% of their genes, on the average). Pairs of biologically related parents and children (who share 50% of their genes) have more similar interests than pairs of adopting parents and the children they adopted in early infancy (who share no genes in common). Although genetic factors do not account for all the variation observed in interests, it seems clear that they make an important contribution. Of course, there is no "hairdresser gene" or "accountant gene," but genetic factors do seem to influence temperament and personality styles. These personality factors then move us in the direction of liking those activities that mesh well with our style and disliking those activities with which we are not compatible.

The family environment also affects adolescents' interests. The interests of parents constitute a range of possible opportunities for their children. As the children develop, they are exposed to the presence of some options and activities as well as affected by the absence of others (Holland, 1973). We all know families in which the mother and father share similar interests (maybe both enjoy sailing, dominoes, or classical music) and other families in which parents have very different interests from each other. Does this parental similarity influence the adolescent's interests? The answer appears to be yes. When parents' interests are very similar to each other, children more often share their interests than when parents prefer different activities (Grotevant, 1978). When parents' interests are dissimilar, children have been exposed to a wider variety of activities with no intense family commitment to any one interest in particular. In these cases, the adolescents tended to develop different interests than their fathers. They were just as similar to their mothers' interests as children in more homogeneous families.

Parents often wonder how strongly they should try to shape or direct their children's interests. If the parents wish to support the development of Identity Achievement in their adolescent, the advice given in the following "Dear Abby" column appears in my opinion, to be sound.

> DEAR ABBY: How does a father who has excelled in sports all his life adjust to a 14-year-old son who has never shown even a normal interest in sports?
>
> I realize that not all boys can be great athletes, but my son has the build for it, and the coordination, too. He could be really good if he wanted to, but he's lazy, and he isn't competitive in anything.
>
> I have done my best to get him interested in sports ever since he was old enough to hold a ball, Abby, but it never caught on. Believe me, it's not easy to be a good father to a boy like this. Any suggestions?
>
> SAD DAD
>
> DEAR DAD: Yes, lay off. A "good" father forgets himself and thinks of his son. He then encourages the boy to grow in the direction he seems inclined.[1]

CONTINUITY AND CHANGE IN ADOLESCENT PERSONALITY

Parents, teachers, and government officials are all interested in understanding and predicting the course of adolescence. Questions like these are

---

[1] *Austin American-Statesman,* May 28, 1978. Reprinted by permission of Abigail Van Buren.

common: How will my child stand up to the increasing peer pressure of junior high and high school? Why do my students seem to be angels one minute and devils the next? What kinds of programs should we plan to keep the rate of juvenile delinquency down? These questions largely boil down to the issue of *prediction*. Is adolescence basically a predictable extension of childhood, or can we do no more than cross our fingers and wait to see what happens? In this section, we will explore evidence that touches on these issues of continuity and change in adolescent development.

Developmental Challenges

Although adolescence is a time of rapid change requiring the mastery of new developmental tasks, the young teenager has had more than a decade in which to develop a distinctive personality. This personality (as seen by Erikson, 1968) has been shaped by the child's response to four significant developmental challenges: establishing a sense of *trust* in caretakers and immediate environment (infancy); beginning to exert an *autonomous* will (toddlerhood); developing a sense of *initiative* and self-directedness (early childhood); and achieving a sense of *industry* by learning to make things and to make them well (middle childhood). In Erikson's (1968) theory of psychosocial development, adolescence is simply the next step in this sequence. The primary developmental task of this period, identity formation, will build on the foundation established in the four earlier stages (see Gallatin's discussion of Erikson in her chapter on adolescent theories).

Continuity in personality development is promoted not only by the individual's developmental history but also by consistency in the adolescent's environment. In most families, young adolescents will live in the same house with the same family members, attend the same school with the same friends, watch many of the same TV shows, and participate in many of the same activities as they did during late childhood. Given this much continuity in the environment, it would be surprising to find that adolescence is always a time of radical personality shifts.

Two investigators recently studied this question of predictability in a longitudinal study of youth (Jessor & Jessor, 1977). They were interested in predicting whether adolescents would participate in various types of "problem behavior," which they defined as drug use, sexual behavior, excessive use of alcohol, protest behavior, or general deviance (aggression, stealing, or lying). The researchers found that these behaviors did not appear suddenly or unpredictably at adolescence. Childhood personality patterns and attitudes were important predictors of problem behavior in youth.

> The adolescent who is less likely to engage in problem behavior is one who values academic achievement and expects to do well academically,

who is not concerned much with independence, who treats society as unproblematic rather than as deserving of criticism and reshaping, who maintains a religious involvement and is more uncompromising about transgression, and who finds little that is positive in problem behavior relative to the negative consequences of engaging in it. (Jessor & Jessor, 1977, p. 237)

The Transactional Model of Development

In order to understand more fully how any specific individual will deal with the developmental tasks and new expectations associated with adolescence, we need to know about the individual's past history as well as about his or her environment. Both the individual and the environment change continually; neither is static. Sameroff (1975) has presented a "transactional model" of development that allows us to consider the simultaneous changes taking place in the adolescent and in the environment. This framework, illustrated in Figure 5.1, will allow us to think more clearly about the issue of continuity in personality development. In Figure 5.1, C_1, C_2, C_3, ... C_n represent characteristics of an individual at different points in time.

Let me illustrate this model with the findings from a study of family decision making by Laurence Steinberg (1977). Steinberg found that, before the onset of puberty, the decision-making process in the families he studied were in a state of relative equilibrium. In other words, patterns of dominance in the family were clearly defined: adolescent boys yielded to their parents' decisions more often than parents yielded to them, and overall levels of conflict were fairly low.

However, when the boy began to experience the physical changes of puberty (a change in C in the diagram), he became more assertive in family discussions. In particular, he began to challenge his mother's power status in the family. The mother responded by becoming more assertive and refusing to yield to her son (a change in E in the diagram, since the mother is a part of her son's environment). As the adolescent became more physically mature (change in C), he continued to attempt to dominate his mother until his father intervened in the situation (change in E). The father's increased assertiveness over his son brought about a modulation of the son's attempt to dominate his mother (change in C).

This example illustrates the developmental interplay between the changing individual and his changing environment. The physical changes experienced by the adolescent modified parents' reactions to his bids for greater self-determination, which, in turn, influenced how the adolescent approached his parents. Increasing physical muturation, coupled with greater confidence in the youth's decision-making ability, will eventually modify initial attitudes and behaviors of the parents.

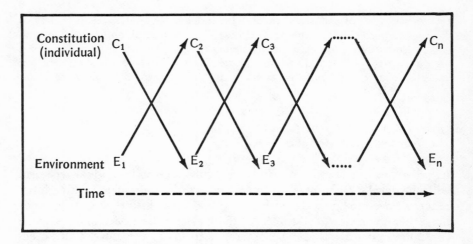

Figure 5.1 The Transactional Model of Development. (From "Early Influences on Development: Fact or Fancy?" by A. J. Sameroff, *Merrill-Palmer Quarterly*, 1975, *21*, 267–294. Reprinted by permission of the author and the Merrill-Palmer Quarterly of Behavior and Development.)

The transactional model is simply a device that allows us to understand how development proceeds as a continuously changing individual is immersed in a continuously changing environment. In my opinion, this perspective is particularly relevant for understanding adolescent development. It conflicts with a long-standing tradition (from Plato to the present) holding that experience in early childhood *irrevocably determines* later behavior. A more reasonable position is that taken by Clarke and Clarke (1976, p. 24) who state:

> A child's future is far from wholly shaped in the "formative years" of early childhood. Rather, human development is a slow process of genetic and environmental interactions with sensitivities (rather than critical periods) for different processes at different times.

Of course, early experiences are important in the development of the individual and help build the foundation on which later growth can occur. However, in order to understand adolescent and adult development completely, it is necessary to examine the individual's current coping skills and cognitive abilities as well as his or her perception of the social environment at that time.

A longitudinal study (Nesselroade & Baltes, 1974) has highlighted the importance of considering changes in both the individual and the environment. A group of 1,849 students from ages 12–17 were each tested for two years with personality and intellectual measures. The historical period during which the study was conducted (1970–1972) was more important in explaining personality changes in these students than were differences in the ages of the subjects. In general, over this 2-year period, all adolescents (regardless of age) became more extroverted, more independent, less anxious, and less achievement oriented. In other words, the experience of being an adolescent during those particular years shaped personality more strongly than the age difference among subjects in the sample.

A second study pointing to the importance of the historical environment (Waterman & Waterman, 1975) investigated the identity status in a sample of adolescent sons and their fathers. Fathers were more likely to be Identity Foreclosures than their sons in both the areas of occupation and religion. Sons were more likely to be in the Moratorium or Diffusion status than their fathers.

The most striking result of this study was the high proportion of Foreclosures and low proportion of Identity Achievers among the fathers. This surprising finding, however, makes more sense when the adolescent experiences of the fathers are taken into account. The fathers were teenagers and young adults during the depression years of the 1930s and the early years of World War II; their sons were adolescents during the more affluent 1960s and the divisive Vietnam War. The authors speculated that these contrasting historical conditions may have contributed to increased Foreclosure (lack of exploration of alternatives) among the fathers and to increased Diffusion and Moratorium (heightened exploration and uncertainty accompanied by lack of commitment) among their sons. Again, we see the importance of considering both the individual and the environment when trying to understand adolescent personality.

The Foundation of Adult Development

The identity established in late adolescence does not represent an ending point in development. Just as identity has its roots in the personality foundation formed in chidhood, adult personality development builds on the achievements of adolescence. The occupational, ideological, and sexual identity that emerged in late adolescence may be modified as the adult faces new challenges. Longer life spans and an increasing emphasis on self-actualization, for example, have contributed to the "midlife crisis" when occupational and family commitments often become challenged. Discovery of a new belief system may call old religious beliefs into question. Divorce, death of a spouse, or the last child's departure from home may prompt an adult to reassess the sexual identity established in early adulthood.

ABNORMAL BEHAVIOR: THE CASE OF
SCHIZOPHRENIA

Any discussion of personality development cannot be complete without consideration of abnormal or atypical outcomes. Although mental disorders are worth studying for their own sake, they can also enrich our understanding of normal processes of development.

Schizophrenia is a serious mental disorder, affecting a significant number of adolescents and adults. The symptoms of schizophrenia often first appear during middle or late adolescence (Weiner, 1970). Holzman and Grinker (1974) reported that the age-specific rate for schizophrenia rises from about 1 case per 100,000 persons under age 15 to about 25 cases per 100,000 between ages 15–24. At present, close to a million Americans either are hospitalized with schizophrenia, are being treated as outpatients, or have active symptoms (Berger, 1978).

In the following discussion of adolescent schizophrenia, three points relevant to both normal and abnormal development will be presented. First, abnormal behavior and normal behavior are not qualitatively different from each other; it is more realistic to think about personality as a continuum from "normal" to "abnormal," with many shades of gray in between (Elkind & Weiner, 1978). Second, although a disorder such as schizophrenia may not become fully manifest until adolescence or adulthood, certain coping patterns evident in late childhood or early adolescence may be predictive of later problems. Third, personality disturbances of adolescents should be taken seriously; these problems will not necessarily disappear by themselves.

The Continuum of Normalcy

From one perspective, schizophrenic behavior looks very different from what most people consider "normal." Some of the most important symptoms include disordered thinking; poor contact with reality; limited ability to maintain relationships with other people; and poor control of emotional responses, thoughts, and behavior (Weiner, 1970). Some of these characteristics of schizophrenic behavior were recalled in the autobiography of Mark Vonnegut, *The Eden Express* (1975). This son of the well-known American writer Kurt Vonnegut vividly described the schizophrenic breakdown he experienced in his twenties. The three passages that follow illustrate the distortion of reality and poor emotional control characteristic of schizophrenia.

> I felt no lack of energy, in fact I had a supersurplus; but my hands, arms, and legs were getting all confused. I'd get all hung up in how per-

fectly beautiful one muscle was, exactly what it did, and get it to do it just right. But then all the others would go off on their own little trip. (p. 105)

My happiness and sadness was all out of proportion to anything that was happening. There were things to be happy about, but not that happy. There were things to be sad about, but not that sad. (p. 108)

I had no idea what I was crying about. Then something would strike me as hysterically funny and I couldn't stop giggling. Then I'd find myself somewhere else wearing completely different clothes or no clothes at all. Time stopped being continuous; it jumped around with lots of blanks. (p. 110)

It is clear that these descriptions do not fit the experiences of most "normal" young adults. However, we can better understand such deviant behavior when we see it as different from normal behavior *in degree* rather than *in kind* (Elkind & Weiner, 1978). In other words, schizophrenia may be thought of as an extreme reaction to the developmental challenges that face most adolescents. Holzman and Grinker (1974) have suggested that the developmental tasks encountered by adolescents place extreme demands on psychologically vulnerable youth. Those who are not able to cope with the challenge may retreat into psychopathology instead. For example, Berger (1978) noted that schizophrenics commonly "feel depersonalized, as if their identity were being dissolved or lost" (p. 975). Weiner (1970) also noted several parallels between acute identity diffusion and borderline schizophrenia: both involve difficulties in establishing satisfying intimate relationships, distortions of time perspective, difficulties with productive activity, and disdain for social roles considered desirable and appropriate by one's family and community.

It is important to note that the behavioral indications predictive of schizophrenia emerge gradually over time. Preschizophrenic children did not appear to be different from their peers until early adolescence (Watt, 1972). As time passed, the pattern of deviant behavior became more and more pronounced.

From Childhood to Adolescence

The search for consistency and continuity of personality has inspired a great deal of theorizing and much research. Some psychologists feel that developmental continuity is a result of consistency in an individual's environment; others feel that the continuity resides more directly in the person. In any case, the evidence for at least moderate stability of personality is strong. Block (1971; cited in Block, 1978) reported that over a 3-year period from junior high school to senior high school, 59% of the personality variables on which his men were rated displayed significant consistency;

57% were consistent for women. From senior high school to the mid-thirties (a 20-year span), 28% of the men's personality characteristics and 30% of the women's characteristics were significantly consistent. Vocational interests are also remarkably stable after mid-adolescence. Strong (1955) reported that correlations between interest profiles across time were .88 for a one-year interval, .82 for a 10-year interval, and .72 for a 22-year interval.

If we take seriously the idea that normal and abnormal behavior form a continuum, we should also expect to find some kind of continuity in abnormal behavior over time. Many researchers who have studied schizophrenia feel that the disorder has its roots in childhood. In one study, teachers described boys who later became schizophrenic with such adjectives as undependable, depressed, maladjusted, egocentric, and antisocial; preschizophrenic girls were described as maladjusted, immature, unsociable, insecure, and egocentric (Watt & Lubensky, 1976). One finding particularly characteristic of these children is that they had a difficult time making and keeping friends. In fact, lack of participation in a social network of peers in early adolescence is a good predictor of social deviance or psychopathology in later adolescence or young adulthood (Hill & Monks, 1977). Both Watt (1972) and Holzman and Grinker (1974) also found that about 50% of their schizophrenic patients exhibited deviant social behavior by early adolescence.

These examples provide evidence that many schizophrenics appeared unusually vulnerable to the stresses of life before they actually exhibited seriously disordered behavior. The transactional model of development presented earlier in this chapter can be used to describe one way in which schizophrenia may come about.

Let us first consider the organism. An extensive body of research has suggested that the vulnerability to schizophrenia may be somehow inherited. Two lines of investigations have led to this conclusion. First, identical (MZ) twins have been found to have a higher concordance rate for schizophrenia than fraternal (DZ) twins (e.g., Gottesman & Shields, 1972). In other words, both members of pairs of MZ twins (who share 100% of their genes in common) are schizophrenic more frequently than both members of pairs of DZ twins (who share 50% of their genes in common, on the average). Second, adoption studies (e.g., Heston, 1966) have followed children who were considered a risk for developing schizophrenia because one or both of their biological parents were schizophrenic. These children were typically placed in early infancy into adoptive homes with no evidence of psychopathology. It was found that these adopted children later developed schizophrenia more frequently than did a control group of adopted children with normal biological mothers.

What happens to these vulnerable individuals once they are placed in a demanding situation, such as dealing with the developmental tasks of adolescence? The genetic vulnerability and environmental stress combine to make coping very difficult. "In the vulnerable person, response is weak, inappropriate, inadequate, avoidant, defiant, absent, apathetic, ineffective, desperate, eccentric, or compliant-at-great-cost" (Holzman & Grinker, 1974, p. 278).

Unless some kind of intervention takes place, the adolescent who initially responds to his or her challenges incompetently will become insecure and will feel ineffective. These feelings will then heighten the adolescent's inability to act in a socially or intellectually competent manner. Eventually, as the adolescent experiences his or her own ineffectiveness, a pattern of pathological symptoms will begin to emerge.

From Adolescent Disturbance to Adult Disturbance

Psychoanalytic theory has had a major impact on the way clinicians view adolescent behavior. The "storm and stress" theory of adolescence has made many professionals expect unusual, semineurotic behavior to be common among youth, and believe that the adolescents would grow out of their problem behavior in time. The diagnostic category "adjustment reaction of adolescence" has been widely used to categorize many young patients who exhibit psychopathological symptoms (Masterson, 1967).

In part, this practice reflects the complex pattern of symptoms that troubled adolescents typically exhibit. For example, the schizophrenic symptoms described earlier are often mixed with other atypical behaviors (Elkind & Weiner, 1978). These may include depression, suicidal thoughts, lack of interest in social activites, or conduct disorders (stealing, fighting, running away), among others.

The belief that adolescence is necessarily a time of storm and stress has been challenged by several large-scale studies of normal adolescents (e.g., Douvan & Adelson, 1966; Offer, 1969). Although some effort is required to accomplish the developmental tasks discussed earlier, most researchers now feel that the transition from childhood to adulthood in America is usually a gradual, relatively smooth process for most youth. In any case, the research suggests that we are not justified in expecting abnormal behavior or psychiatric symptoms from our "normal" young people.

The longitudinal work of Masterson (1967) has underscored the importance of attending closely to adolescent symptoms when they do occur. Out of an initial sample of 18 schizophrenic adolescents, 72% continued to be moderately to severely impaired five years later. Another study followed adolescent patients for a period of ten years. In 62.2% of the cases, the diagnosis of schizophrenia was consistently made at every contact the patient had with a psychiatrist during the ten year period (Weiner & Del-Gaudio, 1976).

> The symptomatic adolescent is believed to step to a different drummer only temporarily under the surge of the adolescent growth process. However, the music to which these adolescents stepped was not a transient melody orchestrated by growth and development but a persistent and pervasive symphony arranged by psychiatric illness. Its somber cadence pursued these patients through their adolescent years into adulthood. (Masterson, 1967, p. 1343)

The prognosis for recovery from schizophrenia that began in adolescence is similar to the prognosis for adult-onset schizophrenia. The general conclusion reached by several studies is that about a fourth of hospitalized adolescent schizophrenics will recover, about a fourth will show some improvement, and about half will fail to improve (Weiner, 1970).

Several factors are predictive of improvement or recovery from schizophrenia. In general, prospects are better if the adolescent is older at the onset of the disturbance, if his or her previous school and social adjustment was adequate, if the disturbance began suddenly rather than gradually, and if the adolescent responded well to initial treatment (Elkind & Weiner, 1978). Most important, however, support from the adolescent's family and the arrangement of satisfactory therapy, work, and school situations can make a significant contribution to a successful adjustment.

Again, in terms of the transactional model, a patient's responsiveness to treatment will depend in part on how his or her initial bids at reestablishing social relationships are met. A supportive family and therapeutic living arrangement can facilitate the patient's adjustment and enhance his or her growing feelings of social competence.

Our knowledge of how to prevent serious disorders such as schizophrenia is quite limited. However, our knowledge of normal adolescent development can guide our thinking about facilitating optimal growth. The advice given 25 years ago by Horrocks (1954, p. 700) still seems most relevant and appropriate:

> If the environment is such that the adolescent can gradually be inducted into experiences for which he is prepared and with which he is able to cope, if he is allowed to assume responsibility and play a mature role when he is ready to do so, and if there is a real effort on the part of adults to accept his interests and, where possible, to meet his needs, the adolescent will find his transition into maturity comparatively smooth and uncomplicated.

In other words, adolescent development can be optimized when a good match is made between the adolescent's personality and his or her social environment.

To return to the beginning analogy of the chapter and to understand the canvas we have called personality, it will be necessary to remind ourselves that personality is complex and multifaceted. We must not restrict our view to one small corner of the painting. We must explore the many detailed aspects of the canvas, and, more importantly, attempt to understand the relations among them.

SUMMARY

Four perspectives have guided the discussion of personality in adolescence: development in one domain (e.g., cognitive, physical, emotional, etc.) affects development in other areas; personality develops as the adolescent actively deals with specific developmental tasks; development must consider the interplay over time between the changing individual and the changing environment; and adolescence is experienced differently in different cultures. Two specific aspects of personality that undergo dramatic change in adolescence, identity formation and vocational–interest development, were discussed in terms of the processes that brought about change. Sameroff's transactional model of development was introduced as an aid to conceptualizing continuities and discontinuities in development. Finally, the development of schizophrenia was discussed as an example of a maladaptive reaction to the developmental tasks of adolescence by a vulnerable individual. Future study of adolescent personality should focus on multiple aspects of personality and their interrelations. Since the study of adolescent personality is multifaceted, the reader of this chapter is encouraged to think of the other chapters within this book—all of which cover topics related to the development of the adolescent personality. It may be possible, in this way, to see far more of the canvas I have called personality than would otherwise be possible.

SUGGESTIONS FOR FURTHER READING

ERIKSON, E. H. *Identity: Youth and crisis.* New York: Norton, 1968.

GOETHALS, G. W., & KLOS, D. S. *Experiencing youth: First-person accounts* (2nd ed.). Boston: Little, Brown, 1976.

HOLLAND, J. L. *Making vocational choices: A theory of careers.* Englewood Cliffs, N.J.: Prentice-Hall, 1973.

VONNEGUT, M. *The eden express.* New York: Praeger, 1975.

WEINER, I. B. *Psychological disturbance in adolescence.* New York: Wiley, 1970.

BIBLIOGRAPHY

ACHENBACH, T. M. *Research in developmental psychology: Concepts, strategies, methods.* New York: Free Press, 1978.

BELL, R. Q., & HARPER, L. V. *Child effects on adults.* Hillsdale, N.J.: Lawrence Erlbaum, 1977.

BERGER, P. A. Medical treatment of mental illness. *Science,* 1978, *200,* 974–981.

BLOCK, J. *Lives through time.* Berkeley, Calif.: Bancroft Books, 1971.

BLOCK, J. Recognizing the coherence of personality. Unpublished manuscript, University of California, Berkeley, 1978.

CAMPBELL, D. P. *Manual for the Strong-Campbell Interest Inventory T325* (Merged Form). Stanford, Calif.: Stanford University Press, 1974.

CARTER, H. D. Twin similarities in occupational interests. *Journal of Educational Psychology,* 1932, *23,* 641–655.

CLARKE, A. M., & CLARKE, A. D. B. *Early experience: Myth and evidence.* New York: Free Press, 1976.

CONGER, J. J. *Adolescence and youth: Psychological development in a changing world.* New York: Harper & Row, 1977.

CRITES, J. O. *Vocational psychology: The study of vocational behavior and development.* New York: McGraw-Hill, 1969.

CROSS, H., & ALLEN, J. Ego identity status, adjustment, and academic achievement. *Journal of Consulting and Clinical Psychology,* 1970, *34,* 288.

DOUVAN, E., & ADELSON, J. *The adolescent experience.* New York: Wiley, 1966.

ELKIND, D. Egocentrism in adolescence. *Child Development,* 1967, *38,* 1025–1034.

ELKIND, D., & WEINER, I. B. *Development of the child.* New York: Wiley, 1978.

ERIKSON, E. H. *Identity: Youth and crisis.* New York: Norton, 1968.

FOX, L. H., PASTERNAK, S. R., & PEISER, N. L. Career-related interests of adolescent boys and girls. In D. P. Keating (Ed.), *Intellectual talent: Research and development.* Baltimore: Johns Hopkins Press, 1976.

GESELL, A., ILG, F. L., & AMES, L. B. *Youth: The years from ten to sixteen.* New York: Harper & Row, 1956.

GINZBERG, E., GINSBURG, S. W., AXELROD, S., & HERMA, J. L. *Occupational choice.* New York: Columbia University Press, 1951.

GOETHALS, G. W., & KLOS, D. S. *Experiencing youth: First-person accounts* (2nd ed.). Boston: Little, Brown, 1976.

GOTTESMAN, I. I., & SHIELDS, J. *Schizophrenia and genetics: A twin study vantage point.* New York: Academic Press, 1972.

GROTEVANT, H. D. Interest development in the context of the family: Assessing environmental influences with behavior genetic methodology. Paper presented at the meeting of the Behavior Genetics Association, Davis, California, June, 1978.

GROTEVANT, H. D., SCARR, S., & WEINBERG, R. A. Patterns of interest similarity in adoptive and biological families. *Journal of Personality and Social Psychology,* 1977, *35,* 667–676.

GROTEVANT, H. D., SCARR, S., & WEINBERG, R. A. Are career interests inheritable? *Psychology Today,* March, 1978, 88–90.

HALL, C. S., & LINDZEY, G. *Theories of personality* (3rd ed.). New York: Wiley, 1978.

HAUSER, S. T. Self-image complexity and identity formation in adolescence: Longitudianl studies. *Journal of Youth and Adolescence,* 1976, *5,* 161–177.

HESTON, L. L. Psychiatric disorders in foster home reared children of schizophrenic mothers. *British Journal of Psychiatry,* 1966, *112,* 819–825.

HILL, J. P., & MONKS, F. J. Some perspectives on adolescence in modern societies. In J. P. Hill & F. J. Monks (Eds.), *Adolescence and youth in prospect.* Guildford, England: IPC Science and Technology Press Limited, 1977.

HILL, J. P., & PALMQUIST, W. J. Social cognition and social relations in early adolescence. *International Journal of Behavioral Development,* 1978, *1,* 1–36.

HILL, J. P., & STEINBERG, L. D. The development of autonomy during adolescence. Paper prepared for the Symposium on Research on Youth Problems Today, Fundación Orbegoza Eizaguirre, Madrid, Spain, 1976.

HOLLAND, J. L. *The psychology of vocational choice: A theory of personality types and model environments.* Lexington, Mass.: Ginn and Co., 1966.

HOLLAND, J. L. *Making vocational choices: A theory of careers.* Englewood Cliffs, N.J.: Prentice-Hall, 1973.

HOLZMAN, P. S., & GRINKER, R. R., SR. Schizophrenia in adolescence. *Journal of Youth and Adolescence,* 1974, *3,* 267–279.

HORROCKS, J. E. The adolescent. In L. Carmichael (Ed.), *Manual of Child Psychology* (2nd ed.). New York: Wiley, 1954.

INHELDER, B., & PIAGET, J. *The growth of logical thinking from childhood to adolescence.* New York: Basic Books, 1958.

JESSOR, R., & JESSOR, S. L. *Problem behavior and psychosocial development: A longitudinal study of youth.* New York: Academic Press, 1977.

JORDAN, D. *Parental antecedents of ego identity formation.* Unpublished master's thesis, State University of New York at Buffalo, 1970.

JORDAN, D. *Parental antecedents and personality characteristics of ego identity statuses.* Unpublished doctoral dissertation, State University of New York at Buffalo, 1972.

KEATING, D. P. Adolescent thinking. In J. Adelson (Ed.), *Handbook of adolescence.* New York: Wiley, 1980.

LOEHLIN, J. D., & NICHOLS, R. C. *Heredity, environment, and personality: A study of 850 sets of twins.* Austin: University of Texas Press, 1976.

MARCIA, J. E. Development and validation of ego identity status. *Journal of Personality and Social Psychology,* 1966, *3,* 551–558.

MARCIA, J. E. *Studies in ego identity.* Unpublished research monograph, Simon Fraser University, 1976.

MARCIA, J. E. Identity in adolescence. In J. Adelson (Ed.), *Handbook of adolescence.* New York: Wiley, 1980.

MASTERSON, J. F. The symptomatic adolescent five years later: He didn't grow out of it. *American Journal of Psychiatry,* 1967, *123,* 1338–1345.

MATTESON, D. R. Alienation vs. exploration and commitment: Personality and family correlates of adolescent identity statuses. *Rapport fra Projekt for Ungdomsforskning.* Denmark, 1974.

MEAD, M. *Coming of age in Samoa.* New York: Morrow, 1961.

NESSELROADE, J. R., & BALTES, P. B. Adolescent personality development and historical change: 1970–1972. *Monographs of the Society for Research in Child Development,* 1974, *39,* Serial No. 154.

OFFER, D. *The psychological world of the teen-ager: A study of normal adolescent boys.* New York: Basic Books, 1969.

ROBERTS, C. A., & JOHANSSON, C. B. The inheritance of cognitive interest styles among twins. *Journal of Vocational Behavior,* 1974, *4,* 237–243.

SAMEROFF, A. J. Early influences on development: Fact or fancy? *Merrill-Palmer Quarterly,* 1975, *21,* 267–294.

STEINBERG, L. *A longitudinal study of physical growth, intellectual growth, and family interaction in early adolescence.* Unpublished doctoral dissertation, Cornell University, 1977.

STRONG, E. K., JR., *Vocational interests of men and women.* Stanford, Calif.: Stanford University Press, 1943.

STRONG, E. K., JR. *Vocational interests 18 years after college.* Minneapolis, Minn.: University of Minnesota Press, 1955.

TYLER, L. E. The antecedents of two varieties of vocational interests. *Genetic Psychology Monographs,* 1964, *70,* 177–227.

VONNEGUT, M. *The eden express.* New York: Praeger, 1975.

WATERMAN, A. S., GEARY, P. S., & WATERMAN, C. K. A longitudinal study of changes in ego identity status from the freshman to the senior year at college. *Developmental Psychology,* 1974, *10,* 387–392.

WATERMAN, A. S., & WATERMAN, C. K. Factors related to vocational identity after extensive work experience. *Journal of Applied Psychology,* 1976, *61,* 336–340.

WATERMAN, C. K., & WATERMAN, A. S. Fathers and sons: A study of ego identity across two generations. *Journal of Youth and Adolescence,* 1975, *4,* 331–338.

WATT, N. F. Longitudinal changes in the social behavior of children hospitalized for schizophrenia as adults. *Journal of Nervous and Mental Disease,* 1972, *155,* 42–54.

WATT, N. F., & LUBENSKY, A. W. Childhood roots of schizophrenia. *Journal of Consulting and Clinical Psychology,* 1976, *44,* 363–375.

WEINER, I. B. *Psychological disturbance in adolescence.* New York: Wiley, 1970.

WEINER, I. B., & DELGAUDIO, A. C. Psychopathology in adolescence: An epidemiological study. *Archives of General Psychiatry,* 1976, *33,* 187–193.

6

COGNITIVE DEVELOPMENT IN ADOLESCENCE

Jeanette M. Gallagher
Richard S. Mansfield

*T*he age of the dreamer . . . the time for theory building . . . the period of the
possible—and impossible. These are popular views of adolescent
thinking. What evidence can be found that, indeed, there is a significant change in the quality of thinking during adolescence? In this chapter
we will center on the theory of cognition, or thinking, proposed by the
Swiss psychologist, Jean Piaget, to search for answers to that question. In
past years, Piaget's theory has been the focus of most research on adolescent
thinking. Since the theory is complex, however, it needs an introduction
and overview. We will discuss some of the central concepts in the theory
and then present Piaget's four stages in the development of thinking. The
last stage, called *formal operations,* which Piaget believes is reached in adolescence, is the focus of this chapter.

We will illustrate the formal operations stage by describing a number
of tasks used in its assessment. The performance of adolescents who have
reached this stage will be contrasted to the thinking of younger children at
a lower stage. Next, we will review some selected areas of contemporary research that hold special appeal, either because they enhance an understanding of adolescent thinking or because they raise critical implications
for education. Finally, we will consider the relationship of adolescent
thinking to creativity, especially as it occurs in the context of scientific discovery. For more comprehensive surveys of research related to Piaget's theory, the reader is directed to Neimark (1975a) and Gallagher and Noppe
(1976).

THE DEVELOPMENT OF THINKING
ACCORDING TO JEAN PIAGET

As an introduction to Piaget's theory, let us consider a task that illustrates a
central theme we will be stressing in this chapter: the development of the
capacity to think in terms of possibilities. This task, as well as most of the
others that will be described in this chapter, is one that you can try out
yourself with children and adolescents.

First, consider a very easy problem that Piaget (1976b) gave to children and adolescents. The subjects, ranging in age from 4 to 12, were

Jeanette McCarthy Gallagher is an Associate Professor of Human Development at
Temple University. She has written a number of research articles on cognitive development and is coauthor of *Knowledge and Development: Piaget and Education* (Vol. 2) and *The
Learning Theory of Piaget and Inhelder.*
Richard S. Mansfield, Associate Professor of Educational Psychology at Temple University, has written on creativity and cognitive development and is coauthor of *Activities
in Child and Adolescent Development* and *The Psychology of Creativity and Discovery.*

placed in a room with a toy car. A simple question was asked: how many possible routes or paths is this car able to travel in this room? The smallest children demonstrated only straight paths with a few deviations to pass around obstacles. Older children began to use some routes that curved or zigzagged. Only at the beginning of adolescence did the subjects make statements that indicated the understanding of an infinite number of possibilities. "You can go further, or not so far, and make as many turns as you want. There's no limit" (p. 2). Note that it was not necessary for the adolescents to attempt to prove all the possible routes. By stating a general rule, they actually went beyond what they observed, indicating an understanding of the *possible*.

A task devised by Peel (1971) in England, although very different from the toy car problem of Piaget, revealed another facet of the adolescent's understanding of the possible. Subjects aged 11 to 15 were asked to read paragraphs and questions such as the following:

> All large cities have art galleries and Italy is exceptionally rich in art treasures. Many people travel to Italy, especially to enjoy these old paintings, books and sculptures. Floods in the Florence area recently damaged many of these great works. Old Paintings are rare, valuable and beautiful and should be kept safely stored.
> Q. Are the Italians to blame for the loss of the paintings and art treasures?
> Q. Why do you say that? (p. 35)

What is being tested is the subject's ability to make judgments based on the information given. Peel found three levels of thinking when he analyzed the judgments. First, a very few of the subjects gave *restricted* answers, such as "No, because they've got lots of treasures." Note that this answer centers on an irrelevant aspect of the problem. At the second level, labeled *circumstantial,* subjects concentrated upon the "here and now," that is, they failed to look beyond content: "I don't think they are to blame. I think it was just the weather, and the rain had to come." Finally, mature answers were labeled *imaginative* when the subjects went beyond the content of the passage and developed possible hypotheses based on their own experience. The introduction of the "possible" is evident in these two answers:

> Well, not entirely, but they were partly because they could have put them somewhere where they weren't damaged by the floods. But if there was nowhere to put them, then they were not to blame.

> Well, they were not completely to blame. They could have been kept safe, unless the floods took them completely by surprise. (Answers modified from Peel, 1971, pp. 35–36)

Both of these judgments were enriched by the subject, that is, possibilities were imagined: lack of a safe place and the element of surprise.

Peel's research revealed that over the age range of 11 to 13 years, the proportion of circumstantial responses slightly declined while imaginative ones greatly increased. At the upper age range of the subjects tested, it was still likely that some circumstantial answers would be given. What is important is the gradual trend away from stress on content or the concrete circumstances to the thinker's own *construction* of the possible.

The Four Factors of Cognitive Development

In both of the examples discussed above, there is evidence of the development of thinking from the restricted *here and now* to the unrestrictive *possible*. Piaget (1970a, 1971, 1975, 1977a) stresses four factors to explain this development. First, it is obvious that biological foundations such as the *maturation* of the nervous system, are necessary. Second, *physical experiences,* such as contact with objects and events in the environment supply information or content as thinking develops. Third, *social transmission,* the role of education and language, highlights the important part that other people play in the development of thinking. Piaget emphasizes that these factors of maturation and environment (physical experiences and social transmission) are not sufficient for cognitive development. A fourth factor, *equilibration* or *self-regulation,* is the fundamental basis of cognitive development and the key to understanding the meaning of Piaget's theory (Piaget, 1975; Gallagher, 1977, 1978b).

Equilibration. Equilibration is the coordinating or organizing factor of cognitive development. Consider again Piaget's task with the toy car. Obviously the gradual maturation of the nervous system is essential if children at any age are to participate in the experiment. In addition, the children had experienced activities with toy cars in the past and had participated in social exchanges with other children. However, these maturational and environmental factors must be coordinated by the child's regulation of the understandings necessary to accomplish the task. At the adolescent level, for example, the understanding of an infinite number of possible routes was not directly experienced from the environment. The understanding of the possible had to be constructed through interactions of the adolescent with what was already known and observations of objects in the environment. Likewise, subjects who gave imaginative answers in Peel's art treasure problem constructed the understanding of the possible. Here again is equilibration, the self-regulation of thinking.

Piaget's Stages of Cognitive Development

The development of thinking, according to Piaget, proceeds through four stages, or periods, which we will briefly outline.[1]

Sensorimotor Stage. Even before the advent of language, infants manifest intelligent behavior while interacting with the environment. For example, infants may draw blankets toward themselves to obtain objects placed on them. Knowledge or knowing about objects has its origin, then, in interactions between persons and such objects and not in language. The sensorimotor period covers the period from birth to about 2 years old.

Preoperational (Representational) Stage. Near the age of 2, children begin to use language symbols with a certain facility. Thus they represent objects in the environment with the use of verbal symbols. They also manifest another type of symbol use by pretending that a box, for example, is a truck. Images and symbols through language and pretend play are the foundations for rapid growth of knowledge in the preschool years.

Concrete Operational Stage. Around the age of 6, the cognitive stage of concrete operations begins. Here the first mental operations exist.

When water is poured from a short, wide glass to a tall, narrow glass, the preoperational child would probably say that there is more water in the taller glass. The child is dominated by what is observed, called the *empirical* features of the event. However, around age 7 the child is able to conserve, that is, to realize that no water was added or taken away and that the quantity of water remains the same regardless of the shape of the container. This operation or internalized understanding becomes reversible because the child mentally reverses the action and can imagine the water poured back to the original container. The psychological criterion for the existence of the reversible operation is the ability to conserve (Piaget, 1966, 1977b).

Other operations develop around the same age. A child begins, for example, to understand class inclusion, that is, how subclasses are related to a class (e.g., cows and horses are both members of the class of mammals). An understanding of seriation, arranging objects systematically from smallest to largest, develops at this stage. All these operations are labeled *concrete* be-

---

[1] These stages are descriptions of behaviors at certain age levels and should not be considered as explanations or predictions of behavior (Piaget, 1975, 1977b). Thus it is possible that the stages could be renamed or grouped differently in revisions of Piaget's theory. Equilibration, however, would remain as the fundamental concept of the theory (Gallagher, 1977).

cause the child acts directly or concretely on objects of content. Recall that the circumstantial answers to Peel's problem of the art treasures centered upon the concrete or the here and now.

Formal Operational Stage. We have already emphasized the key feature of formal operations: the construction of the possible. The formal thinker is capable of thinking not just about the here and now but also about possible variations of the here and now. In problem solving, the formal thinker can consider many possible solutions and can do this according to a systematic plan. In addition, the formal thinker shows flexibility in problem solving. There is an openness to variations of the solution that may be necessary when some facet of the problem changes.

FORMAL OPERATIONS CONTRASTED WITH CONCRETE OPERATIONS

Since the subject of this chapter is formal operations, we will spend some time contrasting formal operational thinking to concrete operational thinking. Piaget and his colleagues (Inhelder & Piaget, 1958; Piaget, 1972a, 1972b, 1976b) have proposed that two fundamental structures of thinking characterize formal operations: the combinatorial structure and a complex mathematical formulation called the four group or INRC group (defined more specifically later). Each of these structures will be illustrated by considering a task used in the assessment of formal operations. Performance on these tasks illustrates the contrast between concrete and formal operational thinking.

The Combination of Colorless Chemicals Task

In this problem, which we will use to illustrate the combinatorial structure, the subject is presented with four numbered flasks, each containing a colorless, odorless liquid (Inhelder & Piaget, 1958). A smaller bottle, also filled with a colorless liquid, is labelled g. The subject is shown that when g is added to an unidentified combination of chemicals from the four numbered flasks, a yellow color results. The subject is instructed to work with the chemicals to produce the yellow color. Only one comination $(1 + 3 + g)$ will do this. Chemical 2 is a bleaching agent which removes the yellow color from the target mixture; chemical 4 is water and has no effect on the color of a mixture.

We will compare the performance on this task of two female subjects, aged 8 and 15. The 8-year-old began by combining g with each of the other liquids in succession. She was at a loss when this strategy failed to produce the yellow color. When it was suggested that she try combinations of three or more chemicals in combination, she proceeded unsystematically, trying combinations such as $(1 + 2 + g)$ and $(2 + 4 + g)$. After several attempts she hit on the correct solution but failed to remember it since she had not been keeping a record of attempted combinations. When she refound the solution, she lost it again by adding chemical 2, the bleaching agent. She suggested that she might have added too much g but made no test of this hypothesis.

Notice two key features of the 8-year-old's approach to this problem. First, she lacked an overall plan: she did not systematically set about testing all possible combinations. Second, she became so centered on the importance of g that she could not decenter, that is, realize the addition of chemical 2 took away the desired color. Because the bottles became all-important as objects or elements in themselves, she did not consider attributing the presence or absence of color to the combination of several elements.

Now consider the strategies of the 15-year-old on the same problem. This subject also began by combining each of the numbered flasks with g. When the desired yellow color did not appear, she repeated these combinations but began to keep a written record of each test and its results. After successively combining g with each bottle, she moved on to triple combinations, tried these systematically, and soon found the correct combination. When questioned about the effects of chemicals 2 and 4, she easily developed tests of their effects (e.g., $1 + 3 + g$ vs. $1 + 3 + g + 2$). She quickly determined that adding chemical 2 to the correct combination eliminated the yellow color, whereas adding chemical 4 had no effect.

What distinguished the thinking of the adolescent from that of the 8-year-old? First, the adolescent systematically proceeded to explore the results of all possible combinations. Only a complete combinatorial system furnishes the total number of possibilities. In addition, the adolescent attempted to determine the effect of one or more liquids upon another, that is, their interrelationships. Relationships can only be understood when variables can be separated.

The Snail and Board Problem

This problem, developed by Piaget and Inhelder (1969), provides a clear example of the INRC group. Imagine a snail that is able to move either left or right on a board. Also imagine that the board may be moved either left or right. Think of the four movements involved: snail to the left; snail to the right; board to the left; and, board to the right. The four movements may be thought of as a double system of reference, for the movements of the snail and board, with reference to a stationary observer, are interrelated.

The movement in one direction may be considered a direct operation. When canceled by a movement in the opposite direction, the direct operation becomes an inverse operation. Children at the level of concrete operations are able to understand the direct and inverse operations of the snail and the board. What they are not able to do is to combine these two operations into one system. Therefore, they cannot understand that the movement of the board could compensate for the movement of the snail so that in actuality, if the snail moved to the right (R) and the board to the left (L), the poor snail would make no progress!

At the formal operational level, however, adolescents gradually understand the double reciprocal relations involved: the movements of the board may cancel out the movements of the snail. The four terms of the INRC structure may be outlined as follows:

I = Identity or Direct Transformation (movement of snail to R)
N = Negation or Inverse Transformation (movement of snail to L)
R = Reciprocity or Reciprocal Transformation (movement of board to L)
C = Correlative of Inverse of the Reciprocal Transformation (movement of board to R)

Every operation is an inverse of another and the reciprocal of a third, so that the four transformations or changes are integrated. Such integration frees the adolescent from the here and now so that various possibilities may be understood. The combinatorial system (the understanding of the possible) and the INRC group (the understanding of complex interelationships working together) provide the foundation for flexibility of thinking.

Descriptions of formal thought often become bogged down in the complexities of the mathematical formulations that Piaget proposed. What is essential for a grasp of what Piaget's theory means for the development of thinking in the adolescent are the notions of the *possible* and *flexibility* of thought. We will return to these characteristics in various sections of this chapter.

Reflexive Abstraction

Later writings of Piaget (1974a, 1975, 1977b, 1978a) on how a person moves from one stage to the next are more useful in understanding adolescent thought than overemphasis on the combinatorial and INRC structures. The mechanism for movement that Piaget proposes is one of reflexive abstraction. When children concentrate on the observable (here and now) aspects of problems, they are making use of empirical or observable abstraction. For enrichment of thinking, it is necessary to go beyond the observable, to reorganize one's thinking, and to project it to a higher level.

Such reorganization and projection is labeled reflexive abstraction. An example may clarify these concepts. If children are presented with six coins, they may simply look at them (empirical abstraction). But if they count them several times, each time in a different order, and thereby conclude that the number of coins does not depend on the order in which they are counted, they have engaged in reflexive abstraction. Reflexive abstraction is the basis for flexibility of thinking and the awareness of the possible.

SELECTED TOPICS OF INTEREST IN FORMAL THOUGHT

Because of space limitations, we will not attempt to review all areas of research on formal operations. You will find references to several more comprehensive review articles among the suggested readings at the end of this chapter. What we will do is to focus on several topics of contemporary interest. The first two topics deal with new tasks. Research and writing in the area of formal thought has traditionally centered on physical science tasks, such as the combination of chemicals, from the original work of Inhelder and Piaget (1958). However, what is central to formal thought are the characteristics of *flexibility* and the understanding of the *possible,* and not any particular set of tasks. We believe that the investigation of new tasks can enhance the understanding of formal thought.

The tasks used to assess formal thought become an important issue when we consider the third topic in this section, sex differences. As we shall see, whether or not sex differences in formal thought are found may depend on the type of task or on the way it is administered. The last two topics, which concern the understanding of proportions and analogies and the relationship of formal operations to the science curriculum, are included because they highlight educational implications of adolescent thinking.

The Hanoi Tower and the Study of Awareness

Piaget and his colleagues (Piaget, 1976a, 1978b) have devised a series of studies to demonstrate that awareness or consciousness of *how* one solves a problem may appear developmentally later than successful solutions or actions. In other words, it is possible to *succeed* with an action apart from what is *understood* to be involved in that success.

For purposes of understanding adolescent thought, these studies are important for two reasons. First, the tasks in these studies are not directly related to possible prior knowledge of scientific concepts. Secondly, the ability to verbalize the rule involved in solution of these problems is the reorganization of a thought phenomenon mentioned earlier as reflexive abstraction. At the adolescent level, this reorganization has the special term of *reflected abstraction,* that is, reflection on the solution with the consequent ability to state the rule involved.

One of the most revealing tasks used to study the effects of awareness on understanding was the Hanoi Tower (Piaget, 1976a). The details of the task are given here to encourage the reader to replicate the study so as to contrast the thinking of children and adolescents. The task consists of three vertical posts, A, B, and C (see Figure 6.1), attached to a base board. On Post A, the starting post, are placed several discs, graduated by size in pyramid fashion so that the largest disc is on the bottom and the smallest on top. The object of the game is to advance, in as few moves as possible, the discs from Post A to Post C following these rules: move only one disc at a time; a large disc may not be placed on a smaller one; discs may not be rested on the table; and discs may not be held in hand while another is moved. (Try to determine the winning strategy before reading the following. Make the game by inserting three colored pencils or sticks into clay or styrofoam. Use graduated rings made from cardboard for discs.)

The key to success in this task is the awareness of the necessity of a storage post while successive moves are made. The difficulty, however, of these successive moves increases dramatically from a 2- to a 3-disc problem (Piaget, 1976a; Byrnes & Spitz, 1977). There are two reasons for this increase in difficulty: first, the number of necessary moves is doubled; second,

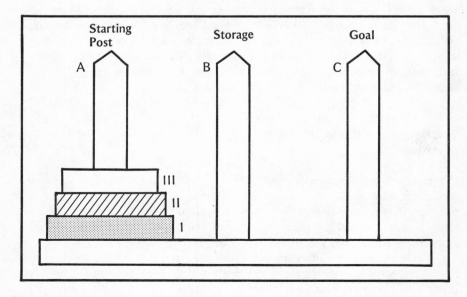

Figure 6.1 The 3-Disc Tower of Hanoi Task.

the first move of the smallest disc changes from the storage post to the goal post.[2]

If we compare actual protocols of children and adolescents as they try to move the 3-disc tower, it is possible to contrast strategies. First, consider the performance of 8-year-old Rob (protocols adapted from Piaget, 1976a, pp. 293–298). Rob first succeeds in 10 moves and then in 8 when working with 3 discs. He starts off well by moving Disc II from A to B, then from B to C, although he wastes one move.

Adult: Does it matter where you put the little one when you start?

Rob: Yes, no, perhaps it will be better like that (Moves disc III from A to C: starts again). Oh, yes, much better.

Adult: Can you do it if you start off that other way (moving disc III from A to B)?

Rob: I don't know. I've never done it. (In actuality, he has done it 3 times.)

Later when the adult experimenter asked Rob how he accomplished the task of moving the discs from Post A to C, he demonstrated all the moves. No general rule or plan was given.

Eric, who is approaching twelve years old, solves the 3-disc tower in 7 moves and then explains his strategy:

Eric: I've understood that it's all right if I put the little one on (Post C): I can put the middle one (on Post B) and then the little one on the middle one, and so Disc I can be placed here (on C).

Adult: Was the 4-disc tower more difficult? (Eric succeeded in 15 moves.)

Eric: A little. There's one more, you have to make more moves; otherwise, it's the same system.

Adult: What system?

Eric: You always take away the smaller one (IV), then the middle one (III), then you put the small one on the middle one and you can get at the big one (II): that makes a small pyramid there, and then the way is clear and I can start all over again; it's the same story afterward (with Disc I). . . . It's the beginning that counts, the first move at the beginning; you've got to be careful, otherwise you can't make it right, or you have to make a lot more moves.

Note Eric's ability to state the general rule (reflected abstraction). It is as if he now has a model that fits any number of discs for the tower prob-

---

[2] To determine the minimum number of moves for each set of discs, use the formula $2^n - 1$ (n equals number of discs): three moves for two discs, seven moves for three discs, fifteen for four, and so forth.

lem. It should be mentioned, however, that Rob and Eric's protocols are somewhat clear-cut. When our graduate students replicated this experiment, several 12-year-olds were in a transitional stage. They may have succeeded, for example, in moving the 4-disc tower but found it difficult to realize the importance of the first move. Therefore, what may be expected in early adolescence is an advanced awareness of a general rule but not necessarily a grasp of all the facets of the problem.

The failure of some children to shift from a 2-disc to a 3-disc solution was based on a strategy of always making the first move to the storage peg. What worked for the 2-disc problem was rigidly applied to the 3-disc problem without an evaluation of other possibilities. Byrnes and Spitz (1977) reported that many of the 8- to 11-year-old normal children (both normal and retarded children were studied) who solved the 2-disc problem could not accommodate to the 3-disc problem.

Natural Experiments

One of the more promising directions in research on formal thought is to study its development using tasks more closely related to everyday experience than the physical science problems used by Inhelder and Piaget (1958). It has commonly been reported (e.g., Neimark, 1977) that many otherwise intelligent and well-educated adults do poorly on the physical science tasks used to assess formal operational thinking. These adults may have difficulty because the content of the problems is unfamiliar. Alternatively, the method of solution may be one that is rarely used by persons in nonscientific fields. For persons in such fields, the traditional tasks used to assess formal thought may yield invalid results. It would therefore be desirable to assess formal thought with tasks more closely related to everyday experience.

Kuhn and Brannock (1977) used what they called "natural experiments" to investigate one aspect of formal thought (the "isolation of variables scheme"). The isolation of variables scheme, as observed in the traditional Inhelder and Piaget tasks, involves constructing and performing a valid experiment by manipulating one variable while holding all other variables constant. We have already encountered this scheme in the chemical combination problem described earlier. If the combination of substances $(2 + 3 + g)$ yields a yellow color, another substance (e.g., 4) can be added to see if the outcome is different. In this case, substance 4 is manipulated, and substances 2, 3, and g are held constant.

Kuhn and Brannock noted that in everyday life people rarely have the opportunity to set up the conditions for a controlled experiment. But there are many occasions in which individuals draw inferences from a series of observations, in which different outcomes are associated with different sets of conditions. Each observation constitutes a "natural experiment."

Kuhn and Brannock developed a special problem to assess the presence of the "isolation of variables scheme" in the context of natural experiments. Subjects were shown four plants on a table. Two of the plants were healthy, and two were obviously in poor condition. Next to each plant were items indicating the conditions under which the plant had grown: a glass of water, either large or small; a dish containing either dark- or light-colored plant food; and the presence or absence of a bottle marked "leaf lotion." The problem was constructed so that only one variable, plant food, influenced the plant's health. Subjects were required to determine which variables influenced the plant's health and which did not. To solve this kind of problem, subjects do not construct an experiment on their own but rather make inferences based on the information provided by a set of "natural experiments."

This problem was used with fourth, fifth, and sixth graders, and college freshmen (all females). These subjects were also given one of the physical science problems used by Inhelder and Piaget to assess the isolation of variables scheme. The latter problem involved experimenting with a pendulum to determine which of several variables influenced the pendulum's rate of oscillation. The same kinds of difficulties in isolating and excluding variables were noted on both problems. Subjects began to be able to solve both problems during the same age range, but the pendulum problem was typically mastered at an earlier age. It is interesting to note that there was not a statistically significant relationship between performance on the two types of problems. Thus Kuhn and Brannock suggested that the two problems may pose different types of obstacles.

More research is needed to evaluate Kuhn and Brannock's hypothesis that natural experiments like the plant problem provide more valid estimates of a person's competence in the domain of formal thought than the physical science tasks. It should be noted, however, that even the plant problem has features that are artificial and unlikely to be found in real-life problems. In the plant problem, there are only three relevant variables, all of which are specified. In problem situations in everyday life there are usually many more potentially relevant variables, and not all of these can be specified in advance. In addition, if several variables jointly influence the outcome, and these variables interact with each other in complex ways, it is difficult to draw inferences in any straightforward way from natural experiments.

Sex Differences in Formal Thinking

The topic of sex differences in formal thinking has recently sparked some intriguing speculation. The nature of sex differences in formal thought is somewhat unclear. Some researchers have found no sex differences, but others have often reported sex differences favoring males (Neimark, 1975a;

Modgil & Modgil, 1976). Do these sex differences mean that males are superior to females in formal reasoning? Perhaps not. Some researchers (Lawson, 1975; Neimark, 1977; Linn, 1978) have hypothesized that the sex differences occur because the tasks used to measure formal thought also measure a dimension of cognitive style for which there are known sex differences: field dependence-independence.

Before explaining this hypothesis, we must briefly define field dependence-independence. This concept, developed by Witkin and his associates (Witkin, Dyk, Faterson, Goodenough, & Karp, 1962), refers to the ability to perceive an object while disregarding the surrounding perceptual field. For example, in one of the tests used to assess field dependence-independence the subject must locate a simple figure that is embedded within a complex design. Field dependent persons have difficulty disembedding the figure. Field independent persons, on the other hand, can locate the target figure because they are not misled by the surrounding perceptual field. Although field dependence was first identified as a perceptual dimension, it appears to reflect a more general cognitive or personality dimension: the degree to which one can think analytically about something while disregarding the context in which it occurs. Thus, if a field-independent person and a field-dependent person saw a movie together, the field-independent person might come out of the theater thinking analytically about the use of visual effects, while the field dependent person might be more concerned with the global emotional impact of the film. Witkin et al. (1962) present extensive evidence for sex differences, with females more field dependent and males more field independent.

How might field dependence-independence be related to the tasks used to measure formal thought? Tasks like the combination of chemicals problem require the subject to consider all the possibilities in the situation, not just those that are immediately obvious in the materials. The subject must consider many things that might be done with the materials. The possibilities in the situation must be disembedded from the subject's global perception of the situation. Therefore, field independent subjects should do better on the tasks than field dependent persons. And males, tending to be more field independent than females, should show higher levels of performance on the tasks. But the males' higher performance could reflect their field independence rather than superiority in logical thinking.

The evidence for this explanation of sex differences in formal operational ability is somewhat limited. A few studies (e.g., Neimark, 1975b; Lawson & Wollman, 1977) have demonstrated relationships between formal thinking and field dependence-independence. But to our knowledge, no one has directly shown that sex differences in formal thought are due to differences in field dependence-independence.

Neimark (1977) suggests several possible directions for further research. First, additional evidence is needed on the relationship between cognitive style and the traditional tasks used to measure formal operational thinking. Second, it may be desirable to develop new tasks that would measure formal thinking without also measuring field dependence-independence. On the basis of the available evidence, Neimark does not think that simply modifying the physical science content of the tasks will be sufficient; it will also be necessary to present the tasks in a much more structured situation in which the subject is told not only the goal of the task but also the alternative means to it and the basis for evaluating performance. Neimark believes that, under these conditions, there is little room for individual differences in cognitive style to manifest themselves, so that performance should more clearly reflect underlying ability. For example, a subject given the snail and board problem would be shown the results of different combinations of movements by the snail and board; different ways of thinking about this problem would be illustrated. If, after all this, the subject still could not predict the snail's movement, we might more confidently explain the failure in terms of a lack of formal thinking abilities, and we might rule out the possibility that the subject was bored with the snail!

Neimark's hypothesis that structuring the presentation of formal operational tasks will enhance performance has received confirmation in a study by Stone and Day (1978). Unfortunately, sex differences in the effects of structuring were not examined.

The Understanding of Proportions

The adolescent who has difficulty understanding proportions (and analogies) is also likely to have difficulty in school. We will discuss proportional reasoning first. Consider a task developed by Karplus, Karplus and Wollman (1974) to assess proportional reasoning. A child is given a chain of paper clips and a sheet of paper displaying a stick figure called Mr. Short. The experimenter tells the child that there is another, larger stick figure, called Mr. Tall, in the office. The experimenter says that when he measured each stick figure with large buttons, Mr. Short's height was four buttons and Mr. Tall's was six buttons. The child is then asked to do three things: measure Mr. Short using paper clips; predict the height of Mr. Tall if he were measured with paper clips; and, explain the prediction. It is the explanation that determines whether the child has used proportional reasoning. For example, one child said, "Mr. Short to Mr. Tall is 4 to 6 buttons; it will be the same with paper clips, 4 is to 6 as 6 is to 9." In the same study, a variety of categories of incorrect explanations was evident. Some children focused on a single difference, uncoordinated with other differences, and dealt with the problem by using addition. One child who used this strategy said, "Mr. Tall was 2 buttons higher than Mr. Short, so I figured he was 2 paper clips higher."

149

Although the paper clip problem involves a relatively simple application of proportional reasoning, most students do not solve it until the last two years of high school. In a large study, involving 727 students from suburban and inner city areas (Karplus & Peterson, 1970), 6% of the suburban children used proportional reasoning at grade 6, 32% at grades 8–10, and 80% at grades 11–12. Very few inner-city children showed proportional reasoning: 3% at grade 6, 5% at grades 8–10, and 9% at grades 11–12. Other researchers, sometimes using different tasks, have confirmed that proportional reasoning is a late acquisition (Brainerd, 1971; Wollman & Karplus, 1974; Chapman, 1975).

Proportional reasoning is needed in many school subjects, including mathematics, physics, and chemistry. But despite its academic importance, proportional reasoning does not emerge in most children until at least the last two years of high school, even though ratio and proportion are typically taught as part of the junior high school mathematics curriculum. Proportionality, like other Piagetian concepts, may be difficult to teach to students who are not cognitively ready for it.

The paper clip problem involves a relatively simple kind of proportional reasoning: There is a direct proportion between the size of a figure in buttons and its size in paper clips. Problems involving inverse proportionality are more difficult (Lunzer, 1965). For example, one of the problems used by Inhelder and Piaget (1958) to assess formal operational thinking deals with the size of a shadow cast by an object on a screen that is illuminated by a point source of light. Solving the problem requires an understanding of the inverse relationship between the size of the shadow and the distance from the light source to the object. Problems involving inverse proportionality are typically solved later than those involving direct proportionality (Lunzer, 1965).

The concept of proportion is closely related to the concept of analogy. Lunzer (1965) points out that the structure of an analogy (Leather is to shoe as wool is to sweater) is exactly parallel to a statement of proportion (3 is to 15 as 4 is to 20). Indeed, analogies may be considered *qualitative* as opposed to *quantitative* proportions.

The Understanding of Analogies

By the time students reach college, they have frequently been asked to solve analogies such as "Rug is to floor as roof is to ———." Such items are included on both intelligence and achievement tests. What students may not realize is that their ability to perform on such items, when vocabulary is controlled, increases dramatically at early adolescence, beginning at approximately twelve years of age. In this section, we examine the evidence and the reasons for this shift.

The developmental study of analogy, that is, how performance changes through time, has been investigated by a number of researchers (Goldstein, 1962; Lunzer, 1965; Orlando, 1971; Gallagher & Wright, 1977, 1979; Piaget, 1977a; Sternberg & Rifkin, 1979). One important finding was that the shift in performance at early adolescence was larger for abstract than for concrete items (Orlando, 1971). Consider the difference between an abstract and a concrete analogy in the following examples adapted from Orlando (1971):

Abstract: Chapter is to book as joint is to *finger.*
Concrete: Leg is to walking as arm is to *throwing.*

Note that the content of the concrete item may be visualized so that the relationships between leg-walking and arm-throwing are readily grasped. However, the solution of the abstract item is complicated by the necessity to search for a higher order relationship. For chapter-book and joint-finger, the higher order relationship is one of part to whole. Such a relationship is grasped in a reordering or reorganizing process of reflexive abstraction (Piaget, 1977a; Gallagher, 1978a) as explained earlier in this chapter. Concrete items may also be linked to the concentration on observables or the here and now. Abstract items, on the other hand, require a search for various possibilities not readily apparent when the items are first read.

Gallagher and Wright (1979), in a study of analogy performance of children in grades 4 through 7, found that concrete item scores did not differ by grade level. Abstract items scores, however, were higher for seventh graders than for fourth and fifth graders.

Another important finding in the study of analogy is that the ability to form a rule is related to successful performance. Sternberg (Sternberg, 1977; Sternberg & Rifkin, 1979) linked analogy solution to the successful search for a rule relating the A term to the C term. Thus, in any analogy with the form, A is to B as C is to D (Rug is to floor as roof is to *house*), the rule connects the first term to the third. For example, it is not sufficient to associate rug with floor just because they "go together." The terms *rug* and *roof* need to be comprehended as coverings or protection for the other terms. Therefore, the concept of covering or protection becomes the *rule* mapping or relating *rug* to *roof,* so that a meaningful fourth term may be chosen from several alternatives.

Asking subjects to explain their selection provides insight into the shift in performance at adolescence. For example, note the written reasons of seventh-grade subjects for this item: Engine is to car as man is to: work, road, speed *bicycle* (Gallagher & Wright, 1979):

Engine and a man make a car and a bicycle move.
Because engine and man power the car and the bicycle.

Because man is a bicycle's "engine."
The first words provide power to the second.
Each powers something.

Each reason is a statement of a rule linking the first (engine) and third (man) terms. In contrast, fourth graders' reasons centered upon the last half of the analogy ("A man rides a bike.") or upon a linear ordering of the observed terms ("Car needs an engine and a bicycle needs a person.") Piaget calls these linear orderings "successive relationships."

In a related study, Petner (1978) listed four alternatives from which the subjects were to select the "best" reason for the given answer. For example, the following reasons were given for the analogy: Picture is related to frame as yard is to ————. Fence is the best answer because:

a. A picture goes inside a frame and a yard inside a fence. (Successive relationship reason)
b. A frame and a fence go around something. (Rule reason)
c. A fence can be built. (Incorrect reason)
d. A yard is inside a fence. (Associative reason)

The selection of alternatives was based on Piaget's (1977a) finding that young children often gave successive relationship and associative reasons, which merely linked terms together with no awareness of the need to relate A to C in an analogy having the form, A is to B as C is to D. Petner, studying children from grades four through seven, found a significant shift at the seventh grade level from successive relationship and associative reasons to rule reasons.

In sum, research on analogies strengthens the notion that adolescent thought extends beyond the here and now to the possible. In addition, the enhanced flexibility of formal thought may be inferred from the adolescent's ability to shift the form of the analogy (A:B as C:D) in such a way as to relate A to C and thereby construct a rule.

The use of analogies is basic to all areas of the curriculum. Analogies appear often in literature as, for example, in metaphors. But analogies, like proportions, may be difficult for many high school students to understand. Herron (1977) states that in high school chemistry courses he often encounters difficulty when he must teach a concept for which there is no readily available, concrete referent. In such cases, he attempts to explain the concept by using an analogy, but regardless of the clarity and appropriateness of the analogy many students cannot use the analogy to understand the concept being taught. Research is needed to determine ways to teach students to understand analogies and proportions, so that high school and college courses may be enriched. We will address these educational issues again, as they relate to the high school science curriculum.

Formal Operations and the Science Curriculum

In the past decade, researchers and educators have devoted much energy to the exploration of the educational implications of Piagetian theory. Not surprisingly, some of this effort has been focused on the educational implications of the acquisition of formal thinking. One area of lively interest and controversy has been the relationship between formal thinking and the science curriculum at the junior high and high school levels. Much of the curriculum, especially in the physical sciences, presupposes that students can reason at the formal level. This was not a deliberate policy of curriculum developers. But an understanding of scientific concepts requires proportional reasoning and the ability to think in terms of relations between relations. In addition, students are expected to be able to use the isolation of variables scheme, discussed earlier, to construct and interpret experiments. The reliance of the secondary science curriculum on formal thinking increased during the 1960s, with the development of new curricula aimed at providing a deeper understanding of scientific concepts and relationships (Lovell & Shayer, 1978). But after a decade of experience with the new curricula, educators began to have some misgivings. Fewer students were enrolling in secondary science courses, and the new curricula were proving to be no more effective than the traditional ones.

Initially, Piagetian theory offered no obvious explanation for the problems with the new curricula. The children studied by Inhelder and Piaget (1958) had begun to show formal operational thinking by about the age of eleven, with most showing evidence of formal thought by early adolescence. If American students acquire formal thought at about the same age, most should be thinking at the formal level by the time they reach high school and encounter the new science curricula.

But Lawson and Renner and their associates (e.g., Lawson & Renner, 1974, 1975; Lawson & Blake, 1976) began to present a considerable amount of evidence that most high school students function primarily at the concrete rather than the formal level. These and other studies are reviewed by Chiapetta (1976), who concludes that most adolescents and young adults have not reached the stage of formal operations. If this conclusion is correct, it would explain students' difficulties with the new science curricula: the science curricula presuppose a level of thinking that many high school students have not attained. In addition, many students who can reason at the formal level on Piagetian tasks function only at the concrete level when dealing with concepts in the science curriculum (Chiapetta, 1976). Herron (1977) points out that even adult formal thinkers revert to the concrete level when confronted with new ideas and concepts. How many adults, encountering the theory of relativity for the first time, would immediately be able to think formally about it, and to relate it to other theories in the physical sciences? Even with numerous concrete examples, the theory of relativity is difficult to grasp. These considerations have led to calls for a reevaluation of the new curricula (e.g., Chiapetta, 1976; Lovell & Shayer, 1978).

One obvious implication would be to eliminate or minimize those concepts that can only be understood by students at the formal level and to keep the curriculum within the limits of concrete operational thinking. Lovell and Shayer even go so far as to suggest that the high school science curriculum be specifically designed to promote concrete operational thinking, since many students will not have extended such thinking over much of a range of experience. Another, more ambitious educational strategy would be to promote the development of formal thinking in the elementary and junior high school years, so that a greater proportion of students would be at the formal level when they encountered the science courses in high school. This strategy presupposes that students can be trained in formal thinking and that this training is effective, long lasting, and can be generalized to tasks that differ from those used in the training. Thus far such evidence is lacking.

The educational implications we have discussed are based on the premises that individuals' formal reasoning ability can be measured and that most high school students are not at the stage of formal operations. These premises were challenged by Emerick and Easley (1978), who objected to the way in which Lawson and Renner and their associates classified individuals with respect to Piagetian stage level. The classification was done by administering interviews or paper and pencil tests and noting the presence or absence of specific explanations reflecting formal operational thinking. Emerick and Easley call Lawson and Renner "operationalists" because they operationally define stage levels in terms of specific behaviors shown in response to problems requiring formal thought. The operationalists, they say, assume that an individual is in all situations at just one of the stages of cognitive development, or else in transition between two stages. Moreover, the operationalists assume that all individuals at a particular stage will show specific behaviors when presented with a given problem.

Emerick and Easley, who call themselves "constructivists," believe that these assumptions reflect a misunderstanding of Piagetian theory. The constructivists believe that each stage represents a new mental equilibrium, which can be reflected in a wide variety of different behaviors. Thus there can be no one-to-one correspondence between stages and behaviors, and it is impossible to delineate a set of behaviors that will be shown by all persons at a particular stage. This problem is especially significant for the assessing of cognitive competence at the formal operational level. They point out that formal operation subjects can reason deductively from thinking about what is possible to actually testing the real; but if subjects deduce /

that a particular result must be obtained, they may not actually test the result. In other words, they may use formal operations but fail to evince that type of thinking in their behavior. Emerick and Easley also argue that in classifying individuals with respect to stage level, the operationalists: ignore idiosyncratic behavior which may give important but unanticipated clues as to the individual's cognitive ability; and, do not allow for the possibility of using alternate strategies to solve the tasks. On the basis of these criticisms, they believe that the operationalists have probably underestimated the proportion of students capable of formal thought.

The position of Emerick and Easley has received important support from two studies (Danner & Day, 1977; Stone & Day, 1978). In both studies, adolescents and younger subjects who did not spontaneously use the isolation of variables strategy when presented with standard Piagetian tasks were given *prompts* (e.g., demonstrations and verbal rules) designed to elicit the strategy. Many of these subjects, especially the adolescents, were then able to use the strategy. Stone and Day (1978) concluded that there are probably a large number of latent strategy users. Thus the operationalists may have underestimated the incidence of at least one formal operational ability among high school students.

More research with adolescents is needed to determine whether simple prompts will elicit other formal operational abilities. It seems doubtful that such prompts will facilitate the performance of most adolescents on many formal operational tasks. If formal thinking were this easy to facilitate, why would teachers be so concerned about the lack of formal thinking skills in their adolescent students? The operationalists' conclusion that many high school students cannot solve problems requiring formal thought is probably accurate. It is consistent with the more general conclusion that the attainment of formal operations is far from universal (Blasi & Hoeffel, 1974; Neimark, 1977).

FORMAL OPERATIONS AND CREATIVITY

Creativity, especially in scientific fields, involves higher level thinking and problem solving. Is there a connection between such thinking and the logical abilities that characterize formal thought? At the present time, we can only speculate about the answer to this question. Eric Lunzer (1978) has suggested two integrative concepts that will aid our speculation. Lunzer has been concerned with the problem of identifying what it is that is common to all tasks requiring formal thought. He suggests that two factors are present in the solution of such tasks: acceptance of lack of closure (ALC) and multiple interacting systems (MIS). We will first define and illustrate these two factors and then suggest ways in which they may facilitate creativity.

Acceptance of Lack of Closure

Acceptance of lack of closure (ALC) is necessary when the initially presented information does not immediately permit solution but does reduce the number of alternative solutions so that the problem may be solved when more information is obtained. In such situations, one must temporarily accept the notion that more than one solution remains possible. As an example of lack of closure, Lunzer (1978) describes a task used in an unpublished study by Pocklington. The tasks involved special apparatus, consisting of a box with one light and with four buttons to press. One button was a switch, causing the light to turn on if it was off and vice versa. A second was an "on" button, causing the light to come on if it was off but having no effect if the light was already on. An "off" button turned the light off if it was on but otherwise had no effect. Finally, a "neutral" button had no effect on the light. The child's task was to determine the function of each button by making as few button presses as possible. On some problems, the children were given labels to tag any of the buttons that they had identified. The labels were *on, off, change, neutral, on or change, on or neutral, off or change,* and *off or neutral.* The last four, called "alternative labels," were provided for use in ambiguous situations occurring when a button was pressed for the first time. Whereas the 11-year-olds studied by Pocklington used the alternative labels frequently, only about half the 9-year-olds used them, and then only infrequently, and the 7-year-olds never used the alternative labels. Lunzer interpreted these results in terms of emerging ALC; that is, the younger children saw no need for the alternative labels because of premature closure; they could not accept the idea that a button could be "on or change," since it must be one or the other. Older children used the alternative labels because they were able to accept lack of closure.

Multiple Interacting Systems

Another feature that Lunzer believes is found in most tasks used to assess formal thought is multiple interacting systems (MIS). MIS are present when the solution of a task involves the interaction of two independent systems of variation. Recall the problem described earlier in this chapter involving the snail on a board. The snail can move to the left or right, as can the board. To predict the progress of the snail, the motion of the snail and of the board, two independent systems, must be coordinated. Lunzer (1978) shows that ALC and MIS are present in many tasks used to assess formal thought. He proposes that ALC and MIS are necessary but not sufficient conditions for formal operational thinking.

ALC, MIS, and Creativity

Are ALC and MIS also involved in creativity? We think so, but before spe-
culating further, we must delimit what we mean by creativity. Unfortunately, the term *creativity* has been applied to a wide variety of phenomena,
ranging from preschool children's art work to Nobel-prize-winning contributions in science. It is not clear that there are common processes underlying these diverse phenomena in different fields and at different levels. For
purposes of this discussion, we will limit our consideration to creativity in
scientific fields. Many of the tasks used to assess formal thinking have scientific content, and it is in the domain of science that links to creativity are
most likely to be found.

What is known about the creative process in science? And how might
the creative process relate to ALC and MIS? Our knowledge about the
creative process in science comes chiefly from retrospective accounts by scientists. On the basis of such accounts, numerous theories have been advanced (See Busse & Mansfield, in press, for a review). We shall focus on
one formulation (Busse & Mansfield, in press; Mansfield & Busse, 1980)
that can easily be linked to ALC and MIS. Busse and Mansfield propose
that creativity in science proceeds through interrelated and overlapping
processes: selection of the problem; extended effort to solve the problem;
setting constraints on the solution of the problem; changing the constraints;
and verification and elaboration. We will briefly consider these processes
and their relationships with ALC and MIS.

Selection of the Problem. Creative breakthroughs result in part from the
selection of important problems, ones which, if solved, would have major
implications for existing theory. To select such problems, a scientist must
be alert to evidence that is difficult to explain in terms of existing theory.
For example, Einstein, in the work that led to the development of the theory of relativity, began by noticing discrepancies between the Newtonian
laws of mechanics and observed phenomena relating to the speed of light.
Sensitivity to problems of this type can be seen in terms of acceptance of
lack of closure; indeed, it may entail a deliberate search for lack of closure.
MIS is also important to the selection of the problem. Relating two previously independent systems of knowledge may lead to an important discovery, such as Einstein's relating Newtonian mechanics and light.

Extended Effort to Solve the Problem. The second process typically precedes major scientific achievements. Einstein spent seven years studying the
velocity of light before he developed his theory of special relativity. This is
a long time to accept lack of closure.

Setting Constraints on the Solution of the Problem. This refers to the initial assumptions made by the scientist that the solution of the problem must explain all relevant empirical observations, must agree with certain theoretical assumptions, and must be found using available instrumentation and methodology. Some of the constraints initially adopted may in time be changed, but in setting constraints the scientist is defining and accepting the problem's lack of closure.

Changing the Constraints. The fourth process often occurs when new evidence makes previously accepted theoretical assumptions untenable. For example, Kepler, after detailed observations of the planet Mars, was forced to abandon the assumption, based on Ptolemaic theory, of circular planetary orbits. Changing the constraints may also occur as a result of considering the problem in relation to a new theory or a new field of inquiry. To cite one well-known example, Darwin was unable to explain evolution satisfactorily until he related the biological evidence to Malthus's principle of the survival of the fittest (part of a theory of human population). The abundance of similar examples in the history of science may explain why Piaget (1979) recommends reading a great deal in related and surrounding fields but not in one's own precise field. By considering the problem from the perspective of another field, the scientist deliberately capitalizes on the chance of a solution through MIS.

Verification and Elaboration. If the changing of constraints leads to a significant discovery, a period of verification and elaboration is necessary. The scientist must insure that the new solution or formulation works under a variety of conditions and that it can provide a satisfactory explanation for all relevant data.

We have seen that ALC and MIS, two principles developed by Lunzer to explain formal thought, can also be related to some of the processes of scientific creativity. In scientific work, ALC and MIS operate at higher levels than in tasks used to assess formal thinking. There is a much greater lack of closure in scientific work than there is in the tasks used to assess formal thought. And although these tasks may require consideration of MIS, the possibilites for MIS in scientific work are virtually unlimited.

SUMMARY

In various sections of this chapter, we have pointed out the implications for education in relationship to the research areas reviewed. In conclusion, it is important to highlight some general educational principles that flow from an evaluation of the significant changes in the quality of thinking at the time of adolescence. In other words, as one considers the characteristics of *flexibility* and *openness to possibilities,* what improvements in education may be suggested for the junior high, senior high, and college levels?

First, recall the meaning of acceptance of lack of closure (ALC) emphasized in the section on formal operations and creativity. Lunzer (1978) stresses that ALC means the realization that more than one solution is possible. Mentally snatching at an obvious solution impedes problem solving for two reasons. First, if more than one solution is possible, the breadth of the problem is not grasped. Second, if an obvious solution is incorrect, yet quickly reached, proper search strategies are neither learned nor appreciated.

Teachers of adolescents, then, face the challenge of fostering flexibility and openness to possibilites. Obvious arenas for such growth are small-group discussions, debates, and critical analyses of social issues. In addition, topics for term papers may be stated as questions that force students to search for possible contradictory views on contemporary issues. According to Piaget (1974b, 1974c), the awareness of contradiction is the key motivating force for growth in understanding. Although a state of contradiction is unsettling, the search process that ensues is the basis of the educational process.

Other educational implications follow from a second issue raised in this chapter: the importance of viewing formal thought in the light of the dynamic model of equilibration. If knowledge is self-regulated, then it seems improbable that any paper and pencil "test" of formal thought can capture the depth and breadth of latent strategies (Stone & Day, 1978). What is needed are interactions between experimenter and subject and between objects and subject with careful analyses of answers to probing questions.

Translated to the classroom, such probing means the ability of a creative teacher to identify and work with students who seem to stress narrow, circumstantial solutions rather than imaginative ones based on the possible (and even the impossible). Instead of labeling these students as "concrete operational" and treating them as such, the creative teacher searches for problems and contradictions that help the student move from the "here and now" perspective to an awareness of possible solutions.

In the final analysis, what is called for is a type of teacher training at all levels that forces an interdisciplinary approach to problem solving. Recall that creativity is fostered by reading outside of one's primary discipline. To know one's own subject matter so well that mental walls impede imaginative solutions may be the result of highly departmentalized institutions of "teacher training." We close with a message to both students and teachers:

> From an educational point of view, it goes without saying that a general lowering of the barriers should be striven for as well as the opening of a

generous number of side-doors which would allow university as well as secondary-school students to pass freely from one section to another and give them the choice of many combinations.

But it would also be necessary for the minds of instructors themselves to become less and less compartmentalized, something which is often harder to obtain from them than from their students. (Piaget, 1972c, pp. 24–25)

SUGGESTIONS FOR FURTHER READING

GALLAGHER, J. M. The future of formal thought research: The study of analogy and metaphor. In B. Z. Presseisen, D. Goldstein & M. H. Appel (Eds.), *Topics in cognitive development: Language and operational thought* (Vol. 2). New York: Plenum, 1978.

GALLAGHER, J. M., & EASLEY, J. A. (Eds.). *Knowledge and development: Piaget and education* (Vol. 2). New York: Plenum, 1978.

GINSBURG, H., & OPPER, S. *Piaget's theory of intellectual development* (2nd ed.). Englewood Cliffs, N.J.: Prentice-Hall, 1978.

NIEMARK, E. Intellectual development during adolescence. In F. D. Horowitz (Ed.), *Review of child development research* (Vol. 4). Chicago: University of Chicago Press, 1974.

PIAGET, J. Intellectual evolution from adolescence to adulthood. *Human Development,* 1972, *15,* 1–12.

PIAGET, J. Creativity. In Gallagher, J. M. & Reid, D. K. (Eds.), *The learning theory of Piaget and Inhelder.* Monterey, Calif.: Brooks/Cole, 1979.

BIBLIOGRAPHY

BLASI, A., & HOEFFEL, E. C. Adolescence and formal operations. *Human Development,* 1974, *17,* 344–363.

BRAINERD, C. J. The development of the proportionality scheme in children and adolescents. *Developmental Psychology,* 1971, *5,* 469–476.

BUSSE, T. V., & MANSFIELD, R. S. Theories of the creative process: A review and a perspective. *Journal of Creative Behavior,* in press.

BYRNES, M. M., & SPITZ, H. H. Performance of retarded adolescents and nonretarded children in the Tower of Hanoi problem. *American Journal of Mental Deficiency,* 1977, *81,* 561–569.

CHAPMAN, R. H. The development of children's understanding of proportions. *Child Development,* 1975, *46,* 141–148.

CHIAPETTA, E. L. A review of Piagetian studies relevant to science instruction at the secondary and college level. *Science Education,* 1976, *60,* 253–261.

DANNER, F. W., & DAY, M. C. Eliciting formal operations. *Child Development,* 1977, *48,* 1600–1606.

EMERICK, B. B., & EASLEY, J. A., JR. A constructivist challenge to the validity of tests of formal operations. Paper presented at the meeting of the American Educational Research Association, 1978.

GALLAGHER, J. M. Piaget's equilibration theory: Biological, cybernetic and logical roots. In M. Appel & L. Goldberg (Eds.), *Topics in cognitive development: Equilibration: Theory, research and application* (Vol. 1). New York: Plenum, 1977.

GALLAGHER, J. M. The future of formal thought research: The study of analogy and metaphor. In B. Z. Presseisen, D. Goldstein & M. H. Appel (Eds.), *Topics in cognitive development: Language and operational thought* (Vol. 2). New York: Plenum, 1978. (a)

GALLAGHER, J. M. Reflexive abstraction and education: The meaning of activity in Piaget's theory. In J. M. Gallagher & J. A. Easley (Eds.), *Knowledge and development: Piaget and education* (Vol. 2). New York: Plenum, 1978. (b)

GALLAGHER, J. M., & NOPPE, I. C. Cognitive development and learning in the adolescent. In J. F. Adams (Ed.), *Understanding adolescence* (3rd. ed.). Boston: Allyn and Bacon, 1976.

GALLAGHER, J. M., & WRIGHT, R. J. Children's solution of verbal analogies: Extension of Piaget's concept of reflexive abstraction. In H. Gardner (Chair), *Thinking with the left hand: Children's understanding of analogy and metaphor.* Symposium presented at the meeting of the Society for Research in Child Development, New Orleans, 1977.

GALLAGHER, J. M., & WRIGHT, R. J. Piaget and the study of analogy: Structural analysis of items. In J. Magory (Ed.), *Piaget and the helping professions* (Vol. 8). Los Angeles: University of Southern California, 1979.

GOLDSTEIN, G. Developmental studies in analogical reasoning. (Doctoral Dissertation, University of Kansas, 1962). *Dissertation Abstracts International,* 1963, *24,* 848–849. (University Microfilms No. 63–5636)

HERRON, J. D. Piaget in the classroom: Guidelines for application. Unpublished manuscript, Purdue University, 1977.

INHELDER, B., & PIAGET, J. *The growth of logical thinking from childhood to adolescence.* New York: Basic Books, 1958.

KARPLUS, E. F., KARPLUS, R., & WOLLMAN, W. Intellectual development beyond elementary school. IV: Ratio, the influence of cognitive style. *School Science and Mathematics,* 1974, *74,* 476–482.

KARPLUS, R., & PETERSON, R. W. Intellectual development beyond elementary school. II: Ratio, a survey. *School Science and Mathematics,* 1970, *70,* 813–820.

KUHN, D., & BRANNOCK, J. Development of the isolation of variables scheme in experimental and "natural experiment" contexts. *Developmental Psychology,* 1977, *13,* 9–14.

LAWSON, A. E. Sex differences in concrete and formal reasoning ability as measured by manipulative tasks and written tasks. *Science Education,* 1975, *59,* 397–405.

LAWSON, A. E., & BLAKE, A. J. D. Concrete and formal thinking abilities in high school biology students as measured by three separate instruments. *Journal of Research in Science Teaching,* 1976, *13,* 227–235.

LAWSON, A. E., & RENNER, J. W. A quantitative analysis of responses to Piagetian tasks and its implications for curriculum. *Science Education,* 1974, *58,* 545–559.

LAWSON, A. E., & RENNER, J. W. Relationships of science subject matter and developmental levels of learners. *Journal of Research in Science Teaching*, 1975, *12*, 347–358.

LAWSON, A. E., & WOLLMAN, W. T. Cognitive level, cognitive style, and value judgment. *Science Education*, 1977, *61*, 397–407.

LINN, M. C. Influence of cognitive style and training on tasks requiring the separation of variables schema. *Child Development*, 1978, *49*, 874–877.

LOVELL, K., & SHAYER, M. The impact of the work of Piaget on science curriculum development. In J. M. Gallagher & J. A. Easley, Jr. (Eds.), *Knowledge and development: Piaget and education* (Vol. 2). New York: Plenum, 1978.

LUNZER, E. A. Problems of formal reasoning in test situations. In P. H. Mussen (Ed.), European research in cognitive development. *Monographs of the Society for Research in Child Development*, 1965, *30*, (2, Whole No. 100), 19–46.

LUNZER, E. A. Formal reasoning: A reappraisal. In B. Z. Presseisen, D. Goldstein & M. Appel (Eds.), *Topics in cognitive development*. New York: Plenum, 1978.

MANSFIELD, R. S., & BUSSE, T. V. *The psychology of creativity and discovery.* Chicago: Nelson-Hall, 1980.

MODGIL, S., & MODGIL, C. *Piagetian research: Compilation and commentary* (Vol. 3). Windsor, Berkshire, Great Britain: NFER Publishing Co., 1976.

NIEMARK, E. D. Intellectual development during adolescence. In F. D. Horowitz (Ed.), *Review of child development research* (Vol. 4). Chicago: University of Chicago Press, 1975. (a)

NEIMARK, E. D. Longitudinal development of formal operations thought. *Genetic Psychology Monographs*, 1975, *91*, 171–225. (b)

NEIMARK, E. D. Toward the disembedding of formal operations from confounding with cognitive style. Symposium paper presented at the meeting of the Jean Piaget Society, Philadelphia, 1977.

ORLANDO, J. E. The development of analogical reasoning ability in adolescent boys. (Doctoral dissertation, University of Michigan, 1971). *Dissertation Abstracts International*, 1972, *32*, 4193B–4194B. (University Microfilms No. 72–4947).

PEEL, E. A. *The nature of adolescent judgment.* New York: Wiley, 1971.

PETNER, C. An investigation of the relationships between the development of understanding analogy and the comprehension of metaphor. Unpublished manuscript, Department of Educational Psychology, Temple University, 1978.

PIAGET, J. A theory of development In D. L. Sills (Ed.), *International encyclopedia of the social sciences.* New York: Macmillan Co. and Free Press, 1966.

PIAGET, J. Piaget's theory. In P. H. Mussen (Ed.), *Carmichael's manual of child psychology* (Vol. 1). New York: Wiley, 1970. (a)

PIAGET, J. *Science of education and the psychology of the child.* New York: Orion, 1970. (b)

PIAGET, J. *Biology and knowledge.* Chicago: University of Chicago Press, 1971.

PIAGET, J. Intellectual evolution from adolescence to adulthood. *Human Development*, 1972, *15*, 1–12. (a)

PIAGET, J. *The principles of genetic epistemology.* New York: Basic Books, 1972. (b)

PIAGET, J. A structural foundation for tomorrow's education. *Prospects*, 1972, *2*(1), 12–27. (c)

PIAGET, J. *To understand is to invent: The future of education.* New York: Grossman, 1973.

PIAGET, J. *Adaptation vitale et psychologie de l'intelligence: La notion de la phenocopie.* Geneve: Droz, 1974. (a)

PIAGET, J. *Recherches sur la contradiction* (Vol. 1). *Les différentes formes de la contradiction: Etudes d'épistémologie genetique* (Vol. 31). Paris: Presses Universitaires de France, 1974. (b)

PIAGET, J. *Recherches sur la contradiction* (Vol. 2). *Les relations entre affirmations et négations: Etudes d'épistémologie génétique* (Vol. 32). Paris: Presses Universitaires de France, 1974. (c)

PIAGET, J. *L'équilibration des structures cognitives: Problème central du développement.* Paris: Presses Universitaires de France, 1975.

PIAGET, J. *The grasp of consciousness: Action and concept in the young child.* Cambridge, Mass.: Harvard University Press, 1976. (a)

PIAGET, J. The possible, the impossible and the necessary. *The Genetic Epistemologist: Quarterly Newsletter of the Jean Piaget Society.* 1976, *6*(1), 1–12. (b)

PIAGET, J. (avec MONTANGERO, J. & BILLETER, J.) Les correlats. In *L'abstraction réfléchissante.* Paris: Presses Universitaires de France, 1977. (a)

PIAGET, J. Problems of equilibration. In M. H. Appel & L. S. Goldberg (Eds.), *Topics in cognitive development: Equilibration: Theory, research and application* (Vol. 1). New York: Plenum, 1977. (b)

PIAGET, J. Correspondences and transformations. In F. B. Murray (Ed.), *Impact of Piaget's theory.* Baltimore, Md.: University Park Press, 1978. (a)

PIAGET, J. *Success and understanding.* Cambridge, Mass.: Harvard University Press, 1978. (b)

PIAGET, J. Creativity. In Gallagher, J. M. & Reid, D. K. (Eds.), *The learning theory of Piaget and Inhelder.* Monterey, Calif.: Brooks/Cole, 1979.

PIAGET, J., & INHELDER, B. *The psychology of the child.* New York: Basic Books, 1969.

STERNBERG, R. J. *Intelligence, information processing, and analogical reasoning: The componential analysis of human abilities.* Hillsdale, N.J.: Lawrence Erlbaum Associate, 1977.

STERNBERG, R. J. & RIFKIN, B. The development of analogical reasoning processes. *Journal of Experimental Child Psychology,* 1979, *27*, 195–232.

STONE, C. A., & DAY, M. C. Levels of availability of a formal operational stategy. *Child Development,* 1978, *49*, 1054–1065.

WITKIN, H. A., DYK, R. B., FATERSON, H. F., GOODENOUGH, D. R., & KARP, S. A. *Psychological differentiation.* New York: Wiley, 1962.

WOLLMAN, W., & KARPLUS, R. Intellectual development beyond elementary school. V: Using ratio in differing tasks. *School Science and Mathematics,* 1974, *74*, 593–611.

7

INDIVIDUAL DIFFERENCES IN INTELLIGENCE

Robert C. Nichols

eople differ greatly in intellectual ability. Civilization provides
abundant evidence of the exceptional intellectual accomplishments
of brilliant researchers, engineers, political leaders, and entrepre-
neurs, while at the other end of the scale about 2% of the population are
considered mentally deficient because they have difficulty coping with the
relatively simple intellectual demands of everyday life. Most people fall
near the middle of the distribution of ability between these extremes, but
even in the middle range individual differences are large and important.

One of the major tasks of late adolescence is the completion of formal
education and entry into the world of work or other adult roles. In this important transition, intelligence plays a more significant role than any other
personal characteristic. The decision whether or not to enter college is perhaps the most critical choice to be made in late adolescence, and the outcome depends more on the student's intelligence than on race, sex, family
circumstances, or any other variable. A study (Peng, 1977) of the high
school graduating class of 1972 showed that the percentage entering a
four-year college from the lowest and highest quarters of the intelligence
distribution was 10 and 54% respectively, a difference of 44%. After intelligence, the next largest influence was family socioeconomic status (SES).
Twenty percent from the lowest quarter in SES and 42% from the highest
quarter entered a 4-year college, a difference of 22%.

Intelligence is also related to occupational achievement, and, in fact,
the social status or prestige of different occupations seems to be largely a
matter of the degree of intelligence required by the occupation (Duncan,
Featherman & Duncan, 1972). The strong relationship of intelligence to
occupation was shown by Harrell and Harrell (1945), who reported the average Army General Classification Test (AGCT) scores of nearly 19,000
Army Air Force enlisted men in World War II by their civilian occupation.
The AGCT is scored on a scale similar to an IQ score with mean of 100 and
standard deviation of 20. The average AGCT scores for several occupations
are as follows:

OCCUPATION	AVERAGE AGCT SCORE
Accountant	128
Chemist	125
Bookkeeper	120
Radio repairman	115
Machinist	110
Mechanic	106

Robert C. Nichols is Professor of Educational Psychology at the State University of New
York at Buffalo. He is coauthor of *Heredity, Environment and Personality: A Study of 850 Sets
of Twins* and has written a chapter in *Methods and Goals in Human Behavior Genetics*. He has
published widely on such topics as the gifted, birth order and intelligence, academic
aptitude and success, psychometrics, and individual differences.

Plumber	103
Cook and baker	97
Barber	95
Miner	91
Teamster	88

An interesting aspect of Harrell and Harrell's data is that the variability of intelligence within occupations was nearly twice as great in occupations for which the average intelligence was low as in occupations for which the average was high. This suggests that people of low intelligence are rarely found in high-ability occupations but that those with high intelligence may be in low-ability occupations.

In addition to educational and occupational achievement for which intelligence is of primary importance, intelligence also plays a role in other important aspects of life. For example, Vandenberg (1972) has shown that intelligence is an important consideration in choice of marriage partner; in fact, he found that spouses resemble each other more in intelligence than in any other trait except height. Reynolds (1974) found that intelligence was also significantly related to a variety of personality characteristics, although he emphasized that none of the relationships was especially strong. His study of the correlates of intelligence among 2500 adolescents indicated that the brighter students tended also to be more nonconforming, aesthetically sensitive, flexible, tolerant, adjusted, and ambitious. They also tended to be less interested in manual activities, in watching television, and in spectator sports.

Findings such as these have attracted the attention of scientists and teachers as well as the general public to individual differences in intelligence. As a result, intelligence has been by far the most intensively studied and also the most controversial of all behavioral differences. In this chapter the present state of knowledge and research in this important variable will be reviewed.

THE NATURE OF INTELLIGENCE

Intelligence is an ancient concept, but useful measures of intelligence are a relatively recent invention. The early mental tests developed in the late 19th century included measures of sensory acuity, reaction time, memory, sensitivity to pain, and color preferences, and they were clearly failures as indicators of the common-sense notion of intelligence.

Development of Intelligence Tests

The first successful intelligence test was developed in Paris by Alfred Binet and Theodore Simon in 1905. The Binet tests differed from their unsuc-

cessful predecessors in two important respects. First, they sacrificed something in precision to measure more global mental abilities such as mem-
orizing sentences, following instructions, distinguishing between abstract
words (such as "liking" and "respecting"), and constructing sentences to
include three given words (such as "Paris," "gutter," and "fortune"). Second, they used age norms for evaluating the performance of a given child
and as the criterion for intelligence itself.

Fortunately, Binet and Simon were working with children, and it became obvious to them that mental capabilities increase rather steadily with
increasing age. This observation provided a criterion for identifying good
tests of intelligence; a good test being one on which older children perform
better than do younger children. It also provided a scale by which a given
child's performance could be evaluated. Each task was assigned an age
level, which was the age at which half the children could correctly perform
the task. Mental performance was thus measured on an age scale, and a
child's mental age could be determined by his or her performance on the
age-graded series of tasks. The test worked. Children who were mentally
advanced, that is their mental age was above their chronological age, generally were considered bright by their teachers, while children whose mental age was below their chronological age generally were considered dull.

The concept of mental age proved to be the key to intelligence. It
provided a scale that corresponded to the common-sense notion of intelligence, and it provided a method of identifying good measures of intelligence without solving the difficult problem of defining exactly what
intelligence is.

Soon after the Binet scales were published, the German psychologist,
William Stern, developed the concept of *intelligence quotient* or IQ. Stern saw
that a child who is a year ahead at age 6 is more advanced than one who is
a year ahead at age 9. The proper measure of intelligence is the ratio of
mental age to chronological age, not the difference. To obtain the IQ, Stern
divided the mental age by the chronological age and multiplied by 100 to
get rid of the decimals. A 5-year-old child who has a mental age of 6 and a
10-year-old who has a mental age of 12 both obtain an IQ of 120. The IQ
is thus a measure of rate of mental growth. A child whose mental abilities
are developing 20% faster than the average child will obtain an IQ of
120.

The Binet tests proved to be remarkably robust when transported to
other countries. It was not only in Paris that the average 7-year-old was
barely able to repeat five digits read to him and to indicate certain omissions in drawings, but in Germany, England, and America as well. This
widespread use of the age scale was one of the first indications that something rather basic was being measured by the IQ. A number of translations
and revisions of the Binet tests were undertaken. The most successful of
these was the Stanford Binet developed by Louis M. Terman and associates
at Stanford University. The Stanford revisions of the Binet published in

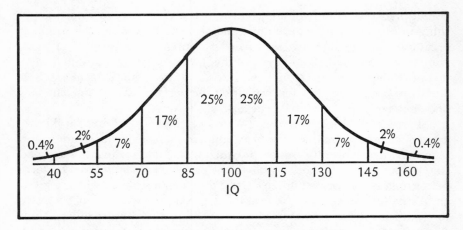

Figure 7.1 Normal Distribution of Intelligence, Showing the Expected Percentages of the Population in Each IQ Range.

1916 and 1937 greatly improved the technology of test construction and standardization while retaining the basic concepts of mental age and IQ as the operational definition of intelligence.

The Stanford Binet became the standard for the evaluation of other tests that were developed, so the mental age concept is at the root of modern conceptions of intelligence. The IQ derived from mental age is no longer used in intelligence measurement, however, because it presents several technical difficulties. One of the major difficulties with the mental age scale is that, like physical growth, mental growth slows during adolescence and then stops altogether by about age 16 or 18. For this reason, the ratio IQ is not a meaningful index of intelligence for adults. Most current tests of intelligence compare the subject's test performance with a representative sample of the population of the same age and express the relative performance in terms of an IQ scale that has a mean of 100, a standard deviation of 15, and a normal distribution in the standardization sample. This procedure produces a distribution of IQs at all ages identical to that shown in Figure 7.1. Although this distribution of IQ scores is now forced in the standardization of most tests, it was originally adopted because this is approximately the distribution actually observed for IQs calculated as 100 times the ratio of mental age to chronological age.

The Structure of Intellect

While the development of intelligence tests was proceeding almost entirely on a pragmatic basis, other psychologists were developing measures of more specific abilities for the investigation of the structure of intelligence. The statistical method of factor analysis was developed to aid in the attempt to infer the structure of intelligence from the inter-correlations of a number of ability tests. Although the statistical method is complex, the basic idea of factor analysis is simple. If several tests tend to correlate more highly with one another than they do with other tests, this is an indication that these tests measure something in common that is not shared by the other tests, at least not as strongly. Such a cluster of highly correlating tests can be considered to be evidence of the operation of some common factor that is causing the tests to vary together. Factor analysis provides a method of determining the number of such common factors in a given collection of tests and the relationship of the tests to the factors so that the underlying factors can be measured.

An early form of factor analysis was developed by Spearman (1927) who was impressed by the fact that almost all mental abilities are positively correlated. People who perform relatively well on one test, such as memory, also tend to perform well on other tests, such as completion of sentences. Spearman interpreted this as evidence of a general factor of intelligence which he called g, and his method of factor analysis was intended to reveal the degree to which each test was saturated with this general factor.

Factor analysis was developed further by L. L. Thurstone (1938), who used the method to identify several ability factors, including verbal comprehension, word fluency, number ability, spatial visualization, rote memory, and reasoning. These factors were all positively correlated with each other, which would fit Spearman's concept of general intelligence; but Thurstone chose to emphasize their separate identity by calling the factors Primary Mental Abilities. The work of Thurstone has been extended by a number of investigators, who have identified ever larger numbers of factors.

A leading figure in this effort has been J. P. Guilford, who organized the known ability factors according to the mental operation, the content, and the product involved in the tests. This three-way classification of factors is displayed in the cube shown in Figure 7.2, which Guilford called the structure-of-intellect model. The front upper-left hand corner of the cube, for example, is cognition of figural units (CFU), which might be measured by a test requiring the subject to identify (cognize) drawings of objects (figural units) that have been partially obscured, or to identify out-of-focus pictures. This model has the advantage of organizing a diverse collection of abilities into a meaningful structure. Such a model is also a useful guide for research, since it predicts the nature of new factors that have not yet been identified. Although the model is a useful organizing schema for a diverse collection of abilities, it does not pretend to be a model of the brain structures that produce these abilities, and it has not yet provided much insight into the underlying causes of differential abilities.

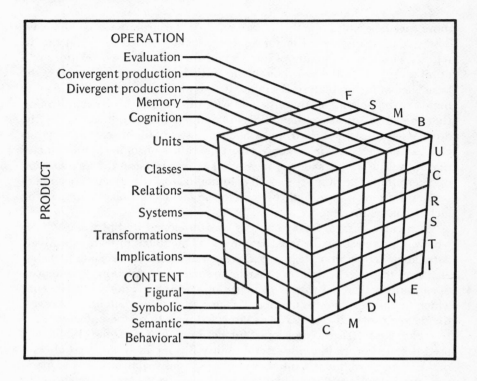

Figure 7.2 Guilford's Structure-of-Intellect Model of Intelligence. (From *The Nature of Human Intelligence* by J. P. Guilford. New York: McGraw-Hill, 1967.)

Most of the 120 abilities represented in the structure-of-intellect model have not yet been adequately identified and measured. The Educational Testing Service has published a kit of reference tests for the ability factors that have been found in more than one laboratory and that are generally accepted as being identifiable factors (Ekstrom, French, Harman & Dermen, 1976). The factors to be represented in the kit were selected with the aid of an advisory committee consisting of leading researchers in the ability field. There was consensus on 23 factors, which are described in Table 7.1.

Examination of Table 7.1 shows that there are indeed a diversity of mental abilities that can be separately identified and measured. A critical question that remains unanswered is why this particular set of differential abilities exists. Are there different biological structures in the nervous system that are used in performing the different mental tasks? Do certain critical experiences or learning opportunities promote the development of abilities represented by the different factors? Currently we do not know.

An indication of how research might proceed in this area is given by the work of Carroll (1976) who has analyzed the detailed mental operations that are required by the tasks involved in each of the factors in Table 7.1. This analysis suggests that each factor may involve operations that depend primarily on a specific aspect of mental functioning. For example, memory span depends primarily on storage and retrieval from short-term memory, the fluency factors involve a scanning of long-term memory, and verbal comprehension depends on the contents of the "lexicosemantic story." It seems reasonable to expect that when the mechanism of storage and retrieval of information in memory and the mechanism of logical mental operations are finally understood, there will be a clear correspondence between the underlying process and the details of overt performance.

TABLE 7.1 *Factors Represented in the Educational Testing Service's Kit of Factor-referenced Cognitive Tests*

FACTOR	CHARACTERIZATION[a]	IDENTIFICATION IN THE STRUCTURE-OF-INTELLECT MODEL[b]
Flexibility of Closure	The ability to hold a given visual percept or configuration in mind so as to disembed it from other well-defined perceptual material. Tests of this factor require the subject to search a distracting perceptual field to find a given configuration.	NFT
Speed of Closure	The ability to unite an apparently disparate perceptual field into a single concept. The ability to recognize ambiguous visual stimuli.	CFV
Verbal Closure	The ability to solve problems requiring the identification of visually presented words when some of the letters are missing, scrambled, or embedded among other letters.	CSU
Associational Fluency	The ability to produce rapidly words which share a given area of meaning or some other common semantic property. A test requires the subject to produce synonyms of given words.	DMR
Expressional Fluency	The ability to think rapidly of word groups or phrases. The emphasis in expressional fluency tests is on producing connected discourse that will fit restrictions imposed in terms of letters, words, or ideas.	DMS

171

TABLE 7.1 (*Continued*)

FACTOR	CHARACTERIZATION[a]	IDENTIFICA-TION IN THE STRUCTURE-OF-INTELLECT MODEL[b]
Figural Fluency	The ability to draw quickly a number of examples, elaborations, or restructurings based on a given visual or descriptive stimulus. A test requires the subject to sketch elaborations or decorations on a given drawing.	DFU, DFI, DFS
Ideational Fluency	The facility to write a number of ideas about a given topic or exemplars of a given class of objects. The quantity of ideas produced rather than the quality is emphasized in this factor.	DMU
Word Fluency	The facility to produce words that fit one or more structural, phonetic, or orthographic restrictions that are not relevant to the meaning of the words. A test of this factor requires the subject to write as many words as possible ending with a given set of letters.	DSU
Induction	This factor identifies the kinds of reasoning abilities involved in forming and trying out hypotheses that will fit a set of data. A measure of this factor requires the subject to mark one of five letter groupings that does not belong with the other four.	CSC, CSS, CFC
Integrative Processes	The ability to keep in mind simultaneously or to combine several conditions, premises, or rules in order to produce a correct response. A test requires the subject to select certain dates on a calendar by following fairly complex sets of directions.	MSR
Associative Memory	The ability to recall one part of a previously learned but otherwise unrelated pair of items when the other part of the pair is presented. Tests are similar to those used in studies of paired-associate learning.	MSI
Memory Span	The ability to recall a number of distinct elements for immediate reproduction. A test requires the subject to repeat a number of digits read to him.	MSU

TABLE 7.1 (*Continued*)

FACTOR	CHARACTERIZATION[a]	IDENTIFICATION IN THE STRUCTURE-OF-INTELLECT MODEL[b]
Visual Memory	The ability to remember the configuration, location, and orientation of figural material. A test requires the subject to indicate the location of a number of buildings seen on a previously studied map.	MFU, MFC, MFR
Number Facility	The ability to perform basic arithmetic operations with speed and accuracy. This factor is not a major component in mathematical reasoning or higher mathematical skills.	MSI
Perceptual Speed	Speed in comparing figures or symbols, scanning to find figures or symbols, or carrying out other very simple tasks involving visual perception.	ESU, EFU
General Reasoning	The ability to select and organize relevant information for the solution of a problem. A test requires the subject to determine what numerical operations are required to solve arithmetic problems without actually having to carry out the computations.	CMS
Logical Reasoning	The ability to reason from premise to conclusion, or to evaluate the correctness of a conclusion. A test requires the subject to indicate whether syllogisms using nonsensical content are true or false.	EMR, EMI
Spatial Orientation	The ability to perceive spatial patterns or to maintain orientation with respect to objects in space. A test requires the subject to identify a figure that has been rotated from among several alternatives.	CFS
Spatial Scanning	Speed in exploring visually a wide or complicated spatial field. Finding one's way through a paper maze requires the ability to scan the field quickly for openings, follow paths with the eye, and reject false leads.	CFI
Verbal Comprehension	The ability to understand the English language. A vocabulary test is a good measure of this factor.	CMU

TABLE 7.1 *(Continued)*

FACTOR	CHARACTERIZATION[a]	IDENTIFICA-TION IN THE STRUCTURE-OF-INTELLECT MODEL[b]
Visualization	The ability to manipulate or transform the image of spatial patterns into other arrangements. A test requires the subject to indicate what a folded paper with a hole in it would look like when unfolded.	CFT
Figural Flexibility	The ability to change set in order to generate new and different solutions to figural problems. A test requires the subject to produce different arrangements of toothpicks according to a given set of rules.	DFT
Flexibility of Use	The mental set necessary to think of different uses for objects. A test requires the subject to think of a common object that could serve as a substitute for another object or purpose.	DFT, NMT

[a] From Ekstrom, R. B., French, J. W., Harman, H. H., & Dermen, D. *Manual for Kit of Factor-Referenced Cognitive Tests.* Copyright © 1976 by Educational Testing Service. All rights reserved. Reprinted by permission.
[b] The three letters giving the structure-of-intellect model identification refer to the operation, content, and product as shown in Figure 7.2. For example, NFT refers to divergent production of figural transformations.

Differential Abilities versus General Intelligence

As we have seen, there are two approaches to the measurement of intelligence. One focuses on a single factor of general ability with little concern for its different aspects. The other emphasizes the analysis of intelligence into component abilities with little concern for the fact that the components tend to be positively correlated. These two approaches may be compared in terms of their contribution to two important goals: prediction and understanding.

Prediction. The general intelligence and aptitude tests have grown up in the prediction arena and are generally considered to have achieved remarkable success, particularly in predicting performance in school and in academically related occupations. If measures of differential aptitudes or more specific abilities are to be useful predictors, they must surpass the high standard established by the general aptitude tests, and this they have not been able to do (McNemar, 1964). Holly and Michael (1972), for example, developed prediction equations representing optimum combinations for selected tests from Guilford's model to predict grades in high school algebra and performance on a standard algebra achievement test. They reported that their cross-validated correlations of .43 for grades and .36 for the test were no better than the uncross-validated correlations for a standard aptitude test.

The presence of a number of specific ability factors along with the preeminently important factor of general intelligence can be seen as analogous to the relationships among a variety of anatomical measurements of a group of people. People differ greatly in size, and large people tend to exceed small people on almost all anatomical measures. Thus there is a general size factor. In addition, people differ in corpulence and in stature, so that longitudinal measurements (such as length of arms, legs, and torso) tend to correlate more highly with each other than with measures of girth (such as circumference of neck, waist, and thigh) which tend to form another homogeneous cluster. Thus instead of describing people as relatively large or small, it is possible to describe the human physique in terms of correlated height and weight factors. Further analysis most likely would identify a long-waisted versus short-waisted factor, and factors specific to particular areas of the body, such as facial physiognomy, hand configuration, and so forth. The relative usefulness of the various anatomical factors for prediction would depend on the performance criteria of most interest. If the criteria all involved breaking through barriers of some sort, the general size factor would probably be most important, even though, for example, the hand factors might seem on the surface to be more relevant for barriers to be broken with the hand.

Understanding. Although differential aptitudes do not contribute appreciably to prediction, they may some day contribute to understanding of the way intelligence works, as Carroll's (1976) analysis suggests. This approach assumes that there are independent individual differences in all of the major mental functions and that the influence of these mental functions on performance can be detected by factor analysis. Since most mental tests are complex and call upon a number of different functions in common, the tests will all be positively correlated, giving the illusion of a general factor.

On the other hand, it is possible that the factors are the result of individual differences in relatively peripheral mental abilities, while the general efficiency of mental functioning may be the major basis for the general factor and for intelligence. Jensen (1978a) has pointed out that the degree of correlation between any task and g is proportional to the complexity of the task, that is, the amount of mental activity involved between stimulus and response. Thus, solving analogy problems has a high g saturation, while repeating digits has a low g saturation. However, the correlation of the digit span task with g is more than doubled, by increasing the mental manipulation by requiring that the digits be repeated backward.

Although early studies attempting to use reaction time as a measure of intelligence were failures, recent studies have shown that the effect on reaction time of small increases in the complexity of very simple tasks is substantially related to intelligence. Increasing complexity increases reaction time less for subjects of high intelligence than for subjects of low intelligence. Hunt, Lunneborg, and Lewis (1975) measured the time required for subjects to determine whether two letters are the same shape (A and A are the same; A and a are different) and the time required to determine whether two letters have the same name (A and a are the same). The latter task involves more mental activity, since the letters must first be identified. The time difference for the two tasks was negatively related to intelligence. Jensen (1978a) found a similar result in a study of time required for reaction to the onset of a light. As complexity was increased by increasing the number of lights from one to four, reaction time increased more rapidly for the less intelligent subjects than for the more intelligent. These findings seem to support the general-mental-efficiency theory of general intelligence.

THE CAUSES OF INDIVIDUAL DIFFERENCES

Whether individual differences in intelligence are determined primarily by genetic differences or primarily by environmental influences has been the subject of controversy since the publication of Francis Galton's *Hereditary Genius* in 1869. The most recent phase of the IQ controversy, as it has been called, began with Arthur Jensen's (1969) provocative paper in the *Harvard Educational Review*.

Genetic Influences

It has not been feasible to interfere with human lives or human reproduction in the ways that would be required to produce conclusive experimental evidence of the degree of genetic determination of individual differences. Instead, investigators have had to rely on indirect evidence and on the analysis of natural experiments that are always unsatisfactory in one way or another. In such circumstances, the answer is to be found in the convergence of evidence from a variety of sources rather than in a single crucial study.

The degree of genetic determination of individual differences is expressed as the *heritability*, which is the proportion of the population variance of a trait that is attributable to genetic differences. It is not an enduring characteristic of a person or of a trait, but is descriptive of a given population at a given point in time. The heritability indicates the relative importance of genetic and environmental influences in bringing about the observed individual differences of the trait in the given population. As such, heritability provides a means of estimating the amount of change in the trait that might result from changing the relevant environmental or genetic factors within the range existing in the population. It does not provide information about the probable effects of changes outside the range of natural variation in the population studied.

Under ideal circumstances, good estimates of the heritability of human traits may be derived from studies of the similarity of various categories of relatives. For example, the correlation between separated identical twins who have had no environmental experiences in common is a direct measure of heritability. Since fraternal twins share about half of the genes on which people differ and since identical twins share all genes, the greater similarity of identical twins represents the effect of half the genetic influence. Thus twice the difference between identical and fraternal twin correlations is a measure of heritability. Since parents and children have about half their genes in common, a measure of heritability may be obtained by doubling the correlation between natural parent and adopted child. There are a number of other special circumstances from which heritability can be estimated.

Unfortunately, the data that are available never conform neatly to all of the assumptions of heritability calculations. Separated identical twins are not assigned randomly to environments; identical twins may be treated more alike than fraternal twins; adopted children may be selectively placed; measurement is often unreliable. In addition, there are a number of genetic complications (such as assortative mating, dominance, epistasis, and gene-environment interaction) that may affect the observed similarity of relatives. Thus, in practice, it is necessary to make a number of corrections and adjustments to the simple heritability calculations, and these adjustments sometimes involve rough estimates of unknown effects. Moreover, the standard errors of heritability estimates tend to be large, since they are usually based on differences among correlations (or among variances), which are subject to large sampling fluctuation. Therefore, one should not have great confidence in the exact heritability coefficients calculated in any given study. Instead, one might hope to narrow the range of probable heritabilities by considering evidence from a number of different studies using different kinds of data with different assumptions.

Twins Raised Together. Twins form a natural experiment in which identical and fraternal twins differ in genetic similarity, yet, when raised together, they do not seem to differ greatly in environmental similarity.

Quantitative estimates may be made of the factors known to affect twin similarity, which permits calculation of the heritability from the observed similarity of the two kinds of twins on a given trait (Jensen, 1967; Jinks & Fulker, 1970).

Almost all studies have found identical twins to be more similar than fraternal twins on tests of intelligence, as well as of most other traits (Nichols, 1978). The median intraclass correlations from 17 of the larger twin studies of intelligence, involving altogether some 6,000 sets of twins, were .85 and .59 for identical and fraternal twins respectively (Loehlin & Nichols, 1976). All 17 studies found substantial differences between the similarity of the two kinds of twins. Depending on assumptions concerning measurement error, assortative mating, errors of twin diagnosis, and so forth, heritabilities calculated from these median correlations can range from about .50 to .80.

The major criticism of these heritability calculations concerns the assumptions of equal similarity of environmental influences for the two kinds of twins. Identical twins spend more time together than do fraternal twins, and because they look more alike they elicit more similar treatment from parents and others. Some studies suggest that this greater environmental similarity for identical twins is not responsible for their greater similarity in intelligence (Loehlin & Nichols, 1976), but they have not satisfied all of the critics.

Identical Twins Raised Apart.   Separated identical twins come close to a true experiment in which genetically identical individuals are placed in different environments. Any similarity of such twins would seem to be due solely to genetic and prenatal environmental influences. However, separated identical twins are rare and difficult to find, and so far they have not satisfied the ideal conditions of a true experiment.

Jensen (1970) reanalyzed the data for the 122 sets of separated identical twins available from the four major studies of twins raised apart and found a correlation for intelligence of .82. However, this impressive correlation has not fared well under the intensive scrutiny of skeptical critics.

The separated identical twin data suffered a severe blow from the recent questioning of the reliability of the data collected by the eminent British psychologist, Cyril Burt (Wade, 1976), which contributed 53 of the 122 sets. The combined correlation for the 69 sets from the remaining three studies is .73; however, Kamin (1974) has cast doubt on the trustworthiness of this figure by pointing out the relatively large effect of age differences (since twins are the same age, any age difference in test scores will produce spurious correlation between twins), the similarity of twin environments, and other flaws.

Adopted Children.   Adoption provides one of the best ways available of separating the environmental and the biological influences of parents on children. Studies of adopted children have been reviewed by Munsinger (1975) and DeFries and Plomin (1978). Munsinger computed the average of the major correlations for IQ from the five adoption studies that he considered to have the fewest methodological defects. These average correlations were: biological parent and adopted-away child (living apart) .48; foster parent and adopted child (living together) .19; and, from control families, parent and own child (living together) .58.

Taken at face value, these results suggest a strong genetic influence causing the adopted child to be more like the biological parent than the foster parent, and a weaker environmental influence causing still greater similarity of parents to their own children and some similarity of adoptive parents to their adopted children. However, these studies are not without methodological problems. As was discussed by Munsinger, and more pointedly by Kamin (1974), there were problems of selective placement, restriction of range, and lack of exact comparability of adoptive and control families.

A large adoption study is currently being conducted by Horn, Loehlin and Willerman at the University of Texas that is reportedly free of some of the defects of earlier studies. Preliminary results, as reported by DeFries and Plomin (1978), show smaller parent-child correlations than those discussed above, but a similar pattern (biological mother and adopted-away child .29, N=342; foster mother and adopted child .18, N=451).

Another adoption study, conducted at the University of Minnesota, has become available since the Munsinger review. This study included a sample of 101 transracial adoptions (Scarr & Weinberg, 1976, 1977a) and another sample of 104 families with 194 children who were adopted in infancy and were teenage (16–22) at the time of the study (Scarr & Weinberg, 1977b). There was also a control group of 120 biological families comparable to the latter sample of adoptive families. The observed correlations followed the usual pattern. For example, in the teenage sample the correlation of biological mother's education with child's IQ was .21 for 150 adopted-away children and .24 for 237 natural children, while the correlations of foster mother's education with adopted child's IQ was .10. The major results were presented in a series of regression equations in which strikingly different effects were observed for biological and adoptive children by adding IQ scores of the rearing parents to an equation including other family demographic characteristics. The parental IQ scores substantially increased the correlation and became the major predictors for the biological children, but had little effect for the adopted children. A similar effect for the adopted children was observed when the natural mother's education was added.

Animal Studies. Although behavioral genetic studies of animals are becoming increasingly sophisticated and focused, only two general lines of evidence for genetic control of animal behavior will concern us here.

Comparison of the behavior of inbred strains provides a simple indication of whether or not genetic differences can affect a given behavioral trait. Dog fanciers need not be told that large strain differences in behavior are typically found. Because of the ease of these comparisons, a large amount of information is available about strain differences. Sprott and Staats (1975) have compiled a bibliography of 1,222 behavioral studies of genetically defined mouse strains. Strain differences are observed for almost every conceivable behavioral measurement.

Selective breeding experiments provide the most unambiguous evidence of the heritability of a behavioral trait. Since Tryon's (1940) classic selection study of maze learning in rats, selection studies have shown substantial heritabilities for a variety of behavioral traits ranging from open-field activity in mice (DeFries, Hegmann & Halcomb, 1974) to geotaxis and phototaxis in *Drosophila* (Polivanov, 1975).

Animal studies have no direct relevance for human intelligence, of course, but the ubiquity of genetic variance in animal behavior makes it seem likely that human behavior also is influenced to some degree by genetic differences.

Analysis of Kinship Correlations. The correlations of intelligence scores among people with various degrees of genetic relationship, raised together and raised apart, which I have discussed separately, form an impressive picture of increasing similarity with increasing genetic relationship when viewed all together. Erlenmeyer-Kimling and Jarvik (1963) presented the results of 52 studies in a chart, shown in Figure 7.3. The median or pooled correlations from this chart, augmented by additional studies, or separate compilations of essentially the same data, have been analyzed by Jencks (1972), Morton (1974), Jinks and Eaves (1974), Eaves (1975), Rao, Morton and Yee (1974, 1976), and others using the method of biometrical genetic analysis. This method involves construction of a model based on theoretical or known genetic and environmental relationships and the calculation of the best-fitting parameters for the model from the observed median correlations. These parameter estimates are said to be superior to those based on a single set of relationships, such as twins or adopted children, because they are derived from a broader observational base and because additional parameters, such as dominance and genotype-environment correlation, may be estimated. The broad heritabilities for intelligence derived from these calculations ranged from .45 for Jencks to .83 for Jinks and Eaves. This is a wide range of values for analyses of essentially the same set of data. Loehlin (1978) repeated the various analyses and found that the discrepant results were due not to differences in the analytic methods or in the data but to differences in the assumptions made by the different groups of investigators concerning such matters as dominance, assortative mating, equivalence of environments, and so forth. The unusually low value obtained by Jencks

Category		0.00 0.20 0.40 0.60 0.80 0.10 0.30 0.50 0.70 0.90	Groups included
Unrelated persons	Reared apart		4
	Reared together		5
Fosterparent-child			3
Parent-child			12
Siblings	Reared apart		2
	Reared together		35
Twins / Two-egg	Opposite sex		9
	Like sex		11
Twins / One-egg	Reared apart		4
	Reared together		14

Figure 7.3 Correlation Coefficients for "Intelligence" Test Scores from Fifty-Two Studies. Some studies reported data for more than one relationship category; some included more than one sample per category, giving a total of ninety-nine groups. Over two-thirds of the correlation coefficients were derived from IQs, the remainder from special tests (for example, Primary Mental Abilities.) Midparent-child correlation was used when available, otherwise mother-child correlation. Correlation coefficients obtained in each study are indicated by dark circles; medians are shown by vertical lines intersecting the horizontal lines which represent the ranges. (From L. Erlenmeyer-Kimling and L. F. Jarvik. Genetics and intelligence: A review. *Science* 1963, *142*, 1477–1479. Copyright 1963 by the American Association for the Advancement of Science. Used by permission.)

appears to be due to a particularly inappropriate set of assumptions (Loehlin, Lindzey & Spuhler, 1975, Appendix 1). When Loehlin (1978) repeated Jencks's analysis, using the assumptions of Jinks and associates, he obtained a value of .68, which is more in line with the other results.

The biometrical genetic method shows promise of being able to yield heritability analyses that will in the future provide a fairly precise and generally acceptable answer to nature-nurture questions; however, claims that this is now the case may be premature. Kamin (1974) has pointed out that the observational data are often not as firmly established as they may seem to be from the number of studies involved. They are sometimes based on arbitrary selections from several correlations reported, they sometimes involve questionable corrections for such distorting factors as restriction of range, there have been errors in calculation and in reporting, and the samples frequently leave something to be desired. Kamin also pointed out that the results of the analyses are particularly sensitive to relatively small fluctuations in certain of the correlations. Until the various issues in dispute are resolved, it may be that more modest attempts to estimate heritability from limited sets of relationships, such as twins and adopted children, may be more convincing than the grand analyses based on all available kinship correlations.

The Heritability of Intelligence. In light of the above evidence, what can one conclude about the heritability of IQ in the European and American Caucasian populations that have been most intensively studied? After the most thorough review and quantitative evaluation of the evidence up to that time, Jensen (1969) concluded that the heritability of IQ was about .80; and subsequent developments have not caused him to revise this estimate. On the basis of a similarly thorough review and analysis, Jencks (1972) arrived at a heritability of .45. Following a critical and one-sided review of much of the same evidence, Kamin (1974) concluded that the available data do not compel us to reject the hypothesis that the heritability of intelligence is zero. Loehlin et al. (1975), in an exceptionally fair and cautious review, focusing primarily on race differences, allowed that the evidence is clearly inconsistent with heritabilities of 0.0 and 1.0. In another review, Lewontin (1975) concluded that the heritability of IQ is utterly trivial and hardly worth the effort necessary to carry out decent studies.

How is one to reconcile such discrepant conclusions from analyses of essentially the same collection of studies? The answer seems to be that the data do allow a rather wide range of interpretations, depending on the method of analysis used and the assumptions and corrections that are employed. For example, Jencks divided the IQ variance into .45 due to heredity, .35 due to environment, and .20 due to covariance of genes and environment on the basis of a path analysis that involved a specific model and specific assumptions about the data. Loehlin et al. (1975, Appendix 1) showed that by changing certain paths in the model to equally (if not more) plausible positions, Jencks's data yield variance estimates of .60 due to heredity, .25 due to environment, and .15 due to covariance of heredity and environment. By a somewhat different selection of assumptions and studies, especially omitting the Burt data, it seems likely that Jensen's calculations could be made to converge on a heritability of .60 as well. Thus, among those honestly attempting to arrive at the best possible estimate of heritability on the basis of available evidence, a range of values from about .45 to about .80 has been reported. As one approaches the upper or the lower limit of this range, it becomes relatively easy to cite reasonably good evidence to pull the estimate back in the other direction. Thus the interested bystander, not wishing to make his or her own calculations and having no reason to prefer one extreme over the other, might reasonably adopt a compromise value of .60 as a working hypothesis, with a confidence interval of about .20 around this value.

The heritability merely indicates in the grossest way that genetic differences are responsible in considerable degree for individual differences in intelligence. Nothing is known about the way in which these genetic influences operate.

The great progress that has been made in the prevention or treatment of the few genetic effects that are known, such as Down's syndrome and phenylketonuria, shows the potential importance of knowledge of the genetic mechanisms.

Environmental Influences

Since all variance that is not genetic may be considered to be environmental, the heritability analyses discussed also provide evidence of environmental effects. As with genetic effects, however, the simple fact that the environment contributes a certain proportion of the variance is of little value unless the mechanism is known by which the environmental effects are produced. Thus evidence is needed concerning specific environmental influences on intelligence to supplement the general evidence from heritability studies that the environment is important.

Nutrition. The literature concerning the effects of nutrition on intelligence has been reviewed by Brozek (1978). Although it seems clear that severe malnutrition in early childhood can have large and lasting deleterious effects on intelligence, the research evidence is not as clear-cut as one might wish. Malnutrition rarely occurs alone; it is typically accompanied by a climate of poverty, apathy, and ignorance, which makes it difficult to isolate the effects of malnutrition from other social effects. Studies in developing countries (such as Birch, Pineiro, Acadlade, Toca & Craviota, 1971) strongly suggest that prolonged severe malnutrition during the first two to four years of life, leading to hospitalization for kwashiorkor, results in lasting intellectual impairment of 10 IQ points or more. The difficulty of obtaining comparable well-nourished controls makes the exact extent of the impairment uncertain. A detailed study of 74 Jamaican children who were severely malnourished in infancy and matched neighborhood comparison cases revealed that the effects of malnutrition depended on the family context in which it occurred (Richardson, 1976). Differences in intelligence between the malnourished and comparison cases were slight when the background history was favorable, but amounted to about 15 IQ points when the history was unfavorable. This suggests that there is not a simple effect of malnutrition but that it interacts with other environmental circumstances.

This is dramatically demonstrated by a study of the results of a severe 6-month famine that occurred in the western part of Holland as a result of a German transportation embargo near the end of World War II (Stein,

183

Susser, Saenger & Marolla, 1972). Rations were drastically reduced, and birth weights of infants declined somewhat. Some 19 years later, almost all Dutch males were being given an intelligence test (Progressive Matrices) on registration for military service, and it became possible to compare the scores of those born before, during, and immediately after the famine in affected cities with those born at the same time in control cities not affected by the famine. No significant differences were found between the approximately 20,000 men affected by the famine early in life and the controls.

Family Socioeconomic Status. As noted at the beginning of this chapter, there is a strong relationship between intelligence and educational and occupational attainment, the major determiners of socioeconomic status (SES). What is more interesting, because it is open to varying interpretations, is the somewhat lower correlation between family SES and the intelligence of children raised in the family. Jencks (1972) reported the average correlation of family SES and the child's intelligence from a number of large studies to be .30, and Coleman et al. (1966) found that eight home background factors (SES indicators) accounted for 23% of the variance in twelfth-grade verbal achievement for whites and 15% for blacks (multiple correlations of .48 and .39 respectively).

Since intelligence has substantial heritability, there must be genetic differences in intelligence between the social classes. If the brightest tend to move up the SES scale and the dullest to move down, they will carry their genes with them, which will maintain genetic differences among social classes. Herrnstein (1973) has pointed out that if IQ is highly heritable, then the greater the equality of opportunity, that is, the greater the chances for individual social mobility, the more social class will become a matter of inherited status. Waller (1971a) has shown that IQ is related to intergenerational social mobility even within families. He found that sons whose IQs were higher than their fathers' IQs (when both were tested at the same age in school) attained by middle age a higher average SES level than their fathers had attained at the same age; sons with lower IQs than their fathers' attained a lower average SES. The correlation between the father-son differences in IQ and in SES was .29.

In spite of the *obvious* genetic linkage, many investigators have considered the strong relationship between intelligence and family SES to be primarily environmental. In fact, parental IQ and SES are probably the most frequently proposed environmental influences on intelligence. Parental IQ or SES, as such, does not have a direct environmental impact on the child, however. The influence must be mediated by specific parental behaviors or other characteristics of the home that the child experiences directly. This idea has spawned a number of studies of the parental attitudes and child-rearing practices of parents of different social classes and of the correlation of parental behaviors with the child's intelligence. These studies have typically found substantial differences in parenting behavior between the social classes. Parents of higher SES tend to be more permissive, to interact verbally with their children more frequently, to encourage them more often, and to be more successful in controlling their children than parents of lower SES.

Although interesting, such observations do not provide strong scientific evidence, since in natural families the parents and children have a genetic as well as a social relationship. Because of this obvious source of ambiguity, it is surprising that more detailed studies of this sort have not been conducted with adopted children. The adoption studies discussed earlier show that the socioeconomic characteristics of the family are much less related to the child's IQ when the child is adopted than when it is not, although there does seem to be a small relationship that cannot be attributed entirely to selective placement.

In the United States and other capitalist countries, low socioeconomic status is usually associated with the grim deprivations of poverty. Since the environmental inadequacies of low-income homes are obvious and distasteful to those in more fortunate circumstances, many observers have become convinced that the unfortunate surroundings are the cause of the low average intelligence generally observed among children of poverty. However, a study by Firkowska, Ostrowska, Sokolowska, Stein, Susser, and Wald (1978) of the mental performance of all 11-year-old children in Warsaw, Poland, suggests that it is not the economic differences themselves that produce socioeconomic differences in intelligence. Warsaw presents an unusual opportunity to study this relationship, since the city was some 70% destroyed during World War II and was rebuilt under a new political system that did not tolerate the old class distinctions. Buildings were constructed and housing was distributed on egalitarian principles so that neighborhoods lost all social class identification.

> In Warsaw today, people of all levels of education and all types of occupations live in apartments that closely resemble each other, shop in identical stores that contain the same goods and share similar catering and cultural centers. Schools and health facilities are equipped in the same way and are uniformly accessible. It is thus quite natural for families of varied occupation and culture to live side by side in the same districts, to occupy buildings and homes of similar standard, and to attend the same schools and medical facilities. (p. 1358)

It is somewhat surprising that in this situation, in which most economic differences have been abolished, the correlations between a child's intelligence and family SES are almost exactly the same as that observed in the United States. The correlation between a mother's and father's educational and occupational levels with their child's intelligence score (progressive matrices) ranged from .27 to .29. The combined family SES index correlated .32 with the child's IQ.

Children Raised in Isolation. Case studies of children raised in extremely deprived environments may provide information concerning the maximum effect of deleterious early environmental influences. There have been several reports (e.g., Gesell, 1940) of feral children who were presumed to have been reared by wolves or other animals. Typically, these children were unable to adapt to human culture; however, these studies have been criticized because the early history of the children was unknown. Bettelheim (1959) suggested that the feral children may have been recently abandoned psychotic, autistic, or severely retarded children.

There have been a few case studies in which the early histories of the children are known, and in these cases the outcome was quite different. These studies were reviewed by Clarke and Clarke (1976), who also included reprints of some of the papers. For example, Isabelle, the illegitimate child of a deaf-mute mother, was kept in almost complete isolation with her mother during her early childhood. When discovered at age 6½, she was unable to talk and had a mental age of 19 months. With compassionate training, she made rapid progress and eventually developed normal intelligence. Similar rapid development after severe retardation due to early deprivation was observed in another case involving twin boys.

In 1970, a 13-year-old girl, Genie, was discovered to have been raised in almost total isolation and had been subjected to considerable abuse (Curtiss, 1977). She suffered from extreme malnutrition and was unable to speak or understand any kind of language. She functioned at about the 2-year-old level on preschool performance scales. Genie was intensively studied over the next 5 years, especially from the point of view of linguistic analysis. She progressed rapidly in language comprehension and could communicate in English; however, tests revealed gaps in her abilities. For example, she was above average in gestalt perception and part-whole judgments, but scored low on tests involving sequential order. Her overall performance on the Raven Progressive Matrices was poor, but she was able to solve certain difficult items. Careful analysis of her linguistic performance suggested that her language was controlled by the right hemisphere of her brain, which is normally a nonlanguage area. Curtiss interpreted these findings as supporting the hypothesis of a "critical period" for normal language acquisition.

These cases show that extreme environmental deprivation can have marked effects, which hardly needs to be demonstrated, but they also suggest that the early stunting of intellectual development is not irreversible. The more detailed analysis in the case of Genie, however, suggests that extreme early deprivation may have permanent effects on certain patterns of abilities.

Massive Intervention. At the other end of the spectrum from children raised in isolation are programs of early environmental stimulation in which children from disadvantaged homes are given massive doses of all environmental inputs that might facilitate intellectual development. Since these programs can be planned deliberately, much better controls are available than for children raised in isolation.

One small program that has been widely cited as showing potent effects of massive early intervention is being conducted in Milwaukee (Garber & Heber, 1977). Forty infants of black slum mothers with IQs below 75 were randomly assigned to experimental and control groups. The experimental families received a massive intervention of 6 years beginning in the first weeks of the infant's life. The 6-year program, consisting of educational and vocational rehabilitation of the mother, provision of adequate nutrition and medical care, and intensive enrichment of the child's environment, is estimated to cost about $30,000 per child (Trotter, 1976). At 6 years of age, the mean IQ of the experimental group was about 112 compared to about 82 for the control group. At age 9, after 3 years of public school, the means were about 106 and 79 for experimental and control groups, respectively.

A similar program being conducted at the University of North Carolina (Ramey & Smith, 1977) has not been in progress as long as the Milwaukee program, but appears to be producing much more modest gains.

McKay, Sinisterra, McKay, Gomez, and Lloreda (1978) reported that an intensive 4-year program involving daylong schooling plus nutritional supplements and health care produced dramatic ability gains in undernourished Columbian preschool children. The 50 children receiving the full 4-year program were superior by almost one standard deviation to the 90 children who were exposed to only the final year, with groups receiving 2 and 3 years of the program falling in between. Most of the group differences remained on a follow-up Stanford Binet test 1 year later.

All three of these studies involved children in extremely deprived environments. It may be that these severely deprived and undernourished children are, like the children raised in isolation, below the threshold of environmental support necessary for the normal development of intelligence and that a special process is involved in reversing the effects of the deficiency. Jensen (1969) proposed such a threshold effect to account for the obviously large influence of extreme deprivation while evidence seems to show only small environmental influences on intelligence in the general population. If this is the case, one would not expect these findings to be generalizable to children in the normal range. On the other hand, it may be that the disadvantaged children in these programs respond to environmental enrichment in the same way as would any other children and that similarly great increments in enrichment would have similarly great effects for the majority of children.

187

Birth Order. It may seem incongruous to discuss such a seemingly innocuous variable as birth order in the context of children raised in isolation and massive intervention; however, birth order has unique advantages for research on early environmental influences. Information about birth order can be easily and reliably obtained from adults and it provides data about an important aspect of early childhood experience that, when family size is controlled, is independent of socioeconomic status.

There is fairly good evidence from several large studies (Belmont & Marolla, 1973; Breland, 1974; Velandia, Grandon & Page, 1978) that the earlier-born children in a family tend to score higher on tests of intelligence and academic achievement than later-born children. The birth-order effects are not large, but they are important because they seem to be clearly environmental in origin. There is no plausible genetic explanation as there is with almost every other observed relationship of intelligence with another variable, although some unknown genetic effect that is correlated with the mother's age (as is Down's syndrome) could conceivably be involved.

Breland (1974) found that the birth order effect is larger for siblings close together in age than for those further apart, as well as a greater effect on verbal than on mathematical tests. These findings seem to suggest that the effect is due to social influences rather than to natal or prenatal biological factors.

Since the birth order effect is so small and its cause is not known, it has no practical significance at present. Small effects can sometimes be of great theoretical importance, however, like the faint clouding of a photographic plate that first indicated the presence of radioactivity. If the critical elements in the birth-order effect could be isolated, their influence might be magnified manyfold.

The Effects of Schooling. The process of schooling is so intimately related to the development of the verbal comprehension and the reasoning abilities measured by most intelligence tests that it seems almost self-evident that formal education is necessary for the development of intelligence as we know it. Indeed, this does seem to be the case.

During World War II, many elementary schools in Holland were closed, and DeGroot (1951) has shown that the IQ scores of children entering secondary school after the war appear to have dropped about 7 IQ points as a result. In another study, 10% of Swedish 13-year-olds were tested in 1961, and 5 years later about 5,000 males from this sample took intelligence tests on enrollment for military service. After control for the test scores of the 13-year-olds and for socioeconomic status, those who had completed the Gymnasium scored between 7 and 8 IQ points above those who had dropped out after only 7 to 9 years of schooling (Härnqvist, 1968). After reviewing these and other studies, Jencks (1972) concluded that each extra year of schooling boosts an individual's adult IQ score about one point above what it would otherwise be.

Differential School Effects. The intimate association between schooling and intelligence also makes it seem reasonable to expect that differences in the quality of schools would be responsible in some degree for individual differences in intelligence and especially in scholastic achievement. The Equality of Educational Opportunity Survey (Coleman, Mood, Campbell, Hobson, McPartland, Weinfield & York, 1966) probably deserves credit for first casting widespread doubt on this expectation, with its conclusion, based on a massive survey of some 600,000 students in 4,000 schools, that "variations in school quality are not highly related to variations in achievement of pupils. . . . The school appears unable to exert independent influences to make achievement less dependent on the child's background" (p. 297). A number of reanalyses of the Coleman data (e.g., Mosteller & Moynihan, 1972) have failed to change the basic conclusion (see chapter 11 by Lovell in this book).

Similar negative results were found at the college level. Astin (1968) discovered that differences in achievement on the Graduate Record Examination area tests were highly related to differences in ability and other student characteristics measured at the time of college entrance. Once the initial characteristics of the students were controlled, however, there was no residual relationship of achievement to measures of college quality.

Averch, Carroll, Donaldson, Kiesling and Pincus (1972) at the Rand Corporation reviewed the existing research on differential school effects for the U.S. Commission on School Finance. This thorough, critical review concluded that ". . . research has not identified a variant of the existing system that is consistently related to student's educational outcomes" (p. 154). The authors explain, "We must emphasize that we are not suggesting that nothing makes a difference, or that nothing 'works.' Rather, we are saying that research has found nothing that *consistently* and *unambiguously* makes a difference in student's outcomes" (p. 145). The report pointed out that what has been investigated are the effects of existing variations within the current system. These findings, of course, say nothing about the potential effects of radical departures from current educational practice.

Effects of Compensatory Education. Even if differences in schooling are not a large source of variance in intelligence and academic achievement for students in general, they may be a potent influence for certain subgroups of students. This seems most likely to be the case for students whose achievement may have been lowered by socioeconomically disadvantaged home backgrounds. Based on this reasoning, a number of compensatory education programs for disadvantaged students were started in the 1960s as part of the "war on poverty." The U.S. Commission on Civil Rights (1967) reviewed the results of these programs and concluded "that none of the programs appear to have raised significantly the achievement of participating pupils as a group, within the period evaluated by the Commission" (p. 138).

Subsequent evaluations of compensatory programs have not been much more encouraging, although the scope and quality of the evaluations have in some cases greatly improved. The Westinghouse Learning Corporation's (1969) evaluation of the effects of Head Start found that children enrolled in both summer and year-round projects of this national preschool compensatory program did, in fact, have a head start when they entered first grade compared with students not in the program. However, by the end of the first grade, all of the advantages produced by the program had been lost. Although the report has been criticized (Cicirelli, Evans & Schiller, 1970; Smith & Bissell, 1970), it seems clear that any lasting effects were small. These findings could be due to the fact that the preschool program increased test-taking ability and social skills rather than having any real effect on cognitive ability. On the other hand, the findings could be due to the fact that real cognitive gains were lost in the allegedly unstimulating atmosphere of public schools enrolling large numbers of disadvantaged children.

To decide between these two interpretations, and possibly others, Project Follow Through was begun in 1969. This compensatory program for grades one through three, plus kindergarten in many cases, of schools enrolling predominantly disadvantaged children was designed as an education experiment. To provide for "planned variation," contracts were awarded for the development of 17 diverse, theoretically relevant, and internally consistent compensatory education curricula called models. One of these models was installed in each of 100 local school districts, and the developers of the model provided consultants to supervise its implementation. In each district, experimental schools that received the program and comparison schools that did not receive the program were identified. Evaluation data, including cognitive (the Metropolitan Achievement Test) and noncognitive outcomes, were collected by an independent agency, the Stanford Research Institute. This is one of the largest educational research projects ever conducted. Over 352,000 children participated during the 4-year evaluation period (although the major analyses were based on considerably smaller samples of children for whom complete data were available), and the data collection alone is reported to have cost approximately $30 million (Marciano & David, 1977).

The results were clearly negative (Stebbins, St. Pierre, Proper, Anderson & Cerva, 1977). After several adjustments to make the outcome measures comparable, a majority of the differences between experimental and control schools were not significant. When significant differences were found, the control school was superior more frequently than was the experimental school. Most models had at least one site in which the experimental school was superior, but all models had at least one site in which the control school was superior. Thus no model was found to be generally superior to the others. Models emphasizing basic skills were reported to be superior to models emphasizing conceptual or affective processes on the basic skills and affective outcomes, but House, Glass, McLean, and Decker (1978) have raised serious questions about this result.

Although the large national compensatory programs have not been shown to be generally effective, there have been notable successes reported by much smaller programs, such as Gray and Klaus (1965). However, in view of the great variation in program effectiveness among local sites found in Project Follow Through, it would seem prudent to require that a program be demonstrated to be transportable to other locations before it is declared an unqualified success.

GROUP DIFFERENCES IN INTELLIGENCE

Whenever identifiable subgroups of the population are compared in reasonably representative samples, significant differences in ability are usually found. These group differences permit a sort of epidemiological analysis that may provide clues to the origin of individual differences. Racial and ethnic differences have received a great deal of attention in the last few years.

The Coleman Report (Coleman et al., 1966), with its large national sample, overrepresenting schools enrolling minority students, tested at five grade levels, provides the best basis for comparisons of the various racial/ethnic groups. This survey showed the following overall rank order of the groups studied: whites (103), Oriental-Americans (101), Mexican-Americans (91), Puerto Ricans (90), Indian-Americans (90), and blacks (84). Numbers in parentheses are average scores for the 12th grade verbal test expressed on an IQ scale (mean=100; SD=15). Mexican-Americans, Oriental-Americans, and Indian-Americans scored somewhat higher on the nonverbal test, with the Oriental-Americans the highest of all groups tested. Studies that have compared religious groups have typically found Jews to score somewhat higher and Catholics somewhat lower than Protestants. It should be pointed out that these are differences among group means. Even though some of the group differences are fairly large, they are not a basis for statements about individuals. The most consistent observation that can be made from comparing distributions of ability in various groups is that there are representatives from all groups throughout the entire range of intelligence.

The difference that has received the most attention is that between blacks and whites, because these are the largest groups and the difference is the largest of all the observed group differences. In the Coleman report, blacks on the average scored about one standard deviation below whites on both verbal and nonverbal tests in rural and metropolitan areas of all regions of the country at all grade levels. It is, thus, a large and pervasive difference. Group differences are most obvious to the casual observer at the extremes, where even relatively small differences between means will have a large effect on the proportional representation of the groups.

The critical question about the racial difference concerns the degree to which it is due to genetic differences. None of the available evidence unambiguously separates genetic and environmental differences between the races. Thus the approach to this question has been one of examining a number of different lines of circumstantial evidence in the attempt to narrow the range of possibilities. For example, controlling for SES and other possible environmental differences does not greatly affect the racial difference in ability (Jensen, 1973), yet the degree of admixture of black and Caucasian genes as determined by blood groups is essentially unrelated to ability measures (Scarr, Pakstis, Katz, & Barker, 1977).

Jensen (1973) reviewed the available evidence in detail and concluded "all the major facts would seem to be comprehended quite well by the hypothesis that something between one-half and three-fourths of the average IQ difference between American Negroes and whites is attributable to genetic factors, and the remainder to environmental factors and their interaction with genetic differences" (p. 363).

After reviewing essentially the same evidence, Loehlin et al. (1975) concluded that the mean IQ differences among racial /ethnic groups in the United States "probably reflect in part inadequacies and biases in the tests themselves, in part differences in environmental conditions among the groups, and in part genetic differences among the groups. . . . A rather wide range of positions concerning the relative weight to be given these three factors can reasonably be taken on the basis of current evidence" (p. 238).

There has been considerable concern about the degree to which the schools may contribute to the group differences. The Equality of Educational Opportunity survey (Coleman, et al., 1966) tested children in grades 1, 3, 6, 9, and 12 specifically to obtain data relative to this issue. If a cumulative deficit, or increasing gap, for minority groups was observed with increasing grade level, it would suggest that the schools or other factors operating during the school years may be involved. The only cumulative deficit found was for blacks in the South and Southwest, where the difference widened by about half a standard deviation over the 12 years. These cross-sectional findings are only suggestive, since they may be affected by differential migration, dropout, and other factors. A more sensitive test of cumulative deficit is provided by comparing scores of older and younger school-age siblings. An age decrement in which the older siblings score lower than the younger siblings would provide evidence for a cumulative deficit. Jensen (1974a) found a slight, but statistically significant, age decrement for verbal IQ, but not for nonverbal IQ, for black siblings, and no age decrement for white siblings in a California school district. Using the same methodology in a rural Georgia school district, Jensen (1977) found a substantial age decrement for both verbal and nonverbal IQ for 826 black siblings, and no age decrement of 653 white siblings. He interpreted these results as most likely due to the markedly greater environmental disadvantages of the Georgia blacks relative to the California blacks.

In addition to the IQ differences between racial/ethnic groups, there appear also to be distinctive group profiles when different ability factors are measured (see Figure 7.4). Typical is the study of Lesser, Fifer and Clark (1965), and a replication by Stodolsky and Lesser (1967), who tested middle- and lower-class first-grade children from several racial/ethnic groups on verbal, reasoning, number, and spatial abilities. The distinctive profile shapes for the various groups were characteristic of both upper- and lower-class children of the group. In other words, the profile shape was characteristic of the racial/ethnic group rather than of SES. Jews and blacks tended to be high in verbal ability relative to the other tests; Puerto Ricans and Chinese tended to be low in verbal relative to the other tests. These general group patterns have tended to be confirmed in other studies.

Jensen (1969) proposed that the major profile difference between blacks and whites consists of relatively small differences in Level I abilities (rote learning and memory) and relatively large differences in Level II abilities (complex cognitive processing). This finding has been replicated in several studies (Jensen & Figueroa, 1975). Jensen (1978b) reported that the magnitude of black-white differences on a variety of tests is directly proportional to the tests' loading on the general factor in factor analytic studies.

Cultural Bias of Intelligence Tests. An explanation frequently offered for group differences in ability is that the tests contain content to which some groups have had greater exposure than others. For example, Block and Dworkin (1974) said, "Standard IQ tests are without any doubt highly culture-loaded. In our view, they are all also clearly culture biased in that they require knowledge of, for example, literary, musical, and geographical facts which are differentially available to people with different sociocultural backgrounds" (p. 461). One can easily find items in most verbal intelligence tests that seem to meet this criterion of culture bias, and the citation of such items has been the major line of evidence presented by those who attribute group differences in whole or in part to biased measurement. This appeal to face validity gains credence from the fact that the groups who obtain lower average scores also seem to be less exposed to the majority culture. Critics of this position, however, can point to certain exceptions, such as Eskimos, who do not score low (MacArthur, 1968), and American

193

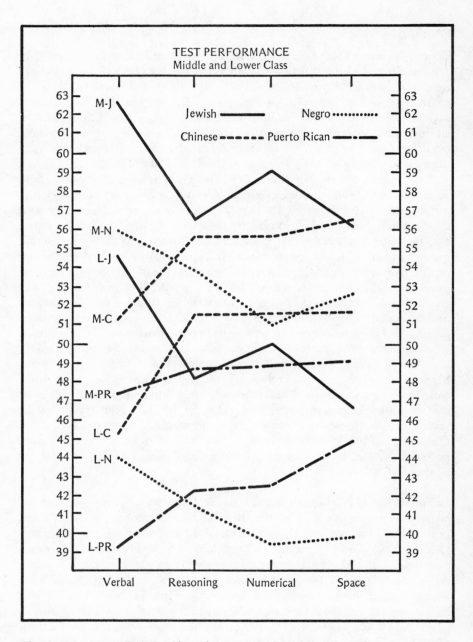

Figure 7.4 Mean Test Profiles of Lower- and Middle-Class First-Grade Children of Four Ethnic Groups. Each profile is the average performance of twenty boys and twenty girls. The tests were specifically constructed to measure these specific abilities at this age level. (From G. Fifer. Social class and cultural group differences in diverse mental abilities. In *Proceedings of the 1964 Invitational Conference on Testing Problems.* Princeton, N.J.: Educational Testing Service, 1965. Used by permission.)

Indians, who score higher than blacks on the average in spite of seemingly greater cultural isolation (Coleman et al., 1966). Also the black-white difference has been reported to be smaller on verbal than on nonverbal, and seemingly less culture-loaded, tests of ability (Jensen, 1974b).

College admissions tests appear to predict college grades equally well for blacks and whites, and they do not underpredict for blacks in integrated colleges as would be expected if the tests were more biased than the college-grade criterion (Cleary, Humphreys, Kendrick & Wesman, 1975). On the other hand, Mercer (1972) has shown that lower-class blacks and Chicanos with IQs below 70 are more capable of self-care than are middle-class whites with similarly low IQ scores.

Jensen (1974b) studied item response patterns on the culture-loaded Peabody Picture Vocabulary Test and the culture-reduced Raven's Progressive Matrices Test in large representative samples of white, black, and Mexican-American California elementary school children. Although there were large mean differences among groups (in the order white, black, Mexican-American on the Peabody; and white, Mexican-American, black on the Raven), the rank order of item difficulties for the tests and the pattern of wrong answers did not differ significantly in the three groups, as would be expected if some items were more culture-biased than others. Equally difficult Raven and Peabody items for whites were also equally difficult for blacks, but the Peabody items became more difficult for the Mexican-Americans, suggesting some culture bias of the verbal Peabody for the largely bilingual Mexican-Americans.

CHANGES OVER TIME

A negative correlation between intelligence and number of siblings on the order of −.20 has long been observed in the United States and in Europe (Anastasi, 1956). Those parents who have lower scoring children, for whatever reason, tend to have more of them than those who have higher scoring children. From this relationship, it was calculated that the average intelligence should decline by about one IQ point in ten years (Cattell, 1950).

Until recently, however, all evidence pointed to an increase in average intelligence (Duncan, 1952; Schaie & Labouvie-Vief, 1974). Tuddenham (1948) reported data for a representative sample of 768 World War II draftees who took the Wells Revision of the Army Alpha examination. This allowed a comparison with the performance of World War I draftees on a similar test. The median score showed an increase of almost 15 IQ points between the two wars. A lack of exact comparability between the tests kept Tuddenham from stating the difference more precisely than that a substantial increase was observed throughout the entire score range. Since the correlation between the test score and years of education was .75, Tuddenham attributed a large part of the gain to increases in the average educational level between the two wars. Somewhat less spectacular gains were observed for children. The 1971 renorming of the Stanford Binet showed increases over the 1937 standardization group for preschoolers and adolescents, but not for ages 7–10. Thorndike (1975) attributed these changes to cultural enrichment for preschoolers brought about by television. The Scottish Council for Research in Education (1949) reported an increase from 1932 to 1947 of about one or two IQ points in the Scottish surveys of 11-year-old children.

The paradox of increasing test scores in the presence of a negative correlation between intelligence and family size was resolved to the satisfaction of many by a series of studies showing that when a total population was studied, including those with childless marriages and individuals never marrying, there was actually a slight positive correlation between intelligence and number of children produced (Bajema, 1963; Higgins, Reed & Reed, 1962; Waller, 1971b). This was primarily because those with very low test scores were particularly unlikely to marry and to have children.

Recently, however, evidence has accumulated that average test scores have been declining. The average score on the Scholastic Aptitude Test (SAT) and the American College Testing Program test has been declining steadily for the past 15 years, and the accumulated decline is substantial— a quarter of a standard deviation or more (Munday, 1976; Advisory Panel, 1977). Figure 7.5 shows that the average SAT verbal score declined from 468 in 1963 to 429 in 1977, the equivalent of about 6 IQ points. During the same period, the average SAT math score declined from 502 to 471, the equivalent of about 5 IQ points. Public attention was first attracted to the decline in scores on the SAT, but subsequent reports have shown that the lower average scores are very widespread. They are found in most state testing programs in secondary schools (although apparently not in primary grades) in both suburban and inner-city areas (Armbruster, 1975). A decline has also been observed in some tests of the National Assessment of Educational Progress and in Canada (Munday, 1976).

The Advisory Panel on the Scholastic Aptitude Test Score Decline (1977) attributed about half of the decline in SAT scores to changes in the composition of the group tested. The remaining half of the decline was attributed to a complex of factors including changes in school curricula, cultural changes, television, and declining academic motivation.

The rise and fall of the average test score appears to be too rapid to be explained by genetic changes that could result from differential birth rates, although heterosis resulting from the large immigration of diverse groups into the United States around the turn of the century might be a factor in the large increase in intelligence from the two world wars, as it apparently was in the increase in average height that occurred at the same time. It seems most likely, however, that cultural factors are the primary source of

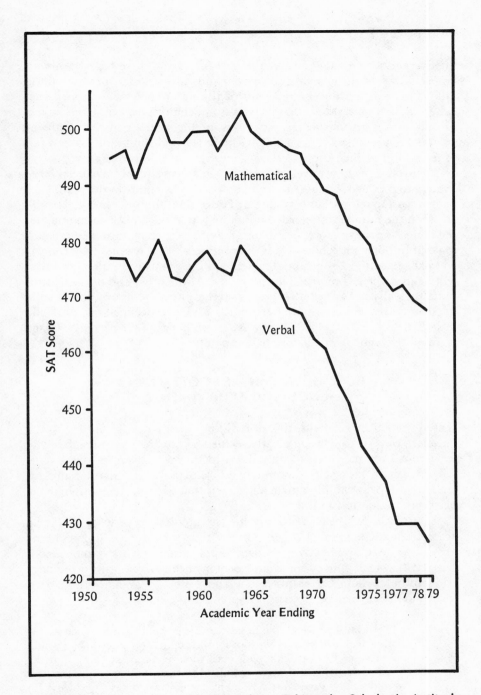

Figure 7.5 Average Score of All Students Taking the Scholastic Aptitude Test for the Academic Years 1952 through 1977. Data from Advisory Panel, 1977.

the average score changes. Over the past fifty years there have been very large changes in the general educational and cultural level that exceed the differences existing for the majority of the population at any one time. Wheeler (1942) has shown that large cultural changes over time can have a substantial effect on average measured intelligence. He reported an increase of ten points in the average IQ in an isolated community over a ten year period in which there were very large cultural improvements.

The changes that have occurred in the average score have been large enough to produce changes of several orders of magnitude in the number of people scoring more than two standard deviations from the mean. The decrease in the number of retarded individuals that most likely accompanied the increasing mean scores of the past may have been obscured by increasing cultural demands; however, if the average score continues to decline, it will likely result in a substantial increase in the number of individuals that will be identified as retarded in the future. At the other end of the continuum, the Advisory Panel (1977) reported that the number of students scoring over 600 on either or both parts of the SAT had declined from 189,300 in 1970 to 108,200 in 1976. There was a corresponding drop in the average score of high school valedictorians and salutatorians.

HOW MUCH CAN WE BOOST IQ AND SCHOLASTIC ACHIEVEMENT?

Jensen's (1969) article with this title did not give a precise answer to the question, but his conclusion clearly seemed to be, "Not very much." The vociferous protests raised in opposition to this pessimistic prospect have faded away in face of the manifest failure of most action programs intended to improve ability and achievement that were started with high aspirations and optimism in the 1960s.

Currently one hears relatively modest predictions of what might be accomplished. Bereiter (1976) estimated that the average IQ might be raised by about 2 points by widespread application of what is known concerning ". . . such conventional and benign means as improved prenatal and postnatal care, better nutrition, and generally greater stimulation throughout the years of growth." He pointed out:

> such a small gain would be imperceptible in small samples such as one would encounter in daily life, but for the population as a whole it would have results of potentially enormous consequence. Assuming that the shape of the IQ distribution remained the same, it would mean there would be only three-fourths as many mental retardates (IQs below 70) as there are now. The number of people with IQs above 130, on whom we depend for most of our professional and highly technical work, would increase by a third." (p. 141)

Bereiter went on to speculate that application of current knowledge might produce greater gains at the lower end of the distribution than at the higher end, although this may not be the case if one considers that only 54% of those in the top quartile of the ability distribution now attend college (Peng, 1977).

Something, or better some things, produce enormous individual differences in intelligence. Currently we are able only to divide these influences roughly into genetic and environmental categories. For practical purposes, this is not much help since we can do little more about unknown environmental influences than about unknown genetic influences. Loehlin et al. (1975) have pointed out the fallacy in the popular supposition that genetic variance is fixed and that only environmental variance provides hope of improvement. They suggest that, when both biological and environmental mechanisms are finally understood, it is probable that the biological will be the easier to change.

There is a way, however, in which large changes in intelligence can be brought about. Since the correlation of intelligence scores of parent and child is about .50, the average ability of a group of children can be determined by selecting the parents. It should be noted that this result follows simply from statistical regression, and it holds true regardless of whether the parent-child correlation is due to genetic or to environmental factors, or to some combination of the two. Reed and Reed (1965), for example, found "that 36.1% of the retarded had one or both parents retarded. Thus mental retardation in one generation would have been reduced by 36.1% if there had been no reproduction of the retardates in the previous generation" (p. 69). They went on to indicate that 93% of the mildly retarded in their large sample had at least one retarded relative.

There have been a great variety of eugenics proposals, and the major papers from Galton to the present have been collected by Bajema (1976). The more ambitious and coercive proposals of the past have not surfaced since the fallacious and brutal racial policies of the Nazis made the danger of misuse of any such program all too painfully obvious. Recent eugenics proposals have been modest in scope and entirely voluntary. The leading positive eugenics proposal (seeking to increase fecundity of the most suitable parents) is the method of germinal choice (Muller, 1965) in which sperm from the most desirable males would be stored and made available to women who voluntarily choose to conceive a child with it. The leading negative eugenics proposal (seeking to restrict reproduction by the least suitable parents) is the voluntary sterilization bonus (Shockley, 1972) in which a bonus amounting to $1,000 for each IQ point below 100 would be offered for voluntary sterilization to nonpayers of income tax. It is interesting to note that the originators of both of these proposals are winners of the Nobel prize and that both have used their prestige to urge public acceptance of the eugenic idea with equally unimpressive results.

———————————— *SUMMARY* ————————————

Individual differences in intelligence play an important role in determining differences in academic and occupational achievement. The history of intelligence testing shows that the IQ and indeed the definition of intelligence derive from the steady mental growth that occurs during the childhood years. Intellectual abilities may be analyzed into a number of component abilities or factors. Although measurement of these more specific abilities does not contribute greatly to prediction of achievement, the study of the component abilities may contribute to understanding the mental basis and organization of intelligence.

Approximately 60% of the variation in intelligence is brought about by genetic differences. This is shown by the greater similarity in intelligence of identical than of fraternal twins, by the striking similarity of identical twins raised apart, and by the greater similarity of adopted children to their biological mother than to their foster mother. Environmental influences are also important. Severe malnutrition in infancy, when combined with an unstimulating environment, results in a lasting intellectual deficit. However, the remarkable recovery shown by children raised in extremely restricted environments when given normal environmental stimulation shows that intellectual development is not easily deflected from its genetically prescribed path.

Although intensive intellectual stimulation of children in deprived circumstances results in lasting intellectual gains, the environmental differences associated with socioeconomic status in developed countries seem not to be a major cause of intellectual differences. Each additional year of schooling raises the IQ about one point over what it would otherwise be. Studies of the effects of different kinds or quality of schools, however, have not found any specific school characteristic or educational experience that is consistently superior to any other.

Differences in average intelligence are usually found whenever representative samples of racial or ethnic groups are studied. The largest of these group differences in the United States is between blacks and whites; evidence suggests that the difference is due in part to genetic and in part to environmental differences between the groups.

The average intelligence of the population increased substantially from 1918, when the first large testing was done, to post–World War II. Since 1960, however, the average intelligence has declined; the cause of these temporal changes is unknown.

There is no known educational or social manipulation that will bring about a large change in intelligence, given the present incomplete understanding of the causes of individual differences.

SUGGESTIONS FOR FURTHER READING

BLOCK, N. J., & DWORKIN, G. (Eds.). *The IQ controversy.* New York: Pantheon Books, 1976.

BRODY, E. B., & BRODY, N. *Intelligence: Nature, determinants, and consequences.* New York: Academic Press, 1976.

BUSS, A. R., & POLEY, W. *Individual differences: Traits and factors.* New York: Gardner Press, 1976.

JENCKS, S. *Inequality: A reassessment of the effect of family and schooling in America.* New York: Basic Books, 1972.

JENSEN, A. R. *Educability and group differences.* New York: Harper & Row, 1973.

LOEHLIN, J. C., LINDZEY, G., & SPUHLER, N. J. *Race differences in intelligence.* San Francisco: W. H. Freeman, 1975.

RESNICK, L. B. *The nature of intelligence.* Hillsdale, N.J.: Lawrence Erlbaum, 1976.

BIBLIOGRAPHY

ADVISORY PANEL ON THE SCHOLASTIC APTITUDE TEST SCORE DECLINE. *On further examination.* New York: College Entrance Examination Board, 1977.

ANASTASI, A. Intelligence and family size. *Psychological Bulletin,* 1956, *53,* 187–209.

ARMBRUSTER, F. *The U.S. primary and secondary education process.* Croton-on-Hudson, N.Y.: Hudson Institute, 1975.

ASTIN, A. W. Undergraduate achievement and institutional "excellence." *Science,* 1968, *161,* 661–668.

AVERCH, H. A., CARROLL, S. J., DONALDSON, T. S., KIESLING, H. J., & PINCUS, J. *How effective is schooling? A critical review and synthesis of research findings.* Santa Monica, Calif.: Rand, 1972.

BAJEMA, C. Estimation of the direction and intensity of natural selection in relation to human intelligence by means of the intrinsic rate of natural increase. *Eugenics Quarterly,* 1963, *10,* 175–187.

BAJEMA, C. J. *Eugenics then and now.* Stroudsburg, Pa.: Dowden, Hutchinson & Ross, 1976.

BELMONT, L., & MAROLLA, F. A. Birth order, family size, and intelligence. *Science,* 1973, *182,* 1095–1111.

BEREITER, C. IQ differences and social policy. In N. F. Ashline, T. R. Pezzullo & C. I. Norris (Eds.), *Education, inequality, and national policy.* Lexington, Mass.: Lexington Books, 1976.

BERG, A. *The nutrition factor.* Washington, D.C.: Brookings Institution, 1973.

BETTELHEIM, B. Feral children and autistic children. *American Journal of Sociology,* 1959, *64,* 455–467.

BIRCH, H. G., PINEIRO, C., ALCALDE, E., TOCA, T., & CRAVIOTO, J. Kwashiorkor in early childhood and intelligence at school age. *Pediatric Research,* 1971, *5,* 579–584.

BLOCK, N. J., & DWORKIN, G. I.Q., heritability, and inequality. *Philosophy and Public Affairs*, 1974, *3*, 331–409 (part 1) and *4*, 40–99 (part 2).

BRELAND, H. M. Birth order, family configuration, and verbal achievement. *Child Development*, 1974,·*45*, 1011–1019.

BROZEK, J. Nutrition, malnutrition and behavior. *Annual Review of Psychology*, 1978, *29*, 157–178.

CARROLL, J. B. Psychometric tests as cognitive tasks: A new "structure of intellect." In L. B. Resnick (Ed.), *The nature of intelligence*. Hillsdale, N.J.: Lawrence Erlbaum, 1976.

CATTELL, R. B. The fate of national intelligence: Test of a thirteen-year prediction. *Eugenics Review*, 1950, *42*, 136–148.

CICIRELLI, V. G., EVANS, J. W. & SCHILLER, J. S. The impact of Head Start: A reply to the report analysis. *Harvard Educational Review*, 1970, *40*, 105–129.

CLARKE, A. M., & CLARKE, A. D. B. *Early experience: Myth and evidence*. New York: Free Press, 1976.

CLEARY, T. A., HUMPHREYS, L. G., KENDRICK, S. A., & WESMAN, A. Educational uses of tests with disadvantaged students. *American Psychologist*, 1975, *30*, 15–41.

COLEMAN, J. S., MOOD, A. M., CAMPBELL, E. Q., HOBSON, C. J., MCPARTLAND, J., WEINFIELD, F. D., & YORK, R. L. *Equality of educational opportunity*. Washington, D.C.: U.S. Government Printing Office, 1966.

CURTISS, S. *Genie: A psycholinguistic study of a modern-day "wild child."* New York: Academic Press, 1977.

DEFRIES, J. C., HEGMANN, J. P., & HALCOMB, R. A. Response to 20 generations of selection for open-field activity in mice. *Behavioral Biology*, 1974, *11*, 481–495.

DEFRIES, J. C., & PLOMIN, R. Behavioral genetics. *Annual Review of Psychology*, 1978, *29*, 473–516.

DEGROOT, A. D. War and the intelligence of youth. *Journal of Abnormal and Social Psychology*, 1951, *46*, 596–597.

DUNCAN, O. D. Is the intelligence of the general population declining? *American Sociological Review*, 1952, *17*, 401–497.

DUNCAN, O. D., FEATHERMAN, D. L., & DUNCAN, B. *Socioeconomic background and achievement*. New York: Seminar Press, 1972.

EAVES, L. J. Testing models for variation in intelligence. *Heredity*, 1975, *34*, 132–136.

ERLENMEYER-KIMLING, L., & JARVIK, L. F. Genetics and intelligence: A review. *Science*, 1963, *142*, 1477–1479.

EKSTROM, R. B., FRENCH, J. W., HARMAN, H. H., & DERMEN, D. *Manual for kit of factor-referenced cognitive tests*. Princeton, N.J.: Educational Testing Service, 1976.

FIRKOWSKA, A., OSTROWSKA, A., SOKOLOWSKA, M., STEIN, A., SUSSER, M., & WALD, I. Cognitive development and social policy. *Science*, 1978, *200*, 1357–1362.

GARBER, H., & HEBER, F. R. The Milwaukee Project: Indications of the effectiveness of early intervention in preventing mental retardation. In P. Mittler (Ed.), *Research to practice in mental retardation: Care and intervention* (Vol. 1). Baltimore: University Park Press, 1977.

GESELL, A. *Wolf child and human child.* New York: Harper, 1940.

GRAY, S. W., & KLAUS, R. A. An experimental preschool program for culturally deprivated children. *Child Development,* 1965, *36,* 887–898.

GUILFORD, J. P. *The nature of human intelligence.* New York: McGraw-Hill, 1967.

HÄRNQUIST, K. Changes in intelligence from 13 to 18. *Scandinavian Journal of Psychology,* 1968, *9,* 50–82.

HARRELL, T. W., & HARRELL, M. S. Army General Classification Test scores for civilian occupations. *Educational and Psychological Measurement,* 1945, *5,* 229–239.

HERRNSTEIN, R. J. *I.Q. in the meritocracy.* Boston: Little, Brown, 1973.

HIGGINS, J., REED, S., & REED, E. Intelligence and family size: A paradox resolved. *Eugenics Quarterly,* 1962, *9,* 84–90.

HOLLY, K. A., & MICHAEL, W. B. The relationship of structure-of-intellect factor abilities to performance in high school modern algebra. *Educational and Psychological Measurement,* 1972, *32,* 447–450.

HOUSE, E. R., GLASS, G. V., MCLEAN, L. D., & DECKER, F. W. No simple answer: Critique of the Follow Through evaluation. *Harvard Educational Review,* 1978, *48,* 128–160.

HUNT, E., LUNNEBORG, C., & LEWIS, J. What does it mean to be high verbal? *Cognitive Psychology,* 1975, *7,* 194–227.

JENCKS, S. *Inequality: A reassessment of the effect of family and schooling in America.* New York: Basic Books, 1972.

JENSEN, A. R. Estimation of the limits of heritability of traits by comparison of monozygotic and dizygotic twins. *Proceedings of the National Academy of Sciences,* 1967, *58,* 149–156.

JENSEN, A.R. How much can we boost IQ and scholastic achievement? *Harvard Educational Review,* 1969, *39,* 1–123.

JENSEN, A. R. IQ's of identical twins reared apart. *Behavior Genetics,* 1970, *1,* 133–146.

JENSEN, A. R. *Educability and group differences.* New York: Harper & Row, 1973.

JENSEN, A. R. Cumulative deficit: A testable hypothesis? *Developmental Psychology,* 1974, *10,* 996–1019. (a)

JENSEN, A. R. How biased are culture-loaded tests? *Genetic Psychology Monographs,* 1974, *90,* 185–244. (b)

JENSEN, A. R. Cumulative deficit in IQ in blacks in the rural South. *Developmental Psychology,* 1977, *13,* 184–191.

JENSEN, A. R. *g:* outmoded theory or unconquered frontier? Invited address given at the American Psychological Association meeting, Toronto, Canada, August 29, 1978. (a)

JENSEN, A. R. The nature of intelligence and its relation to learning. In *Melbourne Studies in Education,* Melbourne, Australia: The University of Melbourne, 1978. (b)

JENSEN, A. R., & FIGUEROA, R. A. Forward and backward digit span interaction with race and IQ: Predictions from Jensen's theory. *Journal of Educational Psychology*, 1975, *67*, 882–893.

JINKS, J. L., & EAVES, L. J. IQ and inequality. *Nature*, 1974, *248*, 287–289.

JINKS, J. L., & FULKER, D. W. Comparison of the biometrical, genetical, MAVA, and classical approaches to the analysis of human behavior. *Psychological Bulletin*, 1970, *73*, 311–349.

KAMIN, L. J. *The science of politics of IQ.* New York: Halstead Press, 1974.

LESSER, G. S., FIFER, G., & CLARK, D. H. Mental abilities of children from different social-class and cultural groups. *Monographs of the Society for Research in Child Development*, 1965, *30*, No. 4.

LEWONTIN, R. C. Genetic aspects of intelligence. *Annual Review of Genetics*, 1975, *9*, 387–405.

LOEHLIN, J. C. Heredity-environment analysis of Jencks' IQ correlations. *Behavior Genetics*, 1978, *8*, 415–436.

LOEHLIN, J. C., LINDZEY, G., & SPUHLER, J. N. *Race differences in intelligence.* San Francisco: W. H. Freeman, 1975.

LOEHLIN, F. C., & NICHOLS, R. C. *Heredity, environment and personality: A study of 850 sets of twins.* Austin, Tex.: University of Texas Press, 1976.

MACARTHUR, R. S. Some differential abilities of Northern Canadian native youth. *International Journal of Psychology*, 1968, *3*, 43–51.

MARCIANO, R., & DAVID, J. Lessons learned in operationalizing the Follow Through planned variation in the field and implications for future research. Paper presented as part of a symposium: The Follow Through planned variation experiment: A report critique and overview. American Educational Research Association Annual Meeting, New York, April 4, 1977.

MCKAY, H., SINISTERRA, L., MCKAY, A., GOMEZ, H., & LLOREDA, P. Improving cognitive ability in chronically deprived children. *Science*, 1978, *200*, 270–278.

MCNEMAR, Q. Lost: Our intelligence? Why? *American Psychologist*, 1964, *19*, 871–882.

MERCER, J. IQ: The lethal label. *Psychology Today*, September, 1972, 44–47, 95–97.

MORTON, N. E. Analysis of family resemblance. I. Introduction. *American Journal of Human Genetics*, 1974, *26*, 318–330.

MOSTELLER, F., & MOYNIHAN, D. P. *On equality of educational opportunity.* New York: Random House, 1972.

MULLER, H. J. Means and aims in human genetic betterment. In T. M. Sonneborn (Ed.), *The control of human heredity and evolution.* New York: Macmillan, 1965.

MUNDAY, L. A. Declining admissions test scores. *ACT Research Report*, No. 71. Iowa City, Iowa: American College Testing Program, 1976.

MUNSINGER, H. The adopted child's IQ: A critical review. *Psychological Bulletin*, 1975, *82*, 623–659.

NICHOLS, R. C. Twin studies of ability, personality and interests. *Homo,* 1978, *29,* 158–173.

PENG, S. S. Trends in the entry to higher education: 1961–1972. *Educational Researcher,* 1977, *6,* No. 1, 15–20.

POLIVANOV, S. Response of *Drosophila persimilis* to phototactic and geotactic selection. *Behavior Genetics,* 1975, *5,* 255–267.

RAO, D. C., MORTON, N. E., & YEE, S. Analysis of family resemblance. II. A linear model for family correlation. *American Journal of Human Genetics,* 1974, *26,* 331–359.

RAO, D. C., MORTON, N. E., & YEE, S. Resolution of cultural and biological inheritance by path analysis. *American Journal of Human Genetics,* 1976, *28,* 228–242.

RAMEY, C. T., & SMITH, E. Assessing the intellectual consequences of early intervention with high-risk infants. *Journal of Mental Deficiency,* 1977, *81,* 318–324.

REED, E. W., & REED, S. C. *Mental retardation: A family study.* Philadelphia: W. B. Saunders, 1965.

REYNOLDS, C. H. *Correlates of mental ability among somewhat superior American adolescents.* Buffalo, N.Y.: Unpublished Ph. D. dissertation, State University of New York at Buffalo, 1974.

RICHARDSON, S. A. The influence of severe malnutrition in infancy on the intelligence of children at school age: An ecological perspective. In R. N. Walsh & W. T. Greenough (Eds.), *Environments as therapy for brain dysfunction.* New York: Plenum, 1976.

SCARR, S., PAKSTIS, A. J., KATZ, S. H., & BARKER, W. B. Absence of a relationship between degree of white ancestry and intellectual skills within a black population. *Human Genetics,* 1977, *39,* 69–86.

SCARR, S. & WEINBERG, R. A. IQ test performance of black children adopted by white families. *American Psychologist,* 1976, *31,* 726–739.

SCARR, S. & WEINBERG, R. A. Intellectual similarities within families of both adopted and biological children. *Intelligence,* 1977, *1,* 170–191. (a)

SCARR, S. & WEINBERG, R. A. The influence of "family background" on intellectual attainment: The unique contribution of adoptive studies to estimating environmental effects. Paper presented at the Mathematical Social Science Board conference on Family Environment and Subsequent Child Development. Stanford University, March 24, 1977. (b)

SCHAIE, K. W. & LABOUVIE-VIEF, G. Generational versus ontogenetic components of change in adult cognitive behavior. *Developmental Psychology,* 1974, *10,* 205–320.

SCOTTISH COUNCIL FOR RESEARCH IN EDUCATION. *The trend of Scottish intelligence.* London: University of London Press, 1949.

SHOCKLEY, W. Dysgenics, geneticity, raceology: A challenge to the intellectual responsibility of educators. *Phi Delta Kappan,* 1972, *53,* 297–312.

SMITH, M. S., & BISSELL, J. S. Report analysis: The impact of Head Start. *Harvard Educational Review*, 1970, *40*, 51–104.

SPEARMAN, C. *The abilities of man.* London: Macmillan, 1927.

SPROTT, R. L., & STAATS, J. Behavioral studies using genetically defined mice— A bibliography. *Behavior Genetics*, 1975, *5*, 27–82.

STEBBINS, L. B., ST. PIERRE, R. G., PROPER, E. C., ANDERSON, R. B., & CERVA, T. R. *Education as experimentation: A planned variation model. Vol. IV-A: An evaluation of Follow Through.* Cambridge, Mass.: Abt Associates, Inc., Report of Contract No. 300–75–0134, prepared for the U.S. Office of Education, 1977.

STEIN, Z., SUSSER, M., SAENGER, G., & MAROLLA, F. Nutrition and mental performance. *Science*, 1972, *178*, 708–713.

STODOLSKY, S. S., & LESSER, G. Learning patterns in the disadvantaged. *Harvard Educational Review*, 1967, *37*, 546–593.

THORNDIKE, R. L. Mr. Binet's test 70 years later. *Educational Researcher*, 1975, *4*, No. 5, 3–7.

THURSTONE, L. L. Primary mental abilities. Psychometric Monographs, 1938, No. 1.

TROTTER, R. Environment and behavior: Intensive intervention program prevents retardation. *APA Monitor*, 1976, *7*, 4.

TRYON, R. C. Genetic differences in maze-learning ability in rats. *Yearbook of the National Society for the Study of Education*, 1940, *39*, (1), 111–119.

TUDDENHAM, R. D. Soldier intelligence in World Wars I and II. *American Psychologist*, 1948, *3*, 54–56.

U.S. Commission on Civil Rights. *Racial isolation in the public schools* (Vol. 1). Washington, D.C.: U.S. Government Printing Office, 1967.

VANDENBERG, S. G. Assortative mating, or who marries whom? *Behavior Genetics*, 1972, *2*, 127–157.

VELANDIA, W., GRANDON, G., & PAGE, E. B. Family size, birth order, and intelligence in a large South American sample. *American Educational Research Journal*, 1978, *15*, 399–416.

WADE, N. IQ and heredity: Suspicion of fraud beclouds classic experiment. *Science*, 1976, *194*, 916–919.

WALLER, J. H. Achievement and social mobility: Relationships among IQ scores, education, and occupation in two generations. *Social Biology*, 1971, *18*, 252–259. (a)

WALLER, J. H. Differential reproduction: Its relation to IQ test score, education, and occupation. *Social Biology*, 1971, *18*, 122–136. (b)

WESTINGHOUSE LEARNING CORPORATION/OHIO UNIVERSITY. *The impact of Head Start.* Springfield, Virginia: Clearinghouse for Federal Scientific and Technical Information, U.S. Department of Commerce, 1969.

WHEELER, L. R. A comparative study of the intelligence of East Tennessee mountain children. *Journal of Educational Psychology*, 1942, *33*, 321–334.

8

MORAL DEVELOPMENT AND MORAL BEHAVIOR

Myra Windmiller

I was led to the question of how an individual forms a coherent value system through my interest in politics and in how to effect political change long before I became a psychologist who was interested in the learning and behavior problems of children and adolescents. I remember the long arguments into the late, late hours with fellow students about the nature of people: were they fundamentally good or evil, did they always act out of self-interest, did they have free will, were their social institutions molded by them or were they molded by their institutions? The ultimate question seemed to be whether or not *just*, social and political institutions could be created by moral individuals, and if so, how then were moral individuals created? ,

I know now that it is the function of late adolescence to reinvent these inquiries over and over again. This process is part of identity formation and, reciprocally, part of consolidating a personal moral position. Moreover, it is necessary to rerun these historical inquiries through a contemporary perspective. It is only in this way that fresh insights emerge and theories continue to be refined. They are the same questions that have been asked through the centuries: "What is the nature of justice?" "What is virtue?" Scholars, teachers, parents, and others also ask these questions, albeit in different forms. For some it is a matter of pure intellectual interest, while for others it is a matter of needing to understand moral development for a purpose: for child-rearing, for educating, for decision making, for generating new hypotheses.

When some people inquire into the moral development of the adolescent, they are really asking whether the child has been socialized into the society and whether the child has assimilated both institutional and personal values. Parents want to know whether they have been successful as parents in rearing "good children." Schools want to know if they have fulfilled their mission of transmitting cultural values and the Western heritage. The church wants to know if it is still a viable force in teaching spiritual and value tenets; while the courts want to be certain that the adolescent will not become a juvenile delinquent and a ward of the state. Everyone seems to have a stake in the outcome of the moral development of the adolescent. What we presently know about moral development, however, suggests that the impact of parents, the church, or the school on direct inculcation of moral principles in the child is questionable.

If one accepts this as true, the problem then becomes one of explaining how the child, and later the adolescent and the adult, acquires what we call

---

Myra Windmiller is a lecturer in the Department of Education and coordinator of the School Psychology Program at the University of California, Berkeley. She is coauthor of *Moral Development and Socialization: Three Perspectives,* and has also written articles on hyperactivity in children, language and cognition, and adaptive behavior and mental retardation.

morality and a system of values. In this chapter, I will explain moral development as described by current psychological theories, together with the significant variables that affect that development. There are other questions that will also be considered: How does one account for the particular qualitative change in moral development that coincides with adolescence? Are there distinctions between moral judgments and moral behavior; that is, can one *say* one thing with respect to moral principles and yet *do* another? Can morality be raised to a higher level or can values be taught?

CURRENT MORAL DEVELOPMENT THEORIES

There are three theories of moral development in contemporary psychological literature: the Freudian or psychoanalytic, the social learning, and the cognitive-developmental or structural-developmental. While the focus of this chapter is on the structural-developmental theory, it is of interest to review all three of the theoretical models to contrast and compare the differences and similarities among them.

Psychoanalytic Theory

The *superego*, or conscience, is Freud's term for that portion of the personality that acts as a guardian or agent of restraint. It is one of the three parts of the personality in psychoanalytic theory and the last to develop, at about age 5. Freud postulated that the individual is born with the *id*, a manifestation of the pleasure principle. The id represents instincts and passions, and is unrestrained and is completely internal to the world of the self. Later as the individual begins to differentiate himself or herself from the environment, the *ego* develops. The ego becomes an important organizer of the self and brings the reality of the outside world to the id. The *superego* next develops out of the ego, coincident with resolution of the Oedipal complex during the so-called *phallic* period. The child forms an *identification* with his or her parents, accepts their values, and *internalizes* these values as controls. In this way, parents are the origin of the individual's moral system, and their influence lasts for a lifetime.

The superego then functions to keep the individual from committing wrongful acts. If a person is tempted to transgress, he or she will begin to experience feelings of guilt. To avoid the guilt, the individual resists temptation. Thus the superego, which continues to be further elaborated during the period of *latency* from ages 6 to 11, becomes the child's mechanism for self-control. Where earlier the child depended on parents to exert overt control, the parents' prohibitions now become the child's. The superego becomes in effect the agent of society, "the moral arbiter of conduct" (Hall & Lindzey, 1957, p. 35), inhibiting the potentially immoral impulses of the id.

At later periods in one's life, at adolescence for example, teachers, authority figures, or heroes may serve as moral models because they are associated with early memories of parents. In the Freudian model of values acquisition, it is difficult to explain the change over time that we know occurs in moral development. Perhaps we must look to other forces operating within the individual and his or her environment to explain these developments.

Social Learning Theory

Social learning theorists like Bandura and Walters (1963) say that morality is learned initially through modeling and imitation. The child has a model in a parent or other significant adult and initially learns through external controls of reward and punishment which kinds of behavior to perpetuate or eliminate. Presumably, those behavior patterns that are reinforced and maintained are later internalized and become a basis for self-controls. In other words, moral behavior is like any other behavior that is learned and retained through reinforcement contingencies.

In social learning theory, it is the internalization of cultural norms as values of right or wrong that determines the moral development of the child. In this approach, the values are relative and are tied to the culture in which one is born and grows up. Later, during adolescence, peer group interactions are important because adolescents look to peers for support and validation. (See chapter 4 by Hamachek for a thorough discussion of this process.) But it is parents who are the vehicles for the cultural transmission of what is moral. In this way, social learning and psychoanalytic theories are alike: they both attribute origins of morality to the internalization of values passed on from parents.

According to social learning theory, the style of parental discipline plays a central role in the child's ability to internalize controls at an early age. Parents who explain and give verbal reasons for approval or disapproval of behavior facilitate the child's understanding of what is expected and help the child to anticipate the consequences of his or her actions. Apparently these children tend to avoid transgressions in order to escape the feelings of guilt that ensue from antisocial acts. Becker (1964) thinks that excessive parental control, hostility, and physical punishment result in increased antisocial behavior and aggression on the part of the child. It seems that aggressive behavior from the parent does not lead to moral learning, but instead makes the child more aggressive. On the other hand, children from warm, loving, nonpunitive homes where constraints are verbalized are more likely to refrain from delinquent behavior.

Staub (1975) has found, for example, that the most important predictor of *prosocial* behavior in a child is the existence of a warm, nurturant, and affectionate relationship between the child and his or her parents. He says that prosocial behavior is the result of previously internalized values. But more important, the process of committing a prosocial act, which positively affects the welfare of others, becomes a reinforcement. In this way, prosocial behavior tends to perpetuate itself, for by being intrinsically rewarding, one prosocial act is apt to lead to another. In addition, Staub says that teaching others, no matter what content is being taught, tends to promote later prosocial behavior. This suggests that teaching in and of itself is a prosocial behavior and contains its own intrinsic rewards. From these clues, it is possible to speculate on the origins of *antisocial* behavior. Sieber (1972) warns that unless a person forms a satisfactory emotional attachment with an adult during the first few years of life, there is little likelihood of internalization of positive social values.

One should note that the social learning theorists speak consistently of moral *behavior* and this approach has built its formulations around the explanation for moral behavior and why people act as they do. Another theory, the structural-developmental theory, is based on how individuals make *judgments* and the way they reason about moral issues.

Structural-Developmental Approach

Building on the initial work of Piaget (1932), Lawrence Kohlberg (1958) has proposed that moral development proceeds in predictable stages in the individual and that it is a part of general cognitive growth and development. The child's cognitive structure establishes the broad limits of moral posture, and these limits change and become more elaborate as the cognitive structure becomes more complex. Within the framework of general cognition, the specifics of moral development may be attenuated by environmental factors, but it is the individual's basic intellectual development that sets the pace for the value system.

One should remember that intellectual development itself results from the constant interaction of the individual and the environment. According to Piaget (1950), human beings are not passive learners; that is, they actively construct their reality and build their mental structures in a kind of spiraling effect, one structure emerging out of the previous one. Thus it is not only simple maturation or environmental experience that affects the cognitive growth of the child but the interplay of the two, with the individual simultaneously assimilating and accommodating to the environment. Sometimes called cognitive-developmental, this approach is identified increasingly as the structuralist or structural-developmental approach (Turiel, 1975; Daman, 1977). In chapter 6 you read about the work of Piaget in some detail which should assist you in understanding what follows.

211

Piaget's Theory. Piaget (1932–1965) formulated a stage theory of moral development in which he assumed a cognitive base for moral judgments. He was able to show that a child acquires a value system in a regularized and systematic manner. He started by looking at children's games and asking them about the rules that governed their conduct of the games. From their responses, he deduced that at the earliest stages children regard rules as immutable and as carrying an inherent authority.

According to Piaget, the child's general acquiescence to obedience without question derives in part from parental authority, which the child sees as all-powerful. Later the child learns that rules can be changed by mutual agreement and that they are no longer sacred. In effect, the child becomes more autonomous. Similarly, the parent is no longer viewed as the ultimate authority, and the child sees that "justice prevails over obedience" (Piaget & Inhelder, 1969, p. 127).

As children become more sensitive to their peer group, Piaget said that they become more autonomous and tend to adopt moral strategies consistent with those of their peers. They do not, however, do this by a modeling or imitative process; rather, they experience a decline in egocentrism and are then able to take the point of view of another and to engage in cooperative and reciprocal behavior. Rules and values then become "interiorized" or internalized and "a new morality follows upon that of pure duty" (Piaget, 1965, p. 404). Adolescent moral development for Piaget is a continuation of the autonomous phase, but it becomes tempered by changes in adolescent cognitive development.

Kohlberg's Theory. Kohlberg (1958) found that by introducing a series of moral dilemmas to subjects ages ten to sixteen and by categorizing the responses he was able to produce a scale from which six discrete stages emerged. The dilemmas he used were similar to the following:

Is it better to save the life of one important person or a lot of unimportant people?

A man's wife is starving to death but the grocer won't give the man any food unless he can pay. He has no money, so should he break in and steal some food? Why?

Should a doctor "mercy kill" a fatally ill woman requesting death because of her pain?

Should a boy tell his father a confidence about a brother's misdeed?

There were no right or wrong answers to these dilemmas, but Kohlberg found that the reasoning behind whatever decisions were made by the subjects fell into discernible patterns usually related to age. He arranged these patterns into three levels and six stages. The first two stages, a *punishment-obedience* orientation and an *instrumental relativist* orientation, form

Level I, which Kohlberg called pre-moral or preconventional. Stages 3 and 4, a *good boy-good girl* orientation and a *law and order* orientation, form Level II, called conventional. The last two stages, a *social contract* orientation and a *value of human life* orientation, form Level III, called postconventional or principled. Table 8.1 shows a matrix of these stages.

Table 8.2 shows the actual responses of children and adolescents to moral dilemmas and the stages to which their responses were assigned (Kohlberg, 1964, p. 401).

Kohlberg has suggested that his moral stages parallel Piaget's *cognitive* (but not Piaget's moral) stages. For example, Kohlberg's conventional level is reached only after Piaget's stage of concrete operations is achieved, whereas Piaget's formal operations stage is necessary before an individual can function at Kohlberg's principled level. It does not necessarily work the other way around, however. In other words, arriving at a particular cognitive stage does not guarantee that an individual will function at a higher level of moral development. Not all individuals progress through all of the stages. While the sequence of stages does not vary and one must go through each stage successively, the stage at which one stops is governed by individual differences and by one's own peculiar interaction with the environment.

The hypothesis that cognitive stages are predictive of moral stages has seemed reasonable, and some investigators have found empirical support for the relationship between Piaget's cognitive stages and Kohlberg's moral stages.

Kohlberg (1976) hypothesizes that role taking is the mechanism by which the individual moves through the moral stages. He makes it clear that these stages reflect ways of thinking and making of moral judgments and are "not a grading of the moral worth of the individual" (p. 46). Role taking is the ability to put oneself in the role of another. It is related to empathy and to the ability to "decenter," that is, to take the point of view of another. Some investigators (Selman & Damon, 1975) contend that role taking proceeds in stages as does cognition, while others (Turiel, 1976) respond that it can occur at any age. Turiel says, for example, that it is the content of the role-taking activity that determines whether the child can perform the role, not just the ability to "role take" per se. Kohlberg says that parents who provide children opportunities for role taking are providing opportunities for moral growth and development. Peers also provide these opportunities, for presumably exposure to other points of view introduces cognitive conflict, which in turn facilitates the onset of new ways of making judgment and thus accelerates development.

Kohlberg (1976) refers to role-taking level as one's level of social cognition and argues that role taking is a prerequisite for moving to a high moral stage. Another explanation for movement through the stages comes from Piaget's work on cognitive development. The general mechanism by

213

TABLE 8.1 *Kohlberg's Stages of Moral Development*

LEVELS	APPROXIMATE AGE	STAGES
I. Pre-Moral or Preconventional	4–5	1. Punishment-Obedience orientation Judgments are made on the basis of avoiding punishment or obtaining rewards.
Reasons given rest on external sanctions, with accommodation to prestige and power	6–9	2. Instrumental Relativist orientation Judgments are made on the basis of reciprocal favors or fulfilling one's needs. A *quid pro quo* view.
II. Conventional	10–15	3. Good Boy–Good Girl orientation Judgments are made on the basis of pleasing others, avoiding criticism, or incurring other's displeasure.
Reasons given reveal conformity, loyalty and support of authority and the social order, and identification with the people involved in it.	15–18	4. Law and Order orientation Judgments are made on the basis of maintaining respect for authority and in obeying the law because it is the law. Social conformity as a way of upholding the social order.
III. Postconventional or Principled	18–20	5. Social Contract orientation Judgments are made on the basis of individual rights and standards which have been agreed upon by the whole society.
Reasons given define values and principles independent of the authority of groups or people holding the values	20–	6. Value of Human Life orientation Judgments are made on the basis of consequence in accord with ethical principles such as justice, equality, reciprocity of human rights, and respect for the dignity of human beings.

TABLE 8.2 *Moral Stages of Children and Adolescents in Response to Moral Dilemma Questions*

STAGE 1:	*Punishment—Danny, age 10:*
	(Should Joe tell on his older brother to his father?)
	"In one way it would be right to tell on his brother or his father might get mad at him and spank him. In another way it would be right to keep quiet or his brother might beat him up."
STAGE 2:	*Exchange and Reward—Jimmy, age 13:*
	(Should Joe tell on his older brother to his father?)
	"I think he should keep quiet. He might want to go someplace like that, and if he squeals on Alex, Alex might squeal on him."
STAGE 3:	*Disapproval Concern—Andy, age 16:*
	(Should Joe keep quiet about what his brother did?)
	"If my father finds out later, he won't trust me. My brother wouldn't either, but I wouldn't have a 'conscience' that he (my brother) didn't." "I try to do things for my parents; they've always done things for me. I try to do everything my mother says; I try to please her. Like she wants me to be a doctor, and I want to, too, and she's helping me to get up there."
STAGE 4:	*Life Sacred Because of a Social and Religious Order—John, age 16:*
	(Should the doctor "mercy-kill" the woman?)
	"The doctor wouldn't have the right to take a life, no human has the right. He can't create life, he shouldn't destroy it."
STAGE 6:	*Self-Condemnation Concern—Bill, age 16:*
	(Should the husband steal the expensive black market drug needed to save his wife's life?)
	"Lawfully no, but morally speaking I think I would have done it. It would be awfully hard to live with myself afterward, knowing that I could have done something which would have saved her life and yet didn't for fear of punishment to myself."

Note. From "Development of Moral Character and Moral Ideology," by Lawrence Kolberg, from Review of Child Development Research, Volume One, by Martin L. Hoffman and Lois Wladis Hoffman, Editors, © 1964 by Russell Sage Foundation.

which development is thought to occur is disequilibrium. Disequilibrium is introduced when the individual is presented with information that contradicts previously held beliefs and for which the individual must make some adjustment. Equilibrium is reestablished when the conflicting views are resolved. This is the way cognitive development is accelerated and provides an explanation for the way moral development advances as well.

Turiel's Theory. The structuralist position is not monolithic, however. The structural-developmental approach is evolving to define moral development more precisely within the confines of general social development.

As the field of social cognition grows, so do the hypotheses about role taking (Selman & Damon, 1975; Turiel, 1977), concepts of justice, sharing, and authority in young children (Damon, 1975, 1977), and the development of social conventional thinking as separate and distinct from that of moral development (Turiel, 1975, 1977).

Turiel argues that concepts of sex roles, social politeness, forms of address, and dress codes are matters of social convention and are products of individual cultures and times. Moral issues, on the other hand, are universal and timeless and involve issues of justice and fairness. Both convention and morality are part of social development but form in different ways and from different developmental structures.

In a series of interviews on social conventional issues, such as whether children should be allowed to use first names to address their teachers, eat with their hands in the presence of company, or whether men could be hired for jobs traditionally filled by women, Turiel found that there are ordered stages of thinking about these social conventional ideas. As the child, and later the adolescent and the adult develops, he or she acquires concepts about society and social rules and expectations in ordered ways. Rather than assuming that conventional ideas are simply less developed conceptions of morality, Turiel demonstrates that this dimension forms a separate kind of thinking with its own particular regularities. In other words, children and adolescents acquire notions about society independent of their acquisition of moral development, although that development may be proceeding simultaneously. This proposition may be useful in helping us account for the specific acceptance or negation of social rules in adolescence.

Kohlberg (1976) has now elaborated his stage theory to incorporate "a social perspective" within each of his three levels of moral development. He suggests that the second stage of all of the three levels is a consolidation of a concern with the *social* of each respective first stage. This consolidation represents a move from a purely personal consideration at the beginning of the level to a concern with the social at the end of each level. For example, Stages 1, 3, and 5 involve personal reasons for moral judgments: At Stage 1, children can view something only from their own perspective and their notion of what is a reward or punishment. At Stage 3, they are concerned with the ability to be a good friend on a person-to-person basis. At Stage 5, the person is concerned with individual rights like those guaranteed by the Bill of Rights.

Now look at the corresponding stage of each level. Stage 2 involves reciprocity with another ("you scratch my back and I'll scratch yours") and takes the other person's perspective into account. Stage 4 involves the individual's compliance with the social and legal system. Stage 6 involves a concern for universal human rights, including the creation of a just society. Within each level, a person moves from a concern with self to a concern with others in society. At the lowest level, the social concern involves a relationship with others. At the higher levels, it involves a concern with society and social principles.

This explanation is interesting, but it is not clear how this reformulation changes Kohlberg's approach to moral development in any significant way. It is a statement of how his stage theory incorporates both personal and social perspectives within one structure. It is his response to social learning theorists who criticize his approach for not taking social influences on behavior into account, and it is his response to other structuralists, like Turiel, who differentiate social conventional stages from those of moral development.

What is of greater potential interest is Kohlberg's move to assign the equivalent of moral stages to institutions in our society. He notes (1976) that institutions like prisons, some schools, and orphanages function at very low levels of moral development with a poverty of opportunities for "role taking" experiences. Individuals assigned to these institutions then are deprived of necessary social interactions that produce movement to higher levels of development. Kohlberg is pursuing empirical research on these ideas, in conjunction with moral education programs in prisons, schools, and orphanages.

In summary, the three major theories in modern psychological thought that purport to explain moral development are the psychoanalytic, the social learning, and the structural-developmental. The first two approaches are concerned with moral behavior, while the third provides an explanation for the development of moral judgments. Social learning theory says that "moral values are beliefs . . . shared in a social group about what is good or right" (Maccoby, 1968, p. 229). The structuralists define morality more narrowly as a concern for justice and fairness, but a concern that is universal to all humankind, regardless of the culture in which one lives. All three of these approaches emanate from historical, philosophical perspectives, and are tied by basic assumptions to major contemporary psychological theories: The psychoanalytic is related, of course, to Freud's personality theory, the social learning approach stems from behaviorism, while the structuralist approach is part of developmental psychology.

The structuralist approach, because it is developmental, offers the best explanation for the unique role of moral development in adolescence.

QUALITATIVE CHANGES IN MORAL DEVELOPMENT AT ADOLESCENCE

Two factors operating in adolescence contribute to significant changes in moral development. One is the onset of formal operations in cognitive development. The second, as pointed out by Erikson (1950, 1968), is the formation of a new identity and a sense of self.

The cognitive stage of formal operations is thought to be a necessary prerequisite for the individual to go beyond a conventional level of morality. For a person to take a principled moral position, that is, to think of social contracts or notions such as the greatest good for the greatest number, equal justice under law, or the value of human life, the individual must be able to think in abstract terms, to go beyond dealing with concrete situations, and to pose hypothetical problems. Formal operations thinking then is a preliminary to this.

Piaget and Inhelder (1969) have said that formal operations affect all facets of adolescent personality, so it is not just moral development that is at issue. Roger Brown (1965) contends that during adolescence there is a powerful emotional attachment to abstract ideas, and that the individual becomes able to visualize alternatives, to see new ways of doing things, and to conceptualize utopias. Piaget (1968, p. 60) argues that "adolescence assures thought and affectivity of an equilibrium superior to that which existed during middle and late childhood." These new thoughts and emotions lead to greater creativity, to intense religious feelings, and to preoccupations with one's self and one's feelings.

All adults, however, do not necessarily develop to a formal operations level. Kohlberg and Gilligan (1971) report findings that show that only 45% of adolescents have reached formal operations by age fifteen. By age thirty, this figure is about 65%. One may conclude that some 35% of adults never reach formal logical thinking, and only 25% reach principled moral thinking! So when we speak of formal operations affecting moral development in adolescence, we must remember that few individuals have the potential to reach Stage 5 by age fifteen. Few reach Stage 6 before age twenty. In fact, most adolescents remain in Stages 2, 3, and 4, as do many adults.

Identity and New Sense of Self

Erik Erikson (1950, 1968) tells us that adolescence is the time when many facets of an individual's personality come together to form a coherent sense of self. There is an integration of the self, an overt realization of who "I" is. This realization becomes an identity. It can also be called an *ego*, and presumably the greater the sense of coherence, the greater the *ego strength*.

As Erikson points out, this process does not necessarily cause a crisis. However, it sometimes does because often it involves a rejection of the family. Where once the child derived his or her identity from the child's integration within the family structure, now in order to achieve his or her own sense of self, there must be at least a psychological separation from the family unit. During the process of identity formation the adolescent is constantly testing out ideas and seeking confirmation of his or her new self.

Erikson reminds us (1968, p. 132) that "to a considerable extent adolescent love is an attempt to arrive at a definition of one's identity by projecting a diffused self-image on another and by seeing it thus reflected and gradually clarified."

There is also a phenomenon in early adolescence that has been labeled "adolescent egocentrism" (Elkind, 1974). According to Piaget (1968, p. 64) adolescent egocentrism is characterized by "belief in the omnipotence of reflection, as though the world should submit to idealistic schemes, rather than to systems of reality ... the self is strong enough to reconstruct the universe and big enough to incorporate it." Adolescent egocentrism thus is tied closely to the search for the self. There is a preoccupation with fulfilling grand schemes and having an impact on the world; to play an "essential role in the salvation of humanity ..." (p. 67). Piaget notes that adolescents are constantly meditating about society and the way they want to go about reforming it. They want to experiment and try different systems, social as well as personal. In effect, they are discovering anew the universal concerns of all humanity. The widespread appeal of a character like Holden Caulfield in Salinger's *Catcher in the Rye* can be explained by the accuracy with which Holden represents the adolescent transition to adulthood. All the manifestations are there: his complete adolescent egocentrism, his concern with establishing his identity, and the obvious formal operational thinking.

In moral development, there is a unique occurrence in late adolescence, which Turiel (1974) labels a *transitional* period between Stage 4, a conventional stage, and Stage 5, the beginning of principled moral thinking. As Turiel (1974, p. 20) comments, "While at Stage 4 moral value is undifferentiated from society's value, these subjects [in transition] distinguish between personal and societal values and view both as valid systems." Social values are, in addition, viewed as the way they ought to be rather than the way they are. Kohlberg (1976) calls this period Stage 4½, since the characteristics of this transition period include a rejection of conventional moral thinking, leading to the eventual adoption of principled moral thinking at Stage 5.

During the transition period, there is a reformulation of thought and a reorganization of structure such that judgments can be made at a higher level. A state of disequilibrium brought on by conflict and confusion, in turn leads to a new equilibrium.

The introduction of formal operational thinking and the quest for the self in adolescence result in a seesaw period of change and conflict that facilitates this development. The adolescent seeks after answers and attempts to find clarifications, not only about the self but also about the world and humanity. This includes the eternal questions of truth, justice, and the good. One's moral position thus becomes important as it is a part of the newly found self.

There have been several attempts to correlate stages of ego development, assumed to be a measure of the strength of the self, with stages of moral development. The results are somewhat equivocal. Sullivan, McCullough, and Stager (1970) administered Loevinger's (1966) scale of ego development and Kohlberg's moral dilemmas to 120 subjects, ages 12, 14, and 17. The correlation between ego development and moral development was .66 overall, with correlations of .19, .48, and .54 at ages 12, 14, and 17, respectively.

This supports the view that ego development becomes more important as age increases in adolescence, and the relationship with moral development becomes greater. Since identity and a new notion of self are beginning to form in early adolescence, the relationship between ego development and moral development should generally be strengthened as age increases.

It is of interest to note that Loevinger (1966) views moral development as a facet of ego development, whereas Kohlberg views ego development as a mediator between moral judgments and moral behavior. The point is that greater ego strength makes it easier for the individual to behave in ways that are compatible with the "conscience" and the person is less susceptible to external influences. Later, Kohlberg (1976, p. 53) has said more strongly that "certain features of ego development are a necessary but not sufficient condition for development of moral structures." Since both ego structures and moral structures assume a cognitive base, it is reasonable to assume that there would be a relationship between them, but we do not know precisely what it is. Both the ego development scale and the moral development scale have six stages through which individuals progress. Loevinger labels her stages as follows: impulse-ridden, opportunist, conformist, conscientious, autonomous, and integrated.

Haan, Stroud, and Holstein (1973) used Loevinger's ego development scale and Kohlberg's dilemmas to study "hippies" and found them to be generally higher in ego development than in moral development. The sample had an ego level consistent with that of most individuals of the same age, while their moral development was less than that of most people of the same age.

Podd (1972) also attempted to measure ego status and morality. He interviewed undergraduate college students in an attempt to assess their ego-identity status and their level of moral development. He found that those with an "ego identity" were at more mature levels of moral judgment, while those with a relative lack of ego identity were at much lower levels. He also found that subjects who were undergoing an "identity crisis" were unstable and inconsistent in their moral reasoning. Finally, Lambert (1972), also using Loevinger's scale and Kohlberg's dilemmas, found that ego development was somewhat ahead of moral development. He was unable to isolate a moral factor in Loevinger's test.

So the empirical evidence is not clear about whether ego development and moral development are strongly related. From two of the studies it would appear that ego development is more accelerated than moral development and perhaps acts to facilitate moral development. This is consistent with the hypothesis that moral *judgments* are influenced by ego development. Ego development then is possibly one variable that determines moral development in adolescence.

THE RELATIONSHIP BETWEEN MORAL JUDGMENTS AND MORAL BEHAVIOR

It is true that the structuralists have attempted to define the way moral judgments are made and have not attempted to explain moral behavior. One of my graduate students, in observing this fact, commented that ". . . behavior cannot be a neglected subject for the science of morality. By all commonsense notions, morality . . . involves how we treat others. It does not involve only how we think about them." This is a reasonable observation to make. Kohlberg has said that it is difficult to separate moral thought from moral action, particularly at higher stages of development:

> To act in a morally high way requires a high stage of moral reasoning. One cannot follow moral principles (Stages 5 and 6) if one does not understand or believe in them. One can, however, reason in terms of such principles and not live up to them. A variety of factors determines whether a particular person will live up to his stage of moral reasoning in a particular situation, though moral stage is a good predictor of action in various experimental and naturalistic settings. (Kohlberg, 1976, p. 32)

Similarly, Turiel (1973, p. 750) has noted that ". . . reasoning is related to action. The two are interrelated in the sense that the way an individual reasons relates to how he acts and the way he acts relates to how he reasons—theoretically a developmental stage reflects these two components and their interrelationship." Both Kohlberg and Turiel, then, say that moral stage is a reasonably good predictor of moral behavior. Turiel and Rothman (1972) and Rothman (1976) have demonstrated that the correspondence between moral behavior and moral reasoning is a function of stage level: The higher the stage, the greater the probability of acting in accord with one's moral reasoning.

This finding was demonstrated in Milgram's (1963) study of obedience to authority in which more subjects at Stage 6 than at lower stages refused to continue to participate in an experiment that required them to shock other subjects in a "learning experiment." It was also found in a fol-

221

low-up study of the Free Speech Movement students at Berkeley (Haan, Smith & Block, 1968) that more participants at Stage 6 sat in and were arrested than were those at lower stages.

What are other variables, however, that affect the relationship between moral judgments and moral behavior? Often it is the *situation* that determines whether or not an individual will behave in accord with his moral principles. Early studies of cheating in individuals (Hartshorne & May, 1930) showed that it is the situation that determines whether or not a person cheats. Most people will cheat in some circumstances, especially if there is no social pressure not to cheat. And different people give different reasons for cheating. Kohlberg and Turiel (1971) report that one cannot predict the later moral behavior of the adolescent who cheats. However, the adolescent who consistently does not cheat has most likely formulated reasons for not cheating and acts on that mature moral judgment. This is an important observation, for it requires moral maturity to refrain from committing antisocial acts where there is social sanction and peer pressure to commit them. This suggests that it may be difficult for many adolescents to behave in "moral ways" because they have not yet reached mature moral reasoning, and there may be no strong social sanction for behaving in "principled" ways. Superficially, the greatest compatibility between judgment and reasoning would seem to be at the conventional level because there are social sanctions for behaving in accord with societal demands; however, as Kohlberg indicates, post-conventional or principled thinking produces the great amount of accord.

Kohlberg and Kramer (1969) report that most people stabilize at functional stages within the conventional level. Men, they say, generally settle at Stage 4 while women settle at Stage 3, a stage compatible with traditional social roles for women. Gilligan (1977) has challenged Kohlberg on his assertion with respect to women, charging that Stage 3 is misplaced in the sequence of stages. She thinks that Stage 3, a concern about people and interpersonal relations, may belong beyond Stage 4 rather than below it; that Stage 3 represents a concern and responsibility for others that transcends the conventional thinking and conformity of Stage 4. Several investigators report no inherent sex differences in moral development, although situational or environmental variables may at times produce differences between males and females in the rate of development.

Information from Rest, Davison and Robbins (1978) reveals that it is primarily level of education that is positively related to moral development in early adulthood. They indicate that moral development appears to progress, however slowly, as long as the individual is acquiring formal schooling. Yet moral stage appears to stabilize with the end of formal education unless the individual is involved in an occupation that "emphasizes moral thinking." This finding suggests implications for whether or not values can be taught.

CAN MORAL VALUES BE TAUGHT?

When our secretary typed an earlier version of this chapter, she mentioned that it was interesting, but not particularly useful. When I asked why not, she responded by saying, "Well, it doesn't tell me how to raise my kids." I have to admit that she is right. There is no formula for producing a moral child or adolescent based on our current theories of moral development or behavior.

If we can formulate the question in a different way, however, and ask whether we can increase our understanding of moral issues and perhaps facilitate growth to higher levels of moral reasoning, then the answer is more hopeful. There are several programs now that seek to teach moral principles indirectly. Most of these use a system based on a developmental psychology approach that relies on introducing disequilibrium. Borrowing from Piaget what is known about cognitive development, the teaching aims to improve problem-solving abilities rather than to provide ready-made answers to concrete situations. An opportunity is provided for the student to engage in confrontations and to see inconsistencies in solutions to moral dilemmas. Rest (1974, p. 245) suggests that the best kind of program is one that presents experiences "which 'stretch' one's thinking and set into motion this search-and-discovery process for more adequate ways to organize experience and action."

For a moral education program to be successful, efforts must be made to approximate the student's current level of moral development. Rest, Turiel, and Kohlberg (1969) exposed students to arguments one stage above, two stages above, or one stage below their actual level of development. They found that the students assimilated more new thinking when the arguments presented were one stage above their current level. While the modes of thinking above their own levels were more difficult to comprehend, they simply rejected arguments that were below their own levels. Rest (1973), in a similar study, showed that students preferred arguments at one stage above their own level. These studies suggest that materials presented in any moral education program should be tailored to, or above, the students' developmental level in order to advance their thinking to a higher moral level.

However, this is not all that is needed to move an individual to a higher moral position. The listener must not only be exposed to an argument but also must be actively involved. In other words, the listener must engage in a struggle or conflict to attempt to resolve competing ideas. As previously discussed, the process of moving to a higher stage requires internal cognitive reorganization rather than a simple acquisition of information from outside.

Many schools have instituted "values clarification" units (Simon,

223

Howe & Kirschenbaum, 1972) that are concerned with the process of valuing rather than with the values themselves. The aim is to develop in students the ability to make choices and decisions and to recognize that this is
an on-going feature in life. Lockwood (1978) has reported on a number of
moral education projects and values clarification projects as well. He concludes that overall the effect of the direct discussion approach in the developmental programs is toward increasing stage development, although
slowly and somewhat tentatively. There were substantial differences in the
effect on the participants, some moving rapidly to new stages, especially in
adolescence, but others not at all. The results of values clarification approaches were less clear, partly because the objectives of many of the studies were less precise. In general, clarification gains seemed to be greater
with younger children and seemed to take the form of increased self-esteem
and variables apart from, although possibly related to, moral development.

Another approach to moral education may lie in our social institutions. As noted earlier, Kohlberg has said that some of our institutions, because of the nature of their functions, manifest a stage level of their own.
Sullivan (1978) has suggested that a reformulation of the aims of education
and a new curriculum must take place before any significant change in
moral education will be evident. As one who has attempted moral education in the schools through the introduction of moral dilemmas for discussion, he is convinced that small increments in development can be induced.
On the other hand, he is less optimistic about any long-term gains, because
of the overriding negative impact of the institution of the school and society itself. An institution that is naturally conservative and that restricts
efforts to confront basic dilemmas in society cannot move individuals to
higher levels of development. Sullivan's perspective argues that more is
needed than a simple determination of the individual's stage level and arguments above that level for the individual to confront. He says that a
major overhaul in our educational institutions is required before any significant change in development will be evident.

Rohwer, Ammon, and Cramer (1974, p. 244) formulate the question
this way:

> Is the goal simply to promote the individual's survival in the world as he
> finds it, or is there more to education than that? Man lives in an en-
> vironment that is largely his own creation. Thus, he has the option of
> changing the environment, instead of simply accepting it the way it is
> and learning to live with it. Man is given the possibility of changing the
> environment in such a way that it will enhance the quality of life for the
> species as a whole. The goal of education might be redefined, then, as
> the facilitation of man's development toward that end.
>
> Piaget's period of concrete operations and Kohlberg's level of con-
> ventional moral judgment represent forms of cognition that permit
> equilibrium with regard to the way things are. On the other hand, for-

mal operations and principled morality permit equilibrium with regard to the way things could be . . . it seems clear that the ultimate goal of education should be to facilitate development to its highest stages.

The solution to this problem requires educational and institutional change as well as general social and political progress. Adolescence is the time when many personal moral issues will be resolved for the individual. It is when a person can move most quickly to new levels of development if opportunities are consistently provided and creative alternatives are proposed. Whether the adult with the potential to do so will move to a principled level or will remain at a conventional level or below is likely to be decided at adolescence. Our task then is to maximize the adolescent's probabilities for achievement of principled levels of development. At the present time, only 25% of the population does reach this level. The paradox is evident: for individuals to change our social institutions so that highly moral individuals emerge, requires thinking at a principled level on the part of those who have come from those same institutions. In other words, can persons from lower-level institutions be expected to think in high level ways? This is an issue for all of us to confront.

SUMMARY

This chapter discusses important elements that contribute to qualitative changes in adolescent moral development. These elements are the onset of formal operations in cognitive development and the formation of identity and a sense of self. It is in adolescence, when one acquires a sense of self, that the individual recognizes the existence of a personal value system.

Three major competing theories endeavor to explain moral development. The first, psychoanalytic, is based on Freudian notions about the superego as the guardian of one's morals. The second comes from social learning theory and states that a child learns morality by modeling and imitation. The third derives from the work of Piaget and Kohlberg and assumes a cognitive or structural-developmental base for moral judgments. This chapter utilizes Kohlberg's six stages of moral development to explain how children and adolescents acquire values.

According to Kohlberg, children proceed successively through these stages in a systematic way, with the child's cognitive development determining the rate of his progress and the stage at which he or she stops. The structuralists define morality as a universal concern for justice.

Adolescence is important in the determination of the individual's lifelong value system, because at that time several variables determine whether the adolescent will adopt a *principled level* of morality or remain at a *conventional level* or below, where judgments are made on the basis of obedience to authority and conformity to the social order. At a principled level the individual makes judgments according to universal ethical principles based on the rights of the individual and the value of human life. It is in this context that the relationship between moral judgments, moral behavior and social conventional thought has been discussed.

Finally, the question of whether or not values can be taught is raised. They cannot be directly inculcated, but if opportunities are provided for the individual to face conflicts and inconsistencies in ideas, then basic cognitive reorganization can occur. This cognitive reorganization, in turn, sets in motion an advance in moral development.

SUGGESTIONS FOR FURTHER READING

DePalma, D., & Foley, J. (Eds.). *Moral development: Current theory and research.* Hillsdale, N.J.: Lawrence Erlbaum Associates, 1975.

Hoffman, M. L. Moral development. In P. H. Mussen (Ed.), *Carmichael's manual of child psychology* (Vol. 2). New York: Wiley, 1970.

Kohlberg, L. *Education for justice: A modern statement of the Platonic view.* In N. F. Sizer & T. R. Sizer (Eds.), *Moral education/Five lectures.* Cambridge: Harvard University Press, 1970.

Kohlberg, L., & Turiel, E. *Moral development and moral education.* In G. Lesser (Ed.), *Psychology and educational practice.* Chicago: Scott, Foresman, 1971.

Likona, T. (Ed.). *Moral development and behavior.* New York: Holt, Rinehart and Winston, 1976.

BIBLIOGRAPHY

Bandura, A., & Walters, R. H. *Social learning and personality development.* New York: Holt, Rinehart and Winston, 1963.

Becker, W. C. Consequences of different kinds of parental discipline. In M. L. Hoffman and L. Hoffman (Eds.), *Review of child development research.* New York: Russell Sage, 1964.

Brown, R. *Social psychology.* New York: Free Press, 1965.

Damon, W. Early conceptions of positive justice as related to the development of logical operations. *Child Development,* 1975, *46,* 301–312.

Damon, W. *The social world of the child.* San Francisco: Jossey-Bass, 1977.

Elkind, D. *Children and adolescents: Interpretative essays on Jean Piaget* (2nd ed.). New York: Oxford University Press, 1974.

Erikson, E. H. *Children and society.* New York: Norton, 1950.

Erikson, E. H. *Identity: Youth and crisis.* New York: Norton, 1968.

Gilligan, C. In a different voice: Women's conception of the self and morality. *Harvard Educational Review,* 1977, *47,* 481–517.

Haan, N., Smith, B., & Block, J. Moral reasoning of young adults: Political-social behavior, family background, and personality correlates. *Journal of Personality and Social Psychology,* 1968, *10,* 183–201.

HAAN, N., STROUD, J., & HOLSTEIN, C. Moral and ego stages in relationship to ego processes: A study of "hippies." *Journal of Personality,* 1973, *41,* 596–612.

HALL, C., & LINDZEY, G. *Theories of personality.* New York: Wiley, 1957.

HARTSHORNE, H., & MAY, M. S. *Studies in the nature of character: Studies in the organization of character* (Vol. III). New York: Macmillan, 1930.

KOHLBERG, L. *The development of modes of moral thinking and choice in years ten to sixteen.* Unpublished doctoral dissertation. University of Chicago, 1958.

KOHLBERG, L. Development of moral character and moral ideology. In M. L. Hoffman & L. Hoffman (Eds.), *Review of child development research.* New York: Russell Sage, 1964.

KOHLBERG, L. Moral stages and moralization. In T. Likona (Ed.), *Moral development and behavior.* New York: Holt, Rinehart and Winston, 1976.

KOHLBERG, L., & GILLIGAN, C. Twelve to sixteen: Earley adolescence. *Daedalus,* Fall, 1971.

KOHLBERG, L., & KRAMER, R. B. Continuities and discontinuities in childhood and adult moral development. *Human Development,* 1969, *12,* 93–120.

KOHLBERG, L., & TURIEL, E. Moral development and moral education. In G. Lesser (Ed.), *Psychology and educational practice.* Chicago: Scott, Foresman, 1971.

LAMBERG, H. A comparison of cognitive development theories of ego and moral development. *Proceedings of the Annual Convention of the American Psychological Association,* 1972, *7,* 115–116.

LOCKWOOD, A. Effects of values curricula. *Review of Educational Research,* 1978, *48,* 325–364.

LOEVINGER, J. The meaning and measurement of ego development. *American Psychologist,* 1966, *21,* 195–206.

MOCCOBY, E. Moral values and behavior in childhood. In J. A. Clausen (Ed.), *Socialization and society.* Boston: Little, Brown, 1968.

MILGRAM, S. Behavioral study of obedience. *Journal of Abnormal and Social Psychology,* 1963, *67,* 371–378.

PIAGET, J. *The moral judgment of the child* (1932). Glencoe, Ill.: Free Press, 1965.

PIAGET, J. *The psychology of intelligence.* New York: Harcourt Brace, 1950.

PIAGET, J. *Six psychological studies.* New York: Vintage, 1968.

PIAGET, J., & INHELDER, B. *The psychology of the child.* New York: Basic Books, 1969.

PODD, N. H. Ego identity status and morality: The relationship between two developmental constructs. *Developmental Psychology,* 1972, *6,* 497–507.

REST, J. Developmental psychology and value education. *Review of Educational Research,* 1974, *44,* 241–259.

REST, J., DAVISON, M., & ROBBINS, S. Age trends in judging moral issues: A review of cross-sectional, longitudinal, and sequential studies of the defining issues test. *Child Development,* 1978, *49,* 263–279.

REST, J., TURIEL, E., & KOHLBERG, L. Level of moral development as a determinant of preference and comprehension of moral judgments made by others. *Journal of Personality,* 1969, *37,* 225–252.

ROHWER, W., AMMON, P. & CRAMER, P. *Understanding intellectual development.* Hinsdale, Ill.: Dryden Press, 1974.

ROTHMAN, G. The influence of moral reasoning on behavioral choices. *Child Development*, 1976, *47*, 397–406.

SELMAN, R., & DAMON, W. The necessity (but insufficiency) of social perspective taking for conceptions of justice at three early levels. In D. DePalma & J. Foley (Eds.), *Moral development: Current theory and research*. Hillsdale, N.J.: Lawrence Erlbaum Assoc., 1975.

SIEBER, J. A social learning theory approach to morality. In M. Windmiller, N. Lambert & E. Turiel (Eds.), *Moral development and socialization*. Boston: Allyn and Bacon, 1980.

SIMON, S. B., HOWE, L. W., & KIRSCHENBAUM, H. *Values clarification*. New York: Hart, 1972.

STAUB, E. To rear a prosocial child: Reasoning, learning by doing and learning by touching others. In D. DePalma & J. Foley (Eds.), *Moral development: Current theory and research*. Hillsdale, N.J.: Laurence Erlbaum, 1975.

SULLIVAN, E., McCULLOUGH, G., & STAGER, M. A developmental study of the relationship between conceptual, ego and moral development. *Child Development*, 1970, *4*, 399–412.

SULLIVAN, E. V. Can values be taught? Unpublished paper, OISE, Toronto, 1978.

TURIEL, E. Stage transition in moral development. In R. Travers (Ed.), *Second handbook of research on teaching*. Chicago: Rand McNally, 1973.

TURIEL, E. Conflict and transition in adolescent moral development. *Child Development*, 1974, *45*, 14–29.

TURIEL, E. The development of social concepts: Mores, customs and conventions. In D. J. DePalma & J. M. Foley (Eds.), *Moral development: Current theory and research*. Hillsdale, N.J.: Lawrence Erlbaum, 1975.

TURIEL, E. Concepts of society in children and adolescents. Paper presented at the Western Regional Conference of the Society for Research in Child Development, Emeryville, California, April 3, 1976.

TURIEL, E. The development of concepts of social structures. In J. Glick & A. Clarke-Stewart (Eds.), *Personality and social development* (Vol. 1). New York: Gardner Press, 1977.

TURIEL, E., & ROTHMAN, G. The influence of reasoning on behavioral choices at different stages of moral development. *Child Development*, 1972, *43*, 741–756.

9

SEX ROLE DEVELOPMENT AND THE ADOLESCENT

Aletha Huston-Stein
Renate L. Welch

Many readers may begin this chapter with questions about how adolescents can avoid traditional sex roles rather than with an interest in cultivating sex role acquisition. The women's liberation movement has drawn attention to the drawbacks involved in defining appropriate and inappropriate activities for individuals on the basis of biological gender. Increasingly, many assumptions that were previously unquestioned have been subjected to careful scrutiny and criticism. Should we teach little boys and little girls to be different? If so, what are we teaching them now? How does the learning of sex roles influence their overall adjustment, ability to function as adults, relations with peers and others? Would we be better off if individuals were permitted by society to develop without regard to gender? Do traditional sex roles provide some useful division of labor in the family or in the society? And, finally, are prevalent sex differences partially based on biological predispositions that are unlikely to be modified by social and cultural changes?

We will be concerned with many of these questions in this chapter on adolescent sex role development. We will raise serious questions about the value of many traditional sex role definitions because we believe they unduly restrict individuals from having a full range of choices in their lives. On the other hand, we see value in some aspects of both masculinity and femininity. The main danger in sex role definitions is the elimination of certain possibilities as options. An artistically talented boy may not develop that talent because he thinks art is feminine or for sissies. Similarly, a girl has to buck a lot of ridicule and self-doubt about her "femininity" if she wants to be a carpenter. Questions about the advantages and disadvantages of traditional sex roles apply to males at least as much as to females. In some respects, the male role in American society is defined more rigidly and with less latitude for deviation than the female role.

WHAT DO WE MEAN BY SEX ROLE?

If you ask a group of friends to name the characteristics that are defined as masculine and feminine in America, you will easily obtain a list on which almost everyone agrees. It will probably correspond closely to the list in Table 9.1 obtained from a sample of adults. Sex role concepts represent one's knowledge of culturally defined sex roles. By the time children reach early adolescence, their sex role concepts are well developed; they can pro-

Aletha Huston-Stein is Professor of Human Development at the University of Kansas. She has published a number of articles and chapters and is particularly interested in the socialization of achievement orientation and sex role development in females as well as the influence of television on children.

Renate L. Welch is a doctoral candidate in human development at the University of Kansas. She has written on androgyny and employment among adult women.

TABLE 9.1 *Male-valued and Female-valued Stereotypic Items*

FEMININE POLE	MASCULINE POLE
Male-valued items (the masculine pole is socially desirable)	
Not at all aggressive	Very aggressive
Not at all independent	Very independent
Very emotional	Not at all emotional
Does not hide emotions at all	Almost always hides emotions
Very subjective	Very objective
Very easily influenced	Not at all easily influenced
Very submissive	Very dominant
Dislikes math and science very much	Likes math and science very much
Very excitable in a minor crisis	Not at all excitable in a minor crisis
Very passive	Very active
Not at all competitive	Very competitive
Very illogical	Very logical
Very home oriented	Very worldly
Not at all skilled in business	Very skilled in business
Very sneaky	Very direct
Does not know the way of the world	Knows the way of the world
Feelings easily hurt	Feelings not easily hurt
Not at all adventurous	Very adventurous
Has difficulty making decisions	Can make decisions easily
Cries very easily	Never cries
Almost never acts as a leader	Almost always acts as a leader
Not at all self-confident	Very self-confident
Very uncomfortable about being aggressive	Not at all uncomfortable about being aggressive
Not at all ambitious	Very ambitious
Unable to separate feelings from ideas	Easily able to separate feelings from ideas
Very dependent	Not at all dependent
Very conceited about appearance	Never conceited about appearance
Female-valued items (the feminine pole is socially desirable)	
Very talkative	Not at all talkative
Very tactful	Very blunt
Very gentle	Very rough
Very aware of feelings of others	Not at all aware of feelings of others
Very religious	Not at all religious
Very interested in own appearance	Not at all interested in own appearance
Very neat in habits	Very sloppy in habits
Very quiet	Very loud
Very strong need for security	Very little need for security
Enjoys art and literature very much	Does not enjoy art and literature at all
Easily expresses tender feelings	Does not express tender feelings at all

Note. Reprinted from Broverman, I. K., Broverman, D. M., Clarkson, F. E., Rosenkrantz, P. S., and Vogel, S. R. Sex role stereotypes and clinical judgments of mental health. *Journal of Consulting and Clinical Psychology,* 1970, 34, 1–7. Copyright 1970 by the American Psychological Association. Reprinted by permission.

vide you with about the same list of attributes that most adults can (Urberg & Labouvie-Vief, 1976). In fact, many sex role concepts are well learned by age six or seven (Kagen, Hosken & Watson, 1961).

Some subtle sex role concepts are learned during middle childhood and adolescence. For example, adults and late adolescents consider reading, verbal skills, artistic skill, and social skill to be feminine forms of achievement, and mechanical, spatial, athletic, and mathematic skills to be masculine. Children entering school have some of these sex role concepts, but others are not yet developed. Second graders, in one survey, considered both mathematics and reading as appropriate for their own gender. That is, boys thought these skills were masculine and girls thought they were feminine. By twelfth grade, both males and females thought that reading was feminine and mathematics masculine (Stein, 1971). It appears then that some changes in sex role concepts about achievement take place as children grow and progress through school. Unfortunately, the changes appear to involve elimination of areas of achievement from those considered appropriate for oneself. Development seems to involve learning what *not* to do, not adding new possibilities of what *to* do.

Not surprisingly, people are generally more interested and motivated in activities that they define as sex-appropriate than those defined as inappropriate. For instance, adolescent females are more motivated to do well in English, verbal skills, social skills, and artistic activities than they are in science, athletics, and mechanical activities. Males have the opposite pattern of interests on the average (Stein & Bailey, 1973).

Not only are students more motivated when they consider a task sex-appropriate, but it appears that they actually perform better as well. In one series of studies, high school and college students performed mathematical and logical problems given in two versions. One version was a standard format, but the other one presented the same problem with "feminine" content. For instance, the following two versions require the same intellectual operations, but differ in *content:*

> Joan, Dorothy, and Barbara together have 36 dresses. Dorothy has twice as many as Barbara, and Joan has as many as Dorothy and Barbara together. How many dresses has Joan?

> John, David, and Robert together have $36. David has twice as much as Robert, and John has as much as David and Robert together. How much money has John?

College students performed better on the version that was "sex appropriate" than on the "inappropriate" version, although high school students did not manifest this difference (Milton, 1958). This correspondence between sex role concepts and performance may be especially important for mathematics in adolescence. In elementary school, children consider mathematics equally appropriate for boys and girls, but in high school, they come to view it as masculine. At the same time, mathematics becomes at least partially an elective subject, and boys more often take elective mathematics courses than do girls. Not surprisingly, males begin to excel in mathematics during high school, and the gap increases during college. Since mathematics forms the basis for many career avenues, this differentiation between boys and girls that begins in adolescence has long-term consequences.

Sex Role Acceptance

Obviously, knowledge about cultural norms does not necessarily lead individuals to adopt those prescriptions for themselves. Knowledge may be a first step, but people vary greatly in the extent to which their behavior, attitudes, personalities, and activities conform to sex role definitions. Some people actively reject cultural stereotypes. The phrase "sex role acceptance" refers to an individual's own acceptance of the sex role prescriptions of the broader society. There are a number of facets of acceptance that may or may not be highly related.

Gender Identity. The most fundamental aspect of sex role acceptance is the simple perception of oneself as male or female, that is, gender identity. Very young children learn to label people as boys and girls, or mothers and fathers, or men and women. During the preschool years, they presumably learn to label themselves as male or female. Initially, however, this label has little meaning. Over time, the child gradually acquires information about what it means to be male or female. For example, children are often 4 or 5 before they recognize that gender does not change. A 3-year-old girl may assert that she is going to grow up to be a daddy, but a 5-year-old girl probably knows that she cannot do that. This knowledge of the constancy of gender over time is important because the child can then begin to organize the world around the fact that he or she is and always will be male or female.

The great majority of people develop gender identities that are congruent with their biological sex, but exceptions do occur. People who are true transexuals actually feel themselves to be the opposite sex, and they often report that they have felt that they are a male residing in a female body (or vice versa) from the time of their earliest memories. Adults for whom surgical changes in gender are successful generally fall in this category. Jan Morris (1974) has written a very perceptive and revealing history of her own life as the successful journalist, James Morris, and of her experiences in surgical and hormonal transformation into the female that she had always felt as her basic gender identity. At this stage, however, we have little information about *why* some individuals develop gender identities that are different from their biological sex.

Masculinity, Femininity, and Androgyny. Perception of oneself as male or female is not the perception of oneself as masculine or feminine. These concepts refer to various aspects of sex role,; this is, the characteristics and activities that are socially defined as appropriate for one sex or the other.

Traditionally, people have considered masculinity and femininity as opposites (Constantinople, 1973). The Femininity Scale of the California psychological Inventory (Gough, 1957) contains a set of true-false items on which one answer signifies femininity and the opposite response is scored as masculine. Unfortunately, this kind of dichotomy encourages one to ignore the likelihood that an individual may possess characteristics stereotypically associated with *both* sexes. For example, enjoying artistic activity does not imply that one does not enjoy athletics. A person may be assertive and independent while also being warm and understanding.

A person with both masculine and feminine characteristics is *psychologically androgynous*. The measures used in recent research allow for androgyny to emerge by including two scales—one for femininity and one for masculinity (Bem, 1974; Spence, Helmreich & Stapp, 1975; Berzins, Welling & Wetter, 1978). Look at Table 9.1 for an idea of what is included in these measures. The femininity scales contain female-valued adjectives; the masculinity scales contain male-valued items. One clear finding from this research is that masculinity and femininity are *not* mutually exclusive; the two scales are generally uncorrelated with each other. That is, people who are highly masculine are not necessarily low in femininity and vice versa. Many people are androgynous (they score high on both masculine and feminine scales), and many are *undifferentiated* (they score low on both scales). We will talk more about androgyny in a later section.

Another traditional assumption is that masculine and feminine personality traits are associated with heterosexual rather than homosexual orientation and with sex-typed patterns of interests and activities. Our stereotype of the masculine male is a dominant, aggressive, independent person who likes sports and working on cars (but not cooking) and who is sexually attracted to women rather than men. It is often assumed that a man with feminine characteristics such as kindness and nurturance is homosexual. Again, research has largely refuted this global conception. These three domains—personality characteristics, sexual orientation, and interests—are largely independent of one another (Constantinople, 1973). To understand masculinity and femininity as an adolescent does, we must consider each of the three areas separately. Unfortunately, most of the earlier research does not include these distinctions, so the discussion that follows will not always follow our own prescription.

One Final Set of Definitions.   Sex role acceptance has at least three components that cut across the three domains we have already discussed. *Sex role identity* refers to the individual's perception of himself or herself as masculine or feminine. It may reflect how much the individual perceives her or his own characteristics as matching sex role concepts. *Sex role preference* indicates the extent to which the individual would *like* to have masculine and feminine characteristics, that is, the value attached to each sex role. *Sex role adoption* indicates how much the individual's behavior conforms to a sex role from an "objective" point of view. How much do others perceive that individual as masculine or feminine?

The components of sex role acceptance are summarized in Table 9.2. Sex role identity, preference, and adoption can be separated within each of the three domains of personality, sexual orientation, and interests. Examples of masculine and feminine characteristics within each are given. Stop for a moment and see if you can think of additional examples.

PATTERNS OF SEX ROLE DEVELOPMENT

Most theories about the way people acquire sex roles agree that the process begins in early childhood. The basis of gender identity appears to be laid in the first 2 years of life. In clinical work with hermaphrodites and individuals who have been labeled as the wrong gender at birth (based on a later assessment of chromosomes), Money and Ehrhardt (1972) have concluded that the socially labeled gender cannot easily be changed after 18 months to 2 years of age. That is, people who are biologically one sex but have been treated as the opposite gender develop an identity that is consistent with the socially defined gender not the biological one.

In middle childhood, consolidation and probably some modification of this early learning take place, but most theories and data suggest considerable continuity, particularly when the early learning fits socially defined norms. Thus, when the child reaches adolescence, sex role concepts and identity are well established. There are, however, a number of hypotheses about changes that take place in early adolescence. In the following section, we will briefly review the major theories about the development of sex roles with a particular focus on their hypotheses about adolescents. The interested reader may wish to review chapter 2 by Gallatin for a greater elaboration of these theories.

Psychoanalytic Theories: Freud and Erikson

In orthodox Freudian theory, children are thought to learn sex roles through identification with the parent of their own gender. The most important period occurs around age 5 when Oedipal conflicts are resolved by

TABLE 9.2 *Examples of Masculine and Feminine Characteristics*

TYPE OF ACCEPTANCE	AREA OF MASCULINITY-FEMININITY		
	PERSONALITY	SEXUAL ORIENTATION	INTERESTS
Identity			
Masculine	Perceives self as assertive, independent	Feels attracted to women	Likes sports, math
Feminine	Perceives self as empathic, kind	Feels attracted to men	Likes art, sewing
Preference			
Masculine	Wants to be dominant, unemotional	Wants to be attracted to women	Wants to be involved in car repair, science
Feminine	Wants to be gentle, tactful	Wants to be attracted to men	Wants to be involved in child care, music
Adoption			
Masculine	Behavior is active, self-confident	Dates, engages in sex with women	Builds things, mows lawn
Feminine	Behavior is expressive, nurturant	Dates, engages in sex with men	Cooks, writes poetry

Note. In each area, the masculine and feminine examples are not mutually exclusive. One person could do both.

the child's identifying with the same-sex parent and internalizing many of the characteristics and values of that parent. Thus sex roles come about through a more general adoption of the attributes of one's mother or father. For the next several years, Freud postulated that children are in a *latency* period. Puberty, however, arouses some of the earlier feelings and conflicts from the Oedipal period, particularly if these were not completely resolved before. Therefore Freud considered early adolescence a time when the child completed the process of emotional maturing, including, presumably, the adoption of mature sexual identification.

Erikson proposed that adolescence is a time for the establishment of identity for both sexes. He was talking about a broad concept of who and what one is, not solely about sex role identity. One of the major issues in this period of identity formation is occupational choice. Adolescents experiment with various roles—occupational and social—in an effort to define themselves. Nevertheless, there are important differences between the sexes in Erikson's view. Identity formation cannot be complete for females, says Erikson, until they know whom they will marry and until they produce children. That is, the central aspect of feminine identity is husband and children; the central aspect of male identity is occupation and other actions in the larger world. One implication of this hypothesis is that identity formation for females will be delayed beyond adolescence.

Whether or not one likes this hypothesis, it does seem to describe a real difference between male and female adolescents. When asked what they expected to do as adults, a large sample of females from ages 11-18 tended to give rather vague or unrealistic answers. They usually expected to have some kind of occupation, but the lack of realistic planning was evident when they have glamorized answers such as movie actress or stewardess. Males who were interviewed had much more concrete and better-thought-out career possibilities even though many of them were uncertain about their final choice (Douvan & Adelson, 1966).

If Erikson's theory is correct, one might expect to get more detailed, concrete answers from females than from males if one asked what sort of spouse, marriage, and family life they expected. So far as we know, this study has not been done. Most of this information is based on people who were adolescents in the 1950s or the early 1960s. It is possible that young women in the current generation of adolescents give more serious consideration to future careers as a component of their identities than earlier generations did, but we suspect the change is not large.

Social Learning Theory

Another major theoretical approach to understanding sex role development is based on social learning theory (Mischel, 1966; 1970). According to this theory, personality and social behaviors develop according to basic learning principles of reward, punishment, imitation, and the like. No stages of development are assumed; instead, sex role learning is considered a continuous process from early childhood throughout life. Sex roles are learned when boys and girls are rewarded and punished for different types of behavior and when they observe models of masculine and feminine behavior. The parents are one set of models, but teachers, admired adults, peers, and siblings may also serve as models. Children and adolescents are especially likely to imitate people who are warm and affectionate, who are powerful and successful in the larger world, and who have high status or who are similar to them in some way.

Social learning principles can be used to encourage nonstereotyped as well as sex-stereotyped behavior. When young people see someone of their own sex doing something nonstereotyped, they are likely to imitate this behavior. This principle has been used to help broaden career possibilities. In one study, for instance, high school students saw and heard two adults (a man and a woman) who described their jobs in computer science. Students who were exposed to women who did different types of computer-science jobs more often considered those jobs appropriate for women than students who saw only male representatives of the same jobs. Experiments with younger children also show that boys will play with cookware or female toys if they see another boy doing so and that girls will show achievement effort when they see another girl doing that (Perry & Perry, 1975; McArthur & Eisen, 1976).

Social learning principles may also account for increased concern with conformity to traditional sex roles that seems to occur in adolescence, particularly for girls. Before they reach puberty, many girls can happily be tomboys, not worrying much about how they look or whether they are sweet, attractive, and feminine. Girls who prefer baseball to dolls are tolerated during elementary school. In some cases, their independence and assertiveness may be valued. This social tolerance is based partly on the assumption that as a girl's body matures she will outgrow tomboyishness naturally.

With the onset of adolescence, a high premium is placed on girls to be socially successful, attractive to boys, and to give up "masculine" activities and interests. The bounds of tolerable behavior are narrowed by both adults and peers. Some girls exhibit a "flight into femininity," perhaps as the beginning of the long-range effort to attract a husband (Douvan & Adelson, 1966). One of the results may be a decline in school achievement if high achievement is considered unfeminine or irrelevant to important goals. In one study, the previous academic records of high school students who were underachievers (i.e., their grades were lower than one would expect on the basis of their intelligence) were examined. The males who were underachievers in high school had histories of poor achievement from the third grade on. However, the females had been performing well until they reached junior high school. During the seventh, eighth and ninth grades, their achievement levels had gradually dropped and had remained low in high school (Shaw & McCuen, 1960). Social pressure toward narrowing of the range of female behavior might work to reduce androgyny for females. In one large survey (Spence & Helmreich, 1978), more high school females were classified as androgynous than college females (35% and 27% respectively).

Males do not experience early tolerance for displaying feminine interests and behavior; from a very early age, adults and peers react very negatively to a boy who likes dolls. Being a sissy is much worse than being a tomboy. Nevertheless, puberty is a time of renewed pressure to be masculine, especially for any boy who has not acquired at least the superficial trappings of the role. In primitive societies, initiation rituals involving pain, deprivation, and challenge are frequent, particularly in societies where boys have been raised largely by their mothers (Burton & Whiting, 1961). In our society, adolescent boys often experience "dares" to do dangerous or impossible feats that prove their courage and masculinity (Harris, 1972). Nevertheless, the latitude for males to acquire at least some aspects of feminine behavior appears to increase rather than decrease through adolescence and adulthood. Qualities such as tact, kindness, and emotional expressiveness become more acceptable as boys grow up. By adulthood, males who combine these qualities fit comfortably into society more often than females do (Block, 1973). In the Spence and Helmreich (1978) survey, androgyny was more frequent in college men than in high school men.

Developmental Theories

Developmental theories have in common the idea that there is a sequence of events through which most people go in a fixed order. The age at which different people go through different stages may be different, but the order is similar.

Two recent theories (Block, 1973; Rebecca, Hefner & Oleshansky, 1976) include descriptions of developmental change in adolescence and adulthood. Both propose that people identify and conform to traditional sex roles before they move beyond those roles to androgyny or to an integration of masculinity and femininity. In Block's theory, the bifurcation of sex roles occurs in middle childhood when children are generally in a period of conformity to external rules and roles. The critical difference between boys and girls in this period is that boys are taught to suppress emotion or overt expression of feeling and girls are taught to suppress aggression and assertiveness. Once again, we find a theme of sex roles dictating that children give up some component of themselves. The suppression of feeling for males and the suppression of assertiveness for females form the core of later definitions of masculinity and femininity.

The next stage is one of introspection. As children move from middle childhood to adolescence, they begin to examine themselves, to compare their behavior with their values, and to become self-critical. One part of this process is to compare themselves to their own internalized concepts of masculinity and femininity.

At the next level, the adolescent (or adult) becomes more autonomous and begins to question the sex role definitions that were accepted earlier while becoming aware of the components of self that do not fit those roles. That is, most individuals have values, attitudes, and behaviors that depart from traditional sex roles. During this period of development, they recognize these and begin to try to integrate them into their self concepts. The final stage, which probably comes only in adulthood, is integration of these components into a new concept of self.

The most important proposition arising from this theory is the notion that identification with traditional sex roles is necessary and normal before one can move on to a departure from those roles or to an androgynous integration of masculine and feminine components of the self.

SOCIALIZATION OF SEX ROLES

Whatever the contribution of biological, hormonal factors to sex differences may be, the principal means by which individuals acquire sex roles is learning. Much of this socialization occurs at a very early age. Parents, siblings, peers, schools, and mass media each contribute to the process. Many of the studies we will discuss were based on the assumption that traditional sex roles were desirable. We will try, however, to see what they imply about socializing nontraditional behavior. As you read, ask yourself, does the literature suggest means by which children may be socialized away from the traditional sex roles as well as toward them? If so, what other consequences for children's development may be entailed in such a pattern?

Parents

Much of the research on parent socialization was guided by the notion that identification with the same-sex parent was the primary source of one's sex role identity. Therefore, the characteristics of parents that were thought to promote strong identification such as warmth, power, and the like have been examined with particular care. In one study of junior and senior high school males (Payne & Mussen, 1956), the boys and their parents each filled out a personality questionnaire that contained one scale measuring masculinity. Identification with the father was determined by the similarity between all of the other personality scales for father and son. Students who were most identified with their fathers (i.e., were the most similar) also had more positive relationships with their fathers and perceived their fathers to be more rewarding than students who showed little father identification. The boys who most identified with their fathers were also the most masculine. This finding is consistent with many other studies of younger children, indicating that more masculine boys have warmer, more positive relations with their fathers than less masculine boys. The interesting twist in this study of adolescents was that the father's own masculinity score was not related to the son's identification. That is, the more highly identified boys, who were more masculine themselves, did not have more masculine fathers with whom to identify. It appears that there is something more general about a positive father-son relationship that permits the boy to acquire masculine characteristics, even when his father is not highly masculine.

For girls, a warm, positive relationship with the mother appears to be central in developing femininity. From the preschool years through preadolescence, at any rate, numerous studies indicate that girls' femininity is highest in families where the mother is very warm, nurturant, and affectionate (Mischel, 1970). Thus for both genders, the warmth and affection of the same-sex parent are associated with high levels of sex role identification. From reading the chapters of Hamachek and Wagner, you can see that these qualities are also important in developing one's self concept and sexuality.

Power or dominance of a parent might also lead to identification. If the child perceives the parent as very powerful, he or she might wish to imitate that parent in order to acquire the same power over the environment. Overall, it appears that dominance or power of the father is associated with high masculinity in sons but has little effect on femininity for daughters (Hetherington, 1967).

One might expect that direct rewards and punishments would be important socializing influences. Surprisingly, boys and girls are often treated quite similarly, especially by mothers (Maccoby & Jacklin, 1974). Fathers treat boys and girls differently more often than mothers do, and their treatment plays an important role in both male and female sex role development (Johnson, 1963). For example, fathers who are themselves quite masculine and who have positive attitudes about their wives tend to reward their daughters for feminine behavior. In turn, their daughters develop femininity.

Parent permissiveness contributes to masculinity for both sexes. Permissiveness means that parents allow the child latitude to do what he or she wishes, that they impose relatively few restrictions on behavior, that they allow independent activity, that they let the child go away from home on his or her own, and the like. It does *not* mean that they do not enforce the rules that they have, but it does mean that there are relatively few restrictions. Given this definition, it is not difficult to understand why permissiveness is associated with masculine behavior for both males and females, at least in childhood (Stein & Bailey, 1973). Aggression, assertiveness, and independence (masculine behaviors) are more likely to develop when parents are fairly permissive. Dependency and passivity (feminine characteristics) are likely when parents are highly restrictive. Thus feminine characteristics are associated with parental restrictiveness, and masculine characteristics with parent permissiveness.

Socialization of Androgyny.   How can parents socialize androgynous children? How can they raise daughters and sons who are independent, assertive, and self-confident as well as kind, nurturant, and tactful? How can they raise children who will feel free to pursue the whole gamut of interests from electronics to child care? For girls, the literature provides some partial answers. Independent, assertive, achieving females often have mothers who are only moderately nurturant, who are permissive, and who encourage independence and achievement (Stein & Bailey, 1973). By adolescence, such females are usually less closely tied to their families than more traditionally feminine girls. For example, in one survey, females with career interests named people outside their families as their models of behavior more often than females with traditional goals (Douvan & Adelson, 1966). In another study, females whose parents were both very warm and rather restrictive (nonpermissive) were lacking in leadership and responsibility at school (Bronfenbrenner, 1961). As one author put it, girls are in some danger of being oversocialized. If parents are very warm and restrictive, girls tend to remain dependent and conforming to their family; as adults, they are likely to shift their dependence to a man rather than becoming independent (Kagan & Moss, 1962).

A second avenue for socialization of androgyny occurs when parents are models of nontraditional behavior. For example, children whose mothers have careers are exposed to a model who combines some aspects of the traditional female role (wife and mother) with nontraditional behavior (pursuing a career). Women with careers are more androgynous than housewives (Welch, 1979), so they exemplify androgyny for their children. Daughters of employed mothers more often aspire to a career and to advanced education themselves than do daughters of nonemployed mothers. In one study of college women, daughters whose mothers had worked outside the home were more dominant and achievement-oriented (masculine attributes) and less likely to be passive and dependent (feminine attributes) than those whose mothers had never been employed. It appears, then, that females develop less traditional feminine patterns when their mothers depart from traditional feminine roles (Stein & Bailey, 1973; Hoffman & Nye, 1974).

We know much less about socializing androgyny in males. Maternal employment does lead males to have less traditional sex role concepts than do children of unemployed mothers. In households where mothers work outside the home, fathers take on more household tasks, so their sons see slightly nontraditional versions of both male and female roles (Hoffman & Nye, 1974).

Father-absence. Another means of determining parental roles in socialization is to examine sex role development in families where one parent is absent. Because most one-parent families are headed by mothers, there is a lot of information about father-absence, but very little about mother-absence. Obviously there are other differences between one- and two-parent families besides the absence of one gender, but studies of father-absent children can provide us with some valuable information about sex role socialization.

Father-absence has a greater impact on the sex role development of males than of females. On the average, father-absent males are less aggressive, less interested in contact sports, more anxious, more impulsive, and less interested in many masculine activities than boys whose fathers are present. When these differences occur for adolescents, they are most likely to result from absence of the father in early childhood. In fact, boys whose fathers left home after the age of five or six generally do not show these patterns (Biller, 1970).

Early father-absence may disrupt the father-child relationship and the son's masculine development, even if the father returns. In two surveys of college students who were born during World War II, individuals whose fathers were away for long periods during the first few years of their lives were compared with those whose fathers were home continuously (Carlsmith, 1964; Nelson & Maccoby, 1966). In most instances, the fathers returned and lived with their families after the children were two or three years old. Males whose fathers had been absent for a long period during their early life had a more "feminine" pattern of abilities on college entrance examinations than those whose fathers had been continuously present. A feminine pattern was defined as the pattern that is characteristic of females (a higher score on the verbal section of the examination than on the quantitative or mathematical section). Father-absent females also had a more feminine pattern than the norm. One reason for the effects of early father-absence is suggested by the fact that the more feminine pattern also occurred for males who reported poor relationships with their fathers. Fathers returning home to children who were 2 or 3 years old often had a difficult time establishing an affectionate relationship with them. Even several years later, they had less close relationships with their sons who had been born during the war than with those who were born after the war (Stolz, 1954).

Some of the affects of father-absence can apparently be counteracted, even for young males, if the mother encourages and rewards masculine behavior. This is likely to occur if the mother has a favorable attitude to the father and to males in general, if she is competent to deal with the many strains of being a single parent, and if there are other males available to whom the child can relate. It is probable that women whose husbands have died will have more positive attitudes toward males and toward the child's father than women who are divorced. Perhaps this is why adolescent males from divorced homes manifest more problems of rebelliousness, irresponsibility, and lack of self control than those whose fathers have died (Douvan & Adelson, 1966).

Although females are less affected by father-absence than males, girls without fathers do appear to have some problems in relating to males. In one study, adolescent females from father-present homes, from father-absent homes separated by divorce, and from homes separated by death of the father were observed extensively in a recreation center. Daughters of divorcées sought out boys, hung around the pool tables and other areas where the boys congregated, were overtly sexy, and dated early. Daughters of widows fell at the opposite extreme; they shied away from boys, appeared uncomfortable around them, dated little, and generally avoided interacting with males. The father-present girls fell between these two extremes.

It appears that both groups of father-absent girls had problems in the area of heterosexual relations, but these were manifested in quite different ways (Hetherington, 1972). Follow-up studies of these girls in early adulthood indicated that the patterns shown in early adolescence continued. Both groups of father-absent women had a somewhat idealized and unrealistic picture of the man they wanted to marry; they often looked for a man who was like their picture of their father. Father-present women were more free to marry someone who differed from their father. Daughters of divorcées married early, and some divorced early; daughters of widows married late (Hetherington & Parke, 1979).

Siblings

You may have detected a suggestion earlier that brothers and sisters can influence sex role development and can often mitigate the effects of father-absence. Opposite-sex siblings may provide a child with opportunities to learn androgyny. For example, in one study of young children (5 and 6 years old), girls with brothers were rated as having more masculine characteristics than girls with sisters, but they had just as many feminine characteristics. Boys with sisters, however, had fewer masculine characteristics and more feminine characteristics than boys with brothers (Brim, 1958). These same differences appeared in college students (Sutton-Smith & Rosenberg, 1965). For father-absent children, both boys and girls who had an older brother were more aggressive and less dependent than those who did not have an older brother (Wohlford, Sandrock, Berger & Liberman, 1971).

It seems, then, that brothers and sisters, particularly when they are older, can teach and support sex role learning. The child who grows up with opposite-sex siblings is exposed to the toys, games, behavior patterns, and expectations for the opposite sex role more than one whose siblings are all the same sex. Consider the difference in atmosphere for a girl who has one or two older sisters and for another who has older brothers. She will take part in less rough and tumble play, the toys and games around her will be different; her parents will take her to different kinds of activities (probably not to a football game); and she will be exposed early to older sisters worrying about clothes, appearance, dates, and boys rather than to older brothers worrying about sports, muscles, and cars.

Opposite-sex siblings often promote the development of androgyny, but same-sex siblings can encourage nontraditional behavior as well, especially in a large family. Some researchers have suggested a process of "de-identification," in which a child deliberately tries to be different from brothers or sisters. For example, a boy with three older brothers might search for interests and behaviors that were distinctive and individual—often these are nontraditional for males. There is some evidence that girls with several older sisters and boys with several older brothers are less traditionally sex-typed than those with fewer same-sex siblings (Grotevant, 1978; Schachter, Gilutz, Shore & Adler, 1978).

Schools as Socializing Agents

The advent of laws and executive rulings against sex discrimination in education has been accompanied by increasing awareness of the ways in which sex role stereotypes and definitions are conveyed throughout the school years (chapter 11, by Lovell, contains a section on this topic that will be of interest to the reader). Some of the more obvious forms of differentiation between males and females in schools are now beginning to be eliminated. In many schools, girls are no longer required to take cooking, sewing, and homemaking courses; and boys are not required to take shop and mechanics courses. Nevertheless, many less obvious forms of differential treatment of the sexes remain.

Differential Teacher Response to Male and Female Students. Although teachers (both male and female) typically report that they treat boys and girls equally, classroom observations fail to confirm this belief (Guttentag & Bray, 1977). Teachers engage in a greater number of interactions with males such as asking questions, criticizing, accepting or rejecting ideas, giving approval and disapproval, and listening (Spaulding, 1963; Felsenthal, 1970; Good, Sykes & Brophy, 1973). Furthermore, although girls volunteer answers more often than boys, they are called on by the teacher less often. Teachers also tend to ignore underachievement in females, but they make active attempts to redirect and assist underachieving boys (Good & Brophy, 1973).

Teachers generally prefer males to females, and they like children who fit sex stereotypes better than those who do not. In one survey, teachers said they liked male students because they were more outspoken, active, willing to exchange ideas, honest, and easy to talk to. The only characteristic that endeared female students to them was their lower frequency of discipline problems (Ricks & Pyke, 1973).

Levitan and Chananine (1972) asked female primary school teachers to rate how typical they thought each of a number of hypothetical students were and also to rate how much they approved of and liked them. Male students described as aggressive were rated by the teachers as more typical than nonaggressive males, whereas female students described as dependent were rated as more typical than independent females. Furthermore, both dependent and achieving female students were rated as being more likable than were the dependent male students. Assuming that these laboratory-assessed attitudes accurately reflect teacher behavior in the classroom, teachers are likely to reward dependent girls and punish dependent boys.

The overall picture indicates that teachers initiate more contact with males, provide them with more evaluative feedback (both positive and negative), and are more likely to reinforce them for independence and achievement. They like boys and girls who fit sex stereotypes of aggression/passivity and independence/dependence. These differences may represent a strong force toward strengthening the independence of the male student and simultaneously weakening or at least failing to reward this characteristic in the female student. Since independence has been shown to be correlated with intellectual ability and achievement (Stein & Bailey, 1973), the implications of this differential treatment for later differences in academic and professional success are clear.

The teacher's method of organizing the classroom can also affect students' sex-typed behavior. On the whole, a classroom in which there is opportunity for individualized, independent work leads children to develop less stereotyped attitudes and behavior and more independence, assertiveness, and positive behavior toward one another than a highly structured, traditional program (Minuchin, 1965).

Sex-biased Instructional Materials.   The Scott, Foresman publishing company has produced a pamphlet entitled *Guidelines for Improving the Image of Women in Textbooks* (1972). In it, the authors labeled textbooks as sexist ". . . if they omit the actions and achievements of women, if they demean women by using patronizing language, or if they show women only in stereotyped roles with less than the full range of human interests, traits and capabilities." Traditionally, elementary and high school textbooks, including not only readers but books on nearly every other subject (e.g., spelling, mathematics, history), have been characterized by sexism (Trecker, 1971; Frazier & Sadker, 1973; Wirtenberg & Nakamura, 1976).

Males serve as the central characters in stories much more frequently than females. Female characters, for the most part, engage in a limited range of activities, often centered in the home, whereas males are involved in more varied, productive, and authoritative activities beyond the domestic scene. For example, in a junior high school spelling book, the following sentences were given as ways of using the words "aerodynamics" and "souffle." "Bill wants to be a pilot. He needs to know about aerodynamics. Cindy wants to be a good homemaker. She needs to learn how to make a souffle." Men and boys are characterized as resourceful, courageous, successful, capable, and achieving. Women and girls, on the other hand, are portrayed as passive, self-sacrificing, and subservient to the male characters.

Separate Curricula for Male and Female Students.   Until very recently, girls in many schools were required to take home economics and boys were required to take shop. Physical education and athletics were segregated by sex; and most of the money, facilities, and glory were lavished on the male teams. In elective courses, girls were more often encouraged to take typing and shorthand; boys were encouraged to pursue automobile repair, mathematics, and science. What effect does this form of tracking have? It may teach students that a person's sex is a legitimate basis for deciding what a person should be interested in doing, regardless of initial interests and aspirations. Perhaps more important, it may suggest that some interests are *illegitimate*. Once again, sex stereotyping may have its most harmful effects by curtailing and restricting exploration of interest areas and opportunities to develop competence. Ultimately, if allowed to persist, sex tracking will produce the very differences in competence that are assumed in sex stereotypes.

In very recent years, changes in curricula have been made in many school systems to reduce sex barriers and inequalities (often after litigation). However, it is much easier to eliminate the formal structure of sexism than the attitudes that originally motivated it. For example, in our local school system, seventh-grade courses in World of Construction and in Designs for Living (what used to be shop and home economics) are officially open to all students. When a sixth-grade daughter of a friend wanted to sign up for World of Construction in seventh grade, she was told by a counselor that she should not take it because the rest of the students would be all boys. Not surprisingly, the "elective" courses remain largely sex-segregated except for a few brave students.

Sexism in Vocational Counseling and Testing. The sex bias of counselors increases when high school students discuss vocational goals. High school counselors tend to direct females into traditional occupations that require little training and a great deal of supervision. The occupations requiring formal education that they suggest are those with low salaries compared to the careers suggested to men (Donahue & Costar, 1977). Furthermore, counselors of both sexes react most favorably to students who hold occupational goals traditional to their sex (Thomas & Stewart, 1971; Abramowitz, Weitz, Schwartz, Amira, Gomes & Abramowitz, 1975).

Women often report that their guidance counselors advised them to become legal secretaries when they proposed becoming lawyers and nurses when they wanted to be doctors (Frazier & Sadker, 1973). The illustrations used in career counseling materials also present outmoded stereotypes by depicting men as chefs, businessmen, and scientists and women as their helpers—waitresses, secretaries, and laboratory assistants (Birk, Cooper & Tanney, 1977). A sample text, directed to women, read: "If you are by nature a helper—reliable, painstaking, accurate—as a laboratory assistant or technician, you could lend a hand to the professional scientist, freeing him for more difficult original work."

Occupational preference tests are often sex-biased. On some commonly used tests (e.g., the Strong Vocational Interest Inventory), there were until recently no scales for females for certain occupations such as engineering. In other words, a female could not obtain a score indicating that her interests were suited for engineering because the test did not permit it (unless she took the male form of the instrument). Gradual changes are being made in these tests—a most important step because they are frequently used in counseling high school students.

If schools want to counteract sexism in career choice, it will not be sufficient simply to remove barriers or to make career counseling more neutral. Children learn sex stereotypes about occupations in the preschool years; even 4- and 5-year-old girls show "occupational foreclosure." When asked "what do you want to be when you grow up?" most little girls say teacher, mother, or nurse. Boys name a much wider range of possibilities. If high school counseling programs are to provide truly nonsexist career counseling, they will have to develop special programs and materials to counteract sex stereotypes actively.

Sexism in the Educational Organization. The status hierarchy in most school systems reflects societal stereotypes. Men run the system while women work in it. Whereas 84% of elementary school teachers are female, only 21% of the principals are women. In fact, the percentage of female principals has declined drastically since 1960. In high school, the percentage of male teachers increases but so does the percentage of male principals (to 97%). Men also dominate the posts of school administrator (74%), superintendent (99%), and chief state school official (96%) (Fact Sheets on Institutional Sexism, 1976). Thus male and female students are exposed throughout their school years to role models who reinforce the notion that men are the policy makers and leaders, and women are the followers.

Changes in Schools. Attempts to change these educational practices were carried out in Sweden during the 1960s, in a complete revamping of the school system to eliminate differentiations of students based on sex. Wood shops, sewing, home economics, and baby care were required for both sexes. Textbooks were revised to eliminate sex stereotypes. For example, a social studies text for eighth and ninth grades contained the following questions: "What kinds of things can a boy with real mechanical interest do in his spare time? And what can a girl who likes to take care of other people do?" "A boy" and "a girl" were replaced by "a person" (Kelman, 1971, p. 22). These changes in the educational system accompanied changes in other aspects of Swedish society, and the ultimate effects remain to be seen. However, initial reports suggest that children like the changes, and one would expect them to grow up with somewhat different views than their elders.

Many efforts to remove sexism from the schools are also being made in this country, but it is difficult to tell how widespread or effective they are. Textbooks are being revised; sex-biased curricula are being reduced; and counselors are instituting programs to encourage both males and females to consider a wide variety of careers. The counseling journals are full of articles on sex stereotyping, and experimental programs are being used in some school systems. Schools are being forced to give equal facilities to male and female athletics or to integrate sports entirely. Little change is apparent, however, in the subtle patterns of teacher approval and disapproval; and the administrative hierarchy remains largely male at most schools.

Peers as Enforcers of Sex Role Conformity

Children who come from families in which nontraditional sex role concepts and expectations have been taught may face a seeming monolith of conventional social expectations when they come in close contact with peers. Peers are among the most traditional and rigid enforcers of stereotypes. Even in nursery school, peers reward boys for masculine behavior and girls for feminine behavior (Fagot & Patterson, 1969). At least until recently, it appears that this pattern continued through adolescence. In the 1950s, the popular leaders in a broad sample of high schools were composed of boys who were good athletes and girls who were pretty and vivacious. The peer culture valued these attributes much more than scholarly achievement (Coleman, 1961).

Adolescent peer norms may change over a short time span. Current generations of adolescents may be sensitized to questions raised by sex role liberation groups, but it is very difficult to tell what real changes are coming about as a result. We doubt that there are very fundamental changes in the values that most adolescent subcultures attach to traditional sex roles. An incident in a large university is a good illustration. The male students in one of the large dormitories set up a table in the dining area from which they held up a sign "rating" the appearance of each female who walked into the dining room on a scale from one to ten. A minority of the women were outraged, but a large number who heard this was happening rushed back to their rooms to change their clothes and comb their hair before entering the dining room.

Mass Media

The mass media, particularly television, are purveyors of conventional sex role stereotypes. The programs that most adolescents watch are replete with he-men who conquer all obstacles by force and violence, who are independent, free of responsibility or close human ties, who are never weak or emotional, and who occupy most of the interesting and prestigious occupations and activities. Females generally appear either as wives and mothers without an outside occupation or as glamorous sex objects who are concerned primarily with their relations with the male heroes. Women rarely have authority and competence. In advertisements, for example, the voice of authority is usually male, even when discussing housecleaning and domestic products (Stein & Friedrich, 1975).

One may be tempted to dismiss television as an important socializing agent on the grounds that adolescents know that the programs and the ads are fictional or a product of Madison Avenue. We believe it is unwise to do so. Many adolescents, particularly those who are poor and who belong to minority groups, say that they use television as a guide for their own behavior. They seek information from television about what to do on dates, how to act with members of the opposite sex, how to dress, and what to do in a whole range of social situations. Even adults who believe that they are not influenced by television show its effects. People who watch a great deal of television believe that the real world is more like the world of television fiction than those who watch little television. Any activity that occupies an average of two or three hours a day, as television does for adolescents, is likely to have some impact. In the case of sex role learning, television reinforces a narrow and rigid view of sex roles while providing little potential range of variation.

Television content has remained basically constant over time, but recent years have seen an increase in active, aggressive, female "heroes." Although most of these females are overtly sexy and often depend on men, they are more aggressive and more active than many previous women characters. One researcher, intrigued by a news report that adolescent girls often named Farrah Fawcett-Majors as the person they would like to be like, conducted a series of studies of adolescents' perceptions of "Charlie's Angels." Most young women admired two of the "angels," Sabrina and Kelly, but they were sharply divided about Jill, the character then played by Farrah. She was perceived as more aggressive and more dominant than the other two women, and the girls who liked her had more androgynous ideals about women than those who did not. The advent of these active, aggressive females on television is a mixed blessing; it appears that the females who liked Jill most were the ones who were most likely to adopt some of her antisocial, aggressive behavior as well as her more acceptable assertiveness (Friedrich-Cofer, Tucker, Norris-Baker, Farnsworth, Fisher, Hannington & Hoxie, 1978).

On quite a different level, a nationally broadcast television program called "Freestyle" has been developed to counteract sex stereotyping in children's career interests. The target age group is 9 to 12, but it may have a wider appeal. It is focused on showing both males and females engaging in a wide variety of activities, interests, and behavior. It is designed for in-school as well as home viewing; there are curriculum materials to accompany it in classrooms and at home.

CONSEQUENCES AND CORRELATES OF SEX ROLE IDENTITY

We can now return in more depth to the questions raised at the beginning of this chapter concerning the value that should be attached to sex role learning. Until recently, it has been assumed by psychologists and lay persons alike that the healthy child should acquire the sex-typed characteristics condoned in the society. Parents express great concern if their children show signs of opposite-sex identity; they often worry that doll play by a boy is a sign of incipient homosexuality or that the tomboy interests of a girl will prevent her from becoming attractive to boys as she grows older. Even parents who dislike sex role stereotypes worry that their children will be social outcasts if they are too different.

An almost opposite view is now being heard from various groups that concern themselves with "sex role liberation" or with androgyny. They argue that imposing limits on the range of interests, activities, and personality characteristics of an individual simply because of biological gender is damaging and pointless. They suggest that all children should be socialized as human beings with the possibility for developing any of their potentials without restraint.

Obviously, various positions can be taken on these issues. What we will do next is examine two questions: What value do members of the current American culture attach to sex roles, and what are the consequences or correlates of adopting different patterns of masculinity and femininity?

Value Attached to Sex Roles

Considerably more value and more status are attached to the male role than to the female role in our American culture. When students or adults are asked whether they would prefer a male or female as their first child or as their only child, the overwhelming majority prefer a son to a daughter. From early childhood, boys consistently show a stronger preference for the male role than girls show for the female role. Masculine play activities and other interests have greater appeal for boys than feminine activities and interests have for girls. In fact, as girls get older, they show increased preference for masculine activities and declining attraction for feminine play (Sherman, 1971; Huston-Stein & Higgins-Trenk, 1978). The mass media reflect the greater interest and appeal of the male role. In adult programs, about three-fourths of the leading characters are male; in children's programs, males constitute 80–90% of the major roles. Furthermore, males engage in a wider range and variety of activities than females (Stein & Friedrich, 1975).

Masculine personality characteristics are more valued than feminine attributes. Look back at Table 9.1. All of the adjectives were judged to be socially desirable characteristics. The male-valued items are those desirable characteristics that people think characterize men; the female-valued items are the desirable attributes that people think women have. Note how many more adjectives appear as male-valued than female-valued. When clinical psychologists were asked to rate "healthy adult," "healthy man," or "healthy woman" on these adjectives, the ratings for healthy men were very similar to those for healthy adults; the ratings for healthy women were different. That is, clinical psychologists thought that masculine characteristics defined mental health for adults in general; feminine characteristics did not fit their concept of a mentally healthy adult (Broverman, Vogel, Broverman, Clarkson & Rosenkrantz, 1972).

Are Sex Roles Functional?

Next we will consider whether sex roles are functional either to the individual or to the society. Some sociologists (e.g., Parsons, 1955) have argued that a division of roles by gender is functional in the family and is therefore functional in the broader society. Within the family, one adult can take primary responsibility for instrumental tasks such as providing income, supplying material goods, and making decisions. The other adult can take primary responsibility for the expressive or emotional aspects of family functioning by being sensitive to the feelings of family members, providing understanding and care to each member, and smoothing the interactions among various people. Obviously, in traditional terms, males are expected to perform instrumental functions and females to perform expressive functions. A number of questions have been raised about this formulation even within the traditional family structure. First, instrumental and expressive activities are not mutually exclusive—one may do both. Second, many of the managerial activities of a housewife are quite instrumental, such as managing a budget, buying clothes and objects for the home, and organizing several sets of carpools, piano lessons, dental appointments, and the myriad of other activities in which modern children are involved. Finally, division of activities may not promote a close husband-wife relationship because it involves few shared interests.

Another view, presented by Bem (1976), is that the androgynous person can function better than either a masculine or feminine person who has only one set of sex-typed characteristics. Bem argues that masculine behaviors are adaptive in some situations and feminine behaviors are adaptive in other situations. Therefore, the person who can show either or both can function better in a wider variety of situations than a person who lacks one or the other.

In a series of studies testing this notion, students were observed in a situation requiring independence (a masculine behavior). Other people pressured the person to conform to their opinion. People who were androgynous or masculine (both men and women) were more independent or non-conforming than feminine people. Two feminine behaviors were observed: taking care of a baby and listening sympathetically to another person's problems. Men who were androgynous or feminine performed these behaviors better than masculine men. Androgynous women also performed these behaviors well. Another study concerned interest or activity rather than personality. Androgynous people were more willing to perform both male and female stereotyped activities (e.g., oil squeaky hinges in a box or prepare a baby bottle by mixing powdered formula with milk) than were masculine or feminine individuals.

On the whole, these studies support the idea that androgynous people can perform better in a wider variety of situations than people who are either masculine or feminine. The implications of this idea for adolescents are clear. Young men can develop feminine qualities such as nurturance or sympathy without sacrificing assertiveness, independence, or masculinity. Similarly, a young woman can show masculine behavior without losing her femininity. For example, students rated one another after a group discussion on two dimensions: instrumental, goal-oriented participation, and expressive responding to others' feelings. Some women were rated high on *both* instrumental behavior (making suggestions, keeping the discussion focused on the task, leading the group) and expressive behavior (smiling, being considerate of others' feelings, smoothing ruffled feathers). That is, they showed plenty of feminine sensitivity but combined it with masculine leadership and goal-direction.

Self-Esteem. You will probably not be surprised that androgynous people have high self-esteem (Bem, 1977; Spence & Helmreich, 1978). Masculinity by itself is more positive than femininity alone. In Table 9.3, the four groups formed by classifying people on masculine and feminine scales are shown. The numbers 1 through 4 show how the four groups are ordered on self-esteem: androgynous people are highest, masculine next, feminine next, and undifferentiated lowest. Perhaps that is why some earlier studies found that feminine girls had relatively poor self-images (Connell & Johnson, 1970; Sears, 1970).

Achievement. Traditional femininity appears to be dysfunctional for many types of intellectual and occupational achievement. Females with androgynous or masculine identities generally perform better in areas of achievement that are defined as masculine such as mathematics, spatial relations, science, and sports. They are also more likely to achieve in the occupational world (Stein & Bailey, 1973; Spence & Helmreich, 1978). Very feminine women and girls are more anxious in school and seek counseling in college more often than those who are less feminine (Webb, 1963; Heilbrun & Fromme, 1965). One reason for feminine females' high anxiety in high school and college may be the inconsistency between the demands for achievement, competition, and independent effort and the feminine role prescription to achieve less well than males, to be cooperative and avoid competition, and to be dependent and oriented to interpersonal relationships.

TABLE 9.3 *Self-Esteem and Masculinity-Femininity*

		MASCULINE SCALE	
		High	*Low*
		Androgynous	Feminine
	High	1	3
FEMININE SCALE			
		Masculine	Undifferentiated
	Low	2	4

Note. Numbers indicate order on self-esteem measures. Androgynous score highest; undifferentiated score lowest.

254

Traditional femininity also conflicts with high achievement because of the very mundane fact that the major feminine role task (being a mother and a wife) makes demands for time, money, and energy that compete with the demands of an advanced education or a career. This conflict is not limited to adult women but is critically important for many adolescents. Adolescent pregnancy, with or without marriage, is very widespread in America. Havighurst, in his chapter on subcultures, indicates that one in ten adolescent girls becomes pregnant. Although some of these young women have abortions or allow the baby to be adopted, many are keeping their babies, and an increasing number are doing so without a husband.

The choice to become a mother, particularly a single parent, is a critical decision with long-term consequences. Teenage mothers often terminate their education early, and they either remain unemployed or work in low-paying jobs. Throughout their lives, women who have had children early stay out of the labor market or work in low-status jobs. By contrast, those women who ultimately get an advanced education or work in high-status occupations are likely to have fewer children and to have them at a later age than their less well-educated and less well-paid peers (Huston-Stein & Higgins-Trenk, 1978). Although these statistical averages do not apply to every person, the choices a teenager makes about *when* to take on adult female role responsibilities have important consequences for her educational and occupational achievement. At the very least, early motherhood makes it much more difficult for a young woman to get an education or to get started in any but the most menial job.

SUMMARY

In modern America, there is good reason to doubt that traditional sex roles are desirable goals toward which children should be socialized. In this chapter, we have attempted to look at the literature on sex role development with attention to its implications for changes in sex role definitions as well as for changes in the learning of traditional roles.

The first thing that children learn about sex roles is simple labels for the people around them as men and women or boys and girls. When they learn to label themselves as boys or girls, they have acquired a *gender identity*. By age two, most children have such a stable gender identity that it cannot be changed without causing serious problems. During the preschool years, children learn many of the culturally defined characteristics that are "masculine" and "feminine." These *sex role concepts* are well formed by the time children reach adolescence. Theory suggests and research has shown that masculinity and femininity are two separate dimensions rather than being opposites.

A person can adopt both masculine and feminine characteristics, a pattern labeled *psychological androgyny*. Some developmental theories suggest that children or young adolescents adopt traditionally stereotyped roles, then gradually evolve toward androgyny. Increased pressure for traditional sex-typed behavior occurs at puberty, especially for girls. When being attractive to boys becomes important, girls may abandon childhood tomboyishness, lose interest in school, and devote their attention to being cute, sexy, and coy. The evolution toward androgyny, when it occurs, appears in later adolescence or early adulthood.

Sex roles are learned from parents, siblings, school, peers, and mass media. For a male, high masculinity is likely when he has a close, warm relation to his father, when his father is dominant, and when both parents are permissive. In a father-absent home, masculinity is greater when the mother directly rewards it and when there are other males around. For females, femininity is promoted by a warm relation to the mother, by restrictiveness, and by rewards from the father. Departures from traditional roles are more likely for females when the mother is employed and is herself androgynous. Children with opposite-sex siblings generally have more androgynous characteristics than those with same-sex siblings. Schools reinforce traditional sex roles by teachers' differential treatment of boys and girls, stereotyped textbooks, sex segregation in certain courses, vocational counseling, and unequal distributions of males and females in high- and low-status jobs. Peers and mass media usually exert pressure toward adoption of traditional sex roles, but they can also be potent forces for change.

In our society, the male role is valued more than the female role, but androgyny seems to be more functional or adaptive for most situations than either masculinity or femininity alone. Androgynous people of both sexes have high self-esteem. Androgynous and masculine females also achieve better in areas like mathematics and science. Feminine females often have low self-esteem and high anxiety, and they frequently seek help for emotional problems in college. Females who take on motherhood, the major feminine role task, during adolescence have a serious handicap in later educational and occupational achievement. If masculine characteristics are adaptive for some situations and feminine characteristics for others, it follows that a person who combines both will fare better than a person who is limited to one or the other. To the extent that androgyny represents combining both roles, it seems that socialization of adolescents for the future should be directed toward this goal.

SUGGESTIONS FOR FURTHER READING

KAPLAN, A. G. & BEAN, J. P. (Eds.). *Beyond sex role stereotypes: Readings toward a psychology of androgyny.* Boston: Little, Brown, 1976.

MISCHEL, W. Sex typing and socialization. In P. H. Mussen (Ed.), *Carmichael's manual of child psychology* (3rd ed.). New York: Wiley, 1970.

MONEY, J. & EHRHARDT, A. *Man and woman: Boy and girl.* Baltimore: Johns Hopkins University Press, 1972.

SPENCE, J. T. & HELMREICH, R. L. *Masculinity and femininity.* Austin, Tex.: University of Texas Press, 1978.

FREIZE, I. H., PARSONS, J. E., JOHNSON, P. B., RUBLE, D. N. & ZELLMAN, G. L. *Women and sex roles: A social psychological perspective.* New York: Norton, 1978.

BIBLIOGRAPHY

ABRAMOWITZ, S. I., WEITZ, L. J., SCHWARTZ, J. M., AMIRA, S., GOMES, B., & ABRAMOWITZ, C. A. Comparative counselor inferences toward women with medical school aspirations. *Journal of College Student Personnel,* 1975, *16,* 128–130.

BEM, S. L. The measurement of psychological androgyny. *Journal of Consulting and Clinical Psychology,* 1974, *42,* 155–162.

BEM, S. L. Probing the promise of androgyny. In A. G. Kaplan & J. P. Bean (Eds.), *Beyond sex-role stereotypes: Readings toward a psychology of androgyny.* Boston: Little, Brown, 1976.

BEM, S. L. On the utility of alternative procedures for assessing psychological androgyny. *Journal of Consulting and Clinical Psychology,* 1977, *45,* 196–205.

BERZINS, J. I., WELLING, M. A., & WETTER, R. E. A new measure of psychological androgyny based on the personality research form. *Journal of Consulting and Clinical Psychology,* 1978, *46,* 126–138.

BILLER, H. B. Father absence and the personality development of the male child. *Developmental Psychology,* 1970, *2,* 181–201.

BIRK, J. M., COPPER, J., & TANNEY, M. F. Is what we see all we can be? In N. K. Schlossberg & J. M. Birk (Eds.), *Freeing sex roles for new careers.* Washington, D. C.: American Council on Education, 1977.

BLOCK, J. H. Conceptions of sex role: Some cross-cultural and longitudinal perspectives. *American Psychologist,* 1973, *28,* 512–526.

BRIM, O. G. Family structure and sex role learning by children: A further analysis of Helen Koch's data. *Sociometry,* 1958, *21,* 1–16.

BRONFENBRENNER, U. Some familial antecedents of responsibility and leadership in adolescents. In L. Petrullo & B. M. Bass (Eds.), *Leadership and interpersonal behavior.* New York: Holt, 1961.

BROVERMAN, I. K., VOGEL, S. R., BROVERMAN, D. M., CLARKSON, F. E., & ROSENKRANTZ, P. S. Sex-role stereotypes: A current appraisal. *Journal of Social Issues,* 1972, *28,* 59–78.

BURTON, R. V., & WHITING, J. W. M. The absent father and cross-sex identity. *Merrill-Palmer Quarterly,* 1961, *7,* 85–95.

CARLSMITH, L. Effect of early father absence on scholastic aptitude. *Harvard Educational Review,* 1964, *34,* 3–21.

COLEMAN, J. S. *The adolescent society.* New York: Free Press, 1961.

CONNELL, D. M., & JOHNSON, J. E. Relationship between sex-role identification and self-esteem in early adolescents. *Developmental Psychology,* 1970, *3,* 268.

CONSTANTINOPLE, A. Masculinity-femininity: An exception to a famous dictum. *Psychological Bulletin*, 1973, *80*, 389–407.

DONAHUE, T. J., & COSTAR, J. W. Counselor discrimination against young women in career selection. *Journal of Counseling Psychology*, 1977, *24*, 481–486.

DOUVAN, E., & ADELSON, J. *The adolescent experience*. New York: Wiley, 1966.

Fact sheets on institutional sexism. New York: The Racism/Sexism Resource Center, 1976.

FAGOT, B. I., & PATTERSON, G. R. An *in vivo* analysis of reinforcing contingencies for sex-role behaviors in the preschool child. *Developmental Psychology*, 1969, *1*, 563–568.

FELSENTHAL, H. Sex differences in teacher-pupil interaction in first grade reading instruction. Paper presented at American Educational Research Association, Minneapolis, 1970.

FRAZIER, N., & SADKER, M. *Sexism in school and society*. New York: Harper & Row, 1973.

FRIEDRICH-COFER, L. K., TUCKER, C. J., NORRIS-BAKER, C., FARNSWORTH, J. B., FISHER, D. P., HANNINGTON, C. M., & HOXIE, K. Perceptions by adolescents of television heroines. Paper presented at the Southwestern Psychological Association, New Orleans, April, 1978.

GOOD, T., & BROPHY, J. Behavioral expression of teacher attitudes. *Journal of Educational Psychology*, 1973, *63*, 617.

GOOD, T., SIKES, J. N., & BROPHY, J. Effect of teacher sex and student sex on classroom interaction. *Journal of Educational Psychology*, 1973, *65*, 74–87.

GOUGH, H. C. *Manual for the California Psychological Inventory*. Palo Alto, Calif.: Consulting Psychologists Press, 1957.

GROTEVANT, H. D. Sibling constellations and sex typing of interests in adolescence. *Child Development*, 1978, *49*, 540–542.

Guidelines for improving the image of women in textbooks. Prepared by the Sexism in Textbooks Committee at Scott, Foresman. New York: Scott, Foresman, 1972.

GUTTENTAG, M., & BRAY, H. Teachers as mediators of sex-role standards. In A. G. Sargent (Ed.), *Beyond sex roles*. St. Paul, Minn.: West Publishing Co., 1977.

HARRIS, D. Discussion in symposium on sex role learning and adolescence. Presented at the Annual Meeting of the American Association for the Advancement of Science, Washington, D. C., December, 1972.

HEILBURN, A. B., & FROMME, D. K. Parental identification of late adolescents and level of adjustment: The importance of parent-model attributes, ordinal position and sex of the child. *Journal of Genetic Psychology*, 1965, *107*, 49–59.

HETHERINGTON, E. M. The effects of familial variables on sex typing, on parent-child similarity, and on imitation in children. In J. P. Hill (Ed.), *Minnesota symposia on child psychology* (Vol. 1). Minneapolis: University of Minnesota Press, 1967.

HETHERINGTON, E. M. Effects of father absence on personality development in adolescent daughters. *Developmental Psychology*, 1972, *7*, 313–326.

HETHERINGTON, E. M., & PARKE, R. D. *Child psychology: A contemporary viewpoint* (2nd ed.). New York: McGraw-Hill, 1979.

HOFFMAN, L. W., & NYE, F. I. (Eds.). *Working mothers.* San Francisco: Jossey-Bass, 1974.

HUSTON-STEIN, A., & HIGGINS-TRENK, A. Development of females from childhood through adulthood: Career and feminine role orientations. In P. B. Baltes (Ed.), *Life-span development and behavior* (Vol. 1). New York: Academic Press, 1978.

JOHNSON, M. Sex role learning in the nuclear family. *Child Development,* 1963, *34,* 319–333.

KAGAN, J., JOSKEN, B., & WATSON, S. Child's symbolic conceptualization of parents. *Child Development,* 1961, *32,* 625–636.

KAGAN, J., & MOSS, H. A. *Birth to maturity.* New York: Wiley, 1962.

KELMAN, S. Sweden's liberated men and women. *New Republic,* March 15, 1971, 21–23.

LEIFER, A. D., & LESSER, G. S. The development of career awareness in young children. Center for Research in Children's Television, Harvard Graduate School of Education, Cambridge, Mass., 1976.

LEVITAN, T. E., & CHANANINE, J. D. Responses of female primary teachers to sex-typed behavior in male and female children. *Child Development,* 1972, *43,* 1309–1316.

MACCOBY, E. E., & JACKLIN, C. N. *The psychology of sex differences.* Stanford, Calif.: Stanford University Press, 1974.

McARTHUR, L. Z., & EISEN, S. V. Achievements of male and female storybook characters as determinants of achievement behavior by boys and girls. *Journal of Personality and Social Psychology,* 1976, *33,* 467–473.

MILTON, G. A. Five studies of the relation between sex-role identification and achievement in problem solving. Technical Report 3, Department of Industrial Administration and Department of Psychology, Yale University, New Haven, Conn., December, 1958.

MINUCHIN, P. Sex-role concepts and sex typing in childhood as a function of school and home environments. *Child Development,* 1965, *36,* 1033–1048.

MISCHEL, W. A social-learning view of sex differences in behavior. In E. E. Maccoby (Ed.), *The development of sex differences.* Stanford, Calif.: Stanford University Press, 1966.

MISCHEL, W. Sex typing and socialization. In P. H. Mussen (Ed.), *Carmichael's manual of child psychology* (3rd ed., Vol. 2). New York: Wiley, 1970.

MONEY, J., & EHRHARDT, A. *Man and woman: Boy and girl.* Baltimore: Johns Hopkins University Press, 1972.

MORRIS, J. *Conundrum.* New York: Harcourt Brace Jovanovich, 1974.

NELSEN, E. A., & MACCOBY, E. E. The relationships between social development and differential abilities on the Scholastic Aptitude Test. *Merrill-Palmer Quarterly,* 1966, *12,* 269–284.

PARSONS, T. Family structure and the socialization of the child. In T. Parsons & R. F. Bales (Eds.), *Family, socialization and interaction process.* Glencoe, Ill.: The Free Press, 1955.

PAYNE, D. E., & MUSSEN, P. H. Parent-child relations and father identification among adolescent boys. *Journal of Abnormal and Social Psychology,* 1956, *52,* 358–362.

259

PERRY, D. G., & PERRY, L. C. Observational learning in children: Effects of sex of model and subject's sex-role behavior. *Journal of Personality and Social Psychology*, 1975, *31*, 1084–1088.

REBECCA, M., HEFNER, R., & OLESHANSKY, B. A model of sex-role transcendence. *Journal of Social Issues*, 1976, *32*, 197–206.

RICKS, F., & PYKE, S. Teacher perceptions and attitudes that foster or maintain sex role differences. *Interchange*, 1973, *4*, 26–33.

SCHACHTER, F. F., GILUTZ, G., SHORE, E., & ADLER, M. Sibling de-identification judged by mothers: Cross-validation and developmental studies. *Child Development*, 1978, *49*, 543–546.

SEARS, R. R. Relation of early socialization experiences to self-concepts and gender role in middle childhood. *Child Development*, 1970, *41*, 267–289.

SHAW, M. C., & McCUEN, J. T. The onset of academic underachievement in bright children. *Journal of Educational Psychology*, 1960, *51*, 103–108.

SHERMAN, J. A. *On the psychology of women*. Springfield, Ill.: Charles Thomas, 1971.

SPAULDING, R. L. Achievement, creativity, and self-concept correlates of teacher-pupil transactions in elementary schools. Cooperative Research Project No. 1352, Washington, D.C.: Department of Health, Education, and Welfare, 1963.

SPENCE, J. T., HELMREICH, R., & STAPP, J. Ratings of self and peers on sex-role attributes and their relation to self-esteem and conceptions of masculinity and femininity. *Journal of Personality and Social Psychology*, 1975, *32*, 29–39.

SPENCE, T. J., & HELMREICH, R. L. *Masculinity and femininity*. Austin, Tex.: University of Texas Press, 1978.

STEIN, A. H. The effects of sex-role standards for achievement and sex-role preference on three determinants of achievement motivation. *Developmental Psychology*, 1971, *4*, 219–231.

STEIN, A. H., & BAILEY, M. M. The socialization of achievement orientation in females. *Psychological Bulletin*, 1973, *80*, 345–366.

STEIN, A. H., & FREIDRICH, L. K. The impact of television on children and youth. In E. M. Hetherington, J. W. Hagen, R. Kron & A. H. Stein (Eds.), *Review of child development research* (Vol. 5). Chicago: University of Chicago Press, 1975.

STOLZ, L. M. *Father relations of war born children*. Stanford, Calif.: Stanford University Press, 1954.

SUTTON-SMITH, B., & ROSENBERG, B. G. Age changes in the effects of ordinal position on sex-role identification. *Journal of Genetic Psychology*, 1965, *107*, 61–73.

THOMAS, A. H., & STEWART, N. R. Counselor response to female clients with deviant and conforming career goals. *Journal of Counseling Psychology*, 1971, *18*, 352–357.

TRECKER, J. Women in U.S. history textbooks. *Social Education*, 1971, *3*, 249–260.

URBERG, K. A., & LABOUVIE-VIEF, G. Conceptualizations of sex roles: A life span developmental study. *Developmental Psychology*, 1976, *12*, 15–23.

WEBB, A. P. Sex-role preferences and adjustment in early adolescents. *Child Development*, 1963, *34*, 609–618.

WELCH, R. L. Androgyny and derived identity in married women with varying degrees of non-traditional role involvement. *Psychology of Women Quarterly,* 1979, *3,* 308–315.

WIRTENBERG, T. J., & NAKAMURA, C. Y. Education: Barriers to changing occupational roles of women. *Journal of Social Issues,* 1976, *32,* 165–179.

WOHLFORD, P., SANDROCK, J. W., BERGER, S. E., & LIBERMAN, D. Older brother's influence on sex-typed, aggressive and dependent behavior in father-absent children. *Developmental Psychology,* 1971, *4,* 124–134.

10

ADOLESCENT SEXUALITY

Carol A. Wagner

Human sexuality, regardless of developmental stage, varies within cultural groups and between cultural groups. Part of this variance can be attributed to the dominant norms of different cultures, part to the impact of social institutions, and part to individual differences in human behavior. Human sexuality is also affected by the historical period in which one lives; societal conflicts about sexuality can have a significant impact on how individuals and subgroups behave, think, and feel. Reiss (1976) has reviewed several major historical patterns that have relevance for the interpretation of sexual behavior in today's adolescents. He believes there were two periods in American history marked by rapid change in sexual attitudes and behaviors. One of those periods was from 1915 to 1920 (World War I); the other was from 1965 to 1970 (Vietnam War). During each of these periods, there were major upheavals in our social institutions as a function of economic and political change.

During both periods there were significant increases in the number of women experiencing premarital intercourse; there were also significant increases in the divorce rate. Reiss believes that the fundamental outcome of the early period was "legitimation of sexual choice" (p. 183). He has characterized the period 1915–1920 as one in which increased communication and openness about sexual ideas and practices were achieved, and one in which the belief that people have a right to choose their own sexual lifestyle became widespread.

The next 50 years saw few major changes in sexual attitudes and behaviors. By the late 1960s, we had entered an era characterized by Vietnam War demonstrations, voting at 18, and legislation on abortion. The courts also established that contraception was a matter of personal privacy (McCoy, 1974). The emphasis on civil rights and women's rights helped to create and sustain a climate conducive to change in sexual behavior.

Hunt (1972), studying a cross section of the American adult population, found a major attitudinal change relating to sexuality. Compared to the Kinsey data collected in the 1930s and 1940s, Hunt records a greater acceptance of sex education, premarital sex, masturbation, and homosexuality. However, other researchers (Alston & Tucker, 1973; Levitt & Klassen, 1973) who used representative national samples, document the maintenance of some of our traditional prohibitive attitudes toward sexual behavior. McCoy (1974) supports these findings by noting that a "sex-negative society" is one of the major problems associated with unwanted pregnancy and venereal disease among American adolescents. It would appear that at the present time our sexual attitudes and behaviors are freer and more

Carol A. Wagner is Associate Professor of Counseling Psychology at Temple University. Dr. Wagner has written on such topics as confidentiality with child clients, group counseling, referral patterns for counseling, and developmental issues at the child and adolescent level.

open than at any time in American history although powerful vestiges of traditional thinking and behaving continue to exist.

THE IMPACT OF SOCIAL INSTITUTIONS ON HUMAN SEXUALITY

Various social institutions contribute to or hinder the achievement of sexual experiences that foster normal growth toward maturity. These institutions include the family, organized religion, the school, and the media.

Family

Every family has standards for what is appropriate in the area of sexual behavior. However, families differ greatly in how these standards are derived, communicated, and treated if violated. Families also differ in the content of the standards, that is, what is permissible and under what conditions. Standards for sexual behavior may come from personal experiences of the parents, from the teachings of a church, from values integrated from previous generations, and from the effects of social change in the dominant culture.

How these standards and attitudes toward sexuality are communicated vary. Frequently the method of communication is covert, that is, taught by omissions, elusive warnings, inattention to sexual inquiries, and nonverbal responses. Overt methods are open and direct and more rare. For example, parents may discuss, even initiate discussions about sexual matters with their children. They may express affection with sexual overtones toward their spouses; they may discuss sexual matters, especially those issues that are controversial and have an impact upon their lives.

Families differ in how rigidly they adhere to prescribed standards and expectations; some families need to exert control and rigid allegiance as a way of coping with their own insecurities. Others are more flexible and adapt to changes and threats to their personal standards. This pattern may be evident in how parents treat violations. Do they become angry, reflective, revengeful, uncommunicative, inquiring, or helpful? In other words, do their responses facilitate communication and understanding, or do they inhibit and discourage further communication?

Another familial impact on the development of healthy sexuality comes from the gender roles of the male and female in the family. If females are expected to be wives and mothers first and to follow a traditional role pattern, there may be standards implicit in that role definition. For example, it may be expected that the daughter gears all dating and sexual behavior to finding a husband. The son, however, may be expected to "sow his oats" before settling down to marriage. In families that achieve greater equity in male and female roles, i.e., in work, home, and leisure activities, one is more likely to find similarity in expectation for the sexual behavior of sons and daughters.

Organized Religion

In the American culture, organized religion has played an important part in the development of attitudes toward human sexuality. As a major social institution, it has wielded tremendous power and influence over the standards of conduct that guide sexual behavior on a daily basis. As is true with families, churches vary greatly in how standards are communicated, how they are adapted to changes in social conditions, and how members are treated if standards are violated. Organized religions are more similar than dissimilar in the *content* of the standards they advocate for sexual behavior. They have traditionally supported the view that all sexual behavior should be confined to the married state. Although this major injunction stands, churches have seemed to tolerate and accept minor violations that might occur in the courtship process—kissing, light petting, heavy petting. Premarital intercourse has, however, been a taboo. Masturbation, homosexuality, extramarital sex, and specific practices (such as oral sex) have also had very strong prohibitive injunctions.

Because some religions hold to their standards more rigorously and purport more serious consequences for violations (i.e., mortal sin, hell, damnation), church members of these groups experience more guilt and self-degradation than members of other churches. Particularly problematic for individuals and families are church teachings on such issues as birth control and abortion.

It is believed by some people that organized religion has been a significant contributor to negative attitudes toward sexuality. Most attention, historically, has been given to sexuality in the context of procreation; what has been underestimated are the joys and pleasures of responsible sexuality, as well as a basic understanding of the normal, healthy process of sexual development from infancy through old age. The churches have had some positive impact by associating sexual behavior with the institution of marriage, thus indirectly teaching the lesson of responsibility.

Today organized religions are attempting to struggle with many of these issues. The advent of safe birth control technology, the human rights movement for women and homosexuals, and adolescents' struggle for increased autonomy have become social pressures that refuse to be ignored. Rigid adherence to standards, admonitions, and "guilt trips" no longer serve to control the behavior of church members, particularly in the evolutionary process of awareness, acceptance, and responsible expression of sexual needs.

265

School

The third social institution in American culture that exerts influence upon the development of sexual attitudes and behavior is the school. Here it seems important to discuss the difference between the formal and informal curriculum. The formal curriculum refers to those planned courses of study that are presented by faculty members in various subject areas. The informal curriculum would include learning how to handle a bully on the playground at lunch time or learning how "to keep your cool" when your first love asks you to go to a movie.

Each curriculum has a special role in affecting the development of human sexuality. The formal curriculum, in my opinion, exerts the least influence. Courses in biology have for many years included a section on the human reproductive system—for the most part, an explanation of the physiological aspects of reproduction.

Some courses in home economics and family life have included units on dating, courtship, marriage, and child development. Health courses and school nurses have frequently been responsible for informing fifth- and sixth-grade girls about menstruation. Few, if any, of these efforts have made human sexuality—its developmental phases and various expressions—the focus of study. It is only within the past 10–15 years that schools have considered the inclusion of a formal sex education curriculum. Many sex education curricula in use today are severely limited in content relevant to student interest and experience. Controversial topics like birth control and homosexuality are often excluded, owing to community opposition. More will be said about this later.

The school is a most important environment for socialization into peer groups. And it is through the informal curriculum that students learn much about sexual thinking, feelings, and behavior. For example, males and females may see peers nude while taking showers at school. Observations of the different rates of physical maturation may prove stressful to some individuals (and educational to others). Slow-maturing students may become worried about the size of their penises or breasts. Fast-maturing students may become self-conscious. In the school environment, girls have many opportunities to chat privately about menstrual characteristics and difficulties; they may discover tampons for the first time.

Social activities sponsored by the school—dances, sports events, class parties—often encourage subgrouping and pairing off. Increased contact with peers of the same or opposite sex increases the probability of physical contact. Boys and girls may express their feelings through holding hands, kissing, and petting. Relationships initiated and developed during school hours usually precipitate additional contact beyond school hours in a more formal ritual of "getting together," "going out," and partying on the week-ends. These additional social experiences provide more opportunities for students to become aware of their sexual identity and to experiment with sexual behavior.

School environments also provide opportunities for students to seek out specific sexual information independent of family, church, and even peers. Libraries frequently purchase books on sex education and human sexuality, which are available for student use. Although such resources are not usually advertised, a few resourceful students will make use of such reading materials.

Media

A final major influence in the development of sexual attitudes and behaviors is the media. By media influence, I mean the exposure to sexual beliefs and practices promulgated by television, films, records, radio, cassette tapes, newspapers, popular sex magazines like *Playboy* and *Penthouse*, and magazines in general. The popular culture is communicated by these media, and today's popular culture is replete with sexual messages. Commercials and printed advertisements play on the sexuality of the viewers and readers, and attempt to seduce them to purchase their goods. Films of good quality freely show nudity and the sexual aspects of interpersonal relationships. Special television programming may focus on homosexuality, birth control, venereal disease, abortion, and aspects of sex education. The changing beliefs about women's roles and rights are well addressed by the media coverage; part of the message conveyed is that women have the right to sexual satisfaction and the responsibility to assert themselves to achieve it in their interpersonal relationships.

I am convinced that the media have done more educating about human sexuality in the past 15 years than the family, the school, and the church combined. We may not like or appreciate the values being covertly taught, but in the absence of more active and realistic efforts on the part of our major social institutions, media messages are filling some obvious gaps in the educating of our young about their sexual selves.

IMPACT OF PHYSIOLOGICAL CHANGES
ON SEXUAL DEVELOPMENT

Now that we have looked at human sexuality in a historical and cultural context, I would like to focus on the adolescent's development in relationship to physiological changes. Physiological changes in boys and girls signify the beginning of puberty, that period in life when sexual maturity is achieved. Usually the onset of puberty occurs prior to the age of 12. These physiological changes involve the production of male and female hormones, the development of primary and secondary sex characteristics, and a growth spurt in height and weight (see chapter 3 on biological development). Reynolds and Wine (1948, 1951) have studied and described the period of pubescence for boys and girls. Among boys, the age of onset varied from 9½ years to 13½ years with the clearest indicators of change being height and testicular growth. First ejaculation occurs about a year after changes and growth in the testes, and accompanies an increase in the size of the penis (Kinsey, Pomeroy & Martin, 1948). Full sexual maturity was achieved for the Reynolds and Wine sample somewhere between 15½ and 18 years of age.

Girls were found to begin these changes earlier, with age of onset varying from 8½ years to 13 years of age. These changes were signaled by the development of breast buds and spurts in height. First menstruation was experienced by these girls on the average of 2 years after the onset of puberty. A modal age of 16–17 years old was suggested as a criterion for sexual maturity among girls. Individual variations in the onset and completion of puberty are enormous. Such individual differences result from a combination of genetic characteristics in interaction with environmental variables. These variations are critically important in understanding a particular adolescent's sexual and social development

Physiological changes result in increased sex drive, as well as increased sexual tension (Garrison, 1976). They also affect the onset and rate of development of heterosexual interests. Various researchers have found that early-maturing boys and girls have more interest in peers of the opposite sex than those who mature late. Early maturers are also more likely to have heterosexual experiences at an earlier age (Stone & Barker, 1939; Sollenberger, 1940; Jones & Bayley, 1950; Jones, 1957).

IMPACT OF PSYCHOLOGICAL NEEDS ON
SEXUAL DEVELOPMENT

It is not just the physiological changes that affect sexual development, but also the psychological needs characteristic of the adolescent period. Relationships to peer group members become increasingly important since it is through these relationships that adolescents begin to test out their identity as unique human beings. Lief (1973) has provided a conceptual framework that I shall follow as we consider the adolescent's search for identity.

The Search for Identity

Adolescents need to test out and experiment with the various social roles they will be expected to assume as adults in American society. For example, adolescents need to find out what it is like to be a worker, a provider, or a club member. They also need to find out what it is like to be a date partner, a kisser, a petter, a lover, a man, or a woman.

Another dimension of the identity search is values and standards, that is, a personalized belief system, as well as an ethical code by which to live one's life. Adolescents test out values and beliefs related to work, religion, leisure, friendship, and family life. They also experiment with values and beliefs related to sexuality and specific sexual practices, i.e., masturbation, homosexual contact, kissing, petting. Some of this testing may be done cognitively, but most is done experientially. Adolescents are likely to question the standards for sexual behavior held sacrosanct by the family and organized religion. They may throw out or modify standards so that they make more sense.

Personality characteristics are another concern in the adolescents' search for identity. Lief (1973) believes that adolescents categorize themselves on bipolar dimensions, e.g., good or bad, ugly or handsome, outgoing or withdrawn. They may also see themselves as sexy or not sexy. They begin to assess their gender identity by asking themselves how masculine or feminine they are in relation to self, peer, and societal expectations.

During this identity search, adolescents begin to formulate goals and expectations. They begin to ask what they want from work, leisure, friendships, and family. And they also begin to formulate sexual behavior preferences, sex object preferences, notions about courtship styles, characteristics of potential marriage partners, and expectations for dating.

Interpersonal attitudes and behaviors are an important component of the identity search. Adolescents begin to examine how they relate to other people, especially their peers. Do they have confidants, or do they feel emotionally and socially isolated? How do they get along with members of the opposite sex? Sexual behavior is examined, experimented with, and evaluated in the context of short- and long-term relationships. Adolescents' sexual behavior may begin to be assessed in terms of its impact on self, partner, and peer status within the group.

The final dimension of adolescents' search for identity relates to self boundaries or the ability to function independently. This means that adolescents must grow in order to assume responsibility for their behavior. They strive to find out what they can handle alone. In the arena of sexual development, adolescents have to learn how to solve problems and make reasonable decisions. Coping with parking and petting, premarital inter-

269

course, masturbation, and guilt resulting from experimentation, provides experience for testing autonomous behavior in conflict situations.

To understand the sexual behavior, attitudes, beliefs, knowledge, and values of adolescents requires a rather comprehensive understanding of the historical and cultural context within which they live. It means that we must examine the specific institutions that impact upon the individual's life, i.e., the family, organized religion, school, and the media. The individual's history, with regard to the onset and rate of puberty, is also essential for assessing the beginning rate of heterosexual development. Finally, all of these variables must be considered in light of the adolescent's search for identity.

SEXUAL DEVELOPMENT IN A SOCIAL CONTEXT: DATING

Since much of what is learned about sexuality in adolescence occurs within the social context of developing and maintaining relationships with the opposite sex, I will spend some time discussing the development of dating behaviors.

Theoretical Aspects of Dating

Skipper and Nass (1966) believe that dating is purposive behavior oriented toward fulfilling four functions. These include dating as recreation, dating as socialization, dating as status achievement, and dating as courtship. Today the courtship function is less prominent, and dating is viewed more as a social experience and as an outlet for heterosexual interests (Rogers, 1969; Smith, 1969). Feinstein and Ardon have proposed a four-stage theory to explain the adolescent's heterosexual development. These stages are outlined as follows:

> Stage I: Sexual awakening (13–15 years old)
> *Characteristics*:
> Friendships with erotic trends
> Dating invitations for movies and parties
> Public acknowledgement of boyfriend or girlfriend
> Kissing and "making out"
> Girls may be able to attract older boys
> Late-maturing boys may experience insecurity
> Stage II: Practicing (14–17 years old)
> *Characteristics*:
> Many short-term relationships accompanied by emotional intensity

Irregular dating either individually or in a group; group dating is popular

May arrive individually to group event, but leave alone, in pairs, or in groups

Stage III: Acceptance of the Sexual Role (16–19 years old)
Characteristics:
Experimentation with various dating styles
Involvement in longer-term dating relationships
More comfortable in heterosexual relationships
More stable and regular dating pattern
Sexual intercourse more often a part of relationships

Stage IV: Development of Permanent Choice (18–25 years old)
Characteristics:
Choice of a more permanent love object is made
Dating couple trust each other more completely
Alternative date and mate choices are given up easily
May result in living together or marriage[1]

Age Characteristics in the Dating Process

Preparation for dating actually begins in preadolescence. In about the fifth and sixth grade, boys and girls begin to show an interest in each other by hitting, teasing, and chasing. This is a clear deviation from previous behavior when girls and boys formed same-sex cliques and showed utter contempt for each other. Broderick (1966a), using a sample of fifth and sixth graders from ten different elementary schools, was able to show a series of developmental steps that these 10 to 12 year olds went through in preparation for their first date. The accomplishment of each step seemed to make more probable the accomplishment of the next step (almost as if a developmental sequence had to occur). Initially, there was a positive attitude toward marriage expressed as a long-range future goal. The second step involved an emotional attachment to some person of the opposite sex, that is, someone was declared a boyfriend or girlfriend. This behavior was followed by a declaration of having been in love. The next step consisted of preferring a movie partner of the opposite sex; and the final step was an actual date.

Broderick (1966b) carried out a similar study with 10–17 year olds to further refine and define developmental trends. He included over 1,000 students in grades 5 to 12. He found support for the notion that negative feelings toward the opposite sex decrease with age and that this pattern

[1] Feinstein, S. C., & Ardon, M. S. Trends in dating patterns and adolescent development. *Journal of Youth and Adolescence*, 1973, *2*, 157–166. Used with permission.

occurs more quickly for females than males (possibly because physiological changes occur earlier for females than males). Using the data from this study (although one needs to be cautious due to the limited sample), it is possible to describe some of the characteristics of heterosexual development. When the youngest group (10–11 years) referred to a date, this usually meant a walk or having a coke. About 30–50% of this group stated that they had an opposite-sex friend. When they spoke of love, it usually referred to an unreciprocated, more than likely undeclared, attachment. Over 25% had begun to date; 50% reported having been in love; and 20% reported they had gone steady.

In the 12- 13-year old group, there was an increased interest in romantic contacts, greater interest in getting married, and greater numbers approving movie love scenes. More students dated, and more reported having girlfriends or boyfriends. Kissing games were popular at this age; boys chose younger girls for dates; and both boys and girls were willing to inform peers about their dating partners and dating experiences. About 50% of the students preferred someone of the opposite sex as a movie partner, and approximately 60% had begun to date. There were no significant increases in the percentages of students who reported "going steady" and having had love experiences.

Among the 14 and 15 year olds, half reported cross-sex friendships. The frequency of dating and the number of dating partners had increased; approximately 90% of the adolescents were dating, and more frequent and meaningful interactions were occurring between partners. Compared to the two younger groups, boys were more likely to consider their girlfriends as friends. At this age, about 75% approved of love scenes in the movies.

The oldest students, 16 and 17 year olds, expressed the most heterosexual interest. Between 60% and 70% reported having a boyfriend or girlfriend. Approximately 70% stated they had gone steady at some time. With almost 97% having begun dating, over half averaged a date a week. Most of the dating was done on the weekends, with single and double dating the preferred styles. Parents and peers of this group were more aware of the adolescents' heterosexual choices than were those of the younger adolescents. Almost all of the adolescents in this age group reported that their affectionate feelings for another were reciprocated. There was more serious kissing and sexual activity among these adolescents.

Although Broderick's sample was extremely limited, a clear pattern of heterosexual development can be discerned. Fantasy and undeclared interest in someone of the opposite sex were followed by the beginning of dating. Infrequent dating associated with a declared interest in another eventually emerges as a more frequent contact with someone who is viewed as date *and friend*. Reciprocated, affectionate feelings between adolescents dating each other seem to become the norm by 16 or 17 years of age.

Values in Date Selection

In a study conducted by Hansen (1977) approximately 350 students, ages 15–19, were surveyed on their dating choices: 25% dated steadily, 25% dated on a random basis, and 33% dated only occasionally. What we can't decipher from these data is the difference in age among those questioned. However, this study does help us to understand the values involved in the selection of dating partners. When the adolescents were asked to rank values they believed important for their date selection, they identified the following: dependability, considerateness, pleasantness, cheerfulness, sense of humor, dress, neatness. There were no differences between the values used by the boys and girls. It was also found that adolescents considered their own date selection process a more serious business than that of their peers. This was reflected by the fact that the subjects believed their peers used primarily external criteria (i.e., good looks, money, car) when choosing a date.

The Experience of Dating

We can gain a better understanding of dating, at least as some adolescent girls experience it, by reviewing some of the descriptive work that emerged from a study of 20 adolescents (Place, 1975). This study involved 15- and 16-year old girls from middle-class families. Although most of the parents of these girls did not expect their daughters to date until the age of 16, many of the girls began negotiating for dating privileges at about 12 and 13 years of age. These negotiations were carried out by nagging, reporting names of peers who were dating, or developing specific strategies for getting their way.

Conflicts continued over dating even after the first date was achieved. Requesting permission to stay out later than parents wanted or asking to go in a car on a date were new hurdles that had to be negotiated. Parents were concerned about safety and their daughters' welfare, whereas the girls struggled to obtain more independence. Many of the girls successfully used peer group pressure to change their parents' beliefs, feelings, or behavior. Siblings were asked to help out in the resolution of conflicts with parents. The girls recounted all the privileges their older brothers and sisters had had in similar situations. The girls also tried to match their behavior to parental expectations as a way of demonstrating that they were mature enough to assume more responsibility.

Most of the girls believed that getting a boy to ask them out was a problem; they developed some rather subtle, but assertive, strategies. They worked at being noticed, at adapting themselves to specific interests of the

273

boys, and learning how to say "no" gracefully. Satisfaction with a date seemed to be a function of mutual expectations about what should occur on the date. These girls reported they had to learn how to discourage unwanted or encourage wanted sexual intimacy. They also had to learn how to provide support and encouragement to boys who felt awkward. The girls valued personality, looks, physique, behavior, and sincerity in date selection (in that order). However, their parents valued appearance, manners, short hair, conversational ability, personality, and intelligence in their daughter's friends (in that order). The girls in this study reported real enjoyment in the dating process; it seemed to provide them with social experiences, fun, companionship, and opportunities to learn from members of the opposite sex.

SEXUAL KNOWLEDGE OF ADOLESCENTS

In this section, I will focus on the sexual knowledge of adolescents—where it comes from, what is known by them, and how it relates to what adolescents want to know.

Where Does Information Come From?

A number of research studies provide evidence that peers are the major source of sex information (Finkel & Finkel, 1975; Reichelt & Werley, 1975); peers seem to be more important for males than females. Additional studies show that independent reading is another major source of information (Commission on Obscenity and Pornography, 1971; Spanier, 1977). One pattern is clear from the literature: Mothers and fathers usually rate poorly in providing meaningful information to their children although mothers seem to be a more important source for girls. Finkel and Finkel (1975) found that less than 11% of their white, Hispanic, and black adolescent urban males received information from their families. Black males listed male and female friends as their two prime sources, whereas white and Hispanic males listed male friends and professionals (doctors, teachers). However, Gebhard (1977) found that adolescents today, as compared to those in the Kinsey research of the 1930s and 1940s, receive more important information from their mothers than from same-sex peers. In addition, he found that sexual learning occurs earlier.

What Is Known?

We do know that much of the information adolescents receive is either inaccurate (Kleinerman, Grossman, Breslow & Goldman, 1971; Thornburg,

1972) or incomplete. For example, adolescents lack basic biological information about the female menstrual cycle, as well as information on the period of greatest risk for conception (Kantner & Zelnik, 1972; Finkel & Finkel, 1975). In the Kantner and Zelnik (1972) study of females, there was evidence that increasing age and sexual experiences were associated with more accurate knowledge about biological functioning. However, Finkel and Finkel (1975) did not find the same to be true for boys.

Many authorities have documented the scarcity of accurate information about contraception among our adolescent population (Furstenberg, Gordis & Markowitz, 1969; Kantner & Zelnik, 1972; Finkel & Finkel, 1975). For example, adolescents may know about the condom or withdrawal as contraceptive methods and little about intrauterine devices. At a more basic level, they may not understand the relationships between intercourse, conception, and venereal disease (VD). Many males do not know that condoms are protection against VD or that male withdrawal doesn't guarantee lack of conception. Among adolescents, there does seem to be widespread knowledge of the pill, the condom, and withdrawal (Kantner & Zelnik, 1972). In the 1930s and 1940s when the Kinsey data was collected, males led females in all aspects of knowledge about sexuality. Today those differences have practically disappeared with males more knowledgeable only in the area of condoms. Females are aware of menstruation and abortion earlier in life than males (Gebhard, 1977).

What Do Adolescents Want to Know?

Adolescents wish to have more information about their sexual selves than is currently available. Gordon and Dickman have listed the questions most often asked by adolescents:

> Is it normal to masturbate?
> Am I masturbating too much?
> Do I have homosexual tendencies?
> Am I abnormal if I have thoughts involving sex with people I know, even members of my family?
> What is a homosexual?
> Are my breasts too small?
> Is the pill safe?
> Is my penis too small?
> How can I get birth control without my parents knowing about it?
> How can you tell if you have VD?
> Is there something wrong with me if I remain a virgin?
> How can you avoid pregnancy?
> How can I say "no"?
> How can I tell if I'm really in love?

How can I know if I have an orgasm?
Is sexual intercourse painful?
Is oral sex normal?
What about having sex with someone you're not in love with?
Where can I get an abortion?
How can I tell if I'm pregnant?
How can I enjoy sex more?
How come I have these unexplained erections?[2]

There certainly is sufficient evidence to indicate that parents, as a group, are negligent about helping their children with such questions. Further evidence (Gordon & Dickman, 1977) suggests that many parents assume that no or little knowledge about sex is advantageous for their children's well-being. However, evidence is accumulating that supports a contrary viewpoint: Informed adolescents (especially if informed by parents) are less likely to engage in premarital intercourse at an early date. And when they do engage in premarital coitus, they are consistently more reponsible in their use of contraceptives (Lewis, 1973; Miller & Simon, 1974; Shah, Zelnik & Kantner, 1975). Although adolescents rank their parents low as sex educators, they do want their parents' knowledge and understanding.

In a study that analyzed the content of books on sexuality in relation to teenagers' interests (Rubenstein, Watson & Rubenstein, 1977), over 30 books were examined for such topics as: pregnancy, sexual intercourse, venereal disease, birth control, love, abortion, prostitution, guilt about sex, and sex offenses. A primary finding was that a large gap existed between the information adolescents want to know and the information provided in these books. The more religious the book was in tone, the less information provided. At the national Wingspread Conference on Adolescent Sexuality and Health Care in 1974, experts identified two of the major problems negatively influencing adolescent sexual development as being "the conspiracy of silence and lack of accurate information regarding human sexuality" and "the influence of a sex-negative society" (McCoy, 1974, p. 19).

ADOLESCENT SEXUAL ATTITUDES AND STANDARDS

It is important to distinguish between attitudes and behavior since each has relevance for understanding adolescent sexuality. By attitudes, I mean how adolescents think and feel about sexual practices and about them-

---

[2] Gordon, S., & Dickman, I. R. *Sex education: The parents' role.* Public Affairs Pamphlet No. 549. New York: Public Affairs Committee, Inc., Copyright © 1977. Used with permission.

selves as sexual beings. By behavior, on the other hand, I refer to what adolescents actually do in the way of sexual expression. There is always the question of whether attitudes affect behavior; that is, are they independent phenomena or are they related, and if so, how?

Attitudes

The amount of research done thus far on adolescent sexual attitudes and behavior is limited. Studies suffer from representativeness of their samples, and so findings need to be interpreted with caution. Offer (1972) studied a random selection of middle-class teens, grouped as young teens (13–14 years old) and older teens (16–18 years old), with respect to attitudes toward sexuality. What Offer found was a significant difference between how the younger and the older teenagers answered his questions: "The younger teen-ager thinks that the opposite sex finds him a bore, finds it harder to know how to handle sex, thinks that dirty jokes are not so much fun, does not attend sexy shows, finds sex more frightening, believes it is important to have a girlfriend, and claims he does not think often about sex" (pp. 83–84). Although there were no differences found between adolescents queried in 1962 and 1970, there were significant differences between males and females. It seems that boys, more than girls, were concerned about having a friend of the opposite sex; were able to report having pleasurable sexual experiences; believed themselves to be a bore to members of the opposite sex; and reported difficulty in knowing how to handle sex appropriately. These differences may reflect the cultural pressure on boys to adopt the traditional male role of aggressor in heterosexual relationships; these pressures may also result in personal conflicts and concerns about whether they will be able to achieve their sexual identity in the traditional male role.

Another important finding of this study was the absence of a uniform attitude toward sexuality. Tremendous variability existed within the boys' and the girls' samples. On the basis of this finding, it was impossible to conclude that a single attitude could be assigned to adolescents and older adolescents; this study is fairly consistent with the patterns noted by Feinstein and Ardon (1973) and Broderick (1966a, 1966b).

Sexual Standards

Much of the work that has focused on sexual attitudes centers around the issue of premarital intercourse. As mentioned earlier in this chapter, premarital coitus has been historically prohibited in the American culture. Therefore, when researchers wish to examine *changes* in sexual attitudes, it is not surprising that attitude toward premarital intercourse would be a prime target. One way of examining attitudinal change is to define standards for premarital intercourse and to determine what percentage of people subscribe to what standards.

Premarital Sexual Standards

Reiss (1967) identified four standards (with subdivisions) for assessing premarital sexual permissiveness: abstinence, double standard, permissiveness with affection, and permissiveness without affection. For example, individuals who adhere to a code of abstinence, that is, no premarital intercourse regardless of circumstances, may accept alternative forms of sexual expression under given circumstances. Some individuals who adhere to an abstinence principle will accept kissing with affection; others will accept kissing without affection. Still others would allow for greater sexual intimacy by accepting petting with affection; others will accept petting without affection. Another subtype for those believing in abstinence will allow the male more rights to kissing or petting than the female; this subtype is called *nonequalitarian.*

The double standard refers to the acceptance of male premarital intercourse while rejecting female premarital intercourse unless the woman is engaged or in love (transitional subtype). The *orthodox* subtype accepts male premarital coitus but prohibits female premarital coitus, regardless of circumstances.

The permissiveness with affection standard allows for premarital intercourse under two conditions: engagement or love, or strong affection. The final standard of permissiveness without affection allows for premarital coitus regardless of circumstances. Each of these standards assumes male-female equity.

Reiss (1967) used these standards and their subtypes to study the sexual behavior of adolescents, college students, and adults. The adolescents included in his study consisted of high school students from junior and senior classes of a white Virginia school and a black Virginia school. His findings are reported in Table 10.1. By scanning the data, one can see a great deal of variability in the sexual standards of 17 and 18 year olds. Furthermore, variability exists between sexes, between races, within sexes, and within races. The predominant white male standard is petting with affection. The predominant white female standards are kissing with affection and petting with affection. The dominant black male standard is permissiveness with strong affection. The predominant black female standard is permissiveness with affection under conditions of love or engagement. Reiss came to the conclusion that males tend to be more permissive than females and that blacks tend to be more permissive than whites; these differences

TABLE 10.1 *Percent Accepting Each Premarital Sexual Standard by Sex in the High School Student Sample (Juniors and Seniors)*

STANDARD	WHITE VIRGINIA HIGH SCHOOL		BLACK VIRGINIA HIGH SCHOOL	
	Male	*Female*	*Male*	*Female*
Abstinence				
Kissing with affection	2	21	3	4
Kissing without affection	5	11	0	4
Petting with affection	22	22	3	8
Petting without affection	3	1	0	0
Nonequalitarian	9	20	3	12
Subtotal percentages	41	75	9	28
Double standard				
Transitional	11	1	19	0
Orthodox	9	10	0	8
Subtotal percentages	20	11	19	8
Permissiveness with affection				
Engaged and/or love	12	1	6	28
Strong affection	6	2	28	12
Subtotal percentages	18	3	34	40
Permissiveness without affection	5	0	25	4
Total percentage[a]	84	89	87	80
Number of respondents	65	82	32	25

Note. Adapted from Reiss, I. L. *The social context of premarital sexual permissiveness.* New York: Holt, Rinehart and Winston, 1967, pp. 25–26. Used with permission.

[a] Error categories omitted

were maintained even when social class was controlled in the study. Variability in sexual standards within any particular social class was mostly attributable to the degree of liberal or conservative thought in nonsexual areas (e.g., religion, economics, politics).

It is important to note that this data was gathered some years ago and attitudes or standards of sexual behavior may have changed. However, it is worth remembering that Reiss's data support different male and female standards. This double standard is symptomatic of the inequity of male and female roles in American culture. Men traditionally have been allowed more rights than have women, including rights related to sexual expression and satisfaction. Women, on the other hand, have been expected to refrain from much sexual expression until they are engaged, married, or at least in love. When one examines Table 10.1, evidence of our cutural patterns can be seen. For example, 43% of the white female adolescents accepted standards of abstinence with kissing or petting with affection, compared to 24% of white, male adolescents. The difference is even greater for the standard of permissiveness with affection.

Although black adolescents are more permissive in standards than their white peers, it is obvious that more black female adolescents expect permissiveness with affection to be contingent upon engagement or love than black male adolescents. It is also obvious that more black females accept a standard of abstinence than do black males. Black males are more accepting of the double standard than black females.

Perhaps a little more should be said about the black experience and attitudes toward premarital sex. Roebuck and McGee (1977) found that permissive attitudes (acceptance of premarital intercourse) was related to family structure. Fifty percent of the black girls from father-dominated homes had permissive attitudes; 62% of the black girls from equalitarian homes had positive attitudes toward premarital intercourse. However, the highest percentage (76%) of black girls with permissive attitudes toward premarital sex came from mother-dominated families. There was also a trend for lower class black female adolescents to be a little more permissive toward petting and premarital intercourse than middle class black female adolescents.

As adolescents have gained increased autonomy, they have assumed more responsibility for evolving sexual standards that make sense to them. Although approximately 65% of the students in Reiss's study (Reiss, 1968) believed their sexual standards were similar to those of their parents, a greater percentage felt their standards were closer to peers (77%) and to close friends (89%). This evolution seems to be even more pronounced at the college level (Ferrell, Tolone & Walsh, 1977). Sexual mores appear to be changing slowly, especially among the young; and *permissiveness with affection* seems to be emerging as *the* standard of choice (Reiss, 1968; Harrison, Bennett & Globetti, 1969; Bell & Chaskes, 1970; Sorensen, 1973; Juhasz, 1976; Ferrell, Tolone & Walsh, 1977).

ADOLESCENT SEXUAL BEHAVIOR

Adolescent sexual behavior, those practices actually engaged in by teenagers, will be discussed next. These will include masturbation, homosexual behavior, and heterosexual behavior, that is, petting and intercourse.

Masturbation

Although many cultures accept masturbation as a normal part of development (Gadpaille, 1976), the American culture has, until recently, maintained a fairly strong injunction against it—particularly for females. All sorts of myths have been propagated to uphold the taboo, for example that acne or mental illness will result. Within the past 20 years, our society has become more accepting of masturbatory behavior. This greater acceptance is probably due to a number of factors: research on sexuality, the women's movement, increased autonomy of the young; and permissive child-rearing practices that date back to the 1960s.

Masturbation is probably the earliest form of sexual expression. Infants explore their bodies in a very natural way; this is the beginning of a lifelong process of knowing one's body and what pleases it. Many children discover this in their play, particularly boys since their genitalia are unprotected by other parts of the body and can be easily stimulated by such activities as climbing a pole or a rope. Johnson (1969) believes that self-stimulation during adolescence aids in the release of sexual tension, in the development of sexual identity, and in learning about one's sexual organs. It can also help individuals discover what they find pleasing, and this can be important knowledge to share with a loved one at a later time in life.

Kinsey, Pomeroy, and Martin (1948) found that many boys learned about masturbation or observed companions masturbating prior to doing it themselves. Self-stimulation often provides boys with their first experience with ejaculation (Shipman, 1971). Although boys joke about it there is evidence to suggest that society's generally negative views toward masturbation continue to cause some concern, that is, guilt or fear of abnormality. It is pretty clear that parents are of little help to adolescent boys in their struggles to cope with wet dreams, ejaculations, and masturbation. In spite of the lack of formal preparation, boys experiment in private and learn that their bodies are a source of pleasure.

A girl's anatomy makes it somewhat less likely that masturbation will occur accidentally. Kinsey, Pomeroy, Martin, and Gebhard (1953) found that most of the females learned self-stimulation through exploration. The fact that few females talk about or observe masturbatory behavior within their own sex suggests less sexual openness. Of course, this is consistent with our differential child-rearing practices and expectations for males and females.

Accurate and representative information on masturbation among adolescents is limited. Kinsey's work, now close to 40 years old, gives us some baseline data. Kinsey et al. (1953) found that 12% of the females and 21% of the males interviewed had experienced masturbation with orgasm by age 12. By 15 years of age about 20% of the females and 82% of the male adolescents had had the same experience; and these figures jumped to 33% and 92% respectively by the age of 20.

The other study that addresses in some detail masturbation among teenagers is Sorensen's (1973) work. Since this study will be referred to frequently in this section, a few preparatory comments seem important. Sorensen's goal was to examine both the sexual attitudes and behavior of today's teenagers. In the process of collecting his sample, he considered it important to obtain parental and adolescent permission for participation in the study; this approach is consistent with the use of ethical guidelines for conducting research on human subjects. However, in the process of getting permission, many in his sample pool were eliminated because parents refused to allow their adolescents to participate. Of those families where parents agreed to cooperate, some of the adolescents themselves refused. The end result was that he lost about 50% of the original random sample. Because of this, the study has been criticized for its liberal bias, that is that those adolescents who participated were the most open and sexually advanced. Even so, I do not believe that the study should be overlooked, because there is so little knowledge on adolescent sexuality. However, it is possible that the figures reported by Sorensen for specific sexual practices are inflated and therefore of limited use in generalizing to the entire American adolescent population.

Sorensen (1973) queried four hundred teens between the ages of 13 and 19. He discovered that adolescents had more difficulty reporting masturbation than any other form of sexual expression. He believed that their defensive reactions were a function of self-esteem, embarrassment, and personal disgust. Sorensen (1973) found that 58% of the boys and 39% of the girls had masturbated at least once; it is difficult to compare these figures directly with the Kinsey data since it is not known if orgasm was achieved. If that is not considered, it appears as if male masturbation has dropped significantly, whereas female masturbation has increased a little. Sorensen believes he may have obtained an under-reporting on this sexual practice (remember that this is supposedly a liberally biased sample).

Sorensen found that most of the girls reporting self-stimulation had their first experience before or at the age of 12; the boys, on the average, had their first experience before or at the age of 13. The younger (13-15 year olds) masturbated earlier in life than did the older adolescents (16-19 year olds). This may reflect changing cultural norms for sexual behavior. Masturbation was more common among nonvirgins than virgins. Although the male-female gap of masturbation experience was much less than in the Kinsey et al. (1953) work, the adolescent boys were more frequent masturbators than the girls. The boys also enjoyed their masturbation more, and the sexually inexperienced enjoyed self-stimulation the most. Almost all adolescents reported the use of fantasy during masturbation; a few reported that it helped them to learn about orgasm and its pleasure. Half of the masturbators reported no guilt or anxiety about their behavior.

It is clear that masturbation has become a more acceptable and normal form of sexual behavior. There are still male-female differences in frequency and enjoyment; these differences probably continue to reflect sex-role stereotypes. No known physical harm can result from masturbation, and the only psychological harm would seem related to the resulting anxiety or guilt if one's personal standards or those of one's family and religion have been violated. There is evidence that guilt is experienced by most people experimenting with new sexual behavior; however, once it is faced and worked through, individuals proceed to the next level of sexual development (Reiss, 1967). The evidence from the Sorensen study (1973) would suggest that fewer young people are experiencing guilt. I agree with Gordon (1973) that adolescents should be taught that masturbation is normal and acceptable behavior if conducted in privacy.

Homosexuality

Societal attitudes toward homosexuality have been anything but kind; some changes now appear evident with the advent of the gay liberation movement and with the decision of the American Psychiatric Association to not consider homosexuality a mental illness. However, large segments of American society still reject homosexual practices.

When discussing homosexuality in relationship to adolescence, it is important to distinguish between a developmental interlude and a lifelong pattern of desiring sexual relations with someone of the same sex. Very little of what is experienced as homosexual contact during adolescence or preadolescence will develop into an adult pattern of homosexuality. Gordon and Dickman (1977) state that 3–4% of the children growing up today will be homosexual as adults. However, many more than this will have some homosexual experience. Schofield (1965a), in his study of homosexual and heterosexual adults, found that homosexual contact in earlier life was *common* to both groups.

Such contact during preadolescence and adolescence is related to curiosity, to testing what is normal, and to coping with anxiety about one's sexuality. It seems to be more common among males than females, and research evidence supports this. Anxiety about homosexuality may result from homosexual thoughts, initiating contacts with or responding to requests for contact by a peer, or being approached by an older adolescent or adult. Gordon and Dickman (1977) believe that homosexual thoughts come more from anxiety and developmental age than they do from a genuine desire to be a homosexual. They suggest that boys and girls be given information about homosexuality as well as increased opportunities for contact with the opposite sex. Another researcher, Finger (1975), has suggested a short-lived period of homosexual behavior as common for males in preadolescence or early adolescence. He states that the first homosexual peer contact occurs on the average about six months before the adolescent's first masturbation and even longer before the male's first nocturnal emission. Data from Kinsey et al. (1948) and Sorensen (1973) suggest that the rate of incidence of homosexual contact takes the biggest jump between the ages of 11 and 15. Kinsey's work showed that 36% of his male sample had had homosexual contact to orgasm by age 18; only 11% of the boys in

Sorensen's (1973) study had had homosexual experience by 19 years of age. These findings indicate a decrease in the amount of contact during adolescence. This is supported by Finger's study (1975) of young, male college students, where he found a drop from 27% to 14% from 1943 to 1973.

It should be obvious that much of the research that has been conducted on homosexuality involves male subjects. This is because the incidences of female homosexual experience are much less. For example, in 1953 Kinsey and coworkers found that 2–3% of his female sample had had orgasm in a homosexual relationship as teenagers compared to 36% for the male sample. Among Sorensen's sample (1973), 6% of the adolescent girls reported a homosexual experience compared to 11% of the boys. Of the few students who reported such behavior, 57% of the girls said their first experience occurred between the ages of 6 and 10; the majority of the boys, however, had their first experience between the ages of 11 and 12. Over three-fourths of the girls had their first experience with a same-aged peer compared to about 55% of the boys. The latter were much more likely to be approached by an older adolescent or an adult.

It is interesting to note that about 40% of the male and female adolescents in Sorensen's study believed it was alright for two people of the same sex to have sexual relationships with each other. They believed that such individuals were fulfilling their needs, that love is unpredictable and could include a same-sex person, that such behavior could be consistent with being one's self, and that behavior and personhood are not synonymous. Although a large proportion of these adolescents were liberal in viewing others' homosexual behavior, almost three-fourths of the same group thought homosexuality unnatural and something they would not choose for themselves.

What can be observed from the data is that homosexual experiences are not uncommon during adolescence and can be a normal part of moving toward an acceptance of one's sexuality and sex-object preference. Adolescent homosexual experiences are not necessarily indicative of a pattern of adult homosexuality.

Adolescents need understanding and knowledge about these issues. They might benefit from learning how to respond to a homosexual advance that they found undesirable. Such experiences could help them cope with their fears and conflicts whether they emerge from developmental changes or in the small number who become aware that their sex-object preference is for someone of the same sex.

Heterosexual Behavior

Several studies conducted in the seventies have attempted to describe heterosexual behavior in adolescents (Kantner & Zelnik, 1972; Sorensen, 1973;

Miller & Simon, 1974; Veneer & Stewart, 1974; Finkel, 1975). A number of patterns emerge from these studies. Male-female differences in specific sexual practices are more evident in those aged 13 to 15 with boys' sexual behavior being more advanced. However, by the age of 16 to 17, these differences begin to disappear and approximately equal numbers of males and females engage in petting and premarital intercourse. The similarity of male-female sexual behavior is occurring earlier than in the past and is attributed to a decrease in male promiscuity and an increase in female permissiveness. This trend also seems related to an increasing number of young people who are adopting the sexual standard of permissiveness with affection.

Among any group of adolescents there is tremendous variability in heterosexual behavior; some of this variability is attributed to sex and age, but other factors interact as well. The rate of heterosexual development seems to occur at a slower pace in adolescents who are religious, who are closer to parents than peers, who are delayed in onset of puberty, and who date at a later age. On the other hand, it is accelerated in adolescents who are closer to peers than parents, who use drugs, who value independence more than achievement, and who are more tolerant of deviant behavior.

Ethnic differences exist in the age at which advanced sexual behaviors are expressed. Black males (Finkel & Finkel, 1975) and females (Kantner & Zelnik, 1972) as well as Hispanic males (Finkel & Finkel, 1975) adopt more sophisticated behaviors earlier than their white counterparts. However, the frequency of intercourse and the number of partners for black adolescent females are less than for their white peers (Kantner & Zelnik, 1972). A study conducted in Mississippi (Roebuck & McGee, 1977) demonstrated that black adolescent girls who came from matriarchal and equalitarian-structured homes, as compared to those from patriarchal homes, were more likely to have engaged in premarital intercourse. The religiosity of these girls was unrelated to sexual permissiveness in behavior; this contrasts sharply with the white culture where increased religiosity relates to decreased sexual permissiveness.

Jessor and Jessor (1975) indicate that adolescent virgins and nonvirgins (both males and females) can be distinguished by a class of social-psychological variables. Taken together, these behaviors suggest that nonvirgins are in transition from reliance on the family and traditional controls to reliance on self and peers. Nonvirgins, as compared to virgins, valued independence over achievement, were more tolerant of deviance, were less religious, and were more susceptible to friends' than to parents' influence. The Jessors believe that transition-proneness represents a pattern of thinking and behaving with sexual expression being only one component; to understand premarital intercourse among adolescents, one must consider the ecological context of the behavior. The research data from several studies suggest that the more advanced forms of sexual communication—petting, intercourse—are occurring at an earlier age (Miller & Stone, 1974; Veneer & Stewart, 1974).

Petting. Petting behavior can be divided into two levels of sexual intimacy. Light petting, distinguished from kissing and necking, refers to touching above the waist. Two studies have investigated this behavior (Miller & Simon, 1974; Veneer & Stewart, 1974). Among 14 and 15 year olds, approximately 50 to 65% of the boys had engaged in light petting compared to 47 to 55% of the girls. As age increases to 16 and 17 years old, 65 to 73% of the boys as compared to 65 to 69% of the girls had engaged in such behavior.

Heavy petting, a more advanced stage of sexual intimacy, is defined as feeling below the waist. From the aforementioned studies, it was found that 28 to 56% of the 14- and 15-year old boys and 24 to 40% of the girls had engaged in heavy petting. When they reached 17 years of age, 50 to 60% of the boys and 46 to 49% of the girls had been involved.

Intercourse. Premarital intercourse, the next level of sexual intimacy, is often used as a criterion for determining the existence of a sexual revolution emanating from the 1960s. Although a number of studies have been conducted in the 1970s (Kantner & Zelnik, 1972; Sorensen, 1973; Miller & Simon, 1974; Veneer & Stewart, 1974; Finkel & Finkel, 1975; Jessor & Jessor, 1975), it is difficult to draw solid conclusions about adolescent rates of premarital coitus because of many sampling problems. Wide differences in male and female rates of premarital intercourse exist across the studies. For example, among 14- and 15-year old adolescent females, the percentages cited range from 50% (Miller & Simon, 1974) to 26% (Jessor & Jessor, 1975). Reported rates for boys of the same age run from 8% (Miller & Simon, 1974) to 94% (Finkel & Finkel, 1975).

Miller and Simon (1974) used a stratified random sample of white adolescents from Illinois, a conservative part of the country. Jessor and Jessor (1975) used a more limited sample of white students from a college town in the Rocky Mountain area and it is possible that the behavior of the high school students was influenced by the college students. (Havighurst, in chapter 12, discusses this study in detail.) The Finkel and Finkel (1975) work involved only adolescent urban males from a city in the Northeast, and was equally represented by blacks, Hispanics, and whites. What evolves from this morass of data is the confounding of reported sexual behavior with the ethnicity of the students and their regional backgrounds. In my opinion, the best sampled female group comes from Kantner and Zelnik (1972); they report a 14% rate of premarital intercourse for 14- and 15-year old girls—with a 32% rate for black females and an 11% rate for white girls. I think the best male sample available comes from Sorensen (1973) who reports a premarital coitus rate of 41% for 14- to 15-year old boys. As noted earlier in the chapter, this study may have a liberal bias; however, it does include black and white adolescents from across the country.

In the 16- to 17-year old bracket, the adolescent female rates of premarital intercourse range from 22% (Miller & Simon, 1974) to 40% (Jessor & Jessor, 1975); the comparable rates for boys are 21% (Miller & Simon, 1974) to 100% (Finkel & Finkel, 1975). Again it seems as if the Kantner and Zelnik (1972) study is the most representative of adolescent females at this age with a reported rate of 27%, and Sorensen (1973) is the most representative of adolescent males with a reported rate of 55%. Compared to the Kinsey et al. (1948) data in which 70% of the males between 16 and 20— and 20% of the females—had premarital intercourse, an analysis of the current data suggests a decline in male and an increase in female premarital intercourse during adolescence.

Sorensen Study

Since Sorensen's (1973) investigation is probably the most exhaustive and most descriptive work yet done on adolescent sexuality, it deserves additional attention. Based on his examination of the sexual attitudes and behaviors of over 400 teenagers, ages 13 to 19, he was able to describe four distinct groups. The *inexperienced* group were virgins who reported no involvement in any of three preintercourse activities: "touching or being touched on the breast, the vagina, or the penis" (p. 458). This group represented 22% of the total sample. Within this group, 55% were females (which means, of course, that 45% were males); the mean age was 14.7 years. Members of this group might describe themselves as follows:

> I am not critical of my parents' attitudes toward sex; in fact, I think my own sexual behavior is consistent with my parents' expectations. I really get along with and respect people of all ages. I would describe myself as somewhat to very religious. Although I am a teenager, I still consider myself a child; I think I would have a difficult time getting along by myself. Drugs that other kids use are not very important to me; I would seldom smoke marijuana. Although I am not very satisfied with my sex life, I believe that intercourse should only occur within marriage. I haven't read any serious sex books, but I think oral sex is abnormal. We really should have laws to restrict certain sexual behaviors.

The second group Sorensen described were the *beginners*. Although these adolescents were virgins, they reported that they had engaged in petting—touching or being touched on the breast, vagina, or penis. Some members of this group had petted to orgasm and were labeled *advanced beginners*. The beginners represented 17% of the total sample; about 57% of the group were female; and the mean age was 16.1 years. Adolescents from this group might typically describe themselves thus:

> I have very stable and happy relations with my parents; they practice what they preach about love and sex. I really can't accept certain practices today like being unfaithful in marriage, having a child outside of marriage, or having an abortion. I tend to be pretty conservative politically.

Sorensen's third group were called *adventurers*. Unlike the other three groups, the adventurers were mostly young men (80%). The group represented 15% of the total sample, and the members' mean age was 16.8 years. Adventurers were described as nonvirgins who had sex on some consistent basis with a number of partners. They would probably describe themselves in the following way:

> I really haven't gotten to know my father or my mother; in fact I can hardly stand to be around them. I really think I could get along on my own. Most of the time I feel as if my abilities are going to waste. I have a hard time obeying laws I don't agree with—or even following standards, e.g., dress codes, pushed on me by our culture. Maybe that's why I'm not too religious, and why I see myself as somewhat of a revolutionary. I think grass is important; it's just a regular part of my life style. Yeh, I have a lot of ideas about sex. Any type of sex is OK with me, as long as the other person is willing and it's someone you dig. I think new and varied sex activities are important; it can help you get to know a new person. I believe you can love more than one person at a time; it's OK to have sex with more than one other person even if it is a little unfaithful. It's good experience. Even if I didn't love the other person, I might say I did so I could have a little sex. I have sex about 5 times a month; up to now I've had about 16 partners. I get a lot of satisfaction from my sex life.

The final group that Sorensen depicts are called the serial *monogamists*. These adolescents are described as individuals who have intercourse on a consistent basis with one person at a time. The average age of the serial monogamists were 17.1 years, and they made up 21% of the total sample. Females dominated the group, accounting for 64% of the membership. The following could well be a self-description of a monogamist:

> When it comes to school I get good to superior grades. I do wish my parents and I could agree more about sex. My friend and I have sex together; we really love each other and try to show caring in our relationship. It's always been this way since I entered my teens. I've had four special relationships where sex was a part—only one at a time, however. My current friend and I have sex about 10 times a month. I

use contraceptives regularly; almost always I have an orgasm. I get a lot of satisfaction from my relationships, as well as satisfaction from my sex life with my partner.

Although 25% of Sorensen's sample falls in none of these groups (unclassifiable by his criteria), the four groups discussed represent some striking differences in school behavior, parental relationships, relationships to authority, independence, and personal autonomy, as well as in their sexual attitudes, beliefs, and practices.

In summary, it appears that a sexual revolution has not occurred; two trends do, however, seem to be observable. The more advanced stages of sexual intimacy are occurring somewhat earlier; and a sexual evolution is occurring characterized by greater equality between adolescent females and males.

PROBLEMATIC SITUATIONS INVOLVING ADOLESCENT SEXUALITY

The expression of the sex drive, regardless of context, requires that young people learn how to manage sex in a responsible way. Without such efforts, problems result that affect others as well as themselves. Such problems include pregnancy and contraceptive behavior, and venereal disease.

Pregnancy and Contraceptive Behavior

Teenage pregnancies are on the increase at a time when the American birthrate is on the decline (McCoy, 1974). In 1973, there was approximately 700,000 unwed pregnant teenagers. Kantner and Zelnik (1972; 1973) found that approximately one-third of the black adolescent females in their sample and one-sixth of the white adolescent females had experienced pregnancy by 19 years of age. Further information on adolescent pregnancy is provided by Jaffe and Dryfoas (1976). One out of every ten females, ages 15 to 19 years, becomes pregnant each year; this represents about one-quarter of those who are sexually active. Another 30,000 girls under 15 years of age also become pregnant each year. In 1974, about 33% of these girls gave birth and about 45% had abortions. (For a more extensive discussion of pregnancy and abortion, see chapter 12 by Havighurst.)

When one begins to examine the data, several factors emerge. Although it is difficult to document a sexual revolution, it is easy to document the greater numbers of adolescent females engaged in premarital intercourse. The pregnancy figures most likely reflect this change. It is also safe to say that the pregnancy rates reflect the haphazard use of contraceptives.

Various figures have been quoted for the number of sexually active adolescents who use birth control methods regularly: 10% (McCoy, 1974), 30% (Kanter & Zelnik, 1977), and 50% or less (Scales, 1977). The concern is, of course, for the many teenagrs who do not use contraceptives to protect themselves. This is in spite of the fact that clinics and physicians are serving more young people: Five times as many teenagers with birth control concerns were served in 1975 compared to 1969 (Jaffe & Dryfoas, 1976).

Intercourse among teenagers tends to be less planned and more sporadic than among the adult population. This is probably a function of changing relationships, the intertwining of romanticism and sexual behavior, the uncertainty about one's sexual identity, the impulsiveness of youth, and the adolescent's level of cognitive and emotional maturity. These characteristics are what make responsible contraceptive behavior difficult. As mentioned earlier, the lack of information or the inaccuracy of information about "safe periods" and contraceptive methods further complicates the problem. In Finkel and Finkel's (1975) sample of urban adolescent males, 60% believed that the use of contraceptives makes sex seem preplanned. About a quarter of the young women in the Shah et al. (1975) study believed contraception interfered with convenience, spontaneity, and pleasure.

I might suggest that when adolescents are struggling with making and keeping themselves attractive and appealing in their new-found heterosexual roles, the likelihood of handling contraception in a sensitive and responsible manner seems a rather high expectation. This is particularly true when we look at the types of birth control being used. The most popular methods (Scales, 1977) are still the condom and withdrawal, although the pill appears to be gaining in popularity. The former two methods necessarily mean an interruption in the lovemaking process; their effective use in a relationship requires both communication and cooperation. And yet there is documented evidence that teenage partners seldom talk to each other about contraception (Scales, 1977).

Although other methods, such as the pill, and IUD, and the diaphragm, are less disruptive, there are various reasons why adolescents fail to use these methods more frequently. Many teenagers believe the pill can be harmful to girls (Sorensen, 1973). The pill requires regular use, and many clinics have had high failure rates in getting adolescents to take the pill every day. The pill seems to be a more successful choice with older adolescents, who have the emotional maturity more characteristic of adults. The IUD has been found to be generally more effective with teenagers (Rauh, Burket & Brookman, 1975). Adolescents have reported difficulty in getting information about effective methods of birth control (Sorensen, 1973; Finkel & Finkel, 1975; Shah et al., 1975). The Wingspread Conference (McCoy, 1974) cited the *lack of access to medical services, including contra-*

ceptives, as one of the four major problems that underlie adolescent sexual difficulties.

Adolescent Irrationality

Another pattern emerges from the research on adolescent contraceptive behavior, which I will label the *irrationality pattern*. There are a sizable number of adolescents across studies who resort to illogical explanations for their failure to use contraceptives. Such responses are "I was trusting my luck," "birth control is unimportant," "I didn't think I could get pregnant," or "I was risking it" would be characteristic of this group. Several authors have hypothesized that this irrational behavior is a function of the adolescent's cognitive stage of development. (See Gallagher and Mansfield's chapter on cognitive development.) Cobliner (1974) believes that many adolescents are functioning with *figurative thinking* (that which is set in motion by sensory input and results in adaptive functioning). Constant sensual press forces a situation or problem into awareness. In adolescents the higher level of functioning referred to as *operative thinking*—the ability to use anticipation in the present for coping with possible future events—is less common. Cobliner believes that all birth control methods, except the IUD, require operative thinking. It is possible that this explanation indicates why the IUD succeeds as a method for most teenagers (Rauh et al., 1975), where the pill fails. It may also explain why pregnant adolescents who had abortions or who carried their babies to term changed their contraceptive behavior, while those who only experienced a pregnancy scare did not (Evans, Selstad & Welcher, 1976).

Some fairly consistent evidence suggests that adolescent sexual behavior will continue and advance, regardless of feelings of personal guilt or society's standards. Fear does not serve as a long-term deterrent to advancing through the stages of sexual development. What we need to do is to help adolescents function responsibly. This means giving them access to knowledge, services, and educational opportunities geared to their social, emotional, and cognitive maturity. Only then can we be assured that children are not conceived out of ignorance and fear, and that young people are not given responsibilities beyond their management capacities.

Since a double standard in contraceptive behavior still seems much in evidence (Scales, 1977), young men need to become more involved in contraceptive, abortive, and childbearing issues (Pannor, Massarik & Evans, 1971; Cohn, 1977; Scales, Etelis & Levitz, 1977). Young women need to become more knowledgeable about effective means of birth control, assertive in pursuing professional assistance, and assertive in encouraging the involvement of their partner.

Venereal Disease

Venereal disease has reached epidemic proportions in the United States, and the young are not excluded. Gonorrhea and syphilis are two common types contracted and carried by sexually active adolescents. Indeed, next to the 20 to 24-year old age group, adolescents from 15 to 19 years old are the major contributors to the epidemic. Adolescents under 14 years of age contribute little to the overall figures.

The prevalence of syphilis and gonorrhea reached a low in 1957 (Darrow, 1976) and then began a rapid upward swing that has continued. Rates for gonorrhea and syphilis among 10 to 14 year olds and 15 to 19 year olds are presented in Table 10.2. The incidence of gonorrhea is more marked than that of syphilis; the cases of gonorrhea among 10- to 14-year old males show a consistent rise from 1956 to 1977. Among girls of the same age, there was a significant increase between 1960 and 1975. The same type of change can be observed for both males and females in the 15- to 19- year group for the same time period. However, the rates for this age group reached a peak in 1975 and have begun to decrease slowly.

The incidence of syphilis, less prevalent among teenagers, continued to increase up through 1975. At that time a small decline began to occur and was maintained through 1977. A significant drop in the rate of syphilis occurred from 1976 to 1977. Of course, we can only hypothesize about the meaning of the data. I think the dramatic rise in the number of adolescent females who contracted gonorrhea from 1960 to 1975 probably reflects the increased numbers of young women who engaged in premarital intercourse. Another contributing cause may be that the increasing reliance on the pill as a birth control method has reduced the use of the condom by male adolescents. The condom, if effectively used, can help prevent VD; this is also true of foams, creams, and gels that contain antibacterial agents.

Syphilis and gonorrhea are mainly passed from person to person via sexual contact since the sexual organs provide the right climate of warmth and moisture in which infection can grow. Males usually have a better opportunity to detect VD early because of their external genitalia. Gonorrhea may be detected as soon as three or four days after the infection has begun. The male may notice pain when he urinates, or he may notice that he is secreting a yellow discharge. Untreated gonorrhea can result in male or female sterility, heart problems, and pelvic disorders, as well as blindness in a baby whose mother had the disease during pregnancy (Planned Parenthood Federation of America, 1975).

Syphilis is even more serious; it is transmitted from person to person via a sore. When the sore comes in contact with another's mouth, penis, rectum or vagina, the disease is communicated. Syphilis is generally thought of in *primary, secondary,* and *tertiary* stages. The primary stage can be

TABLE 10.2 *Rates of Gonorrhea and Syphilis among 10–14 and 15–19 Year Olds*

		1956	1960	1975	1976	1977
AGE						
				Gonorrhea		
10–14	Male	7.1	13.8	21.1	22.2	24.5
	Female	28.7	24.8	74.4	71.2	76.1
	Total	17.7	19.2	47.2	46.2	49.8
15–19	Male	462.9	480.9	1121.5	1061.5	1003.2
	Female	372.0	347.1	1462.4	1445.8	1442.0
	Total	415.7	412.7	1292.2	1253.6	1212.4
				Syphilis (Primary and Secondary)		
10–14	Male	.2	.4	.7	.6	.6
	Female	.8	1.3	1.5	1.2	1.0
	Total	.5	.8	1.1	.9	.8
15–19	Male	10.1	20.4	18.3	18.1	15.0
	Female	11.3	19.2	17.7	16.4	12.6
	Total	10.7	19.8	18.0	17.3	13.8

Note. Cases per 100,000 population. Adapted from *Sexually Transmitted Disease (STD) Statistical Letter*. U.S. Department of Health, Education, and Welfare, Public Health Service, Center for Disease Control, Bureau of State Services, V.D. Control Division, Atlanta, Georgia 30333, May 1978.

detected by the presence of the sore at the place of contact; again the male is more likely to detect this. Within a few days the sore disappears and no new signs reappear until a month has passed. At this time the second stage of infection is characterized by a non-itchy rash that may occur on one's feet, shoulders or around the mouth; in addition some hair may fall out. Again these symptoms disappear; the infection continues over years into its advanced stage and, if undetected, may result in paralysis, blindness, heart disease, and insanity (Planned Parenthood Federation of America, 1975).

Untreated VD is serious business; it requires vigilance, caring, and responsible behavior on the part of those who are sexually active. These diseases can be effectively treated with penicillin or other antibiotics if detected early; however, effective therapy is a problem in the treatment of gonorrhea because the organism becomes resistant to antibiotics (Blount, Darrow & Johnson, 1973). Today most states have laws that permit adolescents to be treated without parental consent (McCoy, 1974).

The Sorensen (1973) study does provide additional information on VD among teenagers. Although only 10% of the nonvirgins reported that they had had VD, *everyone* over 15 years could identify at least one friend who once had VD. Approximately 30% of the adolescents, regardless of intercourse experience, had been informed about venereal disease by their parents. About a third of the teenagers sampled (a higher number among young teens) reported that they would like to be able to talk about VD with their parents. However, they were afraid to ask because they expected a parental sexual inquisition. Over 75% of these adolescents perceived venereal disease to be a serious problem, and over 84% felt responsible for informing a partner if they discovered they had VD.

Assuming that the adolescent rates of sexual intercourse and the trend toward earlier onset of advanced sexual behaviors will not be reversed, it seems logical to examine the steps that adolescents can take to prevent venereal disease. Routine check ups (particularly for females) and awareness of VD symptoms are essential steps for adolescents if they are sexually active. Restricting sexual behavior to solitary masturbation or to one partner who is known to be free of disease is the only sure way to avoid VD. The use of condoms, antiseptic compounds, and the systematic use of antibiotics (Darrow, 1976) are alternative approaches to prevention. Physical health associated with increased sexual activity requires sacrifices. This may mean interruption of the lovemaking process or money for checkups and medication.

Although the data we have examined show the beginning of a decline in gonorrhea and syphillis among young people, there is the ever-present need to inform teenagers about these diseases. A depressing fact is that less than half of urban adolescent males, all of whom were sexually active by 17 years of age, did not know that condoms could help prevent VD (Finkel & Finkel, 1975). Since great numbers of adolescents cannot discuss these issues with their parents or with other significant adults, many are taking health-threatening risks. Family-planning centers, adolescent clinics, and free youth clinics must provide VD testing and counseling in these areas (McCoy, 1974). I believe young people will behave responsibly with regard to their own health and that of their partners if treated with respect at these clinics.

GUIDING THE LEARNING OF
ADOLESCENT SEXUALITY

The impact of societal changes, sexuality as learned behavior, and the role of parents, schools, organized religion, and community services will now be discussed as they relate to guiding adolescent sexual behavior.

Impact of Societal Changes

The argument can be made that the modification of male-female roles, changing family structure, the shifts in the meaning and exercise of authority, the declining influence of organized religion, the increasing diversity of norms, and the increasing autonomy of youth (coupled with few responsibilities) provide the back drop of understanding necessary for those interested in preparing adolescents for the expression of healthy sexuality in the 1980s.

A major evolution is occurring in male and female roles in America; we are moving toward greater equity in responsibilities and behaviors. This evolution is affecting how men and women see and behave toward each other. Dating practices, the expression and management of sexuality, expectations for loving relationships, and living arrangements based on commitment are changing. Desirable characteristics for a marriage partner, attitudes toward marriage, divorce, separation, and remarriage, and the place of children in male-female relationships are also beginning to look different.

More women have begun to challenge the traditionally exclusive role of wife-mother, and new patterns have begun to emerge. It is now estimated that 50% of American women are employed in jobs outside the home. Most of these women also carry out major responsibilities for the family (though some men have assumed more responsible roles for housekeeping and child care chores). The increasing economic independence of women has also encouraged a growth in the divorce rate. Women and men are less likely to stay in a marriage they find destructive or emotionally unsatisfying. These events have had a significant impact on the lives of children. Many spend more time in child-care facilities; child-rearing responsibilities have now been extended to additional adults who exist outside the nuclear or extended family. Furthermore, millions of children today grow up in single-parent families, and many have little ongoing contact with their fathers (or mothers). The end results of these changes are that parental control is more diffuse, parental male-female models are less available, and time demands on available parents are excessive. This leaves minimal time and energy for parent-child communication.

Equally important is the cultural shift in the meaning and exercise of authority. There used to be a time when a parent, a teacher, or a minister stated a request or a standard, and it was followed without question. Blind allegiance to authority is no longer the norm, although many individuals still believe that it is functional. If the civil rights movement, Vietnam, and Watergate taught the young one thing, it was to question "Why?" Asking this question repeatedly and seeking a sound rationale to guide one's behavior when given a command, or even a request, have become learned behaviors. No longer do individuals automatically accept someone else's notion about what behavior is appropriate. This doesn't mean that authority is dead; it simply means that its use requires a more sophisticated set of skills.

A concurrent phenomenon has been the general decline in the influence of organized religion in the daily lives of individuals. It would seem reasonable to believe that this is a result of the inability of organized religion to adapt to a rapidly changing society. As people have experienced the lack of meaning and utility in religious practices and beliefs, especially as they relate to solving twentieth century life problems, they have questioned and rejected much of what organized religion has to offer. This pattern further erodes the traditional controls on sexual behavior. Many young people today do search for meaning in powers beyond themselves; however, the majority are not willing to accept religion as it was once practiced.

A further complicating factor involves the increasing autonomy of adolescents without a concomitant increase in responsible life roles. American adolescents are not needed in the labor market; indeed they are seen as a liability. The age when adolescents marry is increasingly older; many young married people now delay having children or decide to have none. Also quite noticeable is the increased diversity of norms that are acceptable in our culture, including everything from dress to foods, to health practices, to standards for sexual behavior. Regardless of an individual's or family's belief system, it is nearly impossible to be untouched by competing value systems and behaviors. The reality of television and other media reaches into the most isolated communities. Adolescents are confronted with these conflicts and must find ways to sort through the morass of messages to consolidate their own values.

Sexuality: A Learned Repertoire

It seems clear that sexuality, one's repertoire of gender identity, sexual knowledge and values, and sexual behavior, is learned over the course of a lifetime. This learning process is a result of experiencing and requires readiness, time, and practice with other people; it is a developmental sequence that begins at birth. Although longitudinal studies on the development of human sexuality are clearly absent in the research literature, various studies (Broderick, 1966a; Broderick, 1966b; Spanier, 1973; Miller & Simon, 1974; Veneer & Stewart, 1974; Jessor & Jessor, 1975) have begun to provide some descriptive evidence of heterosexual development through late adolescence. Spanier (1975) describes the process of sexualization. He found support for the belief that involvement with a person of the opposite sex begins with kissing behavior and advances in a stepwise progression to intercourse, each step being an advancement in learning prerequisite to the next. Reiss (1976) has maintained that guilt must be worked through with each step prior to advancement and that individuals vary in the length of time it takes them to accomplish this task. What does seem well supported by the data is that the *age of onset* and *rate of progressing* through these learning stages are incredibly varied (Sorensen, 1973). Spanier (1975) notes that the greatest amount of variability between individuals can be attributed to the onset and frequency of dating, that is, opportunity to practice. This is in line with the hypothesis proposed by a number of authorities that coital behavior of teenagers results from dating and courtship (Ehrmann, 1959; Schofield, 1965b; Reiss, 1967; Bell & Chaskes, 1970). It further supports the research of Lewis (1973) that affirmed the hypothesis that coital behavior was related to dating. Although some people marry having only begun this process, others marry having progressed through the entire developmental sequence.

Other contributors to the variability between individuals are physical maturation and attractiveness. However, these seem to be less significant than social-psychological variables, the most important of which are the young person's *current* influences—current values, attitudes, pressure of others, and religiosity. Influences from the past that most affect variability are personal experiences, such as sex play or masturbation. Here again there is the suggestion of a developmental sequence in which experimentation with mature heterosexual behavior rests on prior exploration of one's self and others. Interestingly, formal sex education experiences are the *least* influential in explaining variability between individuals in heterosexual development. Two other factors that are poor contributors are parental sexual conservatism and the adolescent's past religiosity.

Spanier (1975) also found that, as advances were being made in heterosexual development, youth were simultaneously having more exposure to eroticism and were developing greater sexual knowledge and interest. Although formal sex education experiences made no difference in accounting for variability in behavior, significant individuals who provided sex information did explain part of the variability. This is consistent with research cited earlier in the chapter, which showed that those adolescents informed about sex by parents were less likely to engage in premarital intercourse or were more likely to behave responsibly by using contraceptives. Another important finding in Spanier's research was that exposure to sex education and pornography was unrelated, that is, contributed nothing to variability in sexual permissiveness or promiscuity.

Based on knowledge of the developmental sequence of heterosexual behavior, it is possible to identify variables that might be manipulated to either retard or accelerate the rate of heterosexual learning. These include the age of onset of dating, the frequency of dating, current values and attitudes, current interpersonal influences, sexual experiences with masturbation or sex play, physical attractiveness, and sex information that comes from important individuals in the adolescent's life.

Guiding Sexual Learning

Role of Parents. In my opinion, parents should have the primary responsibility for helping children develop attitudes, values, and knowledge for ensuring healthy and responsible sexual behavior. This process begins at birth—not during adolescence. Part of the parental task is to model the process of examining value-laden issues in such a way that values are clarified. A wise parent knows that their children will one day—whether they are age 13 or 53—question and challenge the set of values taught them; some of these will be rejected, some modified, and some accepted. A wise parent further realizes that this is an extremely important process if their children are to estabish themselves as fully functioning adult personalities.

Parents, especially mothers with their daughters, will sometimes discuss biological functioning, such as menstruation; however, discussions on value-laden issues like masturbation, homosexuality, intercourse, birth control, and abortion seldom occur (Scales, 1976). Such discussions are even more lacking in the relationships between mothers and fathers and their sons. Mothers who do discuss such issues with their daughters seem to have daughters who behave more conservatively in their sexual experiences (Shipman, 1968).

There is one word that describes parent-child adolescent communication about sexual issues—absent. I don't believe the intention is to do anything harmful. Avoidance just seems an easier path to take than recognition and the possibility of conflict around uncomfortable issues. The result of this avoidance has been harmful. Of over 400 female adolescents (Cohn, 1977), 18 years of age or younger, who used the services of New York City's Planned Parenthood clinic, less than 30% felt they could discuss their visits with their mothers or fathers; those under 15 years of age told no one—not even friends—about their visits. Ninety percent of these adolescents lived with their parents. Less than a third of the parents were even aware of their daughters' need for help. This is merely one example of the deficit in parent-adolescent communication. In a study that examined unmarried adolescent mothers and fathers (Pannor et al., 1971), researchers asked teenagers what they would have done differently if they had been their parents. Both the boys and girls placed improved relationships and communication between parents and children as their choice for change.

It might be helpful to examine the various reasons that parents have failed to assume their responsibilities as the nation's sex educators. One hypothesis is that parents and adolescents have a difficult time viewing each other as sexual beings (Gagnon, 1965; Pocs & Godow, 1977). This may result from the incest taboo within the family, from the fact that parents transmit the sex-restricted views of their society, or from the adolescents' discomfort and denial of their own emerging sexuality.

It goes without saying that most parents grew up during a period when an open discussion of sexuality and sexual issues was discouraged. What this means is that many adults, including most parents, are uncomfortable and unsure about their own sexuality as well as their values and knowledge around sexual issues. To talk about sexual issues means that parents have to examine their own knowledge, values, feelings and behaviors (Friedman, 1975). This can be very threatening as it may require that parents admit to their limited knowledge. For many adults, this is equivalent to a self-imposed attack on their expertise as parents. What parents fail to recognize is that their children can grow to accept their human limitations if they have the courage and self-respect to allow their humanness to show.

Parents also fail to realize that what is most important and helpful to their children is the *process* of examining important issues with someone who loves them and whom they love. In the long run, this is so much more important than having parents who are "perfectly together" and who have all the answers. In working with a sex education program involving over 1,000 parents, Scales and Everly (1977) found that parents believe: they must be sexual experts to help their children; they must have liberal attitudes or their children won't respect them; and they must feel comfortable discussing any subject related to sexuality. I believe that if this were true there would be no parents involved in sex education; this level of perfection is simply not necessary—and probably not possible.

Parents are aware that changes have occurred in the society and fear that their children will be harmed if they adopt beliefs and values different from their own. Sorensen (1973) and LoPiccolo (1973) suggest that standards and values related to the expression and management of one's sexuality are indeed changing. With these changes, parents have a responsibility to be concerned if their adolescents' sexual behavior is in dissonance with their social and emotional maturity. Parents should also be concerned if their adolescents contract VD, bring unwanted children into the world, or are sexually used or abused by uncaring or immature individuals. But adolescents, too, need to learn to be responsible for their behavior. In the long run, adolescents are the ones that have to make the decisions and that have to live with those decisions. What they need is help in learning a decision-making process that stands them in good stead in time of conflict and that gives a meaningful place to their feelings, thoughts, knowledge, and values.

Role of Schools and Organized Religion. Education and organized religion should have the primary role of helping parents guide the sexual learning of their children. Parents can learn to do a more effective job with encouragement and emotional support. Dr. Mary Calderone, head of the Sex Information and Education Council of the United States, has reported that those sex education programs that have been successful have involved parents (Scales & Everly, 1977). Other efforts involving parents, even families (Rosenberg & Rosenberg, 1973; Scales & Everly, 1977), have been developed to assist in increasing comfort, skills, and knowledge around sexuality issues.

In the past ten years, more responsibility for guiding the sexual learning of adolescents has been placed on the public schools. Although national surveys have reported parental *support* for sex education, parental *behavior* has not been particularly supportive. This behavior has been manifested in political action to control the content of sex education curricula. Of the six states that have required sex education programs, 60% are not allowed to discuss birth control (Gordon & Dickson, 1977). It is not surprising that a school sex eduction program was reviewed in a professional newsletter as follows:

SEX-ED PROGRAM ATTACKED

Teachers at Fairfax County (Va.) high schools, one of the most widely acclaimed school districts in the nation, have attacked the country's year-old sex-education program as a total failure.

One teacher said that only four students finished the course at his school, and they "could have learned as much from a high school biology class."

High school students themselves have complained of the restrictive program since it first began but a recent survey conducted by the county gave the first indication that educators think it is of little use as well.

Many have complained that the program:

—Forbids mention of birth control, homosexuality, abortion and masturbation. Students who have questions in these areas are told to ask their parents.

—Prohibits questions from students unless submitted in writing. Questions are sorted by teachers to determine which can be answered, and their responses must be issued in writing as well.

—Fosters too sterile an approach to sex, using diagrams and outlines to show various sexual functions such as fertilization.

—Teaches boys and girls in separate sessions.

The program, which includes filmstrips, slides and taped lectures, was developed over a 10-year period after parents helped shape its content through testimony at frequent public hearings. It was revised at least twice before it was sent to the schools last fall.

In spite of these less-than-glowing remarks from school staff, Superintendent S. John Davis has recommended that the program remain the same for at least another year "to try it a second year and continue to look at whether changes should be made then."[3]

It seems to me that parental ambivalence about school programs reflects fear that knowledge will lead to increased permissiveness or that adolescents will adopt values different from the family. Parents want *their* values communicated in sex education classes in the schools, whereas adolescents want the freedom to discuss sexual issues openly (Libby, 1970).

---

[3] American Personnel and Guidance Association *Guidepost*, August 31, 1978, p. 8. Used with permission.

What seems to be happening is that parents initially want someone else to do the job—probably because they themselves feel uncomfortable and incompetent to do it. When the schools assume that responsibility, the parents become fearful of losing influence and control over their children's lives and standards.

From my perspective, the responsibility for helping adolescents cope with their sexuality *rests with parents*. Other social institutions need to reinforce this parental role. The school can play a supporting part, as can the church, by offering parent workshops and courses on child and adolescent sexual learning. These workshops and courses need to be led by professional educators, counselors, or psychologists who understand themselves as sexual beings and who can develop a meaningful program that recognizes both the needs of parents and the needs of adolescents.

The content of such programming ought to include knowledge about: the process of heterosexual development; biology; contraception; venereal disease; factors contributing to premarital intercourse; changing values, standards, and behavior in sexual expression; and community support services. As important as this knowledge is, it is equally important to help parents learn and practice the skills necessary for communicating with their children. Such skills include: *listening; clarifying; asking* meaningful questions that guide the definition of problems and the generation of solutions; *using nonjudgmental responses;* and *using restatements* of thoughts, feelings, and beliefs. These skills could be used to explore conflicts and their underlying value issues. The use of these skills requires that parents be able to tolerate ambiguity and uncertainty; be able to trust and respect their adolescents' feelings, and be willing to respect differences between themselves and their children. Meeting with other parents—sharing fears, beliefs, and concerns about sexual issues—is a good way to help parents increase their comfort and self-confidence in discussing value-laden issues. It is recognized that this goal is long-range in nature and may only be achievable through the training of adolescents as future parents.

Role of Community Support Services. Parents have been slow to assume their responsibilities for guiding the sexual learning of their children. Schools and organized religion have been slow to support this parental role. Therefore, community services for adolescents are essential at the present time; they probably will always be needed to some degree. By community services, I mean medical assistance for birth control, venereal disease, and abortion. I also include psychological services that offer counseling and emotional support—in the absence of trusting family relationships and friendships. In addition, legal services need to be available to advise adolescents of their rights and responsibilities in cases of sexual abuse, abortion, or adoption.

Until such time as parents assume more active responsibility for guiding the sexual learning of their children, agencies such as Planned Parenthood will need to expand their efforts to provide the *information* that adolescents need. Adolescents do not have the right to abuse or use another sexually, to bring unwanted children into the world, or to pass venereal disease on to their friends. They do have a right to *information* and *services* that will help them make informal, intelligent decisions. Responsible behavior is not a product of ignorance.

SUMMARY

Sexual development is affected by one's culture at a particular time in history, by family and school experiences, and by the influence of religion and the media. Within the context of these variables, young adolescents experience physiological changes that increase their awareness of their sexual nature. It is also during this developmental period that the search for identity magnifies the need to integrate sexuality into all aspects of life—from standards for behavior to future goals and expectations.

Sexual behavior is learned; the learning varies in content, rate, age of onset, and context for different adolescents. This results in tremendous variability in sexual attitudes, standards, and behaviors. Some variability can be attributed to age and sex, but much is a result of the complex interplay of a multiplicity of variables—such as physical maturation, attractiveness, values, peer influences, religiosity, and dating experiences. Peers are particularly important components of the learning process since they are a major source of sexual information and also provide the social context in which sexual learnings are tested and practiced. The rate of heterosexual development seems to be most affected by the age of onset—and frequency—of dating.

Most adolescents will experience masturbation, kissing, and petting at some time between the ages of 13 and 18. Intercourse is common for many. Adolescent females are still the most likely to experience intercourse within the context of warm, affectionate relationships. Permissiveness with affection appears to be emerging as a standard of choice. Many heterosexual adults have had some homosexual experiences as children or adolescents—although this is more common for boys than girls. For the majority, such experiences represent the testing out of their sexuality and are not to be construed as the acceptance of a future pattern of homosexuality.

Although adolescents have limited accurate knowledge, they want information on all aspects of human sexuality—as well as opportunities to discuss value-laden issues. Increasing evidence suggests that adolescents who receive and discuss sexual information with understanding parents behave more conservatively and responsibly in their sexual practices.

Adolescents need assistance in learning to understand themselves as sexual beings and in learning to use their sexuality responsibly. Disturbing rates of unwanted pregnancy, sporadic use of contraceptives, and venereal disease are clear statements of a society's failure to prepare its youth. Parents should have the primary responsibility for guiding the sexual learning of their children. The school and church can assist in helping parents achieve the education and encouragement needed to fulfill their role. This goal is a long-range one and may be only achievable through the education of adolescents as future parents. Until such time as parents assume their roles more successfully, community agencies such as Planned Parenthood will be needed to provide information and support for adolescents struggling to grow toward responsible behavior.

SUGGESTIONS FOR FURTHER READING

GADPAILLE, W. J. A consideration of two concepts of normality as it applies to adolescent sexuality. *Journal of Child Psychiatry,* 1976, *15,* 679–692.

GORDON, S. *The sexual adolescent.* Belmont, Calif.: Wadsworth, 1973.

GORDON, S. & DICKMAN, I. R. *Sex education: The parent's role.* Public Affairs Pamphlet No. 549. New York: Public Affairs Committee, Inc., 1977.

McCoy, K. Adolescent sexuality: A national concern. *Journal of Clinical Child Psychology,* 1974, *3,* 18–22.

REISS, I. L. *Family systems in America* (2nd ed.). Hinsdale, Ill.: Dryden Press, 1976.

SORENSEN, R.C. *Adolescent sexuality in contemporary America.* New York: World, 1973.

BIBLIOGRAPHY

ALSTON, J. P., & TUCKER, F. The myth of sexual permissiveness. *Journal of Sex Research,* 1973, *9,* 34–40.

AMERICAN PERSONNEL AND GUIDANCE ASSOCIATION. Sex-ed program attacked. *Guidepost,* August 31, 1978, p. 8.

BELL, R. R., & CHASKES, J. B. Premarital sexual experiences among coeds: 1958 and 1968. *Journal of Marriage and Family,* 1970, *32,* 81–84.

BLOUNT, J. H., DARROW, W. W., & JOHNSON, R. E. Venereal disease in adolescence. *Pediatric Clinics of North America,* 1973, *20,* 1021–1033.

BRODERICK, C. B. Socio-sexual development in a suburban community. *The Journal of Sex Research,* 1966, *2,* 1–24. (a)

BRODERICK, C. B. Sexual behavior among preadolescents. *Journal of Social Issues,* 1966, *22,* 6–21. (b)

COBLINER, W. G. Pregnancy in the single adolescent girl: The role of cognitive functions. *Journal of Youth and Adolescence,* 1974, *3,* 17–29.

COHN, J. The needs of adolescent women utilizing family planning services. *The Journal of Sex Research,* 1977, *13,* 210–222.

COMMISSION ON OBSCENITY AND PORNOGRAPHY, Vols. 1–10. Washington, D.C.: U.S. Government Printing Office, 1971.

DARROW, W. W. Social and behavioral aspects of the sexually transmitted diseases. In S. Gordon & R. W. Libby (Eds.), *Sexuality today and tomorrow: Contemporary issues in human sexuality.* North Scituate, Mass.: Duxbury Press, 1976.

EHRMANN, W. W. *Premarital dating behavior.* New York: Holt, 1959.

EVANS, J. R., SELSTAD, G., & WELCHER, W. H. Teenagers: Fertility control behavior and attitudes before and after abortion, childbearing or negative pregnancy test. *Family Planning Perspectives,* 1976, *8,* 192–200.

FEINSTEIN, S. C., & ARDON, M. S. Trends in dating patterns and adolescent development. *Journal of Youth and Adolescence,* 1973, *2,* 157–166.

FERRELL, M. Z., TALONE, W. L., & WALSH, R. H. Maturational and societal changes in the sexual double-standard: A panel analysis (1967–1971; 1970–1974). *Journal of Marriage and the Family,* 1977, *39,* 255–271.

FINGER, F. W. Changes in sex practices and beliefs of male college students: Over 30 years. *The Journal of Sex Research,* 1975, *11,* 304–317.

FINKEL, M. L., & FINKEL, D. J. Sexual and contraceptive knowledge, attitudes, and behavior of male adolescents. *Family Planning Perspectives,* 1975, *7,* 256–260.

FRIEDMAN, R. The vicissitudes of adolescent development and what it activates in adults. *Adolescence,* 1975, *10,* 520–526.

FURSTENBERG, JR., F., GORDIS, L., & MARKOWITZ, M. Birth control knowledge and attitudes among unmarried pregnant adolescents. *Journal of Marriage and the Family,* 1969, *31,* 34–42.

GADPAILLE, W. J. A consideration of two concepts of normality as it applies to adolescent sexuality. *Journal of Child Psychiatry,* 1976, *15,* 679–692.

GAGNON, J. H. Sexuality and sexual learning in the child. *Psychiatry,* 1965, *28,* 212–228.

GARRISON, K. C. Physiological development. In J. F. Adams (Ed.), *Understanding adolescence: Current developments in adolescent psychology* (3rd ed.). Boston: Allyn and Bacon, 1976.

GEBHARD, P. H. The acquisition of basic sex information. *The Journal of Sex Research,* 1977, *13,* 148–149.

GORDON, S. *The sexual adolescent.* Belmont, Calif.: Wadsworth, 1973.

GORDON, S., & DICKMAN, I. R. *Sex education: The parent's role.* Public Affairs Pamphlet No. 549, New York: Public Affairs Committee, Inc., 1977.

HANSEN, S. L. Dating choices of high school students. *The Family Coordinator,* 1977, *26,* 133–138.

HARRISON, D., BENNETT, W. H., & GLOBETTI, G. Attitudes of rural youth toward premarital sexual permissiveness. *Journal of Marriage and the Family,* 1969, *31,* 783–787.

HUNT, M. *Sexual behavior in the 1970's.* Chicago: Playboy Press, 1974.

JAFFE, F. S., & DRYFOAS, J. G. Fertility control services for adolescents: Access and utilization. *Family Planning Perspectives,* 1976, *8,* 167–175.

JESSOR, S. L., & JESSOR, R. Transition from virginity to nonvirginity among youth: A social psychological study over time. *Developmental Psychology,* 1975, *11,* 473–484.

JOHNSON, W. R. Masturbation. In C. B. Broderick & J. Bernard (Eds.), *The individual, sex and society*. Baltimore: Johns Hopkins University Press, 1969.

JONES, M. C., & BAYLEY, N. Physical maturity among boys as related to behavior. *Journal of Educational Psychology*, 1950, *41*, 137.

JONES, M. C. The later careers of boys who were early or late-maturers. *Child Development*, 1957, *28*, 113–128.

JUHASZ, A. M. Changing patterns of premarital sexual behavior. *Intellect*, 1976, *104*, 511–514.

KANTNER, J. F., & ZELNIK, M. Sexual experience of young unmarried women in the United States. *Family Planning Perspectives*, 1972, *4*, 9–18.

KANTNER, J. F., & ZELNIK, M. Contraception and pregnancy. Experience of young unmarried women in the United States. *Family Planning Perspectives*, 1973, *5*, 21.

KINSEY, A. C., POMEROY, W. B., & MARTIN, C. E. *Sexual behavior in the male*. Philadelphia: Saunders, 1948.

KINSEY, A. C., POMEROY, W. B., MARTIN, C. E., & GEBHARD, P. H. *Sexual behavior in the human female*. Philadelphia: W. B. Saunders, 1953.

KLEINERMAN, G., GROSSMAN, M., BRESLOW, J., & GOLDMAN, R. Sex education in a ghetto school. *Journal of School Health*, 1971, *41*, 29–33.

LEVITT, E. E., & KLASSEN, A. D. *Public attitudes toward sexual behaviors*. Paper presented at the meeting of the American Orthopsychiatric Association, New York, 1973.

LEWIS, R. A. Parents and peers: Socialization agents in coital behavior of young adults. *The Journal of Sex Research*, 1973, *9*, 156–170.

LIBBY, R. N. Parental attitudes toward high school sex education programs. *The Family Coordinator*, 1970, *19*, 234–247.

LIEF, H. I. The sexual revolution and the adolescents' search for identity. In S. C. Feinstein & P. L. Giovacchini (Eds.), *Adolescent Psychiatry, Vol. II, Developmental and clinical studies*. New York: Basic Books, 1973.

LoPICCOLO, J. Mothers and daughters: Perceived and real differences in sexual values. *Journal of Sex Research*, 1973, *9*, 171–177.

MASTERS, W. H., & JOHNSON, V. E. *Human sexual response*. Boston: Little, Brown, 1966.

McCOY, K. Adolescent sexuality: A national concern. *Journal of Clinical Child Psychology*, 1974, *3*, 18–22.

MILLER, P., & SIMON, W. Adolescent behavior: Context and change. *Social Problems*, 1974, *22*, 58–76.

OFFER, D. Attitudes toward sexuality in a group of 1500 middle class teenagers. *Journal of Youth and Adolescence*, 1972, *1*, 81–90.

PLACE, D. M. The dating experience for adolescent girls. *Adolescence*, 1975, *10*, 157–174.

PANNOR, R., MASSARIK, F., & EVANS, B. *The unmarried father*. New York: Springer, 1971.

PLANNED PARENTHOOD FEDERATION OF AMERICA, INC. *How to talk to your teenagers about something that's not easy to talk about*. New York, 1975.

POCA, O., & GODOW, A. G. Can students view parents as sexual beings? *The Family Coordinator*, 1977, *26*, 31–36.

RAUH, J. L., BURKET, R. L., & BROOKMAN, R. R. Contraception for the teenager. *Medical Clinics of North America,* 1975, *59,* 1407–1418.

REICHELT, P. A., & WERLEY, H. H. Contraception, abortion, and venereal disease: Teenagers' knowledge and the effect of education. *Family Planning Perspectives,* 1975, *7,* 83.

REISS, I. L. *The social context of premarital sexual permissiveness.* New York: Holt, Rinehart and Winston, 1967.

REISS, I. L. *Family systems in America* (2nd ed.). Hinsdale, Ill.: Dryden Press, 1976.

REYNOLDS, E. L. & WINES, J. V. Individual differences in physical changes associated with adolescence in girls. *American Journal of Diseases of Children,* 1948, *75,* 329–350.

REYNOLDS, E. L. & WINES, J. V. Physical changes associated with adolescence in boys. *American Journal of Diseases of Children,* 1951, *82,* 529–547.

ROEBUCK, J. & McGEE, M. G. Attitudes toward premarital sex and sexual behavior among black high school girls. *The Journal of Sex Research,* 1977, *13,* 104–114.

ROGERS, D. *Issues in adolescent psychology.* New York: Appleton-Century-Crofts, 1969.

ROSENBERG, P. P. & ROSENBERG, L. M. A group experience in sex education for the family. *Journal of Sex and Marital Therapy,* 1976, *2,* 53–67.

RUBENSTEIN, J. S., WATSON, F. G. & RUBENSTEIN, H. S. An analysis of sex education books for adolescents by means of adolescents' sexual interests. *Adolescence,* 1977, *47,* 293–311.

SCALES, P. A quasi-experimental evaluation of a sex education program for parents. Unpublished doctoral dissertation, Syracuse University, 1976.

SCALES, P. Males and morals: Teenage contraception behavior amid the double standard. *The Family Coordinator,* 1977, *26,* 211–222.

SCALES, P., ETELIS, R., & LEVITZ, N. Male involvement in contraceptive decision making: The role of birth control counselors. *The Journal of Community Health,* 1977, *3,* 54–60.

SCALES, P., & EVERLY, K. A community sex education program for parents. *The Family Coordinator,* 1977, *26,* 37–45.

SCHOFIELD, M. *Sociological aspects of homosexuality: A comparative study of three types of homosexuals.* Boston: Little, Brown, 1965. (a)

SCHOFIELD, M. *The sexual behavior of young people.* London: Longmans-Green, 1965. (b)

SHAH, F., ZELNIK, M., & KANTNER, J. F. Unprotected intercourse among unwed teenagers. *Family Planning Perspectives,* 1975, *7,* 39–44.

SHIPMEN, G. The psychodynamics of sex education. *The Family Coordinator,* 1968, *17,* 3–12.

SHIPMAN, G. The psychodynamics of sex education. In R.E. Muuss (Ed.), *Adolescent behavior and society: A book of readings.* New York: Random House, 1971.

SKIPPER, J. K., & NASS, G. Dating behavior: A framework for analysis and an illustration. *Journal of Marriage and the Family,* 1966, *28,* 412–420.

SMITH, E. A. The date. In D. Rogers (Ed.), *Issues in adolescent psychology.* New York: Appleton-Century-Crofts, 1969.

SOLLENBERGER, R. T. Some relationships between the urinary excretion of male hormone by maturing boys and their expressed interests and attitudes. *Journal of Psychology*, 1940, *9*, 179–189.

SORENSEN, R. C. *Adolescent sexuality in contemporary America.* New York: World, 1973.

SPANIER, G. B. Sexual socialization and premarital sexual behavior: An empirical investigation of the impact of formal and informal sex education. Unpublished doctoral dissertation, Northwestern University, 1973.

SPANIER, G. B. Sexualization and premarital sexual behavior. *The Family Coordinator*, 1975, *24*, 33–41.

SPANIER, G. B. Sources of sex information and premarital sexual behavior. *The Journal of Sex Research*, 1977, *13*, 73–88.

SPRINGER, J., SPRINGER, S., & AARONSON, B. An approach to teaching a course of dating behavior. *The Family Coordinator*, 1975, *24*, 13–19.

STONE, C. P., & BARKER, R. G. The attitudes and interests of premenarcheal and postmenarcheal girls. *Journal of Genetic Psychology*, 1939, *54*, 27–71.

THORNBURG, H. D. A comparative study of sex information sources. *Journal of School Health*, 1972, *42*, 88.

U.S. Department of Health, Education, and Welfare, Public Health Service, Center for Disease Control, VD Control Division. *Sexually transmitted disease (STD) statistical letter.* Atlanta, Georgia, May, 1978.

VENEER, A. M., & STEWART, C. S. Adolescent sexual behavior in middle America revisited: 1970–1973. *Journal of Marriage and the Family*, 1974, *36*, 728–735.

ZELNIK, M., & KANTNER, J. F. Sexual and contraceptive experience of young, unmarried women in the United States, 1976 and 1971. *Family Planning Perspectives*, 1977, *9*, 55–71.

11

EDUCATIONAL INSTITUTIONS AND YOUTH

Lloyd Lovell

All societies share a concern for caring for their young and for preparing them for increasingly responsible participation in the community. They share a concern for the regulation of relationships between community members, for control of reproduction and aggression, and for control of the generation and distribution of wealth. Various societies have invented differing regulatory patterns and systems to direct and control those human activities for which public management is essential to the effective maintenance of the society. These guidelines, whether stemming from law, tradition, or general agreement, are the *institutions* of the society. Eisenstadt (1968, p. 409) has said:

> Social institutions are usually conceived of as the basic focuses of social organization, common to all societies and dealing with some of the basic universal problems of ordered social life. Three basic aspects of institutions are emphasized. First, the patterns of behavior which are regulated by institutions (institutionalized) deal with some perennial, basic problems of any society. Second, institutions involve the regulation of behavior of individuals in society according to some definite, continuous, and organized patterns. Finally, these patterns involve a definite normative ordering and regulation; that is, regulation is upheld by norms and by sanctions which are legitimized by these norms.

Institutions, then, are the patterned ways of doing the society's work. They provide continuity between the generations but, though they are generally conservative, they can and do change. As conditions, populations, and events change, existing institutions may be modified or replaced.

Bertrand (1967) indicates that efforts toward social change arise when a sufficient number of influential people become dissatisfied with some aspects of the status quo; this period of dissatisfaction is called the social unrest stage. As the locus of discontent becomes defined and as recruitment of other dissatisfieds takes place, an excitement state develops. If the movement toward change continues, mechanisms for promoting the change are developed during the stage of formal organization. In the final stage, general acceptance of the goal sought is accomplished; the change has become institutionalized.

A society erects a set of "structures," functional groups, to fulfill the norms and expectations of its institutions. Churches and sects are created to meet the norms of religion. Family units are developed to accomplish the regulation of sexual expression and procreation; and educational systems are built to provide for people to come to understand their empirical world and to transmit this knowledge and understanding to others. The functions of a particular group may help to forward several institutional objectives;

Lloyd Lovell is Professor of Educational Psychology at the University of Oregon. He has had a long professional interest in adolescence, sex-role identity, and education of the gifted.

the family, as an example, conducts educational, governmental, and often religious activities in addition to performing its major duties as socializer and protector of the young. Similarly, the main focus of a particular institution (such as education) may be supported by several functional groups. Finally, the relationships between institutions and functional groups change. This has sometimes occurred when the structures of existing functional educational groups have been used to further political, economic, or other noneducational purposes.

EDUCATION AS INSTITUTION

It is taken as a given that people must learn how to live harmoniously and happily in any society. Education is required for the very learning of societal institutions, for the proper performance of a myriad private, noninstitutionalized activities that help to make life complete and fulfilling at best, or endurable at least. The contents of the lessons and the instructional processes vary from society to society, but the requiredness of learning is a universal perception.

What is to be learned has been defined in various ways in various times in various societies; which agencies shall instruct is another question and answered differently in different societies. Typical contemporary statements of the aims of education for the United States seem based on three ideological assumptions:

Faith in education. Education is seen nearly unanimously as foundation of welfare and progress of the individual and of this nation.
The belief in mass education. The several "Right to Education" movements attest to the strength of the belief that everyone is *entitled* to free, appropriate, and adequate education.
The belief that education should be mainly vocational. Education should fit everyone to perform adequately in a work-defined role.

Cremin (1970, p. xiii) defines the aims of education as ". . . the deliberate, systematic, and sustained efforts to transmit or evoke knowledge, attitudes, values, skills and sensibilities." The successful educational institution will fit individuals to their own best selves and to the expectations and opportunities of the larger society. In the United States, it is the formal function of the *schooling system* to act as agency for the accomplishment of the aims of education. And the schools are expected to operate within the ideological framework I have described.

SCHOOL SYSTEMS AS AGENCIES OF THE INSTITUTION OF EDUCATION

Though other institutions such as the family, religion, and the media share in the meeting of the expectations of the institution of education, it is the formal schooling system that has been assigned the major and specific responsibility for the objectives of education described by Cremin (1970). If there is agreement about the American ideology of education, there is also lively dispute about the proper functions of the schools as agents of education (see for example, Ebel, 1972, for a brief discussion of some of the major contentions surrounding this issue). Johnston and Bachman (1976) argue that the schools perform the following functions for a society: caretaking and managing of the populations being schooled; teaching required skills and knowledge; transmitting of cultural values, beliefs, and traditions to its newest members; and sorting, classifying, and grading (evaluating) the members of these populations. McCandless (1970) divides the functions of the schools into two: maintenance-actualization and skills training-cultural transmission. The first function is directed toward making the best provision for the individual's present and future. The second is intended to assure that the individual becomes equipped to contribute to the general maintenance and improvement of the society.

These four (or two) sets of functions are not equally emphasized in any historical period, and the relative value and importance of any one of them is arrived at through a changing balance of compromise between two partially exclusive societal themes reaching back to antiquity. One theme recognizes the need for skilled workers of all sorts and would provide the training necessary to assure the availability of trained persons to do the society's work. Plato's school was designed in part to assure a continuous and ample supply of skilled workers. The other theme views education as a route to self-understanding and human maturity. One remembers Socrates' claim that "the unexamined life is not worth living" (he clearly assumed that the examined life *is*). In his *Republic,* Plato recommended a proper balancing between the two educative goals: the environment should provide "gymnastics for the body and music for the soul" (Muuss, 1975).

A similar effort to balance the provision for technical and for "humane" talents is suggested in the nature of the Chinese civil-service examinations that were begun at about the time of Christ. Government-provided preparatory schools trained prospective government employees; the successive series of competitive examinations assessed the candidates' general knowledge, technical skills, and, until very recently, ability to write poetry.

In this country, the same perplexity about the relative value to be placed on the several potential functions of the schools continues. The first schools in the United States were designed to produce the highly trained leadership required for government, the functioning of the church, and the professions. The schools were small and directly served a minuscule portion of the population. At the same time, increasing numbers of immigrants, many of them unschooled and illiterate, received public attention. A part of that attention centered on the need to incorporate the immigrants into productive activities. Concurrently, the Industrial Revolution had expanded the need for skilled labor exponentially; skilled training for all potential productive workers was an economic necessity.

Another concern was based on philosophical and political beliefs rather than on economic needs. Democracy as a governmental form depended on an informed electorate. This belief was exhibited in the tests of literacy and knowledge that until recently disenfranchised many of our citizens. There was, besides, a growing belief in the value of the assimilation of everyone into the dominant movements of American life. If mainstream American life was the best of all possible lives, if justice would give everyone the opportunity for that life, if education would provide the ways to that admission, then education should be provided for everyone. Before the middle of the last century, Horace Mann and others pled that the right to appropriate education was as inalienable as the infant's right to breathe (Cremin, 1960). The individual would benefit by the improvement of his or her life while society would benefit by the improvement in the characteristics of its members.

The press toward forced assimilation was often stern. Many of the schools established by the Bureau of Indian Affairs forbade the use of any language but English within their confines; similar injunctions existed in some schools having a high proportion of Hispanic-American pupils. Post-Sputnik alarm over American inferiority in military and economic spheres quickly produced changes in the educational requirements students were to meet. And fair treatment of everyone would be provided via the amalgamation of everyone into the educational systems; since *Brown* v. *Board of Education of Topeka* (1954), the schools have been moving slowly away from "separate but equal" educational opportunities and resources. A relatively new voluntary movement among various minority-group participants in the schools, urging an "equal but separate" perspective within the framework of a multicultural rather than assimilated society, is a reflection of a new pride in ethnic identity. Havighurst's chapter provides further documentation of this movement.

These changing values and these changing balances between separable objectives of the educational process have built the present schooling system. Schooling in this country is now nearly universal. Beginning with the passage of the first statewide compulsory attendance law by Massachusetts in 1854, all states have made school attendance mandatory. The impact of that requirement on the schools has been enormous. The schools have radically changed from systems of voluntary education for an elite few, into huge and heterogeneous systems serving nearly everyone. This growth in size and in variability among the students has inevitably led as well to marked increases in the range of student motivations and to mammoth expansion of the variety of school activities as the schools attempt to provide meaningful instruction to captive pupils of enormous diversity. The result is the multiform comprehensive high school, serving over 90% of all adolescents of school age.

How well do the schools serve their pupils and society? The answer to this question depends on whom you ask. We turn now to examining schools' accomplishments, and then to asking what school, pupil, and nonschool characteristics help determine the schools' successes (or failures).

EVALUATING THE SCHOOLS' PERFORMANCE

Determining how well the schools are doing at meeting the expectations held out for education is extraordinarily difficult for several reasons. These expectations are themselves ambiguous and ill-defined, making performance evaluation difficult. Given reasonably clear definitions, developing valid measures of the outcomes of schooling is both conceptually and technically difficult. Many agencies share in meeting the goals of the institution of education; there are overlaps between such instructing bodies as schools, families, churches, and communications media. There is also a notable redundancy of information provided by these instructional groups (with a few exceptions such as mathematics, the sciences, and the creative and performing arts, whose lessons are not widely available outside of the schools). Much of the curricular content of formal schools is widely accessible through other educational channels. Therefore, it is often easier to determine what the pupils know than to decide where they learned it.

One measure of educational accomplishment is the literacy level of a country. In 1969, the United States ranked behind only the USSR and Japan (Baldridge, 1975). Another measure is the amount of information people possess. There is evidence to show that each generation in this country has known more than its predecessor for several decades. Still another measure is the success of school bond measures at voting time. For at least the last few years, more and more schools have opened in the fall without a voter-approved budget; more and more budgets have had to be submitted more than once; and more and more schools have had to close for at least a part of the school year. This particular basis for judging satisfaction with schools is peculiarly difficult to interpret. Economic factors outside the control of the schools obviously have enormous influence on voters' activities in regard to school expenditures. California's Proposition 13 was based on political and economic considerations, but its impact on school resources is enormous. And many voters, distressed by the seemingly increasing distance, impersonality, and unresponsiveness of "big government," seem to vote in protest against *any* local issue, monetary or otherwise.

Another widely used criterion is the satisfaction of the students themselves. Here the evidence is clear: The majority of students are satisfied with their secondary school experiences. The Harris survey (1969) and others (Bachman, 1970) indicate *general* satisfaction with school for most students, though many of them have specific complaints.

The liking for school declines with age, and so does student morale (Yamamoto, Thomas & Karns, 1969). There are several reasons for this decline. The increase in critical abilities during adolescence has been noted by many observers; inevitably these new abilities will be focused upon school. Driving, dating, and similar age-related recreations compete for the time and interests of the older students. Inevitably, the attractions of the nonschool world loom relatively more inviting for many students. It is hardly unexpected that not all students are satisfied with their school experiences. Many remain, but a large minority (25%) drop out. Reasons for dropping out will be mentioned later. We turn now to an evaluation of the functions of the schools.

CARETAKING AND MANAGING OF
SCHOOL POPULATIONS

The schools do keep enormous numbers of people of high school age in school, out of the labor force, and out of contact with many of the daytime activities of the adult world. They keep them (over 90% of the people of school age) in an age-segregated world, offering mainly contact with people of their own age. They provide extracurricular and social opportunities not widely available through other agencies, but these, too, are sharply segregated from similar nonschool activities in terms of the ages of the participants. (In general, the American middle-class family is similarly age-segregated; except for the members of nuclear families, middle-class adults spend most of their social time with people much like themselves in income and in age.) This segregation tends to limit the range of opinion and point of view to those held by acquaintances of similar age status. While it diminishes the influence of parent opinion, it increases the influence of extrafamily attitudes and expectations. Within the age-based acquaintanceships, there exists a wider variety of attitude and opinion than the typical family can present. For a large majority of high school students, school, school-sponsored activities, and acquaintances formed in school occupy the bulk of their time and energies.

For a minority of school-age adolescents, the picture of school-as-universe does not hold. A quarter of the students enrolled in the fifth grade will drop out of school instead of completing it; three times as many boys as girls will do so. Many schools have noticed a U-shaped curve of likelihood of dropping out of secondary school, which curiously parallels the U-shaped curve of escape attempts in correctional institutions. Both leavings tend to occur soon after arrival at the new institution or soon before one would be legally entitled to depart. Voss, Wendling, and Elliott (1966) report that three-fourths of their sample of early dropouts had IQ scores below 85, while only one-third of the later dropouts had IQ scores that low.

314

It is as though the younger dropouts cannot make it in high school, and the older ones refuse to. Other explanations are offered for the dropouts; let us look at their description.

DROPOUTS

Though dropouts tend to have lower intelligence than high school graduates, many have ample intelligence for finishing school. A few leave for reasons of health or economics, but the majority leave because they are not doing well in school and because they are not discouraged from dropping out. Numerous studies such as Bledsoe's (1959) and Cervantes' (1965) report the importance of family factors in the decision to leave school. The families of dropouts tend to have less education and less respect for it than families whose children remain in school. These families are troubled by greater interpersonal strife; commonly, the mother is the dominant parental figure. Family relationships and mutual caring are reported by the dropouts as being distant and unfeeling. Families with warmer and more stable relationships, with more education and with stronger faith in its value, are less likely to have children who leave school before finishing. The interests of the potential dropout are often more closely focused on nonschool than on school-supported activities; frequently their closest friends are dropouts (Elliott, Voss & Wendling, 1966).

Girl dropouts often explain that they are leaving school for marriage. Many dropouts of both sexes report that they felt left out or, worse, excluded from the centers of social prestige and activity; they were self-conscious about their clothing, shortage of money required for participation in the social life of the school, and their lack of social polish.

Socioeconomic factors also predispose students towards early departures. Students of lower socio-economic status have higher dropout rates than middle-class students. Areas of high population density and low average income produce a disproportionately large fraction of high school dropouts.

French and Garden (1968) reported on an unusual population of school dropouts: 125 males and 81 females with IQ scores of at least 110. These students left because they refused to accede to what they thought were the stifling requirements of conformity in the school. Both the boys and girls felt the school was not preparing them for "real" life. They were not college-oriented and were vocationally confused. Personality profiles indicated that they were emotionally healthy.

The consequences of leaving before graduation are generally discouraging. Dropouts tend to suffer chronic unemployment, unstable family lives, and limited future prospects.

One final caution about the "holding power" of the secondary schools is necessary. Some students are retained in school despite their inadequate academic performance. This risk may be greater for certain minority-group members than for other portions of the high school population. These students may be led to overestimate their actual academic performance and capabilities and to set improbably high occupational and educational goals for themselves (Fernandez, Espinosa & Dornbush, 1975). This problem is real for college admissions officers.

TEACHING REQUIRED SKILLS AND KNOWLEDGE

The changing educational attainments of the population are relatively easy to determine; the influence on these changes exerted by the schools is more difficult to decide. The attainments are impressive on a variety of standards. The national literacy rate approaches 98% and is still rising, though slowly of late. The majority of Americans of appropriate age have at least 12 years of formal schooling; over three-fourths of American youth now graduate from high school. Though the percentage of high school graduates among black and other minority groups is rising rapidly, it still lags far behind the rate for Caucasians; these rates are probably more closely related to social class than to ethnicity.

In addition, high school graduates are pursuing further education at a rising rate; over 40% now enroll in college or other formal post-secondary schools. Adult education programs attract students in increasing numbers; the availability of education is seen as continuous for ever-larger portions of the population. The medical and other professions require periodic educational refreshment. Training and retraining programs for executives and other employees of business and government are increasingly an expected part of the job desciption. More and more people receive more and more schooling.

Is more schooling associated with more learning? The answer seems to be a clear affirmative, but the meaning of the answer is unclear. A recent report presented by the U.S. Department of Health, Education, and Welfare (1969) summarizes a number of studies in which comparable tests of information and knowledge were given to successive, representative national samples of respondents. In nearly all comparisons reported, the groups tested later outperformed their earlier-tested comparison samples— for an average superiority of 20%. The population clearly seems to know more than it used to.

However, during the same time that average level of knowledge has been increasing, there has been a disturbing *decrease* in aptitude for advanced education as measured by the Scholastic Aptitude Test, published by the Educational Testing Service of Princeton, New Jersey. Scores have consistently declined for both verbal and mathematical aptitudes and for both men and women, since the mid-1960s. If the tests do measure important aspects of readiness for college, the recent high school juniors and seniors are less ready than their brothers and sisters of ten years ago (see Figure 7.5 in chapter 7 by Nichols).

Explanations for the decline range from arguments that attitudes toward education are changing in this country, that the nationwide increase in the offering of electives as opposed to required academic courses has resulted in inferior preparation for college, and that increases in high school attendance have led to even greater heterogeneity of the student body, which now includes a larger proportion of pupils not interested in, and not seeking, preparation for college.

To confuse the question further, the average grades assigned in undergraduate college courses have risen by a full grade-point over the last decade or so.[1]

If the data generally seem to support the conclusion that people are better educated than past generations, a different question must be asked: Do people presently know *enough?* Colleges the country over deplore the apparent decline in freshman skills in using the English language—particularly in writing it—and in using mathematical procedures and logic. Employers say that high school graduates are not prepared for the minimum computational and communicational requirements of many jobs. The concerns are so widespread and so seriously expressed that entire states are moving toward the requirement of minimum performance on general tests of knowledge and skills as a condition of high school graduation.

These complaints, and the solutions offered for them, are not new in educational circles. "Educational circles" seem really to be spoked wheels, slowly revolving and with a small number of spokes. The demand "back to basics" is not new. It was presented in *The Hoosier Schoolmaster* in 1913 (Eggleston); it reappeared in the post-Sputnik period, and it has now come around again. Busing for educational reasons was adopted by San Francisco in the early forties; and for different reasons, it is a strife-ridden issue now. Attention was to be paid to "the whole child," said Horace Mann before the American Civil War; that spoke was visible again in the Dewey period early in this century, and again, partly in revulsion against the "basics" emphasis of the Sputnik era. What is also not new is that the demand for increased training for industry, government, and the good life *always* far outpaces institutional capabilities for providing it. We must conclude that people know enough to satisfy certain systems of demand.

Finally, the most difficult question of all should be asked. Even if people know more than their predecessors did (though not knowing enough for

---

[1] The explanation for this phenomenon is, of course, clear: The quality of college teaching has improved enormously during that decade.

some societal requirements), do they know the proper things? We attempt to ask this and similar questions when we evaluate the schools' performance on the dimension of transmitting cultural values, beliefs, and traditions.

TRANSMITTING CULTURAL VALUES AND TRADITIONS

Providing an appropriate education for everyone becomes more complicated when "everyone" really comes to mean *every one,* and "appropriate" is taken as a serious requirement of education. Defining these broad objectives becomes increasingly more complicated as the variegation of the school population increases. More interests and more needs are presented to the schools. The schools can be expected, therefore, to transmit an increasingly wide variety of values and traditions—or can they? That the schools try to present values more broadly seems clear, and it is as clear that conflicting values held by different groups entitled to a voice about the schooling processes present opposed views of what the schools should be teaching. Two ancient issues and two relatively new ones illustrate the choices schools must make in this regard: Whether sex education should be offered in the schools (see chapter 10 by Wagner); whether alternatives to scientific explanations of evolution should be offered in the schools; what is the proper place of such subjects as ethnic and women's studies in the schools; and what forms of attention to religious and other nonsecular observances and customs should be paid by the schools. These issues divide communities and educators. Moreover, special interest groups turn ever more often to the courts to make these decisions.

We shall examine the schools' impress on two kinds of value transmission: training people to be able and willing to fit into the work structure and "national character" itself.

Havighurst (1972) and Erikson (Gallatin, 1975) point out that the need to learn the value of industriousness (that need arising from within, in Erikson's view, and from the environment in Havighurst's) assumes particular importance during the early years of schooling and is influenced in its resolution by school experiences. The comfortable incorporation of this need is prerequisite to the satisfaction of the later needs and demands everyone must meet and resolve. More than acquiring work habits is involved in the resolution; one should learn to value work as an essential component of the full life. In Freud's words, *Lieben und Arbeiten* (love and work) are the two divisions of life's activity in which happiness must be sought.

The schools' contribution to the successful resolution of this developmental task is unclear. Many observers deplore the "workaholic climate" of many high schools, oriented around high academic expectation and performance, as indicating a too-successful internalizing of the work ethic (see *Time Magazine,* December 25, 1978, for example). At the same time, many other students wish that the schools were more demanding than they are (Johnston & Bachman, 1976). A fairly large minority of school dropouts cite boredom and lack of challenge as a reason for leaving. Another criticism of the schools' influence on students' attitudes toward work is that the schools mislead the students into believing that better education will guarantee a better job, and that much of the curriculum in general and the credentialing procedures of the schools not merely are irrelevant to successful performance in employment but actually make the students less equipped for that success (Baldridge, 1975).

We recognize that the family and other institutions affect the individual's accommodation to the press toward work. Currently, many middle-aged adult men are praised for deciding to choose a reduction in work pressures, while many women are encouraged to find satisfactions in increasingly challenging work outside the home. Certainly families contribute to youths' acceptance of either under- or overachievement as a value in their own lives. It seems fair to conclude that the school pressures toward satisfaction through accomplishment are appropriate for the majority of its students—but damagingly improper for a minority.

That schools are not preparing their students for the real requirements for work (Berg, 1971) is a serious indictment. An even more serious charge is that the schools are producing not merely the wrong kind of workers, but the wrong kind of *people.* Thoughtful critics lament the schools' rewarding of conformity, docility, dependency, and blandness, and their discouragement of creativity, individuality, and even the taste for independent reflection.

Friedenberg (1959) castigated the American high school of the time for its effeminizing of male youth. The school, he said, does not provide the male-to-male confrontation and comparison vis-à-vis individual strength, talent, and maturity of thought that is essential to the development of personal identity. He urged that opportunities for conflict be deliberately built into the school experiences. (I shall discuss later the opposite criticism of the schools' practices concerning learning sex-role identity, from a more recent perspective.) Riesman, Denny, and Glazer (1950) have already pointed out the dangers of a culture oriented toward conformity (where schools teach lessons in conforming). Goodman (1962) and Holt (1969) describe the inappropriateness of education and the constrictions of the environments in which it is offered. Silberman's influential book, *Crisis in the Classroom* (1970), details the school practices and attitudes that preserve pupil dependency, enforce and reward conformity, discourage initiative, and limit the opportunity to learn independence of thought and decision.

These and other critics understand, of course, that in several senses the schools are tools of the public expectation, but they recognize as well that the teenage pupil is past the period of greatest parent influence and that the school is the only institutional instrument affecting nearly everyone of that age period. If reform is needed to produce a new kind of worker or a new kind of personality, the school seems a likely location to institute the struggle towards change.

The recommended changes for producing creative and autonomous persons capable of productive and independent thought are not the only recommendations about remaking the character of the schools' graduates. *Humanistic* concerns about both the precision and rational-linear methodologies of behaviorism and the (unknown) effects of such instructional procedures have prompted yet another set of proposals: The schools should emphasize the affective and volitional aspects of the complete person and should use humanistic techniques that permit learning instead of forcing it. Luchins (1964) and McDavid and Garwood (1978) describe several models of man that have influenced school goals and activities.

Man is not just *homo mechanicus*—a mechanical individual shaped largely by externally controlled contingent reinforcements—a part of this argument goes. The humanists prefer the model of man as *homo ludens*—a playful individual, with internal direction, who uses strategies and game plans in meeting life. Schools should prize these most human qualities and nourish their development within kindly climates that reassure individuality and foster, by not hampering, feelings.

Rogers (1963) has described his ideal of the attitudinal climate the ideal teacher would create for each student. Krathwohl, Bloom, and Masia (1964) have presented a list of the educational objectives lying within the "affective domain" of school goals. A plethora of helpful authors have been quick to provide guides to teachers and curriculum builders, instructing them in the ways of including lessons about teacher effectiveness training, transactional analysis, and values clarification in the contents and activities of high school instruction.

And the attacks go on. The first ten amendments of the U.S. Constitution, known as the Bill of Rights, were offered as separate "ballot" measures in an opinion survey in the Midwest. As CBS reported, the majority of the representative sample of adults would repeal each of the ten amendments. The critics regard this kind of information as further evidence of the erosion of the American character, and urge schools to reverse this tendency. There is evidence—the disappearance of Independence Day parades from more and more communities, the decrease in the numbers singing the National Anthem at public events, the decline in number of American flags flown on the appropriate national holidays—that Americans indulge less enthusiastically in certain forms of expression of patriotism and respect for their country. Whether the reduced public display signals a real reduction in "Americanism" is difficult to judge.

Sex Inequity

As the redress of racial unfairness was an inspiring and change-provoking matter in and out of the schools during much of the third quarter of this century, the last quarter may well become known as a period of intense effort to correct the wrongs of sex inequity. The inequalities of opportunity and performance, depending on one's sex, have been widely catalogued. It is as well known that these inequalities are not based on relevant differences in capacity between the sexes, but on tradition, prejudice, neglect and, perhaps, masculine defensiveness. In *The Longest War: Sex Differences in Perspective,* Tavris and Offir (1977) present what is perhaps the most complete and accurate description and analysis now available of the documented and imputed sex differences, their sources and their effects. The reader may also wish to review the chapter by Stein and Welch presented earlier in this book.

That the schools have helped perpetuate unfairnesses in sex discrimination is shamefully documentable. That they are not the only preservers of these unfairnesses is equally demonstrable.

Next to skill in language use, skill in the use of mathematics is the single most critically important cognitive ability required for school and for occupational success. The two most widely used predictors of college success, the Scholastic Aptitude Test and the Graduate Record Examination, measure verbal and mathematical abilities. Without four years of high school mathematics, students at the University of California at Berkeley are inadequately prepared for work in twenty-two of the forty-four undergraduate majors offered there (Tobias, 1978). Ninety-two percent of the freshmen women, but only 47% of male freshmen, would have been thus excluded in 1972. Many women possess sufficient mathematical skill for initial selection into a variety of occupations, but not sufficient skill for advancement in those same fields. University women are notorious for avoiding graduate programs placing heavy emphasis on mathematics and statistics.

These facts exist despite the evidence (Tavris & Offir, 1977; Tobias, 1978) that girls equal male performance in mathematics until their junior and senior high school years. Sex differences in mathematical ability do not seem to account for the differences in performance. The differences seem more explainable on the grounds of massive prejudice against mathematics on the part of women, and against women who are "good" at mathematics on the part of everyone. As soon as mathematical training is no longer required, women avoid it (Sells, 1978). Mathematically inclined women hesitate to display their abilities for fear of social ostracism. School textbooks and other materials systematically portray boys as figurers and girls as being mathematical dummies. The social and personal costs of this inequity regarding mathematics are incalculable. As will be seen, efforts are growing to reduce these costs through curative and preventive programs in the schools.

The very tests that students take contribute to the maintenance of destructive sex stereotypes (Saario, Jacklin & Tettle, 1973). Holmen and Docter (1972) report that over 200-million test forms and answer sheets are used annually in the United States. Nearly two-thirds of them are achievement tests; a large minority are tests of aptitude and related areas. Saario et al. report that the majority of the achievement tests reinforced sex-limiting, antifeminine biases.

Items to be used in the first carefully constructed individual tests of mental ability were screened against sex discrimination on *performance* criteria. "From the very beginning, developers of the best known individual scales (Binet, Terman, Weschler) took great care to counterbalance or eliminate from their final scales any items or subtests which empirically were found to result in a higher score for one sex over the other" (Matarazzo, 1972, p. 23). The great success of the use of group tests during World War I prompted the schools to emulate their uses. Though items were still selected in part on their lack of sex bias in performance (making many kinds of study of the existence of real sex differences impossible), attention has been paid only recently to the biases in the content of the test questions. Some of them imply the closure of certain occupations to females; the ratio of masculine to feminine pronouns is huge; activities described in many of the items follow the stereotypes of passive, domestic girls and active, responsible boys.

A final criticism of the schools—and society—voiced by critics is that sex-typing stereotypes, in addition to harming females by restricting their fields of opportunity and narrowing their ranges of interest, are also harmful to males. Whatever utility there may once have been in sex separation of duty and voluntary behavior has long since vanished; its continuation positively damages both males and females. Recent speculation and research suggest that a condition of androgyny—a blending of masculine and feminine traits in the same person—may be the most adaptive condition for both males and females in this society (Douvan, 1975; Singer, 1977; Tavris & Offir, 1977).

This trend toward de-differentiation of the developmental tasks and patterns of males and females has also been furthered by social changes directly affecting male tasks. As we have moved into the postindustrial era, the emphasis in vocational preparation has shifted from production and technical skills to skill in the manipulation of words, ideas, and people. This means, then, that the skills demanded for vocational placement and those required in the traditional socio-emotional and supportive family roles of women are coalescing (Douvan, 1975).

Harari and Kaplan (1977) have summarized a variety of evidence indicating that, though there may be an early advantage in clear sex-typing, extreme sex-typing is disadvantageous to adults. Super-masculine adult males are more anxious and neurotic than their less rigidly stereotyped adult peers, and they have lower self-esteem. Women with high scores on traditional femininity scales tend to be anxious, dissatisfied with themselves, and less popular than females with less extreme scores. Maccoby (1966) reports that general intelligence is associated with cross-sex identification, not with extreme masculinity or femininity. Children who blend the traditionally sex-stereotyped interests and activities score higher on tests of general intelligence and of creativity than do strongly sex-stereotyped children. Bem (1974, 1975) has shown in a series of ingenious experiments that androgynous males and females are more adaptable in a wide range of situations than are strongly stereotyped men and women.

It is difficult to substantiate many of the charges that the transmission of values via the schools is less successful now than in the past. It is even more difficult to determine whether the schools should bear major responsibility and accountability for their transmission. I believe, however, that the schools generally do help most of their pupils understand and choose among the conflicting values held by the larger pluralistic society. The majority of students believe in the values toward country, social obligation and the person, including the value that schools and education can work toward constructive change within the community. However, we must also conclude that the schools still deprive certain classes of students from opportunities that they are entitled to, and that they grant other groups unearned privileges. I shall examine these matters next.

SORTING, GRADING, AND CLASSIFYING STUDENTS

We inevitably categorize each other whenever we form or are placed in groups, and we categorize the groups, and . . . so on. We categorize people because we cannot conveniently manage or interact with them as individuals. We create definitions of combinations of characteristics, and then we assign individuals to membership in the categories on the basis of their apparently possessing the defining characteristics. Some of the definitions we use are precise, while others are more ambiguous. All of us can be placed simultaneously into different categories. We change from one category to another when our defining characteristics change. When our characteristics are fixed, we remain in the categories defined by those characteristics. Further, we almost always rank the various categories on some dimension of prestige or desirability.

The position of member in a defined group is a *status*. We occupy status in two kinds of groups; membership in one kind of group is ascribed or assigned to us, while we earn or achieve membership (status) in the other kind (Landis, 1977). We are ascribed status in groups defined on the basis of sex, or race, or eye color, or nationality. We earn, or achieve, status in other groups defined on such dimensions as occupation, educational level, recreational and social interests. Achieving status (membership) in some groups doesn't take much effort.

The creation of the defined groups is useful for two purposes. It is often convenient to be able to describe numbers of people in terms of the characteristics they share. A very common use of the assignment of individuals to groups is to make predictions; knowing certain characteristics of a group, we predict other (often future) characteristics of that group. The practice of grouping is essential to the reasonable conducting of most of our daily business. The effectiveness of the groups we contrive depends on the usefulness and accuracy of our definitions and on the soundness of the predictions we make. Though no person is completely and precisely described by even the exhaustive list of his or her ascribed and achieved statuses (because the characteristics defining the statuses are "averages"), the descriptions and predictions work adequately most of the time. I shall cite some systematic cases of their *not* working well later.

Outside the military world, the world of the schools is probably the most thoroughly categorized institution we have. Pupils are grouped on age, ethnicity, family membership, achievement, interests, health, social class—on any dimension that seems relevant and useful to the schools. What is more, the pupils themselves use a parallel sorting process, using some of the same sorting dimensions and adding others (e.g., sex appeal, popularity, prowess, income, access to a car or drugs) that seem relevant and useful. Both rank their groupings and the members on some kind of prestige scale.

People learn of the statuses they hold in a variety of direct and indirect ways. Test results and achievement reports inform directly. Assignment of lessons from a particular level of a basal reader, election or appointment to an office, and subtle social cues similarly communicate status and prestige.

Making predictions is the most important use to which schools apply their grouping procedures. How well the procedures work depends on the adequacy of the definitions of the groups, the accuracy of assignment of membership to the groups, and the kinds of predictions made.

How well do they work? It seems that, with certain exceptions, they work rather well. High school achievement is the best single predictor of college success. When curricula and classroom procedures are adjusted appropriately, ability-grouping methods (used as a predictor base) show greater gains for the pupils as compared with similar pupils in heterogeneous classes. Satisfaction of requirements of prerequisite courses is related to success in later courses when the course sequences are arranged on proven instructional and learning factors. The judgments of experts are the best predictors of talented performance in athletics, music, and the performing arts.

School screening and identification procedures are often the first to detect a variety of visual, dental, auditory, and other developmental defects. Schools are usually the first detectors of scholastic underachievement (Shaw & McCuen, 1960).

For most students, then, the procedures seem to work reasonably well. There are famous individual exceptions; Winston Churchill, Albert Einstein and Franklin Roosevelt are among them. There are also, and regrettably, *class* exceptions. That student members of ethnic groups enjoying little prestige in this country are massively misidentified needs little documentation. One example will illustrate the nature, though not the extent, of the difficulty. McCandless, Roberts, and Starns (1972) studied the contributions of race, social class, sex, and estimates of academic ability to teacher grades. Their data reveal that the teachers in the study assigned their grades more accurately (using general achievement and group aptitude score as criteria) to girls than to boys of both races and social classes, and graded white boys more strongly on social and intellectual qualities than on actual achievement. In addition, it should be recognized that the schools are notorious in their failure to identify or accommodate large numbers of creative high school students (French & Carden, 1968). It is also true that girls with high aptitudes in science and mathematics are often not identified or encouraged to develop their capabilities.

What of the screening and evaluating that the students do of each other? Objective information about the accuracy of high school students' assignment of prestige is lacking in the professional literature, but there are many reports of students' reactions to their perceptions of the prestige values they are given. Two recent books find that students are often inaccurate in their perceptions of their fellows' assessment of them, and that they remember with misery their feelings of inferiority, unattractiveness, and uncertainty about their selves during high school. *What Really Happened to the Class of '65* (Medved & Wallechinsky, 1976) and *Is There Life After High School?* (Keyes, 1977) recount the pain, anger, and shame described by the majority of the adults interviewed for the books. The books are revealing about the misperceptions of the actual prestige among many of the respondents in the studies. Other adults remember their high school days as having been the happiest of their lives. Christian Darling, in *The Eighty-Yard Run* (Shaw, 1941), and Rabbit Angstrom, in *Rabbit Run* (Updike, 1960) never again felt the exaltation of their days as high school athletes. High school experiences must all be vivid, it seems, whether accurately perceived or not, and are apparently of lifelong importance.

SCHOOL QUALITY

Massive studies of the relationship between school quality and the "quality" of the students leaving the schools have been conducted. School quality has been judged on such dimensions as the ratio of teachers to pupils, the extent of educational training of the faculty, the largeness and diversity of the library and other supportive facilities, the presence of lunchrooms and lunch programs, and the amount of money spent per pupil per year in the schools. The measures of pupil characteristics center mainly on the students' educational attainments at the end of any given period of school attendance.

In 1964, Congress directed the U.S. Commissioner of Education to conduct a study of "the lack of availability of equal educational opportunities for individuals by reason of race, color, religion or national origin" in the nation's public schools. Two years later, a committee published the famous and influential Coleman Report (Coleman, 1966). It showed the judged quality of the school was almost entirely *unrelated* to the quality of education attained. Family factors, the nature of peer influences, and attitudes toward fatalism were linked more closely to attainment than was school quality itself. A few years later, Jencks (1972) repeated and expanded on the claim that the quality of schooling contributes little to the educational differences between people. These astounding assertions raised controversy that still rages. Both reports have been attacked on grounds of faulty procedures and other technical inadequacies. Both sets of conclusions have been decried and lauded on philosophical and political grounds. The studies seem to deny the overwhelming evidence that more education is associated with greater social mobility (Blau and Duncan, 1967), greater income, and more prestigious employment (Bureau of the Census, 1972). Of course, one needs to be careful in assuming that, because two factors are associated, one causes the other to occur. But does the quality of schooling really not make a difference?

Perhaps it is the amount, not the quality, of schooling that makes the difference. Perhaps the measures of quality used in the Coleman and Jencks studies are inappropriate or insufficiently refined; perhaps the school unit is too insensitive a unit of measure for such study. Heyns (1974) argues that qualitative differences *between* programs *within* schools do affect the outcomes of school attendance. Heyns points out that resources are unequally allocated among the "tracks" within the typical high school.

Consider two other kinds of evidence, each reflecting differences in quality as well as in quantity between schools. First, school size has been shown consistently to be related to certain differential outcomes of education. Beginning with studies by Barker and Gump (1964), evidence has accumulated that students in small schools participate more frequently and in a wider variety of school activities than students in large schools. Students with academic difficulties drop out less frequently from small schools; they feel a sense of obligation to remain with the small population. And students from smaller schools report greater satisfaction with their school experiences, despite attending schools that have fewer and less varied resources, a narrower range of course offerings, and less well-prepared teachers (Willems, 1967; McCowan, O'Reilly & Illenberg, 1968; Wicker, 1968). Perhaps the most interesting finding is one by Glass and Smith (1979), who have reviewed several hundred studies on pupil achievement and class size. Through a procedure called meta-analysis, they have found that when classes contain around 15 students, there is a marked improvement in pupil achievement. It is evident that there are qualitative as well as quantitative differences between schools.

Finally, the success of school integration efforts seems to depend in part on favorable community attitudes, with resulting social and academic benefit to the integrated groups. Eagan (1978) reports that the integration of the Berkeley, California, schools in 1968 has led to improved academic performance for both black and white students when compared with preintegration measures of performance. Increased social equality has led to higher student satisfaction and to improved school morale. White students still surpass the performance of black students, but this difference may be related to social-class differences between the two groups of students. The successful integration and its happy consequences are attributed to the strong support and involvement of government officials, education staffs, and influential community members. There *are* differences between schools that do make a difference. And new developments in the schools promise more differences.

SCHOOL CHANGES

The instrumentality of the schools is often used to further the aims of other institutions. The Soviet urban communal day care and school facilities and the Israeli kibbutz were established primarily for economic reasons. When economic need became less pressing in Russia the structure of the communal schools were retained for political reasons based on their rationale: parents not raised communally cannot educate their children to that way of life; differences of family background and station would give an unfair advantage to some children and penalize others; the communal atmosphere of the schools would equalize opportunity; and, early training in communal living is essential to its success (Gruman, 1978).

American schools have sometimes been borrowed as instruments for other institutions, too. The economically inspired War on Poverty of President Lyndon Johnson is an example. Similarly, some of the changes occurring in schools to be described here, use the schools as a resource in meeting larger societal needs. Others are more closely confined to educational purposes. Two of the changes presented illustrate internal alterations of the schools themselves; the last one describes a change in school leave-taking.

The political and economic activities surrounding the women's movement and the drive toward ratification of the ERA have led to the relatively new Women's Sex Equity Act, passed as part of Public Law 93–380 (Women's Educational Equity Act, 1976). The act authorizes a broad range of actions intended to end sex bias in every area of education. Two examples of recently funded projects indicate the intentions and scope of the activities sponsored by the act. The descriptions are published in *Women's Education Equity Act Program, Annual Report,* published by the U.S. Department of Health, Education, and Welfare (September, 1978, p. 48).

Nonsexist Curriculum for
Pre-Service Teacher Education
American University   Amount: $121,011
School of Education   Duration: Two years
Massachusetts & Nebraska Avenue, N.W.
Washington, D.C. 20016
To develop a sound and coherent model for Nonsexist Teacher Education and to develop instructional materials and training strategies based on the model. Materials will be designed for easy integration into the current core of teacher education courses and programs. Model and materials will be implemented and validated in 10 colleges and universities affiliated in a network of demonstration sites.

Secondary Curriculum Support
Students Create New Images
Region XIII, Education Service Center   Amount: $69,659
7703 North Lamar   Duration: Two years
Austin, Texas 78752
To develop an innovative interdisciplinary course of study for secondary school students which will help them understand and deal with sex role pressures along with developing their own personal definitions of femaleness and maleness. Products will consist of a curriculum package for secondary schools with a teacher manual included, a training manual outlining a workshop design for introducing the curriculum to teachers, and a kit of student creation that compiles exemplary expressions related to sex role identity.

A nationwide organization aimed at concerting efforts to combat "math anxiety" among women and girls has recently been formed by the National Council of Teachers of Mathematics (WEEA, 1978). The Association for the Promotion of Mathematics Education of Girls and Women intends to change female attitudes and achievement in mathematics.

These and acts such as Title IX will affect males as clearly and as intensively as females, and may gradually work toward a reduction in traditional sex stereotyping and toward the development of androgynous personalities adaptive for solving increasingly complex societal problems.

The secondary schools still serve a minority of their students poorly. A dramatic method of working with a portion of that ill-served population was recently developed in California. California Senate Bill 112 (1972) authorized the creation of the California High School Proficiency Examination. Students reaching the age of 16 may, with parental consent, attempt this examination. Those who perform successfully on the test receive a regular high school diploma. The bill intended relief to disadvantaged students whose school performance was borderline at best, but an unexpected use of the availability of the examination is being made by bright students who wish to graduate from high school and enter junior college early. The effects of this awarding of a high school diploma on a challenge-by-examination basis are being carefully studied throughout the United States.

SUMMARY

"If the children and youth of a nation are afforded opportunity to develop their capacities to the fullest, if they are given the knowledge to understand the world and the wisdom to change it, then the prospects for the future are bright. In contrast, a society which neglects its children, however well it may function in other respects, risks eventual disorganization and demise" (Bronfenbrenner, 1970, p. 3).

In one of its efforts to accomplish the goals for children and youth (and through them for the nation) urged by Bronfenbrenner, the United States has built an elaborate educational system. It is rooted in a pervasive faith that a universal, free, vocationally-oriented schooling process is the best way to ensure the fullest actualization of the individual and of the society. It functions through these four kinds of activities in attempting to meet the goals: caretaking and managing of nearly the entire population of school age; teaching required skills and knowledge; transmitting cultural values; and classifying and evaluating the members of the school population. How well does it do toward fulfilling its purposes?

The population of the United States is among the most literate in the world. It has a very high level of educational attainment when judged either on international standards or when judged against its own past educational level. The portion of public funds from local to national levels spent on schools is very high.

The caretaking function is managed well for most people of school age. The majority of children and youth who "should be" in school are in school. But a quarter of the present fifth graders will not graduate from high school, for academic or economic or other reasons. And what is accomplished by those who do remain in school?

Though literacy and knowledge rates are high and rising, a disturbing percentage of the population is inadequately educated for the demand for increasing skill in an increasingly technological society. And the schools' processes contribute to a waste of certain talents; females, for example, are consistently discouraged from developing their mathematical abilities and certain other sex-stereotyped talents.

As to the transmitting of cultural values, the schools do seem to help impart general "American" systems of belief, faith, and value. But as values change, and as they become more numerous, the schools' essential conservativism sometimes leaves them in an old-fashioned state. The schools have helped promote certain aspects of civil rights, but are now only slowly moving to help the expansion of certain individual rights.

The classifying and evaluating functions of the schools are essential. They are better and more fairly performed than formerly, but large minorities of the school age population are still handicapped by school-sustained prejudice and by the inertia characteristic of any huge institution.

On balance, the schools seem to be working mightily and doing well at helping most people as Bronfenbrenner would wish. They are not meeting those wishes perfectly, but to do so is impossible. Although education is mostly a successful institution, it must help and be helped by the family and the other institutions of our society.

SUGGESTIONS FOR FURTHER READING

ELKIND, D. *The child and society.* New York: Oxford University Press, 1979.

FREY, S. H. (Ed.). *Adolescent behavior in school: Determinants and outcomes.* New York: Rand McNally, 1970.

GREGORY, T. W. *Adolescence in literature.* New York: Longman, 1978.

KATZ, M. B. (Ed.). *Education in American history: Readings on the social issues.* New York: Praeger, 1973.

MCKINNEY, J. P., FITZGERALD, H. E., & STROMMEN, E. A. *Developmental psychology: The adolescent and young adult.* Homewood, Ill.: Dorsey Press, 1977.

PEARL, A. *The atrocity of education.* St. Louis: New Critics Press, 1972.

BIBLIOGRAPHY

BACHMAN, G. G. The impact of family background and intelligence on tenth grade boys. *Youth in transition* (Vol. 2). Ann Arbor, Mich.: Ann Arbor Institute for Social Research, University of Michigan, 1970.

BALDRIDGE, J. V. *Sociology: A critical approach to power, conflict and change.* New York: Wiley, 1975.

BARKER, R. G. & GUMP, P. B. *Big school, small school: High school size and student behavior.* Stanford, Calif.: Stanford University Press, 1964.

BEM, S. L. Sex-role adaptability: One consequence of psychological androgyny. *Journal of Personality and Social Psychology,* 1975, *31,* 634–643.

BEM, S. L. The measurement of psychological androgyny. *Journal of Clinical and Consulting Psychology,* 1974, *42,* 155–162.

BERG, L. *Education and jobs: The great training robbery.* Boston: Bearon, 1971.

BERTRAND, A. L. *Basic sociology.* New York: Appleton-Century-Crofts, 1964.

BLAU, P. M., & DUNCAN, O. D. *The American occupational structure.* New York: Wiley, 1967.

BLEDSOE, J. C. An investigation of six correlates of student withdrawal from high school. *Journal of Educational Research,* 1959, *53,* 3–6.

BRONFENBRENNER, U. *Two worlds of childhood.* New York: Russell Sage Foundation, 1970.

BUREAU OF THE CENSUS. *Current population reports.* Washington, D.C.: U.S. Government Printing Office, March, 1972.

CERVANTES, L. F. *The dropout: Causes and cures.* Ann Arbor, Mich.: University of Michigan Press, 1965.

COLEMAN, J. S. *Equality of educational opportunity.* Washington, D.C.: U.S. Government Printing Office, 1966.

CREMIN, L. H. *The republic and the school: Horace Mann on the education of free men.* New York: Teachers College Press, 1960.

CREMIN, L. H. *American education: The colonial experience, 1607–1783.* New York: Harper & Row, 1970.

DOUVAN, E. Sex differences in the opportunities, demands, and developments of youth. In R. J. Havighurst & P. H. Dreyer (Eds.), *Youth: The seventy-fourth yearbook of the national society for the study of education.* Chicago: University of Chicago Press, 1975.

EAGAN, J. C. Berkeley benefitted from integration. Associated Press, December 22, 1978.

EBEL, R. E. What are schools for? *Phi Beta Kappan,* 1972, *54,* 3–7.

EGGLESTON, E. *The Hoosier schoolmaster.* (publisher unknown) 1913.

ELLIOTT, D. S., VOSS, H. L., & WENDING, A. Dropout and the social milieu of the high school: A preliminary analysis. *American Journal of Orthopsychiatry,* 1966, *36,* 808–817.

EISENSTADT, S. Social institutions. In *Encyclopedia of the social sciences* (Vol. 14). New York: Macmillan, 1968.

FERNANDEZ, C., ESPINOSA, R. W., & DORNBUSH, S. M. *Factors perpetuating the low academic status of Chicano high school students.* Palo Alto, Calif.: Stanford Center for Research and Development in Teaching, Stanford University, 1975, *38,* Memorandum No. 1.

FRENCH, J. L., & CARDEN, B. W. Characteristics of high mental ability dropouts. *Vocational Guidance Quarterly,* 1968, *16,* 162–168.

FRIEDENBERG, E. Z. *The vanishing adolescent.* New York: Dell, 1959.

GALLATIN, J. E. *Adolescence and individuality.* New York: Harper & Row, 1975.

GLASS, G. V., & SMITH, M. L. Meta-analysis of research on class size and achievement. *Educational Evaluation and Policy Analysis,* 1979, *1,* 2–11.

GOODMAN, P. *Compulsory mis-education.* New York: Vintage Books, 1962.

GRUMAN, J. Arnatz: A case study of a disturbed child on the Israeli kibbutz. Unpublished manuscript, University of Oregon, 1978.

HARARI, H. & KAPLAN, R. M. *Psychology: Personal and social adjustment.* New York: Harper & Row, 1977.

HARRIS SURVEY. What people think of their high schools. *Life,* 1969, *66,* 22–23.

HAVIGHURST, R. J. *Developmental tasks and education* (3rd ed.). New York: McKay-Longman, 1972.

HEYNS, B. Social selection and stratification within schools. *American Journal of Sociology,* 1974, *79,* 1434–1451.

HOLMEN, M. G., & DOCTER, R. F. *Educational and psychological testing: A study of the industry and its practices.* New York: Russell Sage Foundation, 1972.

HOLT, J. Education for the future. In R. Theobald (Ed.), *Social policies for America in the seventies.* New York: Doubleday, 1969.

JENCKS, C. *Inequality.* New York: Basic Books, 1972.

JOHNSTON, L. D., & BACHMAN, J. G. Educational institutions. In J. F. Adams (Ed.), *Understanding adolescence* (3rd ed.). Boston: Allyn and Bacon, 1976.

KEYES, R. *Is there life after high school?* New York: Warner Books, 1972.

KRATHWOHL, D. R., BLOOM, B. S. & MASIA, B. B. *Taxonomy of educational objectives. Handbook II: Affective domain.* New York: David McKay, 1964.

LANDIS, J. R. *Sociology: Concepts and characteristics* (3rd ed.). Belmont, Calif.: Wadsworth, 1977.

LUCHINS, A. S. *Group therapy.* New York: Random House, 1964.

MACCOBY, E. E. Sex differences in intellectual functioning. In E. E. Maccoby (Ed.), *The development of sex differences.* Stanford, Calif.: Stanford University Press, 1966.

MATARAZZO, J. D. Wechsler's measurement and appraisal of adult intelligence (5th ed.). Baltimore: Williams & Wilkins, 1972.

McCOWAN, R. J., O'REILLY, R. P. & ILLENBERG, G. J. Relation of size of high school enrollment to educational effectiveness. *Child Study Center Bulletin,* 1968, *4,* 73–79.

McCANDLESS, B. R. *Adolescents: Behavior and development.* Hinsdale, Ill.: Dryden, 1970.

McCANDLESS, B. R., ROBERTS, A., & STARNES, T. Teachers' marks, achievement test scores, and aptitude relations with respect to social class, race and sex. *Journal of Educational Psychology,* 1972, *63,* 153–159.

McDAVID, J. W., & GARWOOD, S. G. *Understanding children.* Lexington, Mass.: Heath, 1978.

MEDVED, M., & WALLENCHINSKY, D. *What really happened to the class of '65?* New York: Ballantine, 1976.

MUUSS, R. E. *Theories of adolescence* (3rd ed.). New York: Random House, 1975.

RIESMAN, D., DENNY, R., & GLAZER, N. *The lonely crowd.* New York: Yale University Press, 1959.

ROGERS, C. R. Learning to be free. In S. M. Faber & R. H. L. Wilson (Eds.), *Conflict and creativity: Control of the mind* (Part 2), New York: McGraw-Hill, 1963.

SAARIO, T. H., JACKLIN, C. N., & TETTLE, C. K. Sex-role stereotyping in the schools. *Harvard Educational Review*, 1973, *43*, 386–416.

SELLS, L. Mathematics—a critical filter. *The Science Teacher*, 1978, *45*, 28–29.

SHAW, I. The eighty-yard run. In *Mixed company*. New York: Random House, 1941.

SHAW, M. C., & McCUEN, G. T. The onset of academic underachievement in bright children. *Journal of Educational Psychology*, 1960, *51*, 105.

SILBERMAN, C. E. *Crisis in the classroom: The remaking of American education*. New York: Random House, 1970.

SINGER, J. *Androgyny: Toward a new theory of sexuality*. Garden City, N. J.: Anchor Books, 1977.

TAVRIS, C., & OFFIR, C. *The longest war: Sex differences in perspective*. New York: Harcourt Brace Jovanovich, 1977.

TOBIAS, S. *Overcoming math maxiety*. New York: Norton, 1978.

Trouble in an affluent suburb. *Time*, December 25, 1978, 60.

U. S. DEPARTMENT OF HEALTH, EDUCATION, AND WELFARE. *Toward a social report*. Washington, D.C.: U.S. Government Printing Office, 1969, 66–70.

UPDIKE, J. *Rabbit run*. New York: Knopf, 1960.

VOSS, H. L., WENDLING, A., & ELLIOTT, D. Some types of high school drop-outs. *Journal of Educational Research*, 1966, *59*, 363–368.

WEEA Newsflash, December, 1978, Vol. 2, No. 2.

WICKER, A. W. Undermanning, performances and students' subjective experiences in behavior settings of large and small high schools. *Journal of Personality and Social Psychology*, 1968, *10*, 255–261.

WILLEMS, E. P. Sense of obligation of high school activities as related to school size and marginality of student. *Child Development*, 1967, *10*, 255–261.

WOMEN'S EDUCATIONAL EQUITY ACT. First annual report. Washington, D.C.: U.S. Department of Health, Education, and Welfare, Office of Education, September 30, 1976.

YAMAMOTO, K., THOMAS, C. & KARNS, E. A. School related attitudes in middle-school age subjects. *American Educational Research Journal*, 1969, *6*, 191–206.

12

SUBCULTURES OF ADOLESCENTS IN THE UNITED STATES

Robert J. Havighurst

In a book on adolescence, there is an assumption that the book is devoted to the lives of people within a defined age range—a group who are growing through a social-psychological transition as well as a biological transition. There is also an assumption that the adolescents share in an *adolescent culture* that gives them many similar learning experiences. There are enough common experiences, common developmental problems, and common socialization procedures to permit us to examine the transition from childhood to adulthood in the United States under a number of chapter headings and, thus, to obtain information that helps us to become more effective teachers, employers, parents, and social policy makers.

Most of the chapters in this book are devoted to describing and analyzing one or another area or category of the adolescent experience, such as moral development, cognitive development, sex-role, personality, and career development. While all of this is valuable, we would be remiss if we did not recognize that there are certain subgroups of adolescents who do not fit into the mainstream of the American social life. For example, what have we learned about young American Indians, or Japanese Americans, or Mexican Americans? These and other visible groups of people have subcultures that give their young people a quite different experience from that of the 75% of American adolescents. In this chapter, I will identify a number of adolescent subgroups and describe their differing subcultures.

THE MOST COMMON ADOLESCENT CULTURE

Suppose a stranger to the United States asked us to summarize the typical or modal culture of adolescents, and to describe the processes of socialization that inculcate this culture. We might have considerable difficulty in answering this query, but a good resource would be to turn to the work of a husband-wife team, Richard and Shirley Jessor (1977). The Jessors worked in a university city of 67,000 people in the Rocky Mountain area, a city predominantly white, middle class. They studied longitudinally a sample of 400 public school pupils for three years, from 1969 to 1972, and ended with the same group in grades 10, 11, and 12 of senior high school. They secured, each year, from each boy and girl, a lengthy confidential report on their current life, with a stress on problem behavior and on the persons in the family, community, and peer group with whom he or she associated.

Robert J. Havighurst is Professor of Education and Human Development Emeritus at the University of Chicago. In his distinguished career he has written *Adolescent Character and Personality, Growing Up in River City, Human Development and Education, Developmental Tasks and Education, Comparative Perspectives on Education, Society and Education,* and *400 Losers*. In addition he has published a large number of scholarly articles on such topics as adolescence, adult development and aging, comparative education, urban education, character development, and gifted children.

The Jessors recognized five major sources of socialization: parents, peer group, school, church, and television. They asked questions about five areas of problem behavior for adolescents: drinking alcoholic beverages, smoking marijuana, sexual intercourse, social protest or activism, and a category of delinquency consisting mainly of stealing or aggressive action. In addition, they rated their subjects on such variables as: valuing academic achievement; valuing independence; valuing affection; social criticism; religiosity; and self-esteem. They also measured a number of influences in the social environment: parental control; friends support and control; parent-friends compatibility; parental attitude toward problem behavior; and friends attitude toward problem behavior.

They looked for personality differences between adolescents who were the most and the least likely to engage in problem behavior. Those showing more problem behavior presented a strong concern with personal autonomy, a tolerant attitude toward rule-breaking, little or no interest in the goals of the church and school, and a "jaundiced" view of the larger society.

Those who showed less problem behavior tended to do well academically, were not much concerned with independence, were accepting of society as it is, were involved in religious activity, and could see little that was basically attractive in problem behavior.

Summarizing the developmental changes over the 3-year period ending in grades 10–12 of senior high school, the Jessors (1977, p. 238) note that for the entire group there was:

> ... a growth of independence, a decline in traditional ideology related to achievement value and to society as a whole, the assumption of a more relativistic and more tolerant morality, an attenuation of the hold of conventional norms and controls such as those embodied in religion and the family, an increase in orientation toward peers and in reliance on them as a reference group, an ecological increase in the prevalence of models and supports for transgression, and an increase in problem behavior itself.

The data on the correlation between problem behavior and the pressure of the social environment showed that social pressure was more effective in explaining problem behavior than was personality quality. The problem-prone adolescents "perceive less compatibility between the expectations that their parents and their friends hold for them, they acknowledge greater influence of friends relative to parents, they perceive greater support for problem behavior among their friends, and they have more friends who provide models for engaging in problem behavior" (p. 237).

Some students of adolescence may hesitate to accept the Jessor conclusions as correct for the mainstream of American adolescents, but other chapters in this book will look at various aspects of the question in more detail. Our concern in this chapter is with *atypical* subcultures.

CULTURE AND SUBCULTURE

For the purposes of this chapter, I shall define adolescence as the age period from 12 to 18. I shall use the term "youth" to refer to an overlapping group from 15 through 24 years of age. Since our topic is "subcultures" of adolescents, we also need a clear definition of the key terms *culture* and *subculture*.

A *culture* is a set of common and standard behaviors and beliefs shared by a group of people and taught by them to their children. Different nations have different cultures. Also, within a complex society there are always a number of subcultures. A *subculture* is a culture shared by a subgroup in a complex society and different from the subcultures of other subgroups in that society. For example, the American society has a number of subcultures, including those of Italian-Americans, Mexican-Americans, Japanese-Americans, American Indians, Puerto Ricans, Appalachians, New Englanders, midwesterners, southerners, Texans, blacks, Catholics, Jews, and Protestants. From this list it should be clear that a given American takes part in a number of subcultures, as well as in the common culture shared by all or nearly all citizens of the United States. Thus, a subculture does not include all the learned behaviors and beliefs of its members.

Another form of subculture is that of *social class* which I will describe and discuss later in this chapter. Still another form of subculture is that of *sex*—male or female. Thus we shall see the American adolescent subcultures varying according to ethnicity, social class, and sex. In describing or discussing any particular subculture, we should specify the ethnicity, social class, and sex of the group of adolescents who are in it.

The Adolescent Peer Culture

It is well known that a given age group has its own somewhat truncated culture. While the members of this age group participate in the culture of the larger society, they also have common and standardized ways of behaving and believing that are pretty much limited to their own age group. For instance, the 8-year-old boys of a community are likely to have their own game culture—a set of games with rules handed from one age cohort of 8-year-old boys to the next: rules for games of marbles, hide-and-seek, cops and robbers, etc. To this extent, the 8-year-old boys have a peer culture, that is, a culture of a group who are approximately equal in age. There is a culture of 12-year-olds, one of 14-year-olds, 16-year-olds, 18-year-olds, and one such culture for boys with a different one for girls.

There may also be a more generalized peer culture for teenagers, into which the 13-year-olds enter slowly and unsurely, while the 18-year-olds are dropping their participation in their *adolescent peer culture* in favor of the culture of young adults. The adolescent peer culture is the set of ways of behaving and believing of the age group from 12 to 18, which they pass on to their successors. This is the kind of definition to be found in a modern democratic society, where teenagers are allowed to be "adolescents" with a minimum of control by the adult society.

In a few societies, the adolescent peer culture actually opposes the adult culture at points, and there is a long-drawn-out contest between adults and adolescents. The adolescent peer culture may have certain values and interests that conflict with the values and interests of the adults. In this case, the adult society may seek to put down the adolescent peer culture. This was clearly the case in the United States in the late 1960s, when the adolescent peer culture encouraged boys to let their hair grow long and girls to shorten their skirts. There were a number of battles between the adolescent peer group and the adult generation, which was usually represented by teachers and school principals. More generally, the adolescent peer culture has its own existence more or less outside the ken of adults (although they know it exists), and they make sure it does not interfere with the general adult culture.

In the United States, there has been something of a controversy over the question of whether an adolescent peer culture actually opposes some of the educational values of the high schools, for example, encouraging athletics and social activities at the expense of academic study. In an influential book entitled *The Adolescent Society*, James S. Coleman (1961) reported his study of students in several midwestern high schools. This study appeared to show that adolescent boys and girls in high school were more influenced by their peers than by their parents and teachers.

A critical analysis of Coleman's study and other studies has been written by Gottlieb and Reeves (1963). They concluded that there is a vaguely defined adolescent peer culture made up of varying peer cultures from various groups of adolescents, and that this peer culture has a common basis of disagreement with the adult culture at some points. However, there is no solid monolithic adolescent peer culture that is common to all adolescents in a modern society.

Social Class and Social Mobility

Perhaps the most widespread ambition of adolescents and their families in modern societies during the past century has been the desire to move up the socioeconomic ladder—to rise in social status, to obtain a higher income, to have more prestige. And it was evident that the widest road for upward mobility was through achievement in adolescence and early adulthood. This achievement might take the form of educational progress which opened the way to higher status occupations, or of hard work and cleverness in a series of ever-improving jobs (or of marriage for girls to a man of higher status). To be upwardly mobile, to move from one social class or socioeconomic level to a higher level, means a change from one subculture to another, or a change of life-style.

Research by social anthropologists and sociologists shows that social classes exist as crudely defined subcultures in a number of modern societies. While most of this research has been done in the United States, the social class phenomenon is confirmed by research of the last 25 years in Sweden, Canada, Australia, New Zealand, Brazil, and England (Bendix & Lipset, 1953; Glass, 1954; Havighurst, 1958).

A social class is defined as a group of people who share certain values and attitudes and feel themselves to be similar to each other. It may also be seen as a group of people who share a particular life-style. There is much intermarriage within a social class as well as many informal social relationships. When a social scientist studies a particular community, he observes the various social groupings and economic groupings, and he asks people in the community about the "social structure" of the community. Invariably, if the community contains several thousand people, and if the population has a range of income and occupation, the residents of the community report that there is a hierarchy of social groups, or social classes, with the highest group having the highest prestige and power in the community. The metaphor of vertical distance is used by the residents who speak of "our upper class, our middle class or classes, and our lower class or classes."

The number of visibly different social classes depends on the size and complexity of the community. It may be as many as seven, or as few as three. The American community studies (Warner, Meeker & Eells, 1960) tend to settle on a five-class structure, named as follows: upper, upper-middle, lower-middle, upper-lower, and lower-lower. These five classes can be found in any cross-sectional community of 5,000 or more. The placing of individuals in the class system depends on their social relationships, their occupation, income, educational level, the type of house and area of the community in which they live, and the clubs or church to which they belong. All these social characteristics are judged by people in the community in terms of social prestige.

A democratic society has an "open" class system, with people moving into and out of a given social class on the basis of their performance in various sectors of socioeconomic life. Hence there are always some people at the margin between two classes, and therefore some people cannot be placed as exactly as others in the class structures.

Social mobility is defined as movement within a lifetime by an individual from one class to another. Generally the move is up or down one step on a five-class scale, but sometimes a person moves two or more steps. The degree of social mobility in a society is usually measured by comparing the social class of adult sons and daughters with their fathers. Often the measurement is limited to sons and fathers, since the occupations of males can be easily determined, and occupational level is a very good indicator of social class position all over the world in complex societies.

The proportions of people in the various social classes are substantially as follows in the United States: upper, 3%; upper-middle, 10%; lower-middle, 27%; upper-lower, 45%; lower-lower, 15%. In effect, the white-collar occupations are middle class, and the blue-collar occupations are lower class or working class, with significant exceptions. Some highly skilled handworkers, such as electronic technicians and interior decorators, would be placed by their incomes and their association in the lower-middle class. Also, owners of substantial farms who work their own farms would be placed in one of the middle classes.

ETHNIC AND SOCIAL SUBGROUPS OF ADOLESCENTS

As we look for atypical groups of adolescents, we may place them in Table 12.1, which gives the numbers of youth (age 15–24) in various ethnic subcultures. For the sake of brevity, and because there is not sufficient research on some groups, I will report on only a few of them. Also, I will designate them by social class as well as ethnicity. The following groups will be described: Mexican-Americans—lower-middle class; Puerto Ricans—working class; Japanese-Americans—middle class; American Indians—multitribal; and blacks—middle class. In addition, I will describe two subcultures that are not primarily ethnic, but are isolated from the mainstream of adolescents. They are: street culture males (in slums of big cities); and teenage mothers.

Hispanic Adolescents

A 1972 census publication reports somewhat over 9 million persons of Spanish descent falling into five categories as shown in Table 12.2. They are living mainly in four areas: the Southwest (Texas, Arizona, New Mexico, California); the Northeast (New York, Massachusetts, New Jersey, Pennsylvania); Florida; and the North Central Industrial area. We will focus our attention on the Mexican-Americans and the Puerto Ricans.

Mexican-Americans of the Southwest. What is now the southwestern corner of the United States was a part of Mexico until the Mexican War of

TABLE 12.1   *Youth in Ethnic Subcultures (1970)*

GROUP	NUMBERS OF YOUTH	PERCENT OF YOUTH[a]
Spanish Origin	1,715,000	4.7
Mexican-American	892,000	2.5
Puerto Rican	276,000	0.8
Cuban	76,000	0.2
Other	471,000	1.3
Asian	241,000	0.7
Japanese	96,000	0.3
Chinese	90,000	0.3
Philipino	55,000	0.2
Jews (Est.)	1,500,000	4.1
Southeastern European Ethnics[b]	555,000	1.5
Polish	111,000	0.3
Italian	263,000	0.7
Greek	41,000	0.1
Slav	102,000	0.3
American Indians and Eskimos	157,000	0.4
Blacks	4,300,000	11.8
In metropolitan areas	3,180,000	8.7
Not in SMSAs[c]	1,120,000	3.1
Anglo-European	27,900,000	87.0
In metropolitan areas	18,600,000	59.0
Not in SMSAs	9,300,000	28.0
Total Age Group	36,400,000	100

Note. From U.S. Bureau of the Census, 1970. Series PC(2) 1A, B. C. F. G.

[a] Rounded to nearest .1 percent. The total of this column is more than 100 percent because Spanish Origin, Jews, and European Ethnics are also included in the "Anglo-European" figures.

[b] First and second generation only. Others identify with these groups.

[c] Standard Metropolitan Statistical Areas.

1848. After the war, which resulted in annexation of Texas and the southwestern territory to the United States, the Spanish and Mexican settlers who remained there became American citizens. Thus there is an old American population of Spanish origin which has as long a history of residence in this country as the New England colonists.

Some of these people became business and professional leaders and legislators, so that Spanish surnames figure prominently in the history of the past hundred years in the Southwest. Cities such as Albuquerque, Santa Fe, San Antonio, El Paso, Los Angeles, and San Diego indicate by their names the Spanish influence; and many Spanish surnames are carried on the rosters of the Chamber of Commerce, the upper middle-class service clubs, and the country clubs. In New Mexico, Spanish and English are both official languages.

TABLE 12.2   *United States Population of Spanish Origin, 1972*

Origin	Total	PERCENT OF U.S. POPULA- TION	PERCENT OF POPU- LATION OF SPANISH ORIGIN	AGE DISTRIBUTION (% OF TOTAL)		
				10–17	18–19	20–24
Mexican	5,254,000	2.6	57	20.2	4.3	8.3
Puerto Rican	1,518,000	.7	17	21.5	2.6	8.0
Cuban	629,000	.3	7	13.4	3.8	3.7
Central or South American	599,000	.3	6	—	—	—
Other Spanish	1,178,000	.5	13	—	—	—
Total	9,178,000	4.5	100	—	—	—

Note. From U.S. Bureau of Census. *Current Population Reports,* Series P-20, No. 238, Selected Characteristics of Persons and Families of Mexican and Other Spanish Origin: March 1972.

By far the largest group of Spanish-Americans are those who identify themselves to the census taker as being of Mexican origin, though 83% of them were born in the United States. Over five million strong, they provide more than 20% of the children in Los Angeles public schools. Almost all of them are legally American citizens, though a few have come across the Mexican-American border as wetbacks and are liable to deportation if they should get in trouble with the law and be found to lack citizenship papers.

The Mexican-Americans present a variety of life-styles. They are so heterogeneous in status and racial ancestry that the one thing they have in common is their Mexican heritage. They range in economic status from affluent professionals and businessmen to migrant farm workers and people on welfare in big city barrios.

The period since 1965 has seen the younger

> ... members of the post-World War II Mexican-American generation develop a new political consciousness and a pride in their cultural heritage. The youth cohort has emerged from a fusion of Hispano offspring, who are establishing strong cultural links to Mexican and Indian culture, and dispossessed barrio youth, who are facing prospects of economic marginality and limited realization of aspirations. The politically conscious adolescents call themselves *Chicanos,* a word presumed to be derived from the colloquial speech of northern Mexico but in fact of unknown etiology. (Thornburg & Grinder, 1975, p. 345)

The Chicano is a product of Spanish-Mexican Indian heritage and Anglo influence. "The new dignity of Chicano youth is manifested in the concept of Aztlán, a symbolization for the ethnic unity of the mestizo Mexican American and a rallying point for proclaiming the righteousness of the Mexican-American heritage (Thornburg & Grinder, 1975, p. 345).

Thornburg and Grinder describe the rise of "Chicano power" in the 1960s as a response of Mexican-American youth to the civil rights movement. Their consciousness was stimulated by Mexican-American reform leaders, especially Cesar Chavez who organized the California farm workers; Reies Tijerina who founded the *Alianza Federal de Mercedes,* an organization of New Mexico heirs to old Mexican land grants who claimed ownership of land taken over after the Mexican-American war by the United States government; and Rodolfo "Corky" Gonzales, a youth worker in Denver who organized the Crusade for Justice, a Chicano civil rights organization. In 1969, the Crusade for Justice created the Chicano Youth Liberation Conference, when 2,000 young Chicano delegates, from over 100 Chicano youth groups, called for a revival of traditional cultural values, a re-birth of Chicano nationalism, and the creation of a new political party.

Mexican-American adolescents organized two major school boycotts in East Los Angeles (1968) and Crystal City, Texas (1969). In Los Angeles, they demanded reduction of class size, bilingual counselors, expanded library and industrial arts facilities, reduction of intelligence testing, and more attention by teachers to community problems. In Crystal City, the high school enrollment was 85% Mexican-American, but cheerleaders, elected by a predominantly Anglo faculty panel, were usually Anglo. The Chicanos asked to have cheerleaders and homecoming queen elected by the student body. When the school board refused, a local Chicano leader, Jose Angel Gutiérrez, organized a political campaign that resulted in his election and that of two other Chicanos to the school board. He was elected president of the school board and significant school reforms were instigated.

These Chicano youth activities may have served to increase the interest of the U. S. Commission on Civil Rights to problems of Chicano education. That Commission has held several hearings and issued several reports bearing on Mexican-American education. For example, the 1973 Report by the Commission was entitled *Teachers and Students: Differences in Teacher Interaction with Mexican American and Anglo Students.* This report contains the following conclusions:

> The basic finding of this report is that the schools of the Southwest are failing to involve Mexican American children as active participants in the classroom to the same extent as Anglo children. On most of the measures of verbal interaction between teacher and student, there are gross disparities in favor of Anglos.
>
> It is the schools and teachers of the Southwest, not the children, who are failing. They are failing in meeting their most basic responsibility—that of providing each child the opportunity to gain the maximum benefit of education and develop his capabilities to the fullest extent. In

the Commission's view, the schools of the Southwest will continue to fail until fundamental changes are made. Changes are needed in the way teachers are trained and in the standards by which they are judged, and changes are needed in educational programs and curriculums so that all children may be reached. (p. 44)

Puerto Rican Lower-Class Adolescent Subcultures. Puerto Ricans represent in the industrial North and Northeast what Chicanos represent in the Southwest—a supply of unskilled and semiskilled labor, a growing middle class with political power, and a set of problems and challenges to the schools. Puerto Ricans make up 17% of the population of Spanish descent, slightly over half of whom were born in Puerto Rico. They form a relatively youthful population, and have the lowest amount of schooling among the Spanish-surname groups.

Puerto Ricans come and go freely between the mainland of the United States and the island of Puerto Rico. The number residing on the mainland is about half the number residing on the island. Puerto Rico is a United States "commonwealth" and not a state, but its citizens have the rights of United States citizens, although they are voting citizens only if they reside on the mainland.

More than half of the mainland Puerto Ricans live in the New York City metropolitan area, and there are large populations in Philadelphia, Washington, D.C., and Chicago. Twenty percent of the males have white-collar jobs, very few are farm laborers, and the largest occupational groups are factory and transport workers. Of the New York City public school enrollment, approximately 250,000, or 23% are Puerto Ricans and 35% are blacks.

A considerable proportion of Puerto Rican immigrants have prospered in the United States. Therefore, the Puerto Rican population of the New York metropolitan area is dispersed between middle-class and lower-class residential areas. Two areas of lowest income residents are the South Bronx and Spanish Harlem. These are the areas northeast of Central Park and extending on north into the Bronx. Here there is a street culture that takes charge of the life of a child in spite of parents' efforts, the school, and the church to direct the child into a morally acceptable early adult role. This process is described vividly in the autobiography of Piri Thomas, entitled *Down These Mean Streets.* His Puerto Rican parents did their best to control him, but they lost him to the life of the streets. It started with street games, such as stick ball, and moved on into smoking marijuana, organizing weapons and strategy, to fighting the gang in the next neighborhood, "making out" with the girls on the tenement roof-tops, and on into various forms of delinquency. Piri Thomas summarizes:

> Hanging around on the block is a sort of science. You have a lot to do and a lot of nothing to do. In the winter there's dancing, pad combing,

movies, and the like. But summer is really the kick. All the blocks are alive, like many-legged cats crawling with fleas. People are all over the place. Stoops are occupied like bleacher sections at a game, and beer flows like there's nothing else to drink. The block musicians pound out gone beats on tin cans and conga drums and bongos. And kids are playing all over the place—on fire escapes, under cars, over cars, in alleys, back yards, hallways.[1]

The story of Thomas' adolescence is "dated," of course, since he was born in 1928 and the events he describes took place in the 1940s. But the goal has not changed. He concludes, "It was all a part of becoming *hombre*, of wanting to have a beard to shave, a driver's license, a 'stoneness' which enabled you to go into a bar like a man" (pp. 15–16).

Thomas took the route through drugs to robbery and was sent to prison. After six years, he was paroled and went into drug rehabilitation work. He continues his writing and a variety of community projects in New York City.

Asian-American Adolescents

The Asian-Americans were the fastest-growing immigrant group during the 1970s, and they exhibit a great diversity. Only three groups were visible in the census in 1970—Japanese, Chinese, and Philipinos. But in the last 20 years there has been a rapid growth in three other Asian groups—Koreans, Pacific Islanders (Guam and Samoa), and Vietnamese. In 1975, there were an estimated 215,000 Koreans living in the United States.

We do not yet know enough about the life-styles or even the number of adolescents in the newer groups to be able to describe their adolescent subcultures. Consequently, I will limit my discussion to one group, the Japanese-Americans. Also, I will omit the residents of Hawaii, where the Japanese and Chinese make up a majority of the population, with Philipinos (formerly called Filipinos), native Hawaiians, and Anglos in the minority. What we know about the Japanese-Americans on the mainland may not describe accurately the residents of Hawaii.

Adolescents of Chinese or Japanese origin are found in practically every big city. Although their grasp of the English language is generally good, most of them were raised in a subculture in which family influence and family loyalty are very strong. This has tended to preserve their separate ethnic cultures. The Japanese-Americans are somewhat more integrated into the Anglo life-style than are the Chinese-Americans. These two

---

[1] From *Down These Mean Streets* by Piri Thomas, Copyright © 1967 by Alfred A. Knopf, Inc., New York, p. 14.

groups do very well in school, on the average, and make great use of educational opportunities. Of those males who were 16 years of age and over, the 1970 census indicated that 70% of the Japanese, 62% of the Chinese, and 49% of the Philipinos had completed high school, compared to 32% of blacks and 28% of Mexican-Americans.

The Japanese immigration commenced about 1890 and consisted largely of farm workers and shopkeepers. They rented and then bought small farms in the western states, and the shopkeepers joined them to market their products and to help form mutual aid groups in small and large cities of the West. The "Gentlemen's Agreement" of 1907 between the American and Japanese governments bound the Japanese government to withhold passports from Japanese laborers. This was followed by the Japanese Exclusion Act of 1924, and the Japanese-American population grew very little between 1920 and 1950. Meanwhile, the Japanese-American population was improving its educational and economic status.

Japanese-American Adolescent Subcultures. The *Sansei* (third generation) Japanese group is essentially a post-World War II population group. The adolescents of 1980 were born between 1962 and 1968. They have had educational and occupational opportunities and they have had general social acceptance in the communities where they live.

A subgroup of the Sansei youth have become active politically, though they split into two groups with respect to a Liberal Capitalist versus a Marxist ideology. Another major subgroup does not express a political ideology but works for personal educational and economic success. This analysis has been made by Minako Maykovich (1972) based on interviews with a nonrepresentative sample of Sansei college students in California around 1970. Liu and Yu (1975), in their study of Asian-American youth, see the contemporary Japanese-American youth as *a sweet and sour* generation that is creating new social expectations and a new identity.

Adolescent American Indians

There are about 100,000 American Indian and Eskimo adolescents, aged 12–18, scattered in 30 or more tribal groups and living in considerable numbers in about 20 states. About 90% are enrolled in school. About 15,000 are in boarding schools, mostly maintained by the federal government Bureau of Indian Affairs. Another 45,000 are in public schools on or near Indian reservations where Indians make up more than 50% of the students. The remaining 30,000 are in public schools where they are a minority in the student body. A growing number of this group live in big cities.

In the social anthropological sense, Indian youth do not constitute a subculture because they belong to a number of different tribes, each having its own tribal culture and language. Only one tribal group (the Navaho) is large enough and residentially concentrated enough to provide a clear-cut cultural base for an adolescent subculture. Two others, the Sioux and the Cherokee, have several thousand adolescent members but they are so widely dispersed, and so many of them live in cities, that they do not find themselves associating with fellow tribal members enough to form nuclei of an adolescent tribal subculture.

Furthermore, the young Indians living in the cities and out of contact with their tribal elders are losing their native languages and growing up without knowledge or experience of their tribal religious practices and beliefs. In addition, there is a growing number of marriages with non-Indians.

At the same time, during the decade of the 1970s there was a strong movement for Indian self-determination in economic and educational affairs. This has resulted in the passage by Congress of the Indian Education Act (1972), the Indian Self-Determination and Educational Assistance Act (1975), and the Indian Policy Review Commission Act (1975). These acts of Congress may have been expedited by the growing strength of several Indian rights organizations, which have been led by young adults.

An activist action was undertaken by a multi-tribal group who commenced in 1977 a cross-country march starting from the Pacific Coast. They called this "The Longest Walk" and arrived in Washington on July 15, 1978. Several thousand Indians marched into Washington and held a preaceful mass meeting which was attended by a number of congressmen. The Indian leaders announced their opposition to several bills pending in Congress that they claimed would abrogate some Indian treaty rights and weaken tribal cultures.

Thus during the 1970s, a kind of pan-Indian nationalism was established that might lead the American Indians to think of themselves less as members of different and separate tribes and more as *Indian Americans*. It will be a matter of interest and importance to educators to observe and react to the development of American Indian adolescents' behavior with respect to their diverse tribal identities and to their pan-Indian issues and values.

Black Adolescent Subcultures

The largest easily visible minority group are the blacks, who comprise about 11% of the youth population in the United States. Whether this group, under 1980 conditions, has a significant subculture is a question that will probably be debated by the sociologists for some time to come. Blacks do not have a separate language, or even a separate English dialect. They are distributed through the social class structure, in all five classes, though they have a larger proportion of poor people and therefore of lower-class people, than does the majority white group. There is no cultural characteristic that is common to all or nearly all blacks and absent in whites unless it is the experience of being black, and the elements of ideology that flow from that experience.

In spite of some prejudice against blacks in certain occupations, the proportion of black men and women in middle-class occupations has been increasing since 1940. William Julius Wilson, Black Chairman of the Department of Sociology at the University of Chicago, authored a book published in 1978 entitled *The Declining Significance of Race: Blacks and Changing American Institutions.* He concluded that a substantial and growing proportion of blacks have become middle class and share middle-class attitudes and behavior with white middle-class people. However, the economic structure of the society has changed so as to create a vast underclass of blacks living in poverty-stricken ghettos, so that there are two contrasting black subcultures—one middle class and one characteristic of people below the lower working class, which he calls an *underclass.* He writes:

> A history of discrimination and oppression created a huge black underclass, and the (recent) technological and economic revolutions have combined to insure it a permanent status. As the black middle class rides on the wave of political and social changes, benefitting from the growth of employment opportunities in the growing corporate and government sectors of the economy, the black underclass falls behind the larger society in every conceivable respect. (p. 21)

The U.S. Office of Education reported on racial enrollments in public schools for 1974. In the 100 largest school districts, 68% of the black students were in schools with 80% or more "minority" enrollments. It is safe to assume that the black *underclass* to which Wilson refers is mainly in these ghetto schools in large cities.

On the other hand, the growing number of black middle-class students are mostly in schools with substantial numbers of Anglo students. I will describe this middle-class black adolescent subculture, relying heavily on the chapter entitled *Black Youth* by Doris Wilkinson in the Yearbook on YOUTH (1975) of the National Society for the Study of Education.

The Black Middle-Class Subculture. This group now graduates from high school and enrolls in college to almost as great an extent as do white youth. For example, in 1977, 26% of black youth aged 18 through 21 were enrolled in college, compared with 34% of white youth. Among all black youth, 68% graduated from high school.

The efforts and concerns of middle-class black youth reflect the belief that blacks must continue to confront racial discrimination and to make active protest against various forms of racial injustice. They are caught up in the black power movement that developed in the 1965–70 period. They favor the various forms of black studies that have developed in college and secondary school curriculums. These youth see themselves as pioneers in a new set of social and political roles as well as middle-class occupations. Wilkinson concludes her analysis as follows:

> These youth are unlike their white counterparts not only with respect to placement in the social structure and their definitions of the dynamics of inter-racial relations, but also with respect to the type of attitudinal orientation which emerges from their cultural experiences. They are different in their collective symbolism and self-oriented definitions of who they are and what they wish to become. For they still must contend with social issues that never confront white youth. Because of this and the prevailing differential treatment they experience and the negative myths about their identities, young blacks will not acquiesce passively in the future. (p. 305)

Street Culture Adolescent Subcultures

The slums of big cities present a way of life that is forced on people because of the physical situation in which they live—crowded housing, absence of local neighborhood adult leadership or church influence, low income. When the youth are unemployed and out of school, they are practically forced out on the streets. Life on the streets of the neighborhood constitutes a *street culture*. The adolescents create a subculture for themselves.

I will present a picture of the adolescent subculture of a Chicago slum area which was observed and recorded by Gerald Suttles in 1962–1965. Another example is the Puerto Rican subculture of East Harlem, in New York City, which was described by Piri Thomas in his autobiography.

Adolescent Subculture in a Chicago Slum. The area just southwest of Chicago's downtown district has been a home for immigrant working-class people for a century. Jane Addams established Hull House to serve this area. Since 1965, this area has been changing, due to the fact that the University of Illinois at Chicago was being located on a new campus carved out of the slums.

In the period from 1962 to 1965, this area was a fairly typical Chicago slum known as the Addams area. Suttles was a sociologist who took residence in this area. He became acquainted with the adolescents who lived there and collected data from various available sources. In a section of his book, called *The Boys' World* (1968), he describes the life of the 12- to 18-year-olds which centered around certain street corners in an area of about one square mile.

There were 32 boys' street corner groups with names, examples being the Erls, the Gallants, the Rapids, the Gutter Guys. The average membership was 12-15 boys, with about a 2-year age spread. There were three different age grades, from about 12 to 18. There were also six girls' street corner groups.

Among the boys there were three ethnic groups. One was entirely black, with six or eight street units. One was almost entirely Mexican, with a few Italians, and a dozen street corner units. A third was mainly Italian, with a few Mexicans and a dozen street corner units. The three ethnic groups each lived in a separate territory separated only by streets. The major activities of these groups can be summarized as follows:

Hanging. This consisted of loitering around the particular street corners which constituted the "turf" of the club.
Fighting. This was mainly a matter of guerrilla warfare, though each group had a secret cache with guns and other weapons. Boys who strayed into strange territory would be "jumped" by the group that "owned" the area.
Stealing. This was sometimes organized with expeditions to a target store or warehouse outside of the area, and sometimes a matter of shoplifting in local stores or robbing local adults who had no connection with the group.
Drinking. This was mainly sharing cans of beer or bottles of wine. Only the beginning of marijuana smoking was visible at this time. That came later and was a central characteristic of the equivalent subcultures in the 1970s.

A record was made of the 357 cases in which boys below age 17 were arrested during two years, commencing July, 1963. The main categories were:

Theft, burglary, purse-snatching	54%
Fighting and carrying weapons	15%
Malicious mischief: Property destruction, false fire alarm, opening a city fire hydrant	14%
Drinking, glue sniffing, disorderly conduct	7%
Breaking curfew rules	7%
Sex misdemeanors	3%

Street Gangs Down to Date. An article in the *Chicago Tribune* for August 13, 1978 commences: "Street gangs. They have been around almost as long as there have been cities—roaming the streets of poor neighborhoods, broken kids from broken homes seeking sustenance from their peers. Their members call them 'youth clubs.'" Thus the situation has not changed much since Suttles' study. Police estimate that in Chicago there are at least 150 active street gangs with 5,000 members. There are black gangs, white gangs, and even Chinese gangs, but the largest number are in Chicago's Latino neighborhoods.

Female Subcultures

The discussion and description of adolescent subcultures is almost certain to pay less attention to girls than to boys. This is true of this chapter and it is unfortunate. Girls and women have different roles from boys and men in the several social classes. This is particularly true of the lower classes and the one Wilson (1978) identifies as the underclass. Recognizing this, I have written a section on teenage mothers which deals with a most important and difficult subcultural group.

A Subculture of Teenage Mothers. During the past 20 years there has been a major increase in the numbers of young women under 20 who have borne children. This is true in terms of proportions or percentages of the 5-year age cohort from 15 through 19. The fact is that the proportions of young women having children as teenagers, the proportions of these children born out of wedlock, and the proportions of whites having these experiences have all increased in the past 20 years. Table 12.3 summarizes the relevant data for two periods about 10 years apart.

It should be noted that the median age of marriage for women in the United States has risen more than a year since the low point of 20.1 in 1956. Since 1973, the median age has gone from 21.0 to 21.6 in 1977. The percentages of married women, in relation to age, went steadily upward in 1977 from 15% aged 18 to 47% aged 21. Thus, first marriage is a characteristic experience of the 18–21 age group. This and related experiences might be said to characterize an "early adult subculture" for women who are moving into the typical roles of wife and mother.

There is also an emergent *subculture of teenage mothers* aged 14–17, nearly all of whom are not married and not filling the typical roles of wife and mother. In 1975, only 2.7% of girls aged 14–17 were married. However, as seen in Table 12.3, the birth rate of the 15–17 group was 37 per thousand women, compared with 86 per thousand of the 18–19 age group of whom 21% were married.

Bearing children out of wedlock is a central characteristic of this subculture. As shown in Table 12.4, 86% of births to girls under 15 were illegitimate, 72% for 15-year-olds, and 46% for 17-year-olds. Half of the births to girls aged 15–17 are illegitimate, and a great many of the so-called "legitimate" births were conceived before the girls were married.

Several lines of evidence support the conclusion that this subculture numbers about 10% of adolescent girls. They are sharing a significant set of experiences, and there is some peer-group communication and role-expectation within this group.

Jimmy Breslin wrote an article for the *Chicago Tribune* in 1978 with the title "Having a baby is the only way out—or so it seems." A mother, di-

TABLE 12.3 *Teenage Childbearing in the United States, 1966–1975*

BIRTH RATES (LIVE BIRTHS PER 1,000 WOMEN)			
	1966	*1970*	*1975*
15–17 years			
Total	35.8	38.8	36.6
White	26.6	29.2	28.3
Black	97.9	101.4	86.6
18–19 years			
Total	121.2	114.7	85.7
White	109.6	101.5	74.4
Black	209.9	204.9	156.0
LIVE BIRTHS			
15–17 years			
Total	187,000	224,000	227,000
White	120,000	144,000	148,000
Black	65,000	77,000	75,000
18–19 years			
Total	435,000	421,000	355,000
White	345,000	320,000	262,000
Black	85,000	95,000	86,000
ILLEGITIMACY RATES (LIVE BIRTHS PER 1,000 UNMARRIED WOMEN)			
15–17 years			
Total	13.1	17.1	19.5
White	5.4	7.5	9.7
Black	61.2*	77.9	77.7
18–19 years			
Total	25.8	32.9	32.8
White	14.3	17.6	16.6
Black	110.5*	136.4	126.8
ILLEGITIMACY RATIOS (% OF LIVE BIRTHS THAT ARE ILLEGITIMATE)			
15–17 years			
Total	35	43	51
White	20	25	33
Black	64*	76	87
18–19 years			
Total	16	22	30
White	10	14	17
Black	40*	52	68

Note. From U.S. National Center for Health Statistics. Monthly Vital Statistics Report. Vol. 26, No. 5. Supplement. September 8, 1977. *Teenage Childbearing: United States, 1966–1975.*

  * Black and other nonwhite.

TABLE 12.4 *Illegitimacy Data for 1976*

Age of Mother	NUMBER			RATES PER 1000 UNMARRIED WOMEN			ILLEGITIMATE BIRTHS AS PERCENT OF LIVE BIRTHS		
	Total	White	Black	Total	White	Black	Total	White	Black
All ages	468,000	197,000	259,000	24.7	12.7	83.2	15	8	50
Under 15	10,300	3,500	6,600	—	—	—	86	69	99
15	22,900	9,200	13,200				72	53	95
16	41,700	17,900	22,900	19.3	9.9	74.6	59	40	92
17	51,900	22,900	28,000				46	30	86
18	55,900	24,600	30,200	32.5	17.0	121.6	36	22	76
19	52,600	23,000	28,400				28	16	66
20–24	145,400	58,900	82,400	32.2	16.0	109.3	13	7	46
25–29	55,400	22,800	30,800	27.5	14.4	81.1	6	3	28

Note. From U.S. National Center for Health Statistics. Monthly Vital Statistics Report. *Final Natality Statistics, 1976.* Vol. 26, No. 12 Supplement. March 29, 1978.

vorced and working as a secretary in a law office, was working in her kitchen, making as little noise as possible because she wanted to hear the conversation coming from the living room, where her 15-year-old daughter sat with four of her girl friends.

"School's dragging me down," one of the girls said.

"I told my mother, this is the last time I'm going to school." another girl said.

"What are you going to do next year if you're not in school?" one of them asked.

"Guess I'll have a baby."

"Me, too."

"Hey, we can have babies the same time. Be pregnant together."

The mother lives in a high-rise public housing project that subsidizes rental payments for some families who are on welfare. She told her daughter to stay away from girls who talked about becoming pregnant. But her daughter goes to school with those girls and associates with them in one or another apartment of the project.

One night, coming home from work, she found herself in the elevator with one of the daughter's girlfriends, who was 15 and wearing a maternity blouse.

"I'm going to have a baby and get a pad of my own," the girl boasted.

Then her daughter began to talk about it openly. "I want to have a baby," she said one night.

The mother asked how this would be paid for, since she was barely getting along on her salary.

"I'll get on welfare when I have the baby and get my own pad," the daughter said.

The mother tried to keep an eye on her daughter, especially concerning her contacts with boys in the neighboring junior high school. But the time came when the girl missed her period. The mother said the girl must have an abortion. The daughter ran away, and the mother found her a few days later in the apartment of another 15-year-old. "We're both pregnant," the daughter said. "We're going to have the babies together." The mother took her home, forcibly, and then to an abortion clinic. The girl was crying, but the mother held her by the arm and practically dragged her to the clinic, which was crowded with young girls, some with their boyfriends. The young people were nearly all white.

When the abortion was over, the daughter said to her mother, "I won't have any friends after this."[2]

---

[2] From "Having a baby is the only way out" by Jimmy Breslin. *Chicago Tribune,* February 27, 1978. Syndicated by the Chicago Tribune/NY News Syndicate. Reprinted by permission of The Sterling Lord Agency, Inc. Copyright © 1978 by Jimmy Breslin.

This episode illustrates the way the subculture can work, with peer pressure building up a set of expectations that enables a teenager to resist her parents.

The amount of teenage pregnancy is much greater among black than among white girls, but the gap is narrowing as shown in Table 12.3. Birth-rates for black 15- to 17-year-olds decreased between 1966 and 1975, while the rates stayed constant for white girls. Also, the rates of illegitimate births increased faster for white than for black girls.

The Socioeconomic Status of Teenage Mothers.   The vast majority of teen-age mothers come from working-class families, both those who were mar-ried at the time of the child's birth, and those who were not married. The few attempts to study a cross-section of young women came out clearly with this conclusion. Even in a working-class section of a big city, a com-parison of teenage mothers with agemates who did not become pregnant shows that those who did not become pregnant have mothers and fathers with more education and higher occupational status, as seen in Fursten-berg's Baltimore study (1976).

There appear to be two quite different groups of teenage mothers. The one group, illustrated in Jimmy Breslin's story, are able to build a support-ive peer culture that makes them want to have babies. The other group gets some pleasure from caring for their babies but have very little peer group support.

An example of this other group is Sally, who had her baby at 16. Her middle-class parents wanted to keep this all a secret and pressured her to give away the child for adoption. Sally insisted on keeping the child and then took an apartment with a girl friend who was employed. Sally secured AFDC of $89 a month, but found this arrangement unsatisfactory after a few months. "Just caring for a baby, housework, cooking, and shopping—no way," she said. She found a free day-care center, and went back to an-other high school to try to prepare for a job. Another teenage mother, de-scribed in an article in the *New York Times Magazine* said, "I wondered where in the world I fitted in. With the baby, I felt I no longer belonged with others my age. I lived in the only cheap apartment I could find near my job, and there were middle-aged people all around me. People my age were still in school. I had nothing to talk about to friends who were going to parties. I was into baby things" (Aldridge, 1976, p. 63).

Some social agencies, a few high schools, and some hospitals try to set up groups of pregnant girls for a kind of group therapy. This seems to work out well in the form of helping girls to get through the pregnancy period with less sense of appearing to be deviant and with mutual support for those who have special difficulty.

Partly because it would be against the law in some places, and would be severely criticised by opponents of abortion in all places, groups of pregnant girls do not receive much abortion counseling in the United States. And girls as well as their mothers in working-class families tend to be afraid of abortion. On the other hand, upper middle-class girls are likely to practice birth control and to obtain abortions if they become pregnant.

Teenage Mothers—Comparison of 1976 with 1971. By 1976, four in every ten women aged 15–19 had experienced sexual intercourse while unmarried (Kantner & Zelnik, 1978). This compares with three out of ten in 1971. The percentage increase was greater for whites (41%) than for blacks (19%). There was a substantial decline in the proportion of those women who had an illegitimate birth, due, apparently, to increased abortions. Teenagers account for about one-third of all legal abortions (Green & Potteiger, 1977). The use of abortion was much greater among whites than among blacks, and there was a marked increase in abortions between 1971 and 1976. In 1971, there were 39% abortions among white unmarried women aged 15–19 who became pregnant and did not marry, and 52% live births. In 1976, those proportions had changed to 51% abortions and 31% live births. Abortions were much less frequent (about one-sixth as frequent) among blacks, but the data are not reliable. In any case, it is apparent that abortion is rapidly become the *solution of choice* for unmarried white adolescents who become pregnant. As abortion becomes a more accessible alternative for black girls, it is likely that there will be an increase for this group as well. The most obvious observation which can be made is that birth control information is needed. The points made by Wagner in chapter 10 are relevant to this issue.

SUMMARY

The United States population consists of several minority groups plus one majority group that is white, speaks English, and is largely native-born. There are several minority groups that differ from the majority in one or more of the following: skin color, home language, country of birth or parents' country of birth. Each of these groups has a subculture of adolescents, aged about 13 to 18. There are social class and male and female versions of these subcultures.

This chapter describes the adolescent subcultures of the following groups: Mexican-American, lower-middle class; Puerto-Rican, working class; Japanese-American, middle class; black, middle class; and American Indians. In addition, I have described two subcultures that are not primarily ethnic, but are isolated from the mainstream of adolescents. They are street culture males in slums of big cities and teenage unmarried mothers.

Most members of the ethnic subcultures have been and are still subjected to adverse discrimination with respect to economic and educational opportunity, though this is decreasing due to a widespread policy in this country of democratic culture pluralism. However, the individual adolescent may have difficulty in working out a balance between his associations and his loyalty to his ethnic group on the one side and his desire to move into the economic mainstream of society on the other.

The society in general, minority as well as majority, looks with disfavor at the two small deviant adolescent subcultures—male slum street culture and teenage unmarried mothers. But these life-styles exert a strong attraction for their members and represent a problem and challenge for social workers and educators.

SUGGESTIONS FOR FURTHER READING

DREYER, P. H. Sex, sex roles, and marriage among youth in the 1970s. In R. J. Havighurst & P. E. Dreyer (Eds.), *Youth: The seventy-fourth yearbook of the National Society for the Study of Education.* Chicago: University of Chicago Press, 1975.

LIU, W. T., & YU, E. S. H. Asian American youth. In R. J. Havighurst & P. E. Dreyer (Eds.), *Youth: The seventy-fourth yearbook of the National Society of Education.* Chicago: University of Chicago Press, 1975.

MAYKOVICH, M. *Japanese American identity dilemma.* Tokyo: Waseda University Press, 1972.

THOMAS, P. *Down these mean streets.* New York: Knopf, 1967.

THORNBURG, H. D., & GRINDER, R. E. Children of Aztlán: The Mexican-American experience. In R. J. Havighurst & P. E. Dreyer (Eds.), *Youth: The seventy-fourth yearbook of the National Society for the Study of Education.* Chicago: University of Chicago Press, 1975.

WILKINSON, D. Y. Black youth. In R. J. Havighurst & P. E. Dreyer (Eds.), *Youth: The seventy-fourth yearbook of the National Society for the Study of Education.* Chicago: University of Chicago Press, 1975.

BIBLIOGRAPHY

ACUNA, R. *The story of Mexican Americans.* New York: Litton Educational Publishing, 1967.

ALDRIDGE, L. Kids with kids. *New York Times Magazine,* Feb. 22, 1976.

BARCLAY, A., & CUSUMANO, D. Father-absence, cross-sex identity, and field dependent behavior in male adolescents. *Child Development,* 1967, *38,* 243–250.

BENDIX, R., & LIPSET, S. *Class, status and power: A reader in social stratification.* New York: Free Press, 1953.

BILLER, H., & BORSTELMANN, L. Masculine development: An integrative review. *Merrill-Palmer Quarterly,* 1967, *13,* 253–294.

BURCHINAL, L. (Ed.). *Rural youth in crisis.* Washington, D.C.: U.S. Government Printing Office, 1965.

CASTANEDA, A., JAMES, R. L., & ROBBINS, W. *The educational needs of minority groups.* Lincoln, Nebraska: Professional Educators Publications, 1974.

CLARK, K. B. *Dark ghetto.* New York: Harper & Row, 1965.

COLEMAN, JAMES S. *The adolescent society.* New York: Free Press, 1961.

COLEMAN, R. P., & NEUGARTEN, B. *Social status in the city.* San Francisco: Jossey-Bass, 1971.

DE BLAISSIE, R., & HEALY, G. Self-concept: A comparison of Spanish-American, Negro, and Anglo adolescents across ethnic and socio-economic variables. Las Cruces, New Mexico: ERIC Clearinghouse on Rural Education and Small Schools, 1970.

DERBYSHIRE, R. L. Adolescent identity crisis in urban Mexican Americans in East Los Angeles. In E. B. Brady (Ed.), *Minority group adolescents in the United States.* Baltimore: Williams & Wilkins, 1968.

DREYER, P. H. Sex, sex roles, and marriage among youth in the 1970s. In R. J. Havighurst & P. E. Dreyer (Eds.), *Youth: The seventy-fourth yearbook of the National Society for the Study of Education.* Chicago: University of Chicago Press, 1975.

ERIKSON, E. *Identity: Youth and crisis.* New York: Norton, 1968.

FUCHS, E., & HAVIGHURST, R. J. *To live on this earth: American Indians and their education.* Garden City, N.Y.: Doubleday, 1972.

FURSTENBERG, F., JR., *Unplanned parenthood.* New York: Free Press, 1976.

GLASS, D. R. *Social mobility in Britain.* London: Routledge & Kegen Paul, 1954.

GOTTLIEB, D., & REEVES, J. *Adolescent behavior in urban areas.* New York: Free Press, 1963.

GREEN, C. P., & POTTEIGER, K. Teenage pregnancy: A major problem for minors. Washington, D.C.: Zero Population Growth, August, 1977.

GUTIÉRREZ, A., & HIRSCH, H. The militant challenge to the American ethos: Chicanos and Mexican Americans. *Social Science Quarterly,* 1973, *53,* 830–845.

HAVIGHURST, R. J. Education, social mobility, and social change in four societies. *International Review of Education,* 1958, *4,* 167–185.

HAVIGHURST, R. J., et al. *Growing up in River City.* New York: Wiley, 1962.

HAVIGHURST, R. J., SMITH, F., & WILDER, D. Profile of the big city high school. *Bulletin of the National Association of School Principals,* 1971, *55,* 3–160.

HOLLINGSHEAD, A. B. *Elmtown's youth.* New York: Wiley, 1949.

JESSOR, R., & JESSOR, S. L. *Problem behavior and psychosocial development: A longitudinal study of youth.* New York: Academic Press, 1977.

KANTNER, J. F., & ZELNICK, M. Sexual experience of young unmarried women in the United States. *Family Planning Perspectives,* 1972, *4,* 9–18.

KANTNER, J. F., & ZELNICK, M. Contraception and pregnancy: Experience of young unmarried women in the United States. *Family Planning Perspectives,* 1973, *5,* 21–35.

KANTNER, J. F., & ZELNICK, M. First pregnancies to women aged 15–19: 1976 and 1971. *Family Planning Perspectives,* 1978, *10,* 11–19.

KENISTON, K. *Youth and dissent.* New York: Harcourt Brace Jovanovich, 1971.

LEWIS, OSCAR. *La Vida.* New York: Random House, 1966.

LIU, W. T., & YU, E. S. H. Asian American youth. In R. J. Havighurst & P. E.

Dreyer (Eds.), *Youth: The seventy-fourth yearbook of the National Society of Education.* Chicago: University of Chicago Press, 1975.

MAYKOVICH, M. *Japanese American identity dilemma.* Tokyo: Waseda University Press, 1972.

MCWILLIAMS, C. *North from Mexico: The Spanish-speaking people of the United States.* New York: Lippincott, 1961.

MILLER, W. B. Lower class culture as a generating milieu of gang delinquency. *Journal of Social Issues,* 1958, *14,* 5–19.

SEWELL, W. H., & HALLER, A. Education and occupational perspectives of farm and rural youth. In L. Burchinal (Ed.), *Rural youth in crisis: Facts, myths, and social change.* Washington, D.C.: U.S. Government Printing Office, 1965.

SUTTLES, G. *The social order of the slum.* Chicago: University of Chicago Press, 1968.

THOMAS, P. *Down these mean streets.* New York: Knopf, 1967.

THORNBURG, H. D., & GRINDER, R. E. Children of Aztlán: The Mexican-American experience. In R. J. Havighurst & P. E. Dreyer (Eds.), *Youth: The seventy-fourth yearbook of the national Society for the Study of Education.* Chicago: University of Chicago Press, 1975.

United States Commission on Civil Rights. *The excluded student: Educational practices affecting Mexican Americans in the southwest.* Washington, D.C.: U.S. Government Printing Office, 1972.

United States Commission on Civil Rights. *Teachers and students: Differences in teacher interaction with Mexican American and Anglo students.* Washington, D.C.: U.S. Government Printing Office, 1973.

WARNER, W., MEEKER, M., & EELLS, K. *Social class in America.* New York: Harper, 1960.

WASHBURN, W. E. *Red man's land—white man's law: A study of the past and present status of the American Indians.* New York: Charles Scribner's Sons, 1971.

WILKINSON, D. Y. Black youth. In R. J. Havighurst & P. E. Dreyer (Eds.), *Youth: The seventy-fourth yearbook of the National Society for the Study of Education.* Chicago: University of Chicago Press, 1975.

WILSON, W. J. *The declining significance of race: Blacks and changing American institutions.* Chicago: University of Chicago Press, 1978.

WYNE, M. D., WHITE, K. P., & COOP, R. H. *The black self.* Englewood Cliffs, N.J.: Prentice-Hall, 1974.

YANKELOVICH, D. *The changing values on campus.* New York: Pocket Books, 1972.

ZIRKEL, P., & MOSES, E. Self-concept and ethnic group membership among public school students. *American Educational Research Journal,* 1971, *8,* 253–265.

13

PSYCHOLOGICAL PERSPECTIVES ON DRUGS AND YOUTH

Herbert J. Cross
Randall R. Kleinhesselink

Until the mid 1960s, generally the drug literature that was available was written from the medical point of view which interpreted any nonmedical use of any drug as bad. Most scientific drug literature was drug phobic or at least cautionary about the use of intoxicating substances. Nahas (1973) reviewed much of this literature and carried on the cautionary tradition; he suggested that American youth are unable to control their use of freely available mind-altering substances. He points to the social problem of our inability to control alcohol use to bolster his argument that intoxicating substances are dangerous, especially in a hedonistic society. Specifically, Nahas condemns marijuana because he believes the consumption influences users toward more dangerous substances. He states that drug use is symptomatic of disillusionment and a craving for fulfillment.

Jones and Jones (1977) theorize that drugs are dangerous to youthful users because the drug action mimics some body-system sexual response, either preorgasmic, orgasmic, or postorgasmic. They postulate that the experience associated with the drug becomes conditioned to drug situations and normal sexuality is correspondingly extinguished. Drugs are attractive because of the naturally exciting and reinforcing properties of the sexual excitement or release that they induce.

Nahas and Jones represent a continuing negative tradition in drug literature that insists that any nonmedical use of any drug is detrimental. An extension of this thinking is that any nonmedical use is a crime and should be controlled by law enforcement. This position is essentially the official position of federal, state, and local governments with respect to all illicit drugs, except for marijuana where private possession has been decriminalized in eleven states and in several municipalities.

Other medical writers (e.g., Weil, 1972; Szasz, 1974) imply that there is no simple drug problem that can be controlled by law enforcement or the medical establishment. Szasz believes that the social problem of drug abuse comes from the established powers' need to control the behavior of certain elements within the population. Certain drugs are dangerous only because properties of dangerousness have been attributed to them. When they are no longer perceived as dangerous, their potential for harm will diminish. Until that change in definition occurs, drug users will be stigmatized and punished. Szasz' unusual perspective implies that drug use is a victimless crime and that users' civil rights are being violated when they are arrested or treated against their wishes.

Weil (1972) states that there is an innate drive to alter consciousness

Herbert J. Cross is Professor of Psychology at Washington State University. He has written a number of articles on such topics as the influences of personality development, the generation gap, and alternative life styles.

Randall R. Kleinhesselink, also of Washington State, is Associate Professor of Psychology. His research and writing interests focus on attitude change, interpersonal attraction, drug effects on prosocial behavior, and drug usage.

and experience highs. He believes that mind-altering drugs only trigger states of consciousness that could be reached by other means such as yoga, meditation, or simple concentration exercises. Drugs are short-cut techniques for experiencing the desired states of thinking that are different in kind from ordinary straight thinking. He believes that everyone experiences two types of thought, one *straight* or linear which is a product of the ego-controlled intellect. We use this straight mode of thought to judge, analyze, plan, communicate, and so forth. The other mode is *stoned* thinking which is intuitive, more in touch with unconscious bodily processes, and less dependent on sensory input. Weil suggests that stoned thinking is quite useful in understanding nature which is frequently distorted by uncritical straight perception. Straight thinking is more likely oriented to details of figures which are emphasized in figure-ground gestalts. Stoned thinking de-focuses on details and is more likely to allow unique patterns to emerge when figure and ground reverse.

Weil (1972) provocatively proposes that stoned thinking is deemphasized by adults relating to children, especially teachers, who focus on intellect-dominated experiences. It seems reasonable, as Weil speculates, that we socialize a way of straight thinking and suppress a way of stoned thinking. Drugs are, of course, one method of getting back to this suppressed mentality as well as are alterations associated with hypnosis, yoga, mediation, and other kinds of concentration.

Much of the writing about mystic altered states (Deickman, 1966) implies that mystic experience involves a perceptual refocus on internal events and a withdrawal from ordinary perceptions of reality. Deickman proposes a process of deautomatization which involves a shift of attention and perception from mundane patterns to those that may represent more childlike patterns of perception. He cites perceptual theorists who believe that perceptual development occurs by selecting some stimuli and suppressing others—deautomatization reverses this process and formerly unavailable aspects of reality then enter into awareness. Therefore, individuals who experience mystical states by meditation, hypnotic phenomena, or drugs, frequently feel as if they see things with a freshness or newness that is difficult to describe. However ineffable, or difficult to describe, most subjects agree that this feeling is intense and quite real. We will further discuss alterations in thinking in our social psychological analysis of the drug problem.

We have presented these points of view to illustrate the diverse thinking of some drug experts. With these as background, we turn now to some specific theories of youthful drug use.

THEORIES OF YOUTHFUL DRUG USE

Some specific theories of youthful drug use have been proposed. We will review five of these with the belief that each theory can help us to understand only a small proportion of the total motivation for youthful drug use. However, we believe when these theories are presented together, a significant proportion of the motivation for drug use can be understood.

Peer Influence Theory

The peer influence theory argues that most drug use results from a desire to gain acceptance within the peer group. A more complete analysis of the sources of this influence (Kandel, Kessler, & Margulis, 1978) suggests three ways in which this peer influence can be manifested. Influence can be *direct,* when one person sets an example for another, or provides social reinforcement for another, or provides the drug and teaches another person how to enjoy it. Influence can be manifested indirectly when one person assists in the development of another's personal values, attitudes, and behavior. Finally, influence is conditioned when one source of influence changes another person's susceptibility to being influenced by a third person. Whether through imitation or social reinforcement, the effect of peer influence appears to be much greater for initiation into marijuana use than either hard liquor or any other illicit drug (Johnson, 1973; Kandel et al., 1978).

Parental Influence Theory

Parental influence theory argues that most drug-taking behavior among youths is learned behavior that is directly, indirectly, or conditionally initiated because of their parents. This theory may seem particularly hard to accept in light of the fact that the overwhelming majority of parents don't use and forbid the use of illicit drugs including marijuana (Blane & Hewitt, 1977), or that 68% of parents forbid the use of liquor by their youthful offspring. However, support for a modified version of parental influence comes from an analysis that argues that it is not the parents' attitudes and values toward drugs, but rather the parents' attitudes and behaviors toward their adolescents (as perceived by the adolescent) that shows the strongest correlation with their offspring's behavior (Prendergast & Schaeffer, 1974). Wagner's chapter on the sexual behavior of adolescents contains some interesting support for this theory. Thus, the combination of lax control and parental rejection is associated with youthful drug use. To complicate things a bit more, other evidence (Forsland & Gustafson, 1970; Kandel et al., 1978) indicates that parental drinking behavior is strongly correlated with their offspring's drinking behavior, that parental attitudes and behavior are not strongly related to marijuana use, and that poor parent-child relationships are related to the use of illicit drugs other than marijuana.

363

Anticipatory Socialization Theory

According to this theory, the adolescent is in a transition-prone period between childhood and adulthood where he or she is permitted to "play at" the role behavior associated with what the child perceives to be adult. Because many young people suggest that they use drugs because they like the effects, this has been interpreted by some (Maddox & McCall, 1964; Jessor & Jessor, 1975) as indicating that the young person was exercising "personal discretion" or "independence." Since these are behaviors associated with adult role-playing, they seem to reflect anticipatory socialization. Thus, the initiation of a particular drug leads to a divergence from the characteristics associated with nonusers and a convergence upon the characteristics of established users of that drug.

Drug Prone Personality Theory

This theory suggests that a single personality characteristic or a combination of personality characteristics predispose some young people to use drugs. Critics of this theoretical approach (Josephson, 1974) argue that if there is a drug prone personality, it has not yet been uncovered. However, proponents of this approach (Hogan, Mankin, Conway, & Fox, 1970; Kay, Lyons, Newman, Mankin, & Loeb, 1978) have found some consistent personality differences between young drug users and nonusers. Users were characterized as being nonconforming, independent, and adventure-seeking while nonusers were characterized as being conforming, achievement-oriented, and nonimpulsive. The major controversy surrounding this theory is whether these differences are important and whether these differences cause drug use or are an effect of drug involvement.

Deviance Theory

According to this theory, young people who use drugs are *made* into deviants by the stigmatization, punishment, or harassment imposed upon them (Duster, 1970; Braucht, 1974). Because the social response to youthful drug use is so often irrational, young people may "join" the various drug subcultures in order to survive in a hostile environment (Goode, 1970; Johnson, 1973). Thus, any change in values, attitudes, and personality characteristics are considered to be the *effect* of drug subcultural involvement rather than caused by the drug itself.

Obviously, some of these theories overlap and some explain more lucidly than others. We believe that all may be applicable to one aspect or another of youthful drug use and we will apply some of the ideas in our next section.

A FUNCTIONAL ANALYSIS OF THE PERCEPTIONS OF YOUTHFUL DRUG USERS

Drugs serve a number of functions for different young people and these functions frequently change during a "drug career." The stages of use of any drug may shift from: *experimentation* where the motives for use are curiosity and fun; to *social-reactional* where the motives are to share a pleasurable experience with others; to *circumstantial-situational* where the motives for use are to aid in coping with work, moods, sex, and so on; to *intensified* where the motive for use is a daily desire to escape from emotional distress; and finally to *compulsive* where the motive is to maintain a drug high. We introduce this concept of stages to indicate that not all drug users are the same and that for each individual and each drug the stages of use may be difficult to classify. Nevertheless, from the perception of youthful users, there are several major functions that drugs serve.

Drug Intrinsic Growth Effects

From our point of view (Cross & Kleinhesselink, 1977), many young people use drugs because they expect that the drugs will directly assist them in difficult developmental transitions. One difficult transition in identity is from dependence on parents to independence from them. Another difficult transition is cognitive in nature. According to conceptual systems theory (Harvey, Hunt & Schroder, 1961), individuals experience a transition between a rigid belief system to a more flexible system. Many young people perceive drugs as having intrinsic qualities that will propel them from conventionality to a tolerance and understanding of unconventional behaviors and cognitions.

A final difficult youthful transition is concerned with moral development. Levels of moral reasoning progress from preconventional to conventional to postconventional (Kohlberg, 1969; Kohlberg & Kramer, 1969). While the transition from preconventional to conventional moral reasoning is generally accomplished by the time a young person enters junior high school, the transition between conventional and postconventional moral reasoning, if accomplished at all, occurs during later adolescence. Child

(1973) suggests that this transition period can be characterized as hedonistic in outlook. We contend that there is a connection between this transition in moral reasoning and drug involvement. It is of great moral moment when a young person engages in forbidden or criminal behavior. Growth in moral reasoning comes about from making decisions that are morally post-conventional. For a more detailed discussion of moral development, see chapter 8 by Windmiller.

Inhibitory and Disinhibitory Effects

In addition to any direct pharmacological effects of drugs, there are numerous myths, conceptions, and social rituals associated with drug use. Many of these ideas and rituals provide a rationalization that enables a young person to engage in behavior that would otherwise be inhibited. Acting out fantasy adventure, engaging in sexual experimentation, and expressing hostility and defiance toward parents and authority figures are obvious examples. For example, Kaats and Davis (1972) provide evidence that 90% of college females indicated that they were intoxicated on either alcohol or marijuana at the time they were initiated into sexual intercourse.

On the other hand, drugs may be used to raise inhibitions toward engaging in certain impulsive behavior. Marijuana use, for example, is associated with "being cool" and "hanging loose" (Suchman, 1968). In a study of incarcerated juvenile offenders (Tinklenberg, 1974), it was discovered that marijuana was used to inhibit aggressive impulses and that alcohol and barbiturates were used to bolster one's "nerve" when planning or committing aggressive crimes.

Youth Culture Effects

Even when drugs are used without any expectation of personal growth or effects on inhibitions, they may be perceived to be instrumental in developing and maintaining friendship. Many young people use drugs to obtain status or identity within a subculture of peer group members. For example, it has been found that the single most important attitude in predicting which high school students will become close friends is the congruence of their attitudes toward marijuana use or nonuse (Kandel, 1978). This effect is present, but less pronounced, for alcohol and other illicit drugs. Some researchers have argued that this instrumental function exists because of the development of a youth culture (Johnson, 1973). The youth culture values secrecy from adult supervision, loyalty to friends, and confers status upon those who successfully violate conventional norms.

Perceived Alterations in Thinking

Research (summarized by Hochman, 1972) suggests that many drug users experience a disruption in ability to focus sensory input and that over-learned patterns of perception (the formation of gestalts or consistent fig-ure-ground relationships) are interrupted. If the normal sensory focus of an individual is rapidly shifted to novel aspects of old perceptual patterns, then the meaning associated with the perceptual situation may also be modified. Whether or not this disruption in attention occurs (Delong & Levy, 1974; and Miller, 1974 suggest it does) it is perceived to be an impor-tant effect by users. An effect of the development of altered perception of reality may be questioning cultural traditions and rules.

A SOCIAL PSYCHOLOGICAL ANALYSIS OF DRUG USE

We have proposed an analysis of "the drug problem" (Cross & Kleinhesse-link, 1977) which utilizes conceptual systems theory (Harvey et al., 1961), moral development theory (Kohlberg, 1969), and Heider's balance model (Jordan, 1968).

Conceptual systems theory and moral development theory both imply that most people think in a relatively concrete manner, that is, they fail to perceive information that is discrepant with their beliefs and they make categorical judgments. Zinberg and Robertson (1972, p. 54) offer the fol-lowing excerpt from a physician's interview about drug users: "As a doctor I should be more liberal, but I really think they should all go to jail." Others (Haan, Smith, & Block, 1968; Wrightsman, 1972) have suggested that the public operates on a preconventional level of morality which is fo-cused on rules, traditions, and maintaining the *status quo*. Therefore, the public resists change and reveres established law and order. Kaplan (1970) states that marijuana is a controversial substance because it symbolizes many issues that confront established morality.

In a sense, the moral reasoning of the public is represented by the Na-tional Commission on Marijuana and Drug Abuse (1972). They noted that society is threatened by the perceived association between drugs and youthful "dropping out" or "dropping down." "Some parents make con-siderable sacrifices for their children to go to school and the fears that mari-juana undermines the academic, emotional and vocational development of their young is quite understandable" (National Commission Report, p. 99). The Commission reported a survey which concluded that nearly half (45%) of adults believe that "marijuana is often promoted by people who are en-emies of the United States" (p. 100).

These data and the Commission's interpretations suggest that the public is mainly conventional in morality (as defined by Kohlberg's theory) and perceive illicit drug use as a serious breakdown of law and order. Drugs are specifically feared and hated because they signify that young people flout the very traditions that their elders hold dear.

If the public is unlikely to think abstractly about drugs and users, Heider's balance model would predict conflict between parents and offspring. Heider analyzed social relationships between two people with respect to their perceptions of an outside entity as representing a balanced state between the three or an unbalanced state. For example, if a parent is positive toward his or her offspring, and negative toward marijuana, imbalance will exist if the offspring uses marijuana. Imbalanced states produce tension that motivates the person to restore balance. Balance can be restored by reconceptualizing the dissonant element in the triad, or changing the relationship between one of the pairs, parent and offspring, parent and drug, or offspring and drug.

This model would predict that most parents fear the influence of radical youth on their own offspring and that they see illicit drugs as a menace that is likely to alter the children's motivation to be decent, law-abiding citizens. When confronted with the fact that the offspring uses illicit drugs, some parents would denigrate the offspring. A small minority might reconceptualize the illicit drugs as less harmful than previously thought.

The balance model offers a novel interpretation of the committed drug users' perceptions. If a youthful drug user sees his parents as extensions of a feared authority because of the parents' attitudes toward drugs, a state of imbalance exists. This is difficult to put back in balance by changing either party's attitude toward the drug, so the most likely change will be in the relationship between parent and child. It is likely that older offspring will maintain distance between themselves and parents as long as they use illicit drugs. This allows the offspring to maintain some positive feeling toward the parents but not to be controlled by the parent. In a sense, illicit drugs serve as a socializing force toward independence since parents and drugs do not mix well in most cases. The following is an excerpt from an interview with a college senior:

> When the phone rang I knew it was my mother and I knew she'd found the stuff in my suitcase, and I knew there was no way she could understand, and I had just dropped mescaline, and we had all been smoking, and the car reeked of dope. Well, I went home and survived the hassle, but it was not easy, and since that time my parents have not mentioned it and neither have I. They're not staying here at graduation, they're staying in _____. We'd get on each other's nerves.

The interviewee apparently had some affection for her parents, but could not maintain it if in close proximity.

Drug users' perceptions of the nondrug using world are clearly affected by the users' cognitive structure, which in most cases is quite different from the structure of the nonusing establishment. Conceptual systems theory (Harvey et al., 1961) suggests that much drug use fits into the need for self-distinctiveness and avoidance of influence that young people need to maintain. Kohlberg's theory of moral development suggests that much collegiate drug use is associated with regression to an infantile, hedonistic relativism wherein morality is determined by what serves one's self. Cognitive structures are undoubtedly affected by and interact with the youth cultures (Johnson, 1973; Kandel, 1978) which maintain the generation gap.

Balance and mutuality between the two generations will be difficult to achieve as long as they hold diametrically opposing attitudes about illicit drug use. The intensity of attitudes and the seriousness of criminal involvement have contributed to widening the generation gap. Further intergenerational conflict is engendered by the establishment's acceptance and proselytizing of alcohol and tobacco, both drugs that can be dangerous in certain dosage patterns.

Szasz (1974) suggests that illicit drug use, and attempts to control users, represents a social game that has been occurring and reoccurring for centuries in one form or another. Scapegoating is probably the most descriptive term for a social process whereby behavioral control is maintained in all groups. Drugs represent temptation and rather uniquely symbolize the deeply rooted conflict between self-control and wanton indulgence that has existed in all cultures. Of course, the more socially destructive a given behavior, the more significance it has for an individual whose very identity is built on defying established authority. Illicit drug use meets the criteria of undesirability quite well because, in whatever form, it provokes a reaction from authority.

Analyzing youthful use of drugs from a social psychological viewpoint suggests several conclusions. They are as follows: Youthful drug use is associated with psychological differences between the generations; these differences are similar to differences between the established straight society and various counterculture elements so that they are not strictly associated with age; this situation is complicated by the changing nature of public attitudes and the increasing pluralism in society. Furthermore, drug laws, policies, and attitudes are amazingly contradictory. It is clear that there are no simple solutions to many of the drug problems which will be encountered by society in general and by many individuals.

We are discomforted by the ambiguity associated with the drug problem, but accept it as we turn now to a discussion of specific drugs.

ALCOHOL

Although the use of alcohol has never been primarily associated with young people, there are several aspects of youthful use of alcohol today that have generated a wide spectrum of concerns about patterns of socialization to drink. Korcok (1978b) feels that although the use of alcohol by youth is not a new problem, the concentration of research on youthful drinkers has uncovered new problems. These problems include the documentation of teenage alcoholism and the threat to the future these youthful drinkers represent. Blane and Chafetz (1978) argue that youthful drinking has risen steadily between World War II and 1965, but has remained relatively constant since then. They argue against over-reaction to statistics about alcohol usage and feel that it is inappropriate to define those behaviors which were once seen as transitional between adolescence and adulthood as problems. They are alarmed by the labeling of some young people as alcoholics in the absence of sufficient knowledge to define this entity.

A third point of view (Johnson, Bachman, & O'Malley, 1978) is that alcohol use by youth has been rising slowly and consistently over the past few years. From a nationwide survey of high school students they find that 92.5% of seniors have used alcohol, that 71.9% have used alcohol in the last 30 days, and that 6% are daily users. All these figures are slightly higher than 1975 levels of alcohol use. The primary reasons for this growth appear to be due to the fact that suburban and rural use is catching up with urban use and other regions of the country are catching up with the Northeast which has traditionally been the region with the greatest youthful drinking.

Social Psychological Models of Youthful Involvement with Alcohol

We have found that three kinds of social psychological models have been used to understand youthful alcohol use patterns. Social learning theories have been particularly useful in explaining when and how individuals learn to drink, while social psychological models of deviance seem to be more appropriate for understanding "problem drinking" or "excessive drinking." An important form of social learning is the acquisition of social norms and role expectations. Not surprisingly, when individuals develop the ability to discriminate the occasions appropriate for drinking, they will have learned when and how to drink. The theories that emphasize parental influence, peer influence, and anticipatory socialization all seem to explain this process of socialization.

Social learning theory states that the opportunities to learn when and how to drink correspond closely to the distribution of social practices about alcohol use. While social learning theories are useful in explaining the socialization of drinking, other theories that emphasize personality and social factors are necessary in order to explain individual variations in drinking practices, including "excessive drinking." Excessive or problem drinking is defined by the National Institute of Alcohol as drinking enough to cause frequent intoxication, binge intoxication, symptomatic drinking associated with physical dependence, psychological dependence, or disruption of normal social behavior patterns and is considered by Jessor and Jessor (1977) to be one form of deviant behavior.

The Jessor theory elaborates a set of 14 personality system variables along with a set of nine perceived environmental system variables in order to predict the occurrence of either problem behavior or conventional behavior. The three variables in the personality system which predict problem drinking (Jessor & Jessor, 1977) are tolerance of deviance, a belief that the positive functions of alcohol outweigh the negative functions, and a need for independence. Three variables in the perceived environmental system that significantly correlate with problematic drinking are friends' approval of drinking, friends' modeling of drinking, and lack of parental support.

Risks and Benefits of Alcohol

Surveys of alcohol use (Jessor & Jessor, 1977; Chafetz, 1974) indicate that about 10% of 95 million adult Americans who drink can be classified as "problem drinkers." However, the rate of "problem drinking" by all high school seniors is estimated to be 35%, while the percentage of problem drinkers among all college seniors is estimated to be 30%. Perhaps the most startling statistic on "problem drinking" rates are associated with male college freshmen. An estimate of the amount of "problem drinking" (Jessor & Jessor, 1977) among this group is 49%. Some writers (Fort, 1973; Hafen, 1977) rank alcohol as the number one drug problem because of the potential organ damage and overall social and physical disruptiveness. Fort (1973) estimates that heavy chronic use of alcohol is associated with 11 million accidental injuries a year, 40% of all admissions to mental hospitals, and 50% of all arrests made in the United States. In fact, some research (DeLint, 1974) indicates that as many as 6% of all deaths are attributable to alcohol.

Physical Risks of Alcohol

The physical effects of alcohol can be broken down into acute effects and chronic effects of long-term use. Alcohol is a potent neural depressant and can cause death due to depression of breathing if taken in sufficient quantity. Overdose deaths due to "chugging" large amounts of high proof alcohol are rare and occur mostly in younger age groups. A more serious source of mortality is due to the combined use of alcohol and other depressants. Clinicians (Patel, Roy, & Wilson, 1972) have observed that heavy alcohol use preceded the taking of an overdose of other drugs in 70% of the cases admitted to hospital emergency rooms. In fact, alcohol was involved in over 50% of all dead-on-arrival or sudden deaths occurring in a large city emergency room (Keeley, Kahn, & Keeler, 1974).

The heavy daily use of alcohol is clearly associated with a high incidence of damage to a number of organ systems including the heart, liver, stomach, esophagus, pancreas, muscles, nerves, brain, and blood chemistry (DHEW Report, 1971). Although there is evidence of direct toxic effects of alcohol on the heart (Parker, 1974), the general toxic effects appear to be due to a subtle disruption of the normal chemical processes of the liver (Myerson, 1973). Because the liver gives precedence to the breakdown of alcohol, other systems are depleted of a necessary chemical cofactor (NAD). The resulting compensations by various cells and organ systems produce disruptions that may lead to major damage. Chronic excessive use is harmful because most organs are incapable of reversing these disruptions if damage has progressed too far. Heavy daily use of alcohol leads to the development of tolerance and physical dependence. Abrupt withdrawal from alcohol is considered to be a life-threatening medical emergency with risks far exceeding those seen in withdrawal from narcotic drugs like heroin.

Social Psychological Risks of Alcohol

Two of the best documented deleterious social effects of excessive alcohol consumption are in the area of criminal antisocial behavior and highway safety. In both of these areas young people are more likely to be adversely affected than other segments of the population.

Alcohol and Automobiles. Some of the best estimates are that one-half of the 55,000 traffic deaths each year are directly or indirectly attributable to alcohol (Hafen, 1977). Car drivers are not the only persons adversely affected by alcohol. Nearly half of all pedestrians killed by automobiles have blood alcohol levels of 0.10% (in most states this is the legal definition of intoxication) or more.

Alcohol and Crime. Another important negative social effect is the association between alcohol and violent criminal behavior. This well-documentated relationship has often been overlooked because other drugs have received more sensational press coverage. As an overview of the scope of the association between alcohol and crime, it has been estimated that one-half of all homicides and one-third of all suicides involve alcohol. This alone accounts for 12,000 deaths yearly (Hafen, 1977). In addition, one-half of felons in prison have had alcohol-related problems.

An important study on drug involvement in crime by adolescents was recently reported by Tinklenberg and coworkers (1974). Fifty male adolescents who were detained in a California Youth Authority Facility for assaultive behavior were compared with 80 nonassaultive offenders of similar background who had committed other crimes. Although multiple drug use was common in both groups, nearly two-thirds of the youths in the assaultive group reported that they were under the influence of a drug when they committed physical assaults. Alcohol was linked with 64% of the assaults and secobarbital ("reds") with 36%. When asked which drug would likely enhance assaultive feelings, secobarbital was overwhelmingly selected first. Marijuana was seen as unlikely to enhance assaultiveness, and in fact, the subjects indicated that the use of marijuana would decrease assaultive feelings (Tinklenberg, 1974).

Alcohol in Moderation

After enumerating many of the harmful consequences of alcohol consumption, it may seem ironic that we close this section with a discussion of some potential positive consequences of moderate alcohol consumption. It certainly cannot be maintained that the use of alcohol or any consciousness-altering drug is necessary for good health, social functioning, or vocational adjustment. However, it would be unrealistic to suppose that any sizeable proportion of young people will resist the cultural and social conditioning that accompanies growing up in an environment that encourages the use of alcohol.

According to the National Institute of Alcoholism and Alcohol Abuse (1974), alcohol can be used responsibly if it improves social relationships, is an adjunct to an activity rather than being the primary focus of activity, and promotes human dignity. For example, Chien, Stotsky, and Cole (1973) have found that moderate consumption of beer or wine by elderly persons did not adversely affect physical health. It improved sleep, morale and general well-being. Chafetz (1974), in reviewing several studies of the morality rates of the general population, found that both heavy drinkers *and* abstainers had higher mortality rates than light to moderate drinkers. While the explanation for this finding is far from clear, it appears that the overall life expectancy of moderate occasional and moderate steady drinkers is significantly higher than either high volume drinkers or total abstainers.

MARIJUANA

Most of our social psychological analysis of the generational drug issue applies to marijuana and the hallucinogens. As marijuana has become more acceptable, the intransigence of the establishment abates and the drug loses its symbolic meaning for rebellious youth. Such thinking is part of the motivation behind decriminalization. The National Commission on Marijuana and Drug Abuse recognized this symbolic aspect in 1972 and suggested that removing the stigma would remove some of the social-political influence of the marijuana issue.

Eleven states have now decriminalized marijuana. Decriminalization means that it is no longer a criminal offense, but a civil violation to possess the drug, which is still regarded as contraband and confiscated if it is discovered in public. Offenders are fined but receive no jail sentences or criminal record. This policy is clearly opposed to acceptance of marijuana, but it does remove some element of fear and harrassment for users. It allows the establishment to maintain disapproval, and it frees a great deal of police and judicial efforts for other necessary work. The National Organization for Reform of Marijuana Laws (N.O.R.M.L.) is a national lobby of established citizens, many of them drug researchers and attorneys, which has been instrumental in influencing the decriminalization movement.

Since the early 1960s, marijuana use has increased steadily. Current statistics from the National Survey on Drug Abuse (DuPont, 1978) estimate that 10% of the total population are current users. Only 3% of the group over 26 years old are current users; whereas 27% between 18 and 25, and 17% between 12 and 17 are current users. Many survey estimates point to about half of college students nationwide having tried marijuana and, on some campuses, the figures are as high as 70–80%. It appears that increases in marijuana use are beginning to level off and will remain at the present level (10%) until there is a spectacular change in information available about marijuana or moderate changes in government policy. Almost one-half of the population of the United States lives in areas where decriminalization of private possession is in effect, either by statute or law enforcement policy. It seems possible that softer penalties would encourage use, but research in Oregon (Carr, 1978), the first state to decriminalize, suggests that the proportion of marijuana users is about the same as it was before 1973 when the law was passed.

Psychological and Physical Risks and Effects of Marijuana

Some professional writers might argue that the effects of marijuana are great and even beneficial. We have discussed Weil's proposal that altered consciousness is useful and reinforcing. Users of marijuana state many benefits (Grinspoon, 1971; Hochman, 1972). Several writers (Weil, 1972; Kaplan, 1975) have suggested that marijuana is superior to alcohol and subjective accounts (Slack, 1973) say that it leaves no "hangover."

The risks of using marijuana in most states and foreign countries is great, depending on amount and location. Many states have penalties of up to five years in prison plus a $5,000 fine. Penalties in many foreign countries are extreme as marijuana is classed as a narcotic and believed to be used only by people who are enemies of the state.

Physical risks from moderate marijuana use seems slight except for the effects of the smoke itself, as smoke is a natural irritant to lung and bronchial tissue (Tennant, Preble, Prendergast, & Ventry, 1971; Rubin & Comitas, 1975). Even the cumulative effect of heavy chronic smoking has yielded no clear damage as a function of the drug itself, but only as an effect of smoke (Dornbush, 1974; Rubin & Comitas, 1975; Stefanis, Dornbush, & Fink, 1977). Three excellent reviews of research on possible harmful effects of marijuana have appeared in recent years (Brecher, 1975; Zinberg, 1976; Carr, 1978) in popular magazines. All have concluded that marijuana poses no immediate health risk. That is, of course, different from concluding that the drug is harmless.

There are individual case reports of panic reactions that are most likely to occur when large quantities of marijuana are eaten. Weil (1968) suggests that the method of ingestion by smoking allows the user to moderate his dosage but once a large quantity is eaten, the user cannot control the effect and may experience genuine panic, dizziness, and an inability to control motor movements. Weil notes that passage of time and simple authoritative reassurance is the treatment of choice for marijuana panic. He does not believe that marijuana ever causes psychosis, but allows that altered perceptual effects may frighten an unstable person and push him toward a psychotic break.

Marijuana and Contemporary Cultures

Despite the strong point we have made about the inflexibility of attitudes about marijuana, we do notice regular mention of marijuana by the media and occasionally there are suggestions that attitudes have changed greatly since the late 1960s. Robert C. Carr of the Drug Abuse Council has predicted (1976) that the nation will legally accept marijuana within a generation. He notes that its use is highest among young educated urban dwellers who will have enough political power to decriminalize or legalize their recreational drug.

The U.S. Senate has approved a marijuana decriminalization bill that allows up to three possession offenses of a small amount (up to 10 grams) to be treated as a civil offense which would leave no criminal record. Possession of an ounce would also be a civil offense; whereas greater amounts would be misdemeanors which could result in jail time and heavy fines. The Senate bill seems to reflect the public ambivalence about marijuana so frequently noted (Korcok, 1978a).

The government's difficulties in dealing with marijuana issues are illustrated by events of the spring and summer of 1978. In the spring of 1978, it was discovered that up to 21% of the Mexican marijuana entering the United States was contaminated with Paraquat, a herbicide that might cause lung damage in heavy marijuana smokers. Government spokesman (DuPont, 1978) noted that the Paraquat resulted from a program of the Mexican government. N.O.R.M.L. officially accused the U.S. government of endangering the lives of marijuana users by aiding the Mexican program. N.O.R.M.L. was trying to prod the government into some consumer protection action but the government disclaimed responsibility and noted that marijuana was not only illegal but also dangerous.

HARD DRUGS

In previous work (Kleinhesselink, St. Dennis, & Cross, 1976), we employed the classification of "hard drugs." Indeed, all drugs can be hard on individual users depending on the circumstances, and we have already discussed aspects of drugs that are "hard" for society to deal with. As a medical term, "hard" has suggested addictive potential, but most people would include hallucinogens such as LSD which have no true addictive potential while excluding such substances as tobacco, caffeine, and alcohol which have great addictive potential.

Our classification of "hard" drugs parallels the usage of legal and law enforcement personnel who generally refer to marijuana and alcohol as "soft," and everything else as "hard." The classification seems most relevant in its similarity to legal treatment of drug offenses since illegal possession of any amount of opiate, hallucinogen, amphetamine, barbiturate, or tranquilizer is regarded as a felony in most states. Any drug that can lead to a felony conviction, regardless of its pharmacological properties, is properly regarded as a "hard" drug. We do not mean to downplay the dangerous physical effects of hard drugs, but to emphasize that the social and legal effects of a felony conviction are "hard" on anyone who experiences them.

Furthermore, all psychoactive substances have a direct effect on the nervous system of users. The main direction of effect is speeding up of the nervous activity or a slowing down of nervous activity. No matter what chemical agent causes the nervous system change, the system must come back to its usual normal tempo of operation when the action of the agent ceases by excretion, metabolism, and so on. However, the nervous system does not quickly and easily come back to its regular state. It more frequently "rebounds," that is, goes beyond the normal level in the opposite direction of the drug when the drug wears off. Thus, users coming down from stimulants are frequently depressed and those with hangovers from "downers" are frequently jumpy and hypersensitive. One aspect of addictive potential is nervous system adaptation to drug effect so that more and more of a given agent is necessary to produce the desired effect.

Most "hard" drugs are harder on the nervous system than are marijuana or alcohol because they are potent enough to obtain an effective dose quickly, so that overdose potential is higher and nervous system rebound is painful.

LEGAL DRUGS

Some drugs are classifiable as hard because of their physical effects, such as tobacco, one of the most destructive drugs used in our society. One investigator (Hammond, 1967) has estimated a dose-related decrease in life expectancy of 6 to 7 minutes per cigarette. Nicotine, tars, and carbon monoxide gas account for most of the hazards from smoking tobacco. Nicotine is a stimulant that increases heart rate and blood pressure, decreases blood flow to the skin, and increases stomach acid. The arousal accompanying these changes is pleasant and probably accounts for a major portion of smokers' satisfaction and difficulty in quitting the habit.

Tars are the result of condensation of gases, usually in the lungs. Prolonged exposure produces lung cancer, as is well established. Carbon monoxide is a hazard to people who breathe smokey air, as well as to smokers (Russell, Cole, & Brown, 1973), because it decreases oxygen-carrying capacity of the blood. It probably accounts for shortness of breath and heart disease, as well as many physical disorders in infants delivered from women who smoked during pregnancy (Butler & Goldstein, 1973; DHEW, 1974; Harlap & Davies, 1974).

Former Secretary of Health, Education, and Welfare Joseph Califano has stated (Hagar, 1978) that smoking costs the nation 5 to 7 billion annually in health care and 12 to 18 billion in lost productivity. HEW has initiated a program to educate the public and to restrict smoking in public places. Califano's characterization of smoking as "public health enemy number one" suggests that the government regards tobacco as more dangerous than any other drug.

Legal Highs

A number of substances are being sold, mostly by mail order head shops that advertise in magazines that appeal to the youth culture. Mescal beans, camus root, passionflower, lettuce opium, and yhombine are among these legal substances, all of which are highly touted in advertisements but few of which have the properties their buyers expect. We are acquainted with some teenage users of one of these who stated that they expected to get "ripped off" but were unprepared for the dizziness and nausea. It seems hardly worthwhile to mention the few pharmacological properties that are known for these substances. Some have euphoria-inducing properties but mostly in high dosages, and many have unknown side effects. These substances pose a problem for drug regulatory agencies for their properties are not established clearly enough that they can be made illegal.

Inhalants

Glue, many aerosal propellants, furniture and nail polish, various petroleum products, and some anesthetics are used illicitly to obtain drug effects: mostly a kind of aroused euphoria in low doses and a heavy, uncoordinated drunkenness in high doses. Long-term use has been associated with lung, brain, and liver damage. Numerous deaths have been associated with these substances, many of which are due to the method of ingestion. Usually the agent is placed in a plastic or paper bag or on a rag and inhaled deeply while held over the mouth and nostrils. The immediate effect can be a brief loss of consciousness during which the rag or bag can block breathing. Deaths have occurred from the users being unable to free themselves from the bag. Aerosol propellants that have been associated with sudden deaths are thought to be due to sensitization of the heart and disruption of its rhythm leading to heart failure (Bass, 1970).

The National Institute of Drug Abuse estimates that about 7 million Americans, mostly young, poor, city-dwellers, have used inhalants. In 1976, inhalants caused over 100 deaths and about 2,000 users required emergency room treatment or crisis counseling (DuPont, 1978).

SEDATIVE-HYPNOTIC (DOWNER) DRUGS

The term *downer* is used to describe drugs that depress the general level of activity of the central nervous system. These drugs act to reduce tension and anxiety and to promote sleep. The different classes of sedative-hypnotics include: alcohol, barbiturates, nonbarbiturate sedative-hypnotics, minor tranquilizers, and inhalants. By most estimates, the use of sedative-hypnotic drugs (other than alcohol) by adolescents reached a peak in the early 1970s and has been stable during the mid and late 1970s (Cooper, 1977). Although differences exist between these classes with respect to potency, side effects, and onset and duration of effect, their basic actions are similar. Given in increasing doses, these agents all produce (in this order): sedation, staggering, excitement, intoxication, sleep, anesthesia, coma, death. Upon prolonged dosing, they all produce varying degrees of tolerance, physical dependence, muscle relaxation, and anticonvulsant action. When physical dependence does occur, the withdrawal reactions encountered are the most serious and life-endangering that exist, often progressing to hallucinations, delirium, convulsions, and possible death if allowed to go untreated (Ray, 1978).

Depressant drugs (including alcohol) represent the most commonly used and abused drugs in the United States. Many are available only by prescription from a physician; however, these substances are among the most frequently prescribed drugs in this country and are readily available to the public as sleeping pills and tranquilizers to calm nervous tension.

There is evidence that the use of downers other than alcohol enjoys considerable popularity among today's youth. These agents are readily obtainable and sporadic patterns of heavy use of the currently available "downer of choice" continue to appear from locale to locale with definite regularity (McGlothlin, 1975a). When used recreationally, these drugs are seldom used alone, but they are generally ingested in higher than therapeutic doses mixed with other mind-altering substances. The combination of more than one downer, especially with alcohol, results in additive depression often progressing to overdose and death. Antihistamines such as cold and hay fever remedies are examples of drugs that carry enough depressant action to combine with alcohol and other downers to produce significant drowsiness. Accidents, particularly those involving automobiles, have been reported when this mixture is taken without adequate warning of its consequences.

Barbiturates

Barbiturates represent classical downers and are generally those drugs thought of as sleeping pills by the general public. They are commonly prescribed by physicians to treat insomnia (hypnotic action) and to treat anxiety and nervous tension (sedative action). Many different barbiturates are available and they vary primarily with how long the drug takes to cause an effect and with the duration of drug effects. The short-acting group contains the preferred drugs for nonmedical use. These agents are characterized by both a short onset of action (15 to 30 minutes) and a short duration of effect (2 to 3 hours), that makes it possible, by carefully spacing out doses, to maintain a desired level of intoxication for a prolonged period of time. Examples of this group include: pentobarbital (Numbutal®—yellows), secobarbital (Seconal®—reds), amobarbital (Amytal®—blues), and a mixture of secobarbital and amobarbital (Tuinal®—rainbows).

There is a high individual susceptibility to the mental effect produced by these drugs which is characterized by an intoxication akin to that experienced with alcohol. Inhibitions are lowered and certain individuals experience a strong excitement phase that they may be able to maintain with skillful dosing. Tolerance develops fairly rapidly to the mental effects of these drugs but not to the lethal dose which is about 30 times the normal adult dose used to treat insomnia. Consequently, an escalating dose slowly approaching an overdose level is frequently observed. The addition of any more depressant at this point will lead to overdose and possible death due to depression of breathing. These agents also possess a high potential for the development of physical dependence at daily doses 5 to 10 times that normally prescribed to treat insomnia.

Related Sedative-Hypnotics

This group contains a number of downers that are generally claimed to be nonbarbiturate in action. Although differences do exist, their actions for the most part are similar to the barbiturates. Many of these agents, however, are under much less stringent legal control than barbiturates and are readily obtainable by prescription or on the street. Frequently, fad use of whichever one of these agents has become available will present itself in a given locale.

Examples of this group include: chloralhydrate (Noctec®), paraldehyde (Paral®), ethchlorvynol (Placidyl®), glutethimide (Doriden®), and methaqualone (Quaalude®, Somnos®, Somnafac®, Parest®, Optimil®). The latter compound, methaqualone, enjoyed considerable national popularity in its recreational use until strict federal legislation in the early 1970s severely limited its availability. This drug appeared to combine a long duration of action with pronounced muscle relaxant effects to produce a substance eagerly sought after by youthful users who claimed it to be a potent aphrodisiac and facilitator of sexuality (Jaffe, 1977).

Minor Tranquilizers

These agents represent a newer class of depressants that are usually associated with the treatment of anxiety states. To this end, there are the drugs generally referred to as "tranquilizers" by the general public. Examples include: meprobamate (Miltown®, Equanil®), diazepam (Valium®), chloridazepoxide (Librium®), oxazepam (Serax®), flurazepam (Dalmane®), and chlorazepate (Tranxene®). These agents are definitely safer than the barbiturates in terms of potential for overdose and physical dependence. These properties have prompted physicians to prescribe these drugs in tremendous quantities. Valium® and Librium® are now the number one and number three (respectively) prescribed drugs in the United States (Blackwell, 1973).

The majority of this excessive prescription use is maintained by middle-aged Americans, although recent studies indicate that younger age groups are beginning to experiment with these drugs both medically and illicitly. A recent survey on the drug use of high school seniors from 1974 to 1977 (Johnson et al., 1978) indicates that tranquilizer use has increased steadily. An interesting extension of this tremendous increase in national use of tranquilizers has been pointed out by Goode (1972), in which he discusses numerous studies indicating striking positive correlations between a mother's use of tranquilizers and her children's use of illegal drugs. NIDA estimated that in the year ending in April, 1977, over 57 million Valium® prescriptions were written, and there were enough reactions to Valium® to precipitate over 54 thousand emergency room visits, and 880 deaths (*U.S. Journal*, April, 1978). In spite of these startling figures, Valium® enjoys a good reputation among physicians as a mild tranquilizer with relatively low addictive potential.

Drug-related deaths per million pills are lower for Valium® than for most prescription drugs, which suggests that its danger potential is associated with its availability rather than its potency. An analysis of the statistics on this single drug suggests that it is both safe and dangerous. It is safe enough so that about one-fifth of the population has a prescription in a given year, whereas it is dangerous enough to be associated with more severe reactions than any other drug.

STIMULANT (UPPER) DRUGS

The term *upper* is used to describe drugs that act to increase nervous system activity. Such an action is associated with an increase in arousal and varying degrees of euphoria and excitement depending on the dose of the particular drug being given. The two major classes of stimulants used in the United States include caffeine-containing products and the "speed" group of drugs.

Caffeine

Weil (1974) has noted that caffeine is not generally labeled as a drug, even though it is a potent stimulant with well-known effects such as activation of digestive, circulatory, and nervous systems. In very high doses (generally unobtainable from beverages), the nervous system can become so active as to cause convulsions and death. One investigator (Jick, 1974) has reported a correlation between heavy coffee consumption (more than 5 cups per day) and a high incidence of heart attacks. Tolerance for caffeine develops after several days of heavy use. Sudden withdrawal causes headaches and irritability. In fact, caffeine withdrawal is probably a leading cause of headaches and one reason that headache remedies such as Anacin® and Excedrin® contain caffeine.

Tea and chocolate contain drugs that are similar in structure to caffeine and cola drinks contain caffeine. It is possible to stay aroused all day with a mixture of these commonly available substances. At the same time one is aroused, tolerance is developing for this arousal and the likelihood of depression is increasing because of nervous system rebound.

Cocaine

Cocaine is a white powder extraced from the leaves of the coca bush (erythroxlon coca), which grows almost exclusively in the South American Andes and is smuggled illegally into the United States through Mexico and Colombia. It is available on the street under such names as coke, c, flake, snow, or gold dust, and has become the current status drug in this country. Such notoriety probably centers around its relative scarcity and extremely high cost. Cocaine of varying quality sells for approximately $1,000 per ounce on the West Coast and is frequently adulterated with other substances. Cocaine elicits a strong local anesthetic action resulting in numbness to all mucous membranes to which it is applied. Since the drug is broken down by stomach acid, it is generally taken by forcibly inhaling it through the nostrils (insufflation or "snorting"). Much street cocaine is now being diluted with other more common anesthetics such as lidocaine (Xylocaine®) and procaine (Novocain®) to exploit this effect. Such adulteration is generally not endangering unless the drug is injected.

Taken by inhalation or injection, the subjective effects of cocaine are felt immediately and are over in 15 to 30 minutes at which time it is necessary to repeat the dose to maintain the intense arousal and euphoria associated with its use. Cocaine is a popular social drug because of the rapid onset of symptoms, convenience of use, and status. A National Institute of Drug Abuse study (Peterson, 1977) indicates that about 13% of 18- to 25-year olds and 30% of college students have used cocaine. Those individuals who dose too heavily can develop respiratory depression and cardiovascular collapse. Long-term use can result in a toxic psychosis described as "hallucinosis" (Peterson, 1977).

Amphetamines and Related Drugs

Amphetamines and related stimulants are available in a number of different preparations. Until stringent federal legislation reduced their general availability in 1972, most amphetamines were easily obtainable from physicians as assorted pep and diet pills. Examples of legitimate pharmaceutical grade amphetamines that are still very much in demand include d 1-amphetamine (Benzedrine®—bennies, peaches, cross tops), d-amphetamine (Dexedrine®—dex, horse heart), methaphetamine (Methadrine®—speed, crank, crystal, meth), and a score of related diet preparations such as methylphenidate (Ritaline®), phenmetrazine (Preludin®), Dexamyl®, Eskatrol®, and Desbutal®. Today these agents are hard to obtain and most street-grade speed comes from illicit laboratories. Although the use of these agents among young is declining on a national level, sporadic patterns of episodic use continue to be reported, particularly among students at exam time (McGlothin, 1975a).

These drugs are orally active and the effects last considerably longer than those seen with cocaine. Tolerance develops rapidly to a number of effects with daily use of amphetamines, particularly their ability to produce euphoria, arousal, and decreased appetite. Since these are the usual reasons for taking amphetamines, increasing the dosage is commonly observed and serves as a key factor in producing damaging effects. The only uniformly agreed-on medical uses for amphetamines today are in the treatment of hyperactive children and in treating a pathological sleeping condition known as narcolepsy.

High dose users of amphetamines are restless, irritable, move around incessantly, and verbalize continuously in a rapid fashion, unable to keep their attention focused on any thought for very long. Dosing occurs in "runs" of several days' duration during which intense "rushes" encountered at the time of administration are spaced out. Prolonged high dosing of amphetamine leads to a predictable paranoid psychosis that represents one of the few experimentally demonstrable, drug-induced psychotic reactions known. Persons in this state may experience vivid hallucinations and are capable of physical violence if they feel threatened.

Although medical authorities disagree as to whether or not amphetamines produce physical dependence, there is common agreement that coming off high dosing schedules produces an intense depression that can be suicidal. Often, fear of this effect contributes to users reinitiating their run to avoid this effect. Experienced users have learned to circumvent this problem by injecting depressants or opiates, especially heroin, to smooth out the post-run letdown. It has been noted that many youthful drug users in the Haight-Ashbury section of San Francisco eventually switched over to heroin when the physical damage from the amphetamines began to undermine their health (Sheppard, Gay & Smith, 1971). In this regard, the organ effects of amphetamines combined with lack of sleep and proper nutrition usually result in rapidly deteriorating physical health and possible brain damage. Individuals who manage to kick their speed use at this point are often termed "burnt out" and typically have a hard time regaining previous levels of physical health and mental ability.

OPIATES

Opiates are derivatives of opium, a resin obtained from opium poppies grown mainly in Asia Minor and Southeast Asia. Opiates have been the classic drugs of addiction and many of our stereotypic fears of drugs are based on media portrayals of addicts driven out of their minds with desire for heroin (the major opiate), or experiencing the horrors of "cold-turkey" withdrawal. Heroin is thought of as the most dangerous opiate because its synthesis from raw opium yields the most potent substance per amount of resin. Addict lore states that heroin gives a greater "rush" (surge of pleasant sensation) than any other opiate when injected. So heroin is the drug of choice for most addicts and it is probably the most addicting of all opiates (which are the most addicting of all abused drugs).

Recent estimates of overall social cost of drug abuse (excluding alcohol) suggests that heroin is the most costly (Cruze, 1978) substance and it does account for more drug-related deaths (excluding alcohol) than any other drug. Nevertheless, there is optimism about the opiate problem and addiction rates are thought to be down even since the late 1960s (DuPont, 1978).

While it is clear that physical dependence on all opiates develops quickly with sufficient daily dosing, withdrawal reactions are not nearly so dramatic as is generally believed nor as life-threatening as barbiturate withdrawal. Addiction to opiates is based on more than simple dosing to avoid withdrawal symptoms (Wesson, Smith & Gay, 1972). Physical symptoms of withdrawal are easily treated medically, but rehabilitation seems to depend on a great deal more than drug withdrawal. The principal agent used in treatment programs has been methadone, which is a long-acting, orally-administered, noneuphoric opiate that blocks craving for other opiates.

Successful methadone programs are closely supervised to prevent cheating and may employ many support systems, usually including group therapy to aid addicts. An anti-methadone movement is currently gaining strength, stimulated by the Therapeutic Communities of America, an affiliation of "Daytop-Synanon"-type organizations. This group charges that controlling drug addiction by methadone perpetuates dependency and replaces one narcotic with another. The Therapeutic Community approach assumed that drug-free treatment is possible and workable in a therapeutic community. The two approaches, chemical or therapeutic, seem rooted in a belief that opiate addiction is either permanent or it is not. The Therapeutic Community criticism seems extreme, but it serves to keep methadone programs workably therapeutic rather than allowing the government to curtail support services because of its need to economize.

The chemical approach has been strengthened by the discovery of endorphins, substances in the brain that are structurally similar to opiates, and are involved in neurotransmission (Ray, 1978). Further, effective opiate antagonists are being developed which may supplant methadone (Rawson, 1978).

PHENCYCLIDENE-PCP

PCP, known as the "peach pill," first appeared as an illicit drug in the summer of 1967. When PCP was first developed two decades ago, it was thought to be a revolutionary anesthetic because the patient felt no pain but could remain conscious with most reflexes intact. Bizarre unexplainable hallucinations were discovered to be a "side-effect," and in 1965 the FDA classified the drug as unsafe for humans but allowed its use as an animal tranquilizer. Since 1967, it has been sold as THC or various other drugs, but has lately become known as *angel dust*. PCP has many acute effects. Among those reported are hallucinations that are associated with violent aggressive attacks, many of which have been on unknown bystanders. Unpredictable violent behavior induces fear in almost all individuals who are exposed to it. Consequently, PCP is an important drug for its use has aroused fear even in Congress where two representatives have accused the White House of minimizing the threat of a dangerous drug (Lohr, 1978).

Unfortunately, because PCP has a reputation as a strong hallucinogen, some young people see the drug as a challenge. They try it to test themselves with the strongest of the most forbidden substances. David Smith of the Haight-Ashbury Medical Clinic reports that PCP is the most dangerous drug he has seen. Other drug abuse workers have theorized that psychotic PCP users are all suicidal, trying to provoke attack, or that they hallucinate their own invulnerability and act on every aggressive impulse. The aggression is apparently associated with intense paranoia and a complete loss of "reality-testing" ability (Dellinger, 1978).

Incidence

A National Institute of Drug Abuse survey in early 1977 of 2,750 youths in treatment programs showed that 32% had used PCP. PCP users were most likely to be polydrug abusers, the average age of onset of use was 14.8 years, and 56% state that it is easy to obtain. NIDA reports a 1977 national survey estimate of 6% of the 12- to 17-year olds, and 14% of the 18- to 25-year olds, in the nation have tried PCP. No regular users were estimated in that survey. At least 100 deaths and 4,000 emergency room visits were associated with PCP in 1977 (Dupont, 1978).

Reasons for Use and Risks

PCP users might elevate their status in peer groups of drug users. They might perceive benefits associated with euphoria and feelings of omnipotence that have been reported, or enhanced self-esteem. Risks of chronic use suggest some pattern of neural dysfunction, with speech, memory, and mood disorder as prominent symptoms. Several references have been made to the unpredictability of the behavior of heavy PCP users. Furthermore, most users who have committed violent acts while hallucinating have no memory of the event whatsoever (Dellinger, 1978). It is clear that there are a great many risks associated with PCP use. The lurid stories about the paranoid attacks associated with the drug make sensational news and indirectly contribute to the public risk.

PCP appears to be a serious social problem. We predict that progress in controlling the disorders associated with this drug will come only when the population of users becomes really aware of its dangers. The processing of this necessary information seems unfortunately complicated by the maladaptive thinking of youthful users. As with most drugs, recovered users can be a significant force in educating potential users away from PCP.

HALLUCINOGENIC DRUGS

Of all the drug substances used in this country, none has caught the public's fascination and wrath more than this class of mind-altering drugs. Known under a variety of labels ranging from psychotomimetic (psychosis mimicking) to psychedelic (mind or consciousness expanding), these substances are probably best described as drugs that create vivid alterations in the senses without greatly disturbing many other functions. These alterations vary considerably but may include hallucinations depending on the dose. The prototype drug of this class is lysergic acid diethylamide (LSD). It is one of the most potent drugs known, with effective doses being measured in the millionths of a gram (microgram).

Other pertinent hallucinogens include mescaline (derived from the peyote cactus), psilocybin (derived from the psilocybin, or "magic" mushroom), and DOM (marketed illicitly as STP). Drug analysis services have reported on the extremely poor quality and credibility of hallucinogens sold on the street, pointing out the difficulties associated with trying to evaluate adverse reactions reported with these preparations. One program recently published the results of over 900 samples of street psychedelics analyzed during 1973 and noted a 55.3% credibility of the sample containing what it was sold as containing (Ratcliffe, 1974).

LSD served as a pivotal point in the development of the counterculture of the late 1960s until widespread mass media publicity and strict legislation began to apparently reduce its use in the early 1970s. Although the incidence of hospitalizations for bad reactions to its effects is markedly reduced today compared with the 1960s (McGlothlin, 1975a), some surveys indicate that use is still present in youthful age groups. Blackford (1974) has reported that the incidence of LSD use among high school seniors in San Mateo County has remained stable at around 17% over the last 6 years. Also, many users have switched their preferences to other hallucinogens thought to be safer in their actions than LSD. In particular, mescaline and psilocybin are in great demand on the street, although analysis results indicate that these substances are rare and that LSD is usually what is sold under these names.

Effects encountered with LSD and the other agents in comparable doses include a progressive course of somatic to perceptual to psychic alterations that begin at about 30 minutes following oral ingestion, peak at about 3 to 4 hours, and last up to 10 or 12 hours, depending on the dose ingested. Very low doses produce only the body and perceptual effects and are similar to those seen with amphetamines. Most street LSD has quite low dose levels, averaging around 80 micrograms in lieu of its alleged 200 to 300 micrograms (McGlothlin, 1975a). Commonly reported alterations include the following: somatic effects on major organs resembling those described for amphetamines, in addition to dizziness, tremors, nausea, and prickly sensations in the extremities; perceptual changes of blurred vision, altered shapes and colors, difficulty in focusing, and less discriminate hearing; and psychic changes of mood alteration, distorted time sense, difficulty in expressing thoughts, depersonalization, dream-like feelings, and visual hallucinations. Subjective interpretation of this collective group of effects (trip) varies tremendously with the individual and with each experience. The nature of the trip depends heavily on the expectations the user takes into the experience (set) and the environment in which the drug is taken (setting). Tolerance develops very rapidly to these actions to the extent that nothing will occur if the same dose is taken repeatedly several days in a row. This phenomenon, coupled with the uniqueness of the experience, probably accounts for most users only occasionally taking these drugs. No physical dependence is known to occur with these substances.

Although the controversy linking the use of LSD to chromosomal damage and birth defects in man is not completely resolved, recent reviews

387

of the medical literature are beginning to define these problems in perspective. It now appears that, in people, LSD does not cause lasting chromosome breaks *in vivo* (Long, 1972) and is unlikely to cause adverse effects on future offspring whose parents ingested LSD within the limits of normally encountered doses (Wilson, 1973).

The typical "bad trip" associated with LSD is an acute panic reaction (Ray, 1972) which is probably psychological in nature. There is no particular ill effect on mentation for stable users, but very heavy use has been associated with onset of psychosis in unstable people. "Flashbacks" do occur (Shick & Smith, 1970) and seem to be related to immaturity in the user.

------------------------------ SUMMARY ------------------------------

Surveying a great amount of data and opinion has led us to conclude that drug use in our society cannot be effectively controlled. Law enforcement attempts at controlling opiates and alcohol have probably increased the incidence of addiction and have certainly increased the level of crime in our society. Attempts to control marijuana and psychedelic use by young people have spurred development of the counterculture to the point where startling changes have occurred. There is widespread youthful acceptance of many drugs, yet the established society maintains attitudes that were formed in a bygone era. It seems foolish for the established generation to denigrate the youthful use of illicit drugs and to severely punish the many unfortunte youths who are caught breaking drug laws that are capriciously enforced. It is particularly depressing to note that research data may be suppressed or propagandized to serve ideological goals.

We have offered a social psychological interpretation of generation-gap differences on drug issues, using three cognitive theories to focus on the inflexibility of each side. A social psychological analysis seems especially relevant because of the social nature of the communication problem and the deep psychological attitudes on differing sides of the issue. Clearly, there is a need for tolerance and flexibility on the part of parents, institutions, government agencies, and youth.

Drugs are powerful substances, some of the effects of which are understood and some of which are not. The effect of any mind-altering drug depends on set (characteristics of the user) and setting, as well as on the physical-chemical process. The recreational use of drugs seems much less likely to lead to unfavorable effects than does use based on need. When one is in need of a consciousness-altering substance, the effects of the substance are likely to provide a reinforcement that can lead to personal and social difficulties.

We suggest that young people be aware that moderate use of alcohol is clearly less harmful than continued heavy use. Indeed, some data point to beneficial effects of moderate use (Chafetz, 1974). Smoking any substance in quantity is likely to damage the lungs and circulatory system. Tobacco or marijuana smokers will minimize these difficulties by moderate use, and probably by intermittent periods of abstention. It should be kept in mind that hard drugs are always hard on the people who use them.

Drug education should be helpful to young people if it is directed toward their needs which sometimes seem at variance with the needs of the educator. People who are aware of the effects of various drugs are less likely to abuse them. Therefore, drug education should focus on information, not ideology.

SUGGESTIONS FOR FURTHER READING

GAMAGE, J. (Ed.). *Management of adolescent drug misuses: Clinical, psychological, and legal perspectives.* Beloit, Wis.: Stash Press, 1973.

RAY, O. S. *Drugs, society and human behavior* (2nd ed.). St. Louis: C. V. Mosby, 1978.

RUBIN, V., & COMITAS, L. *Ganja in Jamaica: A medical anthropological study of chronic marijuana use.* The Hague: Mouton, 1975.

RUBIN, V. (Ed.). *Cannabis and culture.* The Hague: Mouton, 1975.

SZASZ, T. *Ceremonial chemistry: The ritual persecution of drugs, addicts, and pushers.* New York: Anchor, 1974.

The U.S. Journal of Alcohol and Drug Dependence, and, *Focus on Alcohol and Drug Issues* (two worthwhile publications).

BIBLIOGRAPHY

BASS, M. Sudden sniffing death. *Journal of the American Medical Association,* 1970, *212,* 2075–2079.

BEAUBRUN, M. H. Cannabis or alcohol: The Jamaica experience. In V. Rubin (Ed.), *Cannabis and culture.* The Hague: Mouton, 1975.

BLACKFORD, L. Student drug use surveys, San Mateo County, California. Preliminary Report. County Department of Health and Welfare, San Mateo, 1974.

BLAINE, H., & CHAFETZ, M. Guard against overreaction. *Focus on Alcohol and Drug Issues,* 1978, *1,* No. 3, 5.

BLANE, H., & HEWITT, L. *Alcohol and youth.* Springfield, Virginia: National Technical Information Service, U.S. Department of Commerce, 1977.

BLUM, R. H., & ASSOCIATES. *Society and drugs.* San Francisco: Jossey-Bass, 1969.

BRAUCHT, G. Psychosocial typology of adolescent alcohol and drug users. In *Proceedings of the third annual alcoholism conference of the National Institute on Alcohol Abuse and Alcoholism.* Washington, D.C.: U.S. Department of Health, Education and Welfare, 1974.

BRECHER, E.M., & the editors of *Consumer Reports.* The "heroin overdose" mystery and other hazards of addiction. In *Licit and illicit drugs.* Boston: Little, Brown, 1972.

BRECHER, E. M., & the editors of *Consumer Reports.* Marijuana: The health questions. Is marijuana as damaging as recent reports make it appear? *Consumer Reports,* 1975, *30,* 143–149.

BUTLER, N. R., & GOLDSTEIN, H. Smoking in pregnancy and subsequent child development. *British Medical Journal,* 1973, *4,* 573–575.

CARR, R. C. The pot vote. *Human Behavior,* 1976, *5,* 56–60.

CARR, R. C. Update/What marijuana does (and doesn't do). *Human Behavior,* 1978, *7,* 20–25.

CHIEN, C. P., STOTSKY, B. A., & COLE, J. O. Psychiatric treatment for nursing home patients: Drug, alcohol, and milieu. *American Journal of Psychiatry,* 1973, *130,* 543–548.

CHILD, J. L. *Humanistic psychology and the research tradition: Their several virtues.* New York: Wiley, 1973.

COOPER, R. *Sedative-hypnotic drugs: Risks and benefits.* Washington, D.C.: U.S. Government Printing Office, 1977.

CROSS, H. J., & KLEINHESSELINK, R. R. Theoretical speculations about marijuana and drug issues. In C. S. Davis & M. S. Schmidt (Eds.), *Differential treatment of drug and alcohol abusers.* Palm Springs, California: ETC, 1977.

CROSS, H., KLEINHESSELINK, R., & ST. DENNIS, C. Contemporary drug issues. In J. F. Adams (Ed.), *Understanding adolescence: Current developments in adolescent psychology* (3rd ed.). Boston: Allyn & Bacon, 1976.

CRUZE, A. M. Estimating the social costs of drug abuse. *The U.S. Journal of Drug and Alcohol Dependence,* 1978, *2,* 7 & 14.

DELLINGER, R. A. High on PCP. *Human Behavior,* 1978, *7,* 38–45.

DHEW Report. *Alcohol and health,* First Special Report to the U.S. Congress from the Secretary of Health, Education and Welfare. Publication No. (ADN) 74–68, formerly No. (HSM) 73-9031, December, 1971.

DHEW Publication No. (ADM) 74–127. The deliberate inhalation of volatile substances report series by the National Clearinghouse for Drug Abuse Information. Series 30, No. 1, July, 1974, 1–17.

DHEW Publication No. (ADM) 76–361. The whole college catalog about drinking, 1976.

DEIKMAN, A. J. Deautomatization and the mystic experience. In R. E. Ornstein (Ed.), *The nature of human consciousness.* New York: Viking, 1973.

DELINT, J. The prevention of alcoholism. *Preventive Medicine,* 1974, *3,* 24–35.

DELONG, F. L., & LEVY, B. I. A model of attention describing the cognitive effects of marijuana. In L. Miller (Ed.), *Marijuana: Effects on human behavior.* New York: Academic Press, 1974.

DORNBUSH, R. L. The long term effects of cannabis use. In L. Miller (Ed.), *Marijuana: Effects on human behavior.* New York: Academic Press, 1974.

Drug related deaths tallied. *U.S. Journal of Drug and Alcohol Dependence,* 1978, *2,* No. 3, 2.

DUPONT, R. L. The drug abuse scene: Past, present, and future. Paper presented at the plenary session of the National Drug Abuse Conference, Seattle, Washington, April 5, 1978.

DUSTER, T. *The legislation of morality: Law, drugs, and moral judgement.* New York: Free Press, 1970.

FORSLUND, M. A., & GUSTAFSON, T. J. Influence of peers and parents and sex differences in drinking by high school students. *Quarterly Journal of Studies in Alcoholism,* 1970, *31,* 868–875.

FORT, J. *Alcohol: Our biggest drug problem.* New York: McGraw-Hill, 1973.

GALLI, N. Patterns of student drug use. *Journal of Drug Education,* 1974, *4,* 237–247.

GLOBETTI, G. A survey of teenage drinking in two Mississippi communities. Report No. 3, Mississippi State University, Social Science Research Center, 1974.

GOODE, E. *Drugs in American society.* New York: Knopf, 1972.

GOODE, E. *The marijuana smokers.* New York: Basic Books, 1970.

GRINSPOON, L. *Marijuana reconsidered.* Cambridge: Harvard University Press, 1971.

HANN, N., SMITH, M. B., BLOCK, J. Moral reasoning of young adults: Political social behavior, family background and personality correlates. *Journal of Personality and Social Psychology,* 1968, *10,* 183–201.

HAFEN, B. *Alcohol: The crutch that cripples.* St. Paul, Minnesota: West Publishing Co., 1977.

HAGER, M. Smoking—Public Health Enemy No. 1. *The U.S. Journal of Drug and Alcohol Dependence,* 1978, *2,* 1 & 4.

HAMMOND, E. C. World costs of cigarette smoking in disease, disability and death. Address to the World Conference on Smoking and Health. New York, September 11, 1967.

HARLAP, S., & DAVIES, A. M. Infant admissions to hospital and maternal smoking. *Lancet,* 1974, *1,* 529–532.

HARVEY, O. J., HUNT, D. E., & SCHRODER, H. M. *Conceptual systems and personality organization.* New York: Wiley, 1961.

HOCHMAN, J. S. *Marijuana and social evolution.* Englewood Cliffs, N.J.: Prentice-Hall, 1972.

HOGAN, R., MANKIN, D., CONWAY, J., & FOX, S. Personality correlates of undergraduate marijuana use. *Journal of Consulting and Clinical Psychology,* 1970, *35,* 58–73.

JAFFE, J. Hypnotic and sedative agents. In M. Jarvik (Ed.), *Psychopharmacology in the practice of medicine.* New York: Appleton-Century-Crofts, 1977.

JESSOR, R., & JESSOR, S. Adolescent development and the onset of drinking. *Journal of Studies on Alcohol,* 1975, *36,* 27–51.

JESSOR, R., & JESSOR, S. *Problem behavior and psychosocial development: A longitudinal study of youth.* New York: Academic Press, 1977.

JESSOR, R., JESSOR, S., & FINNEY, J. A social psychology of marijuana use: Longitudinal studies of high school and college youth. *Journal of Personality and Social Psychology,* 1973, *76,* 1–15.

JICK, H. Report of the Boston Collaborative Drug Surveillance Program—Coffee Drinking and Myocardial Infarction. *Journal of the American Medical Association,* 1974, *227,* 801.

JOHNSON, B. D. *Marijuana users and drug subcultures.* New York: Wiley, 1973.

JOHNSON, L., BACHMAN, J., & O'MALLEY, P. *Drug use among American high school students 1975-1977.* Washington, D.C.: U.S. Government Printing Office, 1978.

JONES, H. B., & JONES, H. C. *Sensual drugs, deprivation and rehabilitation of the mind.* New York: Cambridge University Press, 1977.

JORDAN, N. Cognitive balance as an aspect of Heider's cognitive psychology. In R. Abelson, E. Aronson, W. J. McGuire, J. M. Newcomb, M. J. Rosenberg, & P. H. Tannenbaum (Eds.), *Theories of cognitive consistency: A sourcebook.* Chicago: Rand McNally, 1968.

JOSEPHSON, E. The drug problem. In E. Josephson, & E. Carroll (Eds.), *Drug use: Epidemological and sociological approaches.* New York: Wiley, 1974.

KAATS, G., & DAVIS, K. The social psychology of sexual behavior. In L. Wrightsman (Ed.), *Social psychology in the seventies.* Belmont, California: Wadsworth, 1972.

KANDEL, D. B. Similarity in real-life adolescent friendship pairs. *Journal of Personality & Social Psychology,* 1978, *36,* 306–312.

KANDEL, D., KESSLER, R., & MARGULIES, R. Antecedents of adolescent initiation into stages of drug use: A developmental analysis. *Journal of Youth and Adolescence,* 1978, *7,* 13–40.

KAPLAN, J. Marijuana: *The new prohibition.* New York: World, 1970.

KAPLAN, J. Intersections of anthropology and law in the cannabis area. In V. Rubin (Ed.), *Cannabis and culture.* The Hague: Mouton, 1975.

KAY, E., LYONS, A., NEWMAN, W., MANKIN, D., & LOEB, R. A longitudinal study of personality correlates of marijuana use. *Journal of Consulting and Clinical Psychology,* 1977, *46,* 470–477.

KEELEY, K. A., KAHN, P., & KEELER, M. H. Alcohol and drug use: Causes of sudden death. *Southern Medical Journal,* 1974, *67,* 970–972.

KOHLBERG, L. The cognitive-developmental approach to socialization. In D. A. Goslin (Ed.), *Handbook of socialization theory and research.* Chicago: Rand-McNally, 1969.

KOHLBERG, L., & KRAMER, R. Continuities and discontinuities in childhood and adult moral development. *Human Development,* 1969, *12,* 93–120.

KORCOK, M. NIDA performance review—Dupont responds to critics. *The U.S. Journal of Drug and Alcohol Dependence,* 1978, *2,* 3. (a)

KORCOK, M. Teen alcohol abuse poses threat to future. *Focus on Alcohol and Drug Issues,* 1978, *1,* No. 3, 4. (b)

LOHR, L. Committee attacks Bourne for playing down PCP threat. *The U.S. Journal of Drug and Alcohol Dependence,* 1978, *2,* 1 & 11.

MADDOX, G., & McCALL, B. *Drinking among teen-agers: A sociological interpretation of alcohol use by high-school students.* New Brunswick, N.J.: Rutgers Center of Alcohol Studies, 1964.

McGLOTHLIN, W. H. Drug use and abuse. In M. Rosenzweig & L. Porter (Eds.), *Annual review of psychology.* Palo Alto, California: Annual Reviews Inc., 1975. (a)

McGLOTHLIN, W. H. Sociocultural factors in marijuana use in the United States. In J. Rubin (Ed.), *Cannabis and culture.* The Hague: Mouton, 1975. (b)

MILLER, L. Marijuana: *Effects on human behavior.* New York: Academic Press, 1974.

MYERSON, R. M. Metabolic aspects of alcohol and their biological significance. *Medical Clinics of North America,* 1973, *57,* 925–940.

NAHAS, G. G. *Marijuana—deceptive weed.* New York: Raven, 1975.

NATIONAL COMMISSION ON MARIJUANA AND DRUG ABUSE. *Drug use in America: Problem in perspective.* Washington, D.C.: U.S. Government Printing Office, 1973.

ORCUTT, J. D., & BIGGS, D. A. Perceived risks of marijuana and alcohol use: Comparisons of non-users and regular users. *Journal of Drug Issues,* 1973, *3,* 355–360.

PARKER, B. M. The effects of ethyl alcohol on the heart. *Journal of the American Medical Association,* 1974, *228,* 741–742.

PATEL, A. R., ROY, M., & WILSON, G. M. Self-poisoning and alcohol. *Lancet,* 1972, *2,* 1099–1103.

PETERSON, R. C. Cocaine: An overview. In R. Peterson, & R. Stillman (Eds.), *Cocaine: 1977.* Washington, D.C.: U.S. Government Printing Office, 1978.

PRENDERGAST, T., & SCHAEFFER, E. Correlates of drinking and drunkenness among high school students. *Quarterly Journal of Studies in Alcoholism,* 1974, *35,* 232–242.

RATCLIFFE, B. E. Summary of street drug results 1973. *Pharmchem. Newsletter,* 1974, *3,* No. 3, 11 & 14.

RAWSON, R. A. Use of naltrex for heroin addiction. *The U.S. Journal of Drug and Alcohol Dependence,* 1978, *2,* 7.

RAY, O. S. *Drugs, society and human behavior.* St. Louis, Missouri: C. V. Mosby, 1972.

RAY, O. S. *Drugs, society and human behavior* (2nd ed.). St. Louis, Missouri: C. V. Mosby, 1978.

RUBIN, V., & COMITAS, L. *Ganja in Jamaica: A medical anthropological study of chronic marijuana use.* The Hague: Mouton, 1975.

RUSSELL, M. A. H., COLE, P. V., & BROWN, E. Absorption by non-smokers of carbon monoxide from room air polluted by tobacco smoke. *Lancet,* 1973, *1,* 576–579.

SADAVA, S. W. Patterns of college student drug use: A longitudinal social learning study. *Psychological Reports,* 1973, *33,* 75–86.

SEIDLER, G. Legalization would reap 1.6 billion. *Focus on alcohol and drug issues,* 1978, *1,* 14.

SHAFER, R. National Commission on Marijuana and Drug Abuse. *Marijuana: A signal of misunderstanding.* New York: The New American Library, 1972.

SHEPPARD, C. W., GAY, G. R., & SMITH, D. E. The changing patterns of heroin addiction in the Haight-Asbury subculture. *Journal of Psychedelic Drugs,* 1971, *3,* 22–30.

SHICK, J. F. E., & SMITH, D. E. Analysis of the LSD flashback. *Journal of Psychedelic Drugs,* 1970, *3,* 13–19.

SLACK, C. W. *Timothy Leary, the madness of the sixties and me.* New York: Wyden, 1974.

STEFANIS, C., DORNBUSH, R., & FINK, M. *Hashish: Studies of long-term use.* New York: Raven, 1977.

SUCHMAN, E. A. The "hang-loose" ethic and the spirit of drug use. *Journal of Health and Social Behavior,* 1968, *9,* 146–155.

SZASZ, T. *Ceremonial chemistry: The ritual persecution of drugs, addicts, and pushers.* New York: Anchor, 1974.

TENNANT, F. S., PREBLE, M., PRENDERGAST, T. J., & VENTRY, P. Medical manifestations associated with hashish. *Journal of the American Medical Association,* 1971, *216,* 1965–1969.

TINKLENBERG, J. R. Marijuana and human aggression. In L. Miller (Ed.), *Marijuana: Effects on human behavior.* New York: Academic Press, 1974.

WEIL, A. *The natural mind.* Boston: Houghton Mifflin, 1972.

WEIL, A. Toxic reactions to marijuana. In J. E. Gamage (Ed.), *Management of adolescent drug misuse: Clinical, psychological and legal perspectives.* Beloit, Wisconsin: STASH Press, 1973.

WEIL, A. Letters from Andrew Weil. *Journal of Psychedelic Drugs,* 1974, *6,* 361–363.

WESSON, D. R., GAY, G. R., & SMITH, D. E. Treatment techniques for narcotic withdrawal. In D. E. Smith & G. R. Gay (Eds.), *"It's so good don't even try it once": Heroin in perspective.* Englewood Cliffs, N.J.: Prentice-Hall, 1972.

WESSON, D., & SMITH, D. Cocaine: Its use for CNS stimulation including recreational and medical uses. In R. Peterson, & R. Stillman (Eds.), *Cocaine: 1977.* Washington, D.C.: U.S. Government Printing Office, 1978.

WILSON, J. G. Present status of drugs as teratogens in man. *Teratology,* 1973, *7,* 3–16.

WRIGHTSMAN, L. S. *Social psychology in the seventies.* Monterey, California: Brooks/Cole, 1972.

ZINBERG, N. The war over marijuana. *Psychology Today,* December, 1976, *10,* 44–45 & 102–106.

ZINBERG, N., & ROBERTSON, J. *Drugs and the public.* New York: Simon and Schuster, 1972.

14

CAREER DEVELOPMENT

John O. Crites

If we consider only the sheer amount of time we spend in life activities from childhood to senescence, then clearly our career development stands out literally as our main occupation. For most of our waking hours, particularly from adolescence on but even during the early school years, we are given to either preparing for or engaging in a career. Adolescence is the critical time for career decision making that largely determines the paths we follow in adulthood through the complex and often confusing world of work.

If we consider also the quality of life activities across the life span, then our career development assumes even greater salience as the single most important factor in our personal and social adjustment. In his *Civilization and Its Discontents*, Freud astutely observed that work is our principal point of contact with reality, and he proposed that, in combination with the capacity to love, meaningful and productive work constitutes a hallmark of maturity (*arbeiten und lieben*). How we mature vocationally, therefore, has far reaching ramifications for how we develop generally. To understand how this process gets started and to trace its course across adolescence is the main focus of this chapter, which is divided into several parts: theories of career development, measures of career development, and studies of career development. A final section gives a brief overview of career counseling and career development to indicate the ways in which the adolescent can become more career mature by participating in these interventive and facilitative processes.

THEORIES OF CAREER DEVELOPMENT

It was not until 1950 that career choice was viewed theoretically as a developmental phenomenon. Before that time, it was assumed that an adolescent progressed through high school until the senior year and then made a career choice on the threshold of entering the world of work. Pictured in the popular literature of the 1930s and 1940s as a youth standing at the "crossroads of life" with directional signs pointing toward different careers in engineering, medicine, sales, accounting, and so on, this cross-sectional concept of career choice depicted it as largely epiphenomenal.

The first theorists to propose that career choice is not simply a point-in-time event, but rather a developmental process that embraces at least the period from late childhood through adolescence to early adulthood

---

John O. Crites is Professor of Psychology at the University of Maryland. He has authored or coauthored *Vocational Psychology, Appraising Vocational Fitness, Vocational Development,* and is currently working on *Career Counseling: Models, Methods and Materials,* and *Tests: Measurement of Abilities, Interests and Personality.* He is well known from his books and his many articles on such topics as career development, vocational psychology, career counseling, and testing.

were Ginzberg, Ginsburg, Axelrad, and Herma (1951). This team of an economist, psychiatrist, and two psychologists (one trained by the Buehlers and Piaget) formulated a developmental theory of career choice that has been the prototype for subsequent thinking about how and why adolescents choose careers as they do. The discussion that follows summarizes Ginzberg's theory as well as two others that have stemmed from it, one by Super (1953; 1955; 1957) and the other by Crites (1965; 1971; 1974a).

Ginzberg's Theory of Career Choice

The central proposition in this theory is that *career choice is a process which extends from approximately age 10 to age 21,* encompassing the years of adolescence, principally through high school but also during the upper elementary grades (5 and 6). Ginzberg states that the single most important factor in this process that determines career choice is the series of interlocked decisions the adolescent makes over time.

From this observation, Ginzberg extrapolates his second proposition that *the process of career choice is largely irreversible.* Once launched on a particular career path, it becomes increasingly difficult to change directions. The high school students who elect industrial arts in the ninth grade would find it almost impossible to cross-over to the college prep curriculum in the tenth grade, because they have missed a year of college English and mathematics and probably a year of a foreign language.

Finally, Ginzberg proposes that, partly due to its inherent irreversibility, *the career choice process culminates in a compromise between needs and reality.* Deduced from psychoanalytic theory, this proposition rests upon the assumption that the ego mediates between what the individual wants (id-based impulses) and what reality allows (superego dictates and environmental constraints). Even in the most favored circumstances, the adolescent must make some concessions in choosing a career to gain others. To obtain desired training in architectural engineering, for example, it may be necessary to attend a far-away college.[1]

Ginzberg identified four ego functions the adolescent uses in arriving at a career choice, all of which are more or less highly developed, depending on degree of maturity. One of these is an articulated or differentiated *time perspective.* The more mature adolescent can project further into the psychological future in making a career choice and better anticipate the advantages and disadvantages of different career options than can the individual who conceives time in categorical terms (future = "not now, later").

---

[1] Ginzberg (1972) revised his theory of career choice approximately 25 years after he first introduced it, and he changed some emphases in it, such as placing less importance on irreversibility and extending the period of decision making into adulthood, but the elements of his theory remained substantially the same.

Closely related to time perspective is the second ego function—*delay capacity*. Defined as the ability to postpone immediate need gratification for longer term, more highly valued goals, it represents what Freud called the reality principle, and it produces a more realistic career choice than does the pleasure principle. Capacity to delay interacts with the third ego function, *reality testing*, which is the process of appraising whether one *can* do what one *wants* to do. Even if a young person has outstanding intellectual talent and scholastic achievement, it may be unrealistic to choose a career in medicine which may take more financial resources than are available or obtainable.

The fourth ego function, compromise, is the mechanism by which reality testing is carried out and a realistic career choice (one that can be implemented) is made. More an attitude than a competence in decision making, it is the disposition to "give a little to gain a lot." In contrast to a rigid, inflexible, unbending adherence to a career choice which may be unrealistic, compromise involves an effort to negotiate the best possible career choice with reality. These four ego functions are further defined and explicated in Table 14.1, where the career choice problems and pressures they relate to and the supports available for their use are outlined.

The career developmental process mediated by the adolescent's ego functions is not an unbroken, positively accelerated curve over time. Ginzberg sees it as unfolding in differentiable periods and stages. These are delineated by the factors the young person takes into consideration in making a decision, what Ginzberg calls the "basis of choice." As Figure 14.1 indicates, the bases change from one period to another, the developmental trend being from lesser to greater realism of career choice. Initially, it is based largely on childhood fantasies about "work as play" and the wish to be an adult. During early adolescence, the basis for career choice shifts to intraindividual factors, such as interests, capacities, and values. Then, in late adolescence, the focus is on reality—what it has to offer vocationally and what constraints it imposes. The successive periods and stages in this process of choice determination are outlined in Figure 14.1. What occurs in them is summarized in Table 14.2, where the dynamics of the developmental process underlying career choice can be seen. Also note the complementary, more general facets of development which interact with the making of a career choice. Although career development is a differentiable dimension of the adolescent's increasing maturity, it is interrelated with other growth processes which are on-going at the same time (Super, 1955).

Super's Theory of Career Development

Whereas Ginzberg formulated his explanation of how career choices are made during adolescence primarily from an ego psychological point-of-

TABLE 14.1 Ego Functions in Career Decision Making

PROBLEM	FUNCTION	PRESSURE	SUPPORT
To determine freedom in occupational choice by enlarging knowledge	Reality testing	Immediate gratification of impulses growing out of general maturation, such as emerging sex needs in adolescence	Internal: Values and goals make it possible to relate present activities to future
To distinguish between present, near future, and distant future	Sharpening of time perspective	Time: necessity to make decisions	Prospects of realizing future goals
To postpone current gratifications	Delaying capacity	Parental aspirations and ambitions	Minimum gratification of present needs
To set realizable goals and to choose suitable approaches for their attainment	Ability to compromise	Motivation: work orientation vs. pleasure orientation	External: educational system which sets up intermediate goals; parental guidance; identification with parent

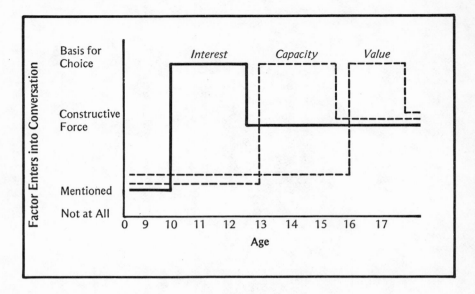

Figure 14.1 Ginzberg's Stages in the Process of Career Choice.

view, Super (1953; 1955; 1957; 1963) has adopted a largely phenomeno-
logical frame-of-reference to conceptualize the process of career development. His basic tenet is that "in choosing an occupation one is, in effect,
choosing a means of implementing a self-concept" (Super, 1951, p. 88).
And, he sees this implementation as a process projected over time, not only
during adolescence but also throughout adulthood as the individual continually adjusts to career.

Unlike Ginzberg, who subscribes to the psychoanalytic interpretation
of adolescence as a period of *Sturm und Drang* ("storm and stress"), characterized by the upheavals of the "return of the repressed," Super (1951) follows the G. Stanley Hall tradition of continuous development from
childhood to adolescence (see chapter 2 by Gallatin on theories of adolescent development), with the self-concept being clarified and crystallized
rather than conflicted. The implication theoretically is that Super posits
synthesis rather than compromise as the outcome of adolescent career development. The elements of the self concept are translated into a compatible
occupational role, without the disruptions and disjunctions in the process
occasioned by the *return of the repressed*. For Super, only when there are deviations in the course of career development, for example, inadequate
learning of coping mechanisms (LoCascio, 1963), is compromise necessary.
In normal career development, there is a progressive interaction of self and
environment which culminates in a career choice based on synthesis.

If the process of career development during adolescence is one of syn-

TABLE 14.2 *Ginzberg's Descriptions of the Periods in the Career Choice Process*

PERIOD	VOCATIONAL ORIENTATION	GENERAL DEVELOPMENT
Fantasy	Shift in basis for choice: 　Function pleasure (ages 4–6) 　Results of work (ages 8–9) Behavioral characteristics: 　Recognition of having to work 　Wish to become an adult 　Distorted time perspective (future: "not now-later") 　No urgency to make a choice, unlimited fantasy 　No means-end cognizance Development toward tentative period: 　Reliance upon parents for choice 　Dissatisfaction with parent's suggestions 　Acceptance of choice as personal responsibility	Increased capacity to accomplish specific tasks Increased objectivity about self Increased concerns with reality Increased pressure from parents to form good working habits
Tentative	Sharpening of time perspective: 　Recognition of continuum between present and future; present and future linked 　Recognition that actions in present will condition those in the future Greater awareness of reality barriers to choice More aware that adult work is same from day to day Desire to choose work which will be continually satisfying Attempts to create image of future self, which tentative choice makes concrete Anticipated satisfactions from tentatively chosen occupations guide present ac-	Increased awareness that self will change Increased awareness that currently pleasurable activities may not be pleasurable in future Increased libidinal pressures which drive individual to immediate gratifications interfere with planning for the future

TABLE 14.2 *(Continued)*

PERIOD	VOCATIONAL ORIENTATION	GENERAL DEVELOPMENT
	tions rather than immediate satisfactions	
	Choices are tentative because:	Increased desire to gain emotional independence from impulses
	They are based upon a self image which is not firm	
	They are often changed in the Realistic period	
	The individual lacks information about training and work	
	As conflicts and tensions are resolved, tentativeness gives way to considerations of reality in choice	Recognition of necessity to resolve early emotional conflicts, particularly with father ("return of the repressed")
Realistic	New approach to problem of choice is brought about by reality pressures, as well as resolution of conflicts	Differentiation of likes and dislikes
	Individual is forced by imminence of school graduation to recognize that he cannot remain undecided any longer	
	Individual looks backward and forward in making a choice and realizes that major changes in self image are costly and unfeasible	Further development of ego functions
	Individual can no longer explore what he would like to do and how he would like to do it	Acceptance of adult responsibilities
	He must now deal with concrete demands, e.g., how to gain admission to a college or advanced training institution	

thesis, then it should describe a curve across time that is essentially linear. And, it is such a model that Super assumes. Super and Overstreet (1960) have hypothesized that there are three progressive (linearly increasing) trends in career development from early to late adolescence toward greater goal direction, independence, and choice realism. They do not identify pe-

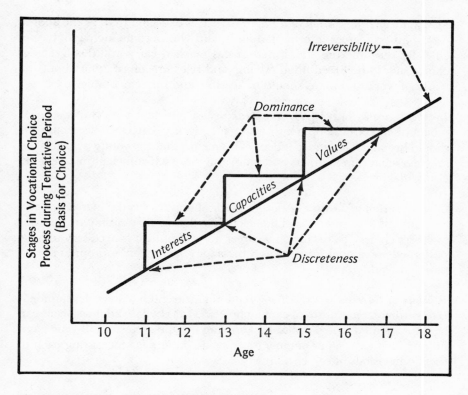

Figure 14.2 Crites' Stages in Career Choice.

riods or stages in this process, but Tiedeman and O'Hara (1963), also from a self-concept orientation, do and they specify three criteria for delineating stages: discreteness, dominance, and irreversibility. Discreteness refers to the limits of a stage, dominance to the basis for choice most salient in a particular time-frame, and irreversibility to the progressive or unidirectional thrust of the career development process. These criteria of stages are graphically represented in Figure 14.2, where they are shown as defining three hypothetical stages in career decision making. These correspond to those enumerated by Ginzberg—fantasy, tentative, and realistic—as well as those proposed by Tiedeman and O'Hara (1963)—anticipation, implementation, and adjustment.

The dimensions of career development cutting across these stages have been ennumerated by Super (1955) as follows.

Awareness of the Need to Choose. It is a mark of career maturity, particularly in early adolescence, to recognize ("be conscious of") the societal expectation that each individual declare a career choice.

Specificity of Information and Planning. It is expected that, as the adolescent matures, career information and plans will become increasingly specific. By the time the young person has reached early adulthood, career choice should be based upon reliable and relevant information about the world of work and plans should be feasible and implementable.

Independence in Career Decision Making. Consistent with Super's linear model of career development during adolescence, career choice behaviors should become more independent. This means that the young person is less and less reliant upon others and more and more self-sufficient in career decision making.

Crystallization of Traits. Another mark of maturity is the increasing pattern of aptitudes, interests, and personality characteristics that are relevant to career choice. To decide on a career, for example, it is necessary to have patterned vocational interests as a basis for selecting an appropriate occupational field.

Wisdom of Career Choice. The predominant trend in career development is toward greater realism of career choice, so that by late adolescence it can be implemented (acted upon) by applying for and securing full-time gainful employment. Super enumerates specific indices for measuring each of these dimensions of career maturity.

Crites' Model of Career Maturity

Combining Ginzberg's focus on ego functions in career decision making with Super's emphasis on the dimensions of career maturity, and adding components from factorial analyses of ability, Crites (1961; 1965; 1974a) has formulated a model of career maturity that encompasses both the *content* and *process* of career decision making. The model has been adapted from the research of British psychologists, notably Vernon (1950) and Burt (1954), on the structure of abilities. They propose that abilities are organized in hierarchical fashion, much as shown in Figure 14.3.

At the lowest level of the hierarchy are the *specific variables* of interest, whether these are intellectual capacities, such as verbal reasoning or spatial perception, or career choice behaviors, such as knowledge of the world of work. At one intermediate level are the so-called *group* factors which are formed by clusters of variables more highly related to each other than to other variables. Thus, all the clerical speed and accuracy variables cluster together and constitute a group. Another, even more inclusive intermediate level which encompasses the group factors, constitutes *dimensions* that converge upon the highest level of the hierarchical model—the *general* factor.

Comparable to Spearman's "g", this supraordinate factor is "degree of career maturity." It can be defined in either: *absolute* terms as "the place reached on the continuum of career development" (Super, 1955); or, *relative* terms with respect to the individual's standing in the appropriate age or grade reference group (Crites, 1961).

This hierarchical model of career maturity is shown in Figure 14.3, where the distinction between career choice *content* and *process* can be recognized as basic. By the content of career choice is meant simply which occupation the adolescent intends to enter after education or training have been completed (as expressed in an occupational title). In contrast, the process of career choice refers to the series of decisions which individuals make before declaring which occupations they intend to enter. It also involves certain attitudes and competencies that mediate the choice process and are part of it. Attitudes are the conative, dispositional variables in career decision making which influence how realistic the adolescent's choices are. They include how involved and independent individuals are in the process, whether they can make compromises, what their orientations are, and how decisive they are in arriving at a career decision. In contrast, competencies are the cognitive, intellective variables which provide the information, comprehension, foresight, and coping mechanisms in career maturation. They embrace how self-appraisals can be made, possession of relevant and reliable occupational information, goal selection faculties, planning abilities, and problem-solving competencies. Together, these attitudes and competencies are the mechanisms by which the career decision making process unfolds.

Following Vernon's (1950) work on the structure of abilities, Crites (1974a) has hypothesized that the interrelationships of the variables within a group, for example, consistency of career choice, are higher than the relationships between groups. The former are expected to average about .50 and the latter approximately .30. Preliminary findings on testing this model of career maturity in adolescence show that it substantially "fits" the data (Westbrook, 1971; Crites, 1978). The correlations within the Career Choice Competencies group are somewhat higher than expectation, being in the .60's, and those within the Career Choice Attitudes somewhat lower, ranging in the mid-.40's. Data on the other two groups, Consistency of Career Choice and Realism of Career Choice, have not as yet been gathered—nor have data been collected on the "differentiation hypothesis."

Similar to Garrett's (1946) notion that intelligence becomes increasingly differentiated with advancing age, Crites (1974a) has proposed that *degree of career maturity,* the general factor in the model, breaks up the four group factors shown in Figure 14.3. This trend seems reasonable, because as the adolescent grows older and is exposed to more and more varied learning experiences, specific factors in career maturity emerge and become more pronounced. Research on the development of career choice attitudes

405

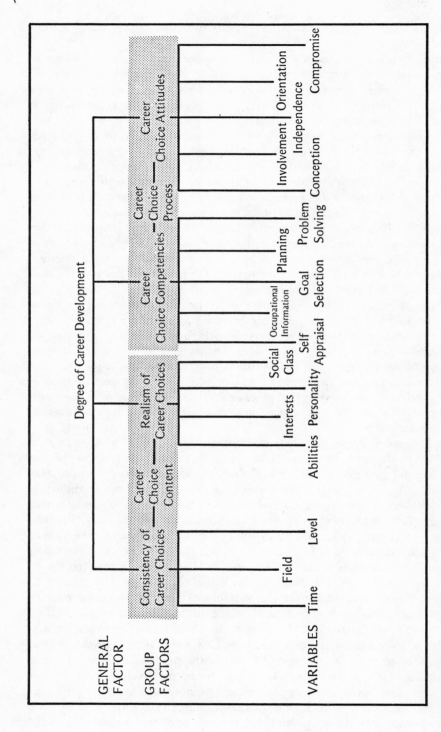

Figure 14.3 A Model of Career Maturity in Adolescence.

summarized in the section on studies of career development confirms this trend, as well as other facets of Crites' model of career maturity.

MEASURES OF CAREER DEVELOPMENT

Stemming from the career development theories of Ginzberg et al. (1951), Super (1953; 1957; 1963), and Crites (1965; 1974a), three approaches to the measurement of the central concepts in the theories have been generated. One of these came directly out of the Career Pattern Study (Super, Crites, Hummel, Moser, Overstreet, & Warnath, 1957), which was launched to test Ginzberg's propositions as well as to extend his theory to other variables. The initial measures, based on a combination of interview ratings and psychometric data, were called the Indices of Vocational Maturity (IVM). Subsequently, they led to the construction of a standardized instrument known as the Career Development Inventory (CDI).

A second approach taken by Gribbons and Lohnes (1968) also was suggested by the Career Pattern Study. This resulted in a semistructured interview schedule termed the Readiness for Vocationsl Planning (RVP) scales, which is more standardized than the IVM but less so that the CDI. The third approach, undertaken by Crites (1965), has been entirely objective (psychometric) and has produced the Career Maturity Inventory (CMI). Each of these approaches, and the measures of career development associated with it, are described in this section.

Career Development Inventory (CDI)

The CDI was constructed largely from studies of the Indices of Vocational Maturity (IVM), which were developed to assess the dimensions of career maturity in Super's (1953; 1957; 1963) theory of career development. The various IVM measures, based on interview and test data, were intercorrelated on the Career Pattern Study sample of ninth grade boys (N = 140) and were factor analyzed to yield three scales for the CDI:

Scale A. Planning Orientation, includes items dealing with concern with choice, specificity of planning, and self-estimated amount of occupational information.

Scale B. Resources for Exploration, involves a self-rated assessment of resources for use in planning. It is a measure of the quality of the actually used and potentially useful resources for career exploration.

Scale C. Information and Decision Making, assesses the individual's possession of actual occupational information and knowledge of how to integrate personal and occupational information into educational and vocational decisions.

Planning Orientation and Resources for Exploration were designed to measure the conative aspects of career maturity, whereas Information and Decision Making were intended to appraise the cognitive dimensions (see Figure 14.3).

Norms for the CDI were gathered principally from its administration to small samples ($N = 80$–90) of tenth graders as part of a broader project on computer-assisted career counseling (Forrest & Thompson, 1974). Comparisons of boys and girls on the CDI scales indicated only negligible sex differences, which suggests that it has some generality psychometrically. However, this is contrary to the results obtained with the Career Maturity Inventory (CMI). Clearly more extensive normative work needs to be done on the CDI to determine its parameters. It appears to be reliable enough for such data collection, its test-retest stability coefficients being .71 to .87 for total score over a 6-month period. No internal consistency evidence is currently available, but the content validity of the scales supports their unidimensionality. As mentioned previously, they were constructed from correlational and factor analyses of the original Indices of Vocational Maturity, which had been purified both rationally and empirically over a long period of time (Super & Overstreet, 1960). From this research, it became apparent that the single most important dimension in the career maturity of ninth graders, at approximately the beginning of the exploratory period in career decision making, was "orientation to planning." In other words, at the beginning of adolescence, those who were more career mature were starting to make vocational plans and project them across the time-span of the high school years.

Other studies on the validity of the CDI are promising, although few in number. In what might be considered an investigation of its criteron-related validity, the CDI was found to increase monotonically across the junior and senior high school years. That is, twelfth graders scored higher than tenth graders and tenth graders scored higher than eighth graders on all three CDI scales. This trend is consistent with a "linear" model of career development during adolescence (Super & Overstreet, 1960; Crites, 1965), but it is not sufficient to establish what the CDI measures. The construct validity of the CDI on this issue is equivocal: the Inventory related to some variables according to expectation, but not to others. In relationship to the CMI-Attitude Scale, for example, scales A and B are essentially uncorrelated, although they presumably assess career choice attitudes. The CMI-Attitude Scale correlates with scale C of the CDI, Information and Decision Making, as would be expected between Career Choice Attitudes and Career Choice Competencies, the two career choice process groups in Figure 14.3, but scale C does not correlate highly with scales A and B. Consequently, the CDI appears to measure some aspect of the cognitive dimension of career maturity, but which one and how strongly remains to be determined.

Readiness for Vocational Planning Scales (RVP)

Also inspired by the Indices of Vocational Maturity (IVM), the Readiness for Vocational Planning Scales (RVP) were developed by Gribbons and Lohnes (1968) to provide a more objective measure of career development variables during adolescence than the open-ended interviews used in the Career Pattern Study. The RVP scales are scored from a 40-minute semi-structured interview in which the subjects are asked 41 questions about their educational and vocational development. Illustrative questions are: "What curricula are there that you can take?" and "What occupations have you thought about as your possible life work?" Responses to these and other questions, with some inquiry by the interviewer for clarification and detail are scored on the following dimensions of career development: Factors in Curriculum Choice; Factors in Occupational Choice; Verbalized Strengths and Weaknesses; Accuracy of Self-Appraisal; Evidence of Self-Rating; Interests; Values; and, Independence of Choice. Some of these variables, such as Interests and Values, were taken from the IVM dimensions, and others, for example, Independence of Choice, were extrapolated from Super's and Ginzberg's theories of career development. The focus upon educational development was added by Gribbons and Lohnes.

Gathering data on a sample of 110 adolescents (56 boys, 54 girls), these investigators pursued a longitudinal study of career development along the school years from the eighth to the twelfth grades. They collected data at these two points in time as well as in the tenth grade. The principal findings were as follows (Crites, 1969):

Interrelationships of the RVP Scales. Studies of how highly correlated RVP variables tended to be were conducted in both the eighth and tenth grades. Contrary to expectation, it was found that they were largely independent of each other, the correlation coefficients being mostly in the .20's and .30's.

Differences between the RVP Scales at the Eighth and Tenth Grade Levels. The tenth grade was significantly higher on all the scales, indicating developmental change on these dimensions during mid-adolescence, but the differences were small. There was considerable overlap in the distributions of RVP scores. The largest "gains" were on Factors in Curriculum Choice and Factors in Occupational Choice.

Interrelationships of RVP Scales across Eighth, Tenth, and Twelfth Grades. Correlational analyses of the RVP scales revealed that the eighth grade variables were related to the twelfth grade scores, as were the tenth grade scales, but the eighth and tenth grade RVP were not appreciably correlated. Other studies of the RVP scales in relationship to a variety of demographic and psychometric variables indicated that they correlated with level of career choice but seldom with other aspects of decision making or personal background, for example, familial socio-economic status.

Of Gribbons and Lohnes' results, those which showed systematic increases in "readiness for vocational planning" across grades are most in accord with a career developmental model of adolescence. Given that this model predicts linear trends across the school years in the maturation of career choice behaviors, their results conform with expectation. (At least, those which trace changes in the *means* on the RVP scales.) The findings on scale intercorrelations, however, are more equivocal. For some reason that is not entirely clear, the RVP in the eighth and tenth grades, respectively, were correlated with the twelfth grade, but the eighth and tenth grades were essentially unrelated.

One explanation for this anomaly (Crites, 1969) is that differential career development resulted in shifts in the ranks on the RVP scales between the eighth and tenth grades which almost perfectly counterbalanced each other in their relationships to the twelfth grade scales. That is, it is possible that individual differences in *rate* of career maturation (Crites, 1961) between the earlier two grades produced sufficient gains and losses to attenuate their intercorrelation. An equally likely, if not more feasible, hypothesis is that the "linear" model of career development is *not* uniformly applicable (Crites, 1978). Some career choice behaviors may mature *nonlinearly* and consequently not fit the model for correlational analysis.

Career Maturity Inventory (CMI)

This measure of career maturity was conceived from the central concepts of career development theories, as proposed by Ginzberg, Super, and others. It was also based on some of the variables assessed by the Indices of Vocational Maturity. There are two parts to the Career Maturity Inventory (CMI), the Attitude Scale and the Competence Test. They were constructed to measure the Career Choice Process variables in the model of career maturity outlined in Figure 14.3.

The Attitude Scale originally consisted of 50 items which yielded only an overall total score for career attitude maturity. Subsequently, it has been expanded and standardized to provide sub-scales for these attitude clusters: Involvement in the Career Decision Making Process; Independence in the Career Decision Making Process; Orientation toward Career

Decision Making; Compromise in Career Decision Making; and, Decisiveness in Career Decision Making. The Competence Test complements the Attitude Scale with the following measures of the more cognitive dimensions of career decision-making: Self-Appraisal; Occupational Information; Goal Selection; Planning; and, Problem-Solving (Crites, 1978). Theoretically, career choice attitudes mediate the use of career choice competencies in making a choice. That is, if individuals have *both* mature attitudes and competencies, then they should make more realistic career choices than if their attitudes were immature.

The principle on which the CMI was constructed and standardized was that, to define and measure a *developmental* variable, each item in it should be related to time (Crites, 1965). Initially, it was assumed that the time function was monotonic as originally proposed by Super and Overstreet (1960). Subsequent conceptual (Goulet & Baltes, 1970) and empirical (Crites, 1978) work on the nature of development suggests that a monotonic (or linear) model for career maturity is too restrictive. Some career choice behaviors are manifest during only certain periods of adolescent career development and consequently they follow nonlinear curves rather than monotonic (or linear) ones. The implication for the CMI was to include not only items that were linear but also nonlinear, given that the latter was systematically (statistically) related to time. In other words, the time functions had to be more than capricious, chance functions. All the items in the CMI, therefore, bear a systematic relationship to time, which was defined in the standardization as school grade, because it yielded more highly differentiated curves (less overlap, steeper slope) than chronological age. The process of career maturation is much more closely related to the structure of the educational system than it is to organismic growth. What might be called *vocationalization* (Crites, 1958), much like socialization, takes place primarily in the schools.

Over 15 years of research on the CMI has established comprehensive psychometric characteristics for it as well as theoretical meaningfulness (Crites, 1974b; 1978). For a measure of a developmental variable, which is expected to change over time, the CMI has acceptable test-retest reliability, the coefficient for a year's interval being .71. When this is corrected for "maturational" variance by using path analysis (Heise, 1969), which is usually allocated to error, the reliability increases to .82, a magnitude comparable to ability and aptitude tests (Super & Crites, 1962). The validity of the CMI has been established in relationship to a variety of variables. It is related to other aspects of the career decisional process, such as decisiveness and realism in choice. It is correlated with level of career choice as well as educational achievement (Crites & Semler, 1967), and it fits into a model of general adjustment in adolescence which encompasses scholastic and vocational development from the beginning of junior high school to the end of senior high school. It is related to several different facets of personality, including locus of control, general adjustment status, temperament characteristics, and personal values (Crites, 1971; 1974). And, it is sensitive to a number of intervention modes, such as individual and group counseling, career educational programs, occupational orientation courses, and other systematic attempts to facilitate career development (Crites, 1978). Thus, it can be concluded that the CMI represents a global measure of many different dimensions of the model of career maturity (Figure 14.3).

STUDIES OF CAREER DEVELOPMENT

Longitudinal research on career developmental processes in adolescence is limited to three large-scale studies: Super's Career Pattern Study; Gribbons and Lohnes' Readiness for Vocational Planning investigation; and Crites' Career Maturity Project. There are numerous cross-sectional studies, including the original work of Ginzberg, but they do not control for cohort differences from one point in time to another (Schaie, 1965; 1970), although they eliminate the reactivity of repeated measurements. There is no substitute for the longitudinal design in studying career development, although ideally it would be combined with the collection of cross-sectional data in what has been called the "cross-sequential" model (Wohlwill, 1970). The Career Maturity Project comes closest to this paradigm, but it is incomplete, and the other studies are solely longitudinal.

Career Pattern Study

Super (1955) initiated this 20-year longitudinal study of 142 ninth grade boys in 1950–1951, principally because Ginzberg's data were cross-sectional and nonrepresentative (small samples from selected backgrounds in New York City). Super also wanted to test hypotheses stemming from Buehler's (1933) research, as well as the so-called "Matching Men and Jobs" orientation in vocational psychology (Crites, 1969). The design of the study was to follow the sample from the ninth to twelfth grade and then to collect data after graduation at ages 25 and 35. While the subjects were still in high school, they were administered extensive batteries of tests, including measures of aptitude, interest, and personality, and they were intensively interviewed about their vocational plans, school activities, extra-curricular pursuits, and family situation.

In addition, when they were in ninth grade their parents were also interviewed. Unfortunately, at the time of the initial testing and interviewing (ninth grade) the concept of vocational maturity had not been formulated (Super et al., 1957) and consequently there were no *direct* measures of it. Post hoc judges' ratings from interviews and derived measures from test scores were used to construct the Indices of Vocational Maturity. Preliminary analyses of them (Super & Overstreet, 1960; Super, 1961) have revealed some artifacts in their interrelationships, possibly because many of them are based on difference scores among interview ratings and test scores. But what results are reliable indicate a general Planning Orientation factor in the ninth grade. High school boys at this stage in their career development are primarily concerned with planning for their vocational futures.

Readings for Vocational Planning

The emphasis of the research by Gribbons and Lohnes (1968) has been largely methodological. As discussed previously, much of their effort was expended on devising the RVP scales to be scored from a semi-structured interview schedule. Their other major focus was on the application of multivariate and stochastic statistical methods in the analysis of their data. They have shown, for example, how a Markov chain analysis can be used in the study of contingencies among series of events in the course of career development (Gribbons, Halperin, & Lohnes, 1966).

The substantive import of their project, however, is less clear-cut. As a standardized measure of career development, the RVP scales are not only time-consuming to administer, but they have disappointing construct validity. The theoretical expectation was that they would be moderately positively intercorrelated, but they tend to be relatively independent of each other. In other words, rather than defining a *construct* of "readiness for vocational planning," they appear to assess fairly specific aspects of career development during the high school years. Moreover, these variables do not enter into relationships generally with the expected correlates of adolescent career development (such as family socioeconomic status). The meaningfulness of "readiness for vocational planning" as a dimension of career development during adolescence, therefore, is less than theory would have predicted, possibly because there seem to be some psychometric anomalies in the RVP scales.

Career Maturity Project

In contrast to the other longitudinal studies of career development, this project encompassed the collection of both cohort-sequential and time-sequential data. The design for the Career Maturity Project is shown in Figure 14.4, where it can be seen that initially the Career Maturity Inventory (CMI) was administered cross-sectionally to grades 5 through 12, and then was repeated each successive year until the fifth graders had graduated. The data generated by this procedure have made possible a variety of anal-

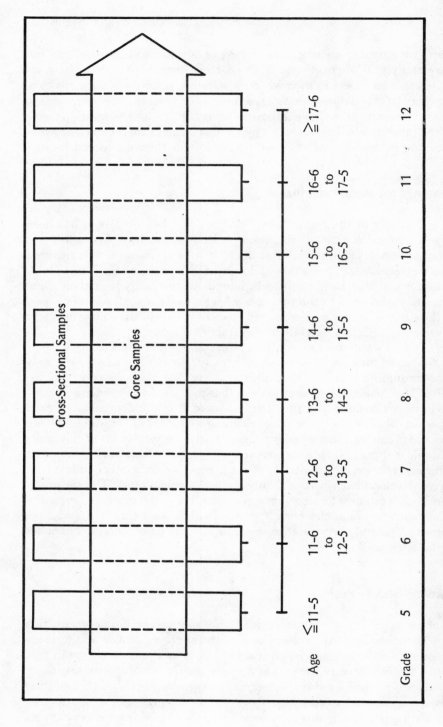

Figure 14.4 Sampling Design for the Career Maturity Project.

yses which cannot be conducted on cross-sectional or longitudinal data alone. Among these have been comparisons of the core and cross-sectional samples at each grade level to determine the effects of cohort differences and the reactivity of repeated measurements. Both of these are potential sources of confounding with developmental changes, although the results in this project indicated that they did not have a significant influence.

In other words, findings from the cross-sectional and longitudinal analyses yielded essentially the same conclusions about career maturation during adolescence, and these were not appreciably affected by the repeated measurements of the core sample. Moreover, it was found that a composite longitudinal gradient based upon one-year interlocking segments from the core sample produced the same trends as the complete longitudinal gradient (Meade, 1974). This is an exciting methodological breakthrough, since it means that longitudinal studies of career development can be based upon only two points-in-time instead of n occasions to span a given developmental period.

CAREER COUNSELING AND CAREER DEVELOPMENT

The process of career development, as it has been described, unfolds across the period of adolescence without intervention. In other words, when its course and nature are studied, no attempt is made to change it. It is investigated as it is. To change an adolescent's career development, other than what would occur through growth and maturation, it is necessary to systematically intervene with career counseling. Over the years, there have evolved five major approaches to career counseling, each of which has had distinctive features and advantages. The oldest of these, *trait-and-factor* career counseling, dates back to the early 20th century, when Frank Parsons (1909), a community worker in Boston, introduced vocational guidance with his book *Choosing a Vocation*. In it he identified what have become recognized as the basic variables in the career decision-making process: the individual who makes the choice; the occupation that is chosen; and the matching of the two for optimal job success and satisfation. With the aid of tests that have been constructed during the past 50 years and occupational information that has been accumulated, trait-and-factor career counselors assist their clients to make career decisions in a largely rational fashion. In contrast, *client-centered* career counseling, inspired by Carl Rogers (1942; 1951), focuses more on the emotional factors that affect career choice. Super (1951) refers to career choice as the implementation of a self-concept, and the client-centered career counselor assists the client in clarifying what this self-concept is and how it might be maximally translated into a compatible occupational role.

Still another type of career counseling is the *psychodynamic*. It adds the dimension of drives, motives, and needs to career choice and deals with how conflicts among them can be resolved in arriving at a decision which best fulfills what the individual wants through work. It traces the psychosexual development of adolescents to identify those stages which have been most salient in their career development (Bordin, Nachmann, & Segal, 1963). The psychodynamic career counselor helps the client resolve conflicts and remove fixations which impede growth toward career maturity. This emphasis upon stages and long-term processes in career choice has been incorporated most thoroughly and completely into the *developmental* approach to career counseling (Super, 1957). Here the career counselor looks first for problems the client may be having in the process of career decision making before moving on at all with career choice content. The Model of Career Maturity discussed previously in the chapter provides the conceptual framework for developmental career counseling. It encompasses the on-going life of the adolescent and the series of interrelated decisions which culminate in a career choice in early adulthood. It stands in sharp contrast to the *behavioral* method of career counseling, which is largely ahistorical, having been developed from the work of B. F. Skinner on operant conditioning (Krumboltz & Baker, 1973). This approach attempts to change the client's career choice behavior through differential reinforcement and punishment of career mature and immature responses. A client would be rewarded, for example, for initiating information-gathering behavior but not for continued indecision.

Each of these approaches to career counseling has its unique impact on the career development of the adolescent, as has been established in many years of research (Crites, 1974c). Each has necessary components to offer to effective career counseling, but none is sufficient for all clients. What has been needed is a comprehensive approach that incorporates the best of each approach and synthesizes their models and methods into a general theory of career counseling that can be applied to all clients whatever their characteristics or problems. Crites (1976) has suggested an outline for such an approach, which is currently being field tested in counseling centers and studied with a variety of criteria, including longitudinal measures of career maturity and adjustment. Preliminary findings indicate that the model and methods of *comprehensive* career counseling are more effective than any one approach. In addition, personal and social development is improved or enhanced.

SUMMARY

Career development is a major dimension of the adolescent period in life. It encompasses those years of career exploration, decision making, and preparation that are so critical for later success and satisfaction in the world-of-work. Increasingly, not only is "career" being viewed as a fulcrum of life, it is being recognized as a developmental phenomenon. No longer is career choice seen as a point in time event that occurs at the end of the high school years. It is rather a maturational process that spans at least a decade from late childhood to early adulthood. The construct of *career maturity* has become a central one in conceptualizing the series of interrelated decisions that culminate in a career choice. Developmentally oriented vocational psychologists have formulated theories of career development during adolescence, constructed measures of the principal variables in this process, and have launched long-term longitudinal studies of how and why adolescents make career decisions.

This chapter reviews the theoretical and empirical work on career development. Three theories are summarized. Ginzberg et al. (1951) have proposed that career development is a process that takes place over a period of approximately 10 years, from age 10 to age 20; that it is largely irreversible, in the sense that once a career decision is made it becomes increasingly difficult to change it; and, that the process culminates in a compromise between the needs of the individual and the realities of the world of work. Super (1957) has extended this theory to incorporate the self concept as a central organizing force in career development and hypothesizes that career choice is a process of implementing a self concept in a compatible occupational role. And, Crites (1965; 1974b) has formulated a Model of Career Maturity which distinguishes between career choice content and the career choice process in decision making and explicates the relationships between them over the course of adolescence. These theories are tested against the empirical research that has been conducted on them and it is concluded that their major propositions accurately describe and explain how and why adolescents make career choices as they do. Measures of career development have been constucted, principally the *Career Maturity Inventory*, and studies with them have established that adolescence is characterized by increasing maturation of attitudes toward making a career choice and by a developing planning orientation that contributes to realism of career choice.

Not all career choices are realistic, however, and adolescents often avail themselves of career counseling as a service to assist them in the decisional process. There are five major approaches to career counseling that have been evolved since the turn of the twentieth century: trait-and-factor, client-centered, psychodynamic, developmental, and behavioral. Each has a somewhat different emphasis, and consequently each is more effective with certain individuals than others (depending on their predispositions and preferences). Crites (1976) has proposed *comprehensive* career counseling applicable to many individuals and special groups. It draws upon the most effective models, methods, and materials of all and attempts to integrate them into an approach which can be adapted to a wide range of adolescent career problems.

SUGGESTIONS FOR FURTHER READING

BOROW, H. (Ed.). *Career guidance for a new age.* Boston: Houghton Mifflin, 1973.
CRITES, J. O. *Vocational psychology.* New York: McGraw-Hill, 1969.
HERR, E. L. (Ed.). *Vocational guidance and human development.* Boston: Houghton Mifflin, 1974.
MIHALKA, J. A. *Youth and work.* Columbus, Ohio: Merrill, 1974.
OSIPOW, S. H. *Theories of career development.* New York: Appleton-Century-Croft, 1973.

BIBLIOGRAPHY

BORDIN, E. S., NACHMANN, B., & SEGAL, S. J. An articulated framework for vocational development. *Journal of Counseling Psychology,* 1963, *10,* 107–116.
BUEHLER, C. *Der menschliche Lebenslauf als psychologisches Problem.* Leipzig: Hirzel, 1933.
BURT, C. The differentiation of intellectual ability. *British Journal of Educational Psychology,* 1954, *24,* 76–90.
CRITES, J. O. Vocational maturity and vocational adjustment. Paper presented at the meeting of the American Personnel and Guidance Association, St. Louis, March, 1958.
CRITES, J. O. A model for the measurement of vocational maturity. *Journal of Counseling Psychology,* 1961, *8,* 255–259.
CRITES, J. O. Measurement of vocational maturity in adolescence: I. Attitude Test of the Vocational Development Inventory. *Psychological Monographs,* 1965, *79,* (2, Whole No. 595).
CRITES, J. O. *Vocational psychology.* New York: McGraw-Hill, 1969.
CRITES, J. O. *The maturity of vocational attitudes in adolescence.* Washington, D.C.: American Personnel and Guidance Association, 1971.
CRITES, J. O. The Career Maturity Inventory. In D. E. Super (Ed.), *Measuring vocational maturity for counseling and evaluation.* Washington, D.C.: National Vocational Guidance Association, 1974. (a)
CRITES, J. O. Career developmental processes: A model of vocational maturity. In E. L. Herr (Ed.), *Vocational guidance and human development.* Boston: Houghton Mifflin, 1974. (b)
CRITES, J. O. Career counseling: A review of major approaches. *The Counseling Psychologist,* 1974, *4,* 3–23. (c)
CRITES, J. O. Career counseling: A comprehensive approach. *The Counseling Psychologist,* 1976, *6,* 3–24.
CRITES, J. O. *Theory and research handbook for the Career Maturity Inventory.* Monterey, Calif.: CTB/McGraw-Hill, 1978.

CRITES, J. O., & SEMLER, I. J. Adjustment, educational achievement and vocational maturity as dimensions of development in adolescence. *Journal of Counseling Psychology,* 1967, *14,* 489–496.

FORREST, D. J., & THOMPSON, A. S. The Career Development Inventory. In D. E. Super (Ed.), *Measuring vocational maturity for counseling and evaluation.* Washington, D.C.: National Vocational Guidance Association, 1974.

GARRETT, H. E. A developmental theory of intelligence. *American Psychologist,* 1946, *1,* 372–378.

GINZBERG, E. Toward a theory of occupational choice: A restatement. *Vocational Guidance Quarterly,* 1972, *20,* 169–176.

GINZBERG, E., GINSBURG, S. W., AXELRAD, S., & HERMA, J. L. *Occuptaional choice.* New York: Columbia University Press, 1951.

GOULET, L. R., & BALTES, P. B. (Eds.). *Life-span developmental psychology.* New York: Academic Press, 1970.

GRIBBONS, W. D., HALPERIN, S., & LOHNES, P. R. Applications of stochastic models in research on career development. *Journal of Counseling Psychology,* 1966, *13,* 403–408.

GRIBBONS, W. D., & LOHNES, P. R. *Emerging careers.* New York: Teachers College Press, 1968.

HEISE, D. R. Separating reliability and stability in test-retest correlation. *American Sociological Review,* 1969, *34,* 93–101.

KRUMBOLTZ, J. D., & BAKER, R. D. Behavioral counseling for vocational decision. In H. Borow (Ed.), *Career guidance for a new age.* Boston: Houghton Mifflin, 1973.

LOCASCIO, R. Delayed and impaired vocational development: A neglected aspect of vocational development theory. *Personnel and Guidance Journal,* 1964, *42,* 885–887.

MEADE, C. The composite longitudinal gradient in career maturity research. Unpublished paper, University of Maryland, College Park, Maryland, 1974.

PARSONS, F. *Choosing a vocation.* Boston: Houghton Mifflin, 1909.

ROGERS, C. R. *Counseling and psychotherapy.* Boston: Houghton Mifflin, 1942.

ROGERS, C. R. *Client centered therapy.* Boston: Houghton Mifflin, 1951.

SCHAIE, K. W. A general model for the study of developmental problems. *Psychological Bulletin,* 1965, *64,* 92–107.

SCHAIE, K. W. A reinterpretation of age related changes in cognitive structure and functioning. In L. R. Goulet and P. B. Baltes (Eds.), *Life-span developmental psychology.* New York: Academic Press, 1970.

SUPER, D. E. Vocational adjustment: Implementing a self-concept. *Occupations,* 1951, *30,* 88–92.

SUPER, D. E. A theory of vocational development. *American Psychologist,* 1953, *8,* 185–190.

SUPER, D. E. The dimensions and measurement of vocational maturity. *Teachers College Record,* 1955, *57,* 151–163.

SUPER, D. E. *The psychology of careers.* New York: Harper & Row, 1957.

SUPER, D. E. Consistency and wisdom of vocational preference as indices of vocational maturity in ninth grade. *Journal of Educational Psychology,* 1961, *52,* 35–43.

Super, D. E., Crites, J. O., Hummel, R. C., Moser, H. P., Overstreet, P. L., & Warnath, C. F. *Vocational development: A framework for research.* New York: Teachers College Bureau of Publications, 1957.

Super, D. E., & Crites, J. O. *Appraising vocational fitness* (Rev. ed.). New York: Harper & Row, 1962.

Super, D. E., & Overstreet, P. L. *The vocational maturity of ninth grade boys.* New York: Teachers College Bureau of Publications, 1960.

Super, D. E., Starishevsky, R., Matlin, N., & Jordaan, J. P. *Career development: Self-concept theory.* Princeton, N.J.: College Entrance Examination Board, 1963.

Tiedeman, D. V., & O'Hara, R. P. *Career development: Choice and adjustment.* Princeton, N.J.: College Entrance Examination Board, 1963.

Vernon, P. E. *The structure of human abilities.* London: Metheun, 1950.

Wohlwill, J. F. Methodology and research strategy in the study of developmental change. In L. R. Goulet & P. B. Baltes (Eds.), *Life-span developmental psychology.* New York: Academic Press, 1970.

15

IN CONCLUSION

James F. Adams

In drawing this volume to a close, it is hoped that you have gained a better *understanding* of adolescence—after all, that is what the book has been all about. The concluding chapter has been written to focus on some of the issues that may have slipped by you as you have been reading. You will find little or no new information on the following pages. The intent of this chapter is to stimulate you in your thinking and discussions, and perhaps to send you in search of information that will help to resolve the questions and issues raised.

If you have read the book carefully, at this point you may have some confusion about exactly what we mean by the term *adolescence*. In the first chapter I defined adolescence as *a holding period in which education, maturation, and waiting to assume an adult role are the major tasks to be faced.* I did not tie it into an age span, for example, from 12 to 20. Rather, I tried to point out that adolescence, as a meaningful concept, is best considered within the broad framework of the total development of the individual. When the child begins to feel less need for the security of familial supervision and protection, at the time when his or her physiological and hormonal development begins to approximate adult maturity, and lastly, at the time when the child's psychological maturity moves him or her in the direction of becoming responsible to society, adolescence has begun.

If we define reaching maturity as becoming a contributing, relatively self-sufficient member of society, it should be apparent that some individuals never grow out of adolescence while others become adults at an early age. The focus of defining adolescence, from my viewpoint, places great emphasis on the psychological development of the individual. Another way of saying the same thing is that adolescence can be considered a social phenomenon, which, because of the influence of society, may and does vary from one culture (or subculture) to another.

There is really no basic conflict in the definitions of adolescence presented by any of the authors within this book. Hamachek gives a good short historical review of the concept and goes on to consider adolescence from the viewpoint of Havighurst's development tasks with a focus on how adolescents come to grips with discovering who they are. Eichorn is concerned more with the biological and hormonal development, which is most certainly a part of adolescence. In fact, these biological and hormonal changes at the onset of adolescence are the only objective and directly measurable signposts that we have with respect to this period. Psychological, sociological, and cultural influences are so fantastically complex in their interaction with the individual that we are forced to conclude that they contribute little to defining just when a person begins or terminates adolescence. For example, in reading Crites' chapter on career development, would you agree that when an individual assumes a responsible work role that he has reached adult status? Think about it. Just what is an adult? If you wish to go through an interesting exercise, ferret out the various definitions (implicit or explicit) of adolescence within the chapters of this book. Then examine a few other textbooks on adolescence. See if you can come up with a better definition than you have found within these pages.

Now, let us take a look a the specific chapters within this book. What conclusions can we draw and what issues do we need to consider further?

UNDERSTANDING ADOLESCENTS

Understanding Adolescence is now in its fourth edition. In the first edition, I focused on the need for greater involvement of youth within the decision-making institutions of our society. In the second and third editions, I continued the same theme but have added the fast-approaching threat of ecological disaster. I have been rather amazed over the number of letters I have received from individuals who have read the earlier editions, who have agreed with the major theses, but who have said, "Even though I agree with you in principle, society has always had problems and it has always solved its problems." Apparently it is inconceivable to many that a child who is born today may not die of old age.

Apparently it is inconceivable to many that the population, pollution, exhaustion of the world's physical resources, and so on, have reached the point where man's survival is in question. Of course, the one major problem the world has not begun to solve is over-population, and this raises some interesting and crucial issues. What are the psychological and sociological pressures that currently encourage individuals to have children? If you were to decide not to have children, what would your family and friends say? What organizations have been formed which focus on these issues? Would you be in favor of a tax structure that would reward people for not having children and penalize those who do have children? What should be the role of the United States in world population considerations? Should food be sent to starving nations (assuming we still have food to send) to continue the process of population growth? These, and many similar such issues, are rapidly moving into the arena of public debate. Where do you stand?

I next discussed the age of menarche with the hypothesis that the earlier age which has developed over the last century can be attributed to the stresses which have been developed via the industrial revolution. Is it also possible that the pressures of a growing population (crowding) have contributed to these stresses? Can you think of other factors that might be involved in this phenomenon of earlier menarche?

The other concern that I discuss in the first chapter is the need to involve youth at a much earlier age in the institutions of our country. I am concerned with what appears to be an increasing detachment of youth from the mainstream of society. In the first two editions of this book there was a chapter on the activism of youth. It was not included in the third and in this edition because the activism of the sixties and early seventies seems largely to have disappeared. The basis for my concern is not so much that wisdom will be found in greater quantities within the youth culture, but that youth present the leadership potential of the future. If we involve young people in societal decision making at an early age, we will have a much greater pool of talent from which to draw for political, industrial, and educational leadership. Would you agree that youth are becoming more detached from society and its institutions? What suggestions do you have for the greater involvement of young people and how would you implement these suggestions?

THEORIES OF ADOLESCENCE

Gallatin considers at some length the evidence for adolescence being a period of *storm* and *stress*. She concludes, quite correctly, that there are wide differences, from culture to culture, on how stormful or stressful adolescence may be, and that even within a given culture there are wide individual variations. As a reader of her chapter, it may be of some interest for you to reflect back on this period within your own life. If you were to write an autobiographical sketch, would it reveal a period of unusual stress?

About 40 years ago, a 13-year-old girl went through what she considered to be a most difficult period with her mother. She decided that she would sit down and write a set of rules so that when she became a mother, she would raise her daughter differently.

Proper Etiquette for Mothers' Relationships
with Their (Teenage) Daughters

Never suggest that they are tired, cranky, hot or cold. Let them tell you of their discomfort themselves.

Never interrupt them when they are telling stories, etc., no matter how important you think it is unless it is simply a *dire necessity*. Do something else until the tale is finished.

Show *absolutely* no partiality to another brother or sister, especially in the matter of running errands. Have it understood that they are taking turns.

No matter how angry or impatient, or surprised you are, never scream, cry, yell, or talk loudly. They'll admire if you keep a cool, matter-of-fact, businesslike manner. It will always do more for results anyway than shouting when nervous. Keep your voice in control.

Don't have it understood as a hard and fast rule, but once in a while plan surprises for your daughter, to remind her that you are constantly thinking of her pleasures, but not hers only. Plan a party, buy a new dress, plan a good movie, and have her take her girlfriend occasionally.

Don't force her confidence, and when she does tell you surprising things, don't make a side show out of it; just answer in a matter-of-fact tone, and she'll tell you more. They don't like emotional outbursts.

It's a good idea to have something nice for her handy, so when she's cross, you just give it to her quietly, and she'll be so ashamed, she'll treat you ten times better. It works better than scolding and sometimes pleadings. Always have an even tone of voice. Don't get emotional and excited. She's liable to be more comrady if you are like this, because she's used to that kind of disposition in her other friends.

Praise her for good work as often as it is rightly due. Don't turn her head though.

Above all things, don't keep referring to "that awful teen age." It makes them self-conscious and they won't confide in you so much for fear you'll say that. Even though you and your friends say it only in fun, it will usually do more harm than good.

Don't contradict your daughter sharply to her face just for something to say. A good example is when your daughter says, "I need a new basketball. My other one is shot to pieces." And you say, "Oh, I don't think it is!" (When you really haven't even looked at it.) If you're trying to save money, tell her so; don't contradict like you know all about it when you don't.

Try to be understanding. When your daughter gets hysterical over a detail, don't just say, "Oh you'll be all right soon." To her, it is a big matter, and you ought to treat it as such. Try to reason it out together and give her your comfort and attention. She will appreciate it more than you know!

Don't govern her too hard; she likes freedom and plenty of it. Let her choose what dress she'll wear, continually, unless it is really absurd. She likes to fly her own wings. Let her make decisions occasionally. Take her into the family secrets, and she'll feel important. She won't tell if you caution her not to. It's really good experience in keeping secrets, and makes her feel you can trust her.

When your daughter's complexion is bad, try to make helpful suggestions, but *don't keep referring to this ailment very often.* It will be a source of friction.

When your daughter's "monthly" comes along, it *isn't* necessary to talk about it *at all* unless she brings the subject up herself. Of course, warn her once that you should be notified at once if she is irregular.

When discussing a serious question (such as morals) with your daughter—no matter how badly you feel she is wrong—*do not get heavy* over your point. Saying "you break my heart" and crying is very annoying no matter how much she loves you.

BE YOUNG IN ACTIONS! BE GAY around her! Act young and you'll always be pals.

MOTTO TO FOLLOW: "Being tired is suicide to HAPPY family relations." Take a day off if you feel this way—go and do something exciting—and rest. Never say "I'm so tired!" if you want to appear young.

When your daughter goes on a short trip (week-end) welcome her back with cheer and a "special supper" for her. Make her feel that you're *especially* happy to have her back. See that you and family are dressed up and neat.

Be *very careful* about imposing yourself on daughter's plans. She likes to feel a certain amount of independence! For instance, if she plans on a picnic with friends, don't invite yourself along. Be backward in this respect. If she really wants you, she'll invite you; of course, in this way you may feel free to go.

A *very important fact* to bear in mind is that a girl doesn't relish her mother's talking of her "personal" and intimate matters within her father's hearing when she is around. If it must be done, for goodness' sake don't let her know about it. *This is extremely important.*

Other than updating this young girl's vocabulary into the vernacular of today, has there been much change in the concerns of girls with their mothers? You might give this list of "rules" to several girls of the same age and get their response; or, perhaps, see if you can generate a similar list for boys. Also, is there a difference in the problems that youth have with their fathers? What percentage of young people go through this period with no problems of this sort with either parent?

In this chapter on theories, after evaluating a number of theorists, Gallatin concludes that Erikson's theory of adolescent development has the most merit. Would you agree? Assuming that you do agree and acknowledging the fact that Erikson focuses primarily on the development of the male, what limitations does this place on understanding the development of the female? Would you predict that, in the absence of sex role training, one theory will adequately cover both males and females? Or, are there some inherent sexual differences that might necessitate the development of a separate developmental theory for females?

BIOLOGICAL DEVELOPMENT

There is much in this chapter, by Eichorn, that the interested reader may wish to pursue further. However, let me focus on several topics and raise some questions for discussion and further consideration. Eichorn gives a rather extensive treatment to the sexual maturation of the adolescent. This raises a rather interesting question of the degree to which the maturational process dictates adult sexual behavior.

What evidence can you find for considering sexuality, or the development of sexuality, within the sphere of its being a learning process (or a cortical function)? We know, for example, that rats will mount and copulate in the absence of prior learning when the female is in her estral period. Imagine, if you will, a human male and female who have been raised in complete isolation of each other and society and, at maturity, are brought together on an uninhabited desert island. If you speculate on the probabilities of copulation taking place, you are facing the issue of whether human sexuality will be determined by hormonal and physiological development versus whether learning is necessary for human sexuality. Is the sexual act instinctive in human beings as it is in most of the lower animals? For the purposes of answering this question, define an *instinct* as a relatively complex pattern of behavior that occurs in all members of a given species in the absence of prior learning. Is there such a thing as instinctive behavior in humans?

Lastly, you will remember that in the first chapter, I discussed the age of menarche in some detail. I presented a stimulation-stress factor hypothesis to account for a number of research findings. If this hypothesis is true, where does the body mediate stress? Eichorn presents you with enough information that you should be able to make some rather reasonable guesses in answer to this question.

PSYCHOLOGY AND DEVELOPMENT OF THE ADOLESCENT SELF

Hamachek defines the *self* as "that part of each of us that we are aware of. It is the sum total of all that a person can consciously call his." Using this definition as well as Hamachek's discussion of the self, how would you describe *your* self? What is there in your description that makes you different from your friends? Have a close friend describe you in writing on the same dimensions that you have used to describe yourself. Compare your description. Are they reasonably similar or are there marked discrepancies? If there are discrepancies, how would you explain them?

As you look back on your life, who has been most influential on your self development: parents, friends, admired adults? While your self is, by and large, a stable concept, there is evidence that change is possible. Are there aspects of your self that you would like to change or are you fairly satisfied with your development? You might wish to survey others of your age and see how they feel about this question. Is there any similarity in terms of desired directions of change? What resources do you have within your community or institution for personal growth?

Seven different parenting styles are discussed and defined in this chapter. Which of these styles would you predict as being the most common within our society (or your culture or subculture)? Conducting a survey to check out your hypothesis could be a very interesting task.

If you were to describe your attitudes toward the best parental emotional and disciplinary climate within which to raise children, what would they involve? Prepare a list and see what experimental support you can find for your list. Consider also that parents are people with their own needs and stresses. Does your optimum environment for raising children take this into consideration?

PERSONALITY DEVELOPMENT

Grotevant states ". . . the adolescent is virtually forced to reevaluate and reorganize the skills, abilities, and identifications of childhood into a new coherent framework or structure, called *identity*." How does, if it does, this reevaluation and reorganization differ from what Hamachek describes in the development of the adolescent *self?* An interesting exercise would be for you to compare and contrast chapters 4 and 5 for similarities and differences.

In the last part of this chapter, the author considers the topic of abnormal behavior. This, of course, is closely tied to the concept of *adjustment* and *maladjustment*. The concept of adjustment is a thought-provoking concept, as it implies that one is adjusted to something, to someone, or to a society as a whole. Actually, we must credit the concept of adjustment to biology. The term comes from "adaptation," which was basic to Darwinian theory. Darwin's theory was that those organisms that could adapt were those that survived; those that could not, perished.

In many respects it is unfortunate that the term adjustment has this etiological connotation. It has meant, to many, that if one does not adapt himself to the demands or mores of society, he is maladjusted. It does not take into consideration that certain types of adjustment for humans may, in fact, be disastrous. Consider the results brought about by those Germans who adjusted themselves to the wishes of Hitler. Six million Jews were massacred. Or consider those organizations, institutions, or nations that have taken a position against birth control. It is impossible to estimate the millions of individuals who have and will be condemned to starvation. The process of adaptation or adjustment to society may or may not facilitate personal adjustment.

Basic to the concept of adjustment, from the viewpoint of mental health, is the necessity for individuals to come to grips with themselves. Such words as self-awareness, self-identity, self-acceptance, and self-regard all focus on self-adjustment. Learning to know one's self has always been a difficult task. However, this is where adjustment begins. The second stage of adjustment turns one outwardly toward one's fellow human beings. Respect for the rights and personal integrity of others is found in this stage of adjustment. In a healthy society, the final stage of adjustment would be reached by becoming a contributing member of that society. At this point we should recognize that we do not have an overly healthy society in many respects. There are things that need to be changed if that society is to survive. What is there in society that you would have difficulty in adjusting to? You may wish to prepare a list and compare it with those of your friends. To what degree do the items on your list reflect societal problems that show individual maladjustment in a collective sense?

COGNITIVE DEVELOPMENT IN ADOLESCENCE

Psychological interest in cognitive development has increased tremendously over the last 25 years—largely as the result of the stimulus provided by the research of Jean Piaget. Gallagher and Mansfield report on the type of research that has been conducted on cognitive development and contrast the types of thinking found at childhood and adolescence.

In several studies of adolescent thought, it has been reported that males are superior to females in formal reasoning. Others have found differences in the same direction in solving conservation of volume tasks. Gallagher and Mansfield suggest that male superiority in formal reasoning may be a result of known sex differences on the variable of field dependence-independence. Piaget has interpreted these types of differences in terms of social environment. What is there in our social environment that might produce these sex differences? In chapter 7, examine Figure 7.4 in which testing results from four cultural groups are examined. Can you explain these results in terms of the social environment, or are there other possible explanations?

Acceptance of lack of closure is considered to be an element in the thinking of creative individuals. Does it disturb you for me to ask questions where there is insufficient evidence for you to form an opinion? Do two contradictory opinions bother you because you don't know which one to believe? If so, you have difficulty with lack of closure. What is there in our environment (if that is where it comes from) that makes individuals uncomfortable if they do not have sufficient facts to obtain closure in their thinking? Can you think of child rearing practices or societal influences which discourage individuals from being comfortable with lack of closure? I certainly can but I think I'll leave you with lack of closure and let you think through these questions yourself.

INDIVIDUAL DIFFERENCES IN INTELLIGENCE

Nichols concludes that individual differences among adolescents are caused in part by differences in native endowment, in part by family and peer influences, and in part by differences in educational opportunities. The available evidence suggests that, in the United States, inherited differences are the most important and educational differences are the least important in bringing about individual differences in intelligence. All measures of intelligence and academic achievement are tied in to the use of test scores. What limitations are there in tying in the concept of intelligence to psychological testing? Can you think of aspects of intelligent behavior that so-called intelligence tests do not measure? Also, when academic achievement is being assessed, can you think of types of learning that are not measured by traditional methods? To what degree would you agree with the following statements: The term *intelligence test* is a misnomer. A more appropriate label would be *test of academic aptitude*.

The existence of widespread abuse and misuse of standardized testing in assessing individuals has been and continues to be a major concern of educators, psychologists, and the public.[1] All too often, testing has been used to make odious comparisons rather than to help the individual to grow and develop. However, short of developing the instrumentation and sophistication necessary to measure individual differences *within* the organism, properly chosen and used tests are the most objective way we have of collecting and imparting information in many areas. These tests have also made substantial contributions to our knowledge of individual and group differences. Can you enumerate some of these contributions? Do you believe, as do some individuals, that the abuse and misuse of testing are sufficient justification to do away with testing entirely? If so, what types of information would you suggest be used in the place of standardized tests?

If you are interested in this topic of individual differences, you may wish to consider cultural, racial, or sex differences in such areas as music, sports, physical characteristics, and disease. What evidence can you find and can you draw any conclusions as to whether such differences are produced by heredity or environment?

MORAL DEVELOPMENT AND MORAL BEHAVIOR

Moral development is a particularly fascinating topic in the years that have followed the throes of Watergate, a presidential resignation, self-examination of foreign policies that have been disastrous in their impact, and legislation to mandate the morals of politicians. Perhaps, never before in our nation's history has there been such an intensive examination of national and personal morality within such a short span of time. Today we are living in a period where public scrutiny has forced politicians to be

---

[1] An excellent resource for your consideration in this area is: Samuda, R. J. *Psychological testing of American minorities: Issues and consequences.* New York: Dodd, Mead & Co., 1975.

more accountable for their behavior. Congressmen who never would have been prosecuted in the pre-Watergate era have found themselves in Federal Courts. A conservative backlash has descended upon our country.

Windmiller states that most individuals stabilize at Stage 4 in moral behavior (which supports conformity to rule, loyalty to authority, and doing what "is right" as defined by society at large). What are the conflicts you can foresee or document between leaders who may be at Stage 5 or 6 and a populace that is at Stage 4? Also, what are the probabilities that we will have leadership at these higher stages when some investigators estimate that only 4% of the population ever reach Stage 6? Windmiller raises many additional questions for discussion within her chapter, so I shall not continue the topic further here. Most certainly, the issue of morality is one that none of us can avoid in our everyday living, and, as Windmiller has pointed out, most of the political questions being asked *are* moral questions.

SEX ROLE DEVELOPMENT AND THE ADOLESCENT

In this chapter, Stein and Welch have examined the literature on sex-role development with its implications for changes in sex-role definitions in American society. During preschool years, children in our culture learn many, if not most, of the culturally defined attitudes toward what is considered to be feminine or masculine. By the time adolescence is reached, sex-role definitions are well implanted within the self-concept and life style of the individual. The women's movement has highlighted the problems of our society that have been caused by inflexible sex role definitions for women (and men). As a result, major revolutions in thinking and life-styles are occurring.

Questioning sex-role definitions raises a number of very interesting questions about the current value of one of the basic structures of American society—the family. How would you expect a redefinition of sex roles to influence the marital adjustment of individuals? As the authors ask, "Would people be better off if individuals were permitted ... to develop without regard to gender?" What pressures to change are currently exerted on individuals who are satisfied with their sex role status?

Little or no attention has been focused by the women's movement on the question of whether there are any innate (genetic) differences between the sexes on such dimensions as personality, aptitudes, etc. Can you find any evidence to support the position that there are or are not innate differences? What implications would such biological predispositions have for the sex role changes and pressures currently being discussed within our society?

ADOLESCENT SEXUALITY

Human sexuality, as a major area of concern to most individuals, is discussed with far more openness today than in the past. Yet, in looking through what has been published, I must admit that very little has been written that is controversial in nature. Presentations on the topic are either a factual narrative of what has been found in studying a given population, a statement of objective facts which describe the development of the human body, or, a statement of opinion which is usually based on personal experiences (and extremely short on "hard" evidence).

Wagner has written a chapter that is quite unusual on two counts. First, she has conducted a very thorough review of the limited research that has examined adolescent sexuality. Secondly, she has had the courage to express her opinions knowing that they would be received with mixed reactions. In fact, I'm not even sure that I agree with some of her conclusions. For example, she believes that sexual education should be conducted in the home. Would you agree? It seems to me that parents have been notoriously poor sex educators (of course, I have to admit that our other social institutions haven't done much better). I really wonder if it is possible to educate parents (or future parents) to help their children in an area that, in all probability, will continue to be emotionally charged. What do you think?

As I write this, the School Board of the Philadelphia Public Schools is debating whether birth control information should be made a part of the curriculum (with permission of a student's parents and as an elective course). What's your prediction of the outcome of this debate? Is the fact that the issue is being debated an encouraging sign? One of the opponents to having birth control information in the schools has expressed his opinion that this will increase premarital sexual experimentation. Is there evidence to the contrary?

My guess is that this chapter will stimulate a great deal of discussion between you and your friends and that it will be a highly charged emotional discussion. If I am right, why am I right?

EDUCATIONAL INSTITUTIONS AND YOUTH

From time to time, discussions develop as to what institution is responsible for what segment of a child's education. The schools of today, as contrasted with those of 50 years ago, are performing many functions that were once considered the responsibility of the family, the church, or society in general. Construct a list of the learning experiences to which you were exposed during your elementary and secondary years of schooling that would *not* be considered to be strictly academic in nature. How many of these experiences would you agree should be relegated to agencies or institutions other than the schools? Is the fact that a child's home does not provide certain necessary learning experiences sufficient justification for the school to assume the responsibility? Is there any limit to the school's responsibility for the learning experiences it provides for youth? Can it do all things well?

Let me give you an example. I filled out a questionnaire which was sent to me by a counselor educator in California. She asked whether or not I thought there should be an educational unit within the schools covering the effects of death and bereavement. I don't believe that anyone would argue that this is an unimportant topic for us all at some point in our lives. The question is, is this one more responsibility that the schools should assume? As a project, you might take your list of learning experiences (non-academic) and have a group of individuals rank them (say, on a five point scale from "very unimportant" to "very important"). Do you find that there is widespread agreement?

SUBCULTURES OF ADOLESCENTS IN THE UNITED STATES

"A *culture* is a set of common and standard behaviors and beliefs shared by a group of people and taught by them to their children." Havighurst has pointed out that different nations have different cultures and that within any culture there are also a number of subcultures. To what cultures or subcultures have you been exposed? To what degree do you find these concepts useful in analyzing the structure of the society of which you are a member?

In examining the universal or quasi-universal aspects of adolescent development, Havighurst has identified seven features that pertain to adolescence: biological development, sex-role differentiation, assumption of adult roles under societal guidance, establishing emotional independence of parents and other adults, acquisition of an ideology, achievement of an identity, and participation in an adolescent peer culture. Eliminating biological development, which is common to all cultures, take one of the other features of development and consider it in the light of the cultures or subcultures with which you are familiar. For example, what value is placed on establishing independence from one's parents and other adults within a Catholic, Jewish, or Protestant religious subculture? Of course, each of these religions can be broken down into smaller subculture units, which will make your task even more complex. Another suggestion for thought is to consider the "rules" for mother-daughter relationships written by the 13-year-old girl. What evidences of the seven aspects of adolescent development do you find?

Havighurst discusses a number of adolescent subcultures. Are there different factors which have produced these groups? Do you think that any of these factors are beginning to disappear from our society and, if so, would you predict that the importance of the related subculture would also disappear? As an example, we know that there is widespread economic discrimination for certain minority groups. Assume that this discrimination disappears. What would you predict would happen to the adolescent subculture of that group?

PSYCHOLOGICAL PERSPECTIVES ON DRUGS AND YOUTH

There is widespread drug usage in our society. In 1972 alone, there were 293,000 arrests for marijuana-related charges. By 1973, this had increased to 420,000. The total number of Americans who are using marijuana is difficult to estimate, but if the more than 50% of college students who have used it is any indication, users must have exceeded several million. When we turn to those who use alcohol, which is clearly more incapacitating, we find that some 95 million Americans are consumers, with the rate rising rapidly in the younger age groups. Adding to this those who use pills of various varieties and those who smoke, it is readily apparent that we have become a nation with a sizable addiction to drugs.

Why do you think this has occurred? Is it economic affluence, increased leisure time, the pressures of an industrialized nation, the divorcement of individuals from society, the acceleration in our life-styles, the failure of religion to meet a person's needs, boredom, crowding, or a combination of some of these factors? It is certainly clear that the abuse or misuse of drugs is most debilitating to the human body; yet, we continue.

The authors of this chapter are of the opinion that attempting to control drug abuse through law enforcement is futile and has probably increased the use of drugs. Would you agree? Their solution is to attempt to educate youth to the harmful effects of many drugs. Would you predict that a massive effort in this area would be effective? Is it equally possible that attempting to change some of the basic directions of society would help? If so, in what directions would you suggest change?

CAREER DEVELOPMENT

It is estimated that 14% of the jobs currently in the labor force are classified as professional or technical. Yet, 62% of high school senior boys and 52% of the girls express occupational preferences within these categories. Our nation has never faced the problem of occupational supply and demand. For example, in my university there was one opening for an assistant professor of history. Over 1,000 applications were received for this position! In certain areas of public school teaching, such as English, the same oversupply of trained personnel exists.

Why do youth strive for a college education? Fifty-one percent reply, "To secure vocational or professional training." The alternative response showing the next highest frequency is, "To develop my mind and my intellectual abilities." If we concentrate on the "vocational" reasoning for attending college for a moment, what responsibility do our universities have for graduating individuals who are unemployable in their chosen professions? As no college student completely pays for his or her education (every student is subsidized from public or private resources), can we justify the waste of the taxpayer's dollar to train an unemployable individual? What are the alternatives? What are the rights of individuals to choose a field even though they are aware of the employment difficulties?

Over a number of years, the U.S. Office of Education has supported career education and encouraged schools (from kindergarten through the adult years) to integrate the *world of work* theme into the classroom. Can you suggest ways in which education can help young people to make more realistic career plans in terms of both their needs and the needs of society? Should every young person who has the ability to go to college be encouraged to plan in that direction? Are there viable alternatives?

SUMMARY

In this last chapter, I have attempted to raise certain issues to stimulate the reader's thinking. Certainly many other issues in *Understanding Adolescence* deserve the same attention, and the topics I have raised may not be the questions you would have asked had you written this concluding chapter. I do hope that the pages of this book have stimulated and furthered your interest and desire to learn more about adolescence and the society within which the adolescent lives. If you are now more understanding of adolescents than you were when you began to read and discuss the issues in the book, then the goals of the editor and the chapter authors have been met.

AUTHOR INDEX

Abraham, D., 100
Abraham, S., 72
Abramowitz, C. A., 248
Abramowitch, S. I., 248
Achenbach, T. M., 111
Adams, J. F., 2n., 14, 20
Adelson, J., 31, 43, 51, 88, 96, 129, 237, 238, 242, 244
Adler, M., 245
Alberti, G., 63
Alcalde, E., 183
Aldridge, L., 355
Allen, J., 116
Alp, H., 8
Alston, J. P., 263
Altland, R., 90
Ames, L. B., 119
Amira, S., 248
Ammon, P., 224
Anastasi, A., 195
Anderson, R. B., 190
Anthony, D., 87
Anthony, E. J., 9, 10
Ardon, M. S., 270, 277
Aries, P., 80
Armbruster, F., 196
Aronson, V., 100
Astin, A. W., 189
Attallah, N. L., 6
Ausubel, D. P., 95
Averch, H. A., 189
Axelrad, S., 119, 397, 407, 417

Bachman, G. G., 313
Bachman, J., 85, 311, 319, 370, 381
Bailey, M. M., 232, 242, 243, 246, 254
Bajema, C., 196, 199
Baker, R. D., 416
Baldridge, J. V., 313, 319
Baltes, P. B., 124, 411
Bandura, A., 31, 43, 45, 47, 210
Barclay, A., 92
Barker, R. G., 268, 326

Barker, W. B., 192
Bass, M., 378
Bath, J. A., 94
Baumrind, D., 91, 92
Bayley, N., 101, 268
Beach, F. A., 62
Becker, W. C., 91, 210
Bell, R. Q., 117
Bell, R. R., 280, 297
Belmont, L., 188
Bem, S. L., 234, 253, 254, 323
Bendix, R., 339
Benedict, R., 42
Bennett, W. H., 280
Bereiter, C., 198, 199
Berg, L., 319
Berger, P. A., 126, 127
Berger, S. E., 245
Bernatova, L., 6
Berscheid, E., 100
Bertrand, A. L., 309
Bertrand, J., 63
Berzino, J. I., 234
Bettelheim, B., 186
Bierce, A., 15
Biller, H. B., 93, 243
Binet, A., 166, 167, 322
Birch, H. G., 183
Birk, J. M., 248
Bissell, J. S., 190
Blackford, L., 387
Blackwell, B., 381
Blake, A. J. D., 153
Blane, H., 363, 370
Blasi, A., 155
Blau, P. M., 326
Bledsol, J. C., 315
Block, J., 93, 127, 222, 239, 367
Block, N. J., 193
Bloom, B. S., 320
Blount, J. H., 293
Bogue, D. J., 4
Bolk, L., 10
Bordin, E. S., 416
Borsos, A., 67
Brainerd, C. J., 150
Brannock, J., 146, 147

Braucht, G., 364
Breland, H. M., 188
Bray, H., 246
Brecher, E. M., 375
Breslin, J., 353–354
Breslow, J., 274
Brim, O. G., 245
Brittain, C. V., 96
Broderick, C. B., 271, 277, 296
Brody, E. G., 98
Bronfenbrenner, V., 96, 242, 329
Bronson, W. C., 85
Brook, D. W., 85
Brook, J. S., 85
Brookman, R. R., 290, 291
Brophy, J., 246
Brouerman, D. M., 252
Brouerman, I. K., 252
Brown, A. C., 100
Brown, E., 377
Brown, R., 218
Brozek, J., 183
Brussel, J., 87
Buehler, C., 412
Burket, R. L., 290, 291
Burt, C., 178, 404
Burton, R. V., 239
Busse, T. V., 157
Butler, N. R., 377
Byrne, D., 100
Byrnes, M. M., 146

Caddini, R., 92
Calderone, M., 299
Campbell, D. P., 118
Campbell, E. Q., 184, 189, 191, 192, 195
Camston, C., 98
Camus, A., 13
Carden, B. W., 315, 325
Carlsmith, L., 243
Carr, R. C., 374, 375
Carroll, J. B., 171, 175
Carroll, J. W., 87
Carroll, M. D., 72
Carroll, S. J., 189

Carter, H. D., 120
Cattell, R. B., 195
Cerva, T. R., 190
Cervantes, L. F., 315
Chafetz, M., 370, 371, 373, 389
Chan, M. M. C., 8
Chananine, J. D., 246
Chang, K. S. F., 8
Chapman, R. H., 150
Chaskes, J. B., 280, 297
Chiapetta, E. L., 153, 154
Chien, C. P., 373
Child, J. L., 365–366
Chinn, S., 6, 8
Chumlea, C., 9
Cicirelli, V. G., 190
Clark, D. H., 193
Clarke, A. D., 124, 186
Clarke, A. M., 124, 186
Clarkson, F. E., 252
Cleary, T. A., 195
Cobliner, W. G., 291
Cohn, J., 291, 298
Cole, J. O., 373
Cole, P. V., 377
Coleman, J. S., 184, 189, 191, 192, 195, 250, 326, 338
Comitas, L., 375
Condry, J. C., Jr., 96
Conger, J. J., 82, 98, 112
Connell, D. M., 354
Constantinople, A., 234
Conway, J., 364
Cooper, J., 248
Cooper, R., 379
Coopersmith, S., 91
Corah, N. L., 9, 10
Corsini, R. J., 85
Costar, J. W., 248
Cramer, P., 224
Cravioto, J., 183
Cremin, L. H., 310, 311, 312
Crites, J. O., 119, 396n., 397, 404–407, 408, 409, 410, 411, 412, 416, 417
Cross, H., 116
Cross, H. J., 361n., 365, 367, 376
Cruze, A. M., 384
Curtis, T., 87
Curtiss, S., 186
Cusumano, D. R., 92

Damon, W., 211, 213, 215
Danner, F. W., 155
Danskin, M. J., 6
Darrow, W. W., 292, 293, 294
Darwin, C., 32, 158
David, J., 190
Davies, A. M., 377
Davis, D. B., 85

Davis, H., 98
Davis, K., 366
Davison, M., 222
Day, M. C., 149, 155, 159
Decker, P. W., 191
DeFries, J. C., 179, 180
DeGroot, A. D., 188
Deickman, A. J., 362
DelGaudio, A. C., 130
DeLint, J., 371
Dellinger, R. A., 385, 386
Delong, F. L., 367
Demirjian, A., 8
Denenberg, V. H., 9
Denny, R., 319
De Peretti, E., 63
Dermen, D., 170
Dickman, I. R., 275, 276, 283, 300
Diers, C. J., 6
Docter, R. F., 322
Donahue, T. J., 248
Donaldson, T. S., 189
Dornbush, R. L., 375
Dornbush, S. M., 316
Douvan, E., 43, 51, 88, 96, 129, 237, 238, 242, 244, 322
Dresser, C. M., 72
Dryfoas, J. G., 289, 290
Ducharme, J. R., 63
Duncan, B., 165
Duncan, O. D., 165, 195, 326
DuPont, R. L., 374, 376, 378, 384, 386
Dusek, J. B., 90
Duster, T., 364
Dworkin, G., 193
Dwyer, J., 99
Dyk, R. B., 148

Eagan, J. C., 327
Easley, J. A., Jr., 154, 155
Eaves, L. J., 180
Ebel, R. E., 311
Edwards, J. A., 96
Eells, K., 339
Eggleston, E., 317
Ehrhardt, A., 235
Ehrmann, W. W., 297
Eichorn, D. H., 55n., 67, 69, 422, 426
Einstein, A., 157
Eisen, S. V., 238
Eisenstadt, S., 309
Ekstrom, R. B., 170
Elder, G. H., Jr., 89
Elkind, D., 84, 116, 127, 129, 130, 219
Elliott, D., 314, 315
Ellis, W. B., 6
Emerick, B. B., 154, 155
Erikson, E., 46–51, 52

Erikson, E., 33, 86–87, 113, 115, 122, 217, 218, 235–237, 318, 426
Erlenmeyer-Kimling, L., 180
Escomel, E., 5, 60
Espinosa, R. W., 316
Etelis, R., 291
Evans, B., 291, 298
Evans, J. R., 291
Evans, J. W., 190
Everly, K., 299

Fagot, B. I., 249
Farnsworth, J. B., 251
Faterson, H. F., 148
Faust, M. S., 60, 67, 102
Featherman, D. L., 165
Feinstein, S. C., 270, 277
Felsenthal, H., 246
Fernandez, C., 316
Ferrell, M. Z., 280
Fifer, G., 193
Figueroa, R. A., 193
Finger, F. W., 283, 284
Fink, M., 375
Finkel, D. J., 274, 275, 285, 286, 287, 290, 294
Finkel, M. L., 274, 275, 285, 286, 287, 290, 294
Finney, D. J., 6
Firkowska, A., 185
Fisher, D. P., 251
Fisher, S., 93
Fitzgerald, H. E., 96
Ford, C. S., 62
Forest, M. G., 63
Forman, G. E., 84
Forrest, D. J., 408
Forsland, M. A., 363
Fort, J., 371
Fox, L. H., 120
Fox, S., 364
Frazier, N., 247, 248
French, J. L., 315, 325
French, J. W., 170
Frend, A., 35–37, 39, 47
Freud, S., 31, 34–37, 39, 46–47, 48, 209–210, 235–237, 396
Friedenberg, E. Z., 319
Friedman, R., 299
Friedrich, L. K., 250, 252
Friedrich-Cofer, L. K., 251
Fromme, D. K., 254
Fulker, D. W., 178
Furstenberg, F., Jr., 275, 355

Gadpaille, W. J., 280
Gagnon, J. H., 298
Gajdusek, D. C., 6
Gallagher, J. M., 136n., 138, 139n., 151, 429

Gallatin, J. E., 2, 31n., 34, 43, 46, 318, 424, 426
Garber, H., 187
Garrett, H. E., 405
Garrison, K. C., 268
Garwood, S. G., 320
Gay, G. R., 384
Geary, P. S., 114
Gebhard, P. H., 274, 275, 281
Gesell, A., 119, 186
Gettys, R., 14
Gibran, K., 17
Gilligan, C., 218, 222
Gilutz, G., 245
Ginsburg, W. W., 119, 397, 407, 417
Ginzberg, E., 119, 397, 398, 400, 401, 407, 412, 417
Girija, B., 8
Glass, D. R., 339
Glass, G. V., 191, 327
Glazer, N., 319
Globetti, G., 280
Godow, A. G., 298
Goethals, G. W., 114
Goldman, R., 274
Goldstein, G., 151
Goldstein, H., 377
Gomes, B., 248
Gomez, H., 187
Good, T., 246
Goode, E., 364, 381
Goodenough, D. R., 85, 148
Goodman, P., 319
Gordis, L., 275
Gordon, I. J., 96
Gordon, S., 275, 276, 283, 300
Gottesman, I. I., 128
Gottlieb, D., 338
Gough, H. C., 234
Goulet, L. R., 411
Grandon, G., 188
Grant, G., 98
Gray, S. W., 191
Green, C. P., 356
Green, L. B., 90
Gribbons, W. D., 407, 409, 410, 412, 413
Grinder, R. E., 342, 343
Grinker, R. F., 126, 127, 128, 129
Grinspoon, L., 375
Grossman, M., 274
Grotevant, H. D., 120, 121, 245, 111n., 428
Gruman, J., 327
Grumbach, M. M., 60, 63
Guilford, J. P., 169, 170
Gump, P. B., 326
Gunders, S. M., 9
Gunther, M., 87, 88
Gustafson, T. J., 363
Guttentag, M., 246

Haan, N., 220, 222, 367
Haeckel, E., 32
Hafen, B., 371, 372, 373
Hagar, M., 377
Halcomb, R. A., 180
Hall, C. S., 111, 210
Hall, G. S., 2, 31–34, 35, 39, 49–50, 400
Hallworth, H. J., 98
Halperin, S., 413
Hamachek, D. E., 72, 79n., 85, 93, 422, 427
Hammond, E. C., 377
Hannington, C. M., 251
Hansen, S. L., 273
Harari, H., 323
Harder, M. W., 87
Harlap, S., 377
Harman, H. H., 170
Harnquist, K., 188
Harper, L. V., 117
Harrell, M. S., 165
Harrell, T. W., 165
Harris, D., 239
Harris, L., 94
Harrison, D., 280
Hartshorne, H., 222
Harvey, O. J., 365, 367, 369
Hauser, S. T., 115
Havighurst, R. J., 81, 255, 318, 335n., 339, 422, 433
Heber, F. R., 187
Hefner, R., 239
Hegmann, J. P., 180
Heilbrun, A. B., Jr., 92, 254
Heise, D. R., 411
Helmreich, R., 234, 239, 254
Herma, J. L., 119, 397, 407, 417
Herrnstein, R. J., 184
Herron, J. D., 152, 153
Hesse, H., 13
Heston, L. L., 128
Hetherington, E. M., 93, 241, 244
Hewitt, L., 363
Heyns, B., 326
Hiernaux, J., 6
Higgins, J., 196
Higgins-Trenk, A., 252, 255
Hill, J. P., 116, 128, 112
Hobson, C. J., 184, 189, 191, 192, 195
Hochman, J. S., 367, 375
Hoeffel, E. C., 155
Hoffman, M. L., 97
Hoffman, L. W., 243
Hogan, R., 364
Holland, J. L., 118, 121
Holly, K. A., 175
Holmen, M. G., 322
Holstein, C., 220
Holt, J., 319
Holzman, P. S., 126, 127, 128, 129

Horn, ., 179
Horrocks, J. S., 130
Hosken, B., 232
House, E. R., 191
Howe, L. W., 224
Hoxie, K., 251
Hraba, J., 98
Hummel, R. C., 407
Humphreys, L. G., 195
Hunt, D. E., 365, 367, 369
Hunt, E., 176
Hunt, M., 263
Huston-Stein, A., 230n., 252, 255

Ilg, F. G., 119
Illenberg, G. J., 327
Inhelder, B., 84, 116, 140, 141, 146, 150, 153, 212, 218

Jacklin, C. N., 241, 322
Jacobs, J., 43
Jaffe, F. S., 289, 290
Jarvik, L. F., 180
Jensen, A. R., 175, 176, 182, 187, 192, 193, 195, 198
Jencks, C., 180, 182, 184, 188, 326
Jenicek, M., 8
Jersild, A. T., 85
Jessor, R., 122, 123, 285, 286, 287, 296, 335–336, 364, 371
Jessor, S. L., 122, 123, 285, 286, 287, 296, 335–336, 364, 371
Jick, H., 382
Jinks, J. L., 178, 180
Johansson, C. B., 120
Johnson, B. D., 363, 364, 366, 369
Johnson, C. L., 12, 72
Johnson, J. E., 254
Johnson, L., 370, 381
Johnson, M., 241
Johnson, R. C., 94
Johnson, R. E., 293
Johnson, W. R., 281
Johnston, J., 85
Johnston, L. D., 311, 319
Jones, H. B., 361
Jones, H. C., 361
Jones, M. C., 101, 102, 268
Jones, T. M., 9
Jordan, D., 116, 117
Jordan, N., 367
Josephson, E., 364
Jourard, S. M., 100
Juhasz, A. M., 12, 280

Kaats, G., 366
Kagan, J., 85, 232, 242

Kahn, P., 372
Kamin, L. J., 178, 179, 181, 182
Kandel, D., 95, 363, 366, 369
Kantner, J. F., 275, 276, 284, 285, 286, 287, 289, 290, 356
Kaplan, J., 367, 375
Kaplan, R. M., 323
Karas, G. G., 9
Karns, E. A., 314
Karp, S. A., 85, 148
Karplus, E. F., 149
Karplus, R., 149, 150
Kashiwazaki, H., 9
Katz, S. H., 192
Kay, E., 364
Keating, D. P., 115, 116
Keeler, M. H., 372
Keeley, K. A., 372
Kelman, S., 249
Kendrick, S. A., 195
Kessler, R., 363
Kett, J. F., 80
Keyes, R., 325
Kiesling, H. J., 189
Kinsey, A. C., 268, 281, 283–284, 287
Kirschenbaum, H., 224
Klassen, A. D., 263
Klaus, R. A., 191
Kleinerman, G., 274
Kleinhesselink, R. R., 361n., 365, 367, 376
Klos, D. S., 114
Kohlberg, L., 211–217, 218, 219, 221, 222, 223, 365, 367, 369
Konopka, G., 51
Korcok, M., 370, 376
Kraines, R. J., 94
Kramer, R., 365
Krathwohl, D. R., 320
Krumboltz, J. D., 416
Kuhn, D., 146, 147
Kuschner, D. S., 84

Labouvie-Vief, G., 195, 232
Lambert, B. G., 90
Lambert, H., 220
Landauer, T. K., 9
Landis, J. R., 324
Landis, P. H., 80
Lawson, A. E., 148, 153, 154
Lee, M. M. C., 8
Lerner, R. M., 100
Lesser, G. S., 95, 193
Levine, S., 9
Levine, V. E., 6
Levitan, T. E., 246
Levitt, E. E., 96, 263
Levitz, N., 291
Levy, B. I., 367
Lewin, K., 41–42

Lewis, E. L., 94
Lewis, J., 176
Lewis, R. A., 276, 297
Lewontin, R. C., 182
Ley, L., 10
Libby, R. N., 300
Liberman, D., 245
Lieft, H. I., 268, 269
Lindzey, G., 111, 181, 192, 199, 210
Linn, M. C., 148
Lipset, S., 339
Liu, W. T., 346
Lloreda, P., 187
LoCascio, R., 400
Lockwood, A., 224
Loeb, R., 364
Loehlin, F. C., 178, 179
Loehlin, J. C., 180, 181, 182, 192, 199
Loehlin, J. D., 120
Loevinger, J., 220
Lohnes, P. R., 407, 409, 410, 412, 413
Lohr, L., 385
London, O., 100
Long, S. Y., 388
LoPiccolo, J., 299
Lovell, K., 153, 154
Lovell, L., 309n.
Lubensky, A. W., 128
Luchins, A. S., 320
Ludford, J., 72
Lunneborg, C., 176
Lunzer, E. A., 150, 151, 155, 156, 159
Lyons, A., 364

MacArthur, R. S., 193
Maccoby, E., 217, 241, 243, 323
MacMahon, B., 5, 6
Maddox, G., 364
Malcolm, L. A., 5
Malina, R. M., 9
Mankin, D., 364
Mansfield, R. S., 136n., 157, 429
Mantell, D. M., 92
Marcia, J. E., 114, 116, 117
Marciano, R., 190
Margulies, R., 363
Markowitz, M., 275
Marolla, F. A., 184, 188
Marshall, W. A., 58
Martin, C. E., 268, 281, 283–284, 287
Masia, B. B., 320
Massarik, F., 291, 298
Masterson, J. F., 129, 130
Masterson, J. G., 5
Matarazzo, J. D., 322
Matteson, D. R., 92, 116
Maurer, K., 69, 70
May, M. S., 222

Mayer, J., 99
Maykovich, M. 346
McArthur, L. Z., 238
McCall, B., 364
McCandless, B. R., 38–39, 45, 47, 311, 325
McClelland, W. J., 8
McCowan, R. J., 327
McCoy, K., 263, 276, 289, 290, 293, 294
McCuen, J. T., 239, 325
McCullough, G., 220
McDavid, J. W., 320
McGee, M. G., 280, 285
McGlothlin, W. H., 379, 383, 387
McKay, A., 187
McKay, H., 187
McKinney, J. P., 96
McKuen, R., 17
McLean, L. D., 191
McNemar, Q., 175
McPartland, J., 184, 189, 191, 192, 195
Mead, M., 42, 90, 112
Meade, C., 415
Medinnus, G. R., 94
Medved, M., 325
Meeker, M., 339
Mercer, J., 195
Michael, W. B., 175
Milgram, S., 221
Miller, A. G., 100
Miller, L., 367
Miller, P., 275, 285, 286, 287, 296
Milton, G. A., 232
Minuchin, P., 246
Mischel, W., 85, 237, 241
Modgil, C., 148
Modgil, S., 148
Money, J., 235
Monks, F. J., 128
Mood, A. M., 184, 189, 191, 192, 195
Morante, L., 92
Moriyama, M., 9
Morris, J., 233
Morton, J. R. C., 9
Morton, N. E., 180
Moser, H. P., 407
Moss, H. A., 85, 542
Mosteller, F., 189
Moynihan, D. P., 189
Mueller, W. J., 85
Muller, H. J., 199
Munday, L. A., 196
Munsinger, H., 179
Mussen, P. H., 92, 93, 102, 240
Muuss, R., 45, 311
Myerson, R. M., 372

Naftolin, F., 9
Nachmann, B., 416

Nahas, G. G., 361
Nakamura, C. Y., 247
Nass, G., 270
Neimark, E. D., 136, 146, 147, 148, 149, 155
Nelson, E. A., 243
Nesselroade, J. R., 124
Neugarten, B. L., 94
Newman, W., 364
Neyzi, O., 8
Nias, D., 100
Nichols, R. C., 120, 165n., 178, 429
Noppe, I. C., 136
Norman, G., 12
Norris-Baker, C., 251
Nye, F. I., 243

Odell, W. D., 67
Offer, D., 43, 46, 129, 277
Offer, J. L., 43
Offir, C., 321, 322
O'Hara, R. P., 403
Oleshansky, B., 239
O'Malley, P., 85, 370, 381
O'Reilly, R. P., 327
Orlando, J. E., 151
Orlansky, H., 86
Ostrowska, A., 185
Overstreet, P. L., 402, 407, 408, 411, 413

Page, E. B., 188
Page, R., 100
Painter, P., 9, 10
Pakstis, A. J.,
Palmquist, W. J., 116
Pannor, R., 291, 298
Parke, R. D., 244
Parker, B. M., 372
Parsons, F., 415
Parsons, T., 252
Pasternak, S. R., 120
Patel, A. R., 372
Patterson, G. R., 249
Payne, D. E., 240
Peck, R. F., 17
Peel, E. A., 137
Peiser, N. L., 120
Peng, S. S., 165, 199
Perry, D. G., 238
Perry, L. C., 238
Peterson, R. C., 382
Peterson, R. W., 150
Petner, C., 152
Piaget, J., 43–45, 50, 84, 116, 136–160, 211–213, 218, 219, 429
Piers, E. V., 85
Pincus, J., 189
Pineiro, C., 183
Place, D. M., 273
Plomin, R., 179

Pocs, O., 298
Podd, N. H., 220
Polivanov, S., 180
Pomeroy, W. B., 268, 281, 283–84, 287
Potteiger, K., 356
Preble, M., 375
Prendergast, T., 363, 375
Proper, E. C., 190
Pyke, S., 246

Ramey, C. T., 187
Rao, D. C., 180
Ratcliffe, B. E., 387
Rauh, J. L., 290, 291
Rawson, R. A., 385
Ray, O. S., 379, 385, 388
Rebecca, M., 239
Reed, E. W., 196, 199
Reed, S. C., 196, 199
Reeves, J., 338
Reeves, K., 100
Reichelt, P. A., 274
Reiss, I. L., 263, 278–280, 283, 296, 297
Renner, J. W., 153, 154
Rest, J., 222, 223
Reynolds, C. H., 166
Reynolds, E. L., 268
Richardson, J. T., 87
Richardson, S. A., 183
Ricks, F., 246
Riesman, D., 319
Rifkin, B., 151
Roffins, S., 222
Roffins, T., 87
Roberts, A., 325
Roberts, C. A., 120
Roberts D. F., 6, 8
Roberts, G. H., 95
Roberts, J., 69, 70, 72
Robertson, J., 367
Roebuck, J., 280, 285
Rogers, C., 320, 415
Rogers, D., 270
Rohwer, W., 224
Roltman, L., 100
Rosenberg, B. G., 245
Rosenberg, L. M., 299
Rosenberg, P. P., 299
Rosenkrantz, P. S., 252
Ross, D., 2
Rothman, G., 221
Rothschild, B. F., 90
Roy, M., 372
Rubenstein, H. S., 276
Rubenstein, J. S., 276
Rubin, V., 375
Russell, M. A., 377
Rutherford, E., 93

Saario, T. H., 322
Sadava, S. W., 12
Sadker, M., 247, 248

Saenger, G., 184
St. Dennis, C., 376
St. Pierre, R. G., 190
Saltzstein, H. D., 97
Sameroff, A. J., 123
Samuda, R. J., 430n.
Sandrock, J. W., 245
Sargent, A. G., 93
Scales, P., 290, 291, 298, 299
Scanlon, J., 71
Scarr, S., 120, 179, 192
Schachter, F. F., 245
Schaeffer, E., 363
Schail, K. W., 195, 412
Schiller, J. S., 190
Schofield, M., 283, 297
Schroder, H. M., 365, 367, 369
Schwartz, J. M., 248
Scottish Council for Research in Education, 196
Sears, R. R., 254
Seckel, H. P. G., 60
Secord, P. F., 100
Segal, S. J., 416
Sells, L., 321
Selman, R., 213, 215
Selstad, G., 291
Selye, H., 8
Semler, I. J., 411
Sempe, M., 63
Shah, F., 276, 290
Shaw, I., 325
Shaw, M. C., 239, 325
Shayer, M., 153, 154
Sheppard, C. W., 384
Sherman, J. A., 252
Shick, J. F. E., 388
Shields, J., 128
Shipman, G., 281, 298
Shock, N. W., 69, 70
Shockley, W., 199
Shore, E., 245
Sieber, J., 211
Sigall, H., 100
Silberman, C. E., 319
Siman, M. L., 96
Simmons, R. B., 87
Simon, S. B., 223
Simon, T., 166, 167
Simon, W., 275, 285, 286, 287, 296
Sinisterra, L., 187
Singer, J., 322
Singh, H. D., 8
Skipper, J. K., 270
Slack, C. W., 375
Smid, I., 67
Smith, B., 222
Smith, D. E., 384, 385, 388
Smith, E., 187
Smith, E. A., 270
Smith, M. B., 367
Smith, M. L., 327
Smith, M. S., 190

Snyder, M., 100
Skolowska, M., 185
Sollenberger, R. T., 268
Sorensen, R. C., 280,
  281–283, 284, 286,
  287–289, 290, 293,
  296, 299
Spanier, G. B., 274, 296, 297
Spaulding, R. L., 246
Spearman, C., 169
Spence, J. T., 234, 239
Spence, T. J., 254
Spitz, H. H., 146
Spitz, R. A., 9
Spock, B., 11
Spranger, E., 45–46, 48, 50
Sprott, R. L., 180
Spuhler, J. N., 181, 192, 199
Staats, J., 180
Stager, M., 220
Stapp, J., 234
Starnes, T., 325
Staub, E., 211
Stebbins, L. B., 190
Stefanis, C., 375
Stein, A., 185
Stein, A., 185, 232, 242, 243,
  246, 250, 252, 254,
  431
Stein, Z., 183
Steinberg, L. D., 112, 123
Stern, J. A., 9, 10
Sternberg, R. J., 151
Stewart, C. S., 285, 286, 296
Stewart, N. R., 248
Stodolsky, S. S., 193
Stolz, L. M., 244
Stone, C. A., 149, 155, 159
Stone, C. P., 268
Stotsky, B. A., 373
Strommen, E., 96
Strong, E. K., Jr., 119, 128
Stroud, J., 220
Stukovsky, R., 6
Suchman, E. A., 366
Sullivan, E. V., 220, 224
Sullivan, H. S., 39–41
Super, D. E., 397, 398–404,
  405, 407, 408, 411,
  412, 413, 415, 416,
  417
Susser, M., 184, 185
Suttles, G., 349
Sutton-Smith, B., 245
Suzuki, T., 9
Sswedloff, R. S., 67
Sykes, J. N., 246
Szasz, T., 361, 369

Takacs, I., 67
Takemoto, T., 9
Tauke, E. D., 100
Tanner, J. M., 8, 60, 68
Tanney, M. F., 248

Tavris, C., 321, 322
Teilhard de Chardin, 13
Tennant, F. S., 375
Terman, L. M., 167, 322
Tettle, C. K., 322
Thomas, A. H., 248
Thomas, C., 314
Thomas, P., 344–345, 349
Thompson, A. S., 408
Thornburg, H. D., 274, 342,
  343
Thorndike, E., 34
Thorndike, R. L., 196
Thurston, D., 9, 10
Thurstone, L. L., 169
Tiedeman, D. V., 403
Tinklenberg, J. R., 366, 373
Tobias, S., 321
Toca, T., 183
Toffler, A., 5, 19
Tolone, W. L., 280
Trecker, J., 247
Troll, L. E., 94
Trotter, R., 187
Tryon, R. C., 180
Tsui, A. A., 4
Tucker, C. J., 251
Tucker, F., 263
Tuddenham, R. D., 195
Turiel, E., 211, 213,
  215–217, 219, 221,
  222, 223
Tyler, L. E., 119

Updike, J., 325
Urbeg, K. A., 232

Valsik, J. A., 6
Vandenberg, S. G., 165
Velandia, W., 188
Veneer, A. M., 285, 286, 296
Ventry, P., 375
Vernon, P. E., 404, 405
Vogel, S. R., 252
Vonnegut, M., 126
Voss, H. L., 314, 315

Wade, N., 178
Wagner, C. A., 263n., 432
Wald, I., 185
Wallenchinsky, D., 325
Waller, J. H., 184, 196
Walsh, R. H., 280
Walster, E., 100
Walters, R. H., 43, 45, 210
Warnath, C. F., 407
Warner, W., 339
Waterman, A. S., 114, 115,
  125
Waterman, C. K., 114, 115,
  125
Watson, F. G., 276

Watson, J., 34
Watson, S., 232
Watt, N. F., 127, 128
Weatherly, D., 102, 103
Webb, A. P., 254
Weil, A., 361, 362, 374, 375,
  381
Weinberg, R. A., 120, 179
Weiner, I. B., 43, 126, 127,
  129, 130
Weinfield, F. D., 184, 189,
  191, 192, 195
Weininger, O., 9
Weiss, R., 95
Weiss, S. D., 93
Weitz, L. J., 248
Welch, R. L., 230n., 242,
  431
Welcher, W. H., 291
Welling, M. A., 234
Wendling, A., 314, 315
Werley, H. H., 274
Wesman, A., 195
Wesson, D. R., 384
Wetter, R. E., 234
Wheeler, L. R., 198
Whiting, J. W. M., 9, 239
Wicker, A. W., 327
Wilen, R., 9
Wilkinson, D. Y., 348–349
Willems, E. P., 327
Williams, J., 86
Wilson, G., 100
Wilson, G. M., 372
Wilson, J. G., 388
Wilson, W. J., 348, 351
Windmiller, M., 208n., 431
Wine, J. V., 268
Wirtenberg, T. J., 247
Witkin, H. A., 148
Wohlford, P., 245
Wohlwill, J. F., 412
Wollman, W. T., 148, 149,
  150
Wright, R. J., 151
Wrightsman, L. S., 367
Wurst, F., 6
Wurtman, R. J., 9

Yamamoto, K., 314
Yankelovich, D., 94
Yee, S., 180
York, R. L., 184, 189, 191,
  192, 195
Young, H., 92
Yu, E. S. H., 346

Zacharias, L., 9
Zarrow, M. X., 9
Zelnik, M., 275, 276, 284,
  285, 286, 287, 289,
  290, 356
Zinberg, N., 367, 375

SUBJECT INDEX

Abilities, hierarchical structure of, 404
Ability factors:
  ETS test kit for, 170–174
  group differences in, 193, 194
  Guilford's classification of, 169–170
  understanding intelligence and,
    175–176, 200
Abnormal behavior, 126–130
Abortion, 289, 355–356
Abstraction:
  reflected, 144
  reflexive, 142–143, 144, 151
Acceptance of lack of closure (ALC),
    155–158, 159, 429
Acne, 72
Adjustment:
  concept of, 428
  social, 97–98. *See also* Peer group
Adolescence, 2, 4, 80–81, 422–423. *See
  also* Adolescents
  anthropological theory of, 42
  anti-"storm and stress" theories of,
    43–52
  developmental tasks of, 81–83, 112,
    122, 123
  discontinuity theme in, 39, 41–43
  drives in, 38
  field theory of, 41–42
  geisteswissenschaftliche theory of,
    45–46, 48, 50
  individual uniqueness in, 46, 48, 50,
    52
  interpersonal theory of, 39–41
  neural-hormonal basis of, 55–58
  nuclear conflicts of, 47–49
  predictability in, 122–123
  psychoanalytic theory of, 34–37, 39,
    46–48, 209–210, 235–237
  psychosexual stages of (A. Freud),
    34–37
  psychosocial theory of, 46–51, 52
  recapitulation theory of, 31–34, 35, 39,
    49–50

social learning theory approach to,
    38–39, 45
"storm and stress" theories of, 31–43,
    52, 129, 400, 424
Adolescents, 12–19
  culture, 98–99, 335–337
  decision-making and commitment,
    114–115
  egocentrism, 84–85, 116, 219
  health and growth, 55–60, 67–68,
    70–73. *See also* Physical (physio-
    logical) development; Sexual
    development
  identification. *See* Identification with
    parents
  identity. *See* Identity; Self
  individual differences. *See* Individual
    differences
  intelligence. *See* Intelligence
  moral development. *See* Moral
    development
  peer group acceptance. *See* Peer group
  personality. *See* Identity; Personality
    development; Self
  physical development. *See* Physical
    (physiological) development
  relationship with parents. *See* Parents
  self. *See* Identity; Self
  sex-role development. *See* Androgyny;
    Sex role development; Sex roles
  sexual development. *See* Sexual devel-
    opment; Sexuality
  social issues and involvement, 20–24
  subcultures. *See* Subcultures
  thinking. *See* Cognitive development;
    Formal operations
  values. *See* Values
Adoptive families:
  interest similarities in, 120
  studies of, 178–179, 185
Adrenal cortex, 56
Adults. *See also* Parents
  mature understanding, 11–12, 15

Adults (*Cont.*)
  nuclear conflicts of, 48, 49
  personality development, 125
Age, maturational, 58–60
Age group culture, 337–338
Age of menarche, 5–10, 64, 65, 423
Alcohol, 20–23, 370–373, 378–379, 434.
    See also Drug use
American Indians, 341, 346–347
Amphetamines, 383–384. *See also* Drug
    use
Analogies, understanding of, 150–152
Anal stage, 35, 48
Androgyny, 234, 239, 253–256, 322–323.
    See also Sex-role development; Sex
    roles
  siblings and, 244–245
  socialization of, 242–245
Angel dust, 385–386. *See also* Drug use
Animal studies:
  of heritability of traits, 179–180
  on stress, 8–9
Anthropological theory of adolescence,
    42
Anxiety, 38, 39
Appearance. *See* Physical appearance
Army General Classification Test
    (AGCT), 165
ARS youth, 21–23
Asian-Americans, 341, 345–346
Association for the Promotion of Mathe-
    matics Education of Girls and
    Women, 328
Authoritarian control, parents', 89–90,
    92
Awareness in problem solving, study of,
    144–146

"Back to basics," 317
Barbiturates, 379–380. *See also* Drug use
Behavior:
  drives and, 38, 39
  moral. *See* Moral behavior
  problem. *See* Problem behavior
  prosocial and antisocial, 211
  standards, internalization of, 16–17
Belief system, commitment to, 114
Birth control. *See* Contraception
Birth order, and intelligence, 188
Births, illegitimate, 255, 351–356
Blacks:
  adolescent subcultures, 341, 347–349
  age of menarche, 6
  differences in IQ and ability factors,
    191–195, 200
  sexual standards and behavior,
    278–280, 285

teenage pregnancy, 352, 353, 355, 356
Blood pressure, volume, 69–70
Body image, and self-esteem, 100–101
Boys:
  gender identity, 233–234, 255–256
  identification with parents, 92–94, 241
  maturation rate and social percep-
    tions, 101–103
  sex-role stereotyping of, 103, 321–323.
    See also Androgyny; Sex-role de-
    velopment; Sex roles

Caffeine, 381–382. *See also* Drug use
California Senate Bill 112, 329
Career counseling, 415–416, 417
  sexism in, 248
Career development (maturity), 117–121,
    128, 396, 434–435
  cognitive development and, 119–120
  commitment to, 114
  Crites' model of, 404–407, 416, 417
  ego functions and, 397–398, 399
  family influences on, 120–121
  Ginzberg's theory of, 397–398, 400,
    401
  intelligence and, 165–166
  measures of, 407–412
  sex role identity and, 237
  stages of, 398, 400, 403
  studies of, 412–415
  Super's theory of, 398–404
  theories of, 396–407
Career Development Inventory (CDI),
    407–409
Career Maturity Inventory (CMI), 407,
    408, 410–412
Career Maturity Project, 412, 413–415
Career Pattern Study, 407, 412–413
Categorization, of groups, 323–325
Caulfield, Holden, 219
Cheating, 222
Chicanos, 342–343
Childbearing, teenage, 255, 351–356
Childhood:
  nuclear conflicts of, 48
  psychoanalytic theory of, 34–35
Child-rearing styles, 89–92. *See also*
    Parents
Chinese-Americans, 341, 345–346
Closure. *See* Acceptance of lack of closure
    (ALC)
Cocaine, 382. *See also* Drug use
Cognitive development, 429. *See also*
    Thinking
  equilibration factor of, 138, 159
  identity formation and, 115–116
  interest development and, 119–120

Cognitive development (*Cont.*)
  operationalists' and constructivists' understanding of, 154–155
  Piaget's stages of, 44, 139–140, 212, 213. *See also* Concrete operations; Formal operations
  Piaget's theory of, 43–45, 50, 116, 136–140, 211, 212, 213
  stages, and Kohlberg's stages of moral development, 211–215
Coleman Report, 189, 191–192, 326
Colleges:
  aptitude for, 316–317
  attendance, 316
  entry, and intelligence, 165
Combinatorial structure, 140–141
Commission on Obscenity and Pornography, 274
Community support services, role in sexual learning, 301–302
Compensatory education programs, 189–191
Conceptual systems theory, and drug use, 367, 369
Concrete operations, 139, 151, 153, 154
  and formal operations, contrasted, 140–143
Conscience, 209
Constructivists, 154–155
Continuity, in adolescent personality, 121–125, 127–128
Contraception, 289–291
  information on, 275
  irrational attitude toward, 291
Counseling. *See* Career counseling
Counterculture movements, 87–88
Creativity:
  formal operations and, 155–158, 159
  teaching of, 319–320
Cults, religious, 87–88
Culture, 337
  adolescent, 335–337. *See also* Subcultures
  bias, in intelligence tests, 194–195
Curricula, sexism in, 247–248

Dating, 270–274
  age characteristics, 271–272
  selection, values in, 273
Dependency drive, 38
Deprivation, and intelligence, 186–187
Developmental tasks of adolescence, 81–83, 112, 122, 123
Deviance theory, drug use, 364, 370
The Devil's Dictionary, 15–16
Discontinuity concept, 39, 41–43

Disequilibrium, in cognitive and oral development, 215
Divorce rate, adolescent, 82
Double standard, 278, 280
Downers, 378–381. *See also* Alcohol; Drug use
Drives, and social behavior, 38, 39
Dropouts, 314, 315–316
Drug prone personality, 364
Drug use, 361–362, 434. *See also* Alcohol; Marijuana; Opiates; PCP
  effects and functions of, 365–367
  hallucinogenic, 386–388
  hard, 376–377
  legal, 377–378
  sedative-hypnotic (downers), 378–381. *See also* Alcohol
  social psychological analysis of, 367–369
  stages of, 365
  stimulant (uppers), 381–384
  theories of, 362–365

Economic differences. *See* Socioeconomic status (SES)
Education. *See also* Schools
  aims of, 310
  attainment, national, 316–318
  compensatory, and intelligence, 189–191
  as institution, and adolescents, 13–14, 310
Educational Testing Service (ETS), 170–174
Ego, 209, 218. *See also* Identity; Self development of, 220–221
Egocentrism, adolescent, 84–85, 116, 219
Ego functions, and career choice, 397–398, 399
Eight Ages of Man (Erikson), 48–49
Employment, preparation for in schools, 319. *See also* Career development (maturity)
Endocrine glands, 55–57
Environment:
  influences on intelligence, 183–191, 199, 200
  personality development and, 123–125
Equality of Educational Opportunity Survey, 189, 191–192, 326
Equilibration concept, 138, 159
Eskimos, 341, 346–347
Ethnic minorities:
  IQ, Coleman Report on, 191–192
  peer group acceptance among, 98
Ethnic subcultures, adolescent, 340–349
Eugenics proposals, 199

Evolution, and human development. *See*
    Recapitulation theory
Examination, High School Proficiency
    (Calif.), 329

Factor analysis, 169–171
Family. *See* Parents; Siblings
Fathers. *See also* Parents
    absence of, 243–244
    identification with, 92, 93, 240–241
Feminine psychology, 50–51. *See also*
    Girls; Women's Liberation
    Movement
Femininity, 234, 255–256. *See also* An-
    drogyny; Sex-role development;
    Sex roles
Feral children, 186
Fertility rate, 2–4
Fetal life, 61
Field dependence-independence concept,
    148
Field theory of adolescence, 41–42
Foreclosure identity status, 114–117, 125
Formal operations, 116, 136, 217–218
    and concrete operations, contrasted,
        140–143
    creativity and, 155–158
    moral development and, 217–218
    new tasks in, 143–147, 149
    prompts in, 155
    science curriculum and, 153–155
    sex differences in, 144, 147–149
    in understanding proportions and anal-
        logies, 149–152
Four group. *See* INRC group

Gangs, street, 344, 349–350
Geisteswissenschaftliche theory, 45–46,
    48, 50
Gender identity, 233–234, 255. *See also*
    Androgyny; Sex-role development;
    Sex roles
General Adaptation Syndrome, 8
Generation gap, 94, 369. *See also* Parents
Genetic analysis, biometrical, 180–181
Genetic factors:
    age of menarche and, 6
    intelligence and, 176–183, 184, 199,
        200
    interest similarity and, 120
Germinal choice, 199
Girls. *See also* Feminine psychology;
    Mothers, teenage
    age of menarche, 5–10, 64, 65, 423
    gender identity, 233–234, 255–256

identification with parents, 93–94,
    241–243
identity formation, and occupation
    choice, 237
maturation rate and social percep-
    tions, 102–103
sex-role stereotyping of, 103, 321–323.
    See also Androgyny; Sex-role de-
    velopment; Sex roles
Gonadotropin secretion, 56–57, 61
Gonorrhea, 292–294
Grading procedures, 325
Grey Marketing and Research Depart-
    ment study, 20–23
Group differences in intelligence,
    191–195, 200
Groups, categorizing, 323–324
Growth spurt, adolescent, 55–60, 67–68,
    73

Hanoi Tower problem, 144–146
Head start program, 190
Health status, of adolescents, 70–72
Heider's balance model, and drug use,
    367, 368
Height:
    stress and, 9
    velocity, peak, 58, 67–68, 73
Heritability, of human traits, 176–183,
    184
Heroin, 384. *See also* Drug use
Heterosexual behavior, 284–287
Heterosexual development, 271–272
    stages, 270–271
Highs, legal, 378. *See also* Drug use
Historical environment, and identity sta-
    tus, 125
Homosexuality, 283–284
Hormones, 55–57
Humanism, 320

Id, 35, 209
Identification with parents, 37, 92–94,
    104, 209, 237, 240–243
    cross-sex, 93–94
Identity. *See also* Moral development;
    Personality development; Self
    concept, 48, 49–50
    "crisis," 46, 49
    formation, 113–117, 218–221, 237
    search, and sexual behavior, 269–270
    status, 114–117, 125
Identity Achievement status, 114–117,
    125
Identity Diffusion status, 114–115, 117,
    125

Ideology. *See* Belief system
Indians. *See* American Indians
Indices of Vocational Maturity (IVM), 407, 409, 413
Individual differences, 176, 200
    environmental, 183–191, 199, 200
    genetic, 176–183, 184, 199, 200
    in intelligence, 165–166, 176–191, 199, 200, 429–430
Individuality, teaching of, 319–320
Infants:
    sexuality. *See* Sexuality, infant
    stress, 8–10
Inhalants, 378, 379. *See also* Drug use
INRC group, 140–142
Institute of Human Development (Univ. of Calif.), 101
Institutions. *See* Education; Social institutions
Instructional materials, sex-biased, 247
Integration, school, 327
Intelligence:
    ability factors in, 169–176
    birth order and, 188
    changes in, 195–199, 200
    college attendance and, 165
    compensatory education and, 189–191
    early deprivation and, 186
    early massive intervention and, 187
    environmental influences on, 183–191
    general, 169, 174–175
    genetic influences on, 176–183
    group differences in, 191–195, 200
    heritability of, 182–184
    individual differences in, 165–166, 176–191, 199, 200, 428–430
    nature of, 166–176
    number of siblings and, 195, 196
    nutrition and, 183–184
    occupation and, 165–166
    peer group acceptance and, 98
    personality characteristics and, 166
    Piaget's theory of, 43–45
    reaction time and, 176
    schooling and, 188–189
    socioeconomic status and, 184–186
    spouse selection and, 166
    structure of, 168–174
Intelligence quotient (IQ), 167–168
Intelligence tests, 166, 430
    Binet, 166–167
    cultural bias of, 193–195
    differential abilities, 174–175
    general, 166–169, 174
    and prediction, 174–175
    Stanford Binet, 167–168
Intercourse, premarital, 277–280, 286–287

Interest development, 117–121, 128. *See also* Career development (maturity)
Interest profiles, 118–119, 128
Interpersonal theory of adolescence, 39–41
IQ:
    group differences in, 192–193
    raising, 198–199
Isolation, children raised in, 186
Isolation of variables scheme, 146–147, 153, 155

Japanese-Americans, 341, 345–346
Judgment. *See* Moral judgments

Kinship correlations, analysis of, 180–182
Knowledge:
    explosion, 4–5
    national level of, 316–317
    required, teaching of, 316–318

Latency period, 35, 48, 209
Learning theory. *See* Social learning theory
Life space concept, 41–42
Literacy rate, national, 316
LSD, 386–388. *See also* Drug use

Malnutrition, 183–184
Marijuana, 361, 366, 367, 373, 374–376, 434. *See also* Drug use
Marriage:
    adolescent, 82
    median age of, 351
    partner, selection of, 166
Masculinity, 234, 255–256. *See also* Androgyny; Sex-role development; Sex roles
Masturbation, 280–283
Mathematics skills ability, sex inequity in, 321–322, 328
Maturation, early vs. late, 101–105. *See also* Physical (physiological) development; Sexual development
Maturational age, determination of, 58–60
Maturity, defined, 4
Media:
    attitudes toward sexuality and, 267
    sex-role stereotypes in, 250–251
Memory span, 171
Menstruation cycle, 66–67. *See also* Age of menarche

Mental age, 167–168. *See also* Intelligence quotient (IQ)
Mental development. *See* Cognitive development
Mental disorders, 126. *See also* Schizophrenia
Metabolic rate, 69
Methadone, 384–385
Methaqualone, 380. *See also* Drug use
Mexican-Americans, 340–344
Minorities. *See* Ethnic minorities
Moral behavior, 430–431
　moral judgments and, 220–222
Moral development, 208–209, 430–431
　disequilibrium and equilibrium in, 215, 219
　drug use and, 365–369
　ego development and, 220–221
　formal operations and, 217–218
　identity formation and, 218–221
　Kohlberg's stages of, 211–217, 219, 222
　Piaget's stages of, 212, 213
　psychoanalytic theory of, 209–210
　qualitative changes in, 217–221
　sex differences in, 222
　social learning theory of, 210–211, 217
　structural-developmental approach to, 211–217
　transitional period in, 219
　Turiel's theory of, 215–217, 219
Moral judgments, and moral behavior, 220–222
Moral values, teaching of, 223–225
Moratorium identity status, 114–115, 117, 125
Mothers. *See also* Parents
　identification with, 93, 241–242. *See also* Identification with parents
　teenage, 255, 351–356
　working, 241–242
Multiple interacting systems (MIS), 155–158
Music, 17

National Commission on Marijuana and Drug Abuse, 367–368
National Council of Teachers of Mathematics, 328
National Organization for Reform of Marijuana Laws, 374, 376
Natural experiments, 146–147
Neural-hormonal basis of adolescence, 55–58
Normalcy, continuum of, 126–127
Normative crisis concept, 47–49
Nuclear conflict concept, 47–49

Nutrition, 72
　age of menarche and, 6
　intelligence and, 183–184

Occupation choice. *See* Career development (maturity)
Oedipus complex, 35, 209
Operationalists, 154–155
Opiates, 384–385. *See also* Drug use
Oral stage, 35, 47
Ovulatory cycle, 66–67

Paper clip problem, 149–150
Parents, 11–12, 15, 427–428. *See also* Fathers; Mothers
　authoritarian, 89–90, 92
　child-rearing styles of, 89–92
　communication and control, 89–92
　discipline, and moral development, 210
　drugs and, 363, 368–369
　identification with, 37, 92–94, 104, 209, 237, 240–243
　identity formation and, 116–117
　mature understanding of, 11–12, 15
　peer groups and, 96
　permissive, 89–90, 241–242
　relationship with adolescents, 88–94, 104
　role of, in sexual learning, 297–299, 301
　sex education and, 299–301
　sexual behavior standards of, 264–265
　single, 243–244
　socialization of sex roles, 240–244
　socioeconomic status of, and intelligence, 184–185
　vocational interests and, 120–121
　warm-controlling vs. warm-restrictive, 90–93
PCP, 385–386. *See also* Drug use
Peer group, 17, 94–99, 104, 210
　acceptance, and social adjustment, 97–98
　as adolescent subculture, 337–338
　drugs and, 363
　functions of, 95–97
　as medium for growth, 98–99, 104
　sex-role conformity and, 249–250
Perceptions:
　alterations in, 367
　deautomatization of, 362
　self-other, and physical appearance, 100–103
Permissiveness, parental, 89–90, 241–242

Personality, 83
  abnormal, 126–130
  adult, 125
  drug prone, 364
  intelligence and, 166
  traits. *See* Traits, heritability of
Personality development, 111–113. *See
    also* Career development (maturity); Identity; Moral development; Self
  continuity and change in, 121–125,
    127–128
  transactional model of, 123–125, 128
  vocational interest theory of, 118–119
Petting, 286
Phallic period, 35, 48, 209
Philipinos, 341, 345–346
Physical appearance, 99–101
Physical (physiological) development,
    67–70, 99, 101–105. *See also* Sexual development; Sexuality
Pituitary gland, 56–57
Plant problem, 147
Poetry, 17–18
Popularity. *See* Peer group
Population growth, 2–4, 423
Possibles, understanding of, 136–138,
    140–143, 152, 159
Predictability, 122–123
Prediction, and tests, 174–175
Pregnancy, adolescent, 255, 351–356
Prenatal life, 61
Preoperational (representational) stage of
    cognitive development, 139
Probit analysis, 6, 7
Problem behavior, 336
  prediction of, 122–123
Problem solving, scientific, 157–158. *See
    also* Formal operations
Project Follow Through, 190–191
Proportions, understanding of, 149–150,
    153
Psychoanalytic theory, 34–37, 39, 46–48
  or moral development, 209–210
  of sex-role development, 235–237
Psychology, published research in, 5
Psychosocial thoery of adolescence,
    46–51, 52
Puberty, 2. *See also* Age of menarche;
    Sexual development; Sexuality
  praecox, 60
  psychoanalytic theory of, 35
Public Law 93–380, 328
Puerto Ricans, 341, 342, 344–345

Reaction time, and intelligence, 176
Readiness for Vocational Planning
    (RVP) scales, 407, 409–410, 413

Reasoning, moral, and moral behavior,
    221, 222
Recapitulation theory of adolescence,
    31–35, 39, 49–50
Religion:
  attitudes toward sexuality and, 265,
    295–296
  role in sexual learning, 299–301
Reproductive system, 60–61, 65–67
Role taking hypothesis, 213–215
Rule formation ability, 151–152

Sansei youth, 346
Schizophrenia, 126–130
Scholastic Aptitude Test, 316–317, 321
  decline in scores, 196–198
Schools, 310–313, 432–433. *See also* Social
    institutions
  caretaking and managing function,
    314–315
  changes in, 327–329
  conformity and dependence in, 319
  educational attainment in, 316–318
  grouping procedures in, 324–325
  humanism in, 320
  as instrument for other institutions,
    327–329
  integration in, 327
  intelligence and, 188–189
  performance evaluation of, 313–314
  quality and size of, 326–327
  screening and identification in, 325
  sex inequity (sex typing) in, 248–249,
    321–323, 328–329
  sex roles and, 245–249, 319
  sexuality and, 266–267
  sexual learning and, 299–301
  values transmission in, 318–323
  work ethic in, 318–319
Science:
  creativity in, 157–158
  curriculum, formal operations and,
    153–155
Self, 83–85, 104–105, 427. *See also* Identity; Personality development
  career choice and, 400, 417. *See also*
    Career development (maturity)
  changes in, 85–88
  concept, 83, 85–86, 91–92, 400, 417
  esteem, 83, 91, 95, 254
  expression, 17–18
  moral development and, 218–221. *See
    also* Moral development
  parents' impact on, 88–94, 104. *See also*
    Parents
  peers' impact on, 94–99, 104. *See also*
    Peer group

Self (*Cont.*)
  physical appearance and development
    and, 99–103
Sensorimotor stage of cognitive develop-
    ment, 139
Sex, as subculture, 337
Sex differences:
  in formal thinking, 144, 147–149
  in moral development, 222
Sex education, 266, 297, 299–301, 432
Sex inequity (sex typing), 103, 247–249,
    321–323
  legislation against, 328–329
"Sexing of the brain," 62
Sexism. *See* Sex inequity (sex typing)
Sex-role development, 431
  developmental theories of, 239–240
  mass media and, 250–251
  parents and, 240–244
  peers and, 249–250
  psychoanalytic theory of, 235–237
  schools and, 245–249, 319
  siblings and, 244–245
  social learning theory of, 237–239
  teachers and, 246
Sex roles:
  acceptance and adoption of, 233–236
  and achievement, 254–255
  concept of, 230–233, 255
  functions of, 252–255
  identity, 235–237, 251, 319. *See also*
    Identity
  preference, 235, 236
  socialization of, 240–251. *See also* Sex-
    role development
  stereotyping. *See* Sex inequity (sex
    typing)
  value attached to, 252
Sex steroids, 56–57
Sexual behavior, 280–289, 302. *See also*
    Dating
  guidance of, 296–302. *See also* Sex
    education
Sexual development. *See* Sexuality
Sexual drive, 38
Sexuality, 19, 263–264, 302, 426–427,
    432
  A. Freud's theory of, 35–37, 39
  attitudes, 276–277
  development of, 18–19, 60–67,
    267–268, 302
  family attitudes toward, 264–265
  infant, 34–35, 39–40, 47, 48
  interpersonal theory of, 39–41
  knowledge, 274–276
  as learned behavior, 294, 296–302
  media and, 267
  preadolescent, 61–63

psychoanalytic theory of, 34–37, 39,
    46–48
psychological needs in, 268–270
religion and, 265, 295–296
school and, 266–267
social learning theory of, 38
societal changes and, 294–296
Sorensen's study of, 287–289, 293
standards, 269, 277–280
Siblings:
  age of menarche and, 6, 10
  number of, and intelligence, 195, 196
  socialization of sex roles and, 244–245
Skeletal age, 58–60
Skills, teaching of, 316–318
Smoking, 377. *See also* Drug use
Snail and board problem, 141–142, 149,
    156
Social adjustment (acceptance), 97–98.
    See also Peer group
Social change, 309
Social class, 337, 338–340
Social convention, and moral develop-
    ment, 215–217, 219
Social expectations, and behavior drives,
    38, 39
Social institutions, 309–310. *See also*
    Schools
  moral development and education in,
    224–225
Socialization, 45, 336
  of androgyny, 242–245. *See also*
    Androgyny
  anticipatory, drug use as, 364
  of sex roles, 240–251. *See also* Sex roles
Social learning theory, 38–39, 45
  of alcohol use, 370–371
  of moral development, 210–211, 217
  of sex-role development, 237–239
Social mobility, 338–340
Social perceptions of adolescents,
    100–103
Socioeconomic status (SES). *See also* So-
    cial class; Social mobility
  age of menarche and, 8
  college entry and, 165
  intelligence and, 184–186
  peer group acceptance and, 98. *See also*
    Peer group
Spanish-Americans, 340–345
Speed, 383–384. *See also* Drug use
Standards. *See also* Belief system; Values
  internalization of, 16–17, 210
  sexual, 269, 277–280
Status, 323–324
Status quo method, 6, **7**
Stereotyping, sex-role. *See* Sex inequity
    (sex typing)

Stimulation stress factor (SSF), 8–10
"Storm and stress" theories of adolescence, 31–43, 52, 129, 400, 424
    anti-, 43–52
Street culture, 344, 349–350
Stress, 8–10. *See also* "Storm and stress" theories of adolescence
Structural-developmental theory. *See* Cognitive development; Moral development
Students, classification and evaluation of, 323–325. *See also* Adolescents
Subcultures, 337, 433–434
    ethnic, 340–349
    peer. *See* Peer group
    social class, 338–340
    street, 344, 349–350
    teenage mothers, 351–356
Successive relationships, 152
Superego, 209–210
Sweden, education in, 249
Symbols, 139
Syphilis, 292–294

Teachers, sex bias of, 246
Television, sex typing in, 250–251
Tests, sex typing in, 249, 322. *See also* Intelligence tests
Textbooks, sex typing in, 247
Therapeutic Communities of America, 384–385
Thinking. *See also* Cognitive development
    alterations in, and drug use, 367
    flexibility of, 142, 143, 152, 159
    formal. *See* Formal operations
    self-regulation of (equilibration), 138, 159
    straight vs. stoned, 362
Thyroid gland, 57
Title IX, 329
Tobacco, 377. *See also* Drug use
Traditions. *See* Social convention; Standards; Values

Traits, heritability of, 177–183, 184
Tranquilizers, 379, 380–381. *See also* Drug use
Transactional model of development, 123–125, 128
Twins:
    age of menarche of, 6
    heritability of traits and, 177–178
    intelligence of, 178
    interests similarity in, 120

U.S. Dept. of Health, Education, and Welfare, 316, 372, 377
Uppers, 381–384. *See also* Drug use

Values. *See also* Moral development; Social convention; Standards
    clarification, 223–224
    internalization of, 16–17, 210
    sexual standards and, 269
    transmission of, in schools, 318–323
Venereal disease, 292–294
Vital and Health Statistics, 70
Vocational counseling. *See* Career counseling
Vocational interest development. *See* Career development (maturity)

WEEA, 328
Women's Educational Equity Act, 328. *See also* Sex inequity (sex typing)
Women's liberation movement, 103
Work, 396. *See also* Career development (maturity)
Work ethic, 318–319

Youth culture, 335–337. *See also* Peer group.
    drug use and, 366
    a medium for growth, 98–99